Foundations of Organizational Behavior:
An Applied Perspective

Andrew J. DuBrin

College of Business
Rochester Institute of Technology

Prentice-Hall, Inc.
Englewood Cliffs, N.J. 07632

HD
58.7
.D79
1984

Library of Congress Cataloging in Publication Data

DuBrin, Andrew J.
  Foundations of organizational behavior, an applied perspective.

  Includes bibliographies and indexes.
  1. Organizational behavior.   I. Title.
HD58.7.D79   1984   658.3   83-13701
ISBN 0-13-329367-X

Editorial/production supervision and text design: Barbara Grasso
Part and chapter opening design: Judith A. Matz
Cover design: Judith A. Matz
Manufacturing buyer: Ed O'Dougherty

Part opening photos by (from top to bottom): Teri Leigh Stratford,
Laimute E. Druskis, Sybil Shelton, and IBM

To Doug, Drew, and Melanie

Printed in the United States of America

10 9 8 7 6 5 4 3 2 1

ISBN 0-13-329367-X

Prentice-Hall International, Inc., *London*
Prentice-Hall of Australia Pty. Limited, *Sydney*
Editora Prentice-Hall do Brasil, Ltda., *Rio de Janeiro*
Prentice-Hall Canada Inc., *Toronto*
Prentice-Hall of India Private Limited, *New Delhi*
Prentice-Hall of Japan, Inc., *Tokyo*
Prentice-Hall of Southeast Asia Pte. Ltd., *Singapore*
Whitehall Books Limited, *Wellington, New Zealand*

Contents

PART ONE
Introduction to Organizational Behavior

CHAPTER **1**

Introduction to Organizational Behavior   3

The Field of Organizational Behavior; Key Characteristics of
Organizational Behavior; A Dimensional Characterization of OB; OB and
Its Related Fields; Sources of Information About Organizational Behavior;
OB and Common Sense; Summary; Questions for Discussion; An
Organizational Behavior Problem; Additional Reading.

CHAPTER **2**

Research Methods in Organizational Behavior   19

The Contribution of Theory and Research; Characteristics of Scientific
Research; Basic versus Evaluation Research; Methods of Data Collection;

Choosing a Method of Data Collection; Methods of Research in Organizational Behavior; Sources of Error in Organizational Behavior Research; The Application of OB Knowledge; Implications for Managerial Practice; Summary; Questions for Discussion; An Organizational Behavior Problem; Additional Reading; Appendix to Chapter 2: Measurement Properties of Tests and Questionnaires.

PART TWO
Understanding Individuals

CHAPTER 3

Perception, Learning, Motives, and Values   49

Individual Differences and Environmental Influences on Behavior; How Perception Influences Behavior; Four Basic Models of Learning; How Needs Influence Behavior; How Values and Beliefs Influence Behavior; Implications for Managerial Practice; Summary; Questions for Discussion; An Organizational Behavior Problem; Additional Reading.

CHAPTER 4

Abilities, Personality, and Attitudes   79

Abilities and Job Performance; Problem-Solving Ability; Intelligence and Job Performance; Other Important Aptitudes and Skills; Personality and Job Behavior; Attitudes and Job Behavior; An Integrative Model of Personality, Ability, and Attitudes; Implications for Managerial Practice; Summary; Questions for Discussion; An Organizational Behavior Problem; Additional Reading.

CHAPTER 5

Motivation in Organizations   103

The Meaning of Work Motivation; Work Motivation and Job Performance; Cognitive versus Reinforcement Models of Motivation; Goal Theory and Work Motivation; The Two-Factor Theory; Job Enrichment: An Application of the Two-Factor Theory; Expectancy/Valence Theory; Equity Theory; Behavior Modification and Positive Reinforcement; Implications for Managerial Practice; Summary; Questions for Discussion; An Organizational Behavior Problem; Additional Reading.

PART THREE
Understanding Small Groups and Interpersonal Influence

CHAPTER **12**

Leadership in Organizations 307

The Meaning of Leadership; Leader Traits and Characteristics; Leadership Behavior and Styles; Situational Influences on Leadership; Fiedler's Contingency Theory; The Path-Goal Contingency Theory; The Situational Leadership Theory; Participative Leadership Style; Entrepreneurial Leadership; Implications for Managerial Practice; Summary; Questions for Discussion; An Organizational Behavior Problem; Additional Reading.

CHAPTER **13**

Conflict in Organizations 345

The Meaning of Conflict; A Systems Model of Intergroup Conflict; Sources of Conflict; Consequences of Organizational Conflict; Intergroup Relations and Conflict; Conflict Resolution Through Conciliation; Conflict Resolution Through Collaboration; Resolving Conflicts Through Organizational Restructuring; Conflict Resolution Through Power Tactics; The Stimulation of Conflict; Choosing the Appropriate Strategy; Implications for Managerial Practice; Summary; Questions for Discussion; An Organizational Behavior Problem; Additional Reading.

CHAPTER **14**

Organizational Power and Politics 375

The Meaning of Power and Politics; Sources of Individual and Subunit Power; Power Exercised by Subordinates; Factors Contributing to Organizational Politics; Power Acquisition Strategies and Tactics; Ordinary Influence Strategies for Acquiring Power; Managerial Awareness of Political Factors; Ethical Considerations; The Control of Organizational Politics; Implications for Managerial Practice; Summary; Questions for Discussion; An Organizational Behavior Problem; Additional Reading.

PART FOUR
Understanding the Macro Structure

Preface

Organizational behavior (OB) has reached its early adulthood. The field now contains specialists who have obtained degrees in OB; it has a body of information that it can call its own; and it is entering the vocabularies of many practicing managers and staff professionals. The field is also now sufficiently large to allow for multiple orientations to its teaching. At the one extreme are the highly quantitative, theoretical, and abstract treatments of the subject, which are of primary interest to researchers and advanced graduate students in the field. At the other extreme are eminently applied treatments that are long on advice giving, experiential exercises, and references to nonacademic sources of information.

Our text falls somewhere midway between these two extremes. The primary goal here, as it has been in several of this author's earlier books about human behavior in organizations, is to present a distinctly applied treatment of OB that is nevertheless buttressed by current research and theory. A four-part rationale underlies the writing of this book.

First, colleagues in the field and students complain that many books about organizational behavior are of relatively low interest to newcomers in the field. An effort has been made in preparing this book to include topics and illustrations of intrinsic interest to students, managers, and staff specialists. For instance, the text contains separate chapters about organizational power and politics and managing job stress. Current case histories collected by the author and his researchers are used as a source of information throughout the book. In addition, information from business and general audience sources is included where appropriate.

Second, an introductory text in organizational behavior should be both read and experienced. Toward this end, the book contains a large number of discussion questions, case problems, self-administering quizzes, and role plays. All are designed to facilitate an effective understanding of the concepts discussed in the text. Virtually all these exercises, or their close equivalents, have been field tested. We sincerely hope that you find few "duds" in the package.

Third, despite the early-adulthood status of the field, many books about human behavior in organizations are overinclusive. Some texts attempt to cover the entire spectrum of OB, personnel and human resource management, organizational psychology, human relations, and management. An unfortunate negative side effect of this mélange has been an overlapping of material among several courses in business school programs. The present book focuses attention on understanding human behavior in organizations. It therefore has implications for the practicing manager or staff specialist, but it is not a book about the principles of management. We also de-emphasize a discussion of personnel techniques and systems such as compensation programs or affirmative action programs.

Fourth, OB can be a difficult subject to study or teach, in part because many of the concepts appear as abstractions to the student. Convenient frames of reference are missing for such abstract concepts as organizational climate and the path-goal theory of leadership. This book is designed to present concepts of organizational behavior at an appropriate level of abstraction. One method of achieving this end is the use of frequent illustrations and examples. Another is the use of a chapter section called "Implications for Managerial Practice." Its purpose is to illustrate how some of the information in the chapter can be used to manage more effectively. Usually, an explanation will be offered as to how the information under consideration relates to productivity (performance) and morale or job satisfaction.

The text is organized in a conventional way that seems to fit the preferences of many instructors in the field. Part I describes the nature of OB; then it explains how information in the field is gathered and how that information is applied by managerial workers and OB specialists. Parts II and III may be considered "micro OB," since they deal with understanding individuals and small groups, respectively. Part IV is "macro OB," understanding the larger organization and its relationship with the external environment. Included in Part IV is an inside look at bureaucracy, since so many readers of this book are now or will be dealing with bureaucratic organizations.

Foundations of Organizational Behavior contains a number of features to enhance its value as a text and an experiential manual. Each chapter begins with a set of learning objectives that headline key chapter topics. The objectives are followed by a chapter opening case that sets the stage for an applications-oriented approach to learning the chapter information. As mentioned, the text is sprinkled with relevant and current examples and illustrations. The section called "Implications for Managerial Practice" guides the reader further toward on-the-job application of OB knowledge.

The summary included in each chapter is designed to serve as a narrative outline of the chapter and an extension of the learning objectives. The "Questions for Discussion" are designed for individual or small-group discussion. All chapters contain "An Organizational Behavior Problem" (including role playing). The selections in the "Additional Reading" sections are from both theoretical and applied sources. We have attempted to cite accessible books and journals.

The reader is invited to make use of the glossary at the end of the book. Part of learning the foundations of any field is to acquire a grounding in its basic terms. The glossary to this text defines key terms that have not already been formally defined in the body of the text. A glossary can also be quite helpful in preparing for an exam.

Acknowledgments

An author of a book of this nature acts as a synthesizer, collector, and integrator of the published and unpublished ideas of many people. Footnotes in the text, however scrupulously inserted, indicate the source of only some of the ideas. Many students of mine at the Rochester Institute of Technology uncovered case illustrations that have worked their way into my writings. Among the groups of people who have furnished me with useful insights into organizational behavior are my colleagues, attendees at my talks and workshops, and clients of mine.

My primary thanks go to the editorial, marketing, and production staffs at the college text division of Prentice-Hall for getting this book into the marketplace. The outside reviewers on this project contributed a number of constructive suggestions that are incorporated into the final draft of this project. By name and organization they are as follows: M. K. Badawy, Cleveland State University; J. Clifton Williams, Baylor University; Angelo S. De Nisi, University of South Carolina; Bernard S. Stern, Villanova University; and Gerald L. Rose, The University of Iowa.

A special note of thanks is due Maria Jeremias, the woman-in-my-life during the heavy work on this project. She has served as my confidante, major source of emotional support, and somebody with whom to share both joy and discouragement.

Andrew J. DuBrin

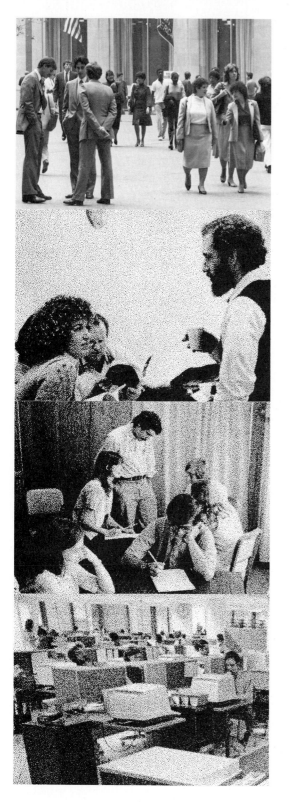

PART ONE

Introduction to Organizational Behavior

Part I has two critical purposes. One is to set a conceptual base for understanding the meaning and nature of organizational behavior. In Chapter 1 we define organizational behavior (OB) and show its relationship to other fields that the student has already or is likely to encounter. Instead of a complicated model of OB that attempts to interrelate all chapters in the text, we provide a state-of-the-art look at key characteristics and dimensions of the field. The second purpose is to explain how the information base of OB is obtained (for example, through experimental research, case observation, and questionnaires) and how that information is applied. By illustration of a career problem, you are shown how a practicing manager may apply a knowledge of OB (see Chapter 2).

The diagnostic model recommended in Chapter 2 for applying organizational behavior knowledge should be reviewed from time to time as you work your way through this text. It represents a sensible game plan for improving one's effectiveness in managing people.

Introduction to Organizational Behavior

The top management of a diversified food manufacturing company was becoming increasingly concerned about its packaging design department. Substantial evidence had accumulated that the company lagged behind the competition in developing new and interesting packages for both established and newer products. As one senior vice president expressed it, "Our packaging design experts are paid to be innovative. But instead of being innovative, they time and time again arrive at ideas that are different, but not particularly useful. Our packaging design people were all carefully chosen for their creative potential. There's no good reason to assume that we hired the wrong people. Maybe it's that we're doing something wrong in the way that we manage them."*

After discussing his concerns with other members of top management, the senior vice president asked a behavioral science consultant working for the company to investigate the problem. The consultant responded, "Your hunch about the company doing something wrong sounds plausible. But it would be professionally unsound for me to agree or disagree with you without first gathering some information about the problem."

The consultant spent the next two weeks interviewing a large cross-sample of people from the packaging design department, including the director and clerical help. She informed the director and other department members that she was gathering information about improving the productivity of the packaging design department. The employees were also told that they would later receive feedback about her study.

The initial report prepared by the consultant suggested strongly that the problem lay with the director of the department. His authoritarian approach to decision making was dampening the creativity of people below him. People throughout the department indicated that although they had considerable respect for the administrative skills and technical expertise of their director, he tended to overedit the ideas coming out of his department.

The consultant shared these perceptions with the director to obtain his reaction to her findings. Rather than being defensive, the director enlisted the help of the consultant in developing a decision-making style that would foster, rather than dampen creativity among subordinates. A six-month follow-up revealed that the director did change his style and several more innovative packaging designs were generated by the department.

THE FIELD OF ORGANIZATIONAL BEHAVIOR

The case just described illustrates how an understanding of human behavior in organizations can contribute to individual satisfaction and organizational effectiveness. By judiciously applying an accepted concept of organizational behavior, the consultant was able to figure out the true nature of the problem facing the company. Despite this isolated successful case, complete answers to why organizations have problems involving people have yet to be found. But a field of study has emerged to help unravel the complexities of organizations and the people in them.

*Innovation is said to refer to original ideas that have an applied value, while creativity refers to ideas that are original, but not developed to the point where they yet have an applied value.

Organizational behavior is generally defined as the study of human behavior in organizations. To confuse matters just a little, the field is sometimes divided into micro and macro OB, as is done in the field of economics. The primary emphasis of micro OB is on the individual and small-group level. In contrast, macro OB (or organizational theory) places its emphasis on the level of the total organization and the interaction of the organization with the outside environment.

From the standpoint of having a formal label, organizational behavior dates back to the early 1960s. However, the two direct roots of OB, social psychology and human relations, extend back to the early 1930s. Today, human relations is essentially a less technical and more applied version of OB. A later section of this chapter briefly examines the relationship of OB to its closely allied fields. You are forewarned that since most fields, disciplines, and professions dealing with people at work overlap considerably, unequivocal distinctions among them are difficult to draw. In addition, the distinctions are not always so vital, particularly when one deals with the application of knowledge. For instance, about twelve different disciplines currently study job stress. It is more important that distressed workers receive help than that the correct discipline receives credit for developing a particular concept about stress.

What Is an Organization?

To understand OB you need to understand the concept of organization as it is used in this context. To many people, an organization is a social or community group such as the YMCA, YWCA, Toronto Birdwatchers Society, or the San Diego Community Center. To a behavioral scientist, manager, or staff professional, an organization is also an entire place of work, or a big chunk thereof. An organization can be defined more formally as "a collection of interacting and interdependent individuals who work toward common goals and whose relationships are determined according to a certain structure."[1]

Even though a family or a scout troup might be classified as an organization, OB typically deals with larger structures whose work is primarily nonrecreational. Thus OB investigations have been carried out in the factory, plant, office, mill, church, synagogue, and library.

What Is Behavior?

Since organizational behavior is the study of human behavior in organizations, it is essential for a student of OB to grasp the concept, "behavior." *Time* magazine regularly runs a section called "Behavior" that deals with relevant topics in psychology or closely related disciplines. Although psychology is considered to be the science of behavior, many other disciplines are also concerned with behavior. Only in rare circumstances can a person avoid dealing with behavior of some sort. One exception would be a stranded astronaut or cosmonaut who was left alone contemplating the moon sur-

[1]W. Jack Duncan, *Organizational Behavior,* 2nd ed. (Boston: Houghton Mifflin, 1981), p. 8.

face and its atmosphere. Behavior is a comprehensive concept referring to almost anything done by living organisms.

A sales representative is behaving when he or she closes a sale; a first-level supervisor is behaving when he or she fires a subordinate; you are behaving when you are reading this book and thinking about the application of this information to your life. Behavior has been formally defined as "the tangible acts or decisions of individuals, groups, or organizations."[2] Thus what you do is your behavior. Some behaviorists would also include inner processes such as thinking, feeling, and dreaming as aspects of behavior.

KEY CHARACTERISTICS OF ORGANIZATIONAL BEHAVIOR

An understanding of the key characteristics of OB will help you to develop a fuller appreciation of the concept. Many of the topics to be discussed in this book reflect these characteristics. Six of them are considered next.[3]

Interdisciplinary Foundation

Similar to most new and emerging fields, OB has borrowed many of its core concepts from other fields and disciplines. For example, many of the topics studied in industrial/organizational psychology courses of yesterday (and today) are found today in OB courses. Among these topics are leadership, motivation, and performance evaluation. The statistical procedures and experimental designs found in the OB literature are quite similar to those used in business research, behavioral sciences, and social sciences.

Behavioral Science Foundation

As already suggested, OB is heavily dependent upon the behavioral sciences for its knowledge base. Psychology, sociology, and anthropology are considered the primary behavioral sciences. Each is concerned with the systematic study of behavior. Of the three fields, psychology has had the biggest impact on OB. Many of the classic contributors to the field (such as Maslow, McGregor, Herzberg, and Likert) are psychologists by training and education. Many courses in organizational behavior are titled "behavioral sciences in management," reflecting further the behavioral science foundation in OB.

---

[2]Andrew D. Szilagyi, Jr. and Marc J. Wallace, Jr., *Organizational Behavior and Performance,* 2nd ed. (Glenview, Ill.: Scott, Foresman and Company, 1980), p. 625.

[3]Ibid., p. 13.

Scientific Method

OB uses many different methods to obtain information, including direct observations of people at work, the case study method, and old-fashioned armchair speculation. However, the use of the scientific method is given top priority in attempting to predict and explain behavior. Several journals in the OB field accept only those articles based on the scientific method. Chapter 2 provides additional information about the use of the scientific method in producing OB knowledge.

Three Levels of Analysis

OB as a field is primarily concerned with an analysis and understanding of individuals, small groups, and organizations. Micro OB concentrates on the first two levels, whereas macro OB concentrates on the third level plus the interface of organizations and the outside environment. About four-fifths of the topics in this text are primarily micro OB; the other fifth is primarily macro.

Contingency Orientation

As illustrated by the consultant in the insurance company, OB takes a contingency approach to most problems. The concept of individual differences dictates that each situation be studied on its own merits, using general principles of behavior as a guide. For instance, we know that in general people respond well to rewards. The task of the applied behaviorist is to discover which rewards will work in a given situation. A team of two researchers and authors put it this way:

> The organizational behavior field has no universally applicable set of prescriptions for managers. Instead, the contingency theme, which encourages the development of action plans that are based on the situation and the people involved, is considered the most relevant.[4]

Concern for Application

OB researchers have always aimed to generate knowledge that the manager and staff professional could put into practice in an organizational setting. The entire behavioral school of management is, in essence, an application of OB knowledge to job settings. A major objective of the current text is to present systematic knowledge about human behavior in organizations that should prove of value to practitioners. To cite one of hundreds of possible examples, if you apply goal-setting theory to your job, your performance (and that of your subordinates) is likely to improve. OB knowledge can be

[4]This and the preceding five subhead topics are from ibid., p. 13.

applied at the individual, group, or organizational level. Since individuals and small groups are easier to control ("get a handle on"), OB has been applied more frequently to those levels than to total organizations.[5]

A DIMENSIONAL CHARACTERIZATION OF OB

Additional insight into the characteristics of the field of OB is provided by Larry L. Cummings' conception of the direction in which the field is evolving (as presented in Figure 1–1). Three dimensions define the conceptual domain of OB (or three characteristics define organizational behavior).[6]

First, OB is *a way of thinking* that can be characterized by five postures: (1) the formulation of problems and questions in a dependent-independent variable framework, (2) an orientation toward change as a desirable outcome for organizations and its members, (3) a distinctly humanistic tone reflected in concern for self-development, personal growth, and self-actualization, (4) a job performance orientation with more studies using performance or productivity as the dependent variable, and (5) use of the discipline imposed by the scientific method.

Second, OB is *a body of constructs, models, and facts.* Support for this notion comes from the fact that most OB texts show a reasonable degree of agreement as to what basic topics should be included in the field. As with any field, there is a shifting of emphasis over time. Some new topics gradually become part of the knowledge of the field, and some others fade from inclusion. Group dynamics and interpersonal communication have always been part of OB. In recent years, organization power and politics have emerged as a topic covered in many current texts.

Third, OB is *a system of technology.* Today, techniques exist for such ends as training leaders, designing jobs, designing organizations, evaluating performances, rewarding behaviors, making people more assertive, and modeling behaviors. New techniques continue to emerge. Unfortunately, not all these techniques have been carefully evaluated before they are offered to the public. The techniques with an admirable batting average—such as programs of positive reinforcement—are based on substantial empirical evidence and an established body of behavioral (or psychological) theory.

As shown in Figure 1–1, three themes span the dimensions defining OB. The relative emphasis given to each theme over time by practitioners and theorists of OB determines our way of thinking, constructs and facts, and the development of techniques.

First is *existentialism,* which among many other tenets, contends that the final responsibility for designing productive and satisfying organizations rests with human beings. Existentialism also contends that all meaning is relative rather than absolute,

---

[5]Ibid.

[6]Based on Larry L. Cummings, "Toward Organizational Behavior," *Academy of Management Review,* January 1978, pp. 90–98.

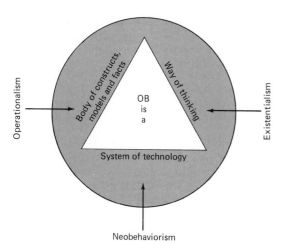

FIGURE 1-1 Dimensions and Themes of Organizational Behavior

Source: Reprinted from Larry L. Cummings, "Toward Organizational Behavior," *Academy of Management Review,* January 1978, p. 93. Used with permission.

which makes OB a complex discipline. Activities and outcomes in a job environment must always be related back to a human purpose. Existentialism might also be considered the philosophical basis for the contingency nature of OB. For instance, what was done (such as a team building session for managers) is good or bad, depending upon with whom it was done and for what purpose.

Second is *operationalism,* the doctrine that the meaning of a proposition consists of the operations performed in proving it or applying it to a specific situation. An operational definition of poor performance would include a list of the actual behaviors engaged in by the person who was said to be performing poorly. To illustrate the operationalism of OB, the literature is beginning to be characterized by such questions as

1. Through what operations is structure actually designed?
2. Through what operations does a leader impact a subordinate?
3. Through what operations do rewards and punishments effect change?
4. Through what operations do groups actually make decisions?[7]

As a consequence of operationalism, the field of OB is highly concerned about the measurement of phenomena. For example, how do you reliably and validly measure whether an employee is motivated, satisfied, or both?

Third is *neobehaviorism,* an offshoot of behaviorism. The behaviorist school of psychology believes that behavior is shaped by its consequences. Thus the rewards that people receive for their actions influence them more than do their inner needs, thoughts, or attitudes. Much of OB today has moved toward a behavioristic orientation, with a simultaneous concern about the cognitions (intellectual processes) of people. Motivation theory, under the influence of behavior modification and expectancy models, has moved in this direction (see Chapter 3). Leadership studies also reflect

[7]Ibid., p. 95.

neobehaviorism. They emphasize the goal-oriented actions of the leader and the fact that what the leader does in the future is shaped to some extent by the consequences of his or her actions.

Another way of communicating the nature of OB is to show the relationships between OB and several of its related fields.

OB AND ITS RELATED FIELDS

By the early 1980s the entire field of studying the human element in organizations had separated into a number of overlapping subfields. The six specialty areas closest to OB are *organizational psychology, organization theory, organization development, personnel and human resource management, personnel psychology,* and *management.* To add a note of confusion, there are other fields that deal with typical OB topics. Among them are psychiatry, industrial engineering, social psychology, and communication theory.

Organizational Psychology

Defined as the study of the interplay of people and organizations, organizational psychology places heavy emphasis on the study of groups. The historic roots of the human relations movement and organizational psychology are almost identical. The focus in organizational psychology is placed on understanding universal principles of human behavior rather than individual differences. Organizational psychology is a major component of OB, as revealed by a comparison of the table of contents of texts in both fields. In short, organizational psychology is almost indistinguishable from organizational behavior except that the latter tends to be taught in colleges of business rather than in departments of psychology.

Organization Theory (OT)

OT attempts to provide an explanatory set of concepts to understand the phenomena of organizations. The field is typically defined by its focus upon the organization as the unit of analysis. In contrast to organizational behavior, which draws primarily from psychology, organizational theory is grounded in the sociology of organizations. OT is sometimes referred to as macro OB, reflecting its emphasis on the total organization and its relationship to the external environment. Among the relevant dependent variables in OT are organizational structure, process, goals, technology, and organizational climate. The independent variables (those manipulated) are typically differences in environmental characteristics such as job design.[8]

Despite the valid distinctions just made, few organizational theorists ignore the

[8]Ibid., p. 91.

influence of people one at a time. And few organizational behaviorists ignore the influence of the total organization. Differences between these two fields—and among any of the fields mentioned in this subsection—are a question of emphasis. We are not dealing with rigid boundaries among OB, OT, OD, and so forth.

Organization Development (OD)

From one standpoint, OD is the application of the concepts and techniques of OB, OT, and related disciplines. Some individuals who apply the concepts, methods, and techniques of behavioral science to improve individual and organizational effectiveness call themselves OD specialists. The term OD is generally taken to refer collectively to an assortment of interventions whose purpose is assumed to be improvement of individuals and its members. OD is so comprehensive in scope and integrates so much information about OB that it is the subject of the final chapter in this text.

Personnel and Human Resource Management (PHRM)

Also referred to as personnel or personnel administration, PHRM is that organizational function that provides specialized concepts, methods, techniques, and professional judgment geared toward effective and efficient utilization of human resources.[9] Thus a personnel specialist would apply a wide variety of techniques to help the organization manage its resources. Among them would be performance evaluation programs, job analysis, personnel testing, and affirmative action programs. OB is considered more basic than PHRM, whereas the latter is more applied in nature. PHRM is much more technique oriented. Nevertheless there is considerable overlap between OB and PHRM. Both fields, for example, are vitally concerned with evaluating and rewarding (or sometimes punishing) employees.

Personnel Psychology

The relationship between OB and personnel psychology is quite similar to that between OB and PHRM. If you glance through several issues of *Personnel Psychology,* you will notice that some of the studies deal with topics of interest to students of OB. Leadership and decision making are two prime examples. Personnel psychology conducts research and offers advice on almost every aspect of human resource management. Personnel psychologists study methods of selection, recruitment, career development, management development, and organization development, among other topics. The field is sometimes considered the scientific underpinnings (or the sibling) of personnel and human resource management.

---

[9]The present scope of PHRM is described in Joyce D. Ross, "A Definition of Human Resource Management," *Personnel Journal,* October 1981, pp. 781–83.

Management

Many readers of this book have taken a course in management principles, management concepts, or introduction to management. Texts in this field usually use the title "management." Most of these management texts contain a good deal of emphasis on OB since organizational behavior can properly be considered to reflect the behavioral school of management. The field of OB represents a critical one-third of the field of management. The behavioral school of management is in essence the application of OB to managing people and organizations. Some introductory management courses are so behaviorally oriented that they use an OB rather than a management text.

The behavioral approach to management followed the classical school, developed originally by production engineers. Among its components was scientific management, a movement advanced by the works of Frederick W. Taylor.[10] In some ways the behavioral approach was a reaction against the "efficiency expert" orientation of Taylor and his disciples. The studies of informal organization and morale conducted at Western Electric by a team of Harvard researchers have been quoted in virtually every book about management, OB, or OT (at least until recently). Their findings were the forerunners of the human relations movement of the late 1940s and 1950s.[11]

Human relations in industry (and part of the roots of OB) was thus founded upon a dramatic example of serendipity. The Hawthorne effect—an increase in productivity stemming from the mere fact that people felt that management cared about them—came about because of experiments designed to investigate the efficacy of modifying physical working conditions.

The third component of management thought, the management science or quantitative approach, has more relationship to OB than is generally recognized. OB relies heavily upon statistical techniques to test hypotheses and conduct surveys. Despite this heavy respect for and involvement in experimental design and statistics, many people regard OB as the qualitative approach to management and management science school as the quantitative approach. No amount of explanation seems to be able to change this perception.

Management Information Systems (MIS)

As an offshoot of the data processing revolution, a new field has emerged that offers systems for coping with the baffling amount of information brought to management's attention. Labeled management information systems, it refers to "The people and equipment used in the selection, storing, processing, and retrieving of information re-

[10]The original source here is Frederick W. Taylor, *Scientific Management* (New York: Harper & Row, 1911). Most management texts of several years ago summarized the works of Taylor at length.

[11]An original source of information about the Hawthorne studies is Elton Mayo, *The Human Problems of an Industrial Civilization* (New York: Viking Press, 1960). A useful summary and synthesis of these classic studies is found in Thomas J. Atchison and Winston W. Hill, *Management Today: Managing Work in Organizations* (New York: Harcourt Brace Jovanovich, 1978), pp. 35–39.

quired in the management decision-making process."[12] Today most large organizations have an MIS department, and many schools of business or computer science offer at least one course entitled "MIS." OB ties in directly with MIS since an MIS practitioner needs an understanding of hardware, software, and the behavioral aspects of processing information. Among the OB topics that tie in with MIS are communication, decision making, creativity, and political factors in the control of information. As Jeffrey Pfeffer explains,

> The design and incorporation of management information systems into the organization is another element of structure than can be analyzed from a political perspective. The existing literature on information systems is primarily normative in orientation, and argues about what file structures, table layouts, and degree of comprehensiveness should be incorporated in order to improve managerial decision making. Yet information and control over information is an important source of power in organizations. Thus, it is inevitable that the design and location of information systems will be entwined with the struggle for power which occurs in many organizations.[13]

In line with its relationship with MIS, OB is also of value to such seemingly unrelated disciplines as accounting and finance. A key linking topic between these disciplines and OB is the management of employee attitudes toward a new control system. The installation of a new system typically encounters resistance to change from employees who are concerned that the system will have negative consequences for them. Unless this resistance is managed properly, the new system will not live up to its expectations.

Again, the student or practitioner should not be overly concerned about the nuances of differences (and the jurisdictional disputes) among OB and its related fields. It is much more important to embrace whatever concepts and techniques are useful in understanding and managing human behavior in organizations.

SOURCES OF INFORMATION ABOUT ORGANIZATIONAL BEHAVIOR

An information explosion is taking place within the field of knowledge that deals with the work behavior of humans. Among the various information sources are general texts, books of readings, speciality texts, trade (nontechnical or general audience) books, films, tape cassettes, trade magazines, newspapers, and scholarly or scientific journals. The references and list of suggested reading at the end of each chapter provide useful guidelines to printed information about OB.

[12]Robert L. Trewatha and M. Gene Newport, *Management,* 3rd ed. (Plano, Tex.: Business Publications, 1982), p. 338.

[13]Jeffrey Pfeffer, *Power in Organizations* (Marshfield, Mass.: Pitman, 1981), p. 275.

Journals

The primary source of information about OB is scholarly and scientific journals. Both general and speciality texts, and sometimes trade books, rely on journal articles as their basic source of information. Scientific studies reported in journals tend to be the basic building block of knowledge in most scientific or scholarly fields.

Listed here are twenty-five journals in which a formal knowledge of OB is found. Many of these journals contain articles that are difficult to comprehend unless the reader has a working knowledge of the scientific method and statistics. Two such journals are *Administrative Science Quarterly* and the *Journal of Applied Psychology*. In contrast, the *Harvard Business Review* is written primarily for the practicing manager or staff professional. Beginners in the field can usually comprehend these articles. The editors of *HBR* consider it a "magazine," not a scientific journal.

1. *Academy of Management Journal*
2. *Academy of Management Review*
3. *Administrative Management*
4. *Administrative Science Quarterly*
5. *Advanced Management Journal*
6. *American Sociological Review*
7. *Business Horizons*
8. *Business Topics*
9. *California Management Review*
10. *Group and Organization Studies*
11. *Human Relations*
12. *Industrial and Labor Relations Review*
13. *Journal of Applied Behavioral Science*
14. *Journal of Applied Psychology*
15. *Journal of Business Administration*
16. *Journal of Management Studies*
17. *Journal of Occupational Psychology*
18. *Organizational Behavior and Human Performance*
19. *Organizational Dynamics*
20. *Personnel*
21. *Personnel Administrator* (formerly, *The Personnel Administrator*)
22. *Personnel Journal*
23. *Personnel Psychology*
24. *Sloan Management Review*
25. *Training and Development Journal*

Trade and General Audience Magazines

A person intent on acquiring knowledge about OB should selectively examine a variety of nontechnical sources. Information in these sources is sometimes based upon scientific research. At other times, such information serves as a stimulus to scientific research. For example, in the later 1960s and early 1970s, trade magazines such as *Industry Week* and *Dun's Review* featured articles about organizational stress and organizational power and politics. In subsequent years, formal OB journals contained research studies about these topics. Listed next is a selection of magazines and nontechnical journals that often contain informative and entertaining articles relevant to organizational behavior.

1. *Business Week*
2. *Dun's Review*
3. *Fortune*
4. *Industry Week*
5. *International Management*
6. *Management Review* (could also be classified in previous list)
7. *Nation's Business*
8. *The New York Times Magazine*
9. *Product Management*
10. *Psychology Today*
11. *Success*
12. *The Financial Post*
13. *The Wall Street Journal*
14. *Time*
15. *U.S. News & World Report*

OB AND COMMON SENSE

A middle manager commented after having read through several chapters of an organizational behavior text, "Why should I study this field, it's just common sense? My job involves dealing with people and you can't learn that through a book." The sentiments expressed by this manager are shared by many other students of management or organizational behavior. However logical such an opinion might sound, common sense is not a fully adequate substitute for knowledge about OB for several reasons.

One reason is that common sense is uncommon. Few people are effective in dealing with people or organizational forces. If common sense (natural wisdom not requiring formal knowledge) were widely held, there would be fewer problems involving people in work organizations.

A second reason for studying organizational behavior is that common sense takes a long time to acquire. Formal knowledge thus helps one to acquire wisdom in a shorter period of time than what might take years by means of trial and error. After reading this book, you might be sensitized to the importance of confronting problems rather than suppressing them. You might achieve the same insight after five years of dealing with conflict. However, five years of mismanaged conflict is a heavy price to pay.

A third reason is that a study of organizational behavior sharpens and refines common sense. You may know through common sense that giving recognition to people is generally an effective method of motivating them toward higher performance. Through a study of organizational behavior you might learn that recognition should be given frequently but not always when somebody attains high performance. Thus formal knowledge enhances your current effectiveness.

Summary

- Organizational behavior is the study of human behavior in organizations. Micro organizational behavior concentrates on the individual and small-group level, whereas macro organizational behavior concentrates on the total organization and its interface with the external environment. An organization is a collection of interacting and interdependent individuals who work toward common goals and whose relationships are determined according to a certain structure. Behavior can be defined as the tangible acts or decision of individuals, groups, or organizations.

- OB as a field of study has certain key characteristics, including (1) an interdisciplinary foundation; (2) a behavioral science foundation; (3) emphasis on the scientific method; (4) analysis at the individual, small-group, and organization levels; (5) contingency orientation; and (6) concern for application.

- Three dimensions define the conceptual domain of OB. First, OB is a way of thinking about people in organizations. Second, OB is a body of constructs, models, and facts. Third, OB is a system of technology (or techniques for application). Three themes influence these dimensions of OB: existentialism, operationalism, and neobehaviorism.

- In understanding the nature and scope of OB, it is helpful to compare it with six closely related fields. Organizational psychology (OP) covers essentially the same information but tends to be taught in psychology departments. Organization theory (OT) is basically macro OB. Organization development (OD) is basically the application of techniques of OB, OT, and related disciplines. Personnel and human resource management (PHRM) is essentially a study of the personnel function in an organization, using some OB knowledge plus knowledge of its own. Personnel psychology is that branch of industrial/organizational psychology that deals with personnel techniques, thus overlapping with OB. Management is a broad field dealing with accomplishing things with and through people. The behavioral school of management is essentially OB applied to managing people and organizations. The fields just mentioned overlap with OB and with each other.

    MIS is an example of a new field that may find the application of OB knowledge useful in carrying out its mission. A management information system refers to the people and equipment used in the selection, storing, processing, and retrieving of information required in the decision-making process.

- Common sense is not a fully adequate substitute for knowledge about organizational behavior for several reasons. One is that common sense is uncommon. Second is that common sense takes a long time to acquire. Third is that the study of OB sharpens and refines common sense.

Questions for Discussion

1. Which levels of management do you think value OB the most? Why?
2. If OB knowledge is so useful, why is it that many successful executives have never even heard of the field?
3. Identify one or two provisions of the psychological contract drawn between you and the instructor in this course.
4. A professor of OB explained to her class that the course would emphasize the application of knowledge. A man seated in class asked, "Why else would anybody take a management course?" How would you answer his question?
5. How would you operationally define a manager?
6. To what extent is OB knowledge useful for a worker not in a managerial position?
7. By the year 1990, the vast majority of managers will have taken an OB course or have studied some form of OB. What effect do you think this will have on the practice of management?
8. In what way has the success of Japanese management given impetus to the use of applied OB in America?
9. How does OB fit into the computer age?

An Organizational Behavior Problem

"We Can't Afford Behavioral Science Around Here"

Todd was happy to be hired by Bradbury Foods as a first-level supervisor in its main processing plant. It was apparent to him that being a supervisor so soon after graduation from business school would be a real boost to his career. After about one month on the job, Todd began to make some critical observations about the company and its management style. He began to wonder if the company was somewhat behind the times in its management practices.

To clarify things in his own mind, Todd requested a meeting with Adam Green, plant superintendent. The meeting between Todd and Adam included dialogue of this nature:

Adam: Have a seat, Todd. It's nice to visit with one of our young supervisors, particularly when you didn't say you were facing an emergency that you and your boss couldn't handle.

Todd: (Nervously) Mr. Green, I want to express my appreciation for your willingness to meet with me. You're right, I'm not facing an emergency. But I do wonder about something. That's what I came here to talk to you about.

Adam: That's what I like to see. A young man who takes the initiative to ask questions about things that are bothering him.

Todd: To be quite truthful, Mr. Green, I am happy here and I'm glad I joined Bradbury Foods. But I'm curious about one thing. As you may know, I'm a graduate of a business college. A few of the courses I took emphasized using behavioral science knowledge to manage people. You know, kind of psychology on the job. It seems like the way to go if you want to keep people productive and happy.

Here at Bradbury it seems that nobody uses behavioral science knowledge. I know you're a successful company. But some of the management practices seem out of keeping with the times. The managers make all the decisions. Everybody else listens and carries out orders. Even professionals on the payroll have to punch time clocks. I've been here for almost two months and I haven't even heard the term participative management used once.

Adam: Oh, I get your point. You're talking about using behavioral science around here. I know all about that. The point you're missing, Todd, is that behavioral science is for the big profitable companies. That stuff works great when business is good and profit margins are high. But around here business is kind of so-so, and profit margins in the food business are thinner than a potato chip. Maybe someday when we get fat and profitable we can start using behavioral science. In the mean time, we've all got a job to do.

Todd: I appreciate your candid answer, Mr. Green. But when I was in college, I certainly heard a different version of why companies use behaviorally oriented management.

Questions

1. What is your evaluation of Adam's contention that OB knowledge is useful primarily when a firm is profitable?
2. To what extent should Todd be discouraged?
3. What should Todd do?
4. Based on your experience, how representative of most managers is Adam Green's thinking?

Additional Reading

HAMNER, W. CLAY, ed. *Organizational Shock.* New York: John Wiley, 1980.

HERSHEY, ROBERT. "Executive Miscalculations." *University of Michigan Business Review,* September 1979, pp. 1–7.

LATHAM, GARY P., LARRY L. CUMMINGS, and TERENCE R. MITCHELL. "Behavioral Strategies to Improve Productivity." *Organizational Dynamics,* Winter 1981, pp. 5–23.

NAYLOR, JAMES C., ROBERT D. PRICHARD, and DANIEL R. ILGEN. *A Theory of Behavior in Organizations.* New York: Academic Press, 1980.

ORGAN, DENNIS W. "Organizational Behavior as an Area of Study: Some Questions and Answers," in Dennis W. Organ, ed., *The Applied Psychology of Work Behavior: A Book of Readings.* Plano, Tex.: Business Publications, 1978, pp. 2–7.

SAUNDERS, CAROL STOAK. "Management Information Systems, Communications, and Departmental Power: An Integrative Model." *Academy of Management Review,* July 1981, pp. 431–42.

SKINNER, WICKHAM. "Big Hat, No Cattle: Managing Human Resources." *Harvard Business Review,* September–October 1981, pp. 106–14.

CHAPTER 2

Research Methods in Organizational Behavior

LEARNING OBJECTIVES

1. To understand how research and theory contribute to knowledge of organizational behavior.

2. To specify at least four different methods of data collection for acquiring knowledge about OB.

3. To explain the essential differences among a case study, field study, and an experiment.

4. To be aware of potential sources of error in OB research.

5. To develop a preliminary strategy for applying OB knowledge in an organizational setting.

John Coleman, agency chief at Sierra County Vocational Rehabilitation Services, spoke with enthusiasm to Irv Chandler, vice president of Human Resources at NATCO Insurance: "Irv, your willingness to let us conduct this research could have nationwide significance for hiring the handicapped. If our results are nearly as good as I think they will be, your company and my agency will be considered leaders in the field of creating better employment opportunities for the handicapped."

"I didn't quite look at your proposed training program and its evaluation as glory building for us, but I am enthused. I've also committed a sizable budget for the project, as we've already discussed. I've read your prospectus on the program and it looks fine. But could you just give me a brief overview of what you intend to do?"

"My overall design is straightforward," said John Coleman. "Based on a careful study of what we know about leadership climate and job performance, I've come up with the following strategy. If the supervisors of handicapped employees give them ample support and reassurance, the job performance of the handicapped employees will be above average. To test this hypothesis, two of my rehabilitation specialists will coach your supervisors of handicapped employees on such matters as giving reassurance and projecting warmth.

"After this supportive climate is in operation for six months, we'll measure the job performance of handicapped workers in several ways. We'll record their performance evaluations, their absenteeism, and their turnover. We will take measures on handicapped workers in the three job categories in which they have been placed at NATCO: professional, technical, and clerical.

"As you are well aware, we'll need to make some comparisons with handicapped workers who do not work in a supportive climate. We can examine the records of another company that hires handicapped workers through our agency. So far we have not approached them about our training program for establishing a supportive leadership climate."

As planned, John and his staff implemented their supportive climate training program. The data for the study were collected within sixty days after the six-month period. John was ecstatic about the results. The average performance rating score for the handicapped workers in all job categories was 3.83 versus 3.01 for employees in general at NATCO. (Under its system, 5 is a maximum performance evaluation and 1 is minimum.) Absenteeism was 6.23 percent versus 7.13 percent for the employees in general. Turnover was 11.23 percent for the handicapped group versus 17.45 percent for employees in general.

The comparisons with handicapped workers in another company served by the agency (but which did not use the supportive training program) were slightly less conclusive. Converted to a comparable scale, the mean performance rating for handicapped employees at the other firm was 3.46, absenteeism was 6.51 percent, and turnover was 10.78 percent.

John then suggested that Irv and he prepare a written report of these findings and make them public knowledge. "We've got to be proud of these results. My agency and your company have taken a big step forward in collecting hard data about hiring the handicapped."

Irv explained patiently, "John, I'm also enthused about what we've done. But let's not rush to print or formulate policy too soon. I've shown this report to Marion Rudolph, our behavioral science consultant. Let's call her in and have her summarize her concerns about our study. I regret somewhat that we didn't think of consulting her when we were planning the study."

Rudolph explained to John and Irv, "I'm as enthusiastic about creating better opportunities for the handicapped as you are. Yet my scientific values have to be reckoned with my humanitarian values. In a nutshell here are some of the concerns I have about the merit of the study:

"First of all, at NATCO you have hired the cream of the crop of handicapped job applicants. So generalizations to the total population of handicapped workers must be made gingerly.

"Second, there may be a big element of subjectivity in the performance evaluations. You have coached the su-pervisors on how to elevate the performance of one group of workers. If the supervisors give high ratings to these workers, it would make them feel they are doing a good job in being supportive. You are creating the conditions for unconsciously manipulating the data in a positive direction.

"Third, we don't know if the supervisors really became more supportive because of your training program. They might have been just as supportive as before.

"I dislike using the oldest cliché in my field, but more research is needed."

THE CONTRIBUTION OF THEORY
AND RESEARCH

The potential contribution of theory and research is illustrated in the NATCO situation. The tentative theory (or perhaps a well-reasoned hypothesis) espoused was that a supportive leadership climate enhances job performance. Several theories of leadership include this proposition or at least emphasize that a leader being considerate of the feelings of subordinates often enhances job performance (see Chapter 12). The NATCO situation also illustrates that research may be necessary to provide answers to applied problems in organizational behavior. In this instance, two top-level managers were willing to pool their resources to investigate whether or not a supportive leadership climate improved the job performance of handicapped employees. Also illustrated is that field research of this nature is fraught with potential errors.

Many people with job experience taking their first course in management or organizational behavior comment, "Skip the theory and research, let's get to the practical applications. I'm taking this course so I can improve my effectiveness on the job." This text is oriented toward the application of behavioral science knowledge to job settings, but we have not capitulated completely to the sentiments expressed in the comment just cited. Sound research, followed by sound theory, leads to generalizations that will enable you to function more effectively as a manager or individual contributor. A case in point is the accumulated wisdom about goal setting. Behavioral scientists have demonstrated through research that the establishment of realistic goals (not too hard, not too easy) leads to improved performance. Practitioners of management can now use such knowledge as a guide to action. Thomas H. Jerdee explains how theory and research contribute to organizational behavior:

> Theory is simply the orderly summarization of verified knowledge about phenomena and their interrelationships. As such, it is the wellspring of human progress in mastering our environment. True theory can be no more inflexible or constraining than reality itself. Furthermore, theory itself is not prescriptive. Prescriptions for action must be derived from theory, and different people may reasonably derive varying prescriptions from the same theory, depending on their values and priorities. Here, perhaps, is where the real gap between theoretician and practitioner develops, rather than in regard to theory itself.
>
> The building of sound organizational behavior theory depends on systematic, verifiable observation of behavioral phenomena, both in the laboratory and in the field. . .
>
> Organizational behavior research, if it is to contribute to the building of good theory, must be cumulative, with each contributor carefully relating his or her own observations to the knowledge gained by others. By employing such procedures during the last 50 years, behavioral scientists have built an impressive theoretical basis for action in the areas of human assessment, development, motivation, group behavior, leadership, negotiation, conflict resolution, and organizational governance. Even greater progress can be expected during the next half century if we continue to devote energy and resources to the task.[1]

These comments should not be interpreted to mean that theory never precedes data collection. In practice, a strong theoretical position can lead to experimentation that sheds light on the adequacy of that particular theory. One researcher might develop a theory based on observation that organizations are effective to the extent that they have good sensing mechanisms to interpret their environments. The researcher might call this theory the "sensor theory of organizational effectiveness." A number of studies might then be conducted comparing organizations that sense the environment well with those that sense the environment poorly. If the latter group tends to be less effective than the former group, support has been found for the theory. As more data are collected, the theory may be further refined. Data collection usually precedes theory, but theory may also precede the collection of data. Good theory leads to good research in organizational behavior as well as in other fields.

An important purpose of the theories presented in this book is to help understand phenomena in organizations. If we merely describe what happens, organizational behavior remains unscientific. For instance, one leadership theory contends that an effective leader shows his or her subordinates the correct path to achieving outcomes they think are desirable. This portion of the theory thus helps to explain why a particular leader is effective. If we merely described an effective leader in action, we would miss out on the unifying principle that helps to explain leadership effectiveness.

[1]Thomas H. Jerdee, "Review of Francis W. Dinsmore, *Developing Tomorrow's Managers Today* (New York: AMACOM, 1975," *Personnel Psychology,* Winter 1976, pp. 655–58. Reprinted by permission.

CHARACTERISTICS OF
SCIENTIFIC RESEARCH

The knowledge of organizational behavior is derived from several different sources. Among them are authoritative opinions, case histories, and scientific research. As mentioned in Chapter 1, the field of organizational behavior is now characterized by a preference for scientific research as the primary source of new knowledge. Many different opinions exist about the true nature of scientific research, yet some generalizations can be drawn about its distinguishing characteristics. Scientific research is empirical, purposeful, cumulative and self-correcting, replicable, communicable,[2] and follows the scientific method.

1. *Empirical.* Conclusions, judgments, and inferences are to be based on empirical observations, not on beliefs or hopes. If a scientist contends that linking pay to performance improves motivation, that scientist should produce some hard data to prove his or her point. (Some data for this conclusion do exist.)

2. *Purposeful.* Scientific research is purposeful; it is focused in a particular direction rather than scattered. There are reasons that some questions are chosen for investigation rather than others. Nevertheless, there is not always some applied purpose in mind when a researcher chooses a problem, since a theoretical question may be just as purposeful. What purposeful does mean in this context is that the choice of a problem is considerably more purposeful than implied by the statement, "I wonder what would happen if . . ." type of choice sometimes used. The vocational rehabilitation director had a specific purpose in mind when he set about to investigate the relationship of emotional support by a leader to job performance.

3. *Cumulative and Self-correcting.* Scientific research builds upon what has taken place before; it is cumulative and self-correcting. "Those who do not know the mistakes of history are doomed to repeat them," Santayana once said. To avoid this mistake, the researcher spends a considerable portion of his or her time reading the scientific literature. The result, it is hoped, is a research investigation that extends what we know about a question rather than a repetition of either the knowledge or the mistakes of previous work. Most articles in scientific journals begin with a review of the relevant literature. A sophisticated study builds upon well-researched information collected in the past.

4. *Replicable.* The procedures undertaken in scientific research are stated with such explicitness that any other qualified researcher could replicate the project if the researcher would so wish. The lead-in case to this chapter does not describe the research in sufficient detail for it to be replicable. Many journal articles do present research in

---

[2]A substantial portion of points 1 through 5 is quoted or is paraphrased from Abraham K. Korman, *Organizational Behavior* (Englewood Cliffs, N.J.: Prentice-Hall, 1977), pp. 17–18. Reprinted by permission.

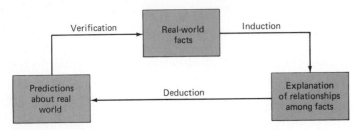

FIGURE 2–1 A Model Depicting the Scientific Method

Source: E. F. Stone, *Research Methods in Organizational Behavior* (Glenview, Ill.: Scott, Foresman and Company, 1978). Reprinted with permission.

sufficient detail for it to be replicable. However, you would probably have to write the authors to obtain a copy of the instruments used and the raw data collected.

5. *Communicable.* The results and conclusions of scientific research can be communicated to other interested parties. The concepts and ideas are not of a private nature but of a kind that may, in principle, be utilized by qualified people.

The five principles just stated may be regarded as an ideal toward which researchers in organizational behavior and related disciplines should strive. Some firms that conduct behavioral research prefer to keep some of their findings confidential for fear of giving away a competitive edge. Among such noncommunicated results have been studies about improving the performance of sales representatives and decreasing turnover among engineers.

6. *Follows the Scientific Method.* A comprehensive characteristic of scientific research is that it, by definition, pays heed to the scientific method. The scientific method will be touched upon later in our discussion of field studies and experimental design. As shown in Figure 2–1, the scientific method in organizational behavior consists of four stages.[3] First is observation of phenomena in the real world. Often the phenomena take the form of facts. It might be observed, for example, that some handicapped workers perform better than others. Second is the formulation of explanations for such phenomena using the inductive process, such as "It could be that supervisors of high-performing handicapped people are doing something different from supervisors of low-performing handicapped employees." Third, predictions or hypotheses about the phenomena are made using the deductive process. At NATCO, "A supportive leadership climate improves the job performance of handicapped employees." Fourth is verification of the predictions or hypotheses using systematic, controlled observation (the essence of an experiment).

---

[3]E. F. Stone, *Research Methods in Organizational Behavior* (Glenview, Ill.: Scott, Foresman and Company, 1978). Referenced in Richard M. Steers, *Introduction to Organizational Behavior* (Glenview, Ill.: Scott, Foresman and Company, 1981), pp. 19–20.

BASIC VERSUS EVALUATION RESEARCH

The OB researcher, similar to other scientists, sometimes conducts studies to learn more about a particular phenomenon such as which job factors really seem to make a difference in terms of employee quality of work life. If the research purpose is primarily to accumulate knowledge about a topic, with no particular application in mind, such research may even be referred to as *pure*. In practice, much of OB research is directed toward the evaluation of a program, technique, method, or intervention. The research example featured in this chapter about the effects of training on motor vehicle employee performance is one example of evaluation research. A more comprehensive example of evaluation research is presented in Chapter 17 about organization development.

Evaluation research is eminently practical because it provides some answers to such nagging questions as, Is this behavioral science intervention really worth its required investment of resources? And are we helping, harming, or simply having no impact on employees by retaining this particular human resource program? The exercise at the end of this chapter invites you to design a program of evaluation research.

METHODS OF DATA COLLECTION

Physical scientists, such as geologists, chemists, and biologists have the edge over researchers in organizational behavior with respect to the collection of precise data. For example, the biologist can readily find a representative plant cell to place under the microscope. The behavioral scientist has to rely upon methods of data collection that are less precise, although often of major significance. A major challenge to the OB researcher is finding ways in which to collect accurate and meaningful data. The four most frequently used measures are questionnaires, interviews, direct observation of behavior, and unobtrusive measures.

Questionnaires

You have probably already filled out dozens of questionnaires (surveys) at school, work, or home. When you dine or stay at a Holiday Inn, for example, you are given the opportunity to complete a brief questionnaire about the quality of the service. One difference between a questionnaire developed by a scientific researcher and the type of everyday questionnaire just mentioned is that scientists collect relevant facts and generate hypotheses before designing the questionnaire. The questions are carefully designed to tap (measure) relevant issues about the topic under survey. One such job questionnaire measuring job satisfaction is shown in Figure 2–2.

Questionnaire construction is a complex art, despite the deceptively straightfor-

After each question circle the number that represents your opinion about the amount of each job aspect being rated. Low numbers represent small amounts and high numbers represent large amounts.

1. The opportunity to earn a comfortable income.
   a. HOW MUCH IS THERE NOW?
      (Minimum) 1 2 3 4 5 6 7 (Maximum)
   b. HOW MUCH SHOULD THERE BE?
      (Minimum) 1 2 3 4 5 6 7 (Maximum)

2. The opportunity to work with pleasant co-workers.
   a. HOW MUCH IS THERE NOW?
      (Minimum) 1 2 3 4 5 6 7 (Maximum)
   b. HOW MUCH SHOULD THERE BE?
      (Minimum) 1 2 3 4 5 6 7 (Maximum)

3. A feeling that my boss will give a fair hearing to my problems.
   a. HOW MUCH IS THERE NOW?
      (Minimum) 1 2 3 4 5 6 7 (Maximum)
   b. HOW MUCH SHOULD THERE BE?
      (Minimum) 1 2 3 4 5 6 7 (Maximum)

FIGURE 2–2 Example of Items from a Job Satisfaction Questionnaire

Source: Andrew J. DuBrin, *Personnel and Human Resource Management* (New York: D. Van Nostrand Company, 1981), p. 228. © 1981 by Litton Educational Publishing, Inc. Reprinted by permission of Kent Publishing Company, a division of Wadsworth, Inc.

ward appearance of one that is well designed. When constructing a questionnaire, the questions that the survey designer should ask include the following:

- Is the question necessary?
- Is the question repetitious?
- Does the question contain more than one idea?
- Should most respondents be able to answer the question?
- Is a given question likely to bias those responding to it?
- Does the sequence maintain respondent motivation? Or is it likely to lose his or her attention?[4]

Since many people in our society are surveyed more than they would prefer, both managers and researchers have to guard against overuse of questionnaires in organizations. As one survey respondent confided to a researcher, "I received the darn thing just when I was about to leave a little early. So I threw down anything without reading it very carefully."

[4]P. L. Erdos, *Professional Mail Surveys* (New York: McGraw-Hill, 1970). As quoted in Andrew D. Szilagyi, Jr., and Marc J. Wallace, Jr., *Organizational Behavior and Performance,* 2nd ed. (Glenview, Ill.: Scott, Foresman and Company, 1980), p. 614.

The appendix to this chapter summarizes some basic concepts about the construction and use of tests and questionnaires. Without such basic knowledge, tests and questionnaires should not be applied to organizational problems.

Interviews

As with anyone whose job involves collecting information, the OB researcher relies heavily upon the interview as a method of data collection. Even when a questionnaire is the primary method of data collection, it is probable that interviews were used prior to designing the questionnaire. The interview provides some useful clues about which questions should be included in the survey. Interviews are also invaluable in uncovering explanations about phenomena and furnishing leads for further inquiry. A researcher conducting interviews about the value of flexible work schedules in one organization spoke with one employee who responded that a disadvantage of flexitime related to the fact that some people were abusing the system (goofing off). Formal questionnaire items would probably have missed this issue. Fill-in questions on written surveys such as "Is there anything else you would like to add?" may also be useful in providing explanations and diagnostic information.

Another advantage of the interview method is that a skilled interviewer can probe for additional information. A *disadvantage* of the interview method is that skilled interviewers operating in an atmosphere of trust are necessary to achieve valid results. Interviews are also time consuming, and fewer people can be reached than through written questionnaires.

Several different types of interviews are used to collect data for acquiring organizational behavior knowledge. One is the *structured interview,* which asks standard questions of all respondents. Highly structured interviews take on the tone of a written questionnaire, particularly when they ask questions calling for pinpointed responses such as "Are you satisfied or dissatisfied with your pay?"

Unstructured interviews encourage the free flow of conversation and appear less scientific than structured interviews. The unstructured interview is used to gather general impressions about the job, firm, or the employee. Television talk-show interviews are often of this nature, asking such questions as, "What is your opinion of life in a prison?" or "How bad are things in Northern Island?"

A third type of interview is the *open-ended, structured interview.* People are asked standard questions, but they are encouraged to answer them with a free response. One example is "What is your opinion of the quality of supervision here?"

Systematic Observation

Much information about OB is collected by the simple expedient of a knowledgeable observer placing himself or herself in the work environment under study. Systematic observations are then made of the phenomena under study. Japanese firms in recent years have been deluged with OB researchers (and media personnel) observing employees and managers in action. A concern some researchers have is that people tend to turn in atypical performances when under observation. For instance, if a friend observed you perform a psychomotor skill such as typing a report or hitting a golf ball, you might perform better (or worse) than usual. Although there is some merit in this comment, most experienced observers tend to "blend into the woodwork" after awhile.

Another form of observation is called participant observation. The observer becomes a member of the group about which he or she is collecting data. Many a newspaper reporter has pretended to be a legitimate member of a group (such as the Ku Klux Klan) to obtain an "inside story." Deception of this nature is generally frowned upon by those subscribing to scientific values. A compromise solution is for the OB researchers to ask somebody to prepare a case about his or her natural work environment. In such situations, it is ethically sound to inform the other members of the group about the case in preparation.

Unobtrusive Measures

One problem with the three methods of data collection mentioned so far is that the researcher interacts with the person providing the data. If you respond to a written or spoken question, or if there is a known observer in your midst, it could color your response. To get around the problem of reactivity—the act of being measured influencing the response—unobtrusive measures are sometimes used. The basic point of an unobtrusive measure is to collect information without people realizing what you are doing.

One organization development specialist was asked to measure customer attitudes about waiting in line at banks. He described his method of data collection as follows:

> For five consecutive business days I waited in line at different locations of the bank. I chose to visit the main office and the branches on their busiest days. I waited in line and even conducted a transaction at the teller's window. I listened to complaints of other customers. As soon as I left the bank I jumped into my car and recorded my observations into a tape recorder. I came away with some information that was very useful to the bank in formulating policy.

CHOOSING A METHOD OF DATA COLLECTION

Many OB research projects use a combination of data collection methods with one method being relied on more heavily than the other. Unstructured interviews are useful in gathering topics about which more structured interviews and a questionnaire can be developed. It is critical to select the method of data collection that seems to best fit your circumstances at the time. Two specialists in the field explain it this way:

Methods of data collection are neither good nor bad, but rather more or less useful in answering particular questions. The scientific study of organizational behavior requires data collection, and which method or combination of methods is used should be selected to test the applicability of knowledge, a theory, or model in a particular setting.[5]

METHODS OF RESEARCH IN ORGANIZATIONAL BEHAVIOR

The methods of data collection just described are basic tools for conducting research in the behavioral sciences (and in business). When these tools or methods are learned, they can be applied to different methods of or strategies for conducting an investigation. Methods of research can be classified into case study, field study, correlational study, and experiment. Almost any OB research study can be placed under one, or a combination, of these methods.

Case Study

Cases are a very popular teaching method in management and organizational behavior, but they are often looked upon critically as a method of conducting research. Some researchers today believe that the case method no longer occupies a legitimate place as a research method, despite its didactic value. Data underlying cases are usually collected by an observer simply recording impressions in his or her head or in a note pad. A natural tendency for human beings is to attend to information specifically related to our own interests or needs. One researcher prepared a case report showing examples of how the initiative of the word processing technicians was hampered by an authoritarian supervisor. Another researcher prepared a report in the same department emphasizing how much the technicians enjoyed not having to make decisions themselves. Both researchers were correct within the limits of their selective perception. Both sets of events probably took place, but each researcher saw only a partial view of reality.

A striking advantage of the case method is that it provides the researcher with a wealth of data about underlying hypotheses and explanations of phenomena. Using the case study method—and working as a participant observer for much of the study—one sociologist arrived at the conclusion that many production workers relieve boredom by informal chatting with one another. A certain amount of "schmoozing" is therefore helpful to the organization.[6] Once the case has been prepared, other researchers can use more rigorous methods to test out the conclusions arrived at by the case method.

Another problem with the case research method is that the original data are lost forever, transformed and twisted around because of the limited information processing

[5]Szilagyi and Wallace, *Organizational Behavior*, p. 617.
[6]Robert Schrank, *Ten Thousand Working Days* (Cambridge, Mass.: M.I.T. Press, 1980).

capabilities of human beings.[7] We are dependent upon the subjective memory of the case investigator. We do not know which data the researcher ignored, nor do we know what "facts" another observer might have noted.

Field Study

Multiple data collection methods are used in a field study. Employees may be observed, interviewed, and surveyed through questionnaires. A critical factor is that employees are asked to express their feelings and opinions about the issue under investigation. A case investigator usually conducts some interviews but relies more heavily upon his or her own perceptions of reality.

An example of a rigorous field study concerned the influence of a safety training program and feedback on safety performance. The study was conducted in the vehicle maintenance division of a large western city's department of public works. One reason the study was undertaken was that the department had one of the highest accident rates in the city, recording 84.2 lost-time accidents per million person hours.

The independent variables in this field study were safety training programs and feedback on safety performance. Of concern here was the type of observations made to measure the dependent variable (the actual safety performance). In place of subjective impressions, researchers had to make relatively objective notations about precise aspects of behavior. The observational procedures included the following:

> Trained raters, identified as interested in the area of safety, served as nonparticipant observers. They coded each item as safe, unsafe, or not observed in full view of the workers. If, for instance, an employee in light equipment repair was seen working under a vehicle, it was observed whether or not he was wearing eye protection. If he was, that item was recorded as "safe"; if he was not, the item was recorded as "unsafe." If no work was being done under a vehicle during the observation period, the item was marked "unobserved." Each observation lasted for a total of 60 minutes.
>
> The percentage of incidents performed safely was calculated as the number of safe items observed divided by the total number of incidents observed, and multiplied by 100.[8]

For the curious, the study found that training plus feedback on safety practices improved safety performance more than training did alone. Although we are concerned here with the type of relatively objective measures possible in a field study, this study is also classified as a field experiment. (We return to the experimental aspects of this study later.) In practice, many large-sized research studies in organizational behavior utilize more than one research method.

---

[7]W. Clay Hamner and Dennis W. Organ, *Organizational Behavior: An Applied Psychological Approach* (Plano, Tex.: Business Publications, 1978), p. 19

[8]Judi Komaki, Arlene T. Heinzmann, and Loralie Lawson, "Effects of Training and Feedback: Component Analysis of a Behavioral Safety Program," *Journal of Applied Psychology*, June 1980, p. 263. Reprinted with permission of the American Psychological Association.

Correlational Study

A widely used research method is organizational behavior to correlate scores on one measure (an independent variable) with scores on some outside criterion (a dependent variable). Often, the dependent variable represents "hard data" such as employee salary, number of units shipped, accident frequency, or number of patents issued. The independent variable is typically measured by a questionnaire. A basic example of this kind of research would be to correlate scores on a test of creativity with number of patents received over a period of time (among a group of engineers and physical scientists). The relationship between these two variables would then be expressed in terms of a correlation coefficient. Most correlational studies published today measure simultaneously the influence of several independent variables upon several dependent variables. In the creativity example just cited, the researcher might take measures of several independent variables such as tests of mental ability, personality, biographical information, and creativity. In addition to patents, the dependent variables might include measures of creativity as perceived by peers, number of journal articles published, and creativity ratings by superiors.

A major limitation of correlational studies is that they can be misinterpreted as implying causation. If we find that a measure of flexibility correlates highly with a measure of creativity, we might conclude that being flexible contributes to or *causes* creativity. In fact, being a creative person might make you more flexible in your outlook. All that can be safely concluded from a correlational study is that the two variables measured vary in a similar fashion. Correlational research has suggested, for example, that sensitivity to people varies with success as a managerial leader. We cannot say that sensitivity is a primary cause of leadership success. Experiments provide more information about causation. But even when a rigorous experiment is conducted, the behavioral scientist is hesitant to say that the cause of a phenomenon has been isolated.

Experiment

The most rigorous research method, and therefore the most desirable from the scientist's viewpoint, is the experiment. The essence of experimentation is to control for factors other than the variable being studied that could be influencing your results. Among the independent variables to be controlled for are intelligence, education, occupational level, type of organization, type of leadership, and salary levels. Variables such as these could have a big influence on the dependent variable. For instance, if you are studying factors that influence work motivation, you must take into account the job levels of the people being studied and the style of leadership under which they are working. There are three basic types of experiments used in organizational behavior research: the laboratory experiment, the field experiment, and the simulation experiment. Each one has its own advantages and disadvantages.

Laboratory experiment.   A major characteristic of the laboratory experiment is that conditions are supposedly under the experimenter's control. A group of people might be brought into a room to study the effects of stress on problem-solving ability. The stress the experimenter introduces is an occasional blast from a siren. In a field setting, assuming that the experiment were permitted, the experimenter might be unaware of what other stresses the employee were facing. A major concern about laboratory experiments is that their results might not be generalizable to the outside world. Among the specific criticisms leading to this general criticism are

- The tasks used are often of a game nature, such as solving Rubik cubes, using puzzle blocks, or designing structures with tinker toys.
- The populations studied are usually college students working without pay or for less than the minimum wage. How motivated or committed could they be under these conditions?
- The independent variable introduced is a poor imitation of that independent variable as it exists in outside organizations. For instance, is a siren a good facsimile of job stress? Does passing messages around a table really duplicate organizational communications?

Sometimes the results from laboratory experiments are generalizable and sometimes they are not.[9] One affirmative example is the early work conducted by psychologists about the influence of stress on performance that has been replicated in organizations. In general, people do perform the best under moderate stress, both in the laboratory and in natural work settings.

Field experiment.   An increasing proportion of the information called organizational behavior is obtained through experimentation in field settings. Field experiments constitute an attempt to apply the experimental method to ongoing, real-life situations. Variables can be controlled more readily in the laboratory than in the field, but information obtained in the field is often more relevant. Suppose that an experimenter were interested in studying the influence of assertiveness training (AT) on the career progress of women in organizations. Assertiveness trainers contend that if people become more direct in expressing what they feel and what they want, they are more likely to achieve their goals. One experimental method to test this contention would be to measure how AT influenced the salary and career progress of women. A conventional research design to study this problem would be set up as shown in Table 2–1.

You would then make statistical comparisons of the salary progress and job-level progress of the experimental and control groups. If the women who underwent AT scored higher in salary and job level, you would tentatively conclude that learning how to be more assertive helped career progress more than did (1) no such training or (2) group discussions about career progress. Using the second control group helps to rule out the possibility that merely talking about improving your career is as effective as AT.

[9]Korman, *Organizational Behavior*, p. 18.

TABLE 2–1 A Conventional Research Design

Procedures and Steps	Experimental Group	Control Group I	Control Group II
Assign women randomly to group	Yes	Yes	Yes
Record current salary	Yes	Yes	Yes
Record current job level	Yes	Yes	Yes
Administer AT program	Yes	No	No
Conduct group discussions about careers	No	No	Yes
Allow time to pass without interacting with participants	Yes	Yes	Yes
Record salary progress at one- and two-year periods	Yes	Yes	Yes
Record job level at one- and two-year periods	Yes	Yes	Yes

A large number of experimental designs has been developed to control for many of the complexities that enter into both laboratory and field experiments.[10] Many of these experimental designs had their origin in agriculture. The designs were set up to answer such questions as "Which combination of fertilizers is the most effective with which kinds of crops?"

In practice, experimental designs follow the general principles just described, but they also allow for ingenuity and innovation as illustrated in the field study about safety mentioned earlier. The researchers needed to design an experiment that would answer the questions: (1) Is training alone sufficient to improve substantially and maintain safety performance on the job? and (2) Is it necessary to provide feedback to maintain safety performance? To answer these questions, the experimenters chose the design summarized in Table 2–2.

The terms "sweeper repair" and so forth refer to the different sections in the vehicle maintenance divisions that participated in the study. "Duration" refers to the length of the experimental phase in weeks that each section received. "Sequence" refers to the week after which the experimental phase was introduced in the section.

The experimenters describe their design as a "multiple-baseline design with a reversal component." The baseline refers to the fact that measurements were taken (by observers) of the accident level at the time the experiment began. Baseline data were collected in all four motor vehicle maintenance sections. The second and third phases were introduced in a staggered sequence. After the twenty-sixth and thirty-sixth weeks, the fourth and fifth phases were introduced. Four different experimental

---

[10]For example, see Fred N. Kerlinger, *Foundations of Behavioral Research* (New York: Holt, Rinehart and Winston, 1973), pp. 300–76.

TABLE 2–2 Duration and Sequence of Experimental Phases Across Sections

| | Section in Vehicle Maintenance Division | | | | | | | |
| | Sweeper Repair | | Preventive Maintenance | | Light Equipment Repair | | Heavy Equipment Repair | |
Experimental Phase	Dura- tion*	Se- quence†	Dura- tion*	Se- quence†	Dura- tion*	Se- quence†	Dura- tion*	Se- quence†
Baseline	9		10		11		11	
Training only 1	5	10	6	11	8	12	8	12
Training and feedback 1	11	15	9	17	6	20	6	20
Training only 2	10	26	10	26	10	26	10	26
Training and feedback 2	10	36	10	36	10	36	10	36

*Length of phase in weeks.

†Week after which the phase was introduced.

Source: Judi Komaki, Arlene T. Heinzmann, and Loralie Lawson, "Effects of Training and Feedback: Component Analysis of a Behavioral Safety Program," *Journal of Applied Psychology,* June 1980, p. 264. Copyright 1980 by the American Psychological Association. Reprinted with permission of the publisher and authors.

"treatments" (the activity assigned to each experimental phase) were used. Note carefully that the same people were in each phase of the experiment.

I *Training Only 1.* Workers attended a safety training session that lasted about thirty-five minutes during their regular workday. A major component of the session was the display of transparencies that showed adherence to or violation of safety rules. Workers were encouraged to discuss these situations.

II *Training and Feedback 1.* In addition to a review of the 35mm slides and safety rules, workers in this group were told that the supervisor would be making a randomly timed safety inspection. As a form of feedback, the results of these inspections were to be posted on a graph. Workers were shown how well they did during the Training Only 1 phases. A goal of 75 percent of incidents performed safely was set for the sweeper and preventive sections and that of the heavy and light sections at 90 percent. The supervisor indicated that performance at the 100 percent level was neither expected nor required.

Before this meeting, supervisors were coached in how to observe and provide feedback. Using the same procedures as the observers, they practiced observations with one of the experimenters until they agreed consistently on over 90 percent of the safety items. Independent observers continued to collect safety data throughout the study.

III *Training Only 2.* In this phase of the experiment, the supervisors ceased conducting observations and providing feedback on safety performance. However, the list of written rules remained posted.

IV *Training and Feedback 2.* During this fourth and final phase of the experiment, feedback was again provided. Depending upon the section, supervisors or co-workers conducted the observations and posted the safety level on section graphs.[11]

When employees received training in the form of a slide presentation, oral explanations, and written rules, performance improved slightly. Performance improved significantly only when feedback was also provided. The experimenters supported their conclusion not through the traditional experimental versus control group design, but through a modern variation thereof. The design chosen was a "reversal component," meaning that the same group was switched back and forth between receiving and not receiving feedback.

Simulation experiment.   Simulation experiments are a combination of the laboratory and field experiment,[12] although some researchers and practitioners would argue that any simulation is a laboratory method. The simulation attempts to duplicate a real-life environment on a small scale. By so doing, changes may be introduced into the environment and measured for effects more easily than they can in real life. The major difference between the laboratory and simulation approach is that the laboratory focuses on one independent variable at a time. With computer-based simulations, many different variables may be introduced at once. For instance, an experimenter might simultaneously examine the influences of leadership style, stress, and functional discipline (such as finance versus marketing) on the quality of solutions to a business problem. Some simulation experiments are so complex that the results are unconvincing.

SOURCES OF ERROR IN ORGANIZATIONAL BEHAVIOR RESEARCH

No science can avoid every potential error in its research. A zoologist taking microphotographs might find that his or her camera reacts differently when the temperature is below zero than when it is over 32°F, thus taking slightly different images of wildlife at those two times. Research in organizational behavior probably has many more problems than does that in most physical and biological sciences. Here we list ten of the most common sources of error and then comment upon the problem of ethics in conducting OB research.

1. *Inaccurate information.* Despite the precise-sounding language and the sophisticated statistical analysis that characterize research in this field, it is sometimes based on inaccurate information. People sometimes respond to questionnaires in a slipshod

---

[11]The informaton about these phases is reprinted and/or paraphrased from Komaki, Heinzman, and Lawson, "Effects of Training and Feedback," pp. 263–64.

[12]Korman, *Organizational Behavior,* p. 20.

manner or, worse, supply inaccurate information. Case investigators may sometimes not attend to the more important aspects of an organizational situation but report back that which interests them the most.

2. *Limited application of results.* Research in organizational behavior is sometimes conducted in organizations where the climate is receptive to such research and where sound human relations is practiced. Thus the results obtained might not be generalizable to environments in which management is less concerned about the needs, feelings, and attitudes of employees. Most OB techniques (such as team building) will work in a well-managed company whose management is genuinely concerned about employee welfare.

3. *Apathy, indifference, and anxiety of subjects.* Related to the first point in this list, the emotional state of the subjects in an experiment or survey can limit the results. One woman was invited to the personnel department to be interviewed as part of a research study. Her name had been randomly selected by the researcher. Before her interview appointment, she asked a friend how she should handle the request. She took the advice of a friend who suggested, "Say as little as possible. Anything negative you say could be held against you."

4. *The social desirability factor.* A normal human tendency is to say things to others that make us look good in their eyes. When interviewed, most managers will explain how they always use participative management, listen to subordinates, and so forth. Similarly, people often answer questionnaires in a socially desirable manner. Virtually everybody will respond "mostly agree" to the questionnaire item "I have above-average skills in dealing with people."

5. *Invalid measures of experimental variables.* Unfortunately for survey research, not every questionnaire is a true measure of what it purports to measure. A given scale may be labeled as a measure of sex discrimination, yet in truth it measures nothing in particular or a general tendency toward conservatism versus liberalism in social attitudes. The researcher who is trying to find correlations between sex discrimination and organizational variables is thus guaranteed no meaningful results.

6. *Reactivity of methods.* A measurement is *reactive* when the attempt to measure something automatically alters that state of the subject being measured.[13] In laboratory experiments, the subjects, being human and friendly, try to figure out the experimental hypotheses and "make the experimenter look good." Some executives are hesitant to conduct morale surveys because they fear that bringing up sensitive issues will trigger employees to think of morale problems.

7. *Extraneous influences.* When conducting an experiment, time often lapses between the first measurement of behavior and later measurements. You might be studying the influence of good management practices on decreasing stress. After the "good management practices" are introduced, and before the second measurement of stress, some of your subjects might take up stress-reducing activities on their own. Unfortunately for your results, many of these people might be in the control group, thus de-

[13]Hamner and Organ, *Organizational Behavior,* p. 31.

creasing the differences you might have found. Or in the time between the treatment and later measurement, people might simply mature in their ability to handle job stress. Since so many external events can influence humans, it becomes necessary to use large numbers of subjects. These extraneous effects would then be randomly distributed between the experimental and control, or contrast, groups.

8.   *Nonrandom selection.* When subjects are assigned to experimental and control groups on any basis other than random selection, the results could be biased. One interesting potential source of bias is that volunteers for a particular program or experiment are sometimes psychologically different from the nonvolunteers. For instance, they might be more adventuresome and self-confident, thus tending to do well in a given training program (or respond well to any treatment). The vocational rehabilitation director who wanted to use another company's handicapped employees as a contrast group may have unwittingly violated the principle of random selection. Perhaps the comparison company hired less skilled workers, thus making the groups noncomparable.

9.   *Loss of subjects.* In field research, particularly, some participants may drop out of the experiment before it is completed. Randomness is thus not assured. In the assertiveness training and career development experiment mentioned earlier, it is conceivable that some of the subjects who responded well to AT may have become so assertive that they left the firm for better opportunities elsewhere.

10.   *Interaction effects.* Any of the sources of error mentioned in this listing might combine with the experimental treatment in such a way as to confound the results. For example, subjects in the experimental group might feel more obliged to give socially desirable responses than might people in the control group.[14] Or the type of people who volunteer to participate in research might not be typical of the population that the experimenter wishes to study. If your intention were to study the work habits of successful executives, you might ask volunteers to record their workday in a specially prepared time-logging device. Truly busy and successful executives might not volunteer because they guard their time so carefully.

Although interaction effects are usually considered to be a source of experimental error, many interaction effects are precisely those of interest to the applied researcher. Throughout this text, we will be making reference to how certain variables have a differential effect upon different people or groups. A third variable influences the relationship between two other variables. There is some evidence, for example, that money does not have the same magnitude of motivational impact on all groups of employees. Upwardly mobile employees, and financially troubled employees are more motivated by the prospects of earning additional income than are less ambitious and more financially secure employees. Thus the variables of ambition and financial status

---

[14]The idea for this list of potential errors is based on James L. Gibson, John M. Ivancevich, and James H. Donnelly, Jr., *Organizations: Behavior, Structure, Processes,* 3rd ed. (Plano, Tex.: Business Publications, 1979), p. 541.

interact with the treatment (money) to influence the relationship between money and performance. Another frequently observed interaction effect is the influence of employee desire on the relationship between job enrichment and job performance (see Chapter 5). Job enrichment does improve the performance of employees who desire an enriched, stimulating job. Yet job enrichment has no particular effect on the job performance of employees who prefer an unenriched job.

It would require extensive knowledge of experimental design and statistics to learn how to overcome or control for all the factors noted. The general strategy is to be aware of such factors and make appropriate adjustments. Conducting careful research follows scientific principles, but it is also an art. Intuition and common sense are required to appreciate what extraneous factor might be influencing your results. In one unpublished experiment, the researcher began to wonder why so many employees from the same department were eager to volunteer. Upon investigation, she discovered that the department was characterized by uncomfortable working conditions. Employees thus welcomed an opportunity to take a break from work by participating in an experiment.

Ethics

Aside from watching for potential sources of error in organizational behavior research, the experimenter must guard against ethical violations of the rights of subjects. Psychologists work under a strict code of ethics in the conduct of research. As common sense would suggest, it is considered unethical to harm or humiliate people (or animals) in any way for the sake of science. In many nonprofit organizations, to get approval for research with humans, your project is scrutinized by a human subjects review committee. Only if they pass favorably upon the ethics of your design will you be allowed to proceed. One research project in OB was voted down by a review board because its design necessitated informing some employees that they were fired. The experimenter was thinking of ways to investigate the impact of being fired on human physiology!

THE APPLICATION OF OB KNOWLEDGE

In a sense, this entire text is about the application of organizational behavior knowledge. Here we focus on a diagnostic model that the manager or staff specialist is advised to use when applying a concept, technique, or method of organizational behavior.[15] After repeated application of the model shown in Figure 2–3, the process becomes relatively automatic, as when an experienced mechanic sizes up an automotive problem and uses the right concept or technique to remedy the situation.

---

[15]The model and accompanying discussion is based on R. Dennis Middlemist and Michael A. Hitt, *Organizational Behavior: Applied Concepts* (Chicago: Science Research Associates, 1981), pp. 35–41. The illustration of the model, however, is original.

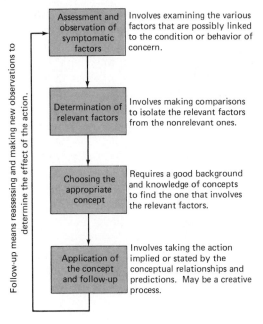

FIGURE 2–3 caption area:

Assessment and observation of symptomatic factors — Involves examining the various factors that are possibly linked to the condition or behavior of concern.

Determination of relevant factors — Involves making comparisons to isolate the relevant factors from the nonrelevant ones.

Choosing the appropriate concept — Requires a good background and knowledge of concepts to find the one that involves the relevant factors.

Application of the concept and follow-up — Involves taking the action implied or stated by the conceptual relationships and predictions. May be a creative process.

Follow-up means reassessing and making new observations to determine the effect of the action.

FIGURE 2–3   The Basic Diagnostic Model

Source: R. Dennis Middlemist and Michael A. Hitt, *Organizational Behavior: Applied Concepts* (Chicago: Science Research Associates, Inc., 1981), p. 37. Reprinted by permission of the publisher.

Assessment and Observation

Behavior in organizations emanates from three types of factors:

1. Factors internal to employees such as skills, personalities, and motivation.
2. Factors in the organizational environment such as the nature of the leadership style, reward systems, and physical surroundings.
3. The interaction between employees and the environment and the way in which environmental factors complement or conflict with factors within the individual.

   In the hypothetical situation used to illustrate the model, Al, a department head, is approached by one of his managers, Luke. The latter states, "Things just haven't been going well for me lately, Al. I feel like I'm headed nowhere. It's the same old routine day after day. I'm on a treadmill, but I'm not even sure if I want to remain on or get off."

   Immediately Al begins to process the information he hears. He questions Luke further with an intent to discover what are some of the many possible factors that might be contributing to his current dilemma.

Determination of Relevant Factors

Dozens of factors could be relevant to the problem at hand. Our purpose here is not to present an exposition of all the reasons Luke might be having career problems. The developers of the diagnostic model suggest that the basic procedure for sorting out relevant from irrelevant factors is through the use of comparison. Here Al might compare Luke's complaints with the dozens of complaints he has heard in his many years as a manager. What Luke has to say seems more pronounced and filled with deeper emotion than do most comments about job dissatisfaction. Al thinks through different organizational behavior concepts in his repertoire. "Is Luke poorly motivated? Is he stifled by my leadership style? Is our reward system faulty? Is Luke facing a problem of a midcareer crisis? Or is he facing burnout?"

Choice of Appropriate Concept

Choosing the correct concept involves much more than making an assessment of the situation and drawing comparisons with other employees and situations. It is also necessary to be familiar with many concepts—one justification for becoming familiar with the broad range of concepts presented in this text. Al begins the process of sorting through the possible factors. Upon reflection, Al says to himself, "My intuition tells me that saying Luke has a motivation problem is too pat. Similarly, my style of leadership doesn't stifle other employees. Our reward system used to work for Luke. From what I hear Luke saying, his situation fits more nearly a midcareer crisis or burnout. Since a manager's role in handling both conditions is about the same, I can't be too far off if the problem is a midcareer crisis *or* burnout.

"If my hunch is correct, I'll offer Luke some job rotation or a special assignment. If that doesn't work, I'll suggest that he speak to our career development department. Perhaps they will send him for outside counseling."

Application of Concept and Follow-up

"The final stage in the diagnostic process is that of applying the concept and following up—to be sure the application accomplished its intended results. Applications often require creativity on the part of a manager, since concepts rarely specify the exact steps for application."[16] To apply his concept, Al decides to discuss his plan with Luke for job rotation and perhaps a special assignment. The theoretical underpinning is that one of the many contributing factors to midcareer stress is a feeling of staleness. New job experiences might give Luke an attitudinal boost that could begin a process of constructive change.

Luke looks favorably upon the prospects of a change in his responsibilities. The idea is implemented, but Al's responsibilities do not end there. He meets with Luke again in several months. Luke is feeling a little less depressed, but a miracle cure has not been effected. Al then suggests that Luke might want to explore the possibility of speaking to the company career development specialist. In turn, the career development specialist will use the basic diagnostic model or a similar mental process.

The diagnostic model follows a similar format to decision making in general, as

[16]Ibid., p. 40.

will be described in Chapter 8. As with any form of decision making, the larger the number of valid concepts in your repertoire, the more likely you will select out a concept particularly relevant to the situation at hand. In the case of Al and Luke, the concept is backed up by an associated technique (job rotation).

IMPLICATIONS FOR MANAGERIAL PRACTICE

1. When you read or hear about a theory of organizational behavior, do not automatically dismiss it as not having relevance for managing human resources. A "theory" in the scientific sense is a systematic explanation of phenomena, not an unsubstantiated hunch. For example, theories about goal setting and positive reinforcement have led to eminently practical ways of improving job performance.

2. Before accepting a research report, you should carefully evaluate the methods by which the data were collected. If questionnaires were used, who constructed them? If interviews were used, how skilled were the interviewers? Under what conditions were the data collected? You might also want to ask if the research is reported in such a way that the study could be replicated.

3. In evaluating a research report, be alert to the many possible sources of error in organizational behavior research (as described on pages 35–38). One way in which to accomplish this end is to discuss these issues with the researcher involved in the project or a few of the participants.

4. The ability to make a sound diagnosis is an essential skill if you are to apply the concepts of organizational behavior to a work setting. After you have made your diagnosis of the problem at hand, or of a relatively healthy situation that you think could stand improvement, choose a valid OB concept to apply. Sometimes the concept will have an associated technique (such as team building); at other times the concept can be applied without a formal technique (such as you clarifying expectations to a subordinate).

Summary

- Sound research in organizational behavior, followed by sound theory, enables you to function more effectively as a manager or individual contributor. Sound theory, in turn, leads to additional research, thus furthering knowledge.
- Scientific research is empirical, purposeful, cumulative and self-correcting, replicable, and communicable and follows the scientific method. The scientific method consists of four stages: (1) observation of phenomena, (2) formulation of explanations, (3) formulation of hypotheses, and (4) verification of the hypotheses.

- Data collection methods in OB include the use of questionnaires, interviews, observations, and unobtrusive measures (the researcher does not interact with the people being studied). Which method or combination of methods is used in a particular research situation should be selected to test the applicability of knowledge, a theory, or model in a particular setting.

- The four general research methods in OB are case study, field study, correlational study, and experiment. Cases are used widely and effectively in teaching but are considered somewhat impressionistic as a research method. Yet cases do provide a rich source of ideas for further research. Field studies use multiple methods of data collection. Employees themselves are interviewed or are asked to complete questionnaires or are observed directly.

- A *correlational study* typically investigates the relationship between independent variables measured by a questionnaire with standing on an outside dependent variable such as productivity or absenteeism. Correlation should not be confused with causation.

- Experiments vary in complexity and type of experimental design. Experiments can be classified as belonging to one of three categories: laboratory, field, and simulation. The experimental method calls for the use of control groups or an experimental manipulation that serves the same purpose (such as the multiple-baseline design with a reversal component illustrated in this chapter).

- Many different sources of error are possible in research about human behavior in organizations. Among them are inaccurate information, limited application of results, the social desirability factor, invalid measures, reactivity of methods, extraneous influences, and nonrandom assignment of subjects to the experimental and control groups. Before research is conducted with humans, ethical issues, such as possible harm to subjects, must be reviewed carefully.

Questions for Discussion

1. Provide an example of how the problem of reactivity could influence the results of a study about consumer preferences for a particular product or service.

2. Why is it that the term "theory" has such a negative connotation among managers in most organizations?

3. What safeguards can any scientific discipline take against the problem of faked results being reported by researchers?

4. How much effort do you think most people put into completing a research questionnaire? Use yourself as a representative case example.

5. If it is true that the case method is a weak scientific tool, what implications does this have for information about organizations that you read in *The Wall Street Journal, Business Week,* and the like?

6. Which methods of data collection would you choose for studying the job satisfaction of computer scientists? of data-entry clerks?

7. Identify several examples of "hard data" that could be used in organizational behavior research.

8. Identify several examples of "soft data" that could be used in organizational behavior research.

An Organizational Behavior Problem

"What Are Word Processors Really Doing for Our Company?"

Barry Rogers, president of NATCO Insurance, called Irv Chandler, vice president of human resources, into his office. Starting the conversation, Rogers said, "I know you've been busy grappling with the problem of investigating our program of creating the right opportunities for handicapped employees. That's a project we certainly think is important. But I have something else in mind that might represent another interesting problem for you to investigate.

"As you know, Irv," Rogers continued, "our firm has invested substantial sums of money in word processing centers in our regional offices. Right now, I'm not concerned about the larger word processing centers that have replaced the steno pools in the home office. Each work station complete with the electronic typewriter, computer, and built-in software costs about $10,000. We decided to take this step as a way of improving productivity in our branches. But lately, we're beginning to wonder what we have bought for our money."

"What specific reservations do you have?" asked Irv.

"The word processing work stations sure look impressive, but what are they really accomplishing for NATCO? Are we investing our money wisely, or are we spending money on a frill? I want to know if employees are any happier or more productive using word processing than they were when using the previous equipment. Maybe electric typewriters combined with the old dictating equipment were just as good.

"Another problem to ponder is that some of the office supervisors think that age seems to make a difference. Younger women may be more favorably inclined toward word processing than older women.

"Other members of the executive committee and I would like the human resources department to provide us some answers to the questions I've asked."

After thinking for a moment, Chandler replied, "Barry, you're asking the right questions. This is just the kind of assignment our people in personnel research should be tackling. I'll have some preliminary thoughts about our approach in a couple of weeks."

Questions

1. Design a study to test for the effects of word processing on satisfaction and productivity among regional office personnel.

2. What interaction effects does Barry Rogers seem to think might be taking place? Your experimental design should attempt to measure these effects.

Additional Reading

BOUCHARD, THOMAS J. "Field Research Methods: Interviewing, Questionnaires, Participant Observation, Systematic Observation, Unobtrusive Measures," in Marvin D. Dunnette, ed., *Handbook of Industrial and Organizational Psychology* (Chicago: Rand McNally, 1976), pp. 363–414.

Cook, Thomas D., and Donald T. Campbell. "The Design and Conduct of Quasi-Experiments and True Experiments in Field Settings," *Handbook of Industrial and Organizational Psychology,* pp. 223–326.

Dubin, Robert. "Theory Building in Applied Areas," in *Handbook of Industrial and Organizational Psychology,* pp. 17–40.

Fromkin, Howard L., and Siegfried Streufert. "Laboratory Experimentation," in *Handbook of Industrial and Organizational Psychology,* pp. 416–65.

Kerlinger, Fred N. *Foundations of Behavioral Research.* New York: Holt, Rinehart and Winston, 1973.

Varela, Jacobo A. "Solving Human Problems with Human Science." *Human Nature,* October 1978, pp. 84–90.

Weick, Karl E. "Laboratory Experimentation with Organizations: A Reappraisal." *Academy of Management Review,* January 1977, pp. 123–27.

Appendix

Measurement Properties of Tests and Questionnaires

References to, or samples of, tests and questionnaires are found throughout this text. Most of these tests are research or self-examination exercises. Before a test or questionnaire is offered to the public, or to psychologists for use with the public, its reliability and validity must be known. It is also helpful to know the type of measurement or scale represented by that test or questionnaire. Here we summarize several of the major concepts dealing with the inner properties of the type of questionnaires widely used in OB research.[17,18]

TYPES OF MEASUREMENT OR SCALES

There are four basic types of measurement or scales, the simplest being nominal scales, followed in complexity or precision by ordinal scales, interval scales, and ratio scales.

A *nominal* scale places things into basic mutually exclusive categories of the

[17]A primary source of information about the psychometric properties of tests and questionnaires is Anne Anastasi, *Psychological Testing,* 5th ed. (New York: Macmillan, 1982), Chapters 5, 6, and 7.

[18]A more concise source aimed primarily at the organizational application of tests and questionnaires is Ernest J. McCormick and Daniel Ilgen, *Industrial Psychology,* 7th ed. (Englewood Cliffs, N.J.: Prentice-Hall, 1980), pp. 106–13.

variable under measurement. Examples include sex, highest educational degree earned, smoker and nonsmoker, and rural and urban. An *ordinal* scale is used to characterize the rank order on some variable of individual cases in a sample such as the ranking of sales representatives with respect to gross sales or commissions. As ordinal scale does not provide information about the distance between adjacent ranks.

Interval scales have the properties of both the nominal and ordinal scales and also provide a measurement of distance. A difference of five points, for example, theoretically means the same thing between any two points on the scale. The difference between scores of 90 and 95 should mean the same thing as the difference between scores of 35 and 40. Most questionnaires are believed to be interval scales. Paper-and-pencil measures of human behavior have yet to go beyond the interval scale. A *ratio* scale is the same as an interval scale with the additional feature of an absolute zero point. Physical measures, such as height and weight are ratio scales. Although such a person has not been located, we know precisely the nature of zero weight or height. Measures of creativity and stress, however, lack a true zero point.

RELIABILITY OF TESTS AND QUESTIONNAIRES

After a scale has been devised, it is essential to know how reliably we are measuring the concept under consideration. Reliability refers to the consistency or stability of whatever measurements are in question. The American Psychological Association recognizes three different types of reliability coefficients: coefficient of stability, coefficient of equivalence, and coefficient of internal consistency.

A *coefficient of stability* is based on the relationship between scores on the same instrument given twice or more times to a sample of people. It is called the test-retest method. Assuming that you have not changed on the variable measured by the questionnaire, today's scores should be about the same as the score you will achieve upon retest in the near future.

A *coefficient of equivalence* measures the equivalence of two or more forms of the same measuring instrument. A clear-cut example of the coefficient of equivalence reliability index would be the correlation between two forms of alternative forms of a test. People should receive about the same scores on the two forms of the test, and the means and standard deviations for the two forms should be approximately the same.

The *coefficient of internal consistency* is an index of the measuring instrument's correlation with itself. A person should achieve approximately equal scores on comparable-size sections of the instrument, if those sections measure the same variable. For example, a person who shows highly favorable attitudes toward the company on one part of a survey should also show highly favorable attitudes in response to another part of the questionnaire. Internal consistency is often measured by the Kuder-Richardson formula 20, which estimates an average of all the split-halves correlations that could have been obtained using all possible ways of dividing the test.

VALIDITY OF TESTS
AND QUESTIONNAIRES

Validity refers to the extent to which a measuring device measures what it purports to measure. Validity is thus more crucial than reliability because it tells us whether or not we are measuring the correct thing. Many written tests consistently measure verbal ability, but they do not measure well what they claim to be measuring. Of particular interest to behavioral researchers are criterion-related validity, construct validity, and content validity.

Criterion-related validity refers to the relationship between scores on a measuring instrument and one or more independent (outside) criteria. Job performance is frequently used as a criterion by which to validate measuring instruments. Suppose that people who score highly on the creativity test presented in Chapter 8 tend to receive high performance ratings on creativity, obtain an above-average number of patents, and win an above-average number of suggestion awards. We would have some evidence that the test shows criterion-related validity, and this relationship would be expressed in terms of a correlation coefficient. If measurements made at one point in time are correlated with standing on a criterion at some point in the future, the criterion-related validity is also referred to as *predictive* validity.

Construct validity refers to the extent to which the measuring instrument measures the construct or variable it claims to measure. If an OB researcher developed an instrument to measure quality of work life, construct validity would be needed to demonstrate that indeed QWL is being measured. Often, the validation proceeds indirectly, such as comparing scores on the QWL instrument with mental and physical health ratings. A person who is experiencing a high QWL should be in good physical and mental health. A construct can also be considered an underlying psychological quality that is presumed to exist, although it cannot be observed directly. Many widely used concepts such as job satisfaction and assertiveness are constructs.

Content validity refers to whether or not a measuring instrument covers a representative sample of the behavior domain to be measured. The tryout for a football player or dancer usually has high content validity—the job applicants are asked to demonstrate many of the skills they would actually be performing on the field or on stage. Frequently, the judgment of experts is used to determine if a test or questionnaire has good content validity. Content validity has also been referred to as "face" validity. If a measuring instrument is to meet with approval from management, it usually needs content or face validity.

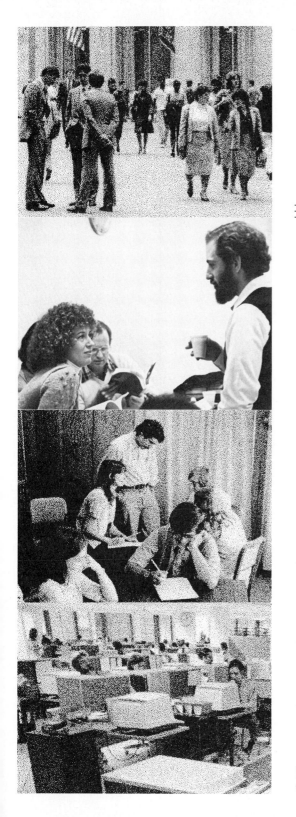

PART TWO

Understanding Individuals

Organizational behavior in reality is the behavior of individuals acting alone or in concert. Without people, organizations would not exist, and if people did not arrange themselves into small groups and organizations, their accomplishments would be severely curtailed. In recognition of the importance of individuals in organizations, this part of the book emphasizes a variety of concepts about individuals relevant to understanding human behavior in organizations.

Chapters 3 and 4 taken together represent a review of selected, cornerstone concepts about the psychology of individual behavior. Combined, these two chapters could be labeled "key determinants of individual behavior." Additionally, Chapter 3 explains the influence of individual differences and environmental factors on behavior. Chapters 5 through 8 deal with a mixture of enduring and current topics in OB. Motivation and job satisfaction are discussed in Chapters 5 and 6, respectively, with an emphasis on modern developments. Chapter 7, on stress and burnout, reflects the emphasis that these topics are receiving in the current literature. Creativity, the subject of Chapter 8, is a topic of particular concern as organizations compete in an environment of scarce resources.

CHAPTER 3

Perception Learning, Motives, and Values

LEARNING OBJECTIVES

1. To understand the implications of individual differences and environmental influences while dealing with people in organizations.

2. To explain some basic concepts about uncomplicated and complicated human learning.

3. To understand how perception, motives, needs, and values may influence behavior in organizations.

4. To be ready to incorporate into one's handling of people some basic concepts about learning, motives, needs, and values.

Rick Rinaldi was happily employed as a software specialist at Mainstream Data Systems. At age twenty-four, he was earning more money and held more responsibility than he anticipated at this stage in his career. Yet his contentment with MDS didn't stop him from at least listening to the scientific recruiter from International Communications Corporation. Both the recruiter and others at International Communications emphasized how much better off Rick would ultimately be at their company. As Rick's prospective boss put it, "I can understand how you enjoy the excitement of that little company you work for. Not a bad idea for a person getting started in his career. But don't you think you'd be better off playing in the big leagues? Don't forget, there's a very high ceiling here. No doubt, there's a very low ceiling at your little firm. Get my point?"

Rick did get the point, and with mixed emotions, he accepted a systems analyst position with ICC. The decisive point for Rick was the jump in job responsibility, combined with a $2,750 annual salary increment. Rick began his new position with a burst of enthusiasm. He visualized himself as someday becoming a high-ranking management information systems executive at ICC. Yet as the weeks passed, Rick began to notice that he was having more trouble with what he perceived as red tape and overly cautious employees.

Rick's concern about a lack of organizational flexibility came to a head over an incident with a malfunctioning display terminal. Rick suggested to the department manager responsible for the terminal, "My opinion is that this broken terminal isn't worth fixing. My old company, MDS, has a terminal that works quite well and is underpriced in today's market."

"Hold on a minute," answered the manager. "We are not authorized to make new purchases in this department. You're stepping way out of line even making the suggestion. Before we could entertain the idea of using a new vendor, the problem would have to be studied quite carefully."

Several days after the incident involving the computer terminal, Ed McNabb, Rick's boss, called him into the office. "Rick, there is something we have to talk about. It seems that you are the high-talent guy we were looking for when we hired you. But you're just not allowing your talent to take hold here. Things aren't going as well as we planned in certain delicate areas."

"What delicate areas are you talking about?" asked Rick. "Well, to be frank, you're beginning to rub people the wrong way. You're too impatient. You overstep your bounds as a systems analyst. You seem to be having some trouble accepting the limits of your job description. We like your talent, but you're creating too many enemies by the way you try to get things done in a hurry."

"I hear what you're saying," responded Rick. "But I'm not so sure if I'm buying it. Back at my old firm, making waves was an asset. Here I feel like a fish out of water. Maybe I'm better suited for a free-swinging small company. Maybe I don't belong in a corporate behemoth like ICC."

"I'm glad we talked about this problem of your rounding off your rough edges. I think things will work out for you here now that you understand the problem."

Two weeks later Rick quit ICC and rejoined MDS in his former capacity.

INDIVIDUAL DIFFERENCES AND
ENVIRONMENTAL INFLUENCES
ON BEHAVIOR

There are many reasons that a talented person such as Rick is unable or unwilling to make the transition from a small informal firm to a large, formal corporation. Underlying Rick's problem was that fact that his individual characteristics (impatience, impulsiveness, and brusqueness with people) interacted poorly with members of a bureaucracy. The bureaucratic form of organization values adherence to rules and cordial transactions among people (see Chapter 16). In managing organizational behavior, relevant individual differences and environmental factors must always be taken into consideration.

A basic proposition of psychology states that behavior is a function of the person interacting with his or her environment.[1] The equation reads

$$B = f(P \times E)$$

where B stands for behavior, P stands for the person, and E represents the environment. One implication of this equation is that behavior is determined indirectly by the effects of the individual and the environment on each other. Rick's tendencies toward impatience may have been intensified when he was placed in a bureaucratic environment. In a small firm, Rick was able to control these tendencies to a level at which they served as an asset to him and the company. Have you ever noticed that some environments, and some people, bring out your worst traits? Or your best traits?

The game of tennis provides a precise illustration of the proposition $B = f(P \times E)$. Some tennis players perform much better on slow than on fast surfaces. Usually those players with more deliberate and less powerful games prosper on slow surfaces. Virtually every concept mentioned in this text can be influenced by differences in individual and environmental factors. At various points we illustrate this influence. A constant reminder of these relationships would suit some people, while others might find it irritating, as implied by the basic proposition under study here.

In the balance of this chapter, we take a general look at individual differences and environmental factors. Then we begin a discussion of determinants of individual behavior that continues into Chapter 4. A key point to remember throughout is that individual differences and environmental factors influence the determinants of behavior. For instance, people of high natural learning ability adapt more quickly to the introduction of new work procedures. But how these procedures are implemented affect how quickly they adapt.

---

[1]This equation traces back to Kurt Lewin, *A Dynamic Theory of Personality* (New York: McGraw-Hill, 1935). The reformulation of its meaning to organizational behavior is based on H. Joseph Reitz, *Behavior in Organizations,* 2nd ed. (Homewood, Ill.: Richard D. Irwin, 1981), pp. 21–23.

Individual Differences

Applied psychology began with the awareness that individual differences in personal characteristics influence how people perform on the job. The challenge to the manager is to (1) find some reliable way of measuring these differences on the job and (2) manage for them. Sometimes the task is straightforward. A first-level supervisor may observe that one employee learns much more quickly than others. The employee would therefore require less guidance than others when a new task was introduced into the department. Among the hundreds of job-relevant variables on which people differ are problem-solving ability, visual acuity, strength, listening acuity, tolerance for ambiguity, report-writing skill, oral communication skill, manual dexterity, tolerance for stress, and creativity.

If individual differences are such an important fact of human behavior, why bother studying generalizations about such topics as motivation, learning, and creativity? One reason is that although people may differ in their relative position on these aspects of behavior (such as which needs they are trying to satisfy), the same processes apply approximately equivalently to all people. It might take one employee only one sitting to learn how to operate a data-entry device. Another employee might require four trials. However, they are both learning by the process called imitation (or modeling). Another reason for studying general principles about human behavior is that they do play a role in understanding individual behavior, particularly when they are combined with an understanding of individual differences.

To illustrate, a general principle of motivation is that people will expend effort to satisfy an important need. Being guided by this principle, the way in which to motivate a given person is to allow for that person's need satisfaction by understanding what needs he or she is trying to satisfy. One must also figure out what reward will satisfy that need. If you believe that a subordinate of yours craves recognition, you might offer that employee a chance to represent the company at an important meeting, providing that his or her work output reached a specified level for a period of time.

Another way of conceptualizing the role of individual differences in job behavior is to say that individual differences *moderate* the way in which people respond to organizational practices.[2] A company might install air conditioning, considered to be badly needed by 80 percent of the work force. Twenty percent of the employees would probably grumble that the workplace is too cold. Four of the many ways in which individual differences have important implications for managing organizational behavior are discussed here.

1. *People differ in their basic energy level and resistance to fatigue.* As one supervisor noted, "When the going gets tough around here, some of my people wilt and stay

---

[2]The basic concept behind this discussion is based on W. Clay Hamner and Dennis W. Organ, *Organizational Behavior: An Applied Psychological Approach* (Plano, Tex.: Business Publications, 1978), p. 186.

home. It's usually the same ones." Some people are poorly suited to the demands of an executive position simply because their bodies cannot take the wear and tear of heavy travel, long hours, and constant meetings. Many people who appear to be unusually well-motivated may in fact simply have more physical and mental energy to expend. Individual differences in energy are noticeable in early childhood, sometimes even in the womb!

2. *People differ in the importance they attach to intrinsic job rewards.* People with a love of work seek out stimulating, exciting, or enriched jobs. Yet about one-third to one-half of the work force are not looking for enriched, intrinsically interesting work. They prefer jobs that require a minimum of mental involvement and responsibility. Some people prefer to daydream on the job and find their self-fulfillment through recreational and family life. For such individuals (the opposite of work addicts), a repetitive job is the most pleasing. In Chapter 5, we return to the topic of job enrichment.

3. *People differ in the style of leadership they prefer and require for good performance.* Many employees prefer as much freedom as possible on the job and can function well under a leader who grants such autonomy. Other individuals want to be supervised closely by the manager. Employees also vary with respect to the amount of supervision they require. In general, less competent, less motivated, and less experienced workers require more supervision. One of the biggest challenges facing a manager is to supervise people who need close supervision but resent it when it is administered.

4. *People differ in their need for interpersonal contact.* As a by-product of their personality traits, psychological needs, and vocational interests, individuals vary widely in how much "people contact" they need on the job to keep them satisfied. Some people can work alone all day and remain highly productive. Others become restless unless they are engaged in business or social conversation with another employee. Sometimes a business luncheon is scheduled more out of a manager's need for social contact than out of a need for discussing job problems.

5. *People differ in their tolerance for responsibility.* Some employees are eager to accept responsibility because they find it inherently pleasant and also because it leads to greater organizational rewards. At the other extreme, some employees prefer accepting to giving orders and dislike being forced to make decisions. A frequently expressed sentiment of such employees is "Who wants the headaches of being a supervisor?"

A day-by-day challenge to management is to find creative ways of managing for individual differences that simultaneously allow the organization to reach its goals. Personnel testing and other selection techniques when used properly to place people in organizations represent one approach to managing individual differences. A modern development that manages for individual differences is flexitime. It allows people to have some say in choosing their own working hours, within limits (see Chapter 6). The individual difference managed for in flexitime is employee preferences about working hours, which in turn may be based on family demands or on individual energy cycles.

In trying to manage for individual differences, the manager is advised to use the diagnostic model described in Chapter 2. Using close observation and discussions with the employee, the manager may estimate how the employee stands on a variable such as tolerance for demanding work. Assignments are then made accordingly.

Intraindividual Differences

Our discussion of individual differences has concentrated on differences between and among different people. *Intra*individual differences are also of significance to both practitioners and researchers. Intraindividual differences refer to the variations within the same person at different points in time. One person may show high motivation under some circumstances but not under others. An environmental factor can sometimes cause this variation in behavior and performance; Rick Rinaldi, for example, experienced intraindividual variations in job performance associated with a difference in organizational climate between his old and new employer. A person's stage in life and/or career can also create intraindividual differences. A person nearing retirement may become much less of a risk taker than he or she was earlier in life. Daily variations in performance and attitude may also be attributed to intraindividual differences. A "morning person" may perform much better before noon than toward the end of the work day, whereas the opposite may be true for a "night person."

Environmental Factors

The E factor in the equation $B = f(P \times E)$ is also significant. Environments can differ in almost as many ways as people. The climate might be supportive or nonsupportive; the working conditions can be comfortable or uncomfortable, safe, or toxic; coworkers can be stimulating or stultifying; and the equipment can be reliable or unreliable. Three particularly significant sets of environmental factors are the physical, human, and structural.[3]

1. *The physical environment.* Much has been studied about the impact of the physical environment on human performance and satisfaction. The entire field of human engineering deals with how performance is influenced by the surrounding physical system. We know that when there is too much noise, or too little, performance will decrease in some kinds of tasks. A competent computer specialist will perform admirably placed in the midst of properly functioning computer software and hardware. The same specialist forced to work with obsolete and frequently breaking-down equipment will perform much less admirably.

The influence of illumination on performance illustrates the amount of research that has been conducted about the physical environment and job performance. In gen-

---

[3]The first two of these factors are based on Reitz, *Behavior in Organizations,* pp. 82–83.

eral, if you have too little illumination for the task at hand, your performance will suffer. A few examples of recommended illumination for job tasks are given here:[4]

Task	Recommended Illumination (in foot-candles)
Surgical operating table	2,500
Very difficult inspection	500
Proofreading	150
General office work	70–150
Food preparation	70
Wrapping and labeling	50
Loading (materials handling)	20

2.   *The human environment.* People themselves can influence the behavior and performance of other people in myriad ways. Supportive, cooperative co-workers can enhance the performance and satisfaction of a person (like most of us) who needs such reassurance. Hostile, competitive co-workers can diminish the work performance and satisfaction of even a self-confident employee. Much of this book is concerned with the human environment in organizations and how the human environment influences behavior. Topics such as leadership, conflict, and organizational effectiveness are aspects of the human environment.

An analysis of how the human environment (or social environment in his terms) can sometimes produce significant changes in performance can be shown by the *social facilitation effect.* When others are around, we tend to perform differently from when we are alone. The presence of an audience, crowd, or co-workers facilitates the performance of well-learned responses. Yet the presence of such people tends to interfere with learning new skills or performing newly learned responses.[5]

An underlying theoretical explanation is that other people increase the arousal level of a performer and make well-learned responses more likely to occur. During the baseball strike of the 1981 season, several of the striking superstars noted that practice sessions in empty ballfields were not adequate to maintain their skills. As Reggie Jackson put it, "I need an audience to do my thing. Empty stands just don't work for me." When you are trying out a new skill, the presence of other people can be a problem. People tend to slip back to well-established behavior patterns when faced with the arousing effects of other people.

An implication of the social facilitation effect for managers is that learning situations should be distinguished from on-the-job performance. Since other people in the

---

[4]Quoted from data gathered by Ernest J. McCormick and Daniel Ilgen, *Industrial Psychology,* 7th ed. (Englewood Cliffs, N.J.: Prentice-Hall, 1980), p. 386.

[5]R. G. Geen and J. J. Gange, "Drive Theory of Social Facilitation: Twelve Years of Theory and Research," *Psychological Bulletin,* Vol. 84, 1978, pp. 1267–88. As referenced in Reitz, *Behavior in Organizations,* p. 84.

environment can inhibit performance, trainees should be given ample opportunity to practice new skills alone. After the new skills are thoroughly learned, trainees can be placed in situations involving other people where their presence might enhance performance.[6]

3. *The structural environment.* Another set of environmental factors that influence behavior in organizations relates to such things as the organization structure, policies, procedures, rules, and regulations. Collectively, these factors make up the formal organization. We saw how rules and regulations about making extemporaneous purchases triggered Rick Rinaldi's impatience. Some organization structures have a stultifying effect on people; others enhance creativity. It is the combination of a given personality type with a given aspect of organization structure that produces a specific aspect of behavior. A cautious person who needs structure would thrive in a work setting where tight rules reduce most of the ambiguity.

A series of studies conducted in one hundred British industries illustrates at a broader level how organizational structure influences business success (an important consequence of human output). One aspect of these classic studies concerned the interrelationships among levels of technical sophistication, organizational structure, and business success. According to Woodward's typology, level of technological sophistication can be divided into three basic types:

Job order (unit) production is the least complex method of manufacturing. Each unit of production is made to customer specifications. Thus, the operations performed on each unit of output is relatively nonrepetitive and noncomparable. A custom printer or a custom automobile manufacturer would fit this category. *Mass-production* manufacturing (such as the production of automobiles or refrigerators) represents the medium level of sophistication. *Process manufacturing* represents the high end of the technology continuum. In this approach, the product is standardized and moves in a predictable and repetitive sequence from one process to the next. The manufacture of chemicals or fertilizers is done by process or continuous-flow manufacturing.

An important finding was that successful job order and process-type manufacturing organizations tended toward certain structural characteristics: (1) less emphasis on precise job descriptions—people were less constrained by rules and regulations—(2) a higher degree of delegation of authority—subordinates were given more decision-making responsibility—(3) a more permissive management style—less emphasis was placed on authoritative management—and (4) less tightly organized work forces.

In the successful firms engaged in mass-production manufacturing (middle ranges of technological complexity), the line versus staff organization was the most highly developed. Other differences between mass-production companies and the other two types studied were found. Mass-production companies (versus the other two broad types studied) were also characterized by (1) more production administration and greater supervision of production operators, (2) more elaborate control proce-

[6]Reitz, *Behavior in Organizations,* p. 85.

dures, (3) more rigid application of sanctions (deviation from company policy was more likely to be reprimanded), and (4) reliance upon written communication.[7]

So far this chapter has explained how individual differences and environmental factors influence behavior. The balance of this chapter and the following chapter discuss several key determinants of individual behavior. The additional reading section should be consulted for more information about these topics.

HOW PERCEPTION INFLUENCES BEHAVIOR

Most of us interpret what is going on in the world outside of us as we see it—not as it really is. A directive might come down from top management that a particular state agency is in for a period of belt tightening. A financial analyst in the agency may perceive this directive as a refreshing bit of good news. She believes that finally more attention will be paid to the financial analysis function. A sixty-year-old supervisor in the motor pool may tremble at the same announcement. He believes that belt tightening will result in his position being declared surplus.

Perception is the process by which people screen, select, organize, and interpret stimuli so that these stimuli have meaning to them.[8] Four aspects of human perception particularly helpful in interpreting job behavior are (1) the conditions under which perceptual problems occur, (2) how people interpret various environmental cues and stimuli, (3) how people act as a consequence of these interpretations, and (4) how people interpret the reasons or causes for their behavior (attribution theory).

Perceptual Problems

People are most likely to encounter perceptual problems when the stimulus or cue to be perceived triggers an emotional response. A manager discussing recruiting plans for his department at a staff meeting casually mentioned that "From now on we are only going to hire fully qualified professionals. We already have our quota of people with less than full credentials." Two weeks later, the manager learned of the negative impact this statement had on several members of the professional staff. One engineer with a bachelor's degree in physics said to a co-worker, "I guess Tom's statement means that I'll never get promoted. I may have a tough career decision to make." Another engineer said, "It sounds as if Tom doesn't think much of our credentials. Maybe he thinks some of us didn't attend the right schools."

The emotional stimulus emitted by the manager was the term "fully qualified professional." Communication and perception form a system. Our perception influ-

---

[7]Joan Woodward, *Industrial Organization: Theory and Practice* (London: Oxford University Press, 1965), pp. 68–80.

[8]Richard M. Steers, *Introduction to Organizational Behavior* (Glenview, Ill.: Scott, Foresman and Company, 1981), p. 98.

ences the messages that we receive and how we interpret them. Perhaps Tom would have elicited fewer perceptual problems from his subordinates if he had removed some of the emotional sting from his message. One possibility would have been, "We are very pleased with the background and credentials of our professional staff. But as technology has changed, we will be looking for a more specific set of credentials in future job applicants." Innocuous messages in staff meetings, such as "We will be getting a new photocopying machine," encounter much fewer perceptual problems.

Characteristics of a Person That Influence Perception

Six factors notably influence perception both on and off the job. One or more of these factors may influence perception at a given time. Sometimes being aware of them can help you to manage another individual; at other times developing a compensatory strategy is beyond ordinary skill.

1. *Anatomical and physiological or chemical condition.* A frail person might perceive lifting a forty-five-pound box to be a difficult task, whereas a stronger person would perceive the task as a pleasant exercise. A cigarette addict would perceive two hours in a meeting room that prohibited smoking as a threatening experience. Thus, anatomy and physiological or chemical conditions exert some influence on job perception and behavior.

2. *Family influences.* A profound influence on the perception and behavior of most people is their family background, both present and past. A person reared in a family where parents have strong authority is likely to perceive an order from a boss as a normal way of life. A person raised in a family where authority and power are shared with parents and children may have a more difficult time perceiving orders as legitimate. That particular employee may have a stronger need for freedom from supervision.

3. *Cultural influences.* A person's cultural background is another major influence on his or her perception of stimuli in a job environment. A young man whose cultural values influence him to perceive work as a necessary evil or as punishment might have a negative attitude toward an extra assignment. Another young man whose cultural values influence him to perceive work as a privilege and a prime reason for living will take a different view of the stimulus of additional work. He may express enthusiasm for the project, whereas his less work-oriented counterpart may show passive resistance (drag his heels).

4. *Motives, needs, and goals.* When people perceive stimuli, they process it into cognitions, which precede, and may influence, their response. The formation of these cognitions (or items of information about the world outside) are influenced by many inner states that are inferred but are not tangible. Atoms were conceptually similar to these inner states until the atomic microscope proved their existence! Among the many inner conditions that influence our cognitions (and, therefore, our perceptions) are mo-

tives, needs, and goals. Consequently, a major determinant of people's perception is their motivation at the time with respect to the object or experience to be perceived (the stimulus or cue).

An employee who believes that her family is deprived because they lack a color television will take an active interest in a suggestion system that offers cash awards. Another woman who is not currently interested in acquiring new possessions or who has a low need for recognition may barely notice the suggestion system box. More will be said about the influence of needs, motives, and goals on behavior later in this chapter and the next two.

5. *Past experiences.* How a person perceives a stimulus today is heavily influenced by what happened when that stimulus was presented in the past. These past experiences contribute to our cognitive structure. An older employee may perceive a younger worker assigned to the department as a threat because in the past he was shown up by an energetic young worker. An employee who demands clarification on the smallest work rules, such as the limits to lunch hour, may be reacting to a past event: her last employer fired her for chronically returning late from lunch.

6. *Personality characteristics.* How a person perceives an event is also influenced by his or her stable traits and characteristics, or personality. An optimistic, adventuresome individual might perceive a new boss as a welcome challenge. The boss represents another influential person to impress with his or her job competence. A pessimistic, cautious individual might perceive the same new boss as a threat—as another influential person who might think critically of his or her job performance.

Devices That People Use to Deal with Sensory Information

Under ideal circumstances, the employee perceives information as it is intended to be communicated or as it exists in reality. A junior accountant examining a set of figures will arrive, it is hoped, at a conclusion that will satisfy both his boss and generally accepted accounting principles. And a union steward offered a promotion to a supervisory position will perceive it as an act of good faith on the part of management, not as a plot to get him out of the union. In reality, people use a number of devices to help them simplify their perception of external events.[9]

1. *Denial.* If the sensory information is particularly painful to us, we often deny to ourselves and others that the information even existed. A secretary confronted with the fact that her use of the office copying machine to make copies of her shrimp creole recipe was against company regulations replied, "I never saw that regulation," even though she had typed the company policy manual just six months previous to the confrontation.

[9]A similar treatment is found in most discussions of perception. The specific reference here is Hamner and Organ, *Organizational Behavior,* pp. 99–100.

2.   *Stereotyping.* A common method of simplifying the perceptual process is to evaluate an individual or thing on the basis of our perception of the group or class to which he, she, or it belongs. One production employee said he preferred not to accept a transfer to the quality-control department, giving as his reason, "I don't want to work for a nitpicker."

3.   *Halo effect.* A tendency exists to color everything that we know about a person because of one recognizable favorable or unfavorable trait. When a company does not insist upon the use of objective measures of performance, it is not uncommon for a supervisor to give a favorable performance rating to people who dress well or smile frequently. The fine appearance or warm smile of these people has created a halo around them.

4.   *Expectancy.* If a person perceives or expects that another individual will behave in a particular way, that person often lives up to such an expectancy. A manager who perceives an employee as being competent will actually help that person to become competent by giving him or her subtle signs of encouragement. Unfortunately, if you expect somebody to fail, he or she will often live down to your expectation.

5.   *Projection.* Another shortcut in the perceptual process is to project our own faults onto others instead of making an objective appraisal of the situation. A manager might listen to a supervisor's request for one additional clerk because of what the supervisor perceives as a heavy work load within her department. The manager might mutter, "Who does she think she is, trying to build an empire for herself?" In reality, the manager might be the empire builder and is projecting this undesirable characteristic onto her supervisor.

6.   *Selective perception.* A person uses this mechanism when he or she draws an unjustified conclusion from an unclear situation. Upon his return from a weekend of hunting, a tool and die maker might see his supervisor's car leaving his block. Once in the door, he confronts his wife with the *fact* that she and his boss are having an affair. Perhaps the tool and die maker in question is looking for an excuse to have a fight with his wife (or his boss). Since human psychology is always complex, it could also be concluded that he is thinking of having an affair himself!

7.   *Perceptual defense.* Once we hold a perception of something or somebody, we tend to cling to that perception by making things that we see, hear, smell, or touch consistent with that belief. All the previous perceptual shortcuts are involved in perceptual defense. Not only do middle managers and individual performers engage in perceptual defense. The president of an American camera company insisted for a period of ten years that Japanese competitors were not a serious threat to his company's high-priced line of cameras. At this writing, that company has been out of business for thirteen years, and the former president owns and operates a hardware store.[10]

---

[10]This discussion follows closely Andrew J. DuBrin, *Effective Business Psychology* (Reston, Va.: Reston, 1980), pp. 28–30.

Attribution Theory: How People Perceive Causation

Attribution theory studies the process by which the individual ascribes causes to the behavior he or she perceives.[11] Your perception of cause and effect in a given situation leads to a cognition (or understanding) about the future. If you perceive that a rival was promoted because that person earned an advanced degree in business, you will tend to follow a similar path. If you attribute your rival's promotion to office politics, you might either quit or develop more skill in political behavior. People have a general tendency to attribute their achievements to their good inner qualities, while they attribute failure to adverse factors within the environment. A shop supervisor thus would take credit for increased productivity but blame low productivity on faulty machinery or inept employees.

Aside from this attribution of the causes of personal success and failure, people tend to put more emphasis on P as the cause of behavior than on E in the equation $B = f(P \times E)$. A commercial artist will thus tend to form the cognition (or develop the insight) that her creativity is the result of inborn talent. In contrast, a behaviorist would tend to argue that this woman has received the right type of reinforcements from her environment (to be discussed shortly).

Locus of control. An offshoot of attribution theory is the concept of locus of control, which classifies the general way in which people look at causation in their lives. Some people perceive their outcomes as controlled internally and therefore believe, to a large extent, that they are in control of their own lives. Some people believe that their outcomes are controlled externally, thus believing that much of what happens to them in life is controlled by circumstances.[12] Employees who perceive an internal locus of control are generally more mature, self-reliant, and responsible. In one study of nine hundred employees in a public utility, it was found that employees with an internal locus of control had higher levels of job satisfaction and were more attuned to a participative management style.[13] They enjoyed participating in decisions as a way of controlling their work environment.

Attribution theory is helpful in managing people because it alerts one to the fact that people look for causes of events and alter their behavior because of these perceptions. For instance, it would be important for morale to explain carefully to members of the work group why a particular employee was fired to avoid serious misinterpretation.

[11]Larry L. Cummings and Randall B. Dunham, *Introduction to Organizational Behavior: Text and Readings* (Homewood, Ill.: Richard D. Irwin, 1980), pp. 86–89.

[12]An original source is Julian B. Rotter, "Generalized Expectancies for Internal vs. External Control of Reinforcement" *Psychological Monographs,* Vol. 80, 1966, pp. 1–28.

[13]Terence R. Mitchell, Charles M. Smyser, and Stan E. Weed, "Locus of Control: Supervision and Work Satisfaction," *Academy of Management Journal,* September 1975, pp. 623–31.

FOUR BASIC MODELS
OF LEARNING

Much of human learning takes place in organizations simply because people spend such a large proportion of their lives in organizational settings. Learning is a relatively permanent change in behavior based on practice or experience. A person does not learn how to grow physically, digest food, hear sounds, or see light. These are innate, inborn patterns of behavior. But a person does learn how to build an industrial robot, program a computer, cut hair, shovel snow, or file a report. Unless new learning takes place, few employees would be able to perform their jobs in a satisfactory manner. Understanding a few basic concepts about learning will assist you as a manager or staff specialist in facilitating the learning of other employees.

The first three types of learning to be described here are based upon a behaviorist (not behavioral) view of how people learn. The essence of this conception of learning is that people learn as a consequence of their actions. Most training programs are based upon principles of learning (such as providing feedback) that originated from a behaviorist view of the learning process. The widely used motivational systems of behavior modification and positive reinforcement (closely related concepts) are also based on behaviorism.

Learning and motivation are related processes. Learning teaches you a skill; a motivational system brings forth that skill sometime in the future. Strictly speaking, you cannot be motivated to perform a task until you have the necessary skill. To add a note of complexity, some people have a desire to learn and therefore learn more readily than others of less desire. Cognitive theories of learning emphasize such factors in the learning process as will be mentioned again in the fourth type of learning discussed in this section.

Classical Conditioning: Learning
of Specific Habits and Reflexes

Classical conditioning focuses on the process by which a bond is developed between a conditioned stimulus and a conditioned response. The bond develops because of the repeated linking of a conditioned stimulus with an unconditioned stimulus, such as hearing a refrigerator open shortly before each time somebody brings you a meal. The formal study of this process began in the late 1890s with the work of a Russian physiologist, Ivan Pavlov, who was conducting a long series of experiments about digestion. While studying a dog, Pavlov noticed that the dog salivated not only to the presence of food in the mouth, but at the sight of the food, the sound of the food trays, and even the footsteps of the experimenter.

The principles of classical conditioning stemming from his experiments help us to understand the most elementary type of learning—how people acquire uncomplicated habits and reflexes. Since most of work behavior involves more than reflexes and simple habits, classical conditioning itself is not of major consequence to the manager or individual contributor. Yet its basic principles and concepts are included in more complicated forms of learning.

Classical conditioning works in this manner. Clyde, a physically normal individual, takes an unskilled, entry-level job in a factory. His first day on the job, a bell rings in his department at 11:45 A.M. Suddenly every other worker stops working and opens a lunch box or heads out to the company cafeteria. Clyde says to himself, "The bell must mean it's time for lunch." By the third day on the job, Clyde develops stomach pangs and begins to salivate as soon as the bell rings. Prior to this job Clyde was in the habit of eating lunch at 1:00 P.M. and did not begin to have stomach pangs until that time.

Looking at the essentials of classical conditioning, here is what happened to Clyde. Since the food naturally and automatically elicits stomach pangs and salivation, it is referred to as the *unconditioned stimulus* (UCS). Salivating to the food in Clyde's lunch box or in the cafeteria occurs automatically without any learning. It is therefore called the *unconditioned response* (UCR). The sound of the department bell was originally neutral with respect to the salivary or hunger pang response, since it did not naturally elicit the UCR. Conditioning has taken place when the previously neutral stimulus (the department bell in Clyde's case) acquires the capacity to bring forth hunger pangs and salivation. The previously neutral stimulus is now called the *conditioned stimulus* (CS), and the hunger pangs and salivation to the sound of the bell are known as *conditioned responses* (CR).

Two other important conditioning concepts are also of major importance. Should the department bell ring frequently when it is not time for lunch, Clyde's hunger pangs and salivation responses will gradually cease or *extinguish*. (An important expectation is that time alone or the empty feeling in his stomach can also serve as a stimulus to Clyde.) As Clyde goes through life, he will learn not to salivate or experience hunger pangs at hearing every bell that sounds like the one used in his department. At first, he may *generalize* his learning by salivating to many different bells and experiencing hunger pangs in response to a variety of bells. After a while, Clyde will *discriminate* and only make such responses to the bell in his department (or any other bell that signals food time).

Classical conditioning helps to explain such elementary job behaviors as how people learn to avoid being conked on the head by cranes and low-hanging pipes and how we learn to step to the side of an aisle when we hear the buzz of a forklift truck behind us. It also explains how people learn to avoid being burned twice by a hot pipe or shocked twice by inserting a screwdriver into an electric outlet.

Operant Conditioning: Learning via Reinforcement

Operant conditioning is learning what takes place as a consequence of behavior. In other words, a person's actions are instrumental in determining whether or not learning takes place. A supervisor asked a darkroom technician how he learned to jiggle the trays of photo chemicals while the prints were being processed. The technician replied,

"I just tried it once and it seemed to help solve the problem of white spots appearing on the finished prints." In this case, the *operant* is the jiggling of the trays. The technician adopted jiggling as a standard practice because he received positive reinforcement—the disappearance of troublesome white spots on the prints—for his initial effort.

The name B. F. Skinner is so closely associated with the development and popularization of information about behaviorism (including reinforcement theory) that advocates of his theories have been referred to as Skinnerians. Operant conditioning differs from classical conditioning in one major respect. In classical conditioning, we can specify the unconditioned stimulus (such as food or water) that elicits the response (such as stomach contractions or salivation). In operant conditioning, somehow the individual tries out a behavior or action. If it leads to a reward, that behavior tends to be repeated. Much human learning proceeds on this basis. Learning how to ride a bicycle, drive a car on ice, surf in the ocean, or order wine in a restaurant is largely attributed to operant conditioning. Through this process we acquire skills that we did not previously know we possessed. Whenever a spontaneous behavior leads to positive reinforcement, it will tend to be repeated.

Spontaneous behavior will also tend to be repeated when it leads to relief from an uncomfortable situation, so-called *negative reinforcement.* A teenager wearing cut-off jeans while riding a motorcycle might suddenly shriek in pain when bare calves touch against an exposed part of the engine. The teenager on future rides might then wear full-length jeans (as undoubtedly recommended by the manufacturer of the motorcycle) and no longer get burned. Negative reinforcement has taken place because something aversive (the burning sensation) has been removed by means of a new behavior (wearing full-length jeans).

Punishment can be an important part of the learning process. While negative reinforcement is the withdrawal of an unpleasant stimulus, punishment is the introduction of an unpleasant stimulus. Or the threat of punishment can be used instead of actually punishing people for making the wrong response in a learning (or motivational) situation. Punishment aids the instrumental learning process because it weakens the particular response—the learner tends not to repeat a response because of its negative consequences.

A common tendency among many beginning (and some experienced) typists is to hit the "v" key when the "b" should be hit. Thus you will find typographical errors such as "livrary." A suitable form of punishment might be for the learner to be forced to retype a page whenever the "b" for "v" or "v" for "b" mistake is made. If the punishment is too severe, such as a humiliating verbal blast or an electric shock, learners may withdraw from the situation, become overly inhibited, or strike back with aggressive behavior of their own.

In practice, learning through operant conditioning proceeds as a sequence of interrelated events, as illustrated in Figure 3–1. A sales representative, for example, receives a memo from his manager to prepare a monthly report of customer inventories on the company's line of ski equipment. The memo is the conditioned stimulus. The

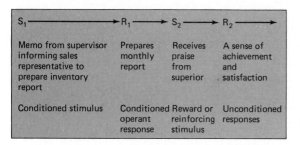

S_1		R_1	S_2	R_2	
Memo from supervisor informing sales representative to prepare inventory report		Prepares monthly report	Receives praise from superior	A sense of achievement and satisfaction	
Conditioned stimulus		Conditioned operant response	Reward or reinforcing stimulus	Unconditioned responses	

FIGURE 3–1 An Example of Operant Conditioning in Practice

sales representative's conditioned operant response is to prepare the report. The operant response is referred to as conditioned because he did not spontaneously think of preparing the report. His boss generously praises the first report for its thoroughness and clarity. Such praise acts as a reward—he has received positive reinforcement. His response is a sense of achievement and self-satisfaction. His unconditioned responses to this reward are feelings of achievement and self-satisfaction. Specific rules for the application of positive reinforcement to motivation are presented in Chapter 5. Operant conditioning is an important part of any manager's job, whether he or she applies these principles systematically or intuitively.

Learning Complicated Skills: Modeling and Shaping

When you acquire a complicated skill such as speaking in front of a group, preparing a budget, or coaching a subordinate, you experience much more than just a single stimulus-response relationship. You learn a large number of these relationships, and you also learn how to put them together in a cohesive, smooth-flowing pattern. Two important processes that help in learning complicated skills are modeling (or imitation) and shaping (learning through approximations until the total skill is learned).

Modeling occurs when you learn a skill by observing another person perform that skill. Many apprentices learn part of their trade just by watching a journeyman practice his (or her) trade. Carefully observing professional athletes on television can improve your own game in that particular sport if you have the right physical equipment and motivation. Modeling or imitation often brings forth behaviors that people did not previously seem to have in their repertoire. A cogent example centers on leadership style.

A long-time foreman with a reputation for a heavy-handed, authoritarian manner was transferred to a section run by a young, well-educated manager. The new manager treated the foreman with a great deal of respect and deference for his knowledge and experience. The foreman was initially uncomfortable in this new relationship because his previous managers, unlike his new manager, had almost never seriously sought his opinion on important matters relating to production operations. Now, the foreman is not only pleased that his opinions are valued and often put into effect, but he has begun to ask *his* subordinates, the line employees, for their views on a number of job-related matters. As the manager has done to him, the foreman also makes it a point to thank his employees for their ideas and lets them know when he implements their suggestions.[14]

Shaping involves the reinforcement of a series of small steps that build up to the final or desired behavior. It is another way in which complicated skills are learned. At each successful step of the way the learner receives some positive reinforcement. Unless the learner receives positive reinforcement at each step of the way, that person will probably not acquire the total skill. As the learner improves in his or her ability to perform the task, more skill is required to receive the reward. A young man might be shaped into an automobile mechanic through a series of small skills beginning with changing tires. He receives a series of rewards as he moves along the path from a garage helper to a mechanic who can diagnose an engine malfunction and repair the problem.

Among the forms of positive reinforcement he received along the way were approval for acquired skills, pay increments, and the feeling of pride as new minor skills were learned. The negative reinforcement he received was fewer bruised knuckles. When this series of small skills has been put together through a complicated pattern of response, the man has been converted from a fledgling garage assistant to a full-fledged mechanic.

When people learn complicated skills through modeling and shaping, the process involved is usually considered an extension of operant conditioning. However, if the learner achieves a high level of skill because he or she arrives at a series of insights or understandings, a cognitive theory of learning can be introduced as an explanation of the underlying phenomena.

Cognitive Learning Theory: Learning by Complex Mental Processes

A cognitive theory approach to learning emphasizes that learning takes place in a much more complicated fashion than can be accounted for by stimulus-response pairings alone.[15] Learners also strive to learn, they develop hunches, they have flashes of insight, they utilize many aspects of their personality in acquiring knowledge. Suppose that a safety and health specialist discovers the cause underlying a mysterious rash on the skin of many employees. It would require rather elaborate theorizing to provide an operant conditioning explanation of how he or she arrived at that conclusion. Cognitive learning theory would emphasize that the specialist may have reached the conclusion by acquiring bits of information from which the conclusion was induced. The cognitive explanation would also emphasize the goal orientation of the safety and health specialist, along with that person's reasoning and analytical skills, dedication to the cause, and problem-solving ability.

[14]Arnold P. Goldstein and Melvin Sorcher, *Changing Supervisor Behavior* (Elmsford, N.Y.: Pergamon, 1974), p. 26.

[15]Steers, *Introduction to Organizational Behavior*, p. 131.

Another example of learning in organizations that fits a cognitive theory explanation is informal learning. The central theme to such learning is that employees seem to pick up important information outside of a formal learning situation. They capitalize upon a learning situation in an unstructured situation where the rewards stemming from learning are not explicit. Informal learning has been defined as "planned learning which occurs in a setting or situation without a formal workshop, lesson plan, instructor, or examination."[16]

A case of informal learning took place at a large diversified manufacturing company whose headquarters were located in a city across the street from a plush restaurant and lounge. At the end of most working days, the lounge became the gathering place for managers from a variety of the company's divisions. While the lounge provided a social outlet, the major topics of conversation were those of mutual concern to all—work-related problems. Managers informally learned aspects of other units important to the effectiveness of their own areas of responsibility. When the lounge went out of business due to poor management, it resulted in such a breakdown in interunit communication among managers that the company seriously considered underwriting the reopening of the business. Fortunately, another restaurateur purchased the lounge and reopened it, reinstating the gathering place where much informal learning was taking place.

HOW NEEDS INFLUENCE BEHAVIOR

Cognitive theories have also contributed to our understanding of why people are motivated to perform on the job. A central idea in most cognitive theories is that people think, plan, and reason about their own behavior. They are driven by internal strivings (such as needs and motives) to accomplish worthwhile ends. Needs and motives are related concepts. A need is a deficit within an individual such as a craving for salt or recognition. A motive is a need or desire coupled with the intention to attain an appropriate goal. The most basic proposition of work motivation is that people work to satisfy needs. You will thus work hard to satisfy needs of yours that are not currently being met.

An elaboration of need satisfaction proposition is presented in Figure 3–2, which represents the central idea to need theory.[17] Assume that a twenty-three-year-old woman has a strong need for self-fulfillment. It will lead to a drive to work toward self-fulfillment. Among the actions or goal-directed behavior she takes is to apply for a position as the department manager. She achieves the position and for now her quest for self-fulfillment is at least partially satisfied. Once she receives this partial satisfaction, two things typically happen. She will soon need a stronger dose of self-fulfillment, or she will begin to concentrate on another higher-level need such as power. In

---

[16]Definition and case history are from Chip R. Bell, "Informal Learning in Organizations," *Personnel Journal,* June 1977, pp. 280–83, 313.

[17]This widely used diagram is presented here as developed by James A. F. Stoner, *Management* (Englewood Cliffs, N.J.: Prentice-Hall, 1978), p. 407.

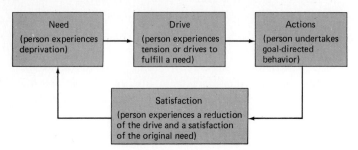

FIGURE 3–2 A Need Theory Model of Motivation

either case, the need cycle will repeat itself. The woman may seek another form of self-fulfillment or satisfaction of her need for power. It is conceivable that she will perceive becoming a manager as a source of satisfaction for both sets of needs.

Need theory is reintroduced in later discussions of personality and motives, motivation, and the causes of political behavior in organizations. Here we summarize the well-known need hierarchy theory because of its historic importance and its contribution to more complex models of motivation. In addition,we describe need achievement theory as another representative explanation of how needs influence human behavior in work settings.

Maslow's Self-actualizing Model of People

Abraham Maslow reasoned that human beings have an internal need pushing them on toward self-actualization (fulfillment) and personal superiority.[18] However, before these higher-level needs are activated, certain lower-level needs must be satisfied. A poor person thus thinks of finding a job as a way of obtaining the necessities of life. Once these are obtained, that person may think of achieving recognition and self-fulfillment on the job. When a person is generally satisfied at one level, he or she looks for satisfaction at a higher level.

A major misinterpretation of Maslow's theory is that people behave as they do because of their quest to satisfy one particular need. In reality, many different motives are dominant at any one time. A design engineer may satisfy a number of needs (for instance, recognition, esteem, and self-satisfaction) by developing a design that works in practice.

Maslow arranged human needs into a five-level triangle (see Figure 3–3). Each level refers to a *group* of needs, not one need for each rung. These need levels are described next in ascending order.

---

[18]Virtually every text on organizational behavior, human relations, introduction to management, or introduction to psychology has a discussion of Maslow's need hierarchy. An original source is Abraham Maslow, *Motivation and Personality* (New York: Harper & Row, 1954), pp. 13 ff.

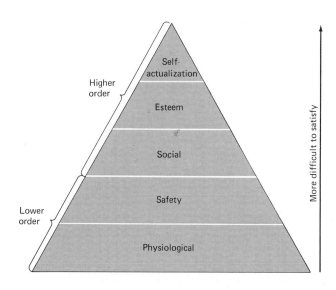

FIGURE 3–3 Maslow's Need Hierarchy

1. *Physiological needs* refer to bodily needs, such as the requirements for food, water, shelter, and sleep. In general, most jobs provide ample opportunity to satisfy physiological needs. Nevertheless, some people go to work hungry or in need of sleep. Until that person gets a satisfying meal or takes a nap, he or she will not be concerned about finding an outlet on the job for creative impulses.

2. *Safety needs* include actual physical safety as well as a feeling of being safe from both physical and emotional injury. Many jobs frustrate a person's need for safety (police officer, taxicab driver). Therefore, many people would be motivated by the prospects of a safe environment. People who do very unsafe things for a living (such as racing-car drivers and tightrope walkers) find thrills and recognition more important than safety. Many people are exceptions to Maslow's need hierarchy.

3. *Social needs* are essentially love, affection, and belongingness needs. Unlike the two previous levels of needs, social needs center on a person's interaction with other people. Many people have a strong urge to be part of a group and to be accepted by that group. Peer acceptance is important in school and on the job. Many people are unhappy with their job unless they have the opportunity to work in close contact with others.

4. *Esteem needs* represent an individual's demands to be seen as a person of worth by others—and to himself or herself. Esteem needs are also called *ego* needs, pointing to the fact that people want to be seen as competent and capable. A job that is seen by yourself and others as being worthwhile provides a good opportunity to satisfy esteem needs.

5. *Self-actualizing needs* are the highest level of needs, including the need for self-fulfillment and personal development. True self-actualization is an ideal to strive for, rather than something that automatically stems from occupying a challenging position. A self-actualized person is somebody who has become what he or she is capable

of becoming. Few of us reach all our potential, even when we are so motivated. Not every self-actualized person is a nationally or internationally prominent individual. A woman of average intelligence who attains an associate's degree and later becomes the owner-operator of an antique store might be self-actualized. Her potential and desire may both have been realized by self-employment as an antique dealer.

The need hierarchy appears to be a convenient way of classifying needs, but it has limited utility in explaining work behavior and is based on very limited empirical support. Its primary value has been the fact that it highlights the importance of human needs in a work setting. When a manager wants to motivate another individual, he or she must offer the individual a reward that will satisfy an important need. Another criticism of the hierarchy approach is that career advancement may be the true factor underlying changes in need deficiencies. Researchers found in one study that, as people advance in organizations, their needs for safety decrease. Simultaneously, they experience an increase in their needs for affiliation with other people, achievement, and self-actualization.

In working with individuals, it is important to recognize that the needs cited by Maslow are only a sample of possible human needs and are really need "categories." Other important needs include power, recognition, intellectual curiosity, and competence. People with such needs will find ways to try to satisfy them on the job.

Achievement Motivation

High levels of accomplishment at work, according to McClelland and his associates, are undergirded by high achievement needs (n Ach). People imbued with a high achievement level are "turned on" by accomplishment for its own sake; money, status, and power are secondary considerations. Accomplishment to the person with a high need for achievement usually means improving something that already exists or creating something entirely new. Extensive research in many different countries and subcultures indicates that the high achiever (1) takes personal responsibility to solve problems, (2) attempts to achieve moderate goals at calculated risks, and (3) prefers situations that provide frequent feedback on results.[19]

Entrepreneurs score quite high on psychological tests of achievement motivation. Patterns of achievement motivation are clearest in small companies. Presidents of smaller companies generally score higher than their associates. In larger companies, lower-ranking management personnel score the lowest and middle-ranking managers are just below the top score. Big-company executives tend to be somewhat average in achievement concern. McClelland notes that possibly they have done well enough to relax a little.

Tentative evidence suggests that entrepreneurs are imbued with the idea of ac-

---

[19]David C. McClelland, "Achievement Motivation Can Be Developed," *Harvard Business Review,* January–February 1965, p. 10.

complishing things, while managers have stronger needs for power. People high in *n* Ach exhibit many antiestablishment tendencies. They are concerned about solving new problems and do not overrely on tradition.

High achievement motivation, similar to any other phenomenon studied in organizational behavior, has some dysfunctional consequences. McClelland made the following comment about high achievers:

> Some psychologists think that because I've done so much on *n* Ach I must like the kind of people who have strong need for achievement. I don't. I find them bores. They are not artistically sensitive. They're entrepreneurs, kind of driven—always trying to improve themselves and find a shorter route to the office or a faster way of reading their mail.[20]

Comment

An important contribution of McClelland's work on achievement motivation is that it has beneficial social consequences. People can learn to become more achievement oriented for the benefit of themselves and society. People can be taught to think, talk, and perceive the role like a person with a high need for achievement. Others have corroborated his belief. For example, an eighteen-month study was conducted of a training program designed to increase entrepreneurial activity among black businessmen.[21] A group that received both achievement motivation training and management development training became significantly more active (hours worked, new investments, employees hired, and the like) than a group receiving only management development training or a control group. As with other studies of achievement motivation, it appeared that an "internal" perception might be a prior condition to increased activity.

The fact that achievement motivation deals almost exclusively with an intrinsic motivator is both a strength and a weakness. On the positive side, once this motive is acquired or strengthened, a person can continue to experience the "joy of accomplishment" for an indefinite period of time. Management thus does not have to be so concerned with providing an increasing number of extrinsic rewards to the individual. On the negative side, it is necessary to change people's motives to increase their output according to need achievement theory. Achievement motivation training, although promising, is time consuming and expensive.

Achievement motivation, as with any theory presented in this chapter or book, has not received unequivocal research support. A basic tenet of achievement motivation is that high levels of *n* Ach propel people toward higher levels of achievement. One study suggested that the opposite is more nearly correct. Achieved occupational level is a better predictor of later achievement motivation than the other way around.

---

[20]"A Conversation with David C. McClelland and T. George Harris," *Psychology Today,* January 1971, p. 70.

[21]Douglas E. Durand, "Effects of Achievement Motivation and Skill Training on the Entrepreneurial Behavior of Black Businessmen," *Organizational Behavior and Human Performance,* August 1975, pp. 76–90.

HOW VALUES AND BELIEFS
INFLUENCE BEHAVIOR

Another group of factors influencing how a person behaves on the job is that person's values and beliefs. A value refers to the importance a person attaches to something. If you believe that religion is one of the most important parts of your life, your religious values are strong. If you pay very little attention to conserving energy, energy conservation is a weak value of yours. Beliefs exert a similar influence on job behavior. If you believe that the company wants to take advantage of you, you might demand that an informal statement made by your manager be put into writing.

How Values Are Learned

A person is not born with a particular set of values. He or she learns them in the process of growing up. One important way in which we acquire values is through observing others or using models. Quite often a person who places a high value on reading was reared among people who valued reading. Models can be parents, teachers, friends, brothers and sisters, and even public figures. Values can be learned through instrumental conditioning or through a cognitive process. If we identify with a particular person, the probability is high that we will develop some of his or her major values.

Another major way in which values are learned is through the communication of attitudes. The attitudes that we hear expressed directly or indirectly help to shape our values. Assume that using credit to purchase goods and services was talked about as an evil practice among your family and friends. You might therefore hold negative values about installment purchases.

Unstated, but implied, attitudes may also shape your values. If key people in your life showed no enthusiasm when you talked about spectator sports, you might not place such a high value on watching sports. If, on the other hand, your family and friends centered their lives on watching sports on television, you might develop similar values. (Or you might rebel against such values because they interfered with other things that you might have wanted to do with your free time.)

Values Lead to Goals and Objectives

The worker's background, composed of job experiences, education, cultural influences, and personality, leads to the formation of values.[22] "Through the lens of those values, the individual will perceive his or her needs." Needs, in turn, lead to the setting of goals and objectives and career plans. As this process continues, the worker carves out a role for himself or herself that is consistent with those values.

> Margot, an intelligent woman with an industrial engineering degree, had long been interested in occupying leadership positions. (She valued being dominant over other people.)

[22]Robert M. Fulmer, *Practical Human Relations* (Homewood, Ill.: Richard D. Irwin, 1977), p. 264.

She became the only woman in her high school graduating class to become an industrial engineer. Upon taking her first job in the industry, she told the employment interviewer that she wanted to become a high-ranking executive in the manufacturing field. She has geared her life toward accomplishing that goal.

Today, Margot is the highest-ranking woman in manufacturing (a second-level manager) in her company, a well-known manufacturer of office machines. Margot now says, "I won't rest until I become an officer of this company. I may be the highest-ranking woman in manufacturing, but I'm still too far down in the company to exert the influence I would like."

Conflict of Values

When the demands made by the organization or a superior clash with the basic values of the individual, that person suffers from *person-role conflict.* He or she wants to obey orders but does not want to perform an act that seems inconsistent with his or her values. A situation such as this might occur when an employee is asked to produce a product that he or she feels is unsafe or is of no value to society.

The Basic Beliefs We Hold About Others

Beliefs, similar to values, influence our actions on and off the job. One of the most influential set of assumptions about the nature of people—Theory X and Theory Y, proposed by Douglas McGregor—illustrates this point. If a manager accepts one of these extreme sets of beliefs (or stereotypes) about people, he or she will act differently toward them than if he or she believed the opposite stereotype.

For those readers not already familiar with the assumptions made about people under Theory X and Theory Y, they are presented here in condensed form:[23]

> *Theory X* assumes that people dislike work and must be coerced, controlled, and directed toward organizational goals. Furthermore, most people prefer to be treated this way, so they can avoid responsibility.

> *Theory Y,* the integration of goals, emphasizes the average person's intrinsic interest in his work, his or her desire to be self-directing and to seek responsibility, and his or her capacity to be creative in solving business problems.

IMPLICATIONS FOR MANAGERIAL PRACTICE

At various points in this chapter we have commented upon the implications for managerial practice of the concepts and ideas under study. Here we highlight a few key points to illustrate how some of the information about organizational behavior can be

---

[23]John J. Morse and John W. Lorsch, "Beyond Theory Y," *Harvard Business Review,* May–June 1970, p. 61.

applied in a work setting. The general message is for the manager, staff specialist, or student to develop the proper mental set for application of this type of knowledge.

1. Every time a manager or staff professional faces a decision about human resources, he or she should reflect upon the concept that $B = f(P \times E)$. It is necessary to make a rough estimate of (a) what characteristics about that person are contributing to how that person is behaving now and (b) what is it about the job environment that could be influencing behavior. Suppose that you are faced with a subordinate who has become overly cautious in recent months. Perhaps the employee seems unwilling to make any significant suggestions. One diagnostic hunch would be that the person is undergoing a personality change (the P factor has been altered). Another more fruitful diagnostic hunch would be that the E factor has been modified; something in the environment is influencing the employee to become a low risk taker. A scanning of environmental factors reveals that the employee is reacting adversely to rumors about a layoff. He or she is backing off from taking chances in order to decrease the chances of making a mistake and consequently being dismissed. You then discuss with the employee the layoff rumors and his or her reaction to them. The employee may then recognize that he or she has become too cautious and makes appropriate adjustments.

2. Almost all the basic concepts about human behavior presented in this chapter could have implications for the proper placement of employees. In any given situation, basic considerations about individual differences in perception, learning, needs, and values could help you to make better job assignments. Assume that you are a restaurant manager, hotel manager, or hospital administrator and therefore have to make work assignments on religious holidays. Instead of assuming that all your employees valued a particular religious holiday (such as Easter Sunday), you might take an informal poll of holiday work preferences. Since your employees may differ in religious values and beliefs, some of them may feel uncomfortable working on Easter Sunday; to others it would be inconsequential. The latter may be quite willing to work on Easter if they could be off duty on another holiday (such as Passover or a major Buddhist holiday).

3. The basic information about learning presented in this chapter has obvious consequences for the training of employees. Assume that you are faced with the task of training a small group of people to learn a new skill, such as leading group discussions on quality improvement (quality circles). You have no funds available for a formal training program so you must do the job inexpensively, but properly. Under these circumstances, your best strategy would be to use modeling or imitation as a learning method. The trainees could observe you in action and follow up with question and answer sessions. Before you begin the process, you are advised to read some additional literature on modeling.

Summary

- Behavior is a function of the individual interacting with the environment, as expressed by the equation $B = f(P \times E)$. Thus individual differences and environmental influences are key determinants of behavior.

- Individual differences moderate behavior in hundreds of ways. Among such differences encountered at work are energy level and resistance to fatigue, the importance that people attach to intrinsic job rewards, preferred leadership style, and tolerance for responsibility.

- Work environments also differ in many ways. The three major sources of differences among work environments are the physical environment, the human environment, and the structural environment (basically, the formal organization).

- Perception is the process by which people select, organize, and interpret stimuli so that these stimuli have meaning to them. Perceptual problems are the most likely to occur when the stimulus to be perceived triggers emotion in people (such as discussions about money or health).

- Characteristics about people that influence perception include (1) physiological and anatomical condition; (2) family influences; (3) cultural influences; (4) motives, needs, and goals; (5) past experience; and (6) personality characteristics.

- People use a number of devices to simplify their perception of external events, including denial, the halo effect (generalizing from one dominant trait about a person or thing), expectancy, projection, selective perception, and perceptual defense.

- Attribution theory studies the process by which people ascribe causes to the behavior they perceive. People then adjust their future behavior to fit these attributions of causality. In general, people place more emphasis on P than on E as a determinant of behavior. In assigning causes for their own outcomes, some people look at internal causation (internal locus of control). Other people look at circumstances beyond their control as bringing about their outcomes (external locus of control).

- The simplest form of learning is classical conditioning, whereby a bond is developed between a conditioned stimulus and a conditioned response. It takes place because of the repeated linking of a conditioned stimulus with an unconditioned (natural) stimulus. The next level of learning, operant conditioning, takes place as a consequence of behavior. If an individual's spontaneous behavior leads to a reward, it tends to be repeated. Negative reinforcement (relief from discomfort) and punishment also contribute to instrumental learning. In practice, learning through operant conditioning proceeds as a sequence of interrelated events.

- Modeling and shaping help to explain how people acquire complicated skills. Modeling occurs when one learns a skill by observing another person perform that skill. The process often brings forth behaviors that people did not seem initially to have in their repertoires. Shaping involves the reinforcement of a series of small steps that build up the final or desired behavior. At each successful step of the way, the learner receives some positive reinforcement.

- According to cognitive learning theory, much of human learning takes place by complex mental processes. Stimulus-response pairings alone are said not to account for all of human learning. For instance, people may develop insights and strive to acquire knowledge. Informal learning fits a cognitive explanation of learning.

- Need theory contends that people are driven by internal strivings to accomplish goals. Maslow's need hierarchy theory contends that people have an internal need pushing them toward self-actualization. But before higher-level needs are activated, certain lower-level needs must be satisfied. In ascending order the classes of needs are physiological, safety, social, esteem, and self-actualizing.

- According to achievement motivation theory, high levels of accomplishment stem from high achievement needs (*n* Ach). People with strong achievement needs (1) take personal responsibility to solve problems, (2) attempt to achieve moderate goals at calculated risks, and (3) prefer situations that provide frequent feedback on results.

- Values and beliefs are also determinants of behavior in organizations. A value refers to the importance that a person attaches to something. Values are learned as part of the maturation process, including the use of models. Values lead to goals and objectives and can be the source of person-role conflict.

- The basic beliefs we hold about others (or the assumptions we make about them) may influence how we relate to them. The Theory X and Theory Y assumptions about people are said to have a profound influence on managerial behavior. Theory X assumes that people dislike work and must be coerced, controlled, and directed toward organizational goals. Theory Y emphasizes the average person's intrinsic interest in work, that person's desire to be self-directing and to seek responsibility.

Questions for Discussion

1. In what ways are you different from most people?
2. In what way do most employee benefit plans neglect the concept of individual differences?
3. Identify several environmental factors that influence, or could influence, your performance in this course.
4. In some business organizations, the two top executives are paid over $600,000 per year, while many clerks are paid about $12,000. What individual differences do you think justify this 50:1 pay ratio?
5. Identify several examples of skills that you have learned through instrumental conditioning (or trial and error).
6. Suppose that your assignment is to lay off three employees in the department you are managing. What perceptual errors should you watch for while delivering your message?
7. "I would have been promoted if it weren't for office politics," say many disgruntled employees. In what way does this comment illustrate attribution theory?

8. How do you explain the fact that so many motorcycle racers, automobile racers, and professional football players are willing to frustrate their needs for safety?
9 What do you see as the relationship between an executive's values and his or her ethical behavior?
10. Describe any job assignment of yours in the present or past that conflicted with your values. What happened as a result?

An Organizational Behavior Problem

The Misplaced Computer Scientist

Reread the lead-in case to this chapter about Rick Rinaldi who left a small firm to join a large company. In the process of analyzing this case, answer the following questions:

Questions

1. Which of Rick's values seemed to be interfering with his effectiveness as a systems analyst at ICC?
2. Which needs does Rick seem to be trying to satisfy through his work?
3. What does Rick's termination tell us about his perception of life in a bureaucracy?
4. In what way might Rick's manager be responsible for his frustration and subsequent termination? Or is this case simply Rick's problem?

Additional Reading

ANDERSON, JOHN R., ed. *Cognitive Skills and Their Acquisition.* Hillsdale, N.J.: Erlbaum, 1981.

BERNSTEIN, PAUL. "The Work Ethic That Never Was." *Wharton,* Spring 1980, pp. 19–25.

COREN, STANLEY, CLARE PORAC, and LAWRENCE M. WARD. *Sensation and Perception.* New York: Academic Press, 1979.

FEDOR, DONALD B., and GERALD R. FERRIS. "Integrating OB Mod with Cognitive Approaches to Motivation." *Academy of Management Review,* January 1981, pp. 115–25.

FELDMAN, JACK M. "Beyond Attribution Theory: Cognitive Processes in Performance Appraisal." *Journal of Applied Psychology,* April 1981, pp. 127–48.

HARVEY, JOHN H., and GIFFORD WEARY. *Perspectives on Attributional Processes.* Dubuque, Iowa: William C. Brown, 1981.

HOWE, MICHAEL J. *The Psychology of Human Learning.* New York: Harper & Row, 1980.

LEFCOURT, HERBERT M. *Research with the Locus of Control Construct,* Vol. 1. New York: Academic Press, 1981.

LOGAN, FRANK A., and WILLIAM C. GORDON. *Fundamentals of Learning and Motivation,* 3rd ed. Dubuque, Iowa: William C. Brown, 1981.

MARTINDALE, COLIN. *Cognition and Consciousness.* Homewood, Ill.: Dorsey Press, 1981.

PETRI, HERBERT L. *Motivation: Theory and Research.* Belmont, Calif.: Wadsworth, 1981.

RACHLIN, HOWARD. *Behaviorism in Everyday Life.* Englewood Cliffs, N.J.: Prentice-Hall, 1980.

CHAPTER 4

Abilities, Personality, and Attitudes

LEARNING OBJECTIVES

1. To acquire knowledge about additional determinants of individual behavior in organizations.

2. To understand how human abilities influence job performance.

3. To explain how human intelligence consists of many components or separate aptitudes.

4. To recognize how personalities and attitudes influence behavior in organizations.

The R. G. Blair Company specializes in the distribution and redemption of grocery store discount coupons. At the heart of its operation is a huge coupon sorting department. The task of sorting coupons into appropriate boxes is performed manually by men and women employees of different ages. Each coupon sorter is surrounded by a never-ending supply of thousands of coupons. Each day, each hour, the work is the same—sorting coupons into their appropriate boxes and sending the boxes on to the next department responsible for their processing.

One day Jennie Kent, manager of the coupon sorting department, was visited by Lance McGraw, her counterpart in another location of the firm. "Thanks so much for allowing me to visit your operation," said Lance. "As I mentioned over the phone, I am really curious about how you folks are running your coupon sorting operation. You seem to be doing well, and we're having lots of trouble."

"Thanks for the compliment," said Jennie. "But what kind of trouble are you having?"

"Our problem is turnover. It's vicious. We're having a tough time keeping people on the job for more than a few months. We only have three satisfactory employees in the department who have stayed with us over a year."

"Lance, what do you see as the basic problem?" said Jennie.

"It must obviously be the job itself. It's a nightmare for the average person. The job isn't even clean. After a while a lot of the ink on those coupons comes off on your hands and clothing. The employees are forced to wear smocks and gloves unless they want stained clothing and hands. The job reminds me of raking leaves after a fall rainstorm. There's no end to it. Just nonstop coupons."

"What screening devices has your personnel department used for the employees?" inquired Jennie.

"We try to be as thorough as we can in terms of the type of people who apply for the job of coupon sorter. We check references. We even use personnel tests. We look for solid citizens who are fairly bright."

Jennie responded, "Lance, I think

I've located your problem. We use personnel tests too. But as we were advised by a personnel psychologist, we look for low scores on the mental ability test. Sorting coupons for a living is not a job for a genius or even a very smart person.

"If an applicant scores too high on the test, we explain that he or she would become bored and frustrated with the job. Yet the person still has to be able to read okay and make some subtle distinctions. We were told to look for applicants of a slightly below-average intelligence. Following this suggestion, we've reduced turnover at least 50 percent."

"Any other tips?" inquired Lance.

"For sure. We ask people if they like to sit still and do the same thing over and over. If they say yes, we ask for an example from their work history or personal life. We find that if the candidate does very little else but watch television in his or her spare time, that candidate doesn't seem to mind sorting coupons. We also try to look for people who are obviously not too energetic."

"What I hear you saying Jennie," said Lance, "is that the ideal candidate for a coupon sorter's job is kind of dull, boring, and physically out-of-shape."

"Exactly," replied Jennie. "And let's you and I keep that a trade secret for the Blair Company. Also, please don't let a written statement like that get into the hands of our coupon sorters. They might not take it as a compliment."

ABILITIES AND JOB PERFORMANCE

This case example about the effective selection of employees for a repetitive, unenriched, and intellectually unstimulating job points to the impact of abilities on job performance. The basic abilities brought to the organization by employees at any level (from coupon sorter to chief executive officer) are an important determinant of their future job performance. A person's abilities are an essential part of his or her makeup. Without core abilities, there would be very little you could contribute to help an organization to reach its goals.

Aptitude and ability are related concepts, and the terms are often used interchangeably. An aptitude is basically a native ability to perform some task, such as singing, dancing, visualizing things in three dimensions, or manipulating mechanical parts. An ability is a current capacity to perform a task or set of tasks. It is partially based on native talent and experience. Abilities thus refer to a broad range of individual characteristics such as problem-solving ability, mechanical ability, and communication skills.[1]

Motivation and Ability

Satisfactory or better job performance will not be attained unless a person has the appropriate abilities to perform the task at hand. Ability is a necessary but not a sufficient condition for achieving performance. Performance is the multiplication of effort (or motivation) and ability, as expressed in the equation $P = (E \times A)$. Ability reflects one's capability to perform; motivation reflects how vigorously one will apply that capability.[2] As inferred from this equation, high motivation can compensate for low ability, but only up to a certain point, which varies for each task. Assume that you have never studied calculus and you were asked to develop a sales forecasting model based on calculus. No matter how hard you tried, your performance would be poor. A believer in the magic of motivation might suggest that a truly motivated person would then embark upon a program of study to learn calculus. The next time around, he or she would be able to handle the forecasting assignment. Again, not entirely true. Some people find some kinds of mathematical (and verbal) tasks beyond their comprehension despite vigorous efforts to learn them.

Selection, Training, and Ability

Since ability is such a critical determinant of job performance, personnel strategies have been developed to elevate ability levels among employees. A good starting point

---

[1] Ernest J. McCormick and Daniel Ilgen, *Industrial Psychology,* 7th ed. (Englewood Cliffs, N.J.: Prentice-Hall, 1980), p. 147.

[2] This discussion and the following one about selection and training are based on Larry L. Cummings and Donald P. Schwab, "Ability as a Performance Determinant," in L. L. Cummings and Randall B. Dunham, eds., *Introduction to Organizational Behavior: Text and Readings* (Homewood, Ill.: Richard D. Irwin, 1980), pp. 195–205.

is to select people into the organization who have the appropriate abilities to perform the task. The ability sought could include a general ability, or aptitude, such as intelligence or problem-solving ability. Employees of high intelligence are especially valuable because they tend to perform complex tasks better than their less intelligent counterparts and they learn new tasks more quickly. Similarly, the owner of a manufacturing firm is well advised to hire production employees with above-average mechanical ability. These employees will perform their assigned tasks better and will adapt more successfully to job reassignment and rotation. Good mechanical ability will help you to solve a variety of mechanical problems.

Training supplements the selection process, as it would be impossible for most organizations to bring people into the organization who could perform all the jobs ever required of them. Besides, the skills and abilities required for jobs may change or people may have to be reassigned to jobs that require different skills and abilities. A manufacturing engineer with twenty years of experience in dealing with primarily mechanical equipment might be faced with implementing a robot system. Substantially increased mathematical ability might be required of that engineer in the present, in addition to intimate knowledge of microprocessors. From a humanitarian and an economic standpoint, it would be better to retrain the engineer than to find a replacement already skilled in robot technology.

Selection and training are interrelated in a way that has considerable implication for making training cost-effective. In general, people of higher ability derive more from training than people of lesser ability. Consequently, much more can be achieved from a training program that begins with a group of high-ability employees screened by way of a valid selection procedure, such as mental ability tests and review of background information.[3] (Sample items of one such mental ability test appear in Figure 4–1.)

PROBLEM-SOLVING ABILITY

Intelligence is one of the major differences among people that affects job performance. Highly abstract work, such as building mathematical models or solving chemical equations, calls for very high levels of intelligence. Effective managers tend to score higher in problem-solving ability than do less effective managers because managerial work involves so many different skills and abilities.[4] As illustrated in the case of the coupon sorters, below-average problem-solving ability is an advantage in uncomplicated, repetitive jobs.

[3]Ibid., p. 202.

[4]Glen Grimsley and Hilton F. Jarrett, "The Relation of Past Managerial Achievement to Test Measures Obtained in the Employment Situation: Methodology and Results—II," *Personnel Psychology,* Summer 1975, pp. 215–31.

Most readers of this book have taken mental ability tests at various stages of schooling or in the process of applying for a job. Nevertheless, there is some value in examining four sample test items of the type that appear on a standardized mental ability test used in business, industry and other work organizations. Question A measures verbal comprehension; question B measures numerical comprehension; question C measures inductive reasoning; and question D measures word fluency. These questions are not taken from the Employee Aptitude Survey, but they follow a similar format.

_____A. A cautious person is
1. wealthy 2. careful 3. ignorant 4. satisfied

_____B. In the following series, which two numbers should come next?
16 18 17 20 18 22
1. 19 and 24 2. 23 and 27 3. 19 and 23 4. 25 and 26

_____C. Read the three statements below:
A is lighter than D.
B is heavier than D.
A weighs more than C.
Which is heaviest? ....

_____D. You will have three minutes to complete the following assignment:
Write down as many words as you can think of beginning with the letter T.

_____ _____ _____ _____

_____ _____ _____ _____

_____ _____ _____ _____

_____ _____ _____ _____

_____ _____ _____ _____

_____ _____ _____ _____

_____ _____ _____ _____

_____ _____ _____

FIGURE 4–1 Sample Mental Ability Test Items

The term "intelligence," as it is used here, refers to problem-solving ability. Intelligence quotient, or IQ, is in reality just one measure of intelligence, just as classifying someone as having "very superior" intelligence is a measure of intelligence. Because the particular test score called IQ is so widely known, many people regard IQ as synonymous with intelligence. Other widely used measures of intelligence include the Scholastic Aptitude Test, the Law School Aptitude Test, the Graduate Management Aptitude Test, and the Employee Aptitude Survey.

Intelligence is not a pure characteristic. It includes a variety of specialized aptitudes that contribute to problem-solving ability. According to the most basic conception, intelligence is composed of verbal and numerical abilities. The Employee Aptitude Survey (EAS) is a representative, highly researched, series of tests designed to measure problem-solving ability in a job environment. An analysis of its underlying meaning shows that it measures eight different factors. These factors might be regarded as basic components of intelligence. It is worth noting these factors or components, because they are a source of individual differences related to job performance. The eight factors are as follows:[5]

1.   *Verbal comprehension:* the ability to use words in thinking and in both spoken and written communications. Good verbal skills are an asset in a wide variety of occupations, including those of sales representatives, executives, and newspaper reporters.

2.   *Numerical comprehension:* the ability to handle numbers, engage in mathematical analysis, and do arithmetic calculations. Among the occupations calling for good numerical comprehension are accounting, computer programming, tax advisor, and engineer.

3.   *Pursuit:* the ability to make quick and accurate scanning movements with the eyes. Occupations calling for quick eye movements, such as proofreader, professional card player, and quality-control inspector, would require relatively high aptitude in pursuit.

4.   *Perceptual speed:* the ability to perceive small details in a rapid manner and "pick out" such details from a mass of material. Most occupations do not call for considerable perceptual speed, but it would seem to be an asset for a computer programmer.

5.   *Visualization:* the ability to visualize objects in three dimensions. Engineers, designers, drafting technicians, and photographers, to some extent, would need an above-average degree of the mental aptitude called visualization.

6.   *Inductive reasoning:* the ability to discover relationships and derive principles by pulling together bits of information. Most higher-level and some medium-level occupations require inductive reasoning. An insurance claims adjuster uses inductive reasoning when he or she pulls together facts to reach conclusions about the probable cause of a fire. So does a mechanic when he or she diagnoses why a car keeps stalling in traffic.

7.   *Word fluency:* the ability to produce words rapidly, without regard to meaning or quality. Fluency alone is not particularly helpful on the job, but it does contribute to a person's ability to communicate in speaking and in writing. Fluency appears to contribute to comprehension. It is important in sales work.

8.   *Syntactic evaluation:* the ability to apply principles to arrive at a unique solution. All higher-level occupations require a good deal of syntactic evaluation. For example,

[5]The Employee Aptitude Survey is published by Psychological Services, Inc., Los Angeles, California. A description of the scales as presented here is found in Marvin D. Dunnette, "Aptitudes, Abilities, and Skills," in Marvin D. Dunnette, ed., *Handbook of Industrial and Organizational Psychology* (Chicago: Rand McNally, 1976), p. 487.

if you are a toy designer, you have to apply principles of mechanical engineering to figure out how to make a particular motorized toy operate efficiently within a certain cost limit.

INTELLIGENCE AND JOB PERFORMANCE

Studies conducted over a fifty-year period present convincing evidence that problem-solving ability is related to good performance in a wide range of occupations. Ghiselli examined the relationship between intelligence and job performance in eight different occupational groups: managers, clerical jobs, salesclerks, salesmen, protective occupations, service occupations, vehicle operators, and trades and crafts.[6] His compendious review took into account all existing published research on the topic. Information was gathered on about 80,000 people in a far-reaching sample of different companies and different measures of job performance (such as sales and production records or supervisory judgments about performance). Intelligence, as measured in paper-and-pencil tests, showed a statistically significant relationship to performance for all these groups except salesclerks—people who sell merchandise to customers in retail stores. Factors such as interpersonal skill may be more important than intelligence for success in selling.

The research in question makes the underlying assumption that intelligence and job performance are linearly related, that job performance increases directly with increases in intelligence. A current approach to the topic suggests that in addition to the magnitude of your intelligence, your style of problem solving also has an impact on job performance.

Problem-Solving Styles and Job Performance

Tentative evidence suggests that some people, on the basis of their problem-solving style, are better suited for intuitive and creative work, whereas others have an easier time solving analytical, logical, and mathematical tasks. About twenty years ago, it was first discovered that one's characteristic problem-solving style may depend on which hemisphere of one's brain is dominant.[7] If a person is right handed, the left side of his or her brain is usually dominant; for left-handed people, the opposite is true. The left hemisphere of the brain controls analytical and logical tasks, along with language and sequential, linear process. Preparing a budget and strategic planning are two activities suited to the person with left-hemisphere dominance.

[6]Edwin E. Ghiselli, "The Validity of Aptitude Tests in Personnel Selection," *Personnel Psychology*, Winter 1973, pp. 461–77.

[7]Our discussion here is based on the synthesis of the literature in Thomas V. Bonoma and Gerald Zaltman, *Psychology for Management* (Boston: Kent, 1981), pp. 111–12.

The right hemisphere of the brain controls intuition. It specializes in detecting patterns, or gestalts, rather than in breaking things down into analytical bits. Within the right cerebral hemisphere lies artistic talents and the ability to handle visual images, creativity, and spatial relations. A small percentage of individual contributors, and an even smaller percentage of managers, are right-brain dominant.

People with high problem-solving ability (or high IQs) tend to be those with highly developed left-brain hemispheres, because it is the left hemisphere's abilities that are frequently called upon in solving the problems on standard IQ tests. Organizations need both left-brain and right-brain types. However, unless the two groups make an effort to understand each other, they will probably clash. The problem is that the "left-brain types are inclined to see the trees and not the forest; right-brain types see the forest and not the trees."[8]

An important implication of this type of brain research is that left-brain people perform better in logical, analytical assignments, and right-brain people perform better in assignments calling for intuitive, creative thought. So far the research evidence is mixed as to which hemisphere is the more dominant among sucessful managers. One problem is that managerial jobs differ with respect to how much logical analytical thought versus intuition is required.

Another implication is that each of us has both analytical and intuitive capabilities. Through practice, one can develop one's creative, intuitive, and holistic thinking. Most people tend to be biased in one direction or the other. It would therefore be helpful to your career to develop more fully the nondominant side of your brain. If you are too left-brained, you might consider creativity-enhancing exercises (see Chapter 8). If you tend to be right-brained, you could develop your analytical skills (as is normally done in the majority of courses in a business curriculum).

OTHER IMPORTANT APTITUDES AND SKILLS

Problem-solving ability is an important determinant of performance in many jobs, but so are other abilities and skills. A skill refers to a specific capability such as driving a car, which is dependent upon a general ability (such as eye-hand coordination). Many higher-level jobs call for nonintellectual abilities such as mechanical ability. For instance, some people can make minor repairs on office machines by themselves, even if it is not part of their job. Others would have to call a maintenance worker to elevate a swivel chair. Sometimes having limited mechanical ability can be a source of embarrassment to an executive, such as being unable to adjust a microphone when giving a talk. Four nonintellectual abilities and skills relevant to job performance and behavior are classified as mechanical ability, psychomotor abilities, visual skills, and physical skills.

[8]Quotation is from Lee Smith, "Too Smart to Be in Business," *Dun's Review,* October 1977, p. 100.

Mechanical Ability

Although most mechanical jobs also require physical skill, mechanical ability refers to the cognitive aspects of those jobs—the mechanic must have some sense of being able to "figure out" the workings of machinery or equipment. Mechanical ability (or aptitude) is said to consist of two classes. One of these is the comprehension of mechanical relations, the recognition of selecting the right tool, and related cognitive abilities. The other class of mechanical ability is the perception and manipulation of spatial relations (the ability to visualize how parts or components fit together).[9] Solving a Rubik cube requires a sense of spatial relations. People with high mechanical ability usually display this talent both on and off the job. It is not unusual for skilled workers to repair their own automobiles and household plumbing.

Psychomotor Abilities

Eye-hand coordination, dexterity, manipulative ability, and the like are important for many skilled and unskilled jobs. People show extreme variations in this ability. Diamond cutters, tool and die makers, dressmakers, and professional golf players are among the workers with considerable psychomotor ability. As with other human abilities, the classification of psychomotor ability can be subdivided into a group of related activities. Following are four of the many components of psychomotor ability that have been derived from factor analysis. (Factor analysis refers to reducing the number of variables in a set based upon the magnitude of their intercorrelation. Highly correlated variables are placed in the same factor.)

1. *Control precision:* tasks requiring finely controlled muscular adjustments, such as moving a gauge to a precise setting.
2. *Manual dexterity:* tasks involving skillful arm and hand movements in manipulating large objects under conditions of speed. Many assembly-line jobs require good manual dexterity.
3. *Reaction time:* the ability to respond to a signal. Fast reaction times are required for truck drivers and process control technicians. (The latter employee observes computerized dials that may indicate when, for example, a malfunctioning machine requires immediate attention.)
4. *Rate control:* the ability to make timed motor adjustments relative to changes in the speed or direction of a continuously moving object. (A person high in this ability would perform well in the computer games placed in retail stores, airports, and amusement arcades!)[10]

---

[9]Leona E. Tyler, *The Psychology of Individual Differences* (New York: Meredith, 1965), pp. 144–45.

[10]Edwin A. Fleishman, "Performance Assessment Based on an Empirically Derived Task Taxonomy," *Human Factors,* September 1967, pp. 349–66.

Visual Skills

Blind people are capable of good performance in a wide range of jobs including quality-control inspector (for instance, searching for burrs on a metal part) or psychotherapist. Yet most jobs involve the use of visual skills such as visual acuity, depth perception, and color discrimination.[11]

Physical Skills

Individual differences in physical skills are pronounced, and these variations have implications for job performance.[12] An X-ray technician, for example, must stand up most of the workday to administer X rays to patients. A licensed practical nurse with a weak back would have great difficulty moving patients in and out of bed. Many physical skills, such as the ability to lift heavy objects, can be developed. In the past women were excluded from certain occupations, such as telephone line rigger, because it was assumed they lacked the appropriate physical skills. It has been demonstrated that with practice, a man or woman can learn to scale a telephone pole.

PERSONALITY AND JOB BEHAVIOR

Personality characteristics such as warmth, extroversion, and assertiveness contribute to success in many jobs. And most failures on the job are not attributed to a person's amount of intelligence or technical competence but to personality characteristics. The subject of personality is therefore of importance to the study of organizational behavior. Despite its importance, considerable controversy centers on the concept of personality. Among the areas of disagreement are the meaning of personality, whether or not it can be accurately measured, and whether it is influenced more by heredity or by environment.

Personality refers to persistent and enduring *behavior patterns* of an individual that tend to be expressed in a wide variety of situations. Your personality is the combination of attributes, traits, and characteristics that makes you a unique individual. Your walk, talk, appearance, speech, creativity, inner values, and conflicts all contribute to your personality. Here we are concerned with several key issues about personality that may help a manager or staff specialist to make better use of human resources.

Determinants of Personality

Many aspects of our personalities are determined early in life, perhaps during the first six years. Many other aspects are determined at other points in life. Your personality

---

[11]McCormick and Ilgen, *Industrial Psychology,* p. 155.

[12]Edwin A. Fleishman, "Evaluating Physical Abilities Required by Jobs," *The Personnel Administrator,* June 1979, pp. 82–90.

is in a continuous process of growth and development, much like a business corporation. General Electric of 1984 is not identical to the General Electric of 1948, yet it is recognizable as the same organization. Some aspects of your personality may even be shaped by a job event facing you in the future, such as receiving a substantial promotion. (Such an event could elevate your self-confidence, thus modifying your personality.) Five major forces influencing personality are heredity, culture, social class and group membership, family relationships, and situational factors.[13]

Heredity directly and indirectly influences personality. Your genes may directly shape vital personal factors that become part of your personality. Among these are energy level, aggressiveness, strength of sex drive, musical ability, mathematical ability, and body type. The personality of a 5' 6" woman with extraordinary musical talent will probably be much different from that of a 5' 1" male with no exceptional inherited talent. Because of these physical characteristics and inherited talents, these two people will probably develop different psychological characteristics. The woman in question will tend to be self-assured while the man may be below average in self-assurance. One way in which a manager can manage for the biological roots of personality is to assign physically and mentally energetic people to demanding tasks.

Culture has a pervasive influence on personality structure. For example, part of the success of Japanese industry is attributable to the personality traits of the majority of Japanese workers, because these people value harmony, team work, and respect for authority. Americans are much more heterogeneous with respect to these characteristics, making management-labor harmony more difficult to achieve. Of course, not every member of the same culture has the same personality structure. Some Japanese workers resent losing their individualism to the group, and some are not as highly cooperative as others.

Social class and other group membership forces are also powerful determinants of personality, and they begin to take hold in early adolescence. One's social class can influence such factors as one's values, beliefs, and opinions (all of which are contributors to personality). Lower-class people, as employees, may have a basic distrust of top management—again with many allowances for individual differences. An employee from an upper-class background might have much less interest in financial incentives than might a lower-middle-class person.

Group membership is related to but can be distinct from social class membership because some groups cut across different social classes. A person may spend four years at a college such as Harvard where students share a strong in-group attitude. A student enrolled at Harvard will sometimes develop enough characteristics in common with other graduates to develop a "Harvard personality" (at least as perceived by friends and employers). Or, if a man joined in a local chapter of the motorcycle club Hell's Angels, he would tend to develop aggressive, socially deviant behaviors. (The

[13]The first four of these factors are based on James L. Gibson, John M. Ivancevich, and James H. Donnelly, Jr., *Organizations: Behavior, Structure, Processes,* 3rd ed. (Plano, Tex.: Business Publications, 1979), pp. 74–76.

counterargument here is that only such people would join Hell's Angels in the first place!)

Family relationships also influence an individual's personality, and these influences may manifest themselves in work behavior. People who are raised in an environment in which there is a low level of competitiveness tend not to be highly aggressive on the job. It has been said that the most aggressive executives were not reared in homes where life was made too easy for them. One theory of occupational choice contends that if one's parents were warm and loving, one may gravitate toward people-helping occupations. Or, if one's parents were cold and distant, one may gravitate toward more data- and "thing"-oriented occupations, such as chemist or operations researcher.[14]

Changes in family relationships may modify an individual's personality to the point where it leads to changes in job behavior. A classic example is the middle-aged college professor whose child enters college. The professor suddenly develops compassion for the foibles of college freshmen.

Situational influences are an intricate, albeit difficult-to-measure, determinant of personality. The situation interacting with the person may trigger certain personality characteristics. An example would be a person with a high need for achievement placed in a large department where individual effort is not recognized. The person may become so frustrated in this environment that he or she appears lethargic. Given a project assignment in that same firm where the employee can directly influence the outcome of his or her work, the person may blossom into a high performer. In the latter situation, an environmental characteristic (opportunity to be recognized for effort) triggered favorable work behavior.

Measurement of Personality

Considerable controversy surrounds personality measurement, especially when it is done through self-report questionnaires. Critics from the general public contend that some statements on personality questionnaires are an invasion of privacy (such as "Do you get a strong urge to strike back when you are criticized?") Many personnel psychologists themselves contend that most personality tests are invalid. Three methods of measuring personality in organizations are direct observation, self-report questionnaires, and experimental procedures.

Direct observation followed by inductive reasoning is the most frequent method through which conclusions about personality are reached. The process proceeds in approximately this fashion: Phil observes Julie, a program analyst, in a staff meeting. During the meeting Julie makes a lucid presentation of the status of the program on which she is working. After the meeting, Phil, Julie, and two other department members have lunch together at a restaurant. The chef salad Julie orders arrives at the table with wilted lettuce and stale-looking cheese. Julie politely asks for a fresh salad,

---

[14]Anne Roe, *The Psychology of Occupations* (New York: John Wiley, 1965).

which is delivered to the table. Next week Phil is discussing his subordinates with his boss. When the subject turns to Julie, Phil says "Keep your eyes on Julie. She's the assertive type of program analyst we need around here. Besides that she's articulate and poised." Phil has observed Julie in two situations and has arrived at a firm conclusion about several of her key personality traits. The accuracy of this method of personality assessment is highly dependent upon the skill and insight of the person making the judgments.

Self-report questionnaires are a standard approach to personality measurement despite whatever problems of validity they encounter. In defense of the better known personality tests, they are backed up by years of research with thousands of subjects before being placed into general use by their publishers. Used as intended, these tests furnish clues to an employee's personality as part of selection, placement, or career development.[15] Thus, one deviant score is not sufficient reason to reject an applicant, demote a present employee, or suggest that somebody switch occupations. Assume that a job applicant scored very low on a scale measuring "energy." The personnel specialist might use that information as a clue to further probing in the employment interview or as a point of inquiry in a reference check.

Following are illustrations of the types of questions (or statements) found on standardized, self-report personality tests and questionnaires:

	YES	?	NO
I become tense and nervous when I am criticized.	_____	_____	_____
If I had my preference, I would be self-employed.	_____	_____	_____
I have had more than my share of good breaks.	_____	_____	_____

Questions such as these are relatively easy to answer in a socially desirable direction. To guard against this problem, several personality tests include a faking index, which provides a rough estimate of your tendency to place yourself in an unreasonably favorable light. Also, when people take personality tests as part of career counseling, their aim is usually to obtain self-insight, not "outwit the examiner."

Experimental procedures show some promise as a way of measuring personality dimensions. The people whose personalities are to be judged are placed in a simulated work environment. While these people are performing their assigned tasks, observers make inferences about their personality. Assessment centers make direct use of this method. In one assessment center exercise, a group of relative strangers is brought together to solve a simulated work emergency, such as a sudden strike during a period of peak work demand. While the participants cope with the problem, the observers make ratings on such personality dimensions as "initiative," dominance, sensitivity to peo-

---

[15]A balanced review of personality measurement is Harrison Gough, "Personality and Personality Assessment," in *Handbook of Industrial and Organizational Psychology,* pp. 571–608.

ple, and personal organization.[16] In this regard, experimental procedures are akin to the direct observation method mentioned earlier. A major difference is that in the assessment center the observers are trained and are given clear definitions of each personality dimension that they will be rating.

Personality, Needs, and Motives

Needs and motives are an important aspect of motivation; they are also a determinant of personality traits, which in turn leads to different types of work behavior. One such need already discussed is the achievement need, which leads a person to gravitate toward entrepreneurial activity. Similarly, a person with a strong need for power would search for ways in which to control resources, such as becoming a business executive, a military general, or a high-ranking elected official. A person with a low need for curiosity and competence would not be particularly interested in intellectually stimulating work. He or she would be more readily satisfied with repetitive work that was not mentally taxing.

Years ago, Murray developed a list of human needs that lead to personality traits. His conceptualization and research on this topic has served as the cornerstone of current information about needs and human behavior.

Ten important needs with direct relevance to work behavior, based on Murray's classification scheme, are described in the paragraphs that follow.[17] Each need or motive results in a propensity to behave in a particular way, thus leading to the formation of a personality trait. Accompanying each trait is a sampling of the type of behavior corresponding to an intense need or pronounced trait of that type.

Achievement.   To accomplish something difficult; to win over others. Such a person tries hard to win in a simulation exercise, looks toward becoming self-employed, and enjoys being measured on the basis of results.

Affiliation.   To seek out close relationships with others; to be a loyal employee or friend. A strong affiliation need would lead a person to form close relationships with co-workers and to identify with his or her work group.

Aggression.   To attack, injure, or punish others; to overcome opposition forcefully. A job manifestation of this need could be an intense desire to beat the competition and make rivals look bad. An aggressive salesperson would use hard-sell tactics.

Autonomy.   To act independently and be free of constraints. People with strong autonomy needs enjoy tackling assignments where they have full responsibility for results. Positions of appeal to them include branch manager, warehouse manager, solitary company representative in the field, and self-employment. A strong autonomy motive also leads a person to dislike being closely supervised.

[16]Andrew J. DuBrin, *Contemporary Applied Management* (Plano, Tex.: Business Publications, 1982), pp. 155–70.

[17]Henry A. Murray, *Explorations in Personality* (New York: Oxford University Press, 1938).

Deference. To admire and support a superior or other person in authority; to conform to custom. A highly deferent employee prefers to call people by title (Ms., Mr., Dr.), makes a respectful subordinate, and respects company organizational traditions.

Dominance. To control one's human environment; to influence others toward one's own way of thinking, often by forceful methods. A person with a high dominance motive will often try to take charge in meetings, will volunteer to be the leader, and will sometimes try to manipulate others for his or her personal advantage.

Exhibition. To make an impression on others; to be seen and heard by others; to excite, entertain, and "get a rise out of" others. People with strong needs for exhibition will spend more time than most people in self-promotion. If emotionally immature, they will sometimes be the office clown or "life of the office party."

Nurturance. To help, support, and take care of needy people. Nurturant people find satisfaction in taking care of disadvantaged employees; they literally enjoy the role of nurse, and they tend to be overprotective of subordinates.

Order. To arrange things carefully, put them in order, and achieve cleanliness and neatness and precision. A person with a high need for order enjoys data collection and analysis and computational work and keeps a neat work station. Employees with very strong motives toward orderliness may not be among the most creative.

Power. To exhibit a strong need to control other people and resources; to desire fame and recognition. People with strong needs for power orient their lives toward attaining high stature in their field. Often they choose clothing, cars, and office furnishing designed to give them a powerful look.

ATTITUDES AND JOB BEHAVIOR

Asked why he was so pleased with his job as manager of Quality-Control Engineering, the manager replied, "It's the attitude of everybody in this department from engineer to file clerk. We all seem to sense that we have an important mission of guaranteeing quality to the public. The positive attitude shows up in little ways like people voluntarily picking up scraps of paper off the floor and not wasting any supplies." This manager has reached a valid conclusion: attitudes are an important determinant of work behavior since they are linked with perception, learning, and motivation.

An *attitude* is a predisposition to respond or a mental state of readiness exerting a specific influence upon a person's response to a person, thing, idea, or situation.[18] Attitudes are complex, having at least three components: the cognitive, the affective, and the behavioral. The *cognitive* component refers to the knowledge or intellectual beliefs that an individual might have about an object (idea, person, thing, or situation).

[18]Gibson, Ivancevich, and Donnelly, *Organizations,* p. 71.

A market researcher might have accumulated considerable factual information about statistics such as specific methods, tests of significance, multiple regression, and so forth, leading to a positive attitude toward statistics.

The feeling or *affective* component refers to the emotions connected with that object. The market researcher in question might bascially like statistical analysis due to some pleasant experiences in college associated with statistics. The *behavioral* component refers to how a person acts. The market researcher might make positive statements about statistical methods or emphasize them heavily in his or her reports.[19]

The cognitive, affective, and behavioral aspects of attitudes are interrelated. A change in one of the components will set in motion a change in the other. If you have more facts about an object (cognition), you form the basis for a more positive emotional response to the object (affective component). In turn, your behavior toward that object would probably become more favorable.

Consistency and Stability of Attitudes

An attitude is consistent when the cognitive, affective, and behavioral aspects are logically related to each other. If a manager has read a statistical report showing the value of OSHA (the Occupational Safety and Health Administration), that manager will tend to develop positive feelings toward OSHA regulations. In addition, the manager's behavior will be positive, for example, enforcing OSHA regulations in the work area. Internally consistent attitudes tend to be stable and thus resistant to change. Furthermore, one attitude is typically linked to another, forming a complex of related attitudes. Often, a major underlying attitude leads to the formation of subordinate attitudes. If a person is generally liberal (a general attitude), that individual will tend to have positive specific attitudes toward such work-related programs as affirmative action and corporate contributions to college.

Attitude Formation

Attitudes are formed in almost as many ways as personality. The previous discussion about the determinants of personality also applies to attitude formation. Even genetic factors can play a role in attitude formation, although somewhat indirectly. For instance, a person born with a birth defect might tend to develop much more tolerant attitudes toward handicapped workers than would people born without birth defects. Culture, social class, and group membership, family relationships, and situational influences also play a role in attitude formation. It is the last factor that is of most immediate concern to the manager.

The work environment is a key situational influence in forming employee attitudes. Atttitudes formed within the first few days of employment can contribute to

---

[19]John P. Campbell and others, *Managerial Behavior, Performance, and Effectiveness* (New York: McGraw-Hill, 1970), p. 263.

employee satisfaction and dissatisfaction. It is therefore helpful for the new employee to spend time with employees who have a positive outlook about the firm. Some truth exists to the adage that attitudes are contagious.

Changing Attitudes

It is frequently necessary to change attitudes because present attitudes are interfering with an important outcome such as job performance, absenteeism, or cost control. In Chapter 6, we deal more specifically with these attitudes toward work, collectively called job satisfaction. The subject of attitude change is a field of knowledge itself. Our purposes are met here by mentioning six methods of attitude change under reasonable control of the manager or staff professional. Attitude change in organizations usually is brought about by using a combination of these methods.

1. *Communicate additional information.* Adding to an employee's knowledge base (the cognitive component of attitudes) is sometimes helpful in bringing about attitude change. Thus providing employees more knowledge about an industrial robot could lead to more positive attitudes about such machinery.

2. *Reinforce desired attitude change.* Rewards and punishments should be reasonably related to desired changes in attitudes. To the extent that subordinates display more positive attitudes toward a work change, they should receive encouragement or other rewards. Should the value of the reward exceed the value of maintaining an original attitude, changes in attitude and behavior may be forthcoming. Similarly, if the magnitude of punishment is too severe (such as delaying a salary increase) to bother clinging to an attitude (such as resisting properly implementing the robot), attitudes and behavior will change. Often, disapproval by the manager is a sufficiently potent form of punishment.

3. *Utilize group influence.* An effective method of attitude change is to hold group discussions about the target topic, particularly if some members of the group share management's positive attitude. Or employees with negative attitudes toward the issue can be brought together in normal work interaction with employees harboring positive attitudes. Group influences will tend to be strongest if an influential group member is sympathetic toward the manager's position on the topic (such as the value of implementing the robot).

4. *Encourage discrepant behavior.* In laboratory studies, subjects have been asked to assume the attitudes of people with opposite viewpoints. Engaging in such discrepant behavior often brings about changes in attitude. A group of laboratory employees who disliked searching for printed information on a microfiche reader might be asked to "At least give it a try for one month."[20]

5. *Adapt change methods to individual differences.* Few work groups are monolithic in their attitudes. One person with negative attitudes toward the object in question

[20]The first four points are based on ibid., pp. 263–64.

might be a normally easygoing, good-natured person. A reasonable attitude change strategy with this person might be to confront him or her directly about the need for change. A highly defensive person with negative attitudes should be approached much more gingerly.

6. *Rely on a trusted and influential source.* If employees trust the sender of the message, they are more likely to change their attitude than if the relationship is characterized by distrust. Employee skepticism toward robots may change if the manager is trusted. Also, if the manager is influential in the organization, the probability of attitude change is enhanced. More will be said about this topic in Chapter 11 in the discussion of interpersonal communication.

AN INTEGRATIVE MODEL OF PERSONALITY, ABILITY, AND ATTITUDES

Job satisfaction and performance generally increase if there is a close correspondence between an employee's personality structure, abilities, and attitudes on the one hand and job demands on the other. As the work adjustment model shown in Figure 4–2 suggests, correspondence leads to both good job performance (as perceived by superiors) and high job satisfaction.[21] Here is how the model would work in practice:

> Brent, an Internal Revenue Service agent, is required by his employer to conduct audits of small firms with questionable income tax returns. The personality requirements of the job call for somebody who can work independently and handle personal criticism. Brent has a strong autonomy need and sufficient ego strength to tolerate criticism. The ability requirements include high problem-solving ability, appreciation for detail, and good oral communication skills. Brent is strong on all three. Among the attitude requirements of the position are a belief in a strong federal government and a positive attitude toward the progressive income tax system. Brent has strong beliefs and attitudes of this nature. Consequently he performs his job well, is highly rated by his boss, and experiences high job satisfaction.

In the right-hand portion of the model, a tentative link is drawn between performance and satisfaction. It suggests that in some cases high job satisfaction leads to good performance. As a result, some people who enjoy their jobs will work hard. In contrast some people are quite content (experience high job satisfaction) when modest work demands are placed upon them (low performance). Also, good job performance sometimes leads to satisfaction. You experience a surge of satisfaction because you have performed a task well. Yet some people dislike their jobs, no matter how well they perform. People of this type have weak work ethics, so good performance is of little consequence to them. More will be said about the relationship of job satisfaction to performance in Chapter 6.

[21]The model presented here is an adaptation of the work adjustment model from Lloyd Lofquist and Rene Dawis, *Adjustment to Work: A Psychological View of Man's Problems in a Work-Oriented Society* (Englewood Cliffs, N.J.: Prentice-Hall, 1969), p. 54.

Job Requirements

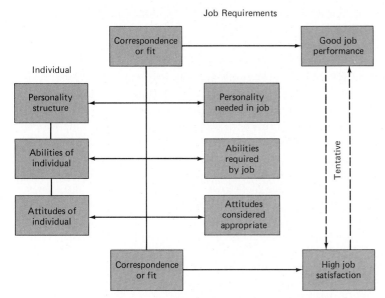

FIGURE 4–2　The Work Adjustment Model: The Relationship of Personality, Abilities, and Attitudes to Job Performance and Satisfaction

Relative Impact of Personality, Abilities, and Attitudes

The general classes of variables listed in Figure 4–2 all have potentially important consequences in terms of job performance and job satisfaction. A perplexing issue concerns which set of variables has the biggest impact on performance and satisfaction.
As mentioned previously, most job failures are attributable to personality problems,
yet this does not really mean that personality is more important than ability as a determinant of job performance. A certain minimum level of ability is required to perform
any job. For instance, no matter how sparkling your personality, or how hard you try
(attitude), you cannot function effectively as an advertising copywriter unless you possess good written communication skills. Yet your attitudes (such as being rigid versus
flexible) can influence your capacity to use your writing skills.

Tentatively, the relative influence of these three sets of independent variables on
performance in higher-level jobs can be viewed in the following terms. Personality has
a potentially bigger negative than positive impact on job performance. You can fail in
almost any managerial, professional, or technical position because of negative personality factors. However, positive personality characteristics are less important than
abilities or attitudes in bringing about good job performance. Abilities represent the
primary success factor for most positions at all levels. If you cannot understand budgeting or communicate your thoughts well, you will fail in almost any executive posi-

tion. Yet the right abilities must be buttressed by the appropriate attitudes (including motivation) and personality characteristics.

Given a reasonable fit between both your personality and abilities, on the one hand, and job requirements, on the other, your attitudes heavily influence both your performance and your satisfaction. Given two people with approximately similar levels of ability and appropriate personality characteristics, the person with a stronger work orientation (set of attitudes) will achieve higher performance.

The specifics of a given situation must be assessed to accurately speculate which set of individual differences will have the biggest impact on job performance and satisfaction. As a given position moves toward more complex interpersonal demands, success in that position is more influenced by personality and attitudinal factors. The more the position demands technical competence (or working with data and things rather than with people), the greater the impact of ability factors. To illustrate, a person with high mechanical aptitude and spatial relations ability will tend to perform well as a mechanical engineer. Also, the engineer will experience high job satisfaction. Without such abilities, the person will perform poorly and be disgruntled (assuming that the individual made it through school and the company selection procedures!).

IMPLICATIONS FOR MANAGERIAL PRACTICE

1. A major implication of individual differences in personality and abilities is that these factors have a critical impact upon the selection, placement, job assignment, training, and development of employees. When faced with a selection, placement, or job assignment decision, the manager should ask such questions as

-   Is this employee intelligent enough to handle the job and deal with out-of-the ordinary problems?
-   Is this employee too intelligent for the assignment? Will he or she become bored relatively quickly?
-   Is this employee's basic personality structure suited to the assignment? For instance, is the employee sufficiently dominant or achievement oriented?

2. Be careful to not overestimate the role of motivation in the job performance. Many employees perform below standard not because they "are not trying" but because their abilities and personality traits are not suited to the job. For instance, an employee who prepares garbled reports may be doing so because of below-average verbal comprehension, not low motivation. Or an auditor may be failing to obtain the necessary information to complete an audit, not out of lack of interest but because he or she is too low in dominance. Careful observation by you as a manager, including a review of the employee's work record, may reveal some of these problems in placement. Training and development programs are useful in making up for deficits that sometimes may appear on the surface to be motivational problems.

3. Although attitudes are intangible and difficult to measure accurately, a manager must take them into account in managing people. At times attitudes must be changed before a new work procedure or system can be implemented successfully. A case in point is affirmative action programs. Unless middle managers develop positive, or at least neutral, attitudes toward affirmative action programs (structured methods of creating good job opportunities for females and minorities), the program will make modest progress. If it appears that employee attitudes toward an important program are negative, the manager should invest time in attempting to change attitudes. The general principles outlined in the chapter subsection "Changing Attitudes" would apply here.

Summary

- The basic abilities possessed by employees are an important determinant of job performance. Abilities refer to a broad range of individual characteristics such as problem-solving ability and mechanical ability. Abilities are enduring traits that come about through both learning and heredity. Skills refer to a level of proficiency on a specific task or job. Ability combined with, or multiplied by, motivation leads to performance.
- Intelligence, or problem-solving ability, is a key determinant of job performance. Eight factors are said to account for intelligence: verbal comprehension, numerical comprehension, pursuit, perceptual speed, visualization, inductive reasoning, word fluency, and syntactic evaluation.
- Problem-solving styles are also related to job performance. People with right-brain dominance are said to be better suited for intuitive and creative work; left-brain dominant individuals have an easier time solving analytical, logical, and mathematical tasks.
- Another important job-related ability is mechanical ability, consisting of mechanical comprehension and the perception and manipulation of spatial relations. Psychomotor abilities such as eye-hand coordination are also a determinant of job performance. Among the components or factors of psychomotor abilities are control precision, manual dexterity, reaction time, and rate control.
- Visual skills also, have different components. Among those most related to job performance are visual acuity, depth perception, and color discrimination. Physical skills are related to performance in a variety of jobs, and wide individual differences exist in these skills. Variations in physical skills, such as strength, also influence performance.
- Personality refers to persistent and enduring behavior patterns of an individual that tend to be expressed in a wide variety of situations. Your personality represents your uniqueness. Among the determinants of personality are heredity, culture, social class and group membership, family relationships, and situational influences. The measurement of personality in organizations is usually accomplished through direct observa-

tions, self-report questionnaires, and experimental procedures such as those used in an assessment center.

- Needs and motives are another determinant of personality traits that, in turn, lead to different types of work behavior. Among the many needs and motives influencing work behavior are achievement, affiliation, aggression, autonomy, deference, dominance, exhibition, nurturance, order, and power.
- An attitude is a predisposition to respond or a mental state of readiness exerting a specific influence upon a person's response to a person, thing, idea, or situation. The components of an attitude are the cognitive, affective, and behavioral. When these components are logically related to one another, the attitude tends to be stable. Attitudes are formed by about the same factors as those that lead to personality formation.
- Strategies for changing attitudes include (1) communication of additional information, (2) reinforcement of desired attitude change, (3) group influences, (4) inducement to engage in discrepant behavior, (5) adaptation of change methods to individual differences, and (6) reliance on a trusted and influential source.
- An integrative model of work adjustment presented here states that job performance and satisfaction will tend to be high if there is a correspondence between (1) an individual's personality, ability, and attitudes and (2) job requirements.

Questions for Discussion

1. How do people ordinarily know which are their best developed abilities?
2. In your opinion, which of the abilities discussed in this chapter are the most important for achieving success in business?
3. Left-handed people are right-brain dominant; therefore, they should be more creative than right-handed people. Have you noticed this to be true?
4. Provide three specific examples of professional-level jobs calling for any type of mechanical ability.
5. Why is being physically fit considered to be so important for holding down an executive position?
6. What difference do you notice between the popular and technical definitions of personality (as presented in this chapter).
7. Which personality traits do you think tend to be the most pronounced in each of the following cultural (or ethnic) groups. Swedish, Asiatic Indians, English?
8. How might an organization tend to change or modify an employee's personality?
9. Should managers be required to inform subordinates of the conclusions they have reached about the subordinate's personality? Explain.
10. How can an organization help employees to satisfy their deference motives?
11. How might a superior document the fact that a subordinate has a negative attitude?
12. What has proved to be an effective method of changing an individual's attitude toward an important issue?

An Organizational Behavior Problem

Ability and Personality Profiles

Different jobs call for a different pattern of ability and personality factors as indicated by the concept of job specification. In this exercise you are asked to draw an ability and trait profile of the ideal incumbent for two different positions. Indicate on the form provided whether you think a successful performer in that position should rate low, medium, or high on the trait or characteristic in question. After you have made your ratings, connect the points with a straight line, forming a profile of the ideal candidate. Check back in the chapter for a definition of each personal trait or characteristic listed.

Questions

1. How might such a position profile be used in the selection of people for jobs?
2. Why do you think these position profiles have not proven as valuable as they appear on the surface?
3. Rate yourself on the same personal traits and characteristics. Use a red pencil and superimpose your profile over those of the airline pilot and the chief financial officer. Based on this self-analysis, are you better suited to be a commercial airline pilot or a chief financial officer? How do you know?

Commercial Airline Pilot, Large Aircraft

	Ideal Standing on Trait or Characteristic		
	Low	Medium	High
Personal Trait or Characteristic			
Numerical comprehension	____	____	____
Verbal comprehension	____	____	____
Inductive reasoning	____	____	____
Syntactic evaluation	____	____	____
Psychomotor ability	____	____	____
Visual skills	____	____	____
Physical skills	____	____	____
Needs and Motives			
Achievement	____	____	____
Affiliation	____	____	____
Autonomy	____	____	____
Deference	____	____	____
Dominance	____	____	____
Order	____	____	____
Power	____	____	____

Chief Financial Officer, Large Firm

Personal Trait or Characteristic	Ideal Standing on Trait or Characteristic		
	Low	Medium	High
Numerical comprehension	___	___	___
Verbal comprehension	___	___	___
Inductive reasoning	___	___	___
Syntactic evaluation	___	___	___
Psychomotor ability	___	___	___
Visual skills	___	___	___
Physical skills	___	___	___
Needs and Motives			
Achievement	___	___	___
Affiliation	___	___	___
Autonomy	___	___	___
Deference	___	___	___
Dominance	___	___	___
Order	___	___	___
Power	___	___	___

Additional Reading

ANASTASI, ANNE. *Psychological Testing,* 5th ed. New York: Macmillan, 1982.

BARRON, FRANK. *The Shaping of Personality: Conflict, Choice, and Growth.* New York: Harper & Row, 1979.

BYRNE, DONN, and KATHRYN KELLEY. *An Introduction to Personality,* 3rd ed. Englewood Cliffs, N.J.: Prentice-Hall, 1981.

EWING, DAVID W. "Discovering Your Problem-Solving Style." *Psychology Today,* December 1977, pp. 69–73, 138.

MADDI, SALVATORE. *Personality Theories: A Comparative Analysis.* Homewood, Ill.: Dorsey, 1980.

MCKIM, ROBERT H. *Thinking Visually.* Belmont, Calif.: Lifetime Learning Publications, 1981.

PETTY, RICHARD E. *Attitudes and Persuasion: Classical and Contemporary Approaches.* Dubuque, Iowa: William C. Brown, 1981.

SAMUEL, WILLIAM. *Personality: Searching for the Sources of Human Behavior.* New York: McGraw-Hill, 1981.

CHAPTER 5

Motivation in Organizations

1. To understand how work motivation is related to performance and satisfaction.

2. To recognize the difference between cognitive and reinforcement theories of motivation.

3. To understand the significance of goal setting to motivation.

4. To summarize the essentials of the expectancy/valence and the equity theories of motivation.

5. To acquire the information necessary to install and implement a behavior modification program.

Sylvia, president and owner of Banner Realty, sighed in minor exasperation as she spoke to Gail, her vice president and partner: "The figures do not look good. Our commercial property sales are down 25 percent over last year's. Residential sales are down 42 percent. I know the real estate business is in a recession, but our decline is worse than the regional average. Any suggestions?"

"This is about the sixth time we've chewed over this problem," said Gail. "But I've done my homework this time. I've been reading some articles about pumping up your sales force when business is bad. I think I have a few novel ideas. Interested?"

"Sure, I'm interested," responded Sylvia. "Let's hear what you have in mind. I'm particularly interested in ideas that will boost motivation but won't bankrupt Banner Agency."

"Here are a few ideas that should pay for themselves," said Gail. "First of all, let's up the ante. On top of the usual 6 percent gross commission, let's give a cash bonus for each completed sale. If the property is sold for less than $125,000, the real estate agent receives $100. If the property is over $125,000 he or she gets $200. And a $300 bonus for any property sold for more than $350,000.

"My second idea gets at the fact that pride is as important as money. Let's spring for a flashy new bulletin board. All agents who make quota for the month get their names posted in large letters on the board. Three straight months of making quota, and the agent gets a good service pin that can be worn on the lapel."

"Anything else?" asked Sylvia. "So far, I'm interested but not overwhelmed."

"Here's a low-priced incentive item that might have a big payoff. I think our office lacks warmth. It's not a very comfortable place. Our staff members tend to hang out in the diner across the street when they want a break. Let's keep a fresh supply of good coffee, donuts, and pastry here. This way our agents will be motivated to stay in the office and prospect for business over the phone."

"All in all, I'm willing to go along with your plan especially since I don't have a better one in mind. But before we implement the program, let's speak to the agents who'll be affected."

During the next two days, Sylvia and Gail informed each real estate agent about the new incentive plan and the program of supplying free coffee, donuts, and pastry. All six agents expressed enthusiasm or at least approval. As one veteran commented, "Who is going to turn down something for nothing?"

The new measures designed to "pump up" the agents were implemented on March 1. After the first thirty days, sales volume had increased 10 percent over the baseline period of December, January, and February. During the next thirty days, sales were down 6 percent. During the third thirty-day period, sales were up 4 percent. During the fourth month of the new motivational program, sales were virtually identical to the three-month baseline average.

At this point Sylvia informed Gail of her decision: "Let's can the sales incentive bonus. It's costing us a bundle of money and neither our sales volume nor our number of closed deals has improved dramatically. We told our people it was only a trial program, so no apologies are in order. But rather than create a morale problem, I'll stay with the coffee and treats idea.

"We may not have learned how to boost the production of our agents but at least we do know that they enjoy receiving extra money and goodies."

THE MEANING OF WORK MOTIVATION

Banner Realty's experience in trying to improve performance through motivation illustrates several key points about the topic of work motivation. Above all, human motivation is a complex phenomenon for which automatic answers are not readily available. Also, the results of motivation are not always easy to measure. If Sylvia and Gail contrasted their sales results to those of other comparable firms, they may have discovered that other firms experienced a greater decline in sales during that period. The case also illustrates that satisfaction and motivation are not identical concepts.

The term *motivation* has two general meanings in the study of management. One use refers to an activity of managers. Thus Sylvia and Gail were trying to motivate a group of real estate agents. Another use refers to a person's internal state that leads to effort expended toward objectives. Work motivation usually means effort expended toward organizational objectives or work accomplishment.

Work motivation is clearly the most widely researched and written about topic in organizational behavior. Here we summarize several key theories of motivation and explain how they are used to enhance motivation and performance in job settings. Some of the information in this chapter is an extension of the basic motivational concepts described in the previous two chapters.

WORK MOTIVATION AND JOB PERFORMANCE

A common misperception is that high motivation almost always leads to good performance. Many people believe that "You can accomplish anything if you want it badly enough" or "Nobody but yourself can stop you from succeeding." Motivation, in fact, is but one set of independent variables that contributes to the dependent variable of performance. It was stated previously that $P = (E \times A)$. However, three other general factors in addition to effort and ability are also involved: nonmotivational and experiential, group, and technological.[1]

Nonmotivational and Experiential Factors

Many hard-working employees fail to achieve high performance because they are deficient in such characteristics as problem-solving ability, special skills, appropriate training, or experience. The last factor is the most readily modified. Your basic abilities set a limit to what you are capable of doing. Skills and training are also important to capitalize upon your basic abilities.

---

[1]Henry L. Tosi and Stephen J. Carroll, *Management,* 2nd ed. (New York: John Wiley, 1982), pp. 405–9.

Group Factors

Sometimes group norms may influence an ordinarily well-motivated person to hold back on performance. A junior chemist was newly hired into the laboratory of a company that made cable insulators. After two weeks, she received a compliment from her group leader about her high productivity. Within a short time, two peers confronted her at lunch and requested that she "quit her showboating and slow down." Her work output then decreased for the next several months. Finally, she decided that peer approval was less important than establishing a good work record.

Technological Factors

Technology also mediates the relationship between motivation and performance. Without the appropriate tools, machines, and equipment, high motivation will rarely lead to high performance. One plant manager showed a 10 percent decrease in salvage rate and a 40 percent decrease in delayed orders in comparison with the previous year's performance. When asked if he were doing a better job of motivating his staff, the manager replied, "Not particularly. I finally received authorization to put in some of the equipment we've needed for years. Now a person can put in a decent day's work without having to worry about machine breakdown."

Despite this disclaimer about the chances of improved motivation always leading to improved performance and productivity, the relationship is still of importance. A number of behavioral science-based methods, techniques, and programs are used to improve productivity in work organizations. Often, the independent variable manipulated is motivation or effort. The accompanying box lists productivity improvement programs that are designed to achieve their ends by improving motivation, satisfaction, or both (see pages 107–108). Many of these programs are discussed in this chapter, elsewhere in this book, or in texts dealing with productivity improvement.[2]

COGNITIVE VERSUS REINFORCEMENT MODELS OF MOTIVATION

The cognitive and reinforcement models (or schools of thought) represent the two major perspectives on motivation in organizations.[3] Cognitive frameworks emphasize that human beings make conscious decisions about their behavior, such as "I'll take on that assignment because it appeals to my desire to solve puzzles." A cognitive model of motivation also contends that people are driven by internal forces that guide their behavior. Among such forces is the quest to satisfy needs for achievement, power, self-fulfillment, and belonging.

[2]Two such books are Andrew J. DuBrin, *Contemporary Applied Management* (Plano, Tex.: Business Publications, 1982), and Gary Dessler, *Improving Productivity: Ten Modern Human Resource Management Techniques* (Reston, Va.: Reston, 1983).

[3]Donald B. Fedor and Gerald R. Ferris, "Integrating OB Mod with Cognitive Approaches to Motivation," *The Academy of Management Review,* January 1981, pp. 115–25.

BEHAVIORAL SCIENCE METHODS CONTRIBUTING DIRECTLY OR INDIRECTLY TO MOTIVATION AND PRODUCTIVITY

Autonomous Work Groups. Small work groups that to a large extent manage themselves. Group members become generalists and have considerable autonomy. Productivity may be enhanced because workers identify with their product, experience increased pride, and therefore expend more effort.

Behavior Modeling. A training method based on behavior modification. The learner acquires new skills by observing a person perform the skill correctly, role playing, reinforcement from others, and transfer of training to the workplace. Productivity increases because a job skill, such as dealing with customer complaints, is developed to a high level.

Behavior Modification and *Positive Reinforcement.* A technique whereby employees are encouraged to repeat productive responses and actions because they are rewarded for such responses. Productivity is enhanced directly, and often dramatically, under careful administration of PR programs.

Brainstorming. The process of gathering a small group of people together to generate alternatives to an operational problem in an atmosphere of encouragement. Productivity is enhanced when a useful solution or course of action is uncovered that might not have been uncovered without brainstorming.

Career Planning and *Development.* A counseling activity that helps individuals to plan their future careers within the enterprise to help both the individual and the organization achieve their objectives. A person with a satisfying career within a firm will tend to stay with the firm, thereby remaining productive and decreasing costly turnover.

Conflict Resolution Techniques. Techniques taught to organization members for identifying and confronting critical problems and arriving at solutions that are functional to the organization. Productivity is enhanced as snags and delays are overcome.

Counseling Problem Employees. Teaching managers how to listen to employee problems, identify causes and contributing factors, and mutually develop action plans to resolve such problems. Productivity is enhanced when the employee overcomes problems and achieves performance standards set for the position.

Employee Assistance Programs (Plans). A formal program, administered by the personnel department, providing help to employees who have become ineffective performers for a variety of personal or work-related reasons, including burnout. Outside agencies perform the actual counseling and rehabilitation programs. Employee returns to productive functioning and turnover costs are reduced.

Employee Attitude Surveys and *Organization Analysis.* Identification of employee concerns and morale problems through questionnaires and interviews. If remedial action is taken, morale and productivity both may increase.

Goal Setting Programs (including MBO). Teaching workers at all levels how to establish useful short-, intermediate-, and long-term goals. Performance increases as a result of setting goals and establishing action plans for their attainment.

Grid Organization Development (Managerial Grid®). A widely used management development and organization development program for teaching leaders the techniques of team management—getting work accomplished through committed people. Productivity increases if the manager applies these techniques successfully over time.

Job Enrichment. The job is redesigned to increase depth and responsibility. Motivation and satisfaction are increased because the employee has an opportunity to satisfy higher-level needs. Improved productivity often results.

Modified Work Schedules (MWS). Modifying working hours into an arrangement favorable to employee preferences. Two popular applications of this strategy are the compressed workweek and flexitime. Morale almost always increases as a result of MWS. Productivity sometimes increases because employees feel more energetic and are less distracted by personal matters that require attention during the normal work day.

Organization Development (OD). An assortment of training or therapeutic interventions whose purpose is to improve the organization and its members. Productivity is increased because OD participants become more adept at solving problems that are blocking the accomplishment of work results (such as interpersonal friction).

Quality of Work Life (QWL). A wide variety of programs giving employees a chance to satisfy important needs through their experiences in the organization. Most QWL programs involve a heavy degree of worker participation. Satisfaction is usually increased, and productivity is sometimes increased, because motivation level is increased through the satisfaction of a wider range of needs.

Scanlon Plan. An organization-wide incentive program that pays incentives for labor-saving suggestions. A network of department and plant screening committees evaluate suggestions from employees and management. Productivity increases since employees perceive a direct link between their implementing suggestions for improvement and higher earnings for themselves.

Stress Management Programs and Techniques. A variety of methods for helping employees prevent and manage the negative effects of distress. Productivity is increased because workers in control of their emotions are able to concentrate better on their work, make fewer errors in judgment, and lose less time from work.

Team Building. A widely used OD technique for helping natural work groups to achieve better internal communication and problem-solving skills, thereby becoming more productive.

Work Habit Improvement and *Time Management*. A group of methods that help people to plan their own work more carefully and be in control of their work schedules. Productivity increases because workers feel less overwhelmed, waste less energy, and focus on more important tasks.

Cognitive models of motivation can be subdivided into content and process models. *Content* theories of motivation are concerned with factors that trigger or arouse motivated behavior. Need theories are considered content theories. *Process* theories of motivation are concerned with both behavioral triggers and the sequence of steps (process), direction, and choice of behavior patterns. Process models of motivation are therefore more complex than are content models. The best developed process model is expectancy/valence theory.

Reinforcement models of motivation have also been labeled "acognitive" or "OB mod," namely, organizational behavior modification. A reinforcement model concentrates on environmental factors rather than on inner strivings. The model contends that employees engage in motivated behavior when their behavior leads to a reward. A manager using reinforcement theory engages in establishing an appropriate set of rewards and punishments rather than trying to analyze the employee's motives or needs.

Despite the controversy between these two schools of thought that exists in the scientific and professional literature, cognitive and reinforcement models of motivation are often integrated in managerial practice. For example, need (cognitive) theory is relied on to help determine which rewards would be useful in a behavior mod program. Based on need theory, you might reward employees by providing them with opportunities for self-fulfillment, such as offering them a challenging assignment.

The cognitive theories discussed in this and the previous chapter are need theory, goal-setting theory, two-factor theory, expectancy/valence theory, and equity theory. Among these five, the first three are considered content theories, whereas the last two are process theories. Considerable overlap exists among the cognitive theories, except that equity theory stands somewhat alone because it focuses on one limited aspect of behavior. Behavior modification represents the reinforcement model of motivation.

GOAL THEORY AND WORK MOTIVATION

Goals have a pervasive influence on behavior in organizations and managerial practice. Programs such as MBO (management by objectives), positive reinforcement, and team building include the establishment of clear-cut goals. Almost every modern business organization has some form of goal setting or planning in operation as illustrated by the comments of the chief executive officer of Chrysler Corporation in the accompanying box (see page 110). Goal-setting theory helps explain both the importance of goal setting and the characteristics of goals that lead to improved performance.

The basic premise of goal-setting theory is that behavior is regulated by values and conscious intentions (goals).[4] A goal is defined simply as what the individual is trying to do. Our values create a desire to do things consistent with them. The organizational behavior problem at the end of this chapter concerns the work ethic value. People with a strong work orientation will tend to set high goals and will work diligently toward their attainment. One way of conceptualizing the behavior of workaholics is to say that their values lead them toward setting and pursuing unattainable goals. The goal-setting theory model works in this sequence:

[4]Gary P. Latham and Edwin A. Locke, "Goal Setting—A Motivational Technique That Works," *Organizational Dynamics,* Autumn 1979, pp. 72–75, and Gary P. Latham and Gary A. Yukl, "A Review of Research on the Application of Goal Setting in Organizations," *Academy of Management Journal,* December 1975, pp. 824–43.

IACOCCA ON GOAL SETTING

"In our corporate life, everything is reported quarterly. I don't know why it's that way rather than daily or monthly or yearly, but that's the way it is. The stockholders want to know what the quarterly dividend is. So in order to make that money and pay that dividend, you must be sure everybody knows his part, his piece of making that dollar share. You have to do that for all your employees, and the way I do it is through setting quarterly objectives.

"I use a simple black book with tabs for each executive who reports to me. Each one files a plan outlining what he expects to accomplish in the next three months. I expect him to do the same thing with his people.

"Once you can get quarterly plans in their minds, get them to write down what they hope to accomplish in the next three months and know they are going to have to report back to their boss at the end of the quarter and tell him how they did, it becomes self-disciplining; it's self-pleasing. They will embarrass themselves if they're at home thinking, 'Jeez, I didn't accomplish anything in the last 90 days.'

"It's tough to do—and if you have to follow everybody like in a military school, bugging them to get their exams in on time or something, then you know you've lost it, they're not responding to that type of plan—but I happen to believe in it. When I left Ford they were making a $1.8 billion profit, and that had something to do with quarterly plans.

"The black book doesn't need to be fancy. The idea is simple—you could do it on the back of an envelope. But it must force self-evaluation.

"It can apply anywhere, even to running a home. In a home, you might not need to write down your goals because you're conscious of them. You know you want to get your kid's teeth straightened and make sure you don't spend more than you're budgeted for or you'll go into hock. But in a big organization, you must get goals written down.

"You have to be sure the guy or the girl knows what is expected. So you ask them.

"They'll say, 'What do you mean? I know my job.' You say, 'Alright then, what is it?' They'll say something like, 'We're supposed to get the penetration of this market up two percent.'

"Now you ask, 'OK, how would you go about doing that?' and you get them to write it down. You have to agree, of course, that those are the objectives and the priorities. How they get there depends on how they want to run. Most managers, it seems, don't let people run. But I tell them to go ahead and tackle these things and see me in 90 days."

Success, January 1982, p. 18.

Values → Emotions and desires → Intentions or goals → Behavior and job performance

Goal-setting theory contends that hard (difficult) goals result in a higher level of performance than no goals at all or generalized goals such as "try hard." The goals toward which the individual works seem to lead to improved performance, whether these goals are set by the person or by the organization. The basics of goal-setting theory have such an impact on managing people that they require elaboration.

Attributes of Goals Influencing Performance

Obviously not all goals work as well as others. It is therefore important to examine several characteristics or attributes of goals that mediate whether or not they lead to improved performance.

Specific versus generalized goals or no goals. Setting specific goals for work performance generally leads to improved productivity. Management by objectives is a system of goal setting and review based on this premise. A specific goal is helpful because it pinpoints where performance should be directed. If you wanted to improve your ability to make oral presentations, it would be of some value to set the goal "Improve my oral presentation skills." It would be more helpful to set specific goals such as (1) decrease vocalized pauses, (2) remember to smile every few minutes, and (3) learn to follow an outline but do not read the presentation to the audience.

One relevant study of the effects of specific goals on performance involved pulpwood workers. The researchers investigated the effects of a one-day training program in goal setting on job performance. Multiple measurements of performance were used, and the study was conducted for twelve consecutive weeks. The results showed that the pulpwood workers who set specific production goals for their crews had higher productivity and lower absenteeism than did those crews in the control group who were told to "do your best."[5]

Difficult goals improve performance. As long as goals are accepted by employees, the more difficult the goals, the higher the performance. A number of laboratory and field studies have supported this conclusion. A limiting factor is that a point of diminishing returns is quickly reached. If a goal is perceived as so difficult that it is virtually impossible to attain, the result will be frustration rather than increased accomplishment. Any goal is subject to some kind of a cognitive process. Consciously, or preconsciously, the person says, "Would I be hitting my head against a brick wall trying to reach that goal?"

Self-confidence mediates the motivational value of difficult goals. Highly self-confident employees are less concerned about not reaching work goals and therefore do not become overly tense in working toward difficult goals. Another mediating factor is the other goals that accompany difficult goals. In many organizations' goal-setting programs, participants will set a series of goals of varying difficulty. If the goal-setter has a few "easy ones" to attain, he or she will be more willing to risk setting a difficult goal. The risk involved is the potential of a low performance evaluation and a blow to self-esteem if the goal is not reached.

---

[5]Gary P. Latham and Sydney B. Kinne III, "Improving Job Performance Through Training in Goal Setting," *Journal of Applied Psychology,* April 1974, pp. 187–91.

Participation sometimes leads to improved performance. Goal-setting theory suggests that employees who participate in setting their own goals will work harder to achieve them than will employees who are simply assigned goals. Although the research evidence is mixed, there seems to be some advantage to employee participation in goal setting. If you are assigned a goal, even if you accept it, you have a tendency to work less diligently than when you set your own goal. Participation in goal setting leads to improved performance because it increases goal acceptance or "ownership."

A study conducted with engineers and physical scientists sheds some light on the participation issue. Participative goal setting showed an edge over assigned goal setting only to the extent that it led to the setting of higher goals. Another finding supported a basic premise of goal-setting theory. Both participative and assigned-goal groups showed superior performance to groups who were simply told to "do your best."[6]

In summary, goal specificity and goal difficulty contribute more consistently to high performance than does participation in goal setting. A review compiled by Gary P. Latham and Gary A. Yukl of twenty-seven research reports on the topic indicated that goal-setting programs were effective over an extended period of time in a variety of organizations at both the managerial and nonmanagerial levels. The evidence from these studies shows some support for both a cognitive (goal setting, in particular) and a reinforcement model of motivation. A conclusion reached was that "Substantial increases in performance were obtained in some of the studies without any special prizes or incentives for goal attainment, although in other studies reward contingencies were an important consideration."[7]

THE TWO-FACTOR THEORY

The two-factor theory of work motivation developed by Frederick Herzberg has had a substantial impact on managerial practice and thought. Underlying this theory was an attempt to answer the age-old question, "What really does motivate or satisfy people?" The original research on this topic centered on in-depth interviews with two hundred engineers and accountants. Herzberg and his associates asked the engineers and accountants to recall two types of work events or circumstances:

1. Those that characterized a marked improvement in work satisfaction, or when they felt exceptionally good about their jobs.
2. Those that characterized a significant reduction in their positive feelings about their jobs.

From an analysis of these interviews, it was concluded that the job factors (or facets of the work situation) that were associated with feelings of satisfaction were different from the factors associated with dissatisfaction. Elements within the *content* of the job are called *satisfiers* because positive feelings toward them provide personal sat-

[6]Latham and Locke, "Goal Setting," p. 74.
[7]Latham and Yukl, "A Review of Research," p. 840.

isfaction. They are also referred to as *motivators* because positive attitudes toward them will elicit motivated behavior. The underlying mechanism is that satisfiers or motivators (the first factor in the two-factor theory) provide people with an opportunity to satisfy their higher-level needs. When satisfiers or motivators are absent, most people will not experience dissatisfaction; the impact is more likely to be neutral.[8]

According to the two-factor theory, the characteristics of the work situation that function as satisfiers or motivators are responsibility, achievement, advancement, the work itself, recognition, and advancement opportunities. Following this conception, if you want to motivate most people, provide them with the opportunity to do interesting work or receive a promotion and recognize their efforts.

In contrast, factors associated with negative feelings about the work are called *dissatisfiers* or *hygiene factors*—the second set of factors in the two-factor theory. Dissatisfiers tend to be noticed primarily by their absence, and they appeal mostly to lower-level needs. For instance, you may grumble about having to work in a hot cramped office without windows. Because of it, you may experience job dissatisfaction or even be demotivated. But a cool, uncrowded office with an ocean view will probably not increase your level of satisfaction or motivation. Dissatisfiers relate mostly to the *context* in which the work is done, including the job setting and the circumstances that surround it.

Characteristics of the work situation that function as dissatisfiers are technical supervision, interpersonal relations with others on the job, salary, working conditions, status, company policy, and job security. Dissatisfiers are called hygiene factors because they prevent the occurrence of dissatisfaction but do not induce people toward extra effort.

The two-factor theory of motivation follows the growth and deficit conceptual scheme of the need hierarchy theory. Factors that have a motivational thrust upon people are *growth* factors—those that provide the worker with a sense of accomplishment through the work itself and thus satisfy higher-level needs. Herzberg criticizes attempts to motivate workers by reliance upon hygiene factors such as paid vacations and cost-of-living adjustments. Employees would certainly rebel if these benefit factors were withdrawn, but their existence does not elicit real motivation from people. Hygiene factors or dissatisfiers appeal to deficit needs, not growth needs. Table 5–1 summarizes these relationships. One major difference between the need hierarchy and two-factor theories is that, according to the former, an appeal to any level need can be a motivator. The latter theory contends that only appeals to higher-level needs can be motivational.

Criticism of the Two-Factor Theory

The two-factor theory has been subjected to extensive testing, but much more in the past than in the present literature of organizational behavior. More studies of the the-

[8]An original source here is Frederick Herzberg, Bernard Mausner, and Barbara Snyderman, *The Motivation to Work* (New York: John Wiley, 1959). See also Herzberg, *Work and the Nature of Man* (Cleveland: World Book Company, 1966).

TABLE 5–1   A Comparison of the Need Hierarchy and
              Two-Factor Theories of Work Motivation

Need Hierarchy of Maslow	Two-Factor Theory of Herzberg
Self-actualization	Motivating factors (satisfiers)
	Responsibility
	Achievement
	Advancement
Self-esteem	The work itself
	Recognition
	Advancement opportunities
Love (belonging and	Hygiene factors (dissatisfiers)
affiliation)	Technical supervision
	Interpersonal relations
	Salary
Safety and security	Working conditions
	Status
Physiological	Company policy
	Job security

ory have produced negative results than positive results. Three consistent sets of criticism have been launched against the motivator-hygiene theory.

First, much of what Herzberg and his followers have observed is simply defensive behavior on the part of people. When people are interviewed, they tend to attribute good things about their job to their own effort and ingenuity. A person thus might say that complex work is a motivator because he or she is performing the complex work. But when things are going poorly, the blame can easily be attributed to somebody else—such as lack of stimulating co-workers.[9]

A second major criticism of Herzberg's conclusions is that they appear to be *method bound.* An interview approach was used in gathering data for the two-factor theory. When questionnaires are used, there is a distinct tendency for researchers to arrive at different conclusions. Soliman reviewed a number of studies testing the motivation-hygiene theory.[10] A telling conclusion he reached was that when Herzberg's methodology was followed, seventeen out of twenty studies were able to replicate his results. However, of more than twenty studies that used a different method, only three supported the theory.

A third major criticism of the two-factor theory is that it does not give consideration to individual differences. Not everybody has the same set of motivators and hygiene factors, and not all people are concerned primarily with satisfying higher-level needs on the job. Salary is a prime example of a job element that acts as a motivator

[9]Victor H. Vroom, *Work and Motivation* (New York: John Wiley, 1964), p. 129.

[10]H. M. Soliman, "Motivation-Hygiene Theory of Job Attitudes," *Journal of Applied Psychology,* December 1970, pp. 452–61. Another comprehensive review of research on Herzberg's theory is Joseph Schneider and Edwin A. Locke, "A Critique of Herzberg's Classification System and a Suggested Revision," *Organizational Behavior and Human Performance,* July 1971, pp. 441–58.

for some people and a dissatisfier for others. When a person is currently worried about money, or has not yet satisfied his or her needs for money, that person will work hard, given the chance to earn the amount of money desired. Another confounding factor is that money satisfies so many different needs. Given enough money, one can purchase status, recognition, and at times even accomplishment. To illustrate, money can lead to accomplishment because it can buy education or a small business venture.

Despite these criticisms, the two-factor theory has revamped management thinking about job motivation, in general, and the design of jobs, in particular. Many a manager has discarded the notion that people work primarily for money as a result of studying the two-factor theory. What the two-factor theory does well is direct attention to the significance of the work itself in the motivation and satisfaction of employees. "And because the message of the theory is simple, persuasive, and directly relevant to the design and evaluation of actual organizational changes, the theory continues to be widely known and generally used by managers of organizations."[11]

JOB ENRICHMENT: AN APPLICATION OF THE TWO-FACTOR THEORY

Job enrichment is a direct application of the two-factor theory to improving productivity and satisfaction. Its basic motivational strategy is to increase an employee's output by providing that person with exciting, interesting, stimulating, challenging, or responsible work. Such work, in turn, gives a person a chance to satisfy higher-level needs and therefore exerts a motivational influence. Managers can enrich jobs on a one-to-one basis or do so as part of a formal program.

Job enrichment is not simply job enlargement whereby a person is given an increased scope of responsibilities. Enrichment implies that the quality of work a person is performing is increased. Job enrichment can take a variety of forms, limited only by the imagination of those attempting to enrich jobs. The constraints of making a profit (or staying within budget), the willingness of people to have enriched jobs, and the acceptance of any labor union involved all influence the potential effectiveness of job enrichment.

A representative illustration of job enrichment took place at Indiana Bell Telephone Company. Thirty-three employees, most of them at a bottom-level clerical category, compiled all telephone directories for the state. The processing from clerk to clerk was laid out in twenty-one steps, many of which involved verifying the work of other clerks. Morale was low and turnover was unacceptably high for employees preparing the directories. In the opinion of supervisors, the employees were indifferent to the task. The job enrichment specialists consulted suggested that the twenty-one steps be combined into fourteen more complex steps. The major enrichment method was to

[11]J. Richard Hackman and J. Lloyd Suttle, eds., *Improving Life at Work: Behavioral Sciences Approaches to Organizational Change* (Glenview, Ill.: Scott, Foresman and Company, 1977).

permit many employees to have virtually complete responsibility (almost all fourteen steps) for thinner telephone directories. The crux of the job redesign took this form:

> In the past, new entries to all directories had moved from clerk to clerk; now all paper-work connected with an entry belonging to a clerk stayed with that clerk. For example, the clerk prepared the daily addenda and issued them to the information or directory assistance operators. The system became so efficient that most of the clerks who handled the smaller directories had charge of more than one.[12]

An Overall Model of Job Enrichment

Greg R. Oldham and J. Richard Hackman have identified five measurable characteristics of jobs that, when present, are said to improve employee motivation, satisfaction, and performance:

1. *Skill variety:* the extent to which a job demands many different skills of the incumbent.
2. *Task identity:* the extent to which the job requires an individual to complete a whole piece of work—doing a job from beginning to end with a tangible and visible outcome. An example would be preparing a tax return from start to finish.
3. *Task significance:* the extent to which the job allows the employee to have a substantial impact on the lives and livelihoods of other people, either in the immediate organization or the external environment.
4. *Autonomy:* the extent to which the job holder has substantial freedom, independence, and discretion in scheduling the work and in determining procedures involved in its implementation. The position of internal or external consultant is high on autonomy.
5. *Feedback:* the extent to which the job allows the individual to obtain direct and explicit information about his or her performance.

The characteristics of variety, identity, and significance contribute to the *meaningfulness* of the job. Autonomy leads to feelings of *responsibility;* feedback contributes to *knowledge of results.* When a job is high on all these characteristics, it is said to have high motivating potential. The model combines these five characteristics into a single index reflecting the overall potential of a job to trigger high internal work motivation among job holders. The index, called the Motivating Potential Score (MPS), is computed as follows:

$$\text{MPS} = \left[\frac{\text{Skill variety} + \text{Task identity} + \text{Task significance}}{3} \right] \times \text{Autonomy} \times \text{Feedback}$$

Numerical values for each of the five job characteristics are obtained by job holders answering the Job Diagnostic Survey, an instrument similar to most job satis-

---

[12]Robert N. Ford, "Job Enrichment Lessons from AT&T," *Harvard Business Review,* January–February 1973, p. 98.

faction questionnaires. According to research evidence, the MPS has been shown to relate positively to a number of desirable work outcomes such as job satisfaction, work motivation, productivity, and attendance.[13]

Comment

When applied from a contingency viewpoint (with the right people in the right work setting), job enrichment has a positive impact on motivation, satisfaction, and performance. Many people at all job levels take pride in their work and welcome autonomy and responsibility. The critical mediating variable seems to be the preference of the job incumbent. As a starting point, job enrichment should be voluntary. Those people who are motivated by extrinsic factors should be left to perform routinized, repetitive work. Support for this generalization was obtained through a survey of 3,053 employees in fifty-three companies throughout the United States. The companies were predominantly involved in manufacturing. Within each company, the sample was stratified to obtain approximately 50 percent employees in production or assembly-line jobs, 20 percent first-level supervisors, and 30 percent middle management, clerical, or staff positions.

Statistical analysis revealed that employees with more enriched jobs generally reported greater job satisfaction and received higher performance ratings from their superiors. The most influential factor in determining whether or not job enrichment was associated with higher performance and satisfaction was the desire for enrichment.[14] If you want to know whether job enrichment will "work" for a given employee, ask "Do you want an enriched job, and if so, what would you like to see changed?"

One's desire for an enriched job is influenced by a host of personal and situational considerations. This complexity is illustrated by the comments of two employees. One thirty-five-year-old woman with three children told the researchers: "I've got too many things to worry about at home. I just don't need any more responsibility here." She was content to perform a routine job since it seemed to add an element of stability and tranquility to her life. On the other hand, a forty-year-old man commented: "My job will probably be phased out in five years from now. If I don't learn how to do other things, I probably won't have a job before too long." His desire for job enrichment was motivated by economic security. He perceived job enrichment as a method of securing further employment.[15]

[13]This model is described in Greg R. Oldham, J. Richard Hackman, and Jone L. Pearce, "Conditions Under Which Employees Respond Positively to Enriched Work," *Journal of Applied Psychology*, August 1976, pp. 395–403.

[14]David J. Cherrington and J. Lynn England, "The Desire for an Enriched Job as a Moderator of the Enrichment-Satisfaction Relationship," *Organizational Behavior and Human Performance*, February 1980, pp. 139–59.

[15]Ibid., pp. 155–56.

EXPECTANCY/VALENCE THEORY

Expectancy/valence theory combines features of other cognitive theories and contributes concepts of its own. Expectancy/valence theory (or expectancy theory) is really a group of theories whose most general assumption is that the amount of effort expended by people depends to a large extent on what return they expect. The theory is based upon a rational-economic view of people. It assumes that people are decision makers who choose among alternatives by selecting the one that appears most advantageous at the time. Although their choice may not prove to be optimum, at least they decide to expend effort within the limits of their decision-making capabilities. The expectancy/valence model is so well accepted by researchers because it takes into account both individual and situational differences. The expectancy/valence model of motivation has three major components: performance-outcome expectancy, valence, and effort-performance expectancy.

Performance-Outcome Expectancy

When people engage in a particular behavior, they do so with the intention that a desired outcome will be forthcoming. Suppose that as part of a job search you mail one hundred firms a copy of your résumé accompanied by a cover letter. You do so because you believe that there is a reasonable chance that you will receive the outcome, or reward, of a job interview and eventually a job. Performance-outcome ($P \rightarrow 0$) expectancies are thus an important determinant of behavior. The stronger your hunch that performance will lead to outcome, the more likely you are to engage in a particular behavior. Since performance is instrumental in causing an outcome, $P \rightarrow 0$ expectancies are also referred to as instrumentalities.

Valence

Each outcome has a value, worth, or attractiveness to an individual called a valence. The same rewards have different valences for different people; you may value the outcome of being assigned to a committee, while another person may even attach a negative valence to that outcome. The valence you attach to a reward or outcome thus influences how willing you are to expend effort. A valence represents your subjective interpretation rather than an inherent quality of the outcome or reward.

Effort-Performance Expectancy

Another question people ask themselves before engaging in a particular behavior is, "If I expend the effort, will I really get the task accomplished?" Each behavior is associated in the individual's mind with a certain expectancy or subjective hunch of the probability of success. Effort-performance ($E \rightarrow 0$) expectancies thus influence whether or not you will even strive for a reward.

Putting these concepts together, people will select a level of performance that seems to have the best chance of achieving a valued outcome. Effort will be expended if the individual believes, or feels confident, that

1. Behavior will lead to outcomes ($P \rightarrow 0$).
2. These outcomes have a positive valence for him or her.
3. He or she can perform at the necessary level to get the task accomplished ($E \rightarrow 0$).

A Basic Expectancy Model

A number of complex expectancy models have been developed, several of them being mathematically based. The Porter-Lawler version presented in Figure 5–1 is widely accepted and fits well the thrust of this chapter. Its theoretical workings proceed in this manner:

> The value of the expected reward to the individual (1) combines with the individual's perception of the effort involved in attaining the reward and the probability of achieving the reward (2) to produce a certain level of effort (3). This effort must be combined with the individual's abilities and traits (4) and his or her perception of the role or activities required for the task (5) in order to reach the performance level (6).
>
> The resulting level of performance leads to intrinsic rewards (or perhaps negative consequences if the performance level is lower than expected). Intrinsic rewards are inherent in the task accomplishment (7A), much like the satisfiers and motivators in the two-factor theory. Taking pride in your accomplishment is an intrinsic reward.

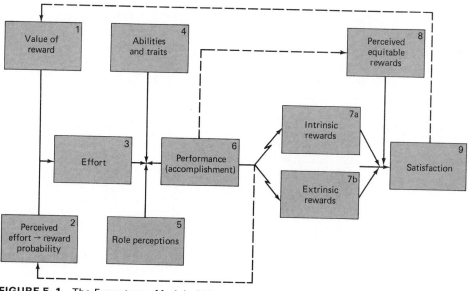

FIGURE 5–1   The Expectancy Model of Motivation

Or, performance may lead to extrinsic rewards (7B) which are external to the task such as receiving a cash bonus or paid vacation for outstanding performance. The wavy line in the model leading to the extrinsic rewards indicates that these rewards are not guaranteed, since they are dependent on assessments of the individual's performance by managers and on the willingness of the organization to reward that performance.

Employees have their own idea about the appropriateness of the total reward received (8), which when measured against the rewards actually received, results in the level of satisfaction experienced by the individual (9). The employee's experience will then be applied to his or her future assessments of the value of rewards for further task accomplishment.[16]

How Motivation Is Calculated

For motivation to be high, expectancies and valence must be high. This relationship can be expressed by the formula

$$\text{Motivation} = (P \to 0) \times (E \to P) \times \text{Valence}$$

An elementary example from small business explains how this process works. The owner believes strongly, on a 1 to 10 scale, that if he wants to he will be able to install an employee suggestion system. He thus has a high $E \to P$ expectancy, perhaps .9. He believes a little less strongly that a suggestion system will lead to useful ideas for organizational efficiency and effectiveness. His $P \to 0$ expectancy is .7. Yet he strongly values organizational improvement. His valence on a scale from -1.0 to $+1.0$ is 1.0. When these three factors are multiplied ($.9 \times .7 \times 1.0 = .63$), it becomes clear that his motivation will be high.

Expectancy/valence theory also helps to explain in mathematical terms why some people engage in behaviors such as playing a lottery or trying to write a best selling novel, although they recognize that the $P \to 0$ expectancy is quite low. The compensating factor is that they place an extraordinary valence upon winning. One winning ticket or one best selling novel and you may become a millionaire!

Implications for Managers
and Organizations

Expectancy/valence theory has many important implications for managing people and organizations. Some of the implications presented in the paragraphs that follow could also be derived from other cognitive models of motivation and from reinforcement theory.

1. *Find out what outcomes are desired by employees.* If managers do not know what "turns employees on," it will be difficult to motivate them and, therefore, to improve performance. Among the techniques for determining the useful motivators are ques-

---

[16]The model is from Lyman W. Porter and Edward E. Lawler III, *Managerial Attitudes and Performance* (Homewood, Ill.: Richard D. Irwin, 1968), p. 165. The quoted verbal translation of the model is from James A. F. Stoner, *Management,* 2nd ed. (Englewood Cliffs, N.J.: Prentice-Hall, 1982), pp. 461–62.

tionnaires, observation of how employees behave in response to specific rewards, and direct questioning, for instance, "What are you shooting for in this job?" or "What does the firm have to offer that you want?"

2. *Define good performance.* The more specifically you define what constitutes good performance, the more likely it will happen. The less structured the job, the more difficult it is to define specific performance standards.

3. *Be sure that the desired performance levels are attainable.* Effort-to-performance expectancy is critical. If employees establish a high subjective probability that their performance targets are unrealistically high, the result will be a decreased expenditure of effort (work motivation).

4. *Link rewards to performance.* Motivation will be increased when employees perceive a link between rewards and performance. It may be necessary to discuss with employees how the two are actually linked.

5. *Analyze the total situation for conflicting expectancies.* Motivation will be high only when employees see many rewards, and few punishments, associated with good performance. For example, if being a high producer gets you assigned to unwanted overtime assignments, or ribbing from your peers, your $P \rightarrow 0$ expectancy may decrease.

6. *Some rewards should be geared to group rather than to individual performance.* Group rewards are especially important when cooperative behavior is required for the task. Managers should also be aware of the kind of expectancies that informal groups establish and check to see if they are in harmony with the expectancies that the organization attempts to create.

7. *Immediate supervisors play a critical role in creating, monitoring, and maintaining the reward structures that will lead to good performance.* The manager's role in motivation becomes one of defining clear goals, setting clear reward expectancies, and providing the right rewards for different workers.

8. *Organizations need to be flexible to accommodate individual differences.* Different employees have different needs and, therefore, different valences. Effective organizations must manage for these individual differences. A germane example is "cafeteria-style" fringe benefit plans that allow employees to choose a package of fringe benefits meeting their personal preferences and current life-styles. (A constraint, however, is that some benefits such as medical insurance are mandatory.)[17]

Comment

A major problem with many versions of expectancy theory is that they have become so complex and esoteric that they are incapable of being properly tested. A synthesis of the literature testing expectancy models shows meager results:

---

[17]This list, and some of our discussion of expectancy/valence theory, is from David A. Nadler and Edward E. Lawler III, "Motivation: A Diagnostic Approach," in J. Richard Hackman et al., eds., *Perspectives on Organizational Behavior* (New York: McGraw-Hill, 1977).

Almost all of the studies purporting to test the full model have been correlational field studies and the correlational "ceiling" seems to be approximately .30 when independent ratings of effort are used as the criterion. The mode seems to be closer to .25. Virtually the only time the *r*'s exceed this ceiling is when self-rated effort is used as a dependent variable.[18]

Another major reservation about expectancy theory is whether or not many people actually engage in detailed cognitive arithmetic before deciding at what level to perform or which organization to join. It has been suggested that upwardly mobile people might engage in such mental arithmetic, whereas less ambitious people merely make impulsive decisions about the expenditure of effort.[19]

EQUITY THEORY

Equity theory posits that employees hold certain beliefs (or formulate cognitions) about the *outputs* they get from their jobs and the *inputs* they invest to obtain certain outcomes. The outcomes of employment include pay, fringe benefits, status, intrinsic job factors, and anything else stemming from the job that people perceive as being useful. The inputs include all the factors that employees perceive as being their investment in the job or anything of value that they bring to the job. Among such inputs are job qualifications, skill, education level, effort, and cooperative behavior.

The crux of equity theory is that employees compare their inputs and outputs with other individuals in the workplace.[20] When employees believe that they are receiving equitable outputs in relation to their inputs, they are generally satisfied. Conversely, when employees believe that they are giving too much as compared with what they are receiving from the organization, a state of tension and dissatisfaction ensues. The people used for reference are those whom the employee perceives as relevant for comparison. For example, a senior chemist would make comparisons with other senior chemists about whom he or she has information.

Comparisons are of two kinds: we consider our own inputs in relation to outputs received; we also evaluate what others are receiving for the same inputs. Equity is said to exist when an individual concludes that his or her own outcome/input ratio is equal to that of other people. Inequity exists if the person's ratio is not the same as that of other persons. All these comparisons are similar to those judgments made by people according to expectancy theory—they are subjective hunches, which may or may not

[18]John P. Campbell and Robert D. Pritchard, "Motivation Theory in Industrial and Organizational Psychology," in Marvin D. Dunnette, ed., *Handbook of Industrial and Organizational Psychology* (Chicago: Rand McNally, 1976), p. 65.

[19]Barry M. Staw and Gerald R. Salancik, eds., *New Directions in Organizational Behavior* (Chicago: St. Clair Press, 1977), p. 77.

[20]M. R. Carrell and J. E. Dettrich, "Equity Theory: The Recent Literature, Methodological Considerations, and New Directions," *Academy of Management Review,* April 1978, pp. 202–10, and Paul S. Goodman, "An Examination of Referents Used in the Evaluation of Pay," *Organizational Behavior and Human Performance,* vol. 10, 1974, pp. 340–52.

be valid. Inequity can be in either direction and of varying magnitudes. One method of expressing the equity ratio is

$$\text{Equity ratio} = \frac{\text{Outcome (high or low)}}{\text{Input (high or low)}}$$

People may choose among five alternatives for resolving a perceived inequity:

1. Distort their perception of their own or others' inputs or outputs. (According to the theory of cognitive dissonance, people typically distort one set of conflicting facts to reduce the tension associated with accepting those facts. If a co-worker were being paid too much in comparison with you, that fact could make you tense. As a coping device you could possibly distort your perception upward of the experience or skill possessed by the co-worker.)
2. Try to bring others toward their own inputs or outputs. (Generally, this is quite impractical, particularly with regard to getting others to accept lower compensation or to work less hard.)
3. Behave in some way to change their own inputs or outputs. (A person might demand a salary increase or expend less effort on the job. Or work harder to justify being overpaid!)
4. Choose another employee as a comparison person. (You might look for another relevant comparison person who is being paid less than you.)
5. Leave the field. (Quit the job in a huff.)[21]

Equity theory has much face validity and has direct relevance for compensation practice. No matter how well designed a program of productivity improvement might be, it must still provide equitable pay. Employees expect to participate in the rewards associated with increased productivity. It also behooves management to determine which reference groups employees are using in making pay comparisons. The accompanying box summarizes two field investigations with equity theory as applied to professional baseball (see pages 124–126).

BEHAVIOR MODIFICATION AND POSITIVE REINFORCEMENT

Behavior modification is the direct application of principles of reinforcement theory to motivation in organizations. Such programs are generally referred to as PR (positive reinforcement) because they rely almost exclusively upon the positive reinforcement component of behavior modification. However, an OB mod program could also use the reinforcement techniques of punishment, extinction, and avoidance learning. Operant conditioning, described in Chapter 3, provides some of the theoretical base for the present discussion. Here we emphasize the application of operant conditioning

[21]Based in part on Stephen P. Robbins, *Personnel: The Management of Human Resources* (New York: Macmillan, 1978), p. 312.

EQUITY AND THE PERFORMANCE OF MAJOR LEAGUE BASEBALL PLAYERS

The two researchers who conducted this study contend that baseball players provide a shrewdly drawn sample to test certain equity theory predictions. First, many accurate and immediately comparable performance measures are available in record form. Second, recent developments in baseball players' contracts have given players an opportunity to get out of contracts they perceive to be inequitable. When his contract expires, a player may elect to play one more season with his team and, at the end of that season, become a free agent and sell his services to another team.

In an earlier study, Lord and Hohenfeld argued that the 1976 season, the first year in which the free agency system was widely used, provides a test of equity theory predictions because (1) there were external referents, (2) players could increase their outcomes by signing with a new team, and (3) most players playing out their options without contracts received pay cuts for 1976, thus intensifying any feelings of undercompensation in the option year.

Lord and Hohenfeld predicted substantial performance decreases for players playing out their options during the 1976 season because the players were believed to have experienced substantial inequity and should have been motivated to reduce tension and restore equity. Examining the batting performance of the nonpitching free agents ($n = 13$) in the year in which they played out their options, Lord and Hohenfeld found a sizable decline in performance in three out of four performance measures. In 1976 the number of home runs, runs scored, and runs batted in were below those of the preceding three years. When playing under new contracts with different teams in the 1977 season, performance was restored to the pre-1976 levels. A second sample of players ($n = 10$) who began the season as free agents, but who signed with their own teams during the course of the season, showed a somewhat similar pattern of performance.

The present study expanded the sample to include free agents who signed with new teams over the first three years of the free agent draft. This study also extends the previous work by including a comparison sample of players who were under contract but were traded. Such a comparison sample allows examination of evidence for any new team adjustment that would be the same for both free agents and traded players. Traded players, unlike free agents, usually do not receive large salary increases with their new team.

Subjects

The subjects were the thirty nonpitching major league baseball players from both big leagues who, during the years 1976 through 1978 (1) played out their options, (2) were claimed by at least one team in the subsequent re-entry draft, (3) signed and played with a new team, and (4) appeared with a major league baseball team at least three seasons before the year they played out their options.

Procedure

Performance data (batting average, home runs, runs batted in, and runs scored) were compiled for each of five baseball seasons (years). In the case of free agents, the fourth year is the one in which they are exercising their option to become free agents. For both free agents and traded players, the fifth year represents the first year's performance with the new team. Home runs, runs batted in (RBIs), and runs scored were made comparable across players by dividing by the number of times at bat.

Results

Mean performance data for free agents, free agents' teammates, and traded players are presented in Table 1. Among the results found were

1.   Equity theory would predict relatively stable performance up to year 4, a decline in year 4, and a recovery in year 5. An analysis of variance with career performance as a covariate revealed no effects for year or for player status when applied to each of the performance measures.

2.   Contrary to the Lord and Hohenfeld prediction, a significant *increase* in runs batted in occurred in the year of undercompensation when compared with the preceding year.

3.   Similar analyses performed on the comparison group of traded players revealed no statistically significant differences when performance in year 4 was compared with performance in other years.

TABLE 1   Batting Performance

Group*	Career Average	Year 1	2	3	4	5
Batting average						
Free agents	.263	.269	.266	.262	.261	.260
Traded players	.258	.251	.275	.264	.253	.260
Teammates		.262	.260	.259	.261	.261
Home runs						
Free agents	.028	.026	.024	.024	.026	.027
Traded players	.022	.022	.020	.021	.023	.024
Teammates		.024	.021	.021	.023	.024
Runs batted in						
Free agents	.129	.124	.123	.117	.133	.122
Traded players	.117	.108	.142	.126	.116	.123
Teammates		.116	.116	.118	.123	.119
Runs scored						
Free agents	.142	.135	.137	.131	.132	.136
Traded players	.126	.171	.203	.134	.121	.122
Teammates		.125	.124	.126	.132	.127

*Free agents: $n = 30$; traded players: $n = 30$. All performance measures were measured on a "per at-bat" basis. Year 4 is the year in which free agents exercised their option; year 5 is the first year of performance with new team for both free agents and traded players.

Discussion

Of most importance, the present investigation failed to support the predictions that perceived inequity among major league baseball players would be translated into a performance decline in the option year (the year of undercompensation) and a return to normal performance in the first year with the new team (the first year under a more lucrative contract).

A separate post hoc analysis performed on only 1976 free agents fully confirmed the original Lord and Hohenfeld result. Other analyses performed on only 1977 and 1978 free agents revealed an opposite pattern of means: performance *increases* in the option year and decreases in the first year with the new team for each of the four performance measures. There are important differences among years that require explanation. For instance, the success of the 1976 free agents in obtaining multimillion-dollar contracts gave players in 1977 and 1978 much greater evidence on which to base an expectation of successful contract negotiations. More certain of the potential costs and benefits of various behavioral alternatives, these players responded to perceived inequity in a manner quite different from their 1976 counterparts. Looking toward the end of the season for their opportunity to restore equity, they exhibited no decline in performance.

Relationship to Both Equity and Expectancy Theory

The existence of many ways of restoring perceptions of equity (adjusting inputs and anticipating adjusted outcomes) makes both the present data and those of Lord and Hohenfeld interpretable in terms of equity theory and, therefore, compatible with each other. Both sets of data also lend themselves to an expectancy theory interpretation. For first-year free agents, the performance-reward expectancies were uncertain. In subsequent years, expectancies were more certain, including the awareness that a season of poor performance might seriously decrease the player's market value and reduce the compensation he could then demand.

Of course without evidence of a player's psychological state, these speculations remain untested. The exclusive reliance on performance data to test equity theory predictions represents a limitation in this type of research.

Baseball owners may wish to note that the data also reveal that free agents as a group do not perform significantly better than do either teammates or traded players. This may suggest that free agents as a group are indeed overcompensated for their relative contribution to the sport or that other players are undercompensated.

Source: Paraphrased and abridged from Dennis Duchon and Arthur G. Jago, "Equity and the Performance of Major League Baseball Players: An Extension of Lord and Hohenfeld," *Journal of Applied Psychology,* December 1981, pp. 728–32. Copyright 1981 by the American Psychological Association. Reprinted by permission of the publisher and authors. See, also, R. G. Lord and J. G. Hohenfeld, "Longitudinal Field Assessment of Equity Effects on the Performance of Major League Baseball Players," *Journal of Applied Psychology,* January 1979, pp. 19–26.

principles to worker motivation programs and introduce several other key concepts. The basic premise of OB mod is the *law of effect:* behavior that appears to lead to a positive consequence tends to be repeated and behavior that appears to lead to a negative consequence tends not to be repeated. By the mid-1970s, hundreds of OB mod programs were in operation in work organizations, and the trend continues today.

Steps in a PR Program

Although behavior modification has become a specialized field of knowledge in and of itself, it has been possible to design simplified PR programs for increasing motivation and productivity in organizations. A generalized model of a PR program is shown in Figure 5–2.[22] Several of the steps are consistent with the implications for managers and organizations drawn from expectancy/valence theory.

1. *Set standards of job performance.* Although performance standards are usually available for most positions, the implementation of an OB mod program provides an opportunity to review these standards. (At Banner Realty, sales quotas served as performance standards.)

[22]These steps are an extension of those presented in W. Clay Hamner and Dennis W. Organ, *Organizational Behavior: An Applied Psychological Approach* (Plano, Tex.: Business Publications, 1978), pp. 243–46.

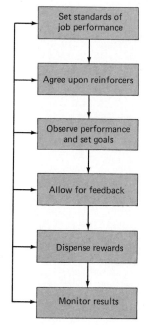

FIGURE 5–2   Steps in a PR Program

TABLE 5–2 A Sampling of Rewards and Punishments of Potential Use in a Job Setting

Rewards

Food related
  Company picnics
  Banquets
  Coffee and pastry
  Holiday turkeys and fruit baskets
  Cocktail party

Visual and auditory
  Office with window
  Feedback on performance
  Favorable performance appraisal
  Improved conditions
  Private office

Durable gifts
  Pen and pencil sets
  Watches
  Trophies
  Small appliances
  Rings and pins

Tokens (secondary reinforcers)
  Money
  Trading stamps
  Profit sharing
  Stocks
  Discount coupons

Social rewards
  Comradeship of boss
  Recognition and praise
  Appreciation
  Privy to confidential information
  Solicitation of advice and suggestions

Intrinsic and Premack*
  Better assignment
  Do more of preferred task
  Presentation to top management
  Afternoon off with pay
  Take over for boss when he or she is away

Punishments

Feedback on undesired behavior
Criticism
Withdrawal of privileges
Probation
Suspension
Fining
Undesirable assignment
Demotion
Documentation of poor performance
Threat of negative sanctions
Withholding any of the rewards listed

*The *Premack principle* states that high-probability behaviors can be used to reinforce low-probability behaviors. For example, if a person gets a least preferred task accomplished, he or she is allowed to move on to a most preferred task. Doing the preferred task serves as a contingent reinforcer for completing the less preferred task. According to the Premack principle, some preferred job activities could always be used to reinforce other job activities. In short, more desired activities are used to reinforce less desired activities.[23]

2. *Have managers, employees, and the labor union (if applicable) agree upon a set of feasible rewards.* A sampling of these potential rewards is listed in Table 5–2, along with a list of potential punishments. By definition, a PR program does not intentionally use negative motivators or punishments.

[23]The description of the Premack principle and the reward categories are from Fred Luthans, *Organizational Behavior,* 2nd ed. (New York: McGraw-Hill, 1977), p. 516. The original source for the Premack principle is David Premack, "Reinforcement Theory," in David Levine, ed., *Nebraska Symposium on Motivation* (Lincoln: University of Nebraska Press, 1965), pp. 123–80.

3. *Observe actual job performance and then set goals for improved performance.* The failure to specify concrete, behavioral goals is a major reason for the failure of many programs. Following the tenets of goal-setting theory, goals should be realistic and set somewhere between present performance and some ideal level.

4. *Allow for employees to obtain their own feedback.* It is essential that participants in the PR program be allowed to measure their own performance. Without feedback, rewards cannot be made contingent upon performance.

5. *Dispense rewards based upon objective performance measures obtained in the fourth step.* A key issue here is how frequently rewards should be administered when employees exhibit the desired behavior. Intermittent (occasional) rewards are the most effective as will be discussed shortly.

6. *Monitor the results of the program.* Sometimes a flaw in the program might be detected that can be remedied. In one company, the PR program had to be modified because too many individual workers and supervisors complained about the excessive paperwork required in keeping track of performance. At another company, praise lost its effectiveness as a reinforcer because it was overused to the point of irritating some employees. As a result, other reinforcers, such as recognition and invitations to business luncheons were then introduced. A related consideration is that too much of one type of reinforcement can satiate a person's need for that type of reinforcement.

The arrow connecting the sixth and preceding steps as illustrated in Figure 5–2 indicates the cyclical nature of the PR system. As results of the program are monitored, evidence might be collected that changes in the other steps are desirable. Among the possibilities are that standards of performance are set too high or too low or that feedback is inaccurate.

Schedules of Reinforcement

An important issue in administering a reinforcement program is how frequently to administer contingent rewards. So much experimentation exists on this topic that reasonably accurate generalizations have been reached about the consequences of the several reinforcement schedules in current use. The two broad classes of schedules are continuous and intermittent.

Under a *continuous* schedule, behavior is reinforced each time it occurs, such as saying "good job" every time a sales person closes a sale. Continuous schedules usually result in the fastest learning, but the desired behavior quickly diminishes when reinforcement stops.

Under an *intermittent* schedule, an employee receives a reward after some instances of engaging in the desired behavior but not after each instance. Intermittent reinforcement is particularly effective in sustaining behavior, because the employee stays mentally alert and interested. At any point in time the behavior might lead to the desired reward. Four specific schedules are included in an intermittent schedule: fixed interval, variable interval, fixed ratio, and variable ratio.

1. *Fixed-interval schedules* are based on time. A reward is administered only after a specified period of time after the last reward was administered. A monthly bonus paid for good performance during the month is an example of a fixed-interval schedule.
2. *Variable-interval schedules* are based on time; however, rewards are administered according to an interval that varies around an average amount of time. Twenty rewards might be dispensed in one month, but on some days the employee would receive two rewards, somedays one, and somedays none.
3. *Fixed-ratio schedules* are based on units of *output* rather than on time, such as giving a real estate agent a 6 percent gross commission on every unit sold. Although the rate remains constant, the total amount of money earned is contingent upon performance.
4. *Variable-ratio schedules* dictate that a certain number of desired behaviors must occur before the reward is dispensed, but the number of behaviors varies around a given average. Gambling casino slot machines are based on a variable-ratio schedule. About 84 percent of the total money played is returned to customers, but the individual player never knows for sure when or if he or she will hit the jackpot. An occasional bonus or act of recognition are both variable-ratio schedules. As the slot machine analogy suggests, variable-ratio schedules are the most effective in sustaining behavior.

The Role of Punishment in OB Mod

Under some circumstances, rewarding people for engaging in constructive behavior does not produce the desired results (as when productivity does not increase despite a well-designed reward schedule). Punishment or the threat of punishment for not improving productivity is another method of increasing motivation.[24] Punishments or negative motivators can theoretically be administered under the same schedules as rewards, although this is rarely done outside hospital and prison settings.

One problem associated with punishments (aside from the bad publicity) is that they may lead to hostile and defensive behavior (such as "accidentally" ruining some paperwork or quitting). Another disadvantage of punishment is that it does not teach the person how to engage in the desired behavior. Instead of being motivated to perform better, the punished employee becomes anxious and tense. Finally, punishment and the threats of punishment are more nearly tied in with lower-level needs, such as security and safety, rather than with higher-level needs. As such, they are weak motivators.

Despite these limitations, the judicious use of punishment does play an important role in organizations, outside of OB mod programs. Many offenses require immediate punishment to maintain discipline in the organization. Among such offenses are alcohol and drug abuse on company premises, sexually harassing other workers, stealing, embezzlement, major disregard of safety and health regulations, and physically attacking other employees. Such behavior calls for summary discipline—immediate suspension or dismissal. Lesser offenses call for corrective or progressive discipline, a gradual approach that allows the person to change his or her behavior in a positive direction. The method is to apply progressively more severe discipline in this order: oral warning, written warning, disciplinary layoff, and discharge.

---

[24]A comprehensive discussion of this topic is Hamner and Organ, *Organizational Behavior,* pp. 73–88.

Intrinsic versus Extrinsic Rewards

PR programs are accused of overemphasizing extrinsic rewards at the expense of intrinsic rewards. According to the *cognitive evaluation* theory of Deci, there are two potential effects associated with extrinsic rewards. First, they can be perceived as a source of competence information, thus appealing to the human need for competence—basically understanding and achieving mastery over one's environment. Or, second, extrinsic rewards can be perceived as a source of behavioral control. As a source of information, extrinsic rewards confirm an employee's feeling of competence and will usually increase intrinsic motivation. If the employee perceives extrinsic rewards as controlling agents, feelings of self-determination may decrease, thus reducing intrinsic motivation.[25]

One conclusion reached in research about the cognitive evaluation theory is that money as an extrinsic reward will sometimes *decrease* intrinsic motivation because it would decrease personal control.[26] One corollary is that, if an employee is paid too much, it will take the self-rewards out of a job, much as would receiving a cash bonus for saving a co-worker in a fire. A practical way around the concerns of extrinsic motivators dampening intrinsic motivation is for managers to rely on the intrinsic and Premack motivators listed in Table 5–2.

Sample Research Evidence

An impressive amount of research evidence has been gathered in support of OB mod as a way of improving productivity and controlling absenteeism in organizations. Two major factors seem to underlie its success. First, PR programs can be implemented after only a modest amount of systematic supervisory and managerial training. Second, these programs are based on sensible management practice and well-proved psychological principles. It will suffice here to mention an example of the use of PR in improving productivity and absenteeism.

At Collins Food International, a PR program was conducted for seventy clerical employees in the accounting area. A determination was first made of the staff's performance in areas such as billing error rates. Supervisors and employees then collaborated to discuss and set goals for improvement. Praise was given to employees who turned in reports containing fewer errors than the norm. Feedback took the form of charting results on a regular basis. According to the company controller, the improvements were dramatic. For example, in the accounts payable department, the error rate fell from more than 8 percent to less than 2 percent.[27]

As a method of improving attendance, a monetary attendance bonus plan was developed for 150 city employees. The plan paid a $10 bonus for each unused sick

[25]Edward L. Deci, "Notes on the Theory and Metatheory of Intrinsic Motivation," *Organizational Behavior and Human Performance*, Vol. 11, 1975, pp. 130–45.

[26]Robert D. Pritchard, K. M. Campbell, and Donald J. Campbell, "The Effects of Extrinsic Financial Rewards on Intrinsic Motivation," *Journal of Applied Psychology*, February 1977, pp. 9–15.

[27]"Productivity Gains from a Pat on the Back," *Business Week*, January 23, 1978, p. 58.

leave day that was not eligible for transfer to accumulated sick leave. Each employee could earn up to a $60 maximum. The bonus was paid on a fixed-interval schedule—once during the last week of the year. In the year before the bonus plan was implemented, the mean number of days absent per employee was 3.59. After the first year of the plan, that corresponding figure was 2.24. It fell to an average of 1.58 over the next three years of the PR program. Although no control group was used, the results appeared to justify the use of OB mod.[28]

Criticism of PR in Organizations

OB mod and PR programs have been stridently criticized on both theoretical and moral grounds. Cognitive theorists are concerned that reinforcement theorists neglect the higher thought processes of people by controlling them with extrinsic rewards. Another argument is that manipulating people against their will strips them of their dignity. Management authority Peter Drucker at one time expressed concern that PR would make workers even more addicted to material rewards than they are today.[29] Another management writer contends that people should not be treated as mice—an argument based on the fact that reinforcement theory was established with infrahuman animals. The same writer looks upon PR as a behavioral approach to scientific management. His reasoning is that for PR to be effective, it is often necessary to break jobs down into subcomponents, just as in scientific management.[30]

The arguments just mentioned are not strong enough to discount the worthwhile outcomes from a sensible application of reinforcement theory to improving productivity and other worthwhile ends. Employees can continue to formulate cognitions under OB mod. They will continue to expend effort only if the rewards from working hard continue to have positive valences for them, and are really rewards. Should increased productivity lead to layoffs and lower pay, the behavior that led to such undesired consequences will be changed by the employees. Another major counterargument is that PR can be used to cultivate intrinsic motivation. Armed with knowledge about reinforcement theory, a manager would become sensitive to the importance of rewarding productivity with the opportunities to engage in such reinforcing experiences as choice assignments.

A desired outcome of a PR program is to make good work itself acquire reinforcing properties. B. F. Skinner has recommended that the organization should design feedback and incentive systems in such a way that the dual objective of getting work accomplished and making work enjoyable is met.[31] Finally, a major problem in

[28]Loretta M. Schmitz and Herbert G. Heneman III, "Do Positive Reinforcement Programs Reduce Employee Absenteeism?" *Personnel Administrator,* September 1980, p. 90.

[29]Peter F. Drucker, "Beyond the Stick and Carrot: Hysteria over the Work Ethic," *Psychology Today,* November 1973, p. 89.

[30]Fred L. Fry, "Operant Conditioning in Organizational Settings: Of Mice or Men?" *Personnel,* July–August 1974, pp. 17–24.

[31]"Conversation with B. F. Skinner," *Organizational Dynamics,* Winter 1973, p. 39.

many organizations is that employees are not systematically rewarded for productive behavior, leading to low satisfaction and productivity. PR programs help to sensitize managers to this problem.

IMPLICATIONS FOR MANAGERIAL PRACTICE

Some of the most important implications of motivation theory for managerial practice have been summarized in the discussion of expectancy/valence theory. A review by Terpstra provides some additional guidelines for applying motivation theory to work settings:

1.   Any motivation attempt must begin by focusing on the needs of the individual employees. Once those needs are identified, one can within limits structure the work experience to accommodate the fulfillment of those needs. Care should be exercised in the selection and use of work rewards and outcomes. The individual's needs dictate which outcomes will have high valence and be reinforcing.

2.   An emphasis on goal setting is advisable. While the nature of the goals should depend somewhat on the individual and his or her needs and abilities, an attempt should be made to provide clear, specific, and somewhat challenging goals. To the extent that goals are clear-cut and unambiguous, employees will be able to more clearly visualize the link between effort and performance ($E \rightarrow P$). Increased motivation should result. Furthermore, the factors related to goal attainment should be under the employee's control to influence positively the $E \rightarrow P$ expectancy component.

3.   Goal attainment and goal-directed behavior should be consistently and positively reinforced by the contingent application of outcomes with high valence. The link between performance and outcomes ($P \rightarrow 0$) expectancy will thus become stronger, serving to increase motivation further.[32]

4.   In general, a manager should select from motivation theory those aspects that appear the most meaningful in terms of a given situation. For example, content and process theories of motivation provide useful clues as to which motivators are likely to be effective in a reinforcement program.

Summary

- Work motivation is effort expended toward organizational objectives. Motivation contributes to performance, but performance also depends upon nonmotivational and ex-

[32]The first three implications are paraphrased from David E. Terpstra, "Theories of Motivation—Borrowing the Best," *Personnel Journal,* June 1979, p. 375.

periential factors, group constraints, and technology. A wide array of behavioral science-based programs attempts to improve productivity via enhancing motivation and satisfaction. They are summarized on pages 107–108.

- Cognitive and reinforcement (OB mod) models represent the two main schools of thought about work motivation. Cognitive models emphasize that people are driven by internal forces that guide their behavior and that they make a series of rational decisions and calculations. Cognitive theories can be divided into content theories (such as the two-factor theory) and process theories (such as expectancy/valence). Reinforcement models concentrate on the environmental contingencies, such as rewards, that govern behavior.

- According to goal-setting theory, behavior is regulated by values and conscious intentions (goals). Difficult goals result in a higher level of performance than no goals at all or generalized goals. Participation in goal setting sometimes improves performance but plays a less critical role than does goal specificity. According to the influential two-factor theory of work motivation, elements within the content of a job are called satisfiers or motivators because positive feelings toward them may increase satisfaction and motivation. Included here are factors such as recognition, challenge, and advancement opportunities, all of which appeal to higher-level needs. Factors associated with negative feelings about the work are called dissatisfiers or hygiene factors because they are noticed primarily by their absence. Included here are physical working conditions, company policy, and job security, all of which appeal to lower-level needs. A major criticism of the two-factor theory is that it neglects individual differences.

- Job enrichment applies the two-factor theory to improving productivity and satisfaction. One specific model of job enrichment attempts to design jobs whereby the employee perceives them as meaningful and responsible, allowing for feedback. Job factors contributing to these feelings are skill variety, task identity, task significance, autonomy, and feedback. Employee desire is a critical variable in job enrichment.

- Expectancy/valence theory assumes that people are decision makers who select the alternative action that appears most advantageous. The theory explicitly accounts for individual and situational differences. The three critical elements in the theory are performance-outcome expectancies, valence, and effort-performance expectancies. A person will expend effort if he or she believes that (1) behavior will lead to outcomes, (2) the outcome has a positive valence, and (3) he or she can perform at the necessary level to get the task accomplished. Subjective hunches about the three critical elements can be multiplied to arrive at a motivational index. Motivation $= (P \to 0) \times (E \to P) \times$ valence.

- Equity theory contends that employees compare their inputs and outputs with other relevant people in the workplace. When employees believe that they are receiving equitable outputs in relation to their inputs, they are generally satisfied. When employees believe they are giving too much in relation to what they are receiving from the organization, tension and dissatisfaction ensue. People will usually take action to bring their equity ratio into balance.

- Behavior modification (OB mod) is the direct application of reinforcement theory to work motivation. The six steps in a PR program are (1) set standards of job performance, (2) agree upon feasible rewards, (3) observe job performance and set goals for improved performance, (4) allow for employees to obtain their own feedback, (5) dispense rewards if earned, and (6) monitor the results of the program. Reward schedules are a crucial factor in a PR program. Intermittent rewards are more likely to lead to sustained performance than are continuous rewards.

- Punishment is used infrequently in OB mod programs, but it can contribute to increased motivation and is often necessary to maintain discipline. It has been argued that an overreliance on extrinsic rewards in OB mod can lead to a decrease in intrinsic motivation (as cautioned by cognitive evaluation theory). Despite its critics, reinforcement programs have good empirical support and help to sensitize managers to the importance of rewarding good performance.

Questions for Discussion

1. What motivators or satisfiers are present in the job of a professional football quarterback? What hygiene factors are present?
2. For prisoners, what sources of need gratification are present in a prison setting? for guards?
3. How might a person use expectancy/valence theory in motivating himself or herself?
4. Assume that you wanted to use reinforcement theory to motivate a subordinate. How might you determine which motivators would be effective for that individual?
5. In what way might socioeconomic status influence which rewards or incentives would be effective in motivating a given employee?
6. Some organizations hire "inspirational speakers" to "rev up" their sales force. Is such an approach to work motivation based more on a cognitive or a reinforcement model? Explain.
7. What key inputs do you place in your equity ratio?
8. How might you use the Premack principle to help you study for examinations?
9. Which motivational strategy should be used with a strongly self-motivated individual?
10. How might training and coaching influence the $E \rightarrow P$ expectancies of employees?
11. What interpretations do you make of the data presented about the batting performance of baseball players? Use some of your knowledge about statistics in making your analysis.

An Organizational Behavior Problem

What Is the Strength of Your Work Orientation?

Self-examination can be helpful in understanding the concept of work motivation. Toward this end, we have developed an exploratory questionnaire for self-administration and interpretation. This questionnaire is not scientifically validated. It is primarily a teaching device to help the reader apply motivational concepts to himself or herself. Answer each question "mostly agree" or "mostly disagree" as it applies to you. Candor on your part might provide you with some clues about the intensity of your orientation toward work.

Work Orientation Questionnaire

	Mostly Agree	Mostly Disagree
1. I find it difficult getting started on Monday morning.	☐	☐
2. Vacations make me tense because they take me away from my work.	☐	☐
3. When engaging in sports I have trouble concentrating because my mind is usually on work.	☐	☐
4. The main reason I engage in physical exercise is to keep me in shape for work.	☐	☐
5. Given the chance, I would leave work early to play with my children (or nephews or nieces).	☐	☐
6. I would cancel a luncheon date with my spouse if that morning my boss asked to have lunch with me.	☐	☐
7. The biggest thrills I get in life are from my work.	☐	☐
8. I work primarily so I can pay my bills and enjoy a few luxuries.	☐	☐
9. When waiting in line in a bank, I get very tense because precious work time is being wasted.	☐	☐
10. Even when at home, I feel guilty just relaxing.	☐	☐
11. An underlying fear I have is that a family emergency will take me away from my work for a period of time.	☐	☐
12. I would enjoy walking leisurely in the park at 10 o'clock on a workday morning.	☐	☐
13. Thoughts of work rarely enter my mind while I'm on vacation.	☐	☐
14. I would like to retire as soon as I could afford it.	☐	☐
15. Having a spouse and chidren is pleasant, but it can prevent you from getting the most out of your career.	☐	☐
16. I work about fifteen more hours per week than do most people in my occupation.	☐	☐
17. Work is meaningless unless it is performed to provide for people close to you.	☐	☐
18. During social activities I often think of unfinished business at the office or school.	☐	☐
19. (Answer 19A or 19B) A. While (or if) my wife was (were) in the delivery room, I brought (would bring) some work into the waiting room	☐	☐
B. If (or when) I gave birth to a child, I would bring (brought) some work to the maternity ward.	☐	☐
20. I keep a notebook (or tape recorder) next to me in my car so I can make use of time that might be lost in stalled traffic.	☐	☐

Scoring the Questionnaire. The answers in the "work is central to life" direction for each question are as follows:

1. Mostly disagree	11. Mostly agree
2. Mostly agree	12. Mostly disagree
3. Mostly agree	13. Mostly disagree
4. Mostly agree	14. Mostly disagree
5. Mostly disagree	15. Mostly agree
6. Mostly agree	16. Mostly agree
7. Mostly agree	17. Mostly disagree
8. Mostly disagree	18. Mostly agree
9. Mostly agree	19. A or B. Mostly agree
10. Mostly agree	20. Mostly agree

Interpreting Your Score. Extremely high or low scores are the most meaningful. A score of 16 or more suggests dominant "work is central to life" orientation. Work addicts or "workaholics" tend to fall into this category. If your biggest thrills (rewards) in life stem from work and vacations make you tense, you display dominant symptoms of a work addict. You may be losing the capacity to stand back from your work long enough to get recharged and take a fresh look at what you are doing.

A score of 6 to 15 suggests that you have a moderate tendency toward an intense work orientation. Under extreme circumstances (such as income tax season for a tax accountant), you may become a temporary or seasonal work addict. Such behavior is usually functional for the organization.

A score of 5 or less suggests that you have a weak work orientation. It may be necessary for you to prompt yourself with external motivators (such as the prospects of a vacation) to keep yourself involved in your work. It is easy for a person of such a weak work orientation to become lethargic and undermotivated.

Additional Reading

ALBER, ANTONE, and MELVIN BLUMBERG. "Team vs. Individual Approaches to Job Enrichment Programs." *Personnel,* January–February 1981, pp. 63–75.

BERNSTEIN, PAUL. "The Work Ethic That Never Was." *Wharton,* Spring 1980, pp. 19–25.

BLAKE, ROBERT R., and JANE S. MOUTON. "Increasing Productivity Through Behavioral Science." *Personnel,* May–June 1981, pp. 59–77.

BURTON, EILEEN KELLY. "Productivity: A Plan for Personnel." *Personnel Administrator,* September 1981, pp. 85–92.

KIRBY, PETER G. "Productivity Increases Through Feedback Systems." *Personnel Journal,* October 1977, pp. 512–15.

LATHAM, GARY P., LARRY L. CUMMINGS, and TERENCE R. MITCHELL. "Behavioral Strategies to Improve Productivity." *Organizational Dynamics,* Winter 1981, pp. 5–23.

MATSUI, TAMAO, AKINORI OKADA, and REIJI MIZUGUCHI. "Expectancy Theory Prediction of the Goal Theory Postulate, The Harder the Goals, the Higher the Performance." *Journal of Applied Psychology,* February 1981, pp. 54–58.

MEDOFF, JAMES L., and KATHARINE G. ABRAHAM. "Are Those Paid More Really More Productive? The Case of Experience." *The Journal of Human Resources,* Spring 1981, pp. 186–216.

MINDELL, MARK G., and LAUREN HITE JACKSON. "Motivating the New Breed." *Personnel,* March–April 1980, pp. 53–62.

MITCHELL, TERENCE R. "Motivation: New Directions for Theory, Research, and Practice." *Academy of Management Review,* January 1982, pp. 80–88.

O'BRIEN, RICHARD M., ALYCE M. DICKINSON, and MICHAEL P. ROSOW, eds. *Industrial Behavior Modification: A Management Handbook.* Elmsford, N.Y.: Pergamon, 1982.

PINDER, CRAIG C. "Concerning the Application of Human Motivation Theories in Organizational Settings." *California Management Review,* July 1977, pp. 384–95.

TOMER, JOHN F. "Worker Motivation: A Neglected Element in Micro-Micro Theory." *Journal of Economic Issues,* June 1981, pp. 351–62.

CHAPTER 6

Job Satisfaction

LEARNING OBJECTIVES

1. To understand the nature of job satisfaction and its relationship to morale, involvement, motivation, and values.

2. To identify several dimensions of job satisfaction and the conditions that contribute to high job satisfaction.

3. To explain how individual and group differences influence job satisfaction.

4. To describe several consequences of job satisfaction and dissatisfaction.

5. To identify several managerial strategies for increasing job satisfaction.

The executive staff at Parkside General Hospital was pleased to hire Lillian Pentworth as their administrative analyst, a newly created position. Although a job description was not yet drawn, it seemed that Lil and her boss understood what needed to be accomplished. The purpose of the position was to improve the administrative procedures in the patient billing and intake departments. Most staff members agreed that the two areas were characterized by confusion and inefficiency (including lost patient records). A hospital administrative committee approved the hiring of a person with a master's degree in hospital administration to fill the position. The committee members agreed unanimously to choose Lil Pentworth over several other candidates. Particularly impressive to them were Lil's enthusiasm and professional manner.

Lil approached her new job with a positive attitude. She arrived at work on time, took brief lunch breaks, and often stayed up to an hour after the end of her official workday. Although Lil had hardly made a dent in the problems facing the billing and receiving departments, she believed that she had at least identified some of the major problems. One day, about three months after Lil's starting date, her boss, Alan Davis, invited her to have lunch with him in the hospital cafeteria. After they were seated, Alan explained why he invited her to lunch.

"Lil, I have a big apology to make. You've been working harder than we ever imagined a person would in this position. You've jumped on every assignment like it meant the difference between the life and death of the hospital. We couldn't be more pleased. And what have you received in return? Nothing. No direction, no instructions, not even a good job description. You've requested a microprocessor and we've stalled you with paperwork delays. Any information you've requested, you've practically had to fetch for yourself. I don't know how you've put up with us for even three months. Again, I apologize for your mistreatment."

"Mr. Davis, I agree with everything but your conclusion," said Lil. "True you don't have me bound up in a tight job description. But I'm not being mistreated. I love it. I love the confusion and the chaos. I'm creating my own job at Parkside. I'm making up the rules and my job description as I go along. I feel like a pioneer, not like an employee plugged into an airtight routine.

"This is a great job. I'm as happy as a kitten chasing a string. Once this mess gets straightened out, I hope you'll give me another one to work on."

As you read this chapter, try to analyze in technical terms why Lil was probably experiencing such a high degree of satisfaction and what her boss was unwittingly doing *right* in terms of creating conditions for job satisfaction.

THE MEANING AND NATURE OF JOB SATISFACTION

Job satisfaction is a specific set of attitudes held by workers. As such, job satisfaction has a cognitive, affective, and behavioral component. Lil believed that confusion is good (cognition); she experienced enthusiasm and elation about her unstructured job (affect); and she acted in a manner consistent with her enthusiasm (behavior). Edwin A. Locke defines job satisfaction as "the pleasurable emotional state resulting from the perception of one's job as fulfilling or allowing the fulfillment of one's important job values, providing these values are compatible with one's needs."[1] In Lil's case, the opportunity to work independently was an important value that was compatible with her obvious need for autonomy.

Satisfaction and Values

Current research and opinion suggest that the job values of the new breed of employees differ in significant ways from the job values of the "old breed." Also, many young employees, in general, have somewhat different values from those of older employees. Nine key job values have been identified that are helpful in drawing comparison between contemporary and traditional employees, as illustrated in Figure 6–1. Guided by the definition just presented, managers could enhance the satisfaction of today's employees by providing them opportunities to fulfill such values as "priorities of fam-

[1]Edwin A. Locke, "The Nature and Causes of Job Satisfaction," in Marvin D. Dunnette, ed., *Handbook of Industrial and Organizational Psychology* (Chicago: Rand McNally, 1976), p. 1342.

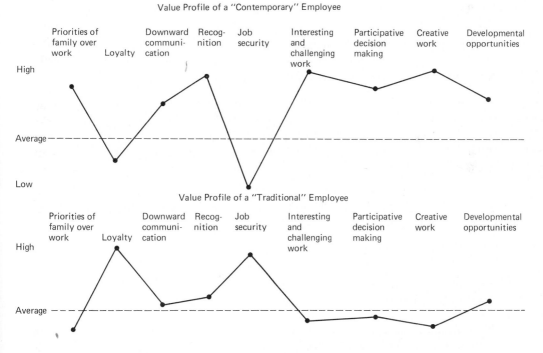

FIGURE 6–1   Nine Key Job Values

Source: Lauren Hite Jackson and Mark G. Mindell, "Motivating the New Breed," *Personnel*, March–April 1980, p. 57. Reprinted with permission from American Management Associations. © 1980 by AMACOM, a division of American Management Associations. All rights reserved.

ily over work" and "creative work." The strategy would work providing that the employees had strong desires to satisfy such needs as affection, competence, or self-fulfillment.

Satisfaction and Motivation

Job satisfaction and job motivation are conceptually related but not identical concepts, although most theoretical positions on the topic do not clearly differentiate between the two variables. Nevertheless, it is useful for the practitioner to differentiate between the two concepts. (You will recall the real estate agents who were *satisfied* with free goodies and extra bonuses, but it had no appreciable impact on their motivation and productivity.) Satisfaction refers to a state of contentment; motivation refers to expending effort toward a goal. One way in which to visualize the relationship between satisfaction and motivation is by use of a four-way diagram indicating the extreme positions, as shown in Figure 6–2. In summary, they are as follows:

Contented, relaxed worker. Some people derive satisfaction from working in a relaxed, nonpressured atmosphere. If they had to work too hard, they would experience job dissatisfaction.

Disgruntled, uninvolved worker. Employees who fit this category are often under stress. They dislike their jobs yet work just hard enough to prevent being fired or receiving serious reprimands. Economic necessity forces them to work.

Dissatisfied, hard-working person. Many people with a professional orientation work hard even if they are currently dissatisfied with their firm or general working conditions. One motive for their motive is that a professionally oriented person would not want to damage his or her reputation by performing poorly, even if a particular job were unsatisfying.

Well-satisfied, hard charger. A person in this category is usually on the path toward self-fulfillment. Lil, the hospital administrative analyst, fits this category as do many branch managers and successful small-business owners.

Satisfaction and Morale

Both satisfaction and morale refer to positive emotional states that may be experienced by job holders, and the terms are often used interchangeably. Morale focuses

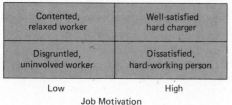

Low   High

Job Motivation

FIGURE 6–2 Four Relationships Among Job Satisfaction and Motivation

Source: Andrew J. DuBrin, *Human Relations: A Job-Oriented Approach,* 2nd ed. (Reston, Va.: Reston, 1981), p. 27. Reprinted with permission of Reston Publishing Company, a Prentice-Hall Co., 11480 Sunset Hills Road, Reston, VA 22090.

Job Satisfaction **143**

more on an employee's interest in helping the organization or going along with its demands. As defined years ago, "Morale is an attitude of satisfaction with, desire to continue in, and willingness to strive for the goals of a particular group or organization."[2] As a consequence of this definition, two distinctions can be drawn between satisfaction and morale. First, morale is oriented toward the future, whereas satisfaction relates to the present and past. Second, morale is a feeling that relates to the group, based on a sense of common purpose and a belief that group and individual goals mesh. Satisfaction typically refers to the assessment made by an individual employee of his or her job situation.

Job *involvement* also differs conceptually from satisfaction. An employee involved in his or her job is one who takes it seriously, for whom important job values are at stake in the job, and who is mentally preoccupied with the job.[3] If you are involved with your job, you are "really into it" and you are more likely to experience job satisfaction or dissatisfaction as a consequence of your involvement. A less involved person would have less acute emotional responses to job circumstances.

COGNITIVE THEORIES OF JOB SATISFACTION

The cognitive theories of work motivation described in previous chapters are virtually identical in format to cognitive theories of job satisfaction. The most obvious example is the two-factor theory, which is really a theory of both satisfaction and motivation. Similarly, the expectancy/valence theory applies reasonably well to satisfaction as well as motivation. In general, people experience satisfaction to the extent that their expectations are met.

Comparison Processes

The most widely accepted theoretical position on job satisfaction is that the degree of affect experienced by the employee is related to a comparison between what the employee would like and what he or she perceives to exist. The bigger the discrepancy between one's ideal and one's actual, the more acute one's job dissatisfaction. One man began looking for a new career shortly after answering the following question on a personal inventory: "The ideal job for me would be _____?" Such a large discrepancy existed between his ideal job (company president) and his actual job (production control analyst) that he concluded it was time to pursue a new field closer to his ideal. He eventually joined a family business where he could at least aspire to a top position. Since the individual subtracts the real from the ideal to gauge the discrepancy, this view has been labeled a *subtractive* theory of job satisfaction.

[2]Morris Viteles, *Motivation and Morale in Industry* (New York: W. W. Norton, 1953), p. 284.
[3]The comparisons among satisfaction, morale, and involvement are from Locke, "The Nature and Causes of Job Satisfaction," p. 1301.

An important issue in a comparison theory of job satisfaction is the specification of what the employee uses as a standard. Needs may be used as a standard, and so may values. The cognitive state of an individual's frame of reference is also used as a comparison.[4] To one sales representative, making cold calls provides excitement and challenge and therefore contributes to job satisfaction. Another sales representative might not consider that aspect of the job to be a source of excitement.

CONSEQUENCES OF JOB SATISFACTION AND DISSATISFACTION

One justification for studying job satisfaction and dissatisfaction is that they have important individual and organizational consequences. One's degree of job satisfaction, however, may be only the manifest cause of the consequence (or outcome). A man may have low job satisfaction, which leads him to quit his firm. His low job satisfaction may stem from his frustration over his inability to perform his job well. His basic problem-solving ability may be deficient for his position. Here we identify several of the consequences of job satisfaction-dissatisfaction of most importance to organizational behavior.

Absenteeism and Turnover

People who dislike their jobs tend to be absent more frequently and are also more likely to quit. People who dislike *work itself* undoubtedly show similar behavioral tendencies. Several major reviews of the technical literature covering this topic indicate that there are significant relationships between job dissatisfaction and absenteeism and turnover.[5] Evidence also suggests that if the cause of discontent is modified, job satisfaction will increase and turnover will decrease.[6] One company reduced turnover 45 percent in one department by installing a giant blower that reduced the temperature from 110°F to 88°F.

Productivity

A popular but discredited view is that productivity or performance varies directly with level of job satisfaction. In fact, the opposite is sometimes true; some dissatisfied people are productive, whereas some satisfied people are fairly unproductive. If your

[4]Ernest J. McCormick and Daniel Ilgen, *Industrial Psychology,* 7th ed. (Englewood Cliffs, N.J.: Prentice-Hall, 1980), p. 306.

[5]A summary of these reviews is found in Locke, "The Nature and Causes of Job Satisfaction," pp. 1331–32.

[6]Charles L. Hulin, "Effects of Changes in Job Satisfaction Levels on Employee Turnover," *Journal of Applied Psychology,* April 1968, pp. 122–26.

work ethic is low (you do not highly value hard work), you might be highly satisfied with a job requiring only modest productivity. It is also true that in many instances highly satisfied workers are productive and highly dissatisfied workers are unproductive.

The performance-reward-satisfaction model provides a reasonable explanation of the relationship between satisfaction and productivity. It contends that high productivity leads to satisfaction. In other words, if you perform well on a useful task, your satisfaction will increase.[7] The conditions under which high satisfaction would subsequently encourage high productivity are complex. Locke concludes that "both logic and research suggest that it is best to view productivity and satisfaction as separate *outcomes* of the employee-job interaction, and to expect causal relationships between them only in special circumstances."[8]

Physical Health and Longevity

An unsatisfying job might be bad for one's physical health. The intervening mechanism seems to be stress. Intense job dissatisfaction leads to an internal stress reaction, which in turn leads to a wide range of psychosomatic disorders such as heart disease, ulcers, and dermatitis (see Chapter 7). A longitudinal study of employees correlated a number of physical and attitudinal measures with a Longevity Quotient. The LQ is the observed years of survival after a physical examination divided by the expected years of survival, based on information contained in actuarial tables. The single best predictor of longevity was work satisfaction.[9] The operational definition of job satisfaction used was a feeling of general usefulness and ability to fulfill a meaningful social role.

Mental Health

Job satisfaction and life satisfaction are inextricably bound. A person who experiences high satisfaction on the job will find some spillover into personal life. By the same token the disgruntled worker will experience a spillover of his or her discontent into personal life. A classic study by Arthur Kornhauser provides empirical evidence for the relationship between job satisfaction and mental health.[10] He derived an index of mental health from six component indices involving anxiety and tension, self-esteem, hostility sociability, life satisfaction, and personal morale. Kornhauser found statistically significant relationships between satisfaction and the total mental health index among three job levels of production workers in Detroit automotive plants.

[7]Edward E. Lawler III and Lyman W. Porter, "The Effects of Performance on Satisfaction," *Industrial Relations,* Vol. 7, October 1967, pp. 20–28.

[8]Locke, "The Nature and Causes of Job Satisfaction," p. 1332.

[9]E. Palmore, "Predicting Longevity: A Follow-up Controlling for Age," *The Gerontologist,* Winter 1969, pp. 247–50.

[10]Arthur W. Kornhauser, *Mental Health of the Industrial Worker: A Detroit Study* (New York: John Wiley, 1965).

Poor Community Relations

A frequently observed consequence of job dissatisfaction, particularly in smaller communities, is for disgruntled employees to verbalize their discontent to others in the community. A number of young people who worked for a popular supermarket chain were dissatisfied with the abrasive management tactics used by the owners. Stock clerks were chastised in front of customers and employees whose shoes were not shined were sent home. Soon a slogan caught on in the community, " _____ Supermarkets are a nice place to shop, but I wouldn't want to work there." Negative publicity of this type can conceivably lead to difficulties in recruiting new employees as well as to loss of business.[11]

Low Quality of Work Life

If a large number of employees experience low levels of job satisfaction, they will interpret their quality of work life as substandard. Aside from the humanistic considerations, an organization that fosters a low QWL is running counter to a contemporary movement throughout North American and Europe. In Chapters 15 and 17 we discuss how organizationwide programs, specifically Theory Z and QWL, can be used to elevate the job satisfaction of large numbers of employees.

JOB SATISFACTION TODAY

"Job discontent among American workers in general is at a 28-year high. Among middle management in particular, discontent is growing for the first time in many years," reported the Opinion Research Corporation in 1981. The conclusion reached is based on the results of surveys conducted with more than 240,000 workers from more than 400 companies and plants in a broad spectrum of industries over a period of twenty-eight years. According to this analysis, the underlying problem of low job satisfaction can be attributed to a shift in values.[12]

Another phase of their study indicated that discontent among hourly and clerical workers seems to be growing. The distinctions that once clearly differentiated clerical and hourly employees are becoming hazy. Both groups attach a high valence to and expect to receive internal satisfactions from work (such as respect, fairness, and enjoyable work) that were formerly reserved for managers, technicians, and professional people. The work force itself and what its members value are changing: "All parts of the work force are beginning to overtly articulate their needs for achievement, recognition, and job challenge."[13]

[11]This consequence and the description of several of these are from Andrew J. DuBrin, *Personnel and Human Resource Management* (Boston: Kent, 1981), pp. 230–31.

[12]Report published by Opinion Research Corporation, North Harrison Street, Princeton, New Jersey 08540, November 1981.

[13]Reported in M. R. Cooper and others, "Changing Employee Values: Deepening Discontent?" *Harvard Business Review,* January–February 1979, p. 117.

Despite the job dissatisfaction revealed in the surveys cited, a large segment of the work force enjoys work. Over sixty years of research about job satisfaction leads to the tentative conclusion that somewhere between 65 and 86 percent of the work force (including all levels of workers) are reasonably satisfied with their jobs. About 10 to 25 percent of the work force seem to be outright discontent with their jobs.[14]

INDIVIDUAL AND GROUP DIFFERENCES IN JOB SATISFACTION

Of more importance to the manager than general levels of job satisfaction in society is how individual and group differences are related to work satisfaction. Among the many factors showing a systematic relationship to job satisfaction-dissatisfaction are personality, age, occupational level, educational level, sex, and race. Situational factors should also be taken into account in understanding employee satisfaction.

Personality

Some people are predisposed to be complainers and malcontents on the basis of their personality traits and characteristics. No matter how hard management tries to please them, they voice dissatisfaction. And these "chronic complainers" and "malcontents" are not necessarily unproductive or disloyal employees. Many are people with personal conflicts that lead them to a pessimistic interpretation of circumstances and job factors that others would perceive as positive. Much systematic research is needed in this area.

Age

A nonlinear relationship exists between age and job satisfaction. Job satisfaction tends to be high when people enter the work force; it plummets and then plateaus for several years up through about age thirty. After the early thirties, there is a steady increase in job satisfaction up through retirement age. A few investigators have noted a slight dip in satisfaction in the later working years due to preretirement apprehension. A plausible explanation for the relationship between age and job satisfaction is that

> People probably tend to begin work with unrealistic expectations about what they will be able to derive from it, and finding that reality falls far short of their expectations, they endure the first decade of work with gradually increasing disillusionment. After some point, expectations are apparently modified and adjusted downward, and the job is seen in a more positive perspective.[15]

[14]A synthesis of this information is found in Dennis W. Organ and W. Clay Hamner, *Organizational Behavior: An Applied Psychological Approach,* rev. ed. (Plano, Tex.: Business Publications, 1982).

[15]Organ and Hamner, 1978 ed., p. 224.

Occupational Level

A consistent finding is that people in high-level jobs experience the highest level of job satisfaction.[16] The most significant underlying reason is that high-level jobs carry the most prestige—self-esteem is enhanced to the extent that other people think one's work is important. It is not uncommon for high-earning sales representatives to seek a managerial assignment despite the anticipated loss of income in the new position. These sales representatives are willing to trade income for prestige (and, therefore, higher job satisfaction). High-level jobs are satisfying for many other reasons as well. They frequently offer opportunities for the expression of the needs for power and autonomy, they reduce financial worries, and they offer task diversity and job enrichment.

Anecdotal evidence from a variety of sources continues to suggest that production workers are often victims of severe job dissatisfaction. An extreme form is assembly-line hysteria, a sudden illness that strikes factory workers in lower-level production jobs. The illness most often afflicts women, it spreads by contagion, and it has no apparent physical cause. Among its most common symptoms are headaches, nausea, and physical weakness.[17]

According to the investigators of assembly-line hysteria, job boredom seems to play a key role. The boredom stems from jobs requiring repetitive tasks performed at fixed work stations with fixed production quotas. One such operation investigated involved workers spending an entire shift soldering transistors onto printed circuit boards that moved down the assembly line at a rapid pace. Psychologist-observers found that the boredom was accompanied by signs of muscular tension, job dissatisfaction, and depression.

Educational Level

With occupational level held constant, there is a negative relationship between the educational level and job satisfaction, particularly with respect to pay.[18] The comparison theory explanation offered most frequently is that people with higher educational levels set higher standards for satisfaction. They use a more stringent reference group than do workers of lower educational levels. In practice, since many people with advanced educational backgrounds are placed in higher-level jobs, the problem often resolves itself.

Sex and Race

Observations of job satisfaction as a function of sex and race tend to be confounded with factors such as occupational level. Undoubtedly, the belief that one is being dis-

---

[16]Abraham K. Korman, *Organizational Behavior* (Englewood Cliffs, N.J.: Prentice-Hall, 1977), p. 223.

[17]Michael J. Colligan and William Stockton, "The Mystery of Assembly Line Hysteria," *Psychology Today,* June 1978, pp. 93 and 94.

[18]The evidence for this conclusion is summarized by Korman, *Organization Behavior,* p. 226.

criminated against would lower one's level of job satisfaction. Women and blacks who are working at occupational levels comparable to their male and nonblack counterparts probably experience similar levels of job satisfaction and dissatisfaction.

Sex differences in job satisfaction have been investigated on the basis of three independently drawn U.S. national samples. In general, almost no significant differences in job satisfaction were found when men and women were equally affected by such determinants of job satisfaction as differential wages, prestige, or supervisory position.[19] A woman placed in a high-paying, prestigious job experiences the same peaks of job satisfaction as does a man in a comparable position.

Transient Situational Factors

The individual and group factors noted exert a stable influence on job satisfaction. Transient situational factors, however, exert temporary influences on satisfaction-dissatisfaction levels. An employee may report a surge in job satisfaction for the duration of an assignment to a high-level task force. Once off the assignment, the employee may experience a decrease in job satisfaction. Among the typical transient situational factors are peaks and valleys in work activity, unusually good or bad temporary assignments, and sudden changes in work conditions (such as cramped quarters during office or plant renovation, a period of "belt tightening," and work problems created by staff shortages).

THE MEASUREMENT OF JOB SATISFACTION

A standard practice for over a half-century has been for large organizations to conduct employee attitude surveys, most of which are designed to measure job satisfaction. These surveys are conducted primarily because many managers implicity or explicity believe that employee satisfaction and morale is an important barometer of organizational effectiveness. Today job satisfaction surveys are often conducted as part of an organization development program. Four methods of measuring job satisfaction are mentioned here: rating scales, individual and group interviews, action tendency scales, and overt behavior.

Rating Scales

Questionnaires based on rating scales are by far the most frequently used formal method of measuring job satisfaction and morale. A rating scale based on comparison theory was presented in Chapter 2 (Figure 2–2). In this approach, measurements are made of the discrepancy between what an employee observes to exist and what he or she thinks should exist. The larger the discrepancy, the greater the dissatisfaction.

---

[19]Charles N. Weaver, "Sex Differences in the Determinants of Job Satisfaction," *Academy of Management Journal,* February 1978, pp. 265–74.

A specific example of a widely used scale to measure job satisfaction is the Job Description Index.[20] The JDI measures attitudes in five areas: work, supervision, pay, promotions, and co-workers. The scale consists of a series of adjectives or statements for each of these five categories. Employees participating in the survey are asked to mark each one as yes (Y), no (N), or cannot decide (?) as it relates to his or her job. Examples are the following:

Work	Pay
_____ Fascinating	_____ Adequate for normal expenses
_____ Endless	_____ Less than I deserve
_____ Gives sense of accomplishment	
	Promotions
Supervision	_____ Promotion on ability
_____ Hard to please	_____ Dead-end job
_____ Praises good work	
_____ Stubborn	**Co-workers**
	_____ Stimulating
	_____ Talk too much

Although the respondents are "describing" their job, they are simultaneously making evaluations of the job. Scores based on this scale have been found to be correlated positively with other measures of job satisfaction, such as turnover, absenteeism, and observations by managers.

In practice most attitude surveys use both questionnaires of the type just described plus write-in comments and interviews with at least a sample of the population surveyed. Typical write-in questions would be "In the space provided below, please feel free to add any other comment you would like to make," or "Is there anything else you would like to tell management?"

Individual and Group Interviews

Interviews have two key purposes in an employee attitude survey. First, they are sometimes used with a small sample of employees to identify in advance critical issues that should be explored. Second, after the questionnaires have been completed, a random sampling of employees may be chosen to explore in depth some of the findings revealed by the job satisfaction scales. For example, if pay receives a low rating, the people interviewed individually or in groups might be encouraged to discuss the topic of pay. In one professional organization, group interviews revealed that what the employees *really* objected to about pay was the salary compression. "New hires" were being paid quite high salaries as compared with "old hires."

---

[20]The Job Description Index is obtained from Bowling Green State University, Department of Psychology, Bowling Green, Ohio 43403.

Aside from clarifying findings, interviews can be a valuable source of additional information untapped by the questionnaires. Interviews used in job attitude surveys have the same advantages and disadvantages and may take the same form as those described in Chapter 2.

Action Tendency Scales

An important clue to our job attitudes is the action we would take if placed in a specific situation. A job-dissatisifed person, for example, might readily accept a job offer from a competitor. Action tendency scales are based more on a reinforcement than on a cognitive theory of behavior. Instead of reporting feelings, the respondent reports on the behavior that he or she would most likely display. Nevertheless, action tendency scales are not devoid of reporting feelings, nor do more conventional scales avoid any mention of behavior. Following are several action tendency items:

1. Are you sometimes reluctant to leave your job to go on a vacation?
2. Do you ever wake up at night with the urge to go to work right then and there?
3. Would you like to find a better job than this one as soon as possible?[21]

Action tendency items have been found to reveal more dissatisfaction than do more direct affect or evaluative ratings. Specifically, the question "If you could start all over again, would you choose the same type of work you are in now or a different type of work?" reveals much more dissatisfaction than a question such as "How well do you like your career?" In one survey it was shown that 24 percent of blue-collar workers would choose the same type of work again.[22] Yet in most surveys, about 65 percent of blue-collar workers are satisfied with their job.

Overt Behaviors

Managers and personnel specialists will often gauge employee attitudes by their behavior in the work setting. Among the behaviors that would suggest low satisfaction and morale are high absenteeism, turnover, scrap, litter, time wasting, tardiness, and reading of classified job ads during working hours. Despite the face validity of linking satisfaction-dissatisfaction and behavior, the two may not be directly related. Employees who display constructive behavior may be nevertheless harboring negative job attitudes. Their motivation (and professional pride) spurs them to high performance, yet their dissatisfaction makes them a turnover candidate. Also, it has been noted that the behavior may not occur with a frequency or intensity that is directly proportional to the intensity of the attitude experienced.[23]

[21]Locke, "The Nature and Causes of Job Satisfaction," p. 1336.

[22]Robert L. Kahn, *The Meaning of Work: Interpretations and Proposals for Measurement,* in A. A. Campbell and P. E. Converse, eds., *The Human Meaning of Social Change* (New York: Basic Books, 1972). Reported in Richard M. Steers, *Introduction to Organizational Behavior* (Glenview, Ill.: Scott, Foresman and Company, 1981), p. 299.

[23]Locke, "The Nature and Causes of Job Satisfaction," p. 1335.

CONDITIONS LEADING TO JOB SATISFACTION

According to one analysis, if there is an ample amount of an important job dimension, or group of dimensions present in a job, it will enhance satisfaction.[24] As with any other generalization about human behavior in a work setting, these factors do not inevitably lead to satisfaction for all employees. Individual differences and situational factors must always be taken into account.

1. *Mentally challenging work.* A minority of employees would prefer to avoid mentally taxing work because of abilities or motivation. The majority of employees, however, crave some intellectual stimulation on the job as implied by the theory and practice of job enrichment.

2. *Personal interest in the work itself.* Job satisfaction often stems from performing work one finds to be intrinsically interesting. Few job elements can be found that are inherently interesting to the majority of people, but factors such as task variety and people contact are appealing to most managers and individual contributors. Also, many people enjoy jobs that enable them to tinker around with problems.

3. *Work that does not place excessive physical demands upon the person.* Work that stretches the physical limits of people tends to become unsatisfying. One reason is that strong physical exertion can act as a stressor. In addition, a person who is physically fatigued is readily frustrated and annoyed by minor disturbances (such as constructive suggestions or a co-worker playing a radio).

4. *Rewards for performance that are equitable, informative, and in line with the employee's goals.* Both equity and expectancy/valence theories would predict this same conclusion. An *informative* reward is one that provides feedback on performance, such as a bonus for error-free work. The performance-reward-satisfaction model predicts that if rewards are to enhance job satisfaction, two conditions must be met. First, there must be an opportunity for intrinsic rewards within the job. Second, the extrinsic rewards available must stem from—or be linked to—good performance. Furthermore, the extrinsic rewards must be perceived by the individual as equitable.[25]

5. *Working conditions that are compatible with one's physical needs and that help make reaching work goals possible.* A sixty-year-old typist with arthritis would find it satisfying to work with an easy-to-manipulate electric typewriter. She (or he) would receive satisfaction from two sources: by using an easy-to-manipulate typewriter, she would avoid some pain in her fingers; also, she would experience satisfaction because the typewriter would help her to reach her goal of typing accurately.

6. *High self-esteem on the part of the individual.* People derive more satisfaction from high- than from low-status occupations. A job that is seen by others as valuable contributes to one's self-esteem. Feelings of self-esteem also stem from doing work that one feels is worthwhile.

[24]The following list, but not the examples, is from ibid., p. 1328.
[25]Lawler and Porter, "The Effects of Performance on Satisfaction," p. 23.

One man owned a gambling parlor that generated enough profits to provide luxuriously for himself, his present and former wives, and his seven children. Yet at age twenty-eight he entered school to earn a degree in business. Asked why he bothered enrolling in school, the gambling entrepreneur replied, "I want to go to law school someday. I don't want my kids to tell people their dad is a hustler."[26]

7. *Helpers in the workplace who "help the employee to attain job values such as interesting work, pay, and promotions, whose basic values are similar to the individual's own, and who minimize conflicting demands and unclear assignments."*[27] Part of job satisfaction stems from having competent managers and staff people who are sensitive to the needs of people.

GENERAL STRATEGIES FOR INCREASING JOB SATISFACTION

A wide range of managerial and applied behavioral science techniques can be used to increase the level of job satisfaction or decrease dissatisfaction. For example, the job enrichment program described in the previous chapter can be used to increase satisfaction as well as motivation. Also, programs offered by the personnel and human resources department are designed in some way to improve satisfaction (and productivity). The general strategy of improving satisfaction is first to assess the nature of the problem creating dissatisfaction. Once an appropriate diagnosis has been made, several straightforward approaches can be helpful in improving job satisfaction. These include remedying substandard conditions, transferring discontented employees, changing the perceptions of employees over a particular issue, and initiating morale building programs.[28]

Remedy Substandard Conditions

The commonsense solution to job satisfaction and morale is to improve those conditions that are organizational sore spots. In a nursing home, job satisfaction was elevated to tolerable levels only after kitchen and janitorial help were given a substantial increase in their hourly wage rate. The strategy of remedial action assumes that the underlying problem has been identified. Early experience with employee attitude surveys indicated that people often focused their complaints on the quality of food served in the cafeteria. In these early studies, improving the food did not lead to improved job satisfaction, because the real problem was often discontent with other job factors such as supervision or general working conditions.

---

[26]Andrew J. DuBrin, *Effective Business Psychology* (Reston, Va.: Reston, 1980), p. 330.

[27]Locke, "The Nature and Causes of Job Satisfaction," p. 1328.

[28]The first three of these strategies are described by Kenneth N. Wexley and Gary A. Yukl, *Organizational Behavior and Personnel Psychology* (Homewood, Ill.: Richard D. Irwin, 1977), pp. 117–19.

Transfer Discontented Employees

In limited cases, it is possible to promote job satisfaction and high morale by transferring employees to achieve a better fit between individual and job characteristics. An important constraint, however, is that a dissatisfied employee is often difficult to transfer. Dissatisfied employees may sometimes be reassigned to form more compatible work groups. An important challenge for managers is to differentiate between employees who are dissatisfied over legitimate issues and those who are chronic complainers. The latter will probably not experience an increase in satisfaction after being transferred or, for that matter, under any circumstances.

Change the Perceptions of
Dissatisfied Employees

Job dissatisfaction sometimes stems from an employee's misperceptions concerning a particular issue. The misconception (or misperception) might be based on inadequate or incorrect information. Assuming that it is trusted, management might remedy the dissatisfaction by providing fresh information. At one college, many of the faculty members openly expressed dissatisfaction about salaries for instructors and assistant professors. The provost gathered salary information from comparable colleges and was able to indicate that the college in question paid above-average salaries to instructors and assistant professors. Discontent over wages consequently subsided somewhat.

Initiate Morale Building Programs

The progressive organization will often improve satisfaction and morale by introducing positive programs even in the absence of discontent. One example would be offering managers a worthwhile new program of management development before they complained about the paucity of offerings in that area. In recent years, hundreds of governmental agencies and business firms have adopted flexible working hours as a method of elevating morale, satisfaction, and to some extent productivity. It is worthwhile examining flexitime in some detail as one example of how organizations can improve the job satisfaction of a large number of employees.

IMPROVING SATISFACTION
THROUGH FLEXITIME

A broad strategy for improving employee satisfaction and productivity is to modify working hours into an arrangement favorable to worker preferences. A modified work schedule that has met with widespread acceptance is flexitime (or flextime or flexible working hours). About 7 percent of the North American work force works flexible hours. At the U.S. Social Security Administration, which employs 80,000 people, about 6,000 employees are on flexitime. Its system is typical. There is a flex band of three hours in the morning and afternoon. The employee has the choice of coming to work anytime between 6:30 A.M. and 9:30 A.M. and leaving between the hours of 3:00 P.M. and 6:00 P.M. All employees must be at work during the core time, which extends from 9:30 A.M. to 3:00 P.M. In addition, every employee must work a full eight hours and must take a half-hour lunch break. Some employees, such as those involved in round-the-clock computer operations, are not included in the flexitime program. Here is an illustration of a typical setup:

```
A.M.               (One-half or one-hour lunch)              P.M.

Flexible                    Core                      Flexible

6:30      9:30                                3:00      6:00
```

Cognitive theory helps to explain why flexitime sometimes improves satisfaction and performance. Employees enjoy being treated as autonomous, mature adults because it provides a partial satisfaction of their needs for autonomy and competence. The element of trust communicated by management can also be beneficial to morale. Employees on flexitime probably form the cognition, "Management must trust us, otherwise the amount of hours we work would be monitored more closely."

Empirical Evidence About Flexitime and Satisfaction

Consistent evidence has accumulated that flexitime usually has a pronounced effect in elevating job satisfaction. According to the reports of seven firms surveyed in one study, flexitime's impact on job satisfaction and/or morale was dramatic. The positive effect ran across industry and organizational lines. "Opinions in four of them ranged from a low of 79 percent (supervisors) to a high of 89 percent (employees) who felt that morale had improved because of flexitime."[29]

At the Social Security Administration, the reaction of personnel to the introduction of flexitime was unusually enthusiastic and their satisfaction with the system grew. Supervisors were slightly less enthusiastic than employees. Of interest, "The impact of flexitime on morale and job satisaction was generally more pronounced in the operational settings than in those dealing with administrative or staff kinds of functions."[30]

Here are two examples of illustrative findings at SSA:

- Prior to flexitime, about 7 percent of employees at Disability Insurance Benefit Authorization had formally requested assignments to new jobs. After flexitime, the figure dropped to 1 percent.

[29]Donald J. Petersen, "Flexitime in the United States: The Lessons of Experience," *Personnel,* January–February 1980, pp. 21–31.

[30]Cary B. Barad, "Flexitime Under Scrutiny: Research on Work Adjustment and Organizational Performance," *Personnel Administrator,* May 1980, p. 70.

- Before-and-after measures of job satisfaction showed that from 6 percent (general administration, equal opportunity, and clerical) of the study participants to 26 percent (clerical, filing, and transcribing) of the study participants enjoyed their work more under flexitime.

The Problem of Interactive Measures in Flexitime Research

A study about flexitime and job satisfaction was conducted with two hundred employees in two firms in central Ohio. Questionnaires were used to measure employee attitudes toward the flexible work hour program. A surprising finding of the study was that no significant differences were found for the flexitime groups compared with the fixed-hour groups on the work satisfaction measures. However, employees working under flexitime did report certain other improvements, including easier travel and parking, a greater feeling of being in control in the work setting, and more opportunity for leisure activities. Also of significance for QWL, employees experienced smaller amounts of interrole conflict (that between the job and home and family demands).

Since most previous studies reported positive results about the relationship between flexitime and job satisfaction, the investigators analyzed why the results were negative. One reason offered was that the study under consideration used nonreactive measures in gathering employee attitudes. Other research on the topic has frequently made reference to flexitime in the process of gathering data. The employees knew that flexitime was the topic under investigation. As suggested by the two researchers,

> Flexitime is valued in this case not because it enhances work satisfaction, per se, but because it makes working a little bit easier. Thus, questionnaires used to gather employee attitudes about flexitime will yield favorable results if the link to flexitime is made obvious. When the link to flexitime is not salient, the traditional relationship may not occur.[31]

CRITICISM OF JOB SATISFACTION RESEARCH

The basic concept of job satisfaction and the attention devoted to it has not gone without criticism. Walter R. Nord believes that we have been beset with incomplete and unrealistic approaches to job satisfaction. Although the general tone of this chapter has been supportive of the literature on job satisfaction, his criticisms merit consideration:[32]

- Job satisfaction researchers have limited themselves to "an incomplete and biased set of dependent variables." Maybe more consequences of job satisfaction should be studied, such as the relationship between job satisfaction and self-confidence.

[31]William D. Hicks and Richard J. Klimoski, "The Impact of Flexitime on Employee Attitudes," *Academy of Management Journal,* June 1981, p. 340. The study is described on pp. 333–41.

[32]Walter R. Nord, "Job Satisfaction Reconsidered," *American Psychologist,* December 1977, p. 1028.

- Researchers have ignored the fact that organizations often have no incentives for experimenting with ways of increasing job satisfaction. For instance, job enrichment is a risky venture to managers in many organizations. If the programs fail, the manager will most probably be held accountable and penalized.
- Almost no consideration has been given to the fact that job satisfaction is to some degree based on the quality of the product produced. Why hasn't the problem of work relevance been incorporated into job satisfaction studies? Sufficient attention has not been given to basic satisfactions such as income, job security, and treatment by one's immediate superior.
- Sufficient attention has not been given to "the relationship of power and control to job satisfaction and alienation." If employees are given more power, they might show higher levels of job satisfaction (see Chapter 14).

IMPLICATIONS FOR MANAGERIAL PRACTICE

1. Job satisfaction and morale are important dependent variables in management. The level of a person's job satisfaction has a significant impact on his or her mental health, physical health, and quality of work life. Aside from these important humanitarian considerations, job satisfaction also has important consequences for organizational effectiveness. For example, low job satisfaction may increase absenteeism, tardiness, and turnover. It is therefore important that the manager examine the job satisfaction consequences of any action before making a final decision.

2. Overall programs of enhancing job satisfaction may have a general value to the organization, but individual differences among employees must be managed for so as to optimize the value of such programs. A program such as flexitime automatically takes into account individual differences because employee preferences are used in assigning work hours. A good starting point in managing for individual differences in satisfiers is to ask employees such questions as "Given a choice, which aspects of your job would you prefer to spend the most of your time doing?"

3. The conditions leading to job satisfaction identified on pages 152–153 can also be considered conditions that may lead to improved productivity and organizational effectiveness. As such, they may be interpreted as ideal working conditions toward which the organization might strive. For example, many worthwhile outcomes would be achieved if an organization were to establish "rewards for performance that are equitable, informative, and in line with the employee's goals."

4. Sometimes managers perceive job satisfaction and job performance as being somewhat incompatible outcomes, so they decide whether it is better to push for satisfaction or productivity. Proper placement of people will often help to create conditions whereby employees will perform at a high level yet also derive adequate job satisfaction. Also of importance, many employees will experience job satisfaction as a consequence of having performed well.

Summary

- Job satisfaction is the pleasurable emotional state resulting from the perception of one's job as fulfilling or allowing for the fulfillment of one's important job values, providing that these values are compatible with one's needs. Contemporary employees tend to have different values from those of more traditional employees, thus influencing which job factors contribute to their job satisfaction.

- Satisfaction and motivation are related but somewhat different concepts; satisfaction refers to a state of contentment, whereas motivation refers to expending effort toward a goal. Workers can be categorized into different combinations of satisfaction and motivation, such as "dissatisfied and hard working" or "disgruntled and uninvolved." Morale refers more to group identification than does satisfaction. Job involvement refers to the intensity of emotion invested in one's work.

- The cognitive theories of job motivation can also be used to explain job satisfaction. The most widely accepted theory of job satisfaction is comparison theory: the degree of affect experienced by employees relates to a comparison between what they would like and what they perceive to exist. The bigger the discrepancy between one's ideal and the actual, the more acute one's job dissatisfaction.

- Among the potential consequences of low job satisfaction are absenteeism and turnover, low productivity, poor physical health, poor mental health, poor community relations, and a low quality of work life as perceived by employees.

- Surveys consistently suggest that somewhere between 65 and 86 percent of the work force are reasonably satisfied with their jobs. About 10 to 25 percent experience outright discontent. Among the individual and group factors that influence levels of job satisfaction are personality differences, age, occupational level, educational level, sex, and race. Transient situational factors, such as peaks and valleys in work load, also influence job satisfaction levels.

- Job satisfaction is typically measured as part of an employee attitude survey or an organization development program. Specific measurement techniques used include rating scales, individual and group interviews, and action tendency scales. Or behavior can be observed directly to make inferences about job satisfaction.

- Certain conditions, when present, are known to contribute to job satisfaction, including mentally challenging work, personal interest in the work itself, work matched to physical needs, work leading to self-esteem, and helpers in the workplace.

- Strategies for improving job satisfaction include remedying substandard conditions, transferring discontented employees, changing the perception of dissatisfied employees, and initiating morale building programs. Flexitime is one example of a program that usually leads to increased levels of job satisfaction. However, some research suggests that flexitime is valued not because it enhances job satisfaction per se, but because it makes working easier (for example, easier traveling and parking).

Questions for Discussion

1. To what extent do you think your level of job satisfaction does, or would, influence your satisfaction off the job?
2. According to one survey, over 93 percent of college professors said that "if they had to do it all over again," they would choose to become college professors. What job dimensions and conditions do you think account for this finding?
3. Which group do you think generally experiences the higher level of job satisfaction—production or clerical workers? Why?
4. How might behavior modification be used to increase job satisfaction?
5. Give two examples of jobs that you think are low paying yet satisfying (for most people).
6. Give two examples of jobs that you think are high paying yet dissatisfying (for most people).
7. Using yourself as a case history, do you see any direct relationship between satisfaction and productivity?
8. What impact do you think dental plans (reimbursement of all or some dental expenses) have on job satisfaction?
9. What steps could a manager take to help employees become "well-satisfied, hard chargers"?
10. Branch managers and small-business owners tend to have high levels of job satisfaction. What factors do you think account for their high satisfaction?

An Organizational Behavior Problem

The Job Satisfaction Interview[33]

The general purpose of this activity is to conduct job satisfaction interviews with a sampling of people in divergent occupations. Each person assigned to the project is responsible for conducting one job satisfaction interview.

Interview Format. Ask questions relating to the variables covered in the chapter sections entitled "Dimensions of Job Satisfaction" and "Conditions Leading to Job Satisfaction." To illustrate, you might ask questions such as "How do you feel about the amount of mental challenge in your work?" "To what extent are you interested in the work itself?" "What is your opinion about the amount of physical demands you face in your job?"

Interviewees. Each interviewer on the team should be responsible for interviewing a member of an occupation not interviewed by any other team member. One person agrees to interview a plumber, one a physician, one a bus driver, one a legal secretary, and so forth.

Comparison of Findings. Each interviewer is responsible for providing a brief summary of the amount of job satisfaction experienced by his or her interviewee. (Interviewees might also be asked, "Overall, how satisfied are you with your job?") The results can be compared in group discussion and by providing summary ratings on the chalkboard. For instance, "Stock clerk in supermarket: very little job satisfaction; mostly aggravation across all the categories studied."

[33]Adapted from DuBrin, *Personnel and Human Resource Management,* p. 238.

It will be particularly significant to look for low satisfaction among higher occupational groups and high satisfaction among lower occupational groups.

Additional Reading

BAIRD, LLOYD. "Managing Dissatisfaction." *Personnel,* May–June 1981, pp. 12–21.

BERNARD, KEITH E. "Flexitime's Potential for Management." *The Personnel Administrator,* October 1979, pp. 51–56.

COLTRIN, SALLY A., and BARBARA D. BARENDSE. "Is Your Organization a Good Candidate for Flexitime?" *Personnel Journal,* September 1981, pp. 662, 712–15.

CURRY, TALMER E., and DEANE N. HAERER. "The Positive Impact of Flextime on Employee Relations." *Personnel Administrator,* February 1981, pp. 62–66.

GINSBURG, SIGMUND G. "The High Achiever's Job Satisfaction." *Personnel Administrator,* January 1981, pp. 78–81.

GRUNEBERG, MICHAEL M. *Understanding Job Satisfaction.* New York: John Wiley, 1979.

JAMES, LAWRENCE R., and ALLAN P. JONES. "Perceived Job Characteristics and Job Satisfaction." *Personnel Psychology,* Spring 1980, pp. 97–135.

KERR, CLARK, and JEROME M. ROSOW, eds. *Work in America: The Decade Ahead.* New York: Van Nostrand Reinhold, 1979.

PEARSE, ROBERT F. *Manager to Manager II: What Managers Think of Their Managerial Careers: An AMA Survey Report.* New York: AMACOM, 1977.

SINETAR, MARSHA. "Management in the New Age: An Exploration of Changing Work Values." *Personnel Journal,* September 1980, pp. 749–55.

CHAPTER 7

Stress and Burnout in Organizations

LEARNING OBJECTIVES

1. To explain the nature and symptoms of stress and burnout.
2. To explain the relationship between stress and job performance.
3. To identify both individual and organizational sources of stress.
4. To describe several consequences of distress.
5. To understand several methods that individuals may use to manage stress.
6. To understand several organizational methods of managing stress.

In the final days of his reign, the pressure had built up to an overwhelming amount. During his two years as president of Continental Airlines, he had been through a lengthy and bitter strike by flight attendants, a tension-producing hijack attempt, and finally an aggressive financial takeover campaign by a competitor, Texas International Airlines. On the second Sunday in August, the president sadly informed key subordinates that a plan to sell the airline to its employees had fallen through. Now it was inevitable that Continental would fall into the hands of its rival, which held close to 49 percent of Continental stock. Several hours later he laid down on a couch in his office and put a bullet through his brain. In his last letter to his children, the fifty-three-year-old executive described the sorrow he had felt since his wife died of cancer a year earlier.

"The constant fighting was wearing us all down," a close associate remarked, "but it was worse for him. In the last month he had become extremely tired. He was alone with the responsibility, and took that responsibility too far. I think on Sunday he saw that there was no resolution (to the takeover troubles) and he felt he was responsible for letting us down."*

As you read this chapter, think about why the events at Continental Airline were so disturbing to the president and how his suicide might have been prevented.

THE NATURE AND MEANING OF STRESS

As could be readily extrapolated from this case incident, the impact of stress on mental health, physical health, and productivity is a growing concern of contemporary organizations. Stress and its related condition, burnout, are sometimes considered the organizational behavior topics of the decade. Executives are becoming increasingly aware of the costs of stress and burnout problems—both in financial and human terms—both to organizations and employees. Stress-induced emotional dysfunctions have resulted in an estimated $17 billion annual decrease in productivity in North American business and industry over the last several years. Other studies have set the cost of stress-related disorders as high as $60 billion annually.[1]

Despite the widespread attention being paid to stress (including hundreds of scientific, professional, and general audience publications on the topic), a disagreement exists about the basic nature of stress. Sometimes stress refers to an external or internal force creating pressure on an individual or group—such as believing that your department may be disbanded in thirty days. Current medical and psychological opinion regards stress as a general physiological and psychological reaction to an external force (stressor). The purpose of stress is to help the individual cope effectively with the environment. But prolonged coping with the environment sometimes hurts the individual and leads to potentially negative consequences.

*Adapted from "Executives Under Stress," *Newsweek*, August 24, 1981, p. 53.

[1]"Stress Management Tools," *Trainer's Bookshelf*, Learning Resources Corporation, Vol. 1, No. 2, p. 1, not dated.

THE SYMPTOMS OF STRESS

An organism facing stressors displays certain signs or symptoms that indicate the experience of stress. Although the categories show some overlap, it is meaningful to classify these symptoms into three groups: physiological, psychological, and behavioral.[2]

Physiological Symptoms

Stress experts agree that the physiological changes within the body seem to be almost identical in reaction to different sources of stress (stressors). All types of stress produce a chemical response within the body, which in turn produces a short-term physiological reaction. Among the most familiar reactions are an increase in heart rate, blood pressure, respiratory (breathing) rate, pupil size, perspiration, skin temperature, blood glucose, blood clotting, and bodily elimination. If stress is continuous (and is accompanied by these short-term physiological changes), certain annoying and life-threatening conditions can occur. Among them are heart attacks, essential hypertension, increased cholesterol levels, migraine headaches, ulcers, allergies, and colitis. The right amount of stress reaction, however, prepares us for meeting difficult challenges and spurs us to new heights of performance. More will be said later about the positive consequences of job stress.

Psychological Symptoms

The psychological or emotional symptoms of stress are far reaching and show wide individual differences. Faced with the same stressor, one person may act impulsively while another person may become depressed. Among the more common psychological outcomes or symptoms of stress are anxiety, tension, depression, discouragement, boredom, complaints about bodily problems, mental fatigue, feelings of futility and inadequacy, and low self-esteem. People may also experience disturbed inner states leading to behavior that is classified as mental disorder. As stress levels increase, job satisfaction decreases. It is also plausible that job dissatisfaction can generate a stress reaction. Thus, stress → job dissatisfaction → more stress.

Anxiety and its accompanying tension are perhaps the most significant psychological symptoms of stress because they in turn lead to other symptoms. The anxious person feels uneasy, nervous, jittery, "up tight," and fidgety. To help combat the adverse effects of anxiety, people resort to defense mechanism that deny, falsify, and distort reality. Among the more typical kinds of defense mechanisms displayed in a job environment are rationalization (substituting acceptable reasons for the real reason) and denial of reality ("You never told me I would be reprimanded if I was late again").

[2]A comprehensive discussion of stress symptoms is found in Arthur P. Brief, Randall S. Schuler, and Mary Van Sell, *Managing Job Stress* (Boston: Little, Brown, 1981), pp. 17–29.

Behavioral Symptoms

Emotional or psychological symptoms point toward how people feel, whereas behavioral symptoms indicate what people actually do under stress. Among the more common job-related behavioral symptoms of stress are

> Impulsive behavior including displays of temper.
> Difficulties in concentration and rapid changing of thoughts.
> Accident proneness.
> Stuttering and other speech difficulties.
> Extremes in appetite.
> Increased cigarette smoking and use of alcohol and illegal drugs.
> Increased use of prescription drugs such as tranquilizers and amphetamines.
> Pacing about and other increased physical movements.

As indicated in the chapter opening case, suicide is yet another behavioral symptom or response to stress. Suicides are often precipitated by severe depression in which the person sees no workable alternative to dealing with the problems at hand. Many suicide notes contain a message to the effect that "There's no way out for me."

STRESS AND JOB PERFORMANCE

An optimum amount of stress exists for most people and in relation to most tasks. A self-confident, well motivated, highly talented computer repair technician may perform best when the stakes are highest—as when a key customer's computer malfunctions. On the other hand, an emotionally insecure, moderately talented repair technician of average motivation might perform the best when conducting routine maintenance on computers. One valid generalization is that job performance tends to be best under moderate amounts of stress. Too much stress causes people to become temporarily ineffective (they tend to "choke"); too little stress causes people to become lethargic and inattentive.

The optimum amount of stress is referred to as *eustress*—a positive force in our lives that is the equivalent of finding excitement and challenge in life.[3] As shown in Figure 7–1, when people experience eustress, positive outcomes for themselves and the organization result. Problem-solving ability and creativity might be enhanced as the right amount of adrenalin flows in our blood to guide us toward maximum performance.

The wrong amount and type of stress is called *distress.* It usually results in negative outcomes for the individual and organization. Placed under unreasonable dead-

---

[3]Hans Selye (interviewed by Laurence Cherry), "On the Real Benefits of Eustress," *Psychology Today,* March 1978, pp. 60–63.

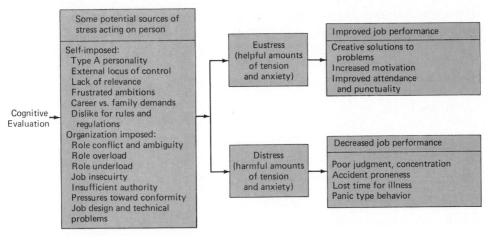

FIGURE 7–1   How Stress Influences Job Behavior and Performance

lines, even the most conscientious and able employee might make errors in judgment and action. Of graver consequence, the distressed employee might succumb to cardiac disease.

The section of Figure 7–1 labeled "Some potential sources of stress acting on person" is a sampling of potential job stressors. With respect to both organization- and self-imposed sources of stress, the individual's cognitive evaluation of the situation helps to determine whether or not it proves to be a stressor.[4] The appraisal process is the most evident in the self-imposed category. The employee who dislikes rules and regulations (a cognitive evaluation of a stimulus), for example, creates his or her own stress by reacting adversely to rules and regulations that may even be a source of comfort to others. Employees who desire high structure do not find tight rules and regulations to be stressors.

A person's past experience heavily influences whether or not stress will be perceived. Suppose that a middle manager had weathered four mergers and acquisitions in the past. The middle manager may not perceive an upcoming merger to be a source of distress. A security guard at an airport may perceive a package emitting a ticking sound as highly stressful. A four-year-old child coming upon the same package may perceive it as entertaining rather than stressful.

INDIVIDUAL DIFFERENCES
AND SOURCES OF STRESS

As the stress model presented here indicates, individual differences help to determine whether or not a given circumstance proves to be a stressor. Personality factors are a major source of these individual differences. Similarly, some things in the job environment prove to be stressors because of personal conflicts and concerns of employees. For example, if you were not ambitious, you would probably not perceive limited advancement opportunities to be a stressor. Here we review two key personality patterns and several individual conflicts that predispose a person to organizational stress.

Type A Personalities

Some people have a basic personality structure that leads them into stressful situations. It is these impatient, demanding, overstriving types that often wind up with heart attacks at an early age. Cardiologists Friedman and Rosenman have identified several personality characteristics of people who are the most prone to heart disease.[5] Such individuals tend to gravitate toward occupations that encourage heavy work. In addition, they are frequently found to be heavy cigarette smokers. Labeled Type A personalities, their distinguishing characteristics are as follows:

- Chronic and severe sense of time urgency. For instance, Type A people become particularly frustrated in traffic jams.
- Constant involvement in multiple projects subject to deadlines. Somehow Type A people take delight in the feeling of being swamped with work.
- Neglectful of all aspects of life except work. *Workaholics* live to work rather than work to live.
- A tendency to take on excessive responsibility, combined with the feeling that "Only I am capable of taking care of this matter."
- Explosiveness of speech and a tendency to speak faster than most people. Type A people are thus prone to ranting and swearing when upset.

Belief in External Locus of Control

Some evidence has accumulated that a person's belief in locus of control is related to susceptibility to job stress. (In review, people with an internal locus of control feel that their fate is pretty much under their control. Externals look to outside forces as controlling their fate.) People with an internal locus of control perceive their jobs as less stressful than do externals. The underlying cognitive mechanism seems to be that if people believe that they can control potential adverse forces in their job environment, they are less prone to the stressor of worrying about them. Simultaneously, the person who believes in an internal locus of control experiences a higher level of job satisfaction.[6]

A natural disaster served as the setting for research about the relationship between locus of control and perceived job stress. The subjects in the study were ninety

[5]Meyer Friedman and Ray H. Rosenman, *Type A Behavior and Your Heart* (Greenwich, Conn.: Fawcett, 1975), pp. 100–103.

[6]H. Joseph Reitz, *Behavior in Organizations,* rev. ed. (Homewood, Ill.: Richard D. Irwin, 1981), p. 245.

small-business owners in a community devastated by a hurricane. Internals—the managers who believed that their fate was mostly under their control—perceived significantly less stress than did externals. A surprising conclusion reached was that the amount of stress perceived by a manager was more closely related to his or her belief in locus of control than to amount of insurance coverage in the business, the percentage of assets destroyed, or the number of business days lost attributed to the hurricane.[7]

Lack of Relevance

Ideals have a strong enough impact upon the psyche to cause stress for some individuals when these ideals cannot be reached. Many managerial and professional people have developed a set of ideals that leads them to interpret their work in organizations as lacking relevance. Today's young businessperson insists on meaning and a sense of social responsibility in his or her job and life in general. Many young managers want to improve the environment and society. Significantly, they insist that their companies work actively toward such goals. Presumably, those more committed individuals suffer actual frustration and stress when their organizations do not comply. Corporations are expected by this new breed of managers to sanction socially relevant activities with financial support or through time off from the job.

Underlying the attempts of many executives, middle managers, and professional people to find teaching positions is a quest for work they perceive as relevant. Again, relevance is a value judgment and a cognition. The individual manager who is managing a manufacturing department must decide for himself or herself whether that work is less relevant than teaching manufacturing management to college students.

Frustrated Ambitions

Cultural pressures dictate—perhaps more so in the recent past than in the present—that members of hierarchical organizations must keep pushing toward a higher position on the corporate ladder. Maintaining yourself at a comfortable plateau, or being demoted, is thus interpreted as failure. Frustrated ambitions and goals are the cause of many psychosomatic reactions. Men and women suffer psychological stress from failure to be promoted even when their financial needs are satisfied at their present level of responsibility. Equally important, many managers experience feelings of failure about not being promoted even when they are poorly qualified for their present responsibilities. Aspirants to greater responsibility far outnumber the positions of responsibility available; "the race to the top" is intensely competitive.

A variation of the stress caused by lack of relevance has been uncovered.[8] People

[7]Carl R. Anderson, Don Hellriegel, and John W. Slocum, Jr., "Managerial Response to Environmentally Induced Stress," *Academy of Management Journal,* Vol. 20, 1977, pp. 260–72.

[8]Robert L. Kahn, "Stress from 9 to 5," *Psychology Today,* September 1969, p. 37.

in creative jobs frequently complained of conflict between their nonroutine creative activities and their routine administrative duties. Paperwork, according to these people, is time consuming, disrupts their creative work, and is generally unpalatable. As such, its relevance is indirectly challenged.

Career versus Family Conflicts

Many managers and professional people experience role conflicts because work and family place overlapping demands upon their time. Conflict occurs because the person wants to devote adequate attention to both family and work. Demands placed upon many managers can be excessive, but the individual—more often than he or she is willing to admit—can opt for a position of lesser responsibility. Frequently, this transition can be made by scaling down one's standard of living. Not every person who is successful in his or her career experiences the career versus family type of stress. One group of these individuals neglects family responsibilities, therefore avoiding conflict. Another group of people, labeled "integrators," is able successfully to resolve the multiple demands of career, family, and concern for self. Underlying the success of such people is a particularly well-organized approach to work.

Dislike for Rules and Regulations

One could argue that excessive rules and regulations are an organizational source of stress. Yet a person's cognitive evaluation plays a key role in determining whether or not being controlled by rules and regulations acts as a stressor. Many people find it stress reducing to turn down requests from customers or other employees because the request is "against regulations." The appeal to rules helps the person to avoid conflict. (See chapter 16 on bureaucracy.)

ORGANIZATIONAL AND ENVIRONMENTAL SOURCES OF STRESS

Stress responses result from the interaction between an individual's predisposition to stress and the force exerted by the environment. The term "environment" includes all factors and forces external to the individual. In this chapter, the organizational portion of the environment is emphasized. Other environmental forces contributing to job stress include economic factors (e.g., recession and inflation), cultural values (e.g., movement up a hierarchy), and marital and family problems (e.g., an adolescent daughter who is pregnant). Environmental factors such as general overcrowding and air, water, and sound pollution create stress for individuals. Stresses exerted by forces outside the job may spill over onto job behavior.

Neither organizational pressures nor individual conflicts exist in isolation. For example, job insecurity is one of the organizational pressures discussed in this section of the chapter. It is much more of a threat to a psychologically insecure (or financially poor) individual than to one who is self-confident (or financially rich). The sources of managerial and professional stress presented next are more nearly problems created by the organization than the product of individual conflicts and perceptions.

Role Conflict and Ambiguity

One form of organization stress extensively studied is that of role conflict and ambiguity. Stress is created under conditions of conflict and ambiguity because under these circumstances people are not sure what to do or which way to turn. *Role conflict* is the "simultaneous occurrence of two or more role sendings such that compliance with one would make more difficult compliance with the other."[9] Four types of role conflict have been identified:

> *Intrasender* conflict occurs when one person asks you to accomplish two objectives that are in apparent conflict. If your boss asks you to hurry up and finish your work but also decrease your mistakes, you would experience this type of conflict (plus perhaps a headache!).
>
> *Intersender* conflict occurs when two or more senders give you incompatible directions. Your immediate superior may want you to complete a crash project on time, but company policy temporarily prohibits authorizing overtime payments to clerical help.
>
> *Interrole* conflict results when two different roles you play are in conflict. Your company may expect you to travel 50 percent of the time (to be promoted) while your spouse threatens a divorce if you travel more than 25 percent of the time.
>
> *Person-role* conflict occurs when the role(s) that your organization expects you to occupy are in conflict with your basic values. Your company may ask you to fire substandard performers, but this could be in conflict with your humanistic values.

Confusing directions (role ambiguity) are closely related to role conflict. A man was hired into a management training program and given the elegant title, Assistant to the General Manager. After three days of reading company manuals and taking plant tours, he pressed for an explanation of what he was supposed to be doing in the assignment. His boss told him, "Just try to make yourself useful. I'll be going out of town for two weeks. If you have any questions, ask my secretary for help."

Role Overload

Employees at all levels sometimes find themselves faced with excessive work demands. Tightly scheduled workdays, cost cutting, and simultaneous demands act as sources of distress. Workweeks of sixty hours or longer are not uncommon in management positions in business and some governmental and educational institutions. Many executives fly over 100,000 miles annually in conjunction with business.

---

[9]The source of this definition and the subtypes of role conflict is Daniel Katz and Robert L. Kahn, *The Social Psychology of Organizations* (New York: John Wiley, 1966), pp. 184–87. (See also the 1978 edition of the same book.)

Fragmentation of a manager's time is an acute source of stress. An executive in charge of a division may answer for the success or failure of 101 simultaneous projects, problems, and operations. Constant interruptions characterize the executive's day. "I change hats every ten minutes," one financial vice president reported. "I act as a tax specialist for a while, a manager for the next few minutes, then a banker, a personnel specialist, and so on."[10]

In an attempt to cope with the multiple demands and interruptions, many managers opt to perform their paperwork at home. This approach to time management succeeds in freeing much of the workday for people-contact activities, but it creates conflict in most family situations. Stressors are thus not eliminated but are displaced from the office to the home.

Role Underload

Feelings of not being challenged, of one's intellectual abilities and formal education being wasted, and of being overqualified for present job responsibilities represent an omnipresent complaint of dissatisfied middle managers and professionals. Some executives also experience role underload. It is not unknown for an executive to be assigned very little work to do as a way of encouraging him or her to resign. Such political tactics may take place after a merger or acquisition. Combining the two companies results in excess executives, yet the acquiring firm is hesitant to lay off redundant managers because of a preacquisition agreement. Instead the surplus executive is left to suffer from role underload, which acts as a stressor.

Job Insecurity

Traditionally, production workers were the first to be laid off during times of business downturn. More recently, top management has looked toward administrative and technical personnel as more dispensable than direct production workers. As expressed by Drucker, "There is not one company I know of where a sharp cut in the number of executives wouldn't be a real improvement."[11] Fear of being fired thus poses another source of stress to the manager and professional.

Job insecurity has both psychological and financial roots. Loss of income, unpaid bills, and abandonment of luxury items constitute only part of the problem of a manager or professional being unemployed. Embarrassment, shame, and guilt are intertwined with the financial losses. Self-images in most cultures are in part dependent upon the type of work an individual performs. Unemployment thus weakens the self-image of those afflicted.

---

[10]George J. Berkwitt, "The Case of the Fragmented Manager," *Dun's Review,* June 1969, p. 49.

[11]Thomas J. Murray, "Peter Drucker Attacks Our Top-Heavy Corporations," *Dun's Review,* April 1971, p. 39. Drucker's comments are still relevant today.

Insufficient Authority

Primers of management contend that authority should be commensurate with responsibility. Yet this axiom is often violated in organization life. This discrepancy between power granted and power needed to accomplish a given task is a source of stress and frustration for many managers and professionals. Insufficient authority sometimes manifests itself in a manager not receiving the backing needed from management to carry out its directives.

Budget control is another key area in which the discrepancy between responsibility and authority creates stress—or at least aggravation—for many managers. Particularly vexing to some people is the lack of authority to expend funds that are already within their budgets. Reacting to the problem of budget control, one manager in a food products company made these comments:

> If we're going to be given budget responsibility, we ought to be given the authority to exercise the judgments we've made on a present budget. If I've budgeted $1,500 for the quarterly period for travel, I ought to be able to use it.

Pressures Toward Conformity

Employees vary widely in their willingness to conform to a norm established by the organization. For some individuals, the pressure to conform represents a stressor. Many managers and professional people, to cite one illustration, object to the pressures placed upon them to contribute to the United Way. Donations, under these circumstances, cease to be voluntary.

Pressures also exist for organizational members to reshape or accommodate their ideas and suggestions to those of their superiors. This represents a more acute source of stress for some people than does conformity in behavior. Creative suggestions are frequently subjected to review by a wide range of people before they can be implemented. Several groups typically add their input to the original suggestion. Stress, or at least job dissatisfaction, can be the result when an original idea is watered down through the process of committee review. According to one young professional in an organization, "Each compromise, each appeasement, and each wording change to satisfy somebody (the infamous 'they') withdraws a little something from your bank of ambition."

Faulty Job Design and Technical Problems

Pressures placed upon individuals discussed so far have dealt primarily with psychological and sociological factors and managerial practices. There also exists within any organization a vast source of stress centering on problems of job design and technology.[12] Automobile dealers, to illustrate, are subject to considerable stress when customers complain about the reliability of automobiles. These same automobile dealers have almost no control over the quality of automobiles purchased from the company. Similarly, there are several jobs in almost any organization that are inherently stressful—often with full awareness on the part of management and the employee. Collection agents for private finance companies rarely have a day that is not stressful.

Stress created by an organization can also be analyzed from the standpoint of the actual interaction patterns that take place between and among individuals. You will be under stress, for example, if your boss gives you orders and directions but you have no opportunity to initiate communication with him or her.

JOB-RELATED CONSEQUENCES OF DISTRESS

Stress can have both functional and dysfunctional consequences to the individual and the organization, as was shown in Figure 7–1. When eustress is experienced, the result is usually improved job performance, which is self-rewarding to an extent, propelling the person to even better performance. This phenomenon is an example of the *success cycle*—each success facilitates an additional success. Of concern here are the consequences of distress (or the dysfunctional consequences of stress). Among them are errors in concentration and judgment, panic-type behavior, absenteeism, managerial defense mechanisms, and preoccupation with busywork.

Errors in Concentration and Judgment

People experiencing distress make frequent errors in attention and judgment. Most readers can probably recall locking themselves out of their cars or living quarters, or losing keys, while under the influence of heavy stressors. An explanation has been provided of the physiology behind such errors. We know, first of all, that stressors bring about a heightened amount of bodily chemical reactions, including the secretion of hormones from the endocrine glands. Second,

> The adaption energy extracted by a higher than normal level of endocrine activity must be replenished sooner or later, and the involuntary "let-down" which seems to be necessary for such replenishment may show up in such trivial, apparently unrelated symptoms as forgetting to lock the garage door, injuring oneself with a power saw, or inadvertently dumping cigarette ashes into one's full cup of coffee.[13]

[12]Brief, Schuler, and Van Sell, *Managing Job Stress,* pp. 152–53.
[13]Dennis W. Organ, "The Meanings of Stress," *Business Horizons,* June 1979, p. 39.

Panic-Type Behavior

Under sufficiently severe distress, employees regress to a more primitive level of functioning and often lose control of the situation. The result can be an impulsive decision (such as firing competent employees to squeeze out additional profits) that overcompensates in terms of the reality of the situation. "Freezing" is another example of panic-type behavior. A typist whose average speed was about 120 wpm entered a typing contest sponsored by an office temporary help organization. While being observed and timed, her speed decreased to 30 wpm. She explained, "Sorry, I just froze. My fingers could hardly move."

Absenteeism

Distress is best escaped by absenting oneself from the source of the stress. Absenteeism is thus another approach to coping with job stress. Part of the psychological dynamics underlying common colds, alcoholism, and minor psychosomatic disorders is the fact that these problems create conditions that legitimize being absent. Even the light-headedness and dizziness that characterize mild attacks of anxiety are sufficient to keep one home from a stressful job situation.

Managerial Defense Mechanisms

An analysis has been made of how the defense mechanisms of illusion and denial relate specifically to executive functioning under stress.[14] *Illusion* as a defense mechanism of managers is illustrated by the comment "I'm doing all I can in these circumstances," in response to criticism of his operation. Consultants frequently face this defensive maneuver when attempting to initiate changes. Managers are unconsciously saying, "Get away from me. Change is a painful, anxiety-provoking thing. If I tell the consultant that I'm already doing all I can, I won't be forced to make any more changes."

Denial of problems is sometimes used by managers to defend against the anxiety produced by a realistic assessment of the situation, as illustrated by the following comment:

> Even though a possibly competitive product was already being market tested, managers of one company convinced themselves that their key customers, many of years' standing, would never be so disloyal as to leave them.[15]

---

[14]Robert H. Schaffer, "The Psychological Barriers to Management Effectiveness," *Business Horizons,* April 1971, pp. 17–25.

[15]Ibid., p. 20.

Preoccupation with Busywork

Many managers expend time on unimportant matters while crucial problems go unresolved. Crucial problems are anxiety provoking and stressful; making decisions about office landscaping is less anxiety provoking than is dealing with creditors. Managers looking for a behavioral escape from the stresses of dealing with important matters can find ample trivial meetings to attend and unimportant memos to read and sort. In any large organization, there are many undermotivated people eager to converse with managers about work-related, albeit unimportant, topics.

Busyness has also been described as an excellent defense against the anxiety often associated with strategic planning. One of management's most frequent rationalizations is: "We've simply got to figure out how to get some time around here to do some more thinking and planning."[16]

BURNOUT: A STRESS-RELATED PROBLEM

Burnout, similar to stress, is a condition that has been observed for many years, yet only recently has it been incorporated into the study of organizational behavior. Burnout refers to a drained-out, used-up feeling that takes place as a consequence of trying to help people in a work situation. It is said to affect mostly conscientious people who after awhile feel that they are not receiving the rewards from helping others that they think they should be receiving. As one caseworker described burnout, "We get burned out in our agency simply because nothing we do is ever enough. If we help one family, that's only a drop in the bucket. There are a thousand other families waiting in line to be helped."

Burnout has been studied primarily in relation to human service workers in such occupations as social work, clinical psychology, secondary school teaching, and police work. Managerial burnout is currently receiving attention. A recent conception of burnout describes the condition as "the total depletion of one's physical and mental resources caused by excessive striving to reach some unrealistic, job related goal or goals."[17] Burnout is akin to prolonged depression. A burnout "checklist" is presented in Figure 7–2.

Relationship to Stress

Stress is often the stepping stone to burnout. If you experience distress for a prolonged period of time, you may suffer the amorphous condition described as burnout. Some cases of teacher burnout are said to result from the long-term stress of having to worry

[16]Schaffer, "The Psychological Barriers to Management Effectiveness," p. 21.

[17]Oliver L. Niehouse, "Burnout: A Real Threat to Human Resource Managers," *Personnel,* September–October 1981, p. 29.

Directions

Answer the following statements as mostly true or mostly false as they apply to you.

	Mostly True	*Mostly False*
1. I feel tired more frequently than I used to.	_____	_____
2. I snap at people too often.	_____	_____
3. Trying to help other people often seems hopeless	_____	_____
4. I seem to be working harder but accomplishing less.	_____	_____
5. I get down on myself too often.	_____	_____
6. My job is beginning to depress me.	_____	_____
7. I often feel I'm headed nowhere.	_____	_____
8. I've reached (or am fast approaching) a dead end in my job.	_____	_____
9. I've lost a lot of my zip lately.	_____	_____
10. It's hard for me to laugh at a joke about myself.	_____	_____
11. I'm not really physically ill, but I have a lot of aches and pains.	_____	_____
12. Lately I've kind of withdrawn from friends and family.	_____	_____
13. My enthusiasm for life is on the wane.	_____	_____
14. I'm running out of things to say to people.	_____	_____
15. My temper is much shorter than it used to be.	_____	_____
16. My job makes me feel sad.	_____	_____

Interpretation

The more of these questions you can honestly answer mostly true, the more likely it is that you are experiencing burnout. If you answered twelve or more of these statements mostly true, it is likely you are experiencing burnout or another form of mental depression. Discuss these feelings with a physical or mental health professional.

FIGURE 7–2 The Burnout Checklist

Source: Andrew J. DuBrin, *Contemporary Applied Management* (Plano, Tex.: Business Publications, 1982), p. 243. Reprinted with permission.

about being physically assaulted by students (among other stressors). It can also be argued that burnout can serve as a stressor. If you feel depleted, apathetic, and washed up, as a consequence you will experience stress.

Stress and burnout are thus overlapping conditions. Similar to stress, the physical and emotional symptoms of burnout are ulcers, high blood pressure, jagged and bitten fingernails, wet palms, twitches, short temper, trembling hands, excessive drinking, impotence, hypochondria, paranoia, depression, and general joylessness.

A comparison of the symptoms of stress and burnout is shown in Table 7–1. It is important to recognize that the symptoms of both conditions vary from person to person and within the same person under different circumstances. One stressor may make you moody; another may trigger profuse perspiration.

Relationship to the Midcareer Crisis

Many people experience stress somewhere between the ages of thirty-five and fifty-five, when they begin to realize that their accomplishments have fallen far short of their aspirations. Referred to as the midcareer crisis, this condition is also related to the physiological slowing down and other life changes that occur in midlife. The condition has many similarities to burnout, as indicated by the following conception of the midcareer crisis:

> [It is the] general feeling of discontent and unhappiness people have concerning their jobs, the feeling of boredom and restlessness, the sense of entrapment, and absence of any significant challenge, and the vague dissatisfaction with the way their careers seem to have turned out. And it's all wrapped up in a distaste for getting up and going to work.[18]

Despite these similarities, burnout is a much more specific problem than is the midcareer crisis. Burnout comes about when one's anticipated rewards from working with people are not forthcoming.[19] The midcareer crisis is tied to midlife physiological and psychological changes. Another crucial distinction is that burnout can take place at any point in a career, whereas the midcareer crisis is believed to occur somewhere between ages thirty-five and fifty-five.

Treatment of Burnout

Since burnout is a stress-related condition, its treatment (and prevention) includes the same processes used to manage stress, a topic to be discussed shortly. In addition, various other strategies have been identified to help managers and others cope with burn-

---

[18]Theodore A. Jackson, "Turned Off by Your Job," *Industry Week,* January 29, 1973, p. 41. See also Manfred F. R. Kets de Vries, "The Midcareer Conundrum," *Organizational Dynamics,* Autumn 1978, pp. 45–62.

[19]Herbert J. Freudenberger, with Geraldine Richelson, *Burn Out: The High Cost of High Achievement* (Garden City, N.Y.: Anchor/Doubleday, 1980), p. 175.

TABLE 7–1 A Comparison of the Symptoms of Stress and Burnout

Stress	*Burnout*
1. Fatigue	1. Chronic fatigue
2. Anxiety	2. Unfulfilled need for recognition
3. Job dissatisfaction	3. Job boredom and cynicism
4. Less commitment	4. Detachment/denial of feelings
5. Moodiness	5. Impatience/irritability, paranoia, and feelings of omnipotence
6. Guilt	6. Depression
7. Poor concentration/forgetfulness	7. Disorientation/forgetfulness
8. Physiological changes (e.g., elevated blood pressure)	8. Psychosomatic complaints

Source: Oliver L. Niehouse, "Burnout: A Real Threat to Human Resource Managers," *Personnel*, September–October 1981, p. 28. Reprinted with permission from American Management Associations. © 1981 by AMACOM, a division of American Management Associations. All rights reserved.

out. Many of these have been presented in "burnout workshops." An outline of some of these strategies is presented next:

1. *Take the problem seriously.* Admit that the problem exists and take remedial action quickly.
2. *Develop realistic expectations.* Burnout arises when you try to accomplish so much that you are bound to fall short of your expectations.
3. *Realign goals.* Closely related to developing realistic expectations is the process of realigning goals once it appears that they might be too difficult to achieve.
4. *Rotate assignments.* Job rotation often brings about a new perspective and new rewards, and it prevents the staleness that often contributes to burnout.
5. *Alter working conditions.* Modify the job conditions so that the primary contributor to the problem is softened in impact, such as decreasing the number of hours worked by air traffic controllers in a given week.
6. *Try new activities.* Recognize that the more well-rounded your life, the more you are protected against burnout.
7. *Find a second career or new job.* For many burnout victims, the only real solution is to place themselves in a new occupational role.
8. *Get close to yourself and others.* Emotional closeness to others and yourself (getting in touch with your feelings) may soften the impact of burnout.
9. *Stroke yourself.* Pampering yourself can sometimes help you to overcome the symptoms of depression.
10. *Maintain a growing edge.* If you maintain a lifelong positive attitude toward self-development and self-improvement, the rewards you receive may help prevent psychological staleness.[20]

[20]The ten suggestions are adapted from Andrew J. DuBrin, *Contemporary Applied Management* (Plano, Tex.: Business Publications, 1982), pp. 236–40.

INDIVIDUAL METHODS OF
STRESS MANAGEMENT

Dozens of specific techniques, methods, and general strategies have been developed to help people cope with the adverse consequences of stress. Almost any experience designed to help people cope with emotional discomfort, from psychoanalysis to yoga, could be interpreted as a stress management technique. So far, the evidence is limited about the effectiveness of such techniques. Here we examine a half-dozen techniques, methods, and strategies that appear to be plausible ways of managing stress.

Fight or Flight

When we experience stress, a signal goes to the brain to either fight the stressor or leave the situation.[21] The stress serves as an energizing force, telling us to do something constructive about the uncomfortable situation. One form of constructive action would be to modify the problem that is creating stress for us. Thus a manager who was being constantly irritated by a tardy subordinate would confront the employee and encourage remedial action. At other times the most constructive action is to flee the situation, such as leaving a job or field you found to be inherently distressful. Many people leave supervisory jobs because they find the responsibility involved to act as a stressor.

Health Assessment and Exercise

Any program of stress management should begin with a thorough medical examination to evaluate the organism's capacity to tolerate stress. A weakened organ or system is the one most likely to be adversely affected by stress. If you have a weak heart, or a pulmonary system damaged by years of smoking, you are a strong candidate to experience heart disease or pulmonary disease (under the influence of a strong enough stressor). Among the useful indicators of susceptibility to stress are cholesterol levels, electrocardiograms, and respiratory capacity. A physician's evaluation of these factors, combined with an analysis of a person's smoking, eating, and exercise habits, may lead to an accurate assessment of a person's capacity to withstand stress.[22]

After the physical evaluation has been completed, a carefully designed program of physical exercise should prove helpful in both reducing and preventing stress. An example of a poorly designed exercise program would be one that makes you tense or places an overload on your cardiac system. For some people an intense, competitive sport such as racquet ball would fit this category. Good physical conditioning helps people to cope with distress. An employee with a cardiac system finely tuned by regular exercise is less likely to have a heart attack when overworked than is an employee whose heart is already weak from lack of exercise.

[21]Reitz, *Behavior in Organizations*, p. 247.
[22]Ibid., p. 246.

Physical exercise helps to prepare the body to withstand the pressures of demanding mental tasks. Jogging, in particular, seems to be effective in this regard for many people. Physical fitness makes people more resistant to fatigue and enables them to handle more challenging physical and mental tasks. A correlated fact is that a person's frustration tolerance is lowered at a time of fatigue and is raised when he or she is feeling energetic. A fatigued person is the more likely to overreact to job frustration. For physical exercise to be an effective stress reducer, however, it must become a positive addiction, not a sporadic measure.[23]

Lifestyle Changes

The holistic view of stress management contends that the best way to reduce and prevent stress is to lead a better all-around life. The person who eats well, sleeps well, exercises regularly, avoids drug and alcohol addiction, and deals constructively with personal problems is likely to minimize personal distress. A proponent of redesigning one's lifestyle to counter the adverse influences of stress recommends the *wellness triad* for coping with stress: relaxation, exercise, and diet.[24]

Relaxation refers to anything you do, including relaxation practice (as discussed later in this chapter) to relieve the stress accumulated through daily activities. *Exercise,* in this context, refers to any physical activity in which you engage to cause you to breath heavily for more than three to five minutes. *Diet* refers to the sum total of food substances introduced into your body. The relaxation, exercise, and diet factors form a Synergistic Wellness Triad, as shown in Table 7–2. Each of the three RED factors influences the other. For instance, if you exercise properly you will develop better food habits.

Improving Work Habits and Time Management

People typically experience stress when they feel that they are losing, or have lost, control of their jobs. Perhaps you are familiar with the distress associated with the feeling that you are hopelessly behind schedule on several important tasks. Conscientious people, in particular, experience distress when they cannot get their work under control. They value orderliness and meeting schedules and thus experience stress because their values are not being fulfilled. Improving your work habits and your management of time will help to relieve this source of stress.[25] Most published information about time management emphasizes similar ideas. Among these are making up lists of

[23]Rose Mary Rummell and John W. Rader, "Coping with Executive Stress," *Personnel Journal,* June 1978, p. 306.

[24]Karl Albrecht, *Stress and the Manager: Making It Work for You* (Englewood Cliffs, N.J.: Prentice-Hall, A Spectrum Book, 1979), pp. 221–27.

[25]Randall S. Schuler, "Managing Stress Means Managing Time," *Personnel Journal,* December 1979, pp. 851–54.

TABLE 7–2 A Synergistic Wellness Triad for Stress Management

This Factor:	Enhances This Factor:		
	Relaxation	Exercise	Diet
Relaxation	Calmer attitude makes living more enjoyable; relaxation and recreation get higher priority.	Changes time priority; makes it easier to make time for exercise.	Reduces anxiety-related eating; increased body awareness and relaxation reduce overeating at meals.
Exercise	Improved physical condition enables the body to consume stress chemicals; makes relaxation skills easier to learn and maintain.	Improved physical condition raises energy level; makes more exercise easier and enjoyable.	Regular exercise burns calories, promotes gradual weight loss, increases metabolic level, reduces appetite.
Diet	Reducing consumption of alcohol, tobacco, and caffeine makes parasympathetic relaxation response easier.	High-quality diet increases energy level; exercise becomes easier as weight decreases.	Good eating habits become easier to maintain over time.

Source: Karl Albrecht, *Stress and the Manager: Making It Work for You* (Englewood Cliffs, N.J.: Prentice-Hall, A Spectrum Book, 1979), p. 227.

activities to be performed, establishing priorities, working at a steady pace instead of spurts, concentrating on important tasks, and identifying and plugging time leaks.[26]

Relaxation Techniques

Various techniques have been developed that aim at helping people cope with stress by teaching them how to relax. The underlying theoretical premise is that if you can reduce the major symptoms of stress (tension), you will be able to function normally or better. Despite the appeal of this notion, the reader is cautioned that to cope with stress over the long term, you must take constructive action about the problem that acts as a stressor. The "fight or flight" strategy includes the idea of working out solutions to vexing problems. Here we sample a group of established and relatively new stress relaxation techniques.

Transcendental meditation (TM). The best known of the relaxation techniques is a process of establishing a physiological state of deep rest. Researchers contend that, during TM, the mind—although awake and able to respond to stimuli—is in a unique state of restful alertness. This state has been described as a fourth major state of consciousness. The other three are wakefulness, dreaming, and deep sleep.

[26]The classic book on this topic is Alan Lakein, *How to Gain Control of Your Time and Your Life* (New York: Peter Wyden, 1973). See also Ross A. Webber, *Time Is Money: The Key to Managerial Success* (New York: Free Press, 1980).

The TM technique is relatively simple once learned.[27] It consists of getting into a comfortable upright position, closing the eyes and relaxing, twenty minutes in the morning and evening. The mind is allowed to drift with no effort or control required. During TM the mind focuses on what is known as a mantra, a meaningless sound assigned to the meditator by his or her teacher. It is considered taboo for people to reveal their mantras. Also, somebody else's mantra supposedly will not help you.

At its best, TM produces deep rest and relaxation, with the meditator showing such distinct physiological changes as a decrease in heart and respiratory rate and lower bodily metabolism. Meditators frequently note that they feel more relaxed or less hurried than before they began to meditate. TM is also said to be useful in preventing future distress from taking place.

The relaxation response. Herbert Benson, a cardiologist at Harvard University, is one of many researchers and practitioners who question the claim of exclusivity made for TM. He offers a simple and workable method of relieving stress. By getting yourself quietly comfortable and thinking of the word "one" (or any simple prayer) with every breath, you can duplicate the tension-reducing effects of TM.[28] One striking advantage of the relaxation response method is that it is absolutely harmless and not time consuming.

The quieting response. Another similar method of stress management is the learning of a quieting response. According to this method, you identify a stressor situation that includes minor annoyances such as being stuck in traffic. You then take two deliberate deep breaths, paying attention to relaxing the jaw, the shoulders, and tongue. You tell yourself "I will not permit my body to get involved in this." This breaks the sequence of the stress response. To manage stress with the quieting response effectively, it will be necessary to repeat the procedure about twenty to forty times a day.[29]

Biofeedback control. Among the most scientific of the relaxation techniques are electronic machines that help you develop an awareness of muscle sensations throughout the body. After awareness comes the ability to control impulses that are ordinarily considered involuntary. For instance, through biofeedback you might be able to slow down your breathing rate. Assume then that you are making a presentation to department heads in your company. As they challenge you, it is apparent that your breathing rate is increasing and that you are losing control of the situation. By slowing down your breathing rate, you may be able to regain your composure and increase your effectiveness in the meeting.

In a typical biofeedback setup, a person is attached to an instrument that continuously measures muscle tension with an electromyograph (EMG). Feedback of this

[27]One applied source is Robert B. Kory, *The Transcendental Meditation Program for Business People* (New York: AMACOM, 1976).

[28]Herbert Benson, *The Relaxation Response* (New York: William Morrow, 1975).

[29]James S. Manuso, "Executive Stress Management," *The Personnel Administrator,* November 1979, p. 24.

type is designed to take continuous measurements of the tension level of particular muscles and to communicate this information to the person attached to the machine. As described by two biofeedback specialists,

> The humlike tone emitted by the EMG will change as it senses changes in the level of muscle tension. When the person tenses, the pitch of the tone rises proportionately. Conversely, when the person relaxes, the pitch falls. By hearing the pitch of the EMG tone, the person is able to learn how to control the tension level of his or her body. The continuous monitoring can allow the person to learn to relax muscle tension by continuously rewarding the desired behavior of relaxing with a lower pitch tone.[30]

Biofeedback control does not eliminate stress but rather, helps the distressed person to relieve the physical symptoms of distress, thus being able to concentrate on the problem situation. Tension headaches are a case in point. Headaches of this type are usually caused by contractions in the scalp and neck muscles. Using EMG biofeedback, a person can learn to relax these muscles even though the tension-producing stress is still present.

Flotation devices. A faddish approach to reducing tension and clearing the mind of thoughts about stressors is the flotation tub or "tension tank." A behavioral scientist originally developed these tanks as a method for studying sensory deprivation. Used as a method of relaxation training, the individual climbs into an enclosed 4-foot by 8-foot tank filled with a 10-inch deep solution of warm water, 800 pounds of epsom salts (which increases buoyancy), and a small amount of chlorine. During about an hour of flotation, the mind is supposed to "debug" itself as distractions are removed. Aside from feeling relaxed, the person in the tank is supposed to think more creatively.[31]

Tension tanks, like TM, jogging, and even napping undoubtedly help many people to relax. Unfortunately, all these methods sometimes become cults, leading their proponents to tell others that nothing else works as effectively, thus ignoring individual and situational differences.

Choosing the Best Method for Yourself

A logical question at this point is whether or not different coping approaches are particularly helpful for different types or sources of stress. In other words, which method is best for coping with which source of stress? This author is not aware of any evidence that answers this question. Coping methods have to be tried until you find one that is effective. Even tranquilizing medication is rarely related to particular sources of stress. People who are tense for many different reasons take the same brand and type of tranquilizer.

[30]Robert C. Ford and Jack Hartje, "Biofeedback and Management Stress," *Human Resource Management,* Fall 1978, p. 12.
[31]"The Great Tank Escape," *Newsweek,* May 4, 1981, pp. 82–83.

ORGANIZATIONAL METHODS
OF STRESS MANAGEMENT

Distress in the organization is often attributed to an employee's perception of an event (such as deciding one's job lacks meaning). Management, therefore, cannot be held accountable for everybody's idiosyncratic appraisal of events. Yet management can carry out actions that will be perceived by *most* of the employees affected as generating a healthy amount of stress. Here we mention several general and specific strategies useful in reducing and preventing distress.

Practice Good Management

Many of the sources of distress described in this chapter could be prevented by an appeal to generally accepted management principles. Conversely, poor management practices of almost any kind can induce stress reactions in people affected by those practices. A specific example is that stress reactions may occur when an individual has no control over people for whose work he or she is responsible (i.e., when his or her authority is not commensurate with responsibility). As mentioned earlier, the most casual observer of organizations will find many instances in which there is a serious gap between what a person is asked to accomplish and the authority given him or her to get it accomplished. Presumably, following the "authority-responsibility" principle would prevent many instances of stress.

Axiomatic to good personnel management is the placement of people in positions for which they are neither over- nor underqualified. Several of the sources of stress described earlier result from selection and placement errors. Mention was made of the stress that results when professional people are given assignments better suited to the qualifications of technicians or clerks. Adherence to elemental principles of selection would have avoided this problem and have eliminated a source of stress.

Participative Decision Making

Some employees find it stressful to be left out of important decisions that directly affect their welfare. Therefore, another managerial action capable of reducing stress reactions in some employees is the use of participative decision making (PDM). A caution is that participation in routine and trivial decisions is transparent to employees and might tend to increase, not decrease, job stress.[32] The underlying psychology to PDM as a stress reducer is perhaps that many people feel better when they believe that they are in control of their jobs. Participating in decision making is one way of gaining more control.

[32]John M. Ivancevich and Michael T. Matteson, *Stress and Work: A Managerial Perspective* (Glenview, Ill.: Scott, Foresman and Company, 1980), p. 212.

Clarify Role Prescriptions

Much organizational stress is created by role problems. Among them are role conflicts, role ambiguity, role overload, and role underload. It follows that clarifying role prescriptions could reduce and prevent many stressful job situations. Sometimes clarification of an employee's responsibility can eliminate the role conflict. A person assigned to a project might experience role conflict because the employee is not sure whose demands receive top priority—the project head or the functional (regular department) boss. The project leader, functional head, and the employee could hold a three-way conference to resolve this conflict. Clarifying role prescriptions (a concept that includes expectations and job descriptions) is a special case of practicing good management. In short, a general strategy for reducing role conflict is to let managers know clearly what is expected of them, by whom, and when.[33]

Improve the Organizational Climate

A macro approach to reducing and preventing distress is to create a healthy organizational climate—the general "feel" or psychological atmosphere of an organization. Research and opinion suggest that a supportive climate tends to increase job satisfaction and productivity and to decrease stress. One key dimension of organizational climate that has relevance for stress management is identification-alienation—the extent to which employees separate themselves psychologically from the organization.[34] Creating an organizational climate where employees at all levels feel more identified than alienated is much like practicing good management. Paternalistic practices, for example giving paychecks early around holiday time or dispensing free turkeys, may contribute to this feeling of identification with the organization.

Closely related to improving the organizational climate is the idea of providing social support to distressed employees. Evidence indicates that employees who do receive emotional support from peers experience fewer stress symptoms such as high blood pressure, escapist drinking, and excessive smoking.[35] An analysis of case histories suggests that emotional support from friends is instrumental in helping people to overcome the distress generated by personal adversity.[36] The relevance of this technique to organizational behavior is therefore not surprising.

Modifying the Organizational or Job Design

Rearranging or modifying the organizational design can sometimes reduce and prevent stress. The objective is to redesign the organizational structure so that the stress-

---

[33]Arthur P. Brief, "How to Manage Managerial Stress," *Personnel,* September–October, 1980, p. 29.

[34]Albrecht, *Stress and the Manager,* pp. 166–67.

[35]Katz and Kahn, *Social Psychology of Organizations,* 1978 ed., p. 603.

[36]Andrew J. DuBrin, *Bouncing Back: How to Handle Setbacks in Work and Personal Life* (Englewood Cliffs, N.J.: Prentice-Hall, A Spectrum Book, 1982).

ful elements in a job are reduced to a healthy level. One example would be to reduce the span of control (number of direct subordinates) of a manager who was overwhelmed with dealing with so many subordinates. The establishment of a complaint department also helps to reduce stress for employees who previously had to deal directly with irate customers. Now all complaints are channeled through one employee who is skilled in resolving conflict.

Stress-Release Activities in the Work Environment

In recognition of the dysfunctional consequences of distress, many organizations provide outlets for accumulated tensions within the work environment. Among the many stress reducers are job counselors, exercise rooms, and meditation rooms. Stress-releasing activities are found primarily in organizations that have a comprehensive approach to employee health, including employee assistance programs (described at the end of this section). Japanese industry has pioneered the "aggressive hostility room." This novel stress reducer is a small room equipped with some punching bags or inflatable figures (symbolic of the offending manager or co-worker?) that bounce back up after being punched or struck with a plastic bat. "Employees—and managers, too—can wander in on a break, take a few enthusiastic swings, and rid themselves of stored-up aggressive or hostile feelings."[37]

Employee Assistance Programs

A comprehensive approach to stress management is the Employee Assistance Program (EAP). Although these programs vary in format, their general purpose is to help employees who have personal problems that may harm job performance and lower attendance. Such problems include alcohol or drug dependency, personal and financial problems, family problems, and physical health problems. Problems such as these are both produced by stress and cause stress. To the extent that the employee is given help in dealing with these problems, he or she can break the cycle of ever-increasing stress. Many of the specialized techniques for dealing with stress already described in this chapter are included under EAP. Equitable Life Assurance, for example, conducts a biofeedback training program in company-owned and -operated laboratories.

The specific form of EAP could include a variety of mental or physical help procedures designed to reduce stress. Among them are psychotherapy to help overcome unresolved hostility, marriage counseling to overcome distracting marital problems, and financial counseling to overcome burdensome financial problems. The responsibility for seeking out assistance is up to the employee.

Most EAPs refer distressed employees to outside agencies that do the actual counseling. Other EAPs have in-house counselors who work with employees on such problems as alcoholism. Still other EAPs use both inside and outside resources.[38] A

[37]Albrecht, *Stress and the Manager,* p. 156.

[38]Edwin J. Busch, Jr., "Developing an Employee Assistance Program," *Personnel Journal,* September 1981, pp. 708–11.

model of a well-designed EAP is shown in Figure 7–3. The box labeled "Employee accepts referral to appropriate professional assistance" could refer to inside or outside assistance.

EAPs have grown in popularity for both humanitarian and economic reasons. They fit the spirit of the movement toward improving the quality of work life, and they have demonstrated their cost effectiveness. Alcoholism referrals are a case in point. EAPs typically report rehabilitation rates of about 60 percent with problem drinkers.[39] For alcoholism and other problems, the work performance of employees

[39]Thomas N. McGaffey, "New Horizons in Organizational Stress Prevention Approaches," *Personnel Administrator*, June 1979, pp. 26–32.

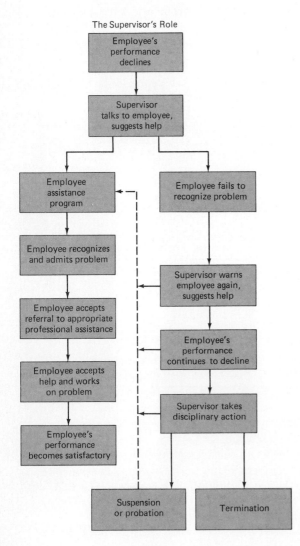

FIGURE 7–3 Employee Assistance Program

Source: Edwin J. Busch, Jr., "Developing an Employee Assistance Program," *Personnel Journal*, September 1981, p. 709. Reprinted with permission of *Personnel Journal*, Costa Mesa, Ca., all rights reserved.

referred to the EAP usually improves and money is saved in terms of time lost from work.

Encouraging Individual Awareness and Physical Fitness

An effective global strategy is for the organization to encourage employees to take care of themselves physically and mentally. Such measures include company-paid physicals, relaxation workshops, exercise facilities, and the sponsorship of stress management seminars. Few people today would deny the importance of stress management, but they may need constant reminders to translate this general awareness into individual action. One stress management consultant believes that proper management of stress is cost-effective. He notes,

> Stress is very expensive to organizations. Stress training is not just "a nice thing to do." It affects the bottom line. Heart attacks are 50% life style caused, of which stress is a major component. General Motors, a company which pays $900 million in health care costs annually—that's more than it spends on steel—estimates the replacement cost of an employee to be equal to 100% of his or her salary plus another 70% for death benefits.[40]

IMPLICATIONS FOR MANAGERIAL PRACTICE

1. Since it is known that an optimal amount of stress facilitates performance, a manager should strive to design the appropriate amounts and kinds of stressors for both individual employees and groups. Manipulating stressors is much like manipulating job challenge. Among the variables that could be manipulated to either increase or decrease stress are amount of job responsibility, goal difficulty, span of control, tightness of deadlines, closeness of supervision, and feedback. For example, increasing the amount of critical feedback serves as a stressor for most people. It is always necessary to consider which of the preceding variables has an effect on a given individual.

2. The organizational stress management strategies described in this chapter all have direct implications for managerial practice. In addition, it is useful for managers (and personnel specialists) to keep alert for the presence of potentially harmful stressors. Virtually any physical, chemical, or human factor is capable of producing harmful job stress. An office manager might discover that the noise level in the office acts as a stressor for some employees, or a plant manager might discover that the first-line supervisors are experiencing role conflict in trying to satisfy the opposing demands of production specialists and line management.

3. Almost no working person can escape the problems of having to manage work-related or nonwork-related stress. It is therefore important for the manager to embark

---

[40]"Dr. John Adams on Stress," *Trainer's Bookshelf,* p. 6.

upon a program of stress management following the type of strategies described in this chapter. At a minimum, every person should have some program of regular physical exercise to treat distress and to prevent further distress. Following this same logic, an important human resource management contribution any manager can make is to encourage his or her subordinates to embark upon a program of stress management.

Summary

- Stress-related disorders and burnout are a major concern to organizations today. Stress is a general physiological and psychological reaction to an external force or stressor. Its purpose is to help the individual cope effectively with the environment. Stress has physiological, psychological, and behavioral symptoms.

- An optimum amount of stress exists for most people in relation to most tasks. An individual's cognitive appraisal of a situation influences whether or not a given factor or stimulus will be stressful. The optimum amount of stress is referred to as eustress, which is a positive force in our lives. The wrong amount and type of stress is called distress. It usually results in negative outcomes for the individual and the organization.

- Individual differences help to determine whether or not a given circumstance proves to be a stressor. Among these differences are personality factors such as Type A personalities—impatient, demanding, overstriving people whose personality structures lead them into stressful situations. People who believe in an external locus of control are also susceptible to job stress. Personal conflicts that predispose people to job stress are perceived as lack of relevance in the work, frustrated ambitions, role conflicts about family versus work responsibilities, and dislike for rules and regulations.

- Organizational and environmental sources of stress include role conflict and ambiguity, role overload, role underload, job insecurity, insufficient authority, pressures toward conformity, and faulty job design and technical problems.

- The job-related consequences of distress take many forms. They include errors in concentration and judgment, panic-type behavior, absenteeism, managerial defense mechanisms, and preoccupation with busywork.

- Burnout refers to a drained-out, used-up feeling that takes place as a consequence of trying to help other people in a formal work role. It is defined as the total depletion of one's physical and mental resources caused by excessive striving to reach unrealistic job goals. Stress leads to burnout, but burnout itself may become a source of stress. Burnout may occur at any stage in a person's career, yet it has many similarities to the midcareer crisis. Techniques for managing burnout are similar to those for managing stress.

- Individual methods of stress management include fighting the problem or problems or leaving the situation, undertaking a health assessment and exercise, changing one's lifestyle (focusing on diet, exercise, and relaxation), and improving work habits and time management. Any program of stress management should also include a relaxation technique such as transcendental meditation, the relaxation response, the quieting response, or biofeedback control.

- Organizational methods of stress management could include almost any practice or technique that minimized stressors in the work environment. Among such strategies and techniques are the practice of good management, participative decision making, clarification of role prescriptions, stress-release activities in the work environment, modification of the organizational design, improvement of the organizational climate, employee assistance programs designed to help people deal with personal problems, and encouraging individual awareness and physical fitness.

Questions for Discussion

1. What symptoms do you experience when you are under heavy stress?
2. Does an employee have to be conscientious to experience job stress? Explain.
3. Provide two examples of low-paying, high-stress occupations.
4. Provide two examples of high-paying, low-stress occupations.
5. What relationship do you think may exist between lack of relevance and burnout for a given individual?
6. It has been observed that middle managers suffer from more stress disorders than do top-level managers, particularly when age is held constant. What do you think accounts for this finding?
7. What should a manager do if it is apparent that a subordinate is experiencing considerable distress?
8. An executive in a community agency asked, "Isn't burnout just another name for being tired?" What is your answer to this question?
9. What could be done to make the job of an air traffic controller less stressful?
10. Describe how income and stress may be linked for some people.
11. Why do some employees who need help fail to take advantage of the EAP?
12. After having read and studied this chapter, what are you going to do differently about dealing with stress?

An Organizational Behavior Problem

The Reluctant Belt Tightener

Recently, top management at the company decided to take decisive steps to "resize" the organization as part of a cost reduction program. A major part of its effort concentrated on reducing payroll costs. One part of the resizing was to lay off the bottom 5 percent of performers. Another was to ask for voluntary layoffs. Each person who volunteered to resign from the company would receive up to one year's severance pay, depending upon seniority. A third part of the reduction-in-force was to encourage early retirement of employees age fifty-five and over. The company also assumed that many employees would leave through normal attrition.

Executive vice president Ted Matthews was assigned overall responsibility for the reduction-in-force program. As Ted reviewed the layoff statistics, a glaring pattern emerged: the southwestern regional office was way behind the others in implementing the program. Ted scheduled an appointment with Conrad Baker, the southwestern regional vice president, to review the figures. Their initial conference took place at Conrad's office. Part of their dialogue was as follows:

Ted: As I suggested on the phone, Conrad, I'm concerned about your progress in carrying out this reduction-in-force. You're way behind the other regions in every category.

Conrad: Statistically that might be true, but I am carefully reviewing the situation. Besides there are humane considerations in our region. We have a close-knit group of employees.

Ted: That excuse won't work. We have a close-knit company in every region. Our other regions are facing the same problems you are.

Conrad: This whole episode is giving me a terrible feeling inside. I feel like the company is falling apart, and I'm being dragged down with it.

Ted: What do you mean, you think you're falling apart?

Conrad: Things are terrible across the board. My armpits are soaked all the time. My wife has asked me to sleep in another room until I can overcome thrashing around in bed. It's hard to sleep knowing that I have to squeeze out a faithful employee the next day. My clothing hardly fits me any longer. I've lost ten pounds in worrying about the situation.

Ted: Do you think you lack the guts to do the job?

Conrad: It's not a question of guts. It's just that the company is putting everybody, including me, under terrific pressure. There are human consequences to what we are doing. But I'll get done what needs to be done. I was hoping normal attrition would take up more of the slack than it has. Maybe if I take a brief vacation, I'll be able to tackle the reduction in force with a fresh perspective.

Ted: Do what you have to, but it sure is a bad time to go off on vacation and get your head together.

As Ted headed back to the home office, he began to wonder if Conrad was under the wrong type and amount of job pressure.

Questions

1. What should Ted do about the problems that Conrad is experiencing?
2. What strategy should Ted use to get Conrad moving on implementing the resizing program?
3. What should Conrad do about his feelings of discomfort?
4. Why should laying off people create stress for Conrad?

Additional Reading

BLAKE, ROBERT R., and JANE SRYGLEY MOUTON. *Grid Approaches to Managing Stress.* Springfield, Ill.: Charles C Thomas, 1980.

COOPER, CARY L., and R. PAYNE, eds. *Current Concerns in Occupational Stress.* New York: John Wiley, 1980.

EDELWICH, JERRY, and ARCHIE BRODSKY. *Burn-Out: Stages of Disillusionment in the Helping Professions.* New York: Human Sciences Press, 1980.

GREENWOOD, JAMES W., III, and JAMES W. GREENWOOD, JR. *Managing Executive Stress: A Systems Approach.* New York: Wiley-Interscience, 1979.

MATTESON, MICHAEL T., and JOHN M. IVANCEVICH. *Job Stress and Health.* New York: The Free Press, 1982.

MCLEAN, ALAN A. *Work Stress.* Reading, Mass.: Addison-Wesley, 1979.

MEGLINO, BRUCE M. "Stress and Performance: Implications for Organizational Policies." *Supervisory Management,* April 1977, pp. 22–28.

NELSON, JOHN G. "Burn Out: Business's Most Costly Expense." *Personnel Administrator,* August 1980, pp. 81–87.

NIEHOUSE, OLIVER L., and KAREN B. MASSONI. "Stress—An Inevitable Part of Change." *S.A.M. Advanced Management Journal,* Spring 1979, pp. 17–25.

PINES, AYALA. *Burnout: From Tedium to Personal Growth.* New York: Free Press, 1980.

RICE, BERKELEY. "Can Companies Kill?" *Personnel Administrator,* December 1981, pp. 54–59.

SELYE, HANS, ed. *Selye's Guide to Stress Research,* Vol. 1. New York: Van Nostrand Reinhold, 1980.

SONNENSTUHL, WILLIAM J. and JAMES E. O'DONNELL. "EAPS: The Why's and How's of Planning Them." *Personnel Administrator,* November 1980, pp. 35–38.

YATES, JERE E. *Managing Stress: A Businessperson's Guide.* New York: AMACOM, 1979.

CHAPTER 8

Creativity in Organizations

LEARNING OBJECTIVES

1. To understand the nature of creative behavior and the stages in creative thought.
2. To recognize the potential benefits and drawbacks of creativity on the job.
3. To describe several major characteristics of creative people and how these characteristics can be measured.
4. To develop a plan for improving your own creativity.
5. To discuss the nature of a creative organization and how organizations can become more creative.

Wallace "Bunny" Bertram, founder of modern skiing in this country, died at Woodstock, Vermont, not far from where he installed the first ski tow in America. Only weeks before his death, at seventy-three, Bertram was elected to the Skiing Hall of Fame.

It was in January 1934 that Bertram put together a Model T Ford engine, a long rope, and some pulleys on a hillside farm near Woodstock to "invent" this country's first ski tow.

Before that time, anyone who wanted to ski spent most of the time climbing for a few minutes of downhill. Bertram's idea caught on rapidly and skiers now have a choice of T-bars, chairlifts, gondolas, tramways, and even such sophisticated combinations as the eight-place chairlift.

Bertram also was one of the early founders of ski resorts, today a multi-billion-dollar business. He developed Suicide Six in Vermont and operated it for twenty-five years. It is still one of the leading small-mountain ski operations in the country. Bertram's love of skiing began at Dartmouth College.*

THE NATURE OF CREATIVITY

The story just presented about the origins of the ski lift illustrates several points about job creativity. Above all, creativity is the ability to process information in such a way that the result is new, original, and meaningful. Finding a way to transport skiers up a mountain has certainly been "meaningful" from a business standpoint. Since creativity is an ability, it must be translated into behavior before the results can help either the individual or the organization. Thus creative behavior results in discovering new and improved means to accomplish our purposes. Just dreaming about a rope tow would not have led to the popularization of downhill skiing—the Model T engine had to actually be linked together with some rope and pulleys.

The news item also illustrates that creative ideas of major significance are sometimes remarkably simple. They can be nontechnical and unrelated to artistic or scientific achievement. A manager at General Motors made an important contribution by suggesting a way of selling more of the houses the company had bought from transferred employees. His solution was to put a new GM car in the driveway of homes sold at or beyond a certain price: the more expensive the home, the more expensive the car. A person buying one of these homes would receive the car as part of the purchase price. Home sales improved significantly as a result of this novel idea.

CREATIVITY AND DECISION MAKING

To make a decision is to choose among alternatives, and the type of decision you face determines how much creativity will be required. A *programmed* decision is one in which specific rules or policies dictate which actions to take, such as deciding which employees are eligible for early retirement when an early-retirement policy has already been formulated. Nonprogrammed decisions are those in which the problems and fac-

*Floyd King, "Business at Resorts Should Peak Today," *Rochester Democrat and Chronicle,* February 15, 1981, p. 11E.

tors involved differ from previous ones and require unique decisions. Creativity is required to make effective nonprogrammed decisions.[1] In this chapter, we emphasize the creative aspects of decision making, but it is important to recognize that creative problem solving is embedded in the decision-making process. The relevance of creative decision making to modern organizations is emphasized in a statement made by a group of managers:

> Creative decision making and problem solving are two of the most important talents that employees can possess, talents that are necessary for the financial health and prosperity of any firm. Unless a firm can respond with unique products/services, innovative marketing strategies and creative responses to complex problems, it may find itself losing sales, shares of the market and profits.[2]

Decision-Making Stages

At the core of the decision-making framework shown in Figure 8–1 are six decision-making stages: problem identification and clarification, finding creative alternatives, weighing alternatives, making the choice, implementation, and evaluation of outcomes. A process of this complicated nature is recommended for nonprogrammed decisions. Faced with a repetitive (programmed) decision, it may not be worth a person's time to use the entire procedure described here.

Problem identification and clarification. An important part of decision making is to recognize that a problem exists—that there is a gap between the desired and the actual. Bunny Bertram, for example, somehow began to realize that skiers were dissatisfied with walking up a mountain. Once a person has discovered or been assigned a problem, the problem must be placed into clearer focus; a more definitive diagnosis is called for. A sound diagnosis of the problem should provide answers to the following questions:

1. Just what gaps exist between the results we desire and the existing or predicted state of affairs?
2. What are the direct root causes and the intermediate causes of the gaps?
3. Does the broader context of the problem place limits within which we should find a satisfactory solution?[3]

Finding creative alternatives. The second stage in the decision-making process will be amplified throughout this chapter. It represents the intellectual freewheeling aspect of decision making. All kinds of possibilities are explored here, even if they seem unrealistic at the outset.

[1]R. Dennis Middlemist and Michael A. Hitt, *Organizational Behavior: Applied Concepts* (Chicago: Science Research Associates, 1981), p. 121.

[2]David R. Wheeler, "Creative Decision Making and the Organization," *Personnel Journal,* June 1979, p. 374.

[3]William H. Newman, E. Kirby Warren, and Jerome E. Schnee, *The Process of Management: Strategy, Action, Results,* 5th ed. (Englewood Cliffs, N.J.: Prentice-Hall, 1982), p. 110.

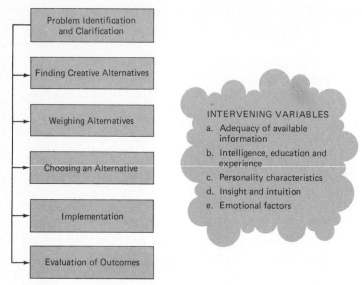

FIGURE 8–1   The Decision-Making Process

Weighing alternatives.   Next, the relative value of the alternatives generated in the previous stage are compared. Pros and cons of each possible decision should be carefully examined.

Choosing an alternative.   "The purpose in choosing an alternative is to solve a problem in order to achieve predetermined goals and objectives."[4] A decision is not an end in itself but a means to an end. A stand has to be taken to solve an individual or organizational problem. Ultimately, every important decision must be made on the basis of values, whether or not these values have been carefully thought through by the decision maker. If a company decides to replace two assembly workers with one robot, a statement of values has been implicitly expressed.

Despite a careful evaluation of alternatives, some ambiguity still exists in most managerial decisions. Even when decision alternatives are supported by charts, figures, statistics, and computer printouts, the decision maker may still be left with a feeling of ambiguity. Personnel decisions are often the most ambiguous of all because of the difficulties in making precise predictions about most aspects of human behavior.

Implementation.   Converting the decision to action is the fifth major stage in the decision-making process. Unless a decision is implemented, it is really not a decision at all. Drucker observes from his consulting experience that "The flaw in so many policy statements, especially those of business, is that they contain no action commitment—to carry them out is no one's specific work and responsibility."[5]

---

[4]James L. Gibson, John M. Ivancevich, and James H. Donnelly, Jr., *Organizations: Behavior, Structure, Processes,* 4th ed. (Plano, Tex.: Business Publications, 1982), p. 423.

[5]Peter F. Drucker, "The Effective Decision," *Harvard Business Review,* January–February 1967, p. 96.

Evaluation of outcomes. The final stage of the decision-making process closely resembles the scientific method. Answering the deceptively simple question, "How good (or bad) was the decision I made?" is a complex activity. Compounding the problem is the difficulty in establishing criteria by which the adequacy of managerial decision can be judged. Nevertheless, without some kind of accurate feedback, decision making can rarely be improved. After feedback has been gathered, the decision quality may be characterized as optimum, satisficing, or suboptimum.

Optimum decisions are those that lead to most favorable outcomes. Alan C. Filley and Robert J. House note that a decision alternative is optimum only if "There exists a set of criteria that permits all alternatives to be compared, and the alternative in question is preferred, by these criteria, to all others."[6] *Satisficing* decisions are those that meet with a minimum standard of satisfaction; they are adequate, acceptable, and passable. Most decision makers discontinue their search for alternatives once they find one that is satisficing.

Suboptimum decisions are those that lead to undesirable outcomes because their consequences are dysfunctional to the system. If a suboptimum decision has been reached, the individual and/or organization is once again faced with a problem. The decision-making process (which is really a method of solving problems) is therefore repeated.

Intervening Variables in Decision Making

Although information about decision making and problem solving has been widely disseminated in the academic and management literature, people still vary widely in their decision-making skills. And some situations are more favorable for making optimum decisions than others. The term "intervening variables" covers those factors that account for individual and situational differences in decision-making capacity. As was shown in Figure 8–1, these intervening variables can include many different aspects of human behavior. Six of the most influential sets of variables are summarized here.

Adequacy of available information. People who have ready access to current, relevant, and vital information are in a good position to identify problems and make decisions. The inventory-control manager who has access to valid computerized information about inventory throughout the company is in a better position to make inventory decisions than is one who lacks or ignores this information.

Intelligence, education, and experience of decision maker. In general, intelligent, well-educated, and experienced managers are in a better position to make decisions than are their counterparts of lesser intelligence, education, and experience. On occasion, an uninformed, naïve person will see a solution to a problem that a more experienced person will miss.

[6]Alan C. Filley and Robert J. House, *Managerial Process and Organizational Behavior* (Glenview, Ill.: Scott, Foresman and Company, 1969), p. 106.

Personality characteristics of decision maker.   Personality factors can also influence decision-making ability. For example, people with a rigid mental set will have difficulty finding problems even when they are intelligent, well educated, and experienced and have access to good information. Perfectionism is another of many behavioral traits that can inhibit decision making. A person who keeps searching for the perfect alternative to a problem may wind up never reaching a decision.

Insight and intuition of decision maker.   Another important intervening variable that influences whether or not problems will be found or effective decisions made is the basic insight and intuition of the decision maker. People who develop a sharp intuitive sense about a certain category of decisions (such as guessing which type of TV show will appeal to next year's audience) accumulate power because of this ability.

Emotional factors.   Nonrational factors play a key role in all stages of decision making. Reason and emotion enter into most decisions. Even when decisions appear to be based almost entirely upon hard data, *which* data are selected for inclusion in the decision-making process are influenced to some degree by emotion. Sometimes an unprofitable product will be carried by a company because that product is a sentimental favorite of one or more key executives.

Unpredictable, uncontrollable factors.   Serendipity, the gift of unexpectedly finding valuable things, is a germane example of an unpredictable factor entering into the decision-making process. Minnesota Mining Company (now **MMM**) originally developed its Scotch Tape as an office product to mend torn documents. The product shortly became a widely known, multipurpose household product. The person who made the decision to develop Scotch Tape probably had no idea of the potential of his or her decision.

DECISION MAKING AND INFORMATION PROCESSING

The conception of decision making just presented is logical and therefore widely accepted. A newer conception of decision making focuses on the person making the decision as a processor of information.[7] If we understand how people process information, it is believed that we can predict the decision they will make and perhaps help people make more accurate decisions. According to Andrew D. Szilagyi, Jr., and Marc J. Wallace, Jr., an information processing approach to decision making asks three basic questions:

1.   What information does a decision maker use in making a decision?
2.   What are the relative weights or importance placed on various pieces of information?

[7]Rene M. Dawis and B. Corrigan, "Linear Models in Decision Making," *Psychological Bulletin,* Vol. 8, 1974, pp. 95–106.

3. In what ways does the decision maker combine information from various sources in arriving at a choice?[8]

The first question involves uncovering the kinds of information actually used in making a decision. Typically, the decision maker wastes considerable data and focuses on a limited sample that seems particularly relevant. For example, many people purchase a new car (an unprogrammed decision) without even asking for a test drive. Presumably, for these people, such information as styling, color, and the trade-in allowance is more influential in making a car-buying decision than is the performance of the vehicle. When people are evaluated for a job, the interviewer often arrives at a yes or no decision within the first five minutes of the interview. Information obtained later in the interview is used to confirm the acceptance or rejection decision arrived at earlier.

The second question is similar to the decision-making stage called weighing alternatives. Individual and situational differences exert a strong influence in determining how much weight is assigned to the same information. Market research conducted by a manufacturer of personal computers revealed that many sales of microprocessors were purchased by managers for home use. Apparently, these managers felt that they had to learn how to use computers to compete favorably with the new generation of college graduates, most of whom are computer literate. The factor given considerable weight by this subset of buyers was "user friendliness." How easy it was for a neophyte to learn the system was more important than many of the more technical features of the microprocessor.

The third question deals the most directly with creativity. A creative person, by definition, processes information in such a way that the result is new, original, and meaningful. Or, more simply, the creative person makes a useful connection between two or more bits of information that less creative people would not notice. Aside from the creative aspect of information processing, three alternative decision processes have been observed:

1. *Compensatory.* A high value on one criterion can offset a low value on another criterion. If an automobile were a convertible, you might purchase it despite the fact that you disliked its color.
2. *Conjunctive.* Minimum standards of acceptability must be achieved on all criteria. A manager might decide that, before hiring an administrative assistant, that individual must pass a set standard on such factors as education, appearance, intelligence, and motivation.
3. *Disjunctive.* A high value on any one of the criteria is acceptable. You might accept a new position, providing that it was outstanding with respect to either salary, growth potential, or geographic location or nature of the work.[9]

[8]Andrew D. Szilagyi, Jr. and Marc J. Wallace, Jr., *Organizational Behavior and Performance,* 2nd ed. (Glenview, Ill.: Scott, Foresman and Company, 1980), p. 411.
[9]Ibid., pp. 412–13.

STAGES IN THE CREATIVE PROCESS

Since the importance of creativity in many aspects of life has been recognized by behavioral scientists for a long time, much effort has been devoted to understanding the process by which creative ideas and creative behavior emerge. In Chapter 4, we discussed the role of the right cerebral hemisphere in facilitating creativity. Here we are concerned with the stages in a person's thinking and behavior that produce a creative result.[10] Several writers on the topic have arrived at conceptions of the creative process similar to the five-stage process described next.

1. *Problem finding or sensing.* The individual discovers that something is worth working on or becomes aware that a problem or disturbance exists. Thus a housing developer might say, "People are getting more and more concerned about the cost of heating and cooling their homes. We've come a long way in offering more efficient cooling and heating systems. What else can we do?"

2. *Immersion of preparation.* The individual concentrates on the problem and becomes immersed in it. He or she will tend to recall and collect information that seems relevant, dreaming up possible alternatives without refining or evaluating them. The housing developer might say, "It seems to me that other industries have been faced with the problem of consumer resistance to the energy costs of using their products."

3. *Incubation or gestation.* After assembling the information, the individual keeps it in the back of his or her mind for a while. It has been postulated that the subconscious mind begins to take over. Although the individual is not actively working on the problem, it is simmering in the back of his or her mind. It would therefore be justifiable for a person to go for a walk outside during working hours to engage in creative problem solving. While the problem is simmering, the subconscious may be trying to arrange facts into a meaningful pattern.

4. *Insight or illumination.* If you have ever experienced a sudden insight about a vexing problem, you will understand this step in the creative process. The new integrative idea flashes into the individual's mind at an unexpected time, perhaps while waking up, going to sleep, eating, or jogging. Experienced creative people often carry idea notebooks to record quickly these flashes of insight. The housing developer achieved his flash of insight while in a shopping mall: "Why not build compact homes to save energy, just like compact cars?"

5. *Verification and application.* The individual sets out to prove by logical argument (including the gathering of supporting evidence) or experimentation that the creative solution has merit. The builder might call for some market research about the marketability of compact houses sold in other locations, at other times. Or he or she might

[10]Two sources are John F. Mee, "The Creative Thinking Process," *Indiana Business Review,* February 1956, pp. 4–9, and Frederic D. Randall, "Stimulate Your Executives to Think Creatively," *Harvard Business Review,* July–August 1955, pp. 121–28. This information has been synthesized by James A. F. Stoner, *Management,* 2nd ed. (Englewood Cliffs, N.J.: Prentice-Hall, 1982), p. 424.

take the plunge and build a few houses for speculation. Tenacity may be required here, since most novel ideas are rejected at first on the grounds of impracticality. Many experienced idea generators recognize that rejection is part of the game. Many inventions and books that later proved to be huge successes were at first rejected by several sources. *Gone with the Wind* and xerography are two historically significant cases in point.

CREATIVITY AND JOB PERFORMANCE

Raw creativity alone may not necessarily lead to productive results. Creativity needs to be buttressed by support from the organization and good administrative skills to obtain good results. Creativity implies "bringing something new into being; innovation implies bringing something new into use."[11] Innovation is considered to be creativity followed up by action to the point where it has economic utility. Erno Rubik, the man who invented the Rubik cube, was not the same person who launched it into a phenomenally successful product.

From the standpoint of many organizations, creative ideas are plentiful. Many employees can think of farfetched ideas for new products or services, but few have the skills and/or motivation to carry these ideas through to fruition. Another reason that raw creativity alone is a mixed blessing is that your creative idea may be something that has been unsuccessfully tried in the past. Unless you are familiar with other people's past experience in your field, you may be wasting time on pursuing ideas that have already proved unworkable.

Cost of Creativity

Another aspect of the relationship between creativity and job performance is that creativity sometimes has dysfunctional consequences. Many creative suggestions are resisted because they are politically inappropriate, as when an employee's suggestion is antithetical to the beliefs of a key executive. Several other costs of creativity have been observed.[12]

1. Time spent on creativity is diverted from time available for other purposes. As one cynical manager put, "I wish my people would spend less time dreaming up new ideas and more time getting the work out."
2. Creatively behaving employees tend to be high-turnover risks. Perhaps they are restless by nature and they may be lured away by other firms because of their ability to be creative.

[11]Lawrence B. Mohr, "Determinants of Innovation in Organizations," *American Political Science Review,* March 1969, p. 112. See also Ross A. Webber, *Management: Basic Elements of Managing Organizations,* rev. ed. (Homewood, Ill.: Richard D. Irwin, 1979), p. 475.

[12]The first three reasons are based on Ramon J. Aldag and Arthur P. Brief, *Managing Organizational Behavior* (St. Paul: West, 1981), p. 293.

3. An organization that emphasizes creativity is less predictable and more changing than is one that emphasizes productivity and efficiency. Some people find these conditions distressing.

4. Nurturing creativity can be an expensive process in terms of carrying people on the payroll whose ideas may not have an economic payout for many years. Many organizations therefore choose to purchase creative ideas from the outside. Most innovations in business and industry follow the pattern of a new idea being developed in a small firm and later introduced into a big firm that launches it to market.[13]

THE CREATIVE INDIVIDUAL

Part of understanding creativity in organizations is understanding the makeup of creative people. A wide range of studies points toward one distinguishing characteristic of creative people. In general they are more emotionally loose, open, and flexible than their less creative counterparts. The accompanying box presents a representative list of traits and characteristics of creative people (see pages 203–204).

Eliciting creative behavior from an individual requires the right interaction between a person and the environment. A psychologist who has researched creativity in organizations concludes that the optimum condition for creativity requires a person of intelligence, that is, a person with a high capacity for learning, for abstracting, for solving problems, and for making discriminations. (Brilliance is not required, but creative people are good at generating many different ideas in a short period of time.) The potentially creative person must also have a strong ego and be confident that he or she can overcome problems.

Next, the person must encounter a need (environmental condition) that stimulates the formulation of a goal. There must be a barrier to reaching this goal (a mild stressor), and there must be no standard way of overcoming the barrier. Finally, the person must have insight, a broad awareness of self and the environment. The researcher concludes that "when these conditions are met, creative behavior is almost a certainty.[14]

Behavioral Characteristics of Leaders Who Encourage Creativity

The accompanying box lists characteristics of creative executives themselves. A related issue is the nature of behaviors engaged in by leaders who elicit creative responses from their subordinates. Research conducted at the Center for Creative Leadership provides some useful clues on this topic as summarized next.

---

[13]This observation is still valid today. Reported by James R. Bright, ed., *Technological Forecasting for Industry and Government* (Englewood Cliffs, N.J.: Prentice-Hall, 1968), p. 381.

[14]This discussion and the quotation are from Daniel G. Tear, as quoted in *Issues & Observations,* February 1981, p. 5 (Center for Creative Leadership, Greensboro, North Carolina).

A CREATIVITY CHECKLIST

The creative executive has distinct characteristics that set him or her apart from less creative colleagues. However, there is no perfect example, because no one executive could have all the attributes of creativity to a uniformly high degree. Thus there are many gradations of attributes and skill levels among creative persons, but all such executives have some measure of these characteristics in common.

The following checklist of behavioral and personality attributes offers further insight into the makeup of the creative executive. It was adapted from a listing by Dr. Ross L. Mooney of Ohio State University, a leading researcher in the field of creativity.

The creative executive:

Is willing to give up immediate gain or comfort to reach long-range goals.

Is determined to finish work even under conditions of frustration.

Has a great amount of energy, which is channeled into productive effort.

Perseveres despite obstacles and opposition.

Has the ability to examine his or her own ideas objectively.

Has great initiative.

Is irritated by the status quo and refuses to be restricted by habit and environment.

Has many hobbies, skills, and interests.

Can open up to experiences and abandon defenses.

Feels that he or she has untapped potentials.

Criticizes himself or herself more than others do.

Is not afraid to ask questions that show ignorance.

Likes ventures involving calculated risks.

Believes, even after repeated failures, that he or she can solve a problem.

Has the confidence to meet new problems, find out new things, and do original things.

Is willing to stand alone if integrity demands it.

Does not blame others or make excuses for errors or failures.

Competes with self rather than with others.

Has neither fear nor resentment toward authority; is nonauthoritarian.

Is open and direct with people and respects their rights.

Wants to examine things from another's viewpoint.

Knows how to give inspiration and encouragement.

Is governed by inner stimulus rather than outer command and has a rising level of aspiration.

Gets the greatest pleasures from creative activities.

Believes that fantasy and daydreaming are not a waste of time.

Has an inherent desire and respect for perfection.

Wants to integrate utility with the aesthetic.

Moves toward solutions using intuition.

Knows that getting stuck on a problem frequently stems from asking the wrong question.

Is alert to new perspectives, and knows that much depends on the angle from which a problem is seen.

Is willing to listen to every suggestion, but judges for himself or herself.

Always has more problems and work than time to deal with them.

Source: Eugene Raudsepp, "Are You a Creative Executive?" *Management Review,* February 1978, p. 15. Reprinted with permission from American Management Associations. © 1978 by AMACOM, a division of American Management Associations. All rights reserved.

1. *Willingness to absorb risks taken by subordinates.* Managers who encourage creativity allow subordinates considerable freedom to be creative. One cost of such freedom is mistakes, which are sometimes expensive. In contrast, managers who are afraid of mistakes restrict the freedom of subordinates to experiment, hoping to eliminate most errors.

2. *Ability to accept half-developed ideas.* Managers of productive research laboratories do not "insist that every *t* be crossed and every *i* be dotted before supporting an idea. They are willing to listen to, and support, 'half-baked,' proposals and encourage subordinates to press on." Creativity-inducing leaders will not graciously welcome every preposterous idea, since they have good intuitive sense about what might work. Yet they are hesitant to discourage the creative flow of ideas or to kill innovation in the bud.

3. *Willingness to "stretch" organizational policy.* Creativity-inducing leaders do not normally disregard rules and policies, but they do know when the rules need to be stretched for the greater good. One manager, for example, allowed a subordinate to take a computer terminal home over the weekend to solve a vexing problem. In the quiet of her home, the programmer arrived at a creative solution to the problem of multiple mailings of the same advertisement to the same household.

4. *Ability to make quick decisions.* Leaders who foster creativity have good track records in recognizing which half-processed idea is worth betting on. They are also courageous enough to immediately commit resources to carrying it out. The creativity-discouraging manager is predisposed to calling for further studies or putting the suggested idea in the hands of a committee.

5. *Good listening skills.* Productive managers listen to their subordinates and build on their suggestions. They seem to have the ability to draw out the best in their personnel and then add to it. A manager who encourages creativity will listen to an idea and then ask a question such as "How might your idea be applied on an even wider scale?"

6. *Refusal to dwell on mistakes.* Creativity-inducing leaders are "willing to begin

with the world as it is today and work for a better future. They learn from experience, but do not wallow in it."

7. *Enjoyment of their job.* Managers who induce creativity among subordinates are enthusiastic, invigorating individuals who like what they are doing. They exude a contagious enthusiasm.[15]

You will note one apparent contradiction about the "creative executive" depicted in the boxed listing versus the creativity-inducing manager just described. Perfectionism is supposedly important to be creative yourself whereas this characteristic inhibits creativity in subordinates. This duality may be true, but in this author's experience, highly creative people are not perfectionists. Or at least they are not obsessed with details. In fact, they are "loose." It is also worth noting that the findings about creativity presented here should not be taken too literally. They represent trends that are true much of the time, but not always.

THE MEASUREMENT OF CREATIVITY

The theoretical and applied importance of creativity has prompted the development of a wide variety of tests and exercises for its measurement. Some of these, such as the one presented at the end of this chapter, are scientifically validated instruments. Others are not much more than captivating parlor games with little merit for predicting job behavior or measuring differences in creative potential. Underlying any attempt at measuring a person's capacity for creative behavior is the assumption that creativity is a dimension of human behavior. If creativity is dimensional, it is false to classify people as creative or uncreative. More accurately, creativity is like height, numerical reasoning, and strength. People vary considerably in these dimensions, but everybody has some height, some numerical reasoning, and some strength. Creative potential appears to be distributed normally. Three ways in which creativity is measured are mentioned here: puzzle problems and tasks, questionnaires, and job behavior.

Puzzles

A popular method of measuring creative potential is by means of puzzles. The assumption is made that a person who readily solves these puzzles is more creative than is a person who cannot solve many of them. One important factor in favor of measuring creativity through puzzles is that they probably do measure ability to overcome routine or conventional thinking. You have to look at these puzzles with an unconventional mental set to solve them. One factor that dissuades us from using such puzzles

---

[15]Reported in *Issues & Observations,* February 1978, pp. 6–7. See also David Campbell, *Take the Road to Creativity and Get Off Your Dead End* (Niles, Ill.: Argus Communications, 1977).

to measure creativity is that many of them correlate too highly with general mental ability (intelligence) or a specific ability such as visualization. Many people who perform well on these puzzles are therefore intelligent, but not necessarily creative. Presented next are three representative examples of the type of puzzle questions used to measure creativity.[16] The answers are found in footnote 17.

    A.   Marie was asked to deliver a box containing nine donuts. The baker marked the box with roman numerals IX to indicate the quantity inside. On her way home Marie was tempted by the donuts and ate three of them. To cover up, she decided to change the marking on the box, but IX was written with a ball-point pen. Nevertheless, Marie figured out a way to alter the numbers without erasing or crossing out. Can you?

    B.   You wish to pour exactly 13 gallons of water into a large drum. However, you only have one 5-gallon bucket and one 6-gallon bucket. How can you do it?

    C.   A doctor and his son are involved in a head-on automobile collision. The doctor is killed and his son is severely injured. When the boy is brought into the operating room, the surgeon says in anguish, "I can't operate on this boy. He is my son." How is this possible?

Questionnaires

Creativity questionnaires are of two general types. One requires the solution of a series of small problems, as shown in Figure 8–2. Although such tests may measure creativity, they are also highly correlated with inductive reasoning ability and abstract thinking. The Creative Personality Test shown in Figure 8–2 illustrates an attempt to measure the potential for creative thinking through a person's attitudes toward important issues related to creative behavior and thinking. For example, creative people do not mind, and may even welcome, vague instructions (see statement 5). They enjoy providing their own structure to situations.

Direct Observation of Job Behavior

Many managers judge the creative potential of subordinates by observing their behavior under actual job conditions. An experienced manager may give a subordinate a

[16]Virtually the same puzzles are found in many articles and books about creativity. The first two presented here are from Harry E. Gunn with Violet C. Gunn, "Test Your Creativity," *Success,* July 1981, pp. 26–27. The third is a widely circulated verbal puzzle.

[17]Answer to A: The solution is to add something to the marking "IX," rather than subtracting. When you add an "S," the marking becomes "SIX."

Answer to B: Fill the large drum twice with the 6-gallon bucket. Then refill the 6-gallon bucket, pour 5 gallons into the 5-gallon bucket, and pour the 1 gallon remaining in the 6-gallon bucket into the large drum.

Answer to C: The surgeon is the boy's mother. This same anecdote has been used as an informal measure of sexist thinking!

trial assignment to measure his or her creativity before giving the subordinate a creative assignment of major consequence. For example, "We need a theme for this year's annual banquet. Could you bring me back an idea by tomorrow?" Or a manager might simply observe how creatively the subordinate handles a variety of assignments. One limitation to using trial assignments and observations of typical job behavior as measures of creativity is that the samples may be unrepresentative. Suggesting a theme for a banquet may not involve the same type of creativity as that required for suggesting new methods of cost cutting.

METHODS OF IMPROVING INDIVIDUAL CREATIVITY

Since creative behavior is generally valued by organizations and individuals, much time, energy, and money has been invested in methods for its improvement or enhancement. Here we describe three methods of improving individual creativity along with a set of creative growth attitudes and behaviors to accomplish the same purpose. In general, the same methods and techniques are used to improve individual and group creativity. Many creativity improvement workshops are conducted with natural work groups or with strangers placed in a group. In Chapter 10 we discuss several methods of improving group decision making, such as the Delphi and nominal group techniques. Such methods can also be considered ways of improving creative decision making in groups. The brainstorming and Gordon methods described in the present chapter are also used to improve both individual and group creativity.

Brainstorming

The term *brainstorm* has become so widely known that it is often used as a synonym for a creative idea. Developed by advertising executive Alex Osburn many years ago, brainstorming really means to use the *brain* to *storm* a problem.[18] Today this technique is used both as a creativity training program and as a method of finding alternatives to organizational and personal problems. In its simplest form, a group of people assemble in a room and spontaneously call out alternatives to a problem facing them. Any group member is free to enhance or "piggyback" or "hitchhike" upon the contribution of any other member of the group. Anything goes, however bizarre it sounds at the time, during the free association portion of brainstorming. Later one person or the group may be assigned the tasks of evaluating (sorting out and editing) some of the unrefined ideas.

Here are some of the new business ventures suggested by the outpourings of several brainstorming sessions: safe deposit box rental centers; survival stores (for nuclear

---

[18]Jack Halloran, *Applied Human Relations: An Organizational Approach* (Englewood Cliffs, N.J.: Prentice-Hall, 1978), p. 214. The original reference is Alex F. Osborn, *Applied Imagination* (New York: Scribner, 1953).

Word Hints to Creativity*

The object of this exercise is to find a fourth word that is related to all three words listed below. For example, what word is related to these?

cookies   sixteen   heart   _____

The answer is "sweet." Cookies are sweet; sweet is part of the word "sweetheart" and part of the phrase "sweet sixteen."

What word is related to these words?

poke   go   molasses   _____

Answer: slow

Now try these words:

1. surprise	line	birthday	_____
2. base	snow	dance	_____
3. rat	blue	cottage	_____
4. nap	rig	call	_____
5. golf	foot	country	_____
6. house	weary	ape	_____
7. tiger	plate	news	_____
8. painting	bowl	nail	_____
9. proof	sea	priest	_____
10. maple	beet	loaf	_____
11. oak	show	plan	_____
12. light	village	golf	_____
13. merry	out	up	_____
14. cheese	courage	oven	_____
15. bulb	house	lamp	_____

If you were able to think of the "correct" fourth word for ten or more of these combinations of words, your score compares favorably with that of creative individuals. A very low score (about one, two, or three correct answers) suggests that performing such remote associations is not yet a strength of yours. Here are the answers:

1. party	5. club	9. high	13. make
2. ball	6. dog	10. sugar	14. Dutch
3. cheese	7. paper	11. floor	15. light
4. cat	8. finger	12. green	

Creative Personality Test†

The following test will help you to determine if certain aspects of your personality are similar to those of a creative individual. Since our test is for illustrative and

*This test, developed by Eugene Raudsepp, is quoted from "Ideas: Test Your Creativity," *Nation's Business*, June 1965, p. 80. Reprinted by permission from *Nation's Business*, Copyright 1965 by *Nation's Business*, Chamber of Commerce of the United States.

†From Andrew J. DuBrin, *Human Relations: A Job-Oriented Approach*, 2nd ed. (Reston, Va.: Reston, 1981), pp. 53–54. Reprinted with permission of Reston Publishing Company, a Prentice-Hall Co., 11480 Sunset Hills Road, Reston, VA 22090.

FIGURE 8–2 Measuring Creative Potential by Questionnaires

research purposes, proceed with caution in mind. Again, this is not a standardized psychological instrument. Such tests are not reprinted in general books.

	Mostly True	*Mostly False*
1. Novels are a waste of time. If you want to read, read nonfiction books.	_____	_____
2. You have to admit, some crooks are very clever.	_____	_____
3. People consider me to be a fastidious dresser. I despise looking shabby.	_____	_____
4. I am a person of very strong convictions. What's right is right; what's wrong is wrong.	_____	_____
5. It doesn't bother me when my boss hands me vague instructions.	_____	_____
6. Business before pleasure is a hard and fast rule in my life.	_____	_____
7. Taking a different route to work is fun, even if it takes longer.	_____	_____
8. Rules and regulations should not be taken too seriously. Most rules can be broken under unusual circumstances.	_____	_____
9. Playing with a new idea is fun even if it doesn't benefit me in the end.	_____	_____
10. As long as people are nice to me, I don't care why they are being nice.	_____	_____
11. Writing should try to avoid the use of unusual words and word combinations.	_____	_____
12. Detective work would have some appeal to me.	_____	_____
13. Crazy people have no good ideas.	_____	_____
14. Why write letters to friends when there are so many clever greeting cards available in the stores today?	_____	_____
15. Pleasing myself means more to me than pleasing others.	_____	_____
16. If you dig long enough, you will find the true answer to most questions.	_____	_____

Scoring the Test

The answer in the *creative direction* for each question is as follows:

1. Mostly False	7. Mostly True	13. Mostly False
2. Mostly True	8. Mostly True	14. Mostly False
3. Mostly False	9. Mostly True	15. Mostly True
4. Mostly False	10. Mostly True	16. Mostly False
5. Mostly True	11. Mostly False	
6. Mostly False	12. Mostly True	

FIGURE 8–2 Measuring Creative Potential by Questionnaires (Cont.)

Give yourself a plus one for each answer you gave in agreement with the keyed answers.

How Do You Interpret Your Score?

As cautioned earlier, this is an exploratory test. Extremely high or low scores are probably the most meaningful. A score of twelve or more suggests that your personality and attitudes are similar to that of a creative person. A score of five or less suggests that your personality is dissimilar to that of a creative person. You are probably more of a conformist (and somewhat categorical) in your thinking, at least at this point in your life. Don't be discouraged. Most people can develop in the direction of becoming a more creative individual.

FIGURE 8–2 Measuring Creative Potential by Questionnaires (Cont.)

accidents, earthquakes, floods, volcanic eruptions); one-stop energy stores; sheepskin seatcovers; omelette shops; post office box rentals; and pet hotel/grooming centers.[19]

Rules for brainstorming. Adhering to a few simple rules or guidelines helps to ensure that creative alternatives to problems will be forthcoming. The activity generally falls into place without frequent reminders about guidelines; nevertheless, some structure helps to prevent brainstorming sessions from becoming an ordinary group discussion. An experience-based set of rules reads as follows:

1. About five to seven people should be present in the group. Too few people and not enough suggestions are generated; too many people and the session becomes uncontrolled.
2. All participants are given the chance to suggest alternatives to the problem without asking permission to speak. Spontaneity is encouraged.
3. No criticism or evaluation is allowed. All suggestions should be welcomed and it is particularly important to refrain from derisive laughter.
4. Freewheeling is encouraged. Outlandish ideas often prove fruitful. It is easier to tone down than originate an idea.
5. Quantity and variety are essential. The greater the number of ideas put forth, the higher the probability of a breakthrough idea.
6. Combinations and improvements are encouraged. Building upon the ideas of others, including combining them, is very productive (the piggyback principle).
7. Notes must be taken during the sessions either manually or with a mechanical device. One group member may act as a recording secretary.
8. Overstructuring by following any of the seven rules too rigidly should be guarded against. Brainstorming is a spontaneous group process.[20]

[19]*New Business Bulletin,* 1982 Winter Business Catalog, American Entrepreneurs Association, 2311 Pontius Avenue, Los Angeles, California 90064.

[20]Andrew J. DuBrin, *Contemporary Applied Management* (Plano, Tex.: Business Publications, 1982), pp. 50–51.

One major criticism of brainstorming is that it may produce superficial ideas and is unsuited for solving complex problems or developing strategies. The technique can be very time consuming including both the idea-generating and evaluation sessions. The primary value of brainstorming seems to be in the generation of specific alternatives to a concrete problem such as finding a name for a new product or suggesting a new business venture.[21]

Group versus individual brainstorming. The founder of brainstorming and his advocates emphasize the value of group participation in brainstorming. It is said to stimulate creative thinking in one member as a result of hearing the ideas of others. A series of experiments has supported the opposite conclusion, namely, that group participation, when brainstorming, inhibits creative thinking—brainstorming by yourself is superior to the group approach. Several explanations have been offered for the inhibiting effects of the group upon the generation of useful ideas:

- There is a tendency for groups to pursue a limited train of thought, thus restricting the diversity that the same number of individuals might generate.
- Time limitations are imposed on group members since they have to share time with other members. Creative group members would then feel compelled to hold back on some good suggestions rather than be perceived as "hogs."
- The social facilitation of dominant (and potentially less creative) responses may take place due to the presence of other group members.

Studies that have attempted to control these three factors have nevertheless replicated the finding that brainstorming works more effectively with individuals than with groups.[22] Despite the pessimism about group brainstorming, some experimental evidence exists that under the right conditions group brainstorming is superior to the individual approach. One of the right conditions is that people make their contributions in sequence rather than simultaneously. By adding the sequencing procedure to typical brainstorming instructions, group performance becomes as good as individual performance.[23] Even if group solutions were slightly inferior to individual solutions, they might be chosen by some organizations. Employees are more willing to implement a solution to a problem that stems from a group meeting than from a unilateral decision.

The Gordon Technique (Synectics)

Another popular way of improving creativity is a group of methods developed by William J. Gordon. The original purpose of synectics was to help in the development of

[21]Henry L. Sisk and J. Clifton Williams, *Management and Organization,* 4th ed. (Cincinnati: South-Western, 1981), p. 119.

[22]The literature on this topic is reviewed in Barbara K. Maginn and Richard J. Harris, "Effects of Anticipated Evaluation on Individual Brainstorming Performance," *Journal of Applied Psychology,* April 1980, pp. 219–20.

[23]Thomas J. Bouchard, "What Ever Happened to Brainstorming?" *Industry Week,* August 2, 1971, p. 29.

new products. While the primary object of brainstorming is to generate a large number of ideas, synectics aims to uncover one radically new idea focused on a specific problem area. The common theme to synectic techniques are two complementary procedures: making the strange familiar and making the familiar strange. Making the strange familiar involves thorough analysis, gathering as much relevant information as possible concerning the problem. Making the strange familiar allows for a new perspective from which to view the world. Synectics relies on the use of four types of analogies to achieve its purpose: personal, direct, symbolic, and fantasy.[24]

1.   *Personal analogy* requires the person to psychologically identify with an object, as in this example: "If the problem is finding a new way to open a particular kind of container, each member of the group in turn plays the role of the container (bottle, box, can) and the remaining members question him or her about the best way to get in."

2.   *Direct analogy* involves looking for parallel facts, knowledge, or technology in a different field or domain from the one being worked on (not unlike the immersion or preparation step in creative thinking). Previous knowledge can come from the most unlikely places, as described by Gordon:

> A Synectics group was faced with the problem of inventing a dispenser that could be used with such products as glue and nail polish. The dispenser was to be in one piece, without a top to be removed and replaced with each use. The mouth of the dispenser would have to be opened for dispensing and closed tightly after each use. The group members considered various analogies in nature and finally designed a dispenser, based on one member's childhood experiences on a farm, modeled after the anal sphincter of a horse.[25]

3.   *Symbolic analogy* incorporates the use of objective and personal images to describe the problem. The development of Pringles (those potato chips packaged like tennis balls) involved symbolic analogy. The synectics group was asked to solve the problem of compressing the potato chips into a small place without squashing them. Part of the creative task was to find an instance in which nature had solved the problem. In the end, the group members found an analogy in leaves. Although fragile, leaves were found compressed and undamaged. This feat is accomplished because the leaves are compressed while moist. It was decided to make Pringles by compressing moist potato chips.[26]

4.   *Fantasy analogy* requires group members to ask, "How in my wildest fantasy can I get this thing to happen?" A problem that plagues many communities—telephone cables that become penetrated with moisture during rainstorms—might be attacked in this manner. Somebody might suggest, "How about some gremlins that take out their

---

[24]William J. J. Gordon, *Synectics* (New York: Harper & Row, 1961). Some of the discussion here is based on an analysis presented in Aldag and Brief, *Managing Organizational Behavior,* pp. 294–95.

[25]Quoted from Aldag and Brief, *Managing Organizational Behavior,* p. 295.

[26]Niles Howard, "Business Probes the Creative Spark," *Dun's Review,* January 1980, pp. 35–36.

mops and sponges during a rainstorm and wipe the cables dry?" Such thinking could lead to the development of a spongelike sheath around the cables.

A unique feature about the Gordon techniques is that in their pure form, only the group leader knows the exact nature of the problem. In this way, people do not stop thinking once they have come up with an immediate solution to a problem. Members continue to search for new ideas, having only a vague description of the nature of the problem.

A very skilled leader is required for synectics, while brainstorming groups require minimal leadership. It would appear that synectic groups require more sophistication on the part of members than do brainstorming groups.

Attribute Listing

An uncomplicated method of finding creative alternatives to a structured problem is the attribute listing technique.[27] The first step is to isolate the major characteristics or attributes of a product, an object, or an idea. Among these attributes might be size, color, shape, and cost. Each major attribute is then considered in turn and is changed or modified in every conceivable way. As in brainstorming, no attempt is made at first to evaluate or criticize the suggestions or limit the suggested changes. Separating evaluation and judgment from creation gives novel and useful ideas a better chance of surfacing. Using the attribute listing method, the question might be asked, "Would a lawn mower be better, bigger, smaller, rounder, slower, faster, with a cutting surface other than metal?" Some of the modern developments in lawn mowers (such as cutting with nylon cord or floating on air) would suggest that at least some variation of the attribute listing method has been used in their development.

Creative Growth Attitudes and Behavior

Based upon his many years of research and observation in the field, Eugene Raudsepp concludes that you can increase your creative ability by heeding the following exercises and principles:[28]

1. *Keep track of your ideas at all times.* Keeping an idea notebook at hand will help you to capture a permanent record of flashes of insights and good ideas borrowed from others.

2. *Pose new questions every day.* "A questioning, inquiring mind is a creatively active mind. It is a mind that constantly enlarges the circumference of its awareness."

---

[27]Herbert G. Hicks and C. Ray Gullett, *The Management of Organizations,* 3rd ed. (New York: McGraw-Hill, 1976), p. 221.

[28]This listing is excerpted and paraphrased from Eugene Raudsepp, "Exercises for Creative Growth," *Success Unlimited,* February 1981, pp. 46–47.

3. *Maintain competence in your field.* The data explosion makes information obsolete quickly. Having current facts in mind gives you the raw material to form creative links among bits of information.

4. *Read widely in fields that are not directly related to your field of interest.* Once you learn how to cross-index the pieces of information you gather, you will be able to cross-fertilize seemingly unrelated ideas.

5. *Avoid rigid patterns of doing things.* Try to overcome fixed ideas and look for new viewpoints. Attempt to push for more than one solution to your problems. Develop the ability to let go of one idea in favor of another.

6. *Be open and receptive to your own as well as to others' ideas.* Be alert to seize on tentative, half-formed ideas and possibilities. Entertain and generate your own far-fetched or seemingly silly ideas. If you are receptive to the ideas of others, you will learn new things that can help you behave creatively.

7. *Be alert in observation.* Look for the subtle aspects of objects, situations, products, processes, and ideas. The greater the number of new associations and relationships you form, the greater your chances of arriving at creative and original combinations and solutions.

8. *Engage in creative hobbies.* Included here are manual hobbies such as arts and crafts and mental hobbies such as doing puzzles and exercises. "Creative growth is possible only through constant and active use of your mind."

9. *Improve your sense of humor and laugh easily.* Humor helps to relieve tension, and most people are more productively creative when they are relaxed.

10. *Adopt a risk-taking attitude.* The fear of failure dampens creativity so be willing to fail on occasion.

11. *Have courage and self-confidence.* Many people surrender just when they are on the brink of a solution, so persist when you are seeking a unique solution to a problem.

12. *Learn to know and understand yourself.* "Creativity is an expression of one's uniqueness. To be creative, then, is to be oneself."

An underlying theme to these suggestions is that self-discipline is required to develop more creative behavior. The advice offered also assumes that the individual has sufficient control over his or her emotions and intellect to develop new habits and break old ones. Although most people would not find following all the advice just given closely, the suggestions are probably more useful in the long run than attending an isolated creativity training program. Nevertheless, programs such as brainstorming help you develop some of the skills needed to follow the twelve suggestions (such as "Avoid rigid patterns of doing things").

IMPROVING ORGANIZATIONAL CREATIVITY

To achieve creative solutions to problems (and to think of new opportunities), an organization needs more than creative people. Creativity is the combined influence of creative people working in a creative environment that encourages, or at least does not discourage, creativity. Again, $B = f(P \times E)$. A valid generalization about creativity-inducing organizations is that they are organic since they have some of the properties of a living organism such as adaptation to the outside environment. A creative organization is much like a creative person in that it is open, loose, adaptive, and free-flowing. Here we are concerned with two issues around which most of the information about creative organizations has centered: the freedom versus structure debate and the characteristics of a creative organization. Both the previous section about creative leaders and the following section about implications for managerial practice provide additional information about creating an environment that fosters individual creativity.

The Freedom versus Structure Debate[29]

One way of encouraging creativity in organizations is to give imaginative people as much time and other resources as feasible to "play around" with ideas. Such freedom often pays big dividends in terms of eliciting creative behavior. Polaroid, which was considered a highly creative organization in its prime, was led by a creative individual, Edwin Land. When one of Polaroid's research staff was asked how he defined research projects, he said "With Dr. Land around, that is no problem." In other words, the researcher had considerable latitude in choosing which problem to investigate.

The counterargument is that the freedom to innovate has its drawbacks. General Electric is reported to have a library filled with ideas it cannot use because of the magnitude of the investment required to implement them or the risk involved. Du Pont, which has researched the topic of creativity extensively, has found that when its most productive people were given the structure of being told which problems to pursue, they produced more than when they were just playing around with ideas. Many other case histories of creative behavior have been collected in response to the necessity of earning money or working under pressure or against deadlines.

The Center for Creative Leadership concludes that there is an element of truth to both sides of the debate. At times, freedom is required for creativity; at other times, structure; and sometimes, a combination of the two. "The playful organization enables people to be more creative; the structured enables the creative to be more productive. The former may be more appropriate for research, the latter for business, but each has elements of the other and neither could succeed without embracing its opposite."

Characteristics of a Creative Organization

Organizations that are able to capitalize upon much of the creative potential of their members generally have certain characteristics in common. As you read the following

---

[29]This discussion follows closely that presented in Center for Creative Leadership, February 1978, pp. 2–3. The quotations are from the same source.

list, notice that many of the characteristics of creative organizations are similar to those of creative people and creativity-inducing managers.[30]

- A trustful management that does not overcontrol people.
- Open channels of communication among members of the organization; a minimum of secrecy.
- Considerable contact and communication with outsiders to the organization.
- Large variety of personality types.
- Willingness to accept change, but not enamored with change for its own sake.
- Enjoyment in experimenting with new ideas.
- Encouragement of people of various education levels and generalists (not only specialists) to contribute new ideas.
- Commitment to retain creative people even during time of financial difficulty.
- Little fear of the consequences of making a mistake.
- Selection and promotion of people primarily on the basis of merit.
- Employment of techniques for encouraging ideas, such as suggestion systems and brainstorming.
- Sufficient financial, managerial, human, and time resources to accomplish its goals.
- An organizational structure flexible enough to bend with whatever strain innovation may bring.
- A process already established for developing new ideas into products or services.
- Managers and leaders at the top of the organization who support innovation.

IMPLICATIONS FOR MANAGERIAL PRACTICE

Eugene Raudsepp has formulated some tips that can be applied by managers to achieve a more creative organization. They fit well the underlying theme of this chapter that a permissive atmosphere is helpful for fostering creativity but that people may also need structure and guidance to help bring about creative behavior. Among Raudsepp's suggestions are the following:

1. Consciously experiment with new forms of organization, searching for suitable ways of maximizing the support that individuals inside the company can give to one another in respect to creativity.

2. Locate individuals in the company who have a capacity for helping others realize their creative potential. Let these individuals become tutors and teachers to promising personnel.

3. As critical incidents of success or failure in creativity occur, write them up and make use of them as subject matter for discussion and analysis.

---

[30]Three sources here are Gary A. Steiner, ed., *The Creative Organization* (Chicago: University of Chicago Press, 1965), pp. 22–23; Maurice I. Zeldman, "How Management Can Develop and Sustain a Creative Environment," *S.A.M. Advanced Management Journal,* Winter 1980, pp. 23–27; and Hubert Jaoui, quoted in *Issues & Observations,* Center for Creative Leadership, February 1981, p. 4.

4.   Create an educational situation in which small discussion groups openly explore their problems and views together. Put creative people in communication with each other, particularly across interdisciplinary lines.

5.   Dramatize problems to which creative solutions are known to be needed and organize brainstorming teams to solve them, using people from different backgrounds.

6.   Analyze the situations surrounding individuals who have gone stale, noting areas in which they will not respond and the opportunities that might be stimulating to them if provided.

7.   Do not regard creativity as a gimmick but as the name for an integral aspect of total management policy.[31]

8.   In addition to all these points, management must stay alert to the importance of keeping a balance between analytic and creative thought.[32] Analytic thought is the application of the scientific research method of problem solving. It helps to bring order out of disorder. Creative thought is relatively undisciplined, and often illogical, but it supplies the new concepts and ideas needed in an organization. Controls can be established after creativity has been unleashed.

Summary

- Creativity is the ability to process information in such a way that the result is new, original, and meaningful. Creative behavior results in discovering an improved means of accomplishing our purpose. Creativity is embedded in the decision-making process, which consists of six stages: problem identification and clarification, finding creative alternatives, weighing alternatives, making the choice, implementation, and evaluation of outcomes. Intervening variables such as emotional factors can influence any stage of decision making. Another conception of decision making is to regard the decision maker as a processor of information.

- The stages in the creative process are (1) problem finding or sensing, (2) immersion or preparation, (3) incubation or gestation, (4) insight or illumination, and (5) verification and application.

- Creativity does not lead inevitably to high job performance. It needs to be buttressed by support from the organization and good administrative skills to improve organizational effectiveness. Innovation is considered to be creativity followed up by action to the point where it has economic utility. Creativity can have dysfunctional consequences, including the diversion of time from other urgent activities, high turnover among creative personnel, and high cost.

- Creative people are more emotionally loose and open and flexible than noncreative

[31]Raudsepp, "Creative Growth Games," p. 47.
[32]Hicks and Gullett, *The Management of Organizations,* p. 231.

people. They also have good problem-solving ability and insight (awareness of self and environment). Creativity is sparked when the creative person is faced with an environmental condition that stimulates the formulation of a goal.

- Leaders who foster creative behavior among their subordinates are characterized by the following behaviors themselves: they are comfortable with half-developed ideas, are willing to stretch organizational policy, are able to make quick decisions, have good listening ability, do not dwell on mistakes, and enjoy their jobs.

- Creativity is normally distributed in people. Among the ways of measuring it are through performance on puzzles designed to measure creative thinking, questionnaires, and direct observation of creative behavior on the job.

- A number of methods have been developed to improve or elicit creative thinking. The best known is brainstorming, which involves the spontaneous generation of ideas in a small-group setting. Brainstorming can also be conducted alone, and the results are generally equal or superior to the group method. The Gordon technique, or synectics, is another popular method of improving creative thinking. It aims to uncover one radically new idea focused on a problem area. The general strategy of synectics is to use analogies to make the strange familiar and the familiar strange. An uncomplicated creativity improvement technique is attribute listing. Each attribute of a product, object, or idea is mentally changed or modified in every conceivable way.

- A general strategy for improving individual creativity is to maintain creative growth attitudes and behaviors. It involves such considerations as keeping track of one's ideas, reading widely, staying flexible, engaging in creative hobbies, adopting a risk-taking attitude, and learning to know and understand oneself.

- Creativity is the combined influence of creative people working in an environment that encourages creativity. Creative organizations, like creative people, are flexible and free-flowing. Yet organizations must provide both freedom and structure to capitalize upon creativity. Among the many characteristics of a creative organization are open channels of communication, willingness to accept change, a willingness to risk mistakes, flexible organization structures, and executives who support innovation.

Questions for Discussion

1. Maurice Zeldman, a management and technical consulting group head, contends that "creativity declines with age and too much education." What is your reaction to his statement?

2. Does your present program of study enhance or inhibit creativity? Discuss the evidence you have for your answer.

3. Think of the most creative person you know. How does he or she fit the conclusions reached about the characteristics of creative people in this chapter?

4. What steps would have to be taken to determine if the creative personality tests presented in this chapter are a valid measure of creativity?

5. Give two examples of higher-level jobs that you think do not require creativity. Explain your reasoning.

6. If you wanted to hire a creative person, how could you determine whether or not that person was creative?

7. Is it important for creative employees to be managed by creative superiors? Why or why not?

8. Some people in so-called "creative fields" claim that they dislike working under deadlines, that creativity cannot be rushed. What is your position on this issue?

9. A few people have mentioned that being creative did them more harm than good on the job. How do you explain their view?

10. Does a person's manner of dress tell you anything about his or her creativity with respect to job behavior? Explain.

An Organizational Behavior Problem

How Creative Are You?*

In recent years, several task-oriented tests have been developed to measure creative abilities and behavior. While certainly useful, they do not adequately tap the complex network of behaviors, the particular personality traits, attitudes, motivations, values, interests, and other variables that predispose a person to think creatively.

To arrive at assessment measures that would cover a broader range of creative attributes, our organization developed an inventory type of test. A partial version of this instrument is featured below.

After each statement, indicate with a letter the degree or extent with which you agree or disagree with it: A = strongly agree, B = agree, C = in between or don't know, D = disagree, E = strongly disagree. Mark your answers as accurately and frankly as possible. Try not to "second guess" how a creative person might respond to each statement.

1. I always work with a great deal of certainty that I'm following the correct procedures for solving a particular problem. _____

2. It would be a waste of time for me to ask questions if I had no hope of obtaining answers. _____

3. I feel that a logical step-by-step method is best for solving problems. _____

4. I occasionally voice opinions in groups that seem to turn some people off. _____

5. I spend a great deal of time thinking about what others think of me. _____

6. I feel that I may have a special contribution to give to the world. _____

7. It is more important for me to do what I believe to be right than to try to win the approval of others. _____

8. People who seem unsure and uncertain about things lose my respect. _____

9. I am able to stick with difficult problems over extended periods of time. _____

10. On occasion I get overly enthusiastic about things. _____

11. I often get my best ideas when doing nothing in particular. _____

*Contributed by Eugene Raudsepp, president, Creative Research, Inc., Princeton, New Jersey. Reprinted with permission from *Personnel Journal,* April 1979, pp. 218, 220, 223.

12. I rely on intuitive hunches and the feeling of "rightness" or "wrongness" when moving toward the solution of a problem. _____

13. When problem solving, I work faster analyzing the problem and slower when synthesizing the information I've gathered. _____

14. I like hobbies that involve collecting things. _____

15. Daydreaming has provided the impetus for many of my more important projects. _____

16. If I had to choose from two occupations other than the one I now have, I would rather be a physician than an explorer. _____

17. I can get along more easily with people if they belong to about the same social and business class as myself. _____

18. I have a high degree of aesthetic sensitivity. _____

19. Intuitive hunches are unreliable guides in problem solving. _____

20. I am much more interested in coming up with new ideas than I am in trying to sell them to others. _____

21. I tend to avoid situations in which I might feel inferior. _____

22. In evaluating information, the source of it is more important to me than the content. _____

23. I like people who follow the rule "business before pleasure." _____

24. One's own self-respect is much more important than the respect of others. _____

25. I feel that people who strive for perfection are unwise. _____

26. I like work in which I must influence others. _____

27. It is important for me to have a place for everything and everything in its place. _____

28. People who are willing to entertain "crackpot" ideas are impractical. _____

29. I rather enjoy fooling around with new ideas, even if there is no practical payoff. _____

30. When a certain approach to a problem doesn't work, I can quickly reorient my thinking. _____

31. I don't like to ask questions that show ignorance. _____

32. I am able to more easily change my interests to pursue a job or career than I can change a job to pursue my interests. _____

33. Inability to solve a problem is frequently due to asking the wrong questions. _____

34. I can frequently anticipate the solution to my problems. _____

35. It is a waste of time to analyze one's failures. _____

36. Only fuzzy thinkers resort to metaphors and analogies. _____

37. At times I have so enjoyed the ingenuity of a crook that I hoped he or she would go scotfree. _____

38. I frequently begin work on a problem that I can only dimly sense and not yet express. _____

39. I frequently tend to forget things such as names of people, streets, highways, and small towns. _____

40. I feel that hard work is the basic factor in success. _____

41. To be regarded as a good team member is important to me. _____

42. I know how to keep my inner impulses in check. _____
43. I am a thoroughly dependable and responsible person. _____
44. I resent things being uncertain and unpredictable. _____
45. I prefer to work with others in a team effort rather than solo. _____
46. The trouble with many people is that they take things too seriously. _____
47. I am frequently haunted by my problems and cannot let go of them _____
48. I can easily give up immediate gain or comfort to reach the goals I have set. _____
49. If I were a college professor, I would rather teach factual courses than those involving theory. _____
50. I'm attracted to the mystery of life. _____

Scoring Instructions. To compute your percentage score, circle and add up the values assigned to each item:

	Strongly Agree A	Agree B	In-Between or Don't Know C	Disagree D	Strongly Disagree E
1.	−2	−1	0	+1	+2
2.	−2	−1	0	+1	+2
3.	−2	−1	0	+1	+2
4.	+2	+1	0	−1	−2
5.	−2	−1	0	+1	+2
6.	+2	+1	0	−1	−2
7.	+2	+1	0	−1	−2
8.	−2	−1	0	+1	+2
9.	+2	+1	0	−1	−2
10.	+2	+1	0	−1	−2
11.	+2	+1	0	−1	−2
12.	+2	+1	0	−1	−2
13.	−2	−1	0	+1	+2
14.	−2	−1	0	+1	+2
15.	+2	+1	0	−1	−1
16.	−2	−1	0	+1	+2
17.	−2	−1	0	+1	+2
18.	+2	+1	0	−1	−2
19.	−2	−1	0	+1	+2
20.	+2	+1	0	−1	−2
21.	−2	−1	0	+1	+2
22.	−2	−1	0	+1	+2
23.	−2	−1	0	+1	+2
24.	+2	+1	0	−1	−2
25.	−2	−1	0	+1	+1
26.	−2	−1	0	+1	+2
27.	−2	−1	0	+1	+2
28.	−2	−1	0	+1	+2
29.	+2	+1	0	−1	−2
30.	+2	+1	0	−1	−2

	Strongly Agree A	Agree B	In-Between or Don't Know C	Disagree D	Strongly Disagree E
31.	−2	−1	0	+1	+2
32.	−2	−1	0	+1	+2
33.	+2	+1	0	−1	−2
34.	+2	+1	0	−1	−2
35.	−2	−1	0	+1	+2
36.	−2	−1	0	+1	+2
37.	+2	+1	0	−1	−2
38.	+2	+1	0	−1	−2
39.	+2	+1	0	−1	−2
40.	+2	+1	0	−1	−2
41.	−2	−1	0	+1	+2
42.	−2	−1	0	+1	+2
43.	−2	−1	0	+1	+2
44.	−2	−1	0.	+1	+2
45.	−2	−1	0	+1	+2
46.	+2	+1	0	−1	−2
47.	+2	+1	0	−1	−2
48.	+2	+1	0	−1	−2
49.	−2	−1	0	+1	+2
50.	+2	+1	0	−1	−2
80 to 100	Very creative				
60 to 79	Above average				
40 to 59	Average				
20 to 39	Below average				
−100 to 19	Noncreative				

Further information about the test "How Creative Are You?" is available from Princeton Creative Research, Inc., 10 Nassau St., P.O. Box 122, Princeton, N.J. 08540.

Additional Class Assignment. For each class member, collect the score on the test just presented and the Creative Personality Test (presented in Figure 8-2) for each individual in the class. Write down your prediction of the correlation coefficient between the two sets of scores; then compute the *r*. How does the result fit your prediction of the magnitude of the correlation? Whatever the actual result, provide an interpretation of the relationship between the two tests that you discover. A class discussion can be held about the relationship found for the group.

If both these tests were measuring the same characteristics, approximately what would be the correlation coefficient between the two?

Additional Reading

AMA FORUM. "Creativity Training: BF Goodrich's New Approach." *Management Review,* March 1980, pp. 28–30.

DENNETT, DANIEL C. *Brainstorms: Philosophical Essays on Mind and Psychology.* Cambridge, Mass.: M.I.T. Press, 1980.

EDWARDS, BETTY. *Drawing on the Right Side of the Brain.* Los Angeles: J. P. Tarcher, 1980.

HUBER, GEORGE P. *Managerial Decision Making.* Glenview, Ill.: Scott, Foresman, 1980.

LEBOEUF, MICHAEL. *Imagineering.* New York: McGraw-Hill, 1980.

MCALINDON, HAROLD R. "Toward a More Creative You: Developing the Whole Person." *Supervisory Management,* March 1980, pp. 31–35.

RAND, JAMES E. "Creative Problem-Solving Applied to Grievance/Arbitration Procedures." *Personnel Administrator,* March 1980, pp. 50–52.

RAUDSEPP, EUGENE. *More Creative Growth Games.* New York: Putman, 1980.

WEISS, BERNARD. "Hiring Creative People: Three Opportunities to Make Better Decisions." *Personnel Administrator,* April 1981, pp. 89–94.

WORTHY, MORGAN. *Aha! A Puzzle Approach to Creative Thinking.* Chicago: Nelson-Hall, 1975.

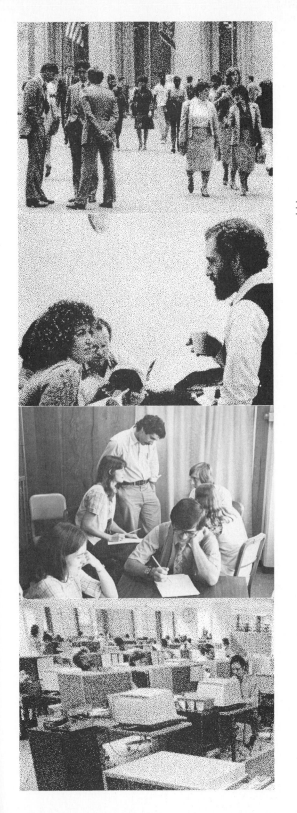

PART THREE

Understanding Small Groups and Interpersonal Influence

This part of the text emphasizes the behavior of people in small groups and interpersonal influence relationships. Many of the key topics relevant to understanding small-group psychology and how people influence each other are included in this section. Chapter 9, Group Dynamics, covers basic concepts about the behavior of people in small groups, such as the characteristics of effective work groups. The chapter is designed to provide a conceptual base for the other chapters in Part III. Chapter 10, Group Decision Making, examines such issues as when and how to make group decisions. A chapter is devoted to this topic because so many decisions today are made by groups.

Chapter 11, Interpersonal Communications, is a study of current theories of leadership in organization. Leadership is perhaps the most important influence process found in organizations. Our leadership chapter is lengthy because of the complexity of the topic, the vastness of the literature and its importance.

Chapter 12, Leadership in Organizations, describes interpersonal communication, the basic process by which most managerial and staff activities are carried out in organizations. The emphasis in this chapter is on understanding the nature of face-to-face, oral communication and how to avoid frequent barriers to effective communication. Chapter 13, Conflict in Organizations, takes the position that the right amount of conflict is helpful to an organization, particularly if it is managed properly. Information is provided about effective techniques for resolving potentially harmful conflict. Chapter 14, Organizational Power and Politics, deals with an influence process of current concern, political behavior in organizations (popularly referred to as office politics).

CHAPTER 9

Group Dynamics

LEARNING OBJECTIVES

1. To understand the nature and types of work groups found in organizations.
2. To analyze why people join work groups and what purposes these groups serve.
3. To identify key factors that influence or determine group behavior.
4. To summarize characteristics and properties of work groups, particularly as they relate to effectiveness.
5. To outline the stages in the formation and development of work groups.
6. To discuss the potential dysfunctional consequences of work groups.

Jim Lyons, the newly appointed manager of operations at Gulf Coast Insurance Company, confided to Wendy McPherson, his executive secretary, "We're going to see a lot of changes around here. Last year the company just about broke even. I don't see any need to lay off people, but I do see a need for us to become more efficient.

"What irks me the most is the time being wasted in the office while people sit around in coffee klatches. Around ten in the morning, the place is deserted. About 90 percent of the staff is down in the cafeteria whiling away time, drinking coffee. We could get by on less staff if we could cut down on those coffee breaks. We could lose about 5 percent of our office staff due to attrition and not have to replace them if we could stop the time leak created by the coffee break."

Jim's first management action to curtail the coffee break was to prepare an edict that from now on no coffee breaks would be allowed in the cafeteria. Instead, coffee- and tea-vending machines would be installed at two key locations in the office building. Any employee who wanted coffee or tea could purchase a beverage in the machine and take it back to his or her work station.

One month later the vending machines were installed and the cafeteria was declared off limits to employees except during their lunch break. Shortly thereafter, Jim received a phone call from Mickey, the head of maintenance.

"Mr. Lyons," said Mickey excitedly, "I think we have a major fire hazard on our hands. Since you ended the cafeteria coffee break and installed the vending machines, the employees have found a new way to serve coffee. All of a sudden we have a collection of hot water heaters, Silexes, and those new coffee makers around the office. I first got on to it when one of them shorted and blew a fuse. I understand that the vending machine is losing money. That's what the route man told me."

"Mickey, I appreciate your having brought this problem to my attention," replied Jim, "I'll get on it right away."

The next day Jim Lyons had a memo affixed to every bulletin board and sent to every supervisor. It read in part, "From now on, no unauthorized coffee- or tea-making equipment will be brought into this office. Any employee caught using unauthorized coffee-mak-

ing equipment will be subject to suspension."

Two weeks later, Jim asked Mickey to make a secretive night inspection of the office. His task was to discover if any coffee pots were still being used in the office. Mickey's investigation turned up no such evidence. Jim also phoned a few supervisors to see if the edict was receiving full compliance. Again, the report was positive. Jim thought to himself that the coffee klatch problem had finally been resolved. Three weeks later, Jody, the personnel manager, came forth with a disconcerting comment:

"Jim, I thought your edict might have been a little heavy handed. And I told you so. I now have evidence that your removal of the coffee pots has created a new problem."

"What's that? I haven't heard of any problems," said Jim.

"Perhaps, then, you haven't been making recent tours of the office at any time from nine to eleven in the morning. You can find little pockets of people drinking coffee in the strangest of places. We found five women from underwriting sitting on the steps of a fire exit. Three fellows and two gals from the claims department were found gathered around the Xerox machine drinking coffee. Worst of all, five people were sitting under a tree on the front lawn with paper cups in their hands. That's hardly what you had in mind with your no coffee pot edict."

"Jody, let me think about this problem for a while longer," mused Jim. Three days later, he sent out a new memo:

"Because of disappointment with certain aspects of the service, the coffee-vending machine will be removed from the building. Therefore, all employees who so desire are allowed a fifteen-minute break per morning to have coffee or other beverage in the cafeteria. Please make sure that this fifteen-minute limit is not exceeded."*

THE NATURE OF WORK GROUPS

As Jim Lyons discovered, groups are a formidable force within an organization and they do not always behave in a manner preferred by management. Work groups are the basic units or modules by which an organization can achieve its goals and objectives. An understanding of behavior in small groups, or group dynamics, is thus essential for an understanding of organizational behavior. A group, in the context used here, is any number of people who interact with one another, are psychologically aware of one another, perceive themselves to be a group, and are working toward a common goal.[1]

Size also must be taken into consideration in defining a group. Two people, technically speaking, are sufficient to comprise a group. Beyond around twenty-five people, group members can no longer interact with each other on a frequent basis, and they begin to lose the feel of being a group. An organization is really an aggregate of many smaller groups.

FORMAL AND INFORMAL WORK GROUPS

Several different methods of classifying work groups have been developed. The most meaningful one from a managerial standpoint is the broad categorization of formal versus informal groups. Both must be understood to manage people in organizations effectively.

Formal Groups

A formal group is one deliberately formed by the organization to accomplish specific tasks and achieve objectives. Its primary purpose is "facilitating, through member in-

---

*Reprinted with permission from Andrew J. DuBrin, *Human Relations: A Job-Oriented Approach,* 2nd ed. (Reston, Va.: Reston, 1981), pp. 188–89. Reprinted with permission of Reston Publishing Company, a Prentice-Hall Co., 11480 Sunset Hills Road, Reston, VA 22090.

[1]This definition is a composite from two sources: Edgar H. Schein, *Organizational Psychology,* 3rd ed. (Englewood Cliffs, N.J.: Prentice-Hall, 1980), p.145, and W. Clay Hamner and Dennis W. Organ, *Organizational Behavior: An Applied Psychological Approach* (Plano, Tex.: Business Publications, 1978), p. 303.

teraction, the attainment of the goals of the organization."[2] Formal groups are designated by the organization chart, by official memo, or by decree from management. The duration of a formal group is an important variable in understanding its nature. Some groups are designed to last for an indefinite period of time (such as an accounting department). Others are designed to stay in existence only until a specific purpose is accomplished, such as a task force to investigate cost savings throughout the firm. Functional groups are usually permanent, whereas task or project groups are usually temporary.

Functional groups.   Also referred to as command groups, functional groups carry out the basic processes of an organization. The formal organization is composed of a group of interconnected functional groups (such as manufacturing, purchasing, engineering, and so forth). The most distinguishing feature of a functional group is that it is hierarchical. A manager supervises subordinates, some of whom may supervise other people.

Task or project groups.   Such groups are composed of a number of employees who are brought together to accomplish a particular purpose or task. Among the different types of task or project groups are ad hoc (special-purpose) committees, project teams, and temporary task forces. In getting their task accomplished, it is necessary for group members to coordinate their efforts. In some instances, members of a functional group have a minimum of interaction. Two clerks in a hospital billing department might be handling work of an independent nature. By definition, the members of a task or project group must work cooperatively. Often, members of these temporary groups are from different functional groups. Most large organizations are composed of both functional and task or project groups. For example, the matrix organization structure is a project form or organization superimposed upon a functional organization.

Standing committees represent an exception to the rule of classifying functional groups as permanent and task or project groups as temporary. Members of the standing committee are assigned a project they work on in addition to their normal duties. The members of the committee may change, but the committee itself is relatively permanent. An auditing and examining committee in a large bank is a germane example of a standing committee.

Informal Groups

Many informal groups evolve naturally from the interaction of people in an organization. These groups take care of people's desire for friendship and companionship and are also formed to accomplish work by filling in the gaps left by the formal organization. At other times, the purpose of the informal group (such as agreeing to return late

---

[2]Andrew D. Szilagyi, Jr., and Marc J. Wallace, Jr., *Organizational Behavior and Performance,* 2nd ed. (Glenview, Ill.: Scott, Foresman and Company, 1980), p. 201.

from lunch on Fridays) may not be congruent with the goals of the organization. Two somewhat related informal groups have been identified.[3]

Interest groups are informal groups that have come together because of some common concern or purpose. A group of laboratory technicians banding together to demand better laboratory uniforms would be one such interest group. These technicians might be from different functional or task groups, yet they have a common interest in comfortable and clean work clothes. Some formal groups such as labor unions or employee associations begin as informal interest groups but eventually become part of the formal organization.

Friendship groups are formed in organizations because members have something in common such as age, political beliefs, similar life-styles (living in mobile homes), or ethnic background. When the employees form friendships with each other on the job, they often extend these relationships to outside activities such as a camping club formed by people who met at work.

Most employees are members of a variety of formal and informal groups within the same total organization. Simultaneously, you might be a member of the financial analysis department of the home office of a bank, the equal opportunity lending advisory committee, the employee recreational association, and the TGIF Club that meets after work on Fridays.

WHY PEOPLE JOIN FORMAL AND INFORMAL GROUPS

People join groups themselves and groups are formed by the organization for two general purposes: task accomplishment and the satisfaction of individual needs. However, the distinction between task accomplishment and need satisfaction is somewhat arbitrary—many people's needs can best be met through accomplishing worthwhile goals.

Assistance in Accomplishing Tasks

Work groups are usually formed by the organization to achieve specific tasks. Aside from these formal arrangements, many informal ones within the group or across groups facilitate task accomplishment. For instance, informal arrangements may be made among a group of design engineers to assist each other with complicated design problems. The end result is equipment design of higher technical integrity than if such informal arrangements did not exist.

In short, work groups are formed to achieve synergy—the group accomplishes something more than or different from that attainable by the same number of people working independently. Synergy appears to come about because of the sharing of ideas and the feedback on these ideas that take place in a cohesive group.

---

[3]James L. Gibson, John M. Ivancevich, and James H. Donnelly, Jr., *Organizations: Behavior, Structure, Processes,* 3rd ed. (Plano, Tex.: Business Publications, 1979), p. 138.

Affiliation and Emotional Support

Both formal and informal work groups serve as direct sources for the satisfaction of the need for affiliation.[4] Somewhat as a consequence, group membership also serves as a means of obtaining emotional support. When an employee within a cohesive group feels emotionally despondent, he or she can rely on the group for some temporary bolstering. Emotional support sometimes takes the form of giving the group member reassurance when he or she has a dispute with management.

Security

Group membership provides a feeling of security to people who would otherwise feel insecure and anxious. The security function of a group is particularly noticeable when somebody first joins a large organization. As Reitz explains, "Joining a group whose members have already experienced and survived the initial period of organizational life is an effective means of reducing such anxiety."[5] New employees will often solicit the advice of older employees on routine matters rather than approach their superiors. Much of this advice seeking relates to the new employee feeling insecure.

Esteem

Groups help individuals to satisfy their esteem needs in two important ways. First, if the group has high status within the firm, the person experiences esteem as a result. Many employees seek out a central headquarter assignment because of its presumed high status. Second, group membership can provide opportunities for recognition and praise that are not available outside the group.[6] This is especially true when one is seeking praise and recognition for technical work that has little meaning to people outside of a small group (such as expertise in building forecasting models).

Power and Protection

People have much more power and protection collectively than individually. The need for both power and protection is an important reason why people join labor unions. The quest to satisfy these needs also helps to explain why people join informal groups within organizations. If you return late from lunch with a group of people, you feel more protected than if you do it alone. Serving as the leader of an informal group within an organization (such as the once-a-month Brown Baggers who discuss professional concerns) may satisfy some of a person's needs for power.

---

[4]Schein, *Organizational Psychology,* pp. 151–52.

[5]H. Joseph Reitz, *Behavior in Organizations,* rev. ed. (Homewood, Ill.: Richard D. Irwin, 1981), p. 262.

[6]Ibid., p. 263.

Identity

Group membership contributes to a person's feeling of identity since much of our identity comes from our relationships with others. People in the group provide feedback that helps a person's self-concept to grow and develop. Groups provide identity in another important way, particularly when the group has high status. To say, "I'm Debbie from Corporate Auditing" may help Debbie feel that she has a strong identity. In reality, this woman may have a strong identity already, but her perceptions are more important than external reality.

Interpersonal Attraction

A basic reason for people electing to join a particular group is that they are attracted to one or more of its members. Much research and theorizing in social psychology has been devoted to explaining what makes people attracted, or not attracted, to each other. Three such theories are the exchange theory, the principle of complementarity, and social comparison theory.[7]

1. *The exchange theory of attraction* explains group interaction in terms of the rewards and costs incurred by the participants in the interaction. A reward is defined as any satisfaction or need reduction (or positive or negative reinforcement) gained from the relationship. Among the costs are punishments resulting from the relationship, including the fear of humiliation, embarrassment, boredom, and anxiety. The individual makes a cognitive evaluation of the trade-offs between rewards and punishments before entering into a relationship with group members.[8] Two standards are used against which each party evaluates his or her reward-cost outcomes:

> The *comparison level* is an average value derived from a person's past experiences and from the person's knowledge of comparable relationships. For example, a worker who has received praise for a given level of performance from the previous supervisor expects similar treatment from the new supervisor.

> The *comparison level of alternatives* is based on the costs and rewards available in the alternative relationships. In the above example, a worker who was nearing retirement and had no acceptable employment opportunities would accept the new supervisor, even if the supervisor were a tyrant compared to the last supervisor.[9]

2. *The principle of complementarity.* Congruent with the notion "opposites attract," this principle contends that people with complementary needs and/or abilities are attracted to each other.[10] You may voluntarily join a group where you thought your

---

[7]Our analysis follows the synthesis in Hamner and Organ, *Organizational Behavior*, pp. 301–2.

[8]One description of exchange theory is contained in George C. Homans, *Social Behavior: Its Elementary Forms* (New York: Harcourt Brace, 1961).

[9]Hamner and Organ, *Organizational Behavior*, p. 301.

[10]R. F. Winch, *Mate-selection: A Study of Complementary Needs* (New York: Harper & Row, 1958).

skills would complement those already present in the group. Often, this exchange is between technical and administrative skills. The principle of complementarity thus fits with exchange theory: people find relationships where their skills and attitudes complement each other to be mutually rewarding. Many business partnerships (a very small group) are formed on this basis. For example, one partner might be adept at administration and control, whereas the other might be adept at selling.

3. *Social comparison* posits that group membership is necessary because people have a need for self-evaluation, defined as "the need to know that one's opinions are correct and to know precisely what one is and is not capable of doing."[11] The individual checks his or her perceptions against others to determine the extent to which the individual's opinions, ideas, and judgments correspond to social reality.

A FRAMEWORK FOR GROUP BEHAVIOR

At this point it will be helpful to integrate much of the information in this chapter around a framework of small-group behavior. As shown in Figure 9–1, there are three sets of variables or forces that influence the outcome of group functioning: individual characteristics, group properties and characteristics, and group development.[12] Individual characteristics and group properties and characteristics themselves influence the development of a group. Also of note, individual characteristics and group properties influence outcomes directly and indirectly through their influence on group development. Many other factors influence group behavior, but the ones summarized here are those most extensively researched by behavioral scientists.

The relationship of individual characteristics to outcomes such as performance has been described in Chapters 3 and 4. Such variables operate essentially the same way in relation to work group outcomes. Group properties and characteristics, and their relationship to work group effectiveness, are discussed extensively in the next section. Group development is also discussed later in this chapter. A brief, hypothetical walk through the framework, touching a few of the possible variables, will help to explain its meaning.

> Kent, a talented and ambitious person (individual characteristics) joins a newly formed, small group of internal consultants within a large organization. The manager of the group assigns Kent to an important project dealing with improving the quality of work life of clerical employees. Other members of the group are cooperative individuals, and the leader uses the right mixture of task and people orientation. Since all these group properties and characteristics are relatively favorable, the group develops quickly and is soon performing its task well. The ultimate outcome is an effective corporate program to enhance quality of work life. Kent and his co-workers experience high morale because of their favorable situation.

[11]Leon Festinger, "A Theory of Social Comparison Processes," *Human Relations,* July 1954, p. 117.
[12]The framework presented here has several similar elements to Szilagyi and Wallace, *Organizational Behavior and Performance,* p. 200.

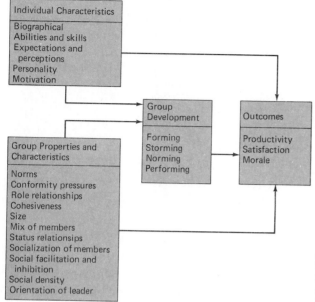

FIGURE 9-1 A Framework for Group Behavior

Source: Adapted from Andrew D. Szilagyi, Jr. and Marc J. Wallace, Jr., *Organizational Behavior and Performance*, 2nd ed. (Glenview, Ill.: Scott, Foresman, 1980), p. 200. Copyright © 1980 Scott, Foresman and Company. Reprinted by permission.

An important conclusion to be reached from examining this framework is that a multitude of factors can influence group performance. Similarly, many factors can influence group performance. Similarly, many factors influence individual or organizational performance.

CHARACTERISTICS AND PROPERTIES OF EFFECTIVE WORK GROUPS

Groups, as do individuals, have properties, characteristics, and traits that give them their uniqueness and have an impact on their effectiveness. In this section of the chapter, we are concerned with major characteristics and properties of groups that make one group different from another and are also relatively enduring aspects of a group. In addition, we will indicate how these properties relate to the outcomes of productivity and satisfaction.

Norms

Every group has some written or unwritten rules of behavior established by group members to provide some order to group activities. Norms can also be considered standards of conduct, such as a code of ethics mutually agreed upon by a small group of consultants. (We will not sell clients more of our services than we think they really need.) Group norms have been studied extensively in terms of their impact on performance. The group as a whole tends to establish both lower and upper limits to productivity. Among professional groups, the norm tends to establish minimum standards, while among production and clerical groups, the norms are set for both minimum and maximum performance. Norms are sometimes learned in this manner:

> When a new member works at too fast a pace the first day on the job, he may be subjected to derogatory comments such as "Look at old speed king there," "Look who's trying to make us look bad," "Look who's trying to impress the foreman," "Look at who's trying to make us lose our jobs," and so on. A little of this goes a long way in obtaining compliance with group norms.[13]

Norms are enforced by punishing deviants (norm violators) in a number of ways. The person who exceeds or does not live up to group norms may find himself or herself ostracized from the rest of the group. Disapproval and even physical attacks are not unheard of in a group's attempt to "keep members in line."

Research conclusions. The nature of group norms and their impact on behavior have been summarized around five major findings.[14]

1. Norms are structural characteristics of groups that summarize and simplify group influence processes. A norm is thus a process that is intended to regulate and standardize group behavior.

2. Norms regulate behavior, not private thoughts and feelings. Not all members may agree with or appreciate a particular norm (such as covering for another person when the latter is sick), but the norm may be obeyed to avoid group sanctions.

3. Norms generally are developed only for behaviors that most group members view as important and relevant. Sometimes the behavior influenced by norms may not in reality be important, but it is perceived by group members to be important. Some groups may enforce the norm of taking off a suit jacket while in the department even though such behavior is largely irrelevant to group effectiveness.

4. Norms usually develop gradually, but the process can be hastened if so desired by the group. The formation of group norms may develop slowly in response to the requirements of the situation, such as giving encouragement to a group member just before he or she leaves to go out on an emergency assignment. At other times, a norm may be instituted instantaneously. Someone might say, for example, "Tony was hospitalized because of that last practical joke. From now on, no more horseplay." Confronted with the grim consequences of their behavior, a new norm (no more horseplay) will be established.

5. All norms are not applicable to all group members. High-status members have more freedom to deviate from a strict interpretation of the norm than do other group

[13]Stephen J. Carroll and Henry L. Tosi, *Organizational Behavior* (Chicago: St. Clair Press, 1977), p. 106.

[14]J. Richard Hackman, "Group Influences on Individuals," in Marvin D. Dunnette, ed., *Handbook of Industrial and Organizational Psychology* (Chicago: Rand McNally, 1976), pp. 1495–96.

members. Also, groups will sometimes establish a norm that applies only to one person, or to a small subset of persons, within a group. One example would be that new group members do a disproportionate share of "dirty work."

Relationship to group effectiveness.   When norms set high standards of performance and behavior, norms lead to high productivity. Conversely, when norms are established that set standards of performance below those desired by management (or the labor union), productivity is lowered. Group norms tend to improve satisfaction and morale for workers who are predisposed to enjoy working in a group effort. If you are very independent in your thinking, however, you may not enjoy having to conform to group norms.

Conformity to Group Norms and Other Pressures

Intertwined with a study of norms is the topic of conformity and nonconformity to norms and other pressures. Members of large organizations, in particular, have been accused of needless conformity in thinking, dress, and living habits. As was noted in Chapter 7, pressures toward conformity create stress for some organization members. And, as documented in the classic experiments conducted by Solomon Asch, some people will change their opinions about highly objective matters (such as the relative length of two lines) in the face of group pressures.

Asch brought together groups consisting of one genuine subject and various numbers of other subjects who were actually confederates of the experimenter. These confederates were told beforehand to deceive the genuine subject by unanimously agreeing on the "wrong answer" in a series of visual judgments. About one-third of the genuine subjects gave judgments distorted in the direction of the false group consensus. The implication of these and similar experiments for small-group behavior outside of a laboratory setting is that groups can generate pressure toward conformity in thinking.[15]

Individual differences in conformity.   People vary widely in their willingness or need to conform to group pressures. Common sense would suggest that independently minded and talented people show a smaller likelihood of conforming to group pressures than do dependent and untalented people. A series of studies provides support for this statement. More than 450 persons participated in a "group pressure situation" in which they were influenced by the groups to change their personal judgments about experimental tasks. Included in the sample were military officers, college students, and medical students. A correlational analysis of a wide variety of personality and intellectual measures with conformity scores revealed the following characteristics of the person who is able to withstand group pressure and remain independent.

---

[15]One good synthesis of these experiments is found in David Krech, Richard S. Crutchfield, and Norman Livson, *Elements of Psychology,* 3rd ed. (New York: Knopf, 1974), pp. 803–4. See also Solomon E. Asch, "Opinions and Social Pressure," *Scientific American,* November 1955, pp. 31–35.

1. Intelligence, as measured by standard mental tests.
2. Originality, as manifested in thought processes and problem solving.
3. "Ego strength," that is, the ability to cope effectively despite stressful circumstances.
4. Self-confidence and absence of anxiety and inferiority feelings.
5. Optimal social attitudes and behavior such as tolerance, responsibility, dominance, and freedom from disturbed and dependent relationships with other people.[16]

People who readily succumb to group pressures (high conformists) are characterized as ranking much lower on these dimensions of behavior. A person characterized as intellectually average, unoriginal, and low in ego strength and self-confidence, and having dependent and disturbed relationships with other people, would probably be a conformist.

Situations that foster conformity.   Individuals show wide variations in conformity to group norms, and situations also show some variation in the extent to which they encourage or precipitate conformity. Under conditions of crisis, for example, conformity to group norms is highly probable. When a firm is financially troubled, for example, employees often show a willingness to conform to a norm of pushing for high quality in the goods they produce or the services they offer.

A set of experiments conducted at the University of Michigan provides some relevant information about the conditions under which people will most probably accept performance goals established by the group and/or the leader. (Adhering to performance goals is one measure of conformity.) According to these research results, susceptibility to a social norm as a determinant of work performance increases with

1. *The ambiguity of the situation.* When people are not certain of what is expected of them, they become somewhat dependent upon whatever norms of behavior might be available.
2. *The necessity of going along with the group for goal achievement.* For example, team members are willing to adhere to norms with regard to computer usage if they need computer time to complete a project.
3. *Decreased self-confidence of the individual.* As mentioned earlier, people low in self-confidence are receptive to conforming to group norms of conduct.
4. *The appropriateness of the goals being offered the individual.* When group goals mesh with individual goals, people are quite willing to adhere to group standards of performance.[17] For instance, a law firm might maintain the group productivity norm of having all lawyers bill an average of 65 percent of their time to clients. Members of the firm will probably accept this norm because this level of billing will place them at a desired level of income.

Relationship to effectiveness.   Conformity is functional when the norms, rules or regulations, or policies conformed to are valuable. Conformity to health and safety regulations is one example of functional conformity. Dysfunctional conformity takes place when there is something inherently wrong with the standard of conduct to

---

[16]Krech, Crutchfield, and Livson, *Elements of Psychology,* pp. 804–6.

[17]Abraham K. Korman, *Organizational Behavior* (Englewood Cliffs, N.J.: Prentice-Hall, 1977), p. 81.

which group members conform. Suppose that the stockbrokers in one office all agree to make the same buy or sell recommendation for the same stocks and bonds. A given stock or bond may represent a sound investment for most people but not for a few other people in light of their unique financial situation. Conformity to the group policy thus detracts from work group effectiveness because several clients are being ill-served.

Role Relationships

To carry out their work, groups differentiate the work activities of members, referred to as role differentiation. A role is a set of activities expected of a person holding a particular position within the group.[18] It defines and clarifies members' responsibilities on behalf of the group. The leader has several roles to perform and so do subordinates. One way of understanding how roles operate is to differentiate among expected, perceived, and enacted roles.[19] The *expected role* is close to being a formal role. It is defined by such means as one's job title, job description, or policy manual. The manager of a restaurant is expected to carry out such activities as purchasing food and hiring and firing staff.

The *perceived role* is the set of activities in the group that an individual believes that he or she should perform. Sometimes there is a difference between the expected and the perceived role. A restaurant manager might be expected by the owner to influence his or her relatives and friends to dine at the restaurant, while the manager may not perceive that to be true. The *enacted role* is the way in which the group member or leader actually behaves. It stems from the perceived role. As discussed under the topic of stress, various confusion about roles is a pervasive stressor in organizations. Among the stressors are role ambiguity, role conflict, role underload, and role overload.

Relationship to effectiveness. Role clarity, but not role rigidity, seems positively related to the group outcomes of productivity and satisfaction. If a given individual has optimum role clarity, as desired by that individual, it leads to positive outcomes. A manager, therefore, has to introduce the right amount of role conflict, role ambiguity, and role load to group members.

Cohesiveness

A cohesive group is one in which the members possess a feeling of closeness (literally adhering to each other) that shows up in their attitudes, performance, and behavior. Some groups are much more cohesive than others. Group cohesiveness is increased under the following conditions:

- The group agrees on its goals or the purpose and direction of its activities.
- The group members interact frequently with each other and meet regularly, but not to

[18]John R. Schermerhorn, Jr., James G. Hunt, and Richard N. Osborn, *Managing Organizational Behavior* (New York: John Wiley, 1982), p. 453.

[19]Szilagyi and Wallace, *Organizational Behavior and Performance*, p. 218.

the point of diminishing returns. Groups can run stale, and therefore lose some cohesiveness, by meeting too frequently.

- Group members are mutually attracted to each other and particularly enjoy working together.
- Intergroup competition exists, particularly to the extent that group members perceive a common enemy. Group members consistently draw more closely to each other when an external threat exists.
- When a group performs well and therefore receives a favorable evaluation, group members tend to become more cohesive. The U.S. Olympic hockey team that eventually won the gold medal in 1980 was a remarkably cohesive group during its brief life. Some of its cohesiveness could be attributed to the lavish praise heaped upon the squad.

Groups decrease in cohesiveness when the opposite conditions and certain other relationships exist:

- The group disagrees on its goals, leading to dissension and infighting.
- The group size increases to the point that the frequency of interaction each member has with others decreases.
- The group members are not attracted to each other, and consequently the relationships with each other become uncomfortable.
- Intragroup competition exists to the point that members are in conflict with each other and no longer emphasize cooperation with each other.
- The group performs poorly and therefore receives an unfavorable evaluation. The finger-pointing and blaming that takes place erodes group cohesiveness.
- When one or more of the group members try to dominate, cohesiveness cannot adequately develop. Cliques sometimes form as a result, further detracting from overall group cohesiveness.[20]

Work group effectiveness. Group cohesiveness contributes to increased productivity, provided that the goals of the group are aligned with those of management. When the group norm does not favor the goals of management, decreased productivity is the result. Cohesive work groups are high in productivity when group members have high confidence in management. When confidence is low, productivity also tends to be low. Experimental evidence collected some years ago helps to explain these relationships. It was shown that group cohesiveness acts as a determinant of whether or not the individual will go along with the group with respect to task performance. Members of cohesive groups tend to accept group goals whether they reflect high or low productivity.[21]

Size

Work groups are arranged into many different sizes, usually according to management's perception of what the right size should be for a given task. When it appears

---

[20]The discussion of factors increasing and decreasing cohesiveness follows closely ibid., pp. 221–22.

[21]Abraham K. Korman, *Industrial and Organizational Psychology* (Englewood Cliffs, N.J.: Prentice-Hall, 1971), p. 59.

that the group is becoming too large to supervise adequately, the logical step is to divide the group and appoint a new leader. Research evidence suggests that group size has a noticeable influence on certain important variables. As group size increases, we find that

1. Increased tension release takes place and more suggestions and information are exchanged among group members.
2. Job satisfaction decreases because the majority of people prefer working in small groups. People seem to enjoy the greater attention and feeling of importance they receive in a small group.
3. Absenteeism tends to increase among blue-collar (production) workers, but this relationship does not exist for white-collar workers.
4. Turnover tends to increase, possibly because with increased group size, each worker feels less crucial to the group's effort. When the group size is small, each member tends to feel that he or she plays a vital role.[22]

Relationship to productivity. Productive work groups come in different sizes. The optimum size of a work group depends upon the nature of the task to be performed. All things being equal, smaller groups are less subject to problems of coordination, but certain qualifying conditions must be considered. In a straight "additive" task, such as accountants preparing income tax returns, each new worker can produce additional units. In tasks where coordination among group members is essential, productivity is dependent upon the most or least competent worker. In the former case, an increase in size increases the chances of getting a competent individual.[23] Unfortunately, increased group size also increases the probabilities of adding an incompetent person to the group.

The old adage "Too many cooks spoil the broth" has relevance for understanding effective work groups. As group size increases, a point of diminishing returns is reached whereby coordination becomes quite difficult and productivity decreases. This is often true when the group size exceeds five people. The negative effects on coordination are most marked when the task involves no clear and objective criterion for judging the quality of performance.[24]

Cautiously, the observation is offered that a group of five, six, or seven members is the most effective size for accomplishing tasks of a general nature (e.g., devising a campaign strategy for a local candidate). A group of five is most effective, in part because of three characteristics. First, no deadlock is possible with an odd number of group members. Second, a group member does not feel as deviant being in the minority as he or she would in an even smaller group. Third, a group of five is large enough for members to shift roles easily.[25]

---

[22]This research evidence is summarized in Richard M. Steers, *Introduction to Organizational Behavior* (Glenview, Ill.: Scott, Foresman and Company, 1981), pp. 188–90.

[23]William G. Scott and Terence R. Mitchell, *Organization Theory: A Structural and Behavioral Analysis,* 3rd ed. (Homewood, Ill.: Richard D. Irwin, 1976), p. 165.

[24]Alan C. Filley, Robert J. House, and Steven Kerr, *Managerial Process and Organizational Behavior,* 2nd ed. (Glenview, Ill.: Scott, Foresman and Company, 1976), p. 417.

[25]Paul A. Hare, *Handbook of Small Group Research* (New York: Free Press, 1962), pp. 243–44.

The safest generalization about group size is that group size is contingent on the situation. Key situational variables are (1) amount of coordination required among members—with less coordination required, the group can be larger—(2) task complexity—larger groups are better equipped to handle more complex tasks—and (3) urgency of the problem—all things being equal, smaller groups accomplish their mission more quickly.

Mix of Members

The mix or variety of group members is another group property of note. We ordinarily think of group homogeneity as leading to cohesiveness, yet some groups whose members have diverse backgrounds become highly cohesive. War novels and movies frequently include the theme of a group of people with radically different backgrounds developing a closeness to each other. The common enemy faced by group members may contribute more to cohesiveness than does member diversity.

Group composition and work group effectiveness. Sometimes groups composed of people of different opinions and abilities lead to high effectiveness, whereas in other situations homogeneous groups are the most effective. Evidence for this conclusion is supported by a variety of laboratory experiments reviewed by Bernard M. Bass.[26]

Homogeneous groups tend to be the most productive under three conditions: first, when the task is relatively simple and a variety of resources is not needed to complete the task; second, when considerable cooperation is required to complete a task (e.g., homogeneous groups are effective because there is less conflict and competition in such groups); third, where a chain of reactions is required of a group (e.g., a group of people erecting a bridge).

Three conditions can also be identified under which heterogeneous groups tend to be the most productive. First, heterogeneous groups are well suited to completing complex tasks because of the diversity of opinion and capability in such groups. Second, when a speedy solution has potentially unfavorable consequences, a heterogeneous group has merit. Homogeneous groups tend to work more rapidly because of the congruence of opinion. A heterogeneous jury takes longer to reach a decision, thus allowing for a more intensive analysis of the testimony. Third, where creativity is required, groups of dissimilar people have the advantage. Varied resources tend to enhance creativity.

An optimum balance of homogeneity versus heterogeneity probably exists for each task. If group members are too heterogeneous, their difficulties in interacting smoothly with each other may inhibit productivity. Conversely, if the group is too homogeneous, agreement is reached too readily and the resources of the group are sparsely utilized.

---

[26]Bernard M. Bass, *Organizational Psychology* (Boston: Allyn & Bacon, 1965), pp. 204–9.

Status Relationships

Most groups are composed of members of unequal status. The status of a given member comes about through formal position or individual qualities. A superstar in any group may have more status than the leader who may be occupying primarily an administrative role. In general, an individual's job title defines status within a group. A senior programmer has more status than a junior programmer and an executive vice president has more status than does a department head. Since the fact that people vary in status is an accepted way of life, the existence of status differentials within a group usually does not create problems.

Status differentials can have a direct influence on group productivity through *status congruence,* which reflects the agreement among group members on the level of status of individual group members. If group members bicker over who has more status than whom, efforts are diverted from task accomplishment and invested in resolving the conflict. In mental health settings, for example, it is not unknown for psychiatrists, clinical psychologists, and psychiatric social workers to argue about their relative pecking order. (And sometimes occupational therapists enter the fray.)

Socialization of Members

Socialization refers to the varied process by which an individual acquires the attitudes, values, beliefs, and norms necessary to function smoothly as a group member.[27] Socialization into society is a long, complicated process that approximates in complexity the development of personality. Here we are concerned with the process whereby a new member becomes socialized into the group. "Learning the ropes" may be achieved in a variety of ways:

1. Older group members "explain the ropes" to the newcomer, including the formal and informal structure of the group. As one clerk said to a recruit, "Don't worry about the boss. His bark is worse than his bite. You don't have to knock your brains out in this department."
2. The new member quietly observes what is going on within the group and reaches conclusions about expected behavior, such as what needs to be done to be regarded as a standout performer.
3. The new member is exposed to considerable ribbing, joshing, and undesirable assignments just to test out his or her toughness. Once this hurdle has been overcome, the new member is officially accepted into the group. Athletic teams and some construction crews are notorious for this type of behavior.

Socialization enhances group effectiveness when the norms and practices conveyed are congruent with organizational objectives, similar to the relationship of cohesiveness to productivity.

[27]Reitz, *Behavior in Organizations,* p. 458.

Social Facilitation and Inhibition

In Chapter 3 we described the effect of the presence of others upon learning. A more general case of social facilitation is that a person's level of performance increases in the context of a group. It takes place more often when people are performing tasks they have previously learned. Therefore, where people are doing things in which they are already competent, group membership facilitates performance, providing that the people involved care about the evaluation they receive from others.

Social inhibition takes place when the presence of others inhibits or lowers performance.[28] Such inhibition will most likely take place when group members are learning new tasks or are trying things in which they are not yet competent. The underlying mechanism is that the presence of others makes some people anxious. As some people say, "Please don't look at me when I'm trying to work, it makes me nervous."

Social Density

The extent to which a person is in close physical proximity with other group members is another group property that influences output. People dislike the feeling of being crowded and cramped, but they do work better when they have ready interaction with people they need to consult about their work. For instance, in one research and development unit, the frequency of flow of technical information increased when the distance between desks was decreased.[29] When the work being performed is of a more independent nature, there should be fewer people within a certain walking distance (the precise meaning of social density).

Social facilitation and social density are sometimes correlated factors. Stockbrokers have reported, for example, that they are stimulated by the sounds of co-workers chattering on the phone and work best under such conditions. Journalists, too, have reported the same phenomenon. In effect, a socially dense workplace has an arousal social density that allows for social facilitation (and sometimes social inhibition).

Task Accomplishment versus People Orientation of Leader

A factor of major significance upon group accomplishment and effectiveness is the style of the leader. If the manager emphasizes goal accomplishment, productivity will tend to be higher. If the manager emphasizes the interpersonal aspects of leadership, morale will be elevated, sometimes at the expense of productivity. Since neither task accomplishment nor the feelings and attitudes of people can be completely ignored, the group leader must strive for achieving the right balance.

[28]Elliott McGinnies, *Behavior in Small Groups* (Boston: Houghton Mifflin, 1970).

[29]T. J. Allen and D. I. Cohen, "Information Flow in R & D Laboratories," *Administrative Science Quarterly*, 1969, pp. 12–25. Cited in Szilagyi and Wallace, *Organizational Behavior and Performance*, p. 218.

One way of gaining perspective on the concept of an effective work group is to examine autonomous work groups—units designed with effectiveness in mind. They are described in the box appearing on pages 246–247.

STAGES IN GROUP FORMATION AND DEVELOPMENT

A group is a dynamic organism, much like a person, that gradually changes throughout its lifetime. One useful conception of group formation and development is that shown in Figure 9–2.[30] The first stage is *forming* (testing and dependence). In testing, the group members attempt to discover from the reactions of other group members what interpersonal behaviors are acceptable within the group. The new group member wants to know, "What can I do that will be liked by others?" "How far can I push them?" While testing takes place, the new member forms certain dependencies on the leader, other group members, and rules and regulations. He or she must depend on these sources for information about topics such as "Which rules will be enforced?" "How do I get a favorable assignment?" In summary, the forming stage is used to establish ground rules for the new member.

Storming or intergroup conflict is the second stage in the development of group structure. Group members may become hostile toward one another and/or the leader. Such behavior is prompted by a desire to express individuality and to resist the formation of a group structure. During this stage, goals set by the leader may be ignored and resistance to task requirements is common. The storming stage may be more evident in informal than in formal work groups. People tend to be more predisposed to accept authority in an organizationally prescribed group.

During the *norming* stage of group development, in-group feelings and cohesiveness develop, new standards evolve, and new roles are adopted. Group members begin

---

[30]B. W. Tuckman, "Development Sequence in Small Groups," *Psychological Bulletin,* 1965, pp. 384–99, as described in Hamner and Organ, *Organizational Behavior,* pp. 304–5.

FIGURE 9–2 Stages of Group Formation and Development

AUTONOMOUS WORK GROUPS: THE DESIGN
OF EFFECTIVE WORK GROUPS

In recent years much attention has been paid to combining the principles of job enrichment and group dynamics to form work groups whose outcomes are high productivity and high morale. This approach to job design gaining increasing acceptance is the internally led, self-regulating, autonomous work group. The general format is for teams of eight to twelve workers to cover a full set of tasks, and team members to decide which people will perform which tasks. In essence the team becomes a small group of generalists rather than an equivalent number of employees performing specialized, narrow tasks. An attempt is made to optimize jointly both the technical and social components of work in order to optimize the production system and enhance morale.

Characteristics of the Autonomous Work Group

The design of autonomous groups begins with the specification of the minimal set of boundary and task control conditions needed to create a self-regulating work system for a given task environment. The remaining task and control variables are permitted to vary with the needs of the situation, thus giving the work group latitude to handle nonroutine work. The minimal set of task and boundary conditions necessary for self-regulation varies with the situation, but a few generalizations can be reached:

> Inclusion within a single social unit responsibility for the total production unit.
> Inclusion within the unit of all functions and technical skills necessary for process control, maintenance, and adjustment.
> A clearly definable way of measuring output.
> Joint commitment by individual members of the social unit to optimize the functioning of the unit with respect to achieving its production goals.

To be effective, members of the autonomous work group must possess the requisite job skills. Members are able to self-regulate and control the group task best where the members are multiskilled, all-around workers. Ideally, each worker should be able to perform a wide variety of tasks and be able to switch jobs, replacing co-workers when they are tired, bored, or absent. As with individual forms of job enrichment, the workers must desire to be part of a team effort. Comprehension of the workers of a variety of job skills along with job switching (or rotation) tends to reduce the likelihood of prestige and status differences within the group.*

---

*The first part of this box is based on Melvin Blumberg, "Job Switching in Autonomous Work Groups: An Exploratory Study in a Pennsylvania Coal Mine," *Academy of Management Journal,* June 1980, pp. 287–89.

Sample Results

Sherwin-Williams designed an entire automotive paint manufacturing plant along the autonomous work group concept. The plant chosen for the job redesign was in a rural town in Kentucky. Considerable human judgment and intuition is required in the manufacture of high-quality automotive paint. The comprehensive team approach to group structure was carefully designed and implemented, including employee training in teamwork skills. Such care led to a number of worthwhile results for the plant, including the following:

1. Efficiencies in the utilization of human resources: despite an original estimate of a necessary work force of 200, 160 employees proved to be adequate to accomplish the job.
2. Absenteeism for work-team members is 2.5 percent in comparison with the all-plant average of 6.7 percent. Turnover is reported to be negligibly low.
3. Productivity is objectively measured to be 30 percent higher than in sister plants. The cost per gallon of paint made in the facility is 45 percent lower than in other plants manufacturing automotive paint. Plant management attributes 75 percent of the cost reduction to human factors, not to the physical structure of the plant or new technology.
4. The Richmond facility came to produce the highest-quality paint manufactured by Sherwin-Williams. Ninety-four percent of its production is rated excellent by the technical department in contrast to a 75 percent all-plant average.
5. The quality of work life has increased as measured by the results of the first two annual attitude surveys since the inception of the work group restructuring programs. It is not unusual for employees to tell visitors, "This is the best place I've ever worked. Management cares about you and the work is fun."†

†The results section of this box is from Ernesto J. Poza and M. Lynne Markus, "Success Story: The Team Approach to Work Restructuring," *Organizational Dynamics*, Winter 1980, pp. 3–25.

to feel free to express personal opinions about task accomplishment such as "We'll never get done if we have to wait for a solution that everybody accepts."

Performing is the fourth stage of group development. By now the group has created a network of interpersonal relationships that allows for task accomplishment. Roles become flexible and functional, and the group channels most of its energy into getting on with the job. (It would be a rare circumstance for a group not to divert some energy into political maneuvering or internal bickering.) By this final stage, structural issues have been resolved and structure now supports task performance.

According to the model shown in Figure 9–2, groups can be in any one stage of these four stages of development at any time. Group effectiveness is a function of how close the group is to the performing stage. An experienced manager recognizes that it takes time to ease a new team of workers into a high-performing unit. The process cannot be rushed.

POTENTIAL DYSFUNCTIONS
OF GROUP EFFORT

Despite their many functional consequences, groups sometimes create problems for management and group members. Almost every advantage of group membership described in the section "Why People Join Groups, Formal and Informal" could also be a disadvantage in some situations. For instance, people might find the affiliation with peers so satisfying that they neglect to concentrate on their work. Here we mention six potential dysfunctions of group effort. One, suboptimum decision making, is examined in more detail in the following chapter.

1. *Restriction of work output.* When the group norm is away from high productivity, and the group is cohesive, lowered productivity is usually the result. An almost identical phenomenon is that groups create pressures toward mediocre performance and conformity to standards of behavior that are less than optimum. To avoid being perceived as a deviant, some people will hold back on their output; thus dysfunctional conformity has taken place.

2. *Suboptimum decision making.* Committees have been widely criticized for arriving at compromise decisions that prove to be of little value. One example would be constructing an inferior building because agreement could not be reached on spending the amount of money required to build an adequate one. When group members try too hard to be cohesive, *groupthink* is often the result. The group thinks as a unit rather than as a collection of individuals, and much critical evaluation of group ideas is lost. Also, groups tend to make much riskier (and sometimes hazardous) decisions than do individuals acting alone.

3. *Suboptimum performance on complex tasks.* A group may be superior to the best individual when a meaningful division of labor is possible. But when the task is very complex (such as designing an insurance program), the group often performs less well than either the best or average member. Basically, this is based on the notion that a chain is only as strong as its weakest link.[31]

4. *Groups often waste time.* When a task is uncomplicated and straightforward, it may simply be a waste of time for people to convene. Much more could be accomplished if each person were assigned a segment of the total task and worked independently. One appliance manufacturer had developed a committee to meet regularly to review complaints from dealers and individual customers. Although the system worked well, the company switched to having individuals handle the complaints. Much time saving resulted.

5. *Breeding of political infighting and other forms of intragroup and intergroup conflict.* When people work in close proximity to each other and compete for the same resources, it often leads to political behavior (see Chapter 14). Intergroup conflict oc-

---

[31]Thomas V. Bonoma and Gerald Zaltman, *Psychology for Management* (Boston: Kent, 1981), pp. 225–26.

curs when group members develop the attitude that their work group is more important than the organization as a whole. Rivalries develop, and "beating the opposition" becomes more important than reaching organizational objectives.

6. *Shirking of individual responsibility.* For those people with a weak work ethic, group assignments are sometimes an invitation to shirk responsibility. Unless assignments are carefully drawn and both group and individual objectives are established, undermotivated members can often squeeze by without contributing their fair share.

IMPLICATIONS FOR MANAGERIAL PRACTICE

A general strategy for applying the information in this chapter to the practice of management would be to review how a particular group characteristic or property relates to effectiveness and then manage accordingly. For instance, you would try to select a group size that is optimum for a particular task, given the information presented about group size and effectiveness. A few additional implications of group dynamics are presented next.

1. Be aware of group norms and the extent to which they facilitate or inhibit attaining organizational objectives. Reward systems must be developed that encourage high group performance. For instance, if a group performs well on a given task, and management then elevates performance standards, a norm toward lowered productivity may result.

2. When overconformity to group behavior and thinking develops (such as unanimous decisions being reached too often), it may be time to disband cliques by across-group rotation. The heterogeneity of the new groups may result in a better cross-fertilization of ideas and less groupthink.

3. When it appears that the work group is too cohesive or not cohesive enough, the leader can manipulate certain variables toward the right amount of cohesiveness. Among the variables related to cohesiveness potentially under a manager's control are establishing clear goals, selecting compatible group members, encouraging or discouraging intergroup competition, and evaluating group performance. (Refer to the discussion of group cohesiveness presented earlier.) In general, it is not a good idea to encourage cohesiveness when the prevailing attitude in the group is antimanagement.

4. When forming a new work group, it should be recognized that time is needed before the group will be able to achieve its maximum performance. The leader should be alert to the somewhat predictable stages of group formation and development termed forming, storming, norming, and performing.

5. Selecting the appropriate leadership style is an important requirement for group effectiveness. Generally, the manager must give some emphasis to both the task accomplishment and interpersonal aspects of leadership. Intuition combined with trial

and error may reveal the correct combination of task and people orientation for the situation at hand.

Summary

- A group is any number of people who interact with one another, are psychologically aware of one another, perceive themselves to be a group, and are working toward a common goal. An organization is an aggregate of many smaller groups. Formal groups are those deliberately formed by the organization to accomplish specific tasks and achieve objectives. Two types of formal groups are functional, or command, groups and task, or project, groups. Generally, functional groups are more permanent than task groups.

- Informal groups evolve naturally in an organization to take care of people's desire for friendship and companionship. Also, they accomplish work by filling in the gaps left by the formal organization. Two major types of informal groups are interest and friendship groups.

- People join informal groups, and such groups are formed by management for many reasons, including assistance in accomplishing tasks, affiliation and emotional support, security, esteem, power and protection, and identity and because they are attracted to one another. Several theories have been advanced to explain the basis for interpersonal attraction. Exchange theory says that people evaluate the trade-offs between rewards and punishments before joining a group. The principle of complementarity contends that opposites attract, and social comparison theory holds that people join groups for purposes of self-evaluation.

- Work groups have a wide variety of characteristics, traits, and properties that gives them uniqueness. Those described here are generally related to work group effectiveness. Following is a list of these properties with a comment about the relationship of each to group effectiveness.

  1. Norms lead to high productivity when they set standards of behavior desired by management.
  2. Conformity, similarly, can be functional or dysfunctional, depending upon the specific standards to which group members conform.
  3. Role relationships in groups lead to productivity and satisfaction when roles are clear, but not rigid. If a given individual has sufficient role clarity for him or her, it leads to positive outcomes.
  4. Cohesiveness leads to high member satisfaction and may lead to increased productivity, provided that the goals of the group are aligned with those of management.
  5. The optimum group size is contingent upon the situation. When less coordination is required, group size can be larger; larger groups are better equipped to handle more complex tasks; and smaller groups get tasks done more quickly.

6. Homogeneity of group member background increases performance when (a) the task is relatively simple and a variety of resources is not needed to complete the task, (b) considerable cooperation is required to complete the task, and (c) a chain of reactions is required from the group.

7. Status relationships are related to productivity through status congruence, the agreement among group members on the level of status of individuals. Low congruence diverts time from task accomplishment.

8. Socialization ("learning the ropes") enhances group effectiveness when the norms and practices conveyed are congruent with organizational objectives.

9. Social facilitation and inhibition relate to productivity, because the presence of other members can either enhance or inhibit performance. When workers are performing tasks in which they are already competent, group membership facilitates performance, providing that they care about the evaluation received from others.

10. Social density, the extent to which one is in close physical proximity with other group members, should be less when work is of an independent nature.

11. The leadership style should reflect the appropriate balance between task accomplishment and people orientation. Heavy emphasis on people at the expense of task accomplishment may improve morale but cause productivity to decline.

- A group passes through various stages of formation and development. In order, they are forming (testing and dependence), storming (intergroup conflict and power tactics), norming (development of cohesiveness and norms), and performing.

- Among the potential disadvantages of group efforts are restriction of work output, suboptimum decision making (such as groupthink), suboptimum performance on complex tasks, time wasting, breeding of intragroup and intergroup conflict, and shirking of individual responsibility.

Questions for Discussion

1. Is the class for which you are reading this book a group? Explain your reasoning.
2. Would you prefer to work in an individual or a team effort? Why?
3. Is an employee credit union a formal or informal group. Explain.
4. Athletic teams tend to be more cohesive than industrial work groups. What do you think are some of the factors responsible for these differences?
5. From the standpoint of management, what are several disadvantages to having highly cohesive work groups at lower and middle levels of the organization?
6. Many winning athletic teams do not have superstars. What does this fact tell you about group dynamics?
7. Why are novels almost never written by more than one person whereas texts and other scientific books are frequently written by groups of two or three people?
8. Give an example of how the concept of an autonomous work group might be used with professional-level employees.
9. What characteristics of people have you observed to be related to their preference for working in groups rather than by themselves?
10. Describe any informal group to which you belong. How did it come into being?

An Organizational Behavior Problem

The Unbalanced Team

Rob called his task force together for their first meeting. Cheerfully, he said to the group, "I hope the rest of you are as excited as I am about having been chosen to work on one of the Pure Waters Agency's most pressing problems. As explained to me by the director, the Pure Waters Agency has an image problem. People resent paying money for water pollution services. Part of their resistance is because they don't know what we do. They don't understand how important we are to their health. Our job is to develop some guidelines for informing the public. But first we have to learn how big a problem we really have. What are your thoughts, Ginger, Derek, Gil, and Willie?"

Ginger spoke first: "So long as you mentioned my name first, I thought I would contribute before the good ideas were used up. It seems like a marketing research assignment to me. We have to go out into the field and find out how we are perceived by the public. After we get a clear picture of our strengths and weaknesses as the public sees us, we can plan some remedial action."

Willie commented, "I couldn't have said it better myself. But first we'll have to design a questionnaire and figure out whom we are going to interview. We have some experts in the department of statistics who can help us select the right kind of sample."

"I have a question, Rob," said Gil. "It sounds as if this task force will be pretty time consuming. Will we be getting enough time off from our regular jobs to do justice to this assignment?"

"The ground rules state that each member of this task force will be excused from twenty hours of regular work per week for up to three months," replied Rob. "I don't think we have to put that in writing."

Derek commented, "We haven't even begun and there goes Gil, trying to ensure that he's not overworked. For me, I couldn't be more pleased to be assigned to this project. I've done some depth interviewing for a course I took in consumer psychology."

"Good enough, team, let's make up a tentative list of questions right now. We still have a couple of hours till quitting time."

"Hey, I've got an idea," said Gil. "While you four are working on the questionnaire, I'll run over to the statistical department and see if they can help us draw up a sample."

Two weeks later the Public Relations Task Force was ready to begin field interviewing. Each member was assigned twenty-five interviews to be conducted in a ten-day period. After the interviewing project was one-week old, Derek received a phone call from Willie:

"Derek, I've got something confidential to tell you."

"What is it, you're not in any trouble are you?"

"Not me exactly, Derek," said Willie. "But I think our team is headed for some trouble. I've just spoken to Ginger and she agrees. Gil has been goofing off since the start of the project. He finds the cutest ways to avoid work. He was supposed to meet me one day to do a group interview. Instead he left a message in my department that he was tied up with some urgent business matters."

"That's right, Willie, I remember the first day of our meeting, he took two hours to ask the statistical department a few questions. Have you noticed any other problem?"

"For sure. Not only is Gil behind in his interviews but I think he made up most of the ones that he plans to turn in. I think he is going to single-handedly ruin the output of the group."

"Okay, Willie, what are you telling me? What should we do about the problem?"

"That's why I've called you. Ginger doesn't have any good suggestions either. She thinks we should just let the issue ride. But if we turn in a mediocre or incomplete report, everybody on the task force will look bad. This is supposed to be a team effort. I'm afraid we're stuck with a team member who won't carry his weight."

Questions

1. What alternatives do you see facing Willie, Ginger, and Derek?
2. What would the advisability be of Ginger, Willie, and Derek calling a private meeting with Rob to discuss the situation?
3. What should Rob's role be in making sure that the team members make an equal contribution?
4. What does this case incident tell us about the functioning of task forces?
5. Is Gil being given a fair chance? Explain.

Additional Reading

BAKER, H. KENT. "Tapping into the Power of Informal Groups." *Supervisory Management,* February 1981, pp. 18–24.

BERTCHER, HARVEY J., and FRANK F. MAPLE. *Creating Groups.* Beverly Hills, Calif.: Sage Publications, 1977.

DESSLER, GARY. *Human Behavior: Improving Performance at Work.* Reston, Va.: Reston, 1980, Chapter 10.

DOUGLAS, TOM. *Basic Groupwork.* New York: International Universities Press, 1978.

HARE, PAUL A. *Handbook of Small Group Research,* 2nd ed. Riverside, N.J.: Free Press, 1976.

JEWELL, LINDA N., and H. JOSEPH REITZ. *Group Effectiveness in Organizations.* Glenview, Ill.: Scott, Foresman and Company, 1981.

JOHNSTAD, TRYGVE. *Group Dynamics and Society: A Multinational Approach.* Cambridge, Mass.: Oelgeschlager, Gunn & Hain, 1980.

PAULUS, PAUL B. ed. *Psychology of Group Influence.* Hillsdale, N.J.: Erlbaum, 1980.

SHAW, MARVIN E. *Group Dynamics: The Psychology of Small Group Behavior,* 3rd ed. New York: McGraw-Hill, 1981.

"Small Groups: An Agenda for Research and Theory," a special issue of *American Behavioral Scientist,* May 1981.

ZANDER, ALVIN. *Groups at Work: Unresolved Issues in the Study of Organizations.* San Francisco: Jossey-Bass, 1977.

CHAPTER 10

Group Decision Making

LEARNING OBJECTIVES

1. To be able to apply the model for deciding when to use group decision making.

2. To explain the nature of groupthink and the risky-shift phenomenon.

3. To know how to increase the effectiveness of meetings.

4. To be familiar with two methods for making group decisions without face-to-face interaction.

5. To explain the quality circle technique for improving product quality and productivity.

6. To discuss several advantages and disadvantages of group decision making.

Maria, director of County Social Services, looked forward to her Monday afternoon staff meeting. Eager to receive acceptance for her new program, she opened the meeting with these words, "I'm not one for long-winded introductions to important topics. I have a major program for your approval that could make us pacesetters in the social services field. By following my basic program, we will demonstrate that the government means business about moving into the modern age.

"I'm proposing that effective July 1 of this year, our Social Services Agency make the switch from the decimal to the metric system. No more hesitation; no more blocking the inevitable.

From July 1 forward, we think metric around here. When I read files about clients I want to see their height and weight expressed in centimeters and kilograms. When you tell me they need heating fuel, I want to know how many liters, not how many gallons."

Nomenee, director of housing, was the first to react: "Maria, I hear what you're saying, but I'm not in total agreement. I would think you would need ten levels of approval to make the switch you're talking about. We still receive a big chunk of our funding from state and federal sources. If we fall out of line with their official procedures, we could get penalized. Maybe even lose some of our funding."

Jean, director of administrative services, spoke next: "Maria, I wish you and I had thrashed this out before you made up your mind on this topic. Are you aware of the administrative nightmare you would be creating by converting to the metric system? We'd have to calculate metric equivalents for all the data in our files. Any time we sent files to out-of-county agencies we'd get a barrage of complaints."

Maria replied, "I hear some resistance from the group surfacing. But any worthwhile change will have its critics. So I won't be dissuaded by a few negative comments."

Ron, director of income maintenance, commented, "Maria, you're dealing with more than a few negative comments. You're trying to buy into one of the biggest government flops of the decade. So far the metric conversion program has had its biggest impact on diary and calendar makers. Engagement calendars and the like now all contain metric conversion tables. And a small proportion of gas pumps dispense liters rather than gallons. So why bother with a program that is dying on its launching pad? Up in Canada it's a different story. But we're in the States."

Helen, director of child services, spoke next: "I make a motion that we table the idea of a metric conversion program at this time. Perhaps we should set up a task force to study the issue more carefully."

Reluctantly, Maria said, "Okay, who seconds the motion of tabling the metric conversion program? After we vote on this motion, we will introduce the motion of setting up the necessary task force."

As the group considered the motion, Maria thought to herself, "What did I do wrong? Maybe I should have just issued an edict to convert to the metric system."

Depending upon your commitment to the metric system, the case just described is an example of the functional or dysfunctional aspects of group decision making. Maria thought she had a good idea, but when she brought it up for group consideration it was swiftly torpedoed. Another conclusion you may have reached about the vignette presented is that Maria did not use the appropriate leadership tactics to get her idea implemented. She "told" instead of "sold," or perhaps she allowed the group to move too quickly toward a formal motion. Whatever analysis you make of the incident, it does illustrate that many decisions made in organizations are in fact group decisions. A good starting point in understanding the group decision-making process is to examine a model that tells a manager whether or not group decision making is appropriate for a given situation.

THE VROOM-YETTON MODEL FOR DECIDING WHEN TO USE GROUP DECISION MAKING

Vroom and Yetton have developed a model (or set of guidelines) to help the group leader decide how much to allow subordinates to participate in making decisions.[1] The same model can also be presented as a method of selecting the appropriate leadership style for a given situation. Since the focus on the model is upon decision making, we discuss it here rather than in the leadership chapter. The anchor points on the continuum of leader decision-making behavior are autocratic, consultative, and group or consensus decisions. (Maria tried to be unilateral, but somehow the group did not accept her authority.) The different management decision styles are described in the following listing. As the decision approach moves from AI, the amount of subordinate influence over the final decision increases. ("A" stands for autocratic, "C" for consultative, and "G" for group.)

Types of Management Decision Styles

AI	Manager solves the problem or makes the decision alone, using currently available information.
AII	Manager obtains necessary information from subordinates. Then manager decides on the solution to the problem alone. Manager may or may not tell subordinates what the problem is in getting the information from them (as in synectics). The role played by subordinates in making the decision is clearly one of providing the necessary information rather than generating or evaluating the alternative solutions.
CI	Manager shares problems with relevant subordinates individually, obtaining their ideas and suggestions without bringing them together as a group. Manager then makes the decision that may or may not reflect subordinates' influence.
CII	Manager shares the problem with subordinates as a group, collectively obtaining their ideas and suggestions. Then manager makes the decision, which may or may not reflect the subordinates' influence.
GII	Manager shares the problem with subordinates as a group. Together they generate and evaluate alternatives and attempt to reach agreement (consensus) on a solution. The manager's role is much like that of a chairperson. The manager does not try to influence the group to adopt his or her solution and is willing to accept and implement any solution that has the support of the entire group. Other options also exist such as delegating the problem to a subordinate or the group and letting them make the decision by themselves.

[1]The information presented here, including the types of decision styles discussed in this chapter, is based on Victor H. Vroom, "A New Look in Managerial Decision Making," *Organizational Dynamics,* Spring 1973, pp. 66–80, and Victor H. Vroom and Philip W. Yetton, *Leadership and Decision Making* (Pittsburgh: University of Pittsburgh Press, 1973).

The model is a contingency one, taking into account characteristics of the situation that influence which of the five decision styles should be used. Seven questions are presented that the leader can ask himself or herself, along with a set of decision rules put in the form of a decision tree that leads to the most desirable option to be used (see Figure 10–1). The seven questions are arranged so that a leader can analyze his or her immediate problem situation and, by answering yes or no to each question, arrive at feasible decision alternatives.[2]

For many paths through the decision tree the answer generated may still reflect a viable choice between an essentially autocratic or essentially participative alternative. In that case, the leader can assess whether he or she wants to use a short-run model to maximize short-term efficiency (by using an autocratic solution) or a long-run developmental model that maximizes the ability of subordinates to learn how to solve problems themselves. The underlying decision rules (contingency factors) that lead to the feasible alternatives are described next.

[2]This particular explanation of the V-Y model is excerpted and paraphrased from Edgar H. Schein, *Organizational Psychology,* 3rd ed. (Englewood Cliffs, N.J.: Prentice-Hall, 1980), pp. 118–22. Reprinted with permission.

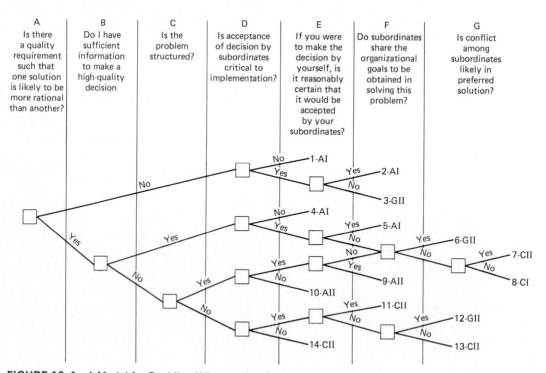

FIGURE 10–1 A Model for Deciding When to Use Group Decision Making

Source: Reprinted from *Leadership and Decision Making* by Victor H. Vroom and Philip W. Yetton, pp. 41–42, by permission of the University of Pittsburgh Press. © 1973 by the University of Pittsburgh Press.

Rules to Enhance Decision Quality

1. *The information rule.* If the quality of the decision is important and if the leader does not possess sufficient information or expertise to solve the problem alone, AI is eliminated from the feasible set. Its use risks a low-quality decision.

2. *The trust rule.* If the quality of the decision is important and if the subordinates cannot be trusted to base their efforts to solve the problem on organizational goals, GII is eliminated from the feasible set. Alternatives that eliminate the leader's final control over the decision reached may jeopardize the quality of the decision.

3. *The unstructured problem rule.* Assume that the quality of the decision is important. If the leader lacks the information or expertise to solve the problem alone, and if the problem is unstructured (ill-defined), the method chosen must allow for productive methods of collecting information. Methods that involve interaction among all subordinates with full knowledge of the problem are likely to lead to a high-quality solution. Under these conditions, AI, AII, and CI are eliminated from the feasible set. For example, AI does not give the leader the opportunity to collect the necessary information.

Rules to Enhance Decision Acceptance

4. *The acceptance rule.* If subordinate acceptance of the decision is critical to implementation, AI and AII are eliminated from the feasible set. Neither provides an opportunity for subordinates to participate in the decision and both risk the necessary acceptance.

5. *The conflict rule.* AI, AII, and CI are eliminated from the feasible set if (a) the acceptance of the decision is critical and (b) an autocratic decision is not certain to be accepted. The method used in solving the problem should enable those in disagreement to resolve their differences with full knowledge of the problem. For this reason also, AI, AII, and CI are excluded because they involve no opportunity for those in conflict to resolve their differences. Using them runs the risk of leaving some of the subordinates with less than the necessary commitment to the final decision.

6. *The fairness rule.* If the quality of the decision is unimportant, but acceptance is critical, and not certain to result from an autocratic decision, AI, AII, CI, and CII are eliminated from the feasible set. In contrast, GII tends to generate more acceptance and commitment.

7. *The acceptance priority rule.* If acceptance is critical, but not assured by an autocratic decision, and if subordinates can be trusted, AI, AII, CI and CII are eliminated from the feasible set. Methods that provide equal partnership in the decision process can provide greater acceptance without risking decision quality. Use of any methods other than GII results in an unnecessary risk that the decision will not be fully accepted or receive the necessary commitment by subordinates.

An example of using the decision tree.   Suppose that Bud, a maintenance manager, wants to change the work schedule to have at least one maintenance engineer on duty at all times between 9 A.M. and 9 P.M., six days a week, constituting a change from previous work schedules. He has several alternatives facing him. Bud starts with question A in Figure 10–1, "Is there a quality requirement?" Bud decides that there is none since he will be satisfied with a wide variety of work schedules so long as there is coverage from 9 to 9, six days a week. Because he answered "No" to question A, he must proceed to question D, "Is acceptance of decision by subordinates critical to effective implementation?" Suppose Bud thinks that the answer to question D is "Yes" since acceptance of the schedule is critical to successful implementation.

Because he answered "Yes," Bud must next answer question E, "If I were to make the decision by myself, is it reasonably certain that it would be accepted by my subordinates?" A "No" answer to question E leads to the recommendation that the approach for making this type of decision is GII. It requires the decision maker to share the problem with the group and to agree to accept any alternative that the group supports.[3]

Comment

The Vroom and Yetton model is time consuming, yet it does provide a useful framework for making systematic decisions about the extent of employee participation in group decision making. Research results show that if managers follow the prescriptions of the model, they are likely to improve the success rate of their decisions.[4] A useful spinoff from the model is that it has generated a rule of thumb that can readily be followed to improve decision making:

> If acceptance of a decision by subordinates is critical to effective implementation and it is reasonably certain that subordinates would not accept autocratic decisions, but they share organizational goals (or decision quality is not important), use GII. Otherwise, use CII.[5]

CREATING THE RIGHT ATMOSPHERE FOR GROUP DECISION MAKING

Group decision making and creativity are similar processes in two important respects: first, they are more relevant for nonprogrammed than programmed decisions, and, second, they are helped along by a leadership climate that encourages people to ex-

---

[3]This illustration follows closely that provided by Henry L. Tosi and Stephen J. Carroll, *Management,* 2nd ed. (New York: John Wiley, 1982), p. 372.

[4]Victor H. Vroom and Arthur G. Jago, "On the Validity of the Vroom-Yetton Model," *Journal of Applied Psychology,* April 1978, pp. 151–62.

[5]George R. H. Field, "A Critique of the Vroom-Yetton Contingency Model of Leadership Behavior," *The Academy of Management Review,* October 1979, pp. 249–57, as quoted in Tosi and Carroll, *Management,* p. 373.

press their ideas, opinions, and feelings. The findings about creativity-inducing leaders summarized in Chapter 8 apply also to providing an atmosphere that facilitates group decision making. Table 10–1 presents a set of guidelines for establishing the permissive atmosphere known to enhance group decision making. Although a few of these guidelines would also apply to brainstorming, the desirable outcome from group decision

TABLE 10–1   Creative Group Decision Making

Group Structure

The group is composed of heterogeneous, generally competent personnel who bring to bear on the problem diverse frames of reference, representing channels to each relevant body of knowledge (including contact with outside resource personnel who offer expertise not encompassed by the organization), with a leader who facilitates creative process.

Group Roles

Behavior is characterized by each individual exploring with the entire group all ideas (no matter how intuitively and roughly formed) that bear on the problem.

Group Processes

The problem-solving process is characterized by
 Spontaneous communication between members (not focused on the leader).
 Full participation from each member.
 Separation of idea generation from idea evaluation.
 Separation of problem definition from generation of solution strategies.
 Shifting of roles, so that interaction, which mediates problem solving (particularly search activities and clarification by means of constant questioning directed both to individual members and the whole group), is not the sole responsibility of the leader.
 Suspension of judgment and avoidance of early concern with solutions, so that emphasis is on analysis and exploration rather than on early solution commitment.

Group Style

The social-emotional tone of the group if characterized by
 A relaxed, nonstressful environment.
 Ego-supportive interaction, where open give and take between members is at the same time courteous.
 Behavior that is motivated by interest in the problem rather than concern with short-run payoff.
 Absence of penalties attached to any espoused idea or position.

Group Norms

 Are supportive of originality and unusual ideas and allow for eccentricity.
 Seek behavior that separates source from content in evaluating information and ideas.
 Stress a nonauthoritarian view, with a realistic view of life and independence of judgment.
 Support humor and undisciplined exploration of viewpoints.
 Seek openness in communication, where mature, self-confident individuals offer "crude" ideas to the group for mutual exploration without threat to the individuals for "exposing" themselves.
 Deliberately avoid credence to short-run results, or short-run decisiveness.
 Seek consensus, but accept majority rule when consensus is unobtainable.

Source: Andre L. Delbecq, "The Management of Decision Making Within the Firm: Three Strategies for Three Types of Decision Making," *Academy of Management Journal,* December 1967, pp. 334–35.

making is to specify a recommended course of action. Brainstorming is usually concerned more with specifying a number of alternatives to a problem.

GROUPTHINK

Although it is important to create the right atmosphere for group decision making, at times the atmosphere is so comfortable that group members cease to think independently. Loss of independence in thinking occurs most often when the group is highly cohesive. The group thinks as a unit rather than as a collection of individuals. Called groupthink, it is an extreme form of consensus. The concept was formulated by Janis while he was reading about the United States' foreign policy mistakes at the Bay of Pigs.[6] The Central Intelligence Agency (CIA) developed a plan to invade Cuba and eventually overthrow Fidel Castro. A seriously flawed plan, it ended in embarrassment to the U.S. government.

At first, Janis wondered how intelligent people like John F. Kennedy and his advisors could accept the irrational plan offered by the CIA. Later he realized that the behavior of the decision makers fit a pattern of concurrence seeking that also takes place in other cohesive groups. The original Watergate break-in appears to have been a product of groupthink. Similarly, when a group of workers jointly decides to sabotage an assembly line, groupthink is probably an important underlying process. Eight main symptoms of groupthink have been identified:

1. An illusion of invulnerability shared by group members, which leads to overoptimism and encourages high risk taking.
2. Collective efforts at rationalization so as to discredit warnings that might lead members to question their policy decisions.
3. An unquestioned belief in the group's morality, leading group members to ignore the ethical or moral consequences of their decisions.
4. Stereotyped views of the opposition as too evil to warrant genuine attempts to negotiate or as too inept to counter whatever attempts are made to defeat their purposes.
5. Direct pressure on any member who expresses strong arguments against any of the group's thinking, making clear that dissent is contrary to what is expected of loyal members.
6. Self-censorship of deviations from the apparent group consensus.
7. A shared illusion of unanimity concerning judgments and opinions conforming to the majority view.
8. "The emergence of self-appointed mind guards, defined as members who protect the group from information that might shatter their shared complacency about the effectiveness and morality of their decisions."[7]

[6]The original source here is Irving J. Janis, *Victims of Groupthink* (Boston: Houghton Mifflin, 1972). Our discussion is also based on the formulation prepared by Thomas V. Bonoma and Gerald Zaltman, *Psychology for Management* (Boston: Kent, 1981), pp. 206–8.

[7]This list is based on and the quotation is from Janis, *Victims of Groupthink*, p. 198.

Although the major group characteristic leading to groupthink is cohesiveness, not all cohesive groups succumb to this dysfunction. Group leaders can follow several suggestions to defeat the occurrence of groupthink in policy and decision-making groups.

> Encourage all group members to express doubts and criticisms of proposed solutions to problems. (For example, a White House advisor observed that if one cabinet member had opposed the Bay of Pigs fiasco, it would never have happened.)
>
> Show by example that you are willing to accept criticism.
>
> Divide the group into subgroups to develop ideas. Then have the subgroups confront one another to examine why they differ.
>
> Periodically invite qualified outsiders to meet with the group and provide suggestions.
>
> If groupthink seems to be emerging, bring it to the attention of the group. A comment of this nature might be effective: "I get the impression that we are too eager to think as one. What is your reaction to the problem?"
>
> Assign at least one group member to the role of devil's advocate at meetings in which alternatives are evaluated.[8]

RISK-TAKING BEHAVIOR
WITHIN GROUPS

As mentioned in connection with groupthink, many people shift their behavior toward greater risk taking placed in a group setting.[9] According to the *risky-shift* concept, people who belong to stock investment clubs might recommend that the group invest in a stock of higher risk than those that they would purchase individually. An exercise follows that has been used to demonstrate the risky-shift phenomenon.[10]

> Julie, a commercial artist employed by an automobile manufacturer, inherits $20,000 (after inheritance taxes) from her parents' estate. Julie is divorced and has two children, ages nine and twelve, who live with her. Her former husband has moved out of state and infrequently sends his child-support payments.
>
> Julie discusses her inheritance with Rod, a salesman who sells ad space for magazines. The two of them have been dating regularly for three months but do not have an exclusive relationship. One week after the discussion, Rod suggests that Julie and he open a commercial art studio, using $15,000 of her inheritance as the initial investment. According to Rod's plan (1) Julie will be president of the studio, (2) Rod will be the administrator and be responsible for soliciting business for the studio, (3) Julie will perform the art work assisted by as many artists (on a subcontract basis) as the work load requires, (4) Julie will retain 75 percent of the profits and Rod 25 percent, and (5) they will each receive an equal salary, geared to cover their basic living expenses.

---

[8]David R. Hamptom, *Contemporary Management* (New York: McGraw-Hill, 1977), pp. 184–85.

[9] James A. F. Stoner, "Risky and Cautious Shifts in Group Decisions: The influence of Widely Held Values," *Journal of Experimental Social Psychology,* Vol. 4, 1968, pp. 442–59.

[10]Exercise from Andrew J. DuBrin, *Human Relations: A Job-Oriented Approach,* 2nd ed. (Reston, Va.: Reston, 1981), p. 179.

Which one of the following alternatives should Julie choose?

1. Tell Rod to get lost and forget the deal.
2. Wait until Rod makes a marriage proposal before even considering entering into a business relationship with him.
3. Agree to the general idea except that she invest $5,000, and that they begin business on a part-time (evenings and weekends) basis. Neither would resign his or her position until the studio was big enough to justify a full-time effort.
4. Accept the general idea, but insist that Rod put up one-half of the investment. He could then share equally in the profits.
5. Totally accept Rod's proposition, recognizing that "opportunity only knocks once." And, of course, have a lawyer scrutinize the formal partnership contract.

In experiments such as these, people tend to choose a less risky course of action when they choose the alternatives individually. When such problems are discussed in small groups, the average risk-taking score tends to be higher. Several reasonable explanations have been advanced for the risky shift. First, in an open environment, groups are able to share information. If the information seems optimistic, you are more willing to take a risk than if you were less informed. Second, cultural values favor risk taking. In a group setting, a person may be embarrassed to appear too conservative and would therefore act more bullish. Third, responsibility for the possible loss is spread out over a few people. People are more willing to take chances when they will not be totally responsible for things that may go wrong—others are present to share in the blame.

INCREASING THE EFFECTIVENESS OF MEETINGS

As implied by most of the lead-in cases presented in this text, much of organization behavior takes place within the context of a meeting. Managers spend much of their time in meetings, with some managers conducting virtually all their work in small groups. Technical and professional employees also devote much of their work time to meetings. Since most work in organizations involves the coordinated effort of people, meetings cannot be eliminated. A more realistic strategy is to observe some of the guidelines that have been formulated by researchers for the more effective management of committees and meetings in general. The accompanying box contains a representative set of prescriptions for the leader who wants to improve the outcome of meetings (see page 265). Presented next is an explanation of the kinds of behaviors by a committee head that will facilitate a productive meeting.

1. *Committees work most effectively when they have the properties of effective work groups in general.* As discussed in the previous chapter, this includes considerations such as optimum size, cohesiveness, mix of people, and a norm structure that encourages high productivity.

2. *The committee chairperson should be directive and task oriented in his or her behavior, but not necessarily authoritarian.* As noted in a *Harvard Business Review* sur-

CHECKLIST FOR MEETING LEADERSHIP SKILLS

In preparing for meetings, do you   Yes   No   Sometimes

1. Write out your goals and objectives in advance of the meeting? ☐ ☐ ☐
2. Evaluate the meeting and members in attendance for cost effectiveness? ☐ ☐ ☐
3. Determine the number of topics that can be discussed productively within the time limit? ☐ ☐ ☐
4. Send those who will attend a clear, descriptive agenda prior to the meeting? ☐ ☐ ☐
5. Review possible procedures for conducting the meeting (for example, brainstorming or buzz groups) and then select the most appropriate? ☐ ☐ ☐

In conducting meetings, do you

1. Temper your own role in the meeting so that others feel free to fully contribute? ☐ ☐ ☐
2. Employ effective listening skills? ☐ ☐ ☐
3. Match your leadership and decision-making style to the needs of the particular situation? ☐ ☐ ☐
4. Recognize the strengths in what others are saying as well as the weaknesses? ☐ ☐ ☐
5. Help group members to voice their criticisms in an open, constructive manner? ☐ ☐ ☐
6. Feel equipped to handle the problem roles of such members as monopolizers, aggressors, quiet types, and chronic complainers? ☐ ☐ ☐

Source: William Kirkwood and Janice Wilson, "Leadership Strategies for Successful Meetings," *Supervisory Management,* October 1981, p. 5. Reprinted with permission from American Management Associations. © 1981 by AMACOM, a division of American Management Associations. All rights reserved.

vey, "the problem is not so much committees in management as it is the management of committees."[11] Considerable empirical evidence and common sense underscore the importance of an effective leader for productive committee functioning. Although the task orientation is crucial, the chairperson or someone else must take care of the social leadership role as well.[12]

[11]Rollie Tillman, Jr., "Problems in Review: Committees on Trial," *Harvard Business Review,* May–June 1960, p. 171.

[12]Alan C. Filley, Robert J. House, and Steven Kerr, *Managerial Process and Organizational Behavior,* 2nd ed. (Glenview, Ill.: Scott, Foresman and Company, 1976), p. 417.

3. *The committee chairperson should encourage constructive ideas by sharing power and acting as a collaborator with members.* In most meetings the superior makes many statements that inhibit creative responses from group members. Learning to be more accepting of ideas from participants tends to spur on creativity. Considerable skill is required to modify or resist suggestions from the group without inhibiting creativity or further contributions. Concerns and flaws should be noted as subproblems to be worked on to keep the group's energy focused on building a solution. Here is a sample interchange of this approach:

> *Mr. A:*   You know, if we decentralize our manufacturing, we could cut shipping costs.
>
> *Manager:*   Decentralizing would do some nice things for us. It would save on shipping and it would give us smaller, faster-moving manufacturing units. Another thing I like about the idea is that it would break up this huge, centralized operation and spread responsibilities in the organization. (Having acknowledged the value in Mr. A's thinking and revealed some of his values too, the manager shifts to his own concerns.) I have some problems here to consider—how to decentralize without any capital expense, for one. Another is how to retain both economies of scale and the advantages of small plants.[13]

4. *Committee members should be technically and personally qualified to serve on the committee, and they should also have an appropriate interest in serving.* As obvious as this principle sounds, it is frequently violated. Many people are appointed to committees who either cannot or do not wish to make a contribution. Some people are technically knowledgeable about the subject matter under discussion but lack the face-to-face communication skills necessary to be an effective participant. Often communication skills can be acquired in training programs or by serving on committees of lesser importance. One company president's analysis of the technical and personal qualifications for committee membership is relevant here:

> Committee members should be selected on the basis of their knowledge, their responsibility, and their interest in the areas in which the committee is to function. They should bring knowledge and information to the committee; . . . they should be interested, active participants. To my way of thinking, the appointment of a person to a committee for the sole purpose of conferring some sort of status to that person, or building his or her ego and prestige, is a bad move.[14]

5. *The leader should not dominate the discussion.* Related to the first suggestion, the leader should not become the dominant person in the meeting. If you are conducting a problem-solving meeting, your main task is to elicit ideas from the group, not supply

---

[13]George M. Prince, "Creative Meetings Through Power Sharing," *Harvard Business Review,* July–August 1972, p. 53.

[14]Tillman, "Committees on Trial," p. 171.

them. A natural tendency exists for the head of a meeting to try to sell his or her ideas to other members and to argue against contrary opinions. Such behavior curtails the free exchange of ideas.[15]

GROUP DECISION MAKING WITHOUT MEETINGS

Since group decision making is such a critical process, substantial resources have been committed to its improvement. Two techniques have been developed that provide for the input of several people on a project but do not require face-to-face interaction of those people involved. Both methods, the nominal group technique (NGT) and the Delphi technique, are designed to capitalize upon the value of collective thought without incurring the problems that may arise when people interact to solve a problem, particularly groupthink.

The Nominal Group Technique

The opposite of an interacting group is a nominal or coaching group whose distinguishing characteristic is silent effort in a group setting. A basic illustration would be for group members to individually write down their solutions to a problem. In this way no one person would dominate and nobody would feel embarrassed. The steps in the NGT are straightforward:

1. Members of the target group are chosen and brought together.
2. If the group is overly large, it is divided into subgroups of eight members or less.
3. The group leader presents a specific question.
4. Individual members silently and independently record their ideas in writing.
5. Each group member (one at a time, in turn, around the table) presents one idea to the group without discussion. The ideas are summarized and recorded on a chalkboard, a flipchart, or a sheet of paper on the wall.
6. After all members have presented their ideas, a discussion takes place to clarify and evaluate the ideas.
7. The meeting terminates with a silent, and independent, voting on priorities by individuals through a rank ordering or rating procedure. The nominal group decision is the pooled outcome of the individual votes.[16]

The NGT is widely used and reported generally to meet with success. Experiments have shown it to be equal to or better than an interacting group for the purposes

[15]Gary Dessler, *Human Behavior: Improving Performance at Work* (Reston, Va.: Reston, 1981), p. 276.

[16]Andrew H. Van de Ven and Andre L. Delbecq, "The Effectiveness of Nominal, Delphi, and Interacting Group Decision-Making Processes," *Academy of Management Journal,* December 1974, p. 606.

of generating a large number of alternatives, minimizing errors, and satisfying group members.[17]

The Delphi Technique

In some instances, group input is needed, yet it is difficult to bring people together because of the cost or time away from the office involved. The Delphi technique is ideal for these purposes, and it offers most of the advantages of the NGT. As outlined in Figure 10–2, the Delphi technique incorporates a carefully structured sequence of questionnaires to each group member. Each person answers the questionnaire about the problem at hand and mails along his or her responses and thoughts to the coordinator. As the questionnaires go through successive iterations, feedback is provided to the different people working on the problem. Problem-solving ordinarily improves with each successive input. In the last round of questionnaires, group members are asked to vote for their choice of solutions. Responses are sometimes averaged; at other times, some people's choices are given more weight than others.[18]

The Delphi technique is excellent in terms of obtaining multiple inputs to a problem (such as designing a new distribution system). A striking disadvantage is that the technique is hampered by the normal human tendency to procrastinate.

The relative advantages, disadvantages, and distinguishing features of interacting groups, nominal groups, and the Delphi technique are summarized in Table 10–2. Which technique you use to solve a particular problem depends upon which dimension (such as time required to obtain group ideas) you value highly.

QUALITY CIRCLES

Considerable attention has been paid in recent years to a group decision-making approach to improving product quality and productivity called quality circles (QCs). In general format, they are teams of workers, including supervisors and individual contributors, who meet regularly to solve production and quality problems and sometimes to brainstorm ways to improve productivity. QC groups attempt to solve operational problems traditionally handled by management alone. Both products and services (such as health care delivery systems) can be improved by the QC method. The impetus behind the QC movement in the United States has been its identification as an important contributor to the success of Japanese industry.[19] Paradoxically, an American statistician named Deming introduced quality circles to Japan! Although QC programs vary from company to company, a representative format follows the diagram

---

[17]Ramon J. Aldag and Arthur P. Brief, *Managing Organizational Behavior* (St. Paul: West, 1981), p. 281.

[18]Norman Dalkey, *The Delphi Method: An Experimental Study of Group Opinions* (Santa Monica, Calif.: Rand Corporation, 1969).

[19]Gerald D. Klein, "Implementing Quality Circles: A Hard Look at Some of the Realities," *Personnel,* November–December 1981, p. 11.

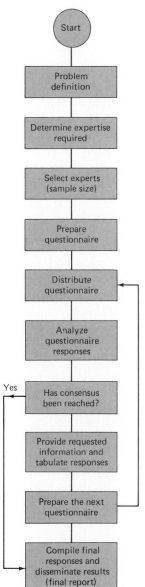

FIGURE 10–2 Steps in the Delphi Process

Source: R. J. Tersine and W. E. Riggs, "The Delphi Technique: A Long-Range Planning Tool," *Business Horizons,* April 1976, p. 53. Copyright © 1976 by the Foundation for the School of Business at Indiana University.

shown in Figure 10–3. Successful QC programs appear to have certain elements in common. Those elements most related to group dynamics and group decision making, plus one research-oriented suggestion, are as follows:[20]

---

[20]This list is based on two sources: Ed Yager, "Examining the Quality Control Circle," *Personnel Journal,* October 1979, p. 684, and Robert J. Barbato and Richard E. Drexel, "Americanizing Quality Circles," in Sang M. Lee and Gary Schwendeman, *Management by Japanese Systems,* (New York: Praeger, 1982), pp. 491–94.

TABLE 10–2 Comparison of Qualitative Differences Among Three Decision Processes Based upon Evaluations of Leaders and Group Participants

Dimension	Interacting Groups	Nominal Groups	Delphi Technique
Overall methodology	Unstructured face-to-face group meeting High flexibility High variability in behavior of groups	Structured face-to-face group meeting Low flexibility Low variability in behavior of groups	Structured series of questionnaires and feedback reports Low variability respondent behavior
Role orientation of groups	Socioemotional Group maintenance focus	Balanced focus on social maintenance and task role	Task-instrumental focus
Relative quantity of ideas	Low; focused "rut" effect	Higher; independent writing and hitch-hiking round robin	High; isolated writing of ideas
Search behavior	Reactive search Short problem focus Task-avoidance tendency New social knowledge	Proactive search Extended problem focus High task centeredness New social and task knowledge	Proactive search Controlled problem focus High task centeredness New task knowledge
Normative behavior	Conformity pressures inherent in face-to-face discussions	Tolerance for nonconformity through independent search and choice activity	Freedom not to conform through isolated anonymity
Equality of participation	Member dominance in search, evaluation, and choice phases	Member equality in search and choice phases	Respondent equality in pooling of independent judgments
Method of problem solving	Person-centered Smoothing over and withdrawal	Problem-centered Confrontation and problem solving	Problem-centered Majority rule of pooled independent judgments
Closure decision process	High lack of closure Low felt accomplishment	Lower lack of closure High felt accomplishment	Low lack of closure Medium felt accomplishment
Resources utilized	Low administrative time and cost High participant time and cost	Medium administrative time, cost, preparation High participant time and cost	High administrative
Time to obtain group ideas	1½ hours	1½ hours	5 calendar months

Source: Used with permission from Andrew Van de Ven and Andre Delbecq. "The Effectiveness of Nominal, Delphi, and Inter-acting Group Decision-Making Processes," *Academy of Management Journal,* December 1974, pp. 605–21.

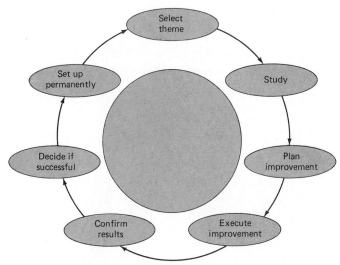

FIGURE 10–3 Representative Model of a Quality Circle

1. *Membership should be voluntary.* As with all other forms of participative management and job enrichment, employee preference is an important contingency factor. Employees who desire to contribute their ideas will generally perform better than will employees who are arbitrarily assigned to the QC program.

2. *QCs are group efforts, not individual efforts.* Recognizing this factor decreases dysfunctional competition and increases cooperation and the value of interdependence within the group. Quality circles, not individual employees, should receive credit for innovations and suggestions for improvement.

3. *Participation from all members is essential.* The leader's central responsibility is therefore to encourage all members of the circle to contribute and to facilitate free expression of ideas.

4. *Creativity is encouraged.* Group brainstorming, or a slight variation thereof, fits naturally into the quality circle method and philosophy. For example, it is important to maintain an attitude of "anything goes." If half-developed ideas are discouraged by the leader or other members, idea generation will extinguish quickly.

5. *Involvement of line managers in all aspects of the program.* The success of the program is enhanced when line managers through education and involvement perceive a QC as an aid to accomplishing results rather than as an annoying and unproductive human relations program.

6. *Effectiveness is measured using baseline data.* A team that helped to design and implement a QC program observes that it is important to measure and report success in terms that are directly related to productivity. Baseline measures of value include

amount of scrap, amount of rework, rate of absenteeism, rate of turnover, and attitude change.[21]

Properly implemented, quality circles are a highly profitable form of group decision making. Over 10 million Japanese workers are active in QC programs. Thousands of American workers in well-established American firms are also involved in such programs. The Quality Circle Institute (perhaps not an unbiased source of information) reports that QCs have been known to save substantial amounts of money for firms. On balance, they represent a low-cost, efficient vehicle for unleashing the creative potential of employees. Counterarguments regarding QC include the assertions that sometimes the wrong group members dominate, people may volunteer for the wrong reason (such as getting time off from regular work), and too much reliance is put upon the ideas of people without advanced technical training. A delicate problem is the issue of how much QC participants should share in the cost savings stemming from their suggestions. QCs provide intrinsic rewards such as the opportunity to express creativity but many employees also demand extrinsic rewards.

ADVANTAGES AND DISADVANTAGES OF GROUP DECISION MAKING AND PROBLEM SOLVING

At times groups are superior to individuals in solving problems and making nonprogrammed decisions; at other times individuals have the edge. (Programmed decisions are rarely brought before a group.) The topic of group versus individual superiority has already been touched upon in several places including the discussion of brainstorming in Chapter 8 and the analysis of potential disadvantages of group effort in Chapter 9. Of greater validity than the debate of individual versus group superiority is a specification of the conditions that favor group versus individual decision making. A broad generalization is that group decision making and problem solving tend to be better when the group involved has the characteristics of an effective work group. Also, it only makes sense to compare group and individual decision making when dealing with people of comparable caliber acting alone or in groups. With these general points in mind, there is merit in summarizing the advantages and disadvantages of group decision making and problem solving.[22]

Advantages

- A greater sum total of knowledge and information is accessible in a group than in any of its members. Members are often able to fill in each others' information gaps.

[21]Barbato and Drexel, "Americanizing Quality Circles."

[22]This analysis is based upon the author's own analysis and Norman R. F. Maier, "Assets and Liabilities in Group Problem Solving: The Need for an Integrative Function," *Psychological Review*, Vol. 47, 1967, pp. 239–49.

- Groups provide a greater number of approaches to a problem because individuals are more likely to get into ruts in their thinking. "Since group members do not have identical approaches, each can contribute by knocking others out of ruts of thinking."
- Participation in decision making and problem solving increases acceptance of the decision or the solution to the problem (this is the best documented fact in group dynamics).
- Group effort increases comprehension of the decision. Since group members have been involved in the decision, further information about the decision does not have to be relayed to them. Also, people understand the decision better because they saw and heard it develop.
- Groups are more effective at establishing objectives, identifying alternatives, and evaluating alternatives because of the increased knowledge and viewpoints available to them.
- Since group members evaluate each other's thinking, major errors, bloopers, and "glitches" tend to be avoided by groups.

Disadvantages

- Groups create pressures toward conformity, groupthink, and mediocrity in decision making.
- In a group setting there is a distinct tendency to accept the first satisficing (just acceptable) decision that emerges. As research shows, "If the number of negative and positive comments for each solution are algebraically summed, each may be given a valence index. The first solution that receives a positive valence of .15 tends to be adopted to the satisfaction of all participants about 85 percent of the time, regardless of its quality."[23]
- Dominant members sometimes make the major decisions in a group setting, thus eliminating the potential contributions of nonassertive members.
- Winning an argument sometimes becomes a secondary goal of aggressive group members. Decision-making and problem-solving quality consequently suffer.
- Individuals are vastly superior to groups at the implementation phase of a decision.
- In general, group processes interfere with decision making and problem solving when the situation calls for a sequence of multiple stages, when the problem is not easily divisible into distinct and separate parts, and when the correctness of the solution is not easily demonstrated.[24]

Some Field Research About the Effectiveness of Group Decision Making

According to Bernard M. Bass, a great many laboratory studies demonstrate that group decisions are better than those made by its average member. However, few non-laboratory examples of group superiority are available. A survey was therefore conducted of the decisions of U.S. firms over a five-year period about overseas locations for 118 plants. Two of the research questions asked were

1. Overall, looking back on it, how would you evaluate the decision to locate the plant where you did?

[23]This and the previous quotation are from Maier, "Assets and Liabilities," p. 241.
[24]H. Joseph Reitz, *Behavior in Organizations,* rev. ed. (Homewood, Ill.: Richard D. Irwin, 1981), p. 353.

2. Who made the final decision in selecting each site?

For the 118 sites, 26 percent had been decided by an individual executive (including the chief executive officer), 47 percent had been decided by the board of directors, and 27 percent by a task force, operating committee, or executive committee. Decision quality was rated on a three-point scale: "Best possible" decisions were scored as 2, "satisfactory" decisions as 1, and "less than satisfactory" decisions were scored as 0. The overall mean effectiveness rating for the 118 decisions was 1.51—midway between "satisfactory" and "best possible." A statistically significant difference was found between the effectiveness ratings for group and individual decision making:

1. Decisions made by individual executives had a mean rating of 1.32.
2. Decisions made by boards of directors had a mean rating of 1.51.
3. Decisions made by committees or task forces had a mean rating of 1.66.

It was concluded that plant location decisions made by groups such as a committee of executives or the board of directors were perceived as more effective than those made by an individual executive. "These results would appear to be a practical demonstration of the extent that group decision making is superior to that of its average member."[25]

Bass's study is best interpreted as a demonstration of how under ideal conditions a complex organization decision is better made by a group than an individual. The subjects in this study were probably well-motivated, experienced, and intelligent individuals. Quite often people lacking in such qualities are asked to participate in group decision making.

IMPLICATIONS FOR MANAGERIAL PRACTICE

1. Be cautious of the tendency for organizations to give all important decisions automatically to the group. Before the organization decides to rely upon group decision making, it should be confident that the group can capitalize upon its advantages and that these advantages merit the cost of the group decision-making process.[26]

2. When accepting advice from a group, recognize that the group's decision may involve a higher degree of risk than the members would take individually.

3. If you are convinced of the rightness of your decision, be cautious about submitting it for group discussion. As Maria discovered, the group may defeat your proposal. To implement your decision, you would then have to overrule your approach to participative decision making.

[25]Bernard M. Bass, "Group Decision," *American Psychologist,* March 1977, pp. 230–31.
[26]Reitz, *Behavior in Organizations,* p. 371.

4.   If you wish to choose among authoritarian, consultative, or group decision-making methods, take the time (perhaps thirty minutes) and effort required to follow the Vroom and Yetton model.

5.   A rule of thumb for making the same choice is as follows: if acceptance of a decision by subordinates is critical to effective implementation and it is reasonably certain that subordinates would not accept autocratic decisions, but they share organizational goals (or decision quality is not important), use GII, the consensus solution. Otherwise, use CII, the shared-responsibility approach.

6.   An early strategic step in implementing a QC is to clarify relationships between the quality circle and the formal quality-control department and perhaps the suggestion system coordinator. If this step is not taken, the quality-control and employee suggestion departments may perceive the circle as a redundancy or threat. One effective arrangement is for the QC to complement the quality-control and suggestion departments rather than to take away some of their authority.

7.   Management must implement many of the suggestions forthcoming from the quality circle, yet still define the limits of the power and authority of the circle. If none of the circle's suggestions are adopted, the QC will lose its effectiveness as an agent for change. However, if the quality circle has too much power and authority, it will be seen as a governing body for technical change.[27]

Summary

- The Vroom-Yetton model described in considerable detail in this chapter helps a leader or manager to decide how much the group should participate in decision making. Key points on the continuum of decision-making style are autocratic, consultative, and group or consensus. The model is a contingency one, taking into account characteristics of the situation that influence which of five decision styles should be used. Seven questions are presented that the leader can ask himself or herself, along with a decision tree that leads to the most desirable option to be used (review Figure 10-1). The seven questions are arranged so that a leader can analyze his or her immediate problem situation and, by answering "Yes" or "No" to each question, arrive at feasible decision alternatives.

- Group decision making is facilitated by creating a leadership climate that encourages people to express their ideas, opinions, and feelings. In general, the same kind of permissive atmosphere that enhances creativity enhances group decision making.

- Groupthink is an extreme form of consensus in which the group thinks as a unit rather than as a collection of individuals. A leader can minimize groupthink by such mea-

[27]Points 6 and 7 are from DuBrin, *Contemporary Applied Management*, p. 122.

sures as (1) encouraging all group members to express doubts and criticisms of proposed solutions to problems, (2) showing a willingness to accept criticism, (3) using subgroups to develop ideas, and (4) assigning at least one person the role of devil's advocate at meetings in which alternatives are evaluated.

- Many people shift their behavior toward greater risk taking when placed in a group setting. Among the explanations offered for the risky-shift phenomenon are the information sharing that takes place in a group, the desire not to appear too conservative in front of others, and the possibility that blame for potential errors can be shared with other group members.

- Committee meetings, and meetings in general, tend to be more productive under the following conditions. (1) Chairperson is directive and task-oriented. (2) Chairperson shares power and acts as a collaborator with members. (3) Members are technically and personally qualified and are motivated to serve. (4) Chairperson does not dominate the discussion.

- The nominal group technique and the Delphi technique are designed to capitalize upon the value of collective thought without incurring the problems that may arise when people interact to solve a problem, particularly groupthink. Using the NGT, each person writes ideas on a pad of paper and later shares ideas with the group. The list of ideas is discussed, and finally a decision is reached by ranking or rating the individual ideas. Using the Delphi technique, the people contributing to the decision do not even meet. Instead each person answers a questionnaire about the problem at hand, and his or her imput is passed along to others. In the last round of questionnaires, group members are asked to vote for their choice of solutions.

- Quality circles are teams of workers who meet regularly to solve production and quality problems, sometimes using the brainstorming method. Successful QC programs have certain elements in common, including voluntary membership, participation of all members, the encouragement of creativity, involvement of line management in all phases of the program, and using baseline data to measure effectiveness.

Questions for Discussion

1. What proportion of managers do you think would be willing to devote the time and effort necessary to using the Vroom-Yetton model?
2. If you were about to purchase an automobile, would you use group or individual decision making? Why?
3. Identify two examples of groupthink in work or nonwork settings that you have observed or read about.
4. What fringe benefits not apparent on the surface do you think are provided by meetings?
5. Provide an additional suggestion for conducting a meeting that was not mentioned in this chapter.
6. Identify three services provided by a profit or not-for-profit organization that you think might be improved via a QC.
7. Why do you think it is usually unnecessary to use groups to make programmed decisions?

8. Why do ambitious people sometimes prefer individual over group decision making?
9. Both the Delphi and nominal group techniques have met with much success in situations where they have been applied. What factors do you think contribute to their success?
10. How might the Delphi technique be applied to helping you prepare an effective job résumé?

An Organizational Behavior Problem

Selecting the Most Appropriate Decision-Making Style

The purpose of this exercise is to gain experience in applying the Vroom-Yetton model to a decision-making situation. For the first exercise, refer to the case of Maria and the metric conversion. Based upon the information contained in the case, provide "Yes" or "No" answers to the seven questions asked in Figure 10-1. Next, proceed through the decision tree to arrive at a decision-making strategy that Maria should use (AI, GII, and so forth). Summarize your analysis on paper. Several class members will be asked to present their findings to the class. A group discussion will be held over such points as (1) Did we all agree on the best strategy for Maria? If not, why not? (2) Did Maria take the right action, as described in the case?

Second, create your own scenario for a decision-making situation to run through the V-Y Model. You might want to use a decision-making situation you recently faced on the job or in a domestic situation (such as Should we paint the apartment? If so, what color?).

Additional Reading

"A Personnel Journal Conference Report: Corporate Approaches to the Quality of Work Life." *Personnel Journal,* August 1980, pp. 632–34, 636–38.

BRADFORD, LELAND P. *Making Meetings Work: A Guide for Leaders and Group Members.* La Jolla, Calif.: University Associates, 1981.

DELBECQ, ANDRE, ANDREW H. VAN DE VEN, and DAVID H. GUSTAFSON. *Group Techniques for Program Planning.* Glenview, Ill.: Scott, Foresman and Company, 1975.

JENKINS, KENNETH M., and JUSTIN SHIMADA. "Quality Circles in the Service Sector." *Supervisory Management,* August 1981, pp. 2–7.

JEWELL, LINDA N., and H. JOSEPH REITZ. *Group Effectiveness in Organizations.* Glenview, Ill.: Scott, Foresman and Company, 1981, Chapter 5.

KIRKWOOD, WILLIAM, and JANICE WILSON. "Leadership Strategies for Successful Meetings." *Supervisory Management,* October 1981, pp. 2–8.

ROSS, JOEL E., and WILLIAM C. ROSS. *Japanese Quality Circles and Productivity.* Englewood Cliffs, N.J.: Prentice-Hall, 1982.

SHAW, ROBERT J. "Tapping the Riches of Creativity Among Working People." *Management Focus,* September–October 1981, pp. 24–29 (published by Peat, Marwick, Mitchell & Co.).

TROPMAN, JOHN E., HAROLD R. JOHNSON, and ELMER J. TROPMAN. *Essentials of Committee Management.* Chicago: Nelson-Hall, 1977.

VON BERGEN, CLARENCE W., Jr., and RAYMOND J. KIRK. "Groupthink: When Too Many Heads Spoil the Decision." *Management Review,* March 1978.

CHAPTER 11

Interpersonal Communication

LEARNING OBJECTIVES

1. To know the meaning of communication and identify the basic steps in the interpersonal communication process.

2. To understand the various directions in which communication takes place and the pathways over which messages travel.

3. To be aware of important barriers to communication and how they may be overcome.

4. To understand the role of nonverbal communication in organizations.

A machine tool company arranged a trade show exhibit to feature a recently developed computer-assisted manufacturing (CAM) system that the company thought would have a major impact on the industry. The company president believed that the trade show would be a sound advertising investment. Brochures were printed, material for the booth was purchased, and a trade show exhibitor was hired. Two weeks before the exhibit opened, the manager of manufacturing announced to the president, "As I told you one month ago, this CAM system will not be ready for shipment by the date of the show. I'm not superman and neither are any of my people."

The director of public relations at an Eastern university requested permission to hire an administrative assistant on the basis of a heavy work load. Her superior, the provost, carefully reviewed the situation and agreed that an administrative assistant would be justified from the standpoint of work load. Budgetary considerations, he cautioned, would still weigh heavily in his thinking. Whenever the director of community affairs met with the provost in the normal course of events, the latter did not take the initiative to mention hiring an administrative assistant. In response to a direct question about the topic, the provost would reply, "The matter is being given careful consideration." Next, the director of public relations took to writing memos about the disposition of the case. Finally, one year later, the provost mentioned casually, "This is a tough year for the school financially. Bring up your staffing needs again next year."

These two cases represent the type of communication problems among people frequently found in organizations. By studying interpersonal communication, you may develop the level of awareness and understanding required to overcome many of these problems. Because the reasons for communication breakdowns are so complex, and the process of communication encompasses so many different facets of behavior, such problems can be minimized but never eliminated.

THE MEANING AND FUNCTIONS OF COMMUNICATIONS

Communication is the basic process by which everything between and among people happens in an organization. Unless people transmit information to each other, processes such as motivation, leadership, and conflict resolution cannot take place. In this chapter, we emphasize face-to-face or interpersonal communication. We use the term "interpersonal communication" to also include organizational communication, because all messages in organizations are sent from one or more persons to one or more other persons.

Interpersonal communication is an interactive process that results in the exchange of information between and among people. It involves transmission and reception of verbal and nonverbal signs and symbols that come from another person and the environment of both sender and receiver.[1] The important functions performed by interpersonal communication include emotive, motivation, information, and control.[2]

[1]Lyman W. Porter and Karlene H. Roberts, "Communication in Organizations," in Marvin D. Dunnette, ed., *Handbook of Industrial and Organizational Psychology* (Chicago: Rand McNally, 1976), p. 1558.

[2]Our discussion of these factors is based on William G. Scott and Terence R. Mitchell, *Organization Theory: A Structural and Behavioral Analysis,* 3rd ed. (Homewood, Ill.: Richard D. Irwin, 1976), pp. 192–203.

Emotive

Some of the communication in organizations is almost unrelated to the rational aims of management. Rather, it involves human feeling and emotion. Communication thus serves people's basic need for affiliation. It also helps them to reduce some of the ambiguity in human relationships. One employee may start a conversation with another simply to help clarify the nature of their relationship. The conversation may take time because the transmitter of the message will approach the issue indirectly, "Am I really supposed to be accepting work from you?" The informal socializing that takes place in organizations ("schmoozing") is related to the emotive function of communication. Employees find it emotionally comforting and tension reducing to converse with each other about nonwork-related matters.

Motivation

A vital function of interpersonal communication is to influence others to accomplish goals in a work setting. The words used to serve the motivational functions must be chosen with care. An experienced communicator has learned the difference between motivational and demotivational words. For example, most people in most situations respond better to "Would you be able to get this done by three today?" than "Since you're not doing anything important anyway, I wish you would get this done for me by three today."

Information

Communication provides the data for making decisions and carrying out orders and instructions. For example, a management information system is designed to facilitate the communication of useful, objective information. Conclusions about interpersonal communication could be made more accurately if the topic dealt only with its information function. In this chapter, we are much more concerned with the psychological nuances involved in communication.

Control

Without adequate communications, the control function in organizations would not be possible. Management sets standards, observes performance, and makes corrections for deviations from standards by communicating with people. Another form of control refers more to the regulation of behavior. By establishing both formal and informal communication networks (such as organization charts), transmission paths for certain messages are established.

Suppose that a first-level supervisor in a large organization had a suggestion about long-range planning for the total organization. He or she would have to follow a rigid hierarchical pattern for communicating that message to the executive committee. The individual's behavior has therefore been controlled or regulated. Formal communication channels are said to represent a major structural means of control in organizations.[3]

A PROCESS MODEL OF INTERPERSONAL COMMUNICATION

Communication between and among people is a complicated process as shown in Figure 11–1. The process involves the following sequence of events: ideation, encoding, transmission over a medium, receiving, decoding, understanding, and finally, taking action.[4] The clouds above and below the diagram symbolize barriers to communication (or noise, roadblocks, and so forth) that can take place at any stage in communication. Barriers to communication and strategies for overcoming them are discussed later in this chapter.

The communication process is cyclical. Upon decoding a message, understanding it, and then taking action, the receiver sends out his or her own message and the cycle is repeated at least once. Assume that Vera, a clothing company executive, thinks that her leading stylist, Jules, should develop something more adventuresome for the upcoming season.

Step 1 is *ideation* by Vera. She organizes her thoughts about this sensitive problem. This stage is both the origin and the framing of the idea in the sender's mind. She is perhaps motivated by the recognition that business needs a boost. Step 2 is *encoding*. Vera perceives her experiences and formulates a series of symbols for expressing them. The "code" part of encoding means that symbols are used to represent something else. Here the ideas are organized into a series of symbols (words, hand gestures, body movements, or even drawings) designed to communicate to the intended receiver. Vera says, "Jules, there is something I would like to talk to you about if you could arrange to have the time available today . . .".

Transmission takes place next. Vera has encoded her message and she must deliver it to Jules. Her past experience with Jules tells her that he prefers spoken to written communications. Vera also knows from her experience that Jules is sensitive to criticism and, therefore, must be approached diplomatically. Her planned opening comment is, "Jules, I want you to give free rein to your creative mind in this assignment." As Vera encodes, neural impulses are sent from the brain to the abdominal muscles for air power, the larynx for phonation, and the articular organs (tongue, glottis, lips, and jaw). Vera is now transmitting.

Vera's message is transmitted over a medium. Spoken messages are transmitted over air. Other modes of transmission include writing, gesturing, and telephoning. Vera's vibrations now reach Jules's hearing organs, allowing for the *receiving* of the

---

[3]Andrew D. Szilagyi, Jr., and Marc J. Wallace, Jr., *Organizational Behavior and Performance,* 2nd ed. (Glenview, Ill.: Scott, Foresman and Company, 1980), p. 428.

[4]Variations of this general model are found in many textbook discussions of interpersonal communication. Our model shows some similarities to H. R. Smith, Archie B. Carroll, Asterios G. Kefalas, and Hugh J. Watson, *Management: Making Organizations Perform* (New York: Macmillan, 1980), pp. 370–74.

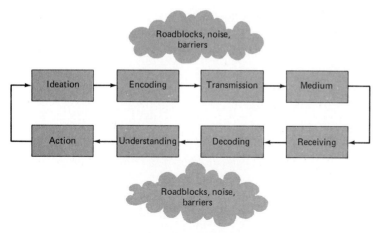

FIGURE 11–1 A Process Model of Interpersonal Communication

message, providing that Jules has been attentive. Technically, these vibrations are physical stimuli that are relayed to the brain via an intricate set of processes in the form of neural impulses.[5]

Decoding, the next stage, is both a neural and a psychological process. Jules converts the impulses sent to his brain into symbols and the symbols into meaning. Decoding can be considered a form of perception. Many variables mediate Jules's responses to these neural impulses, including his intelligence, personality characteristics, and past experiences with Vera (or other authority figures). Communication barriers are the most prominent in the decoding stage of interpersonal communication. If communication has been successful, decoding by the receiver matches the encoding by the sender.

Understanding takes place after the decoding process. Jules understands that Vera wants him to be more adventuresome in his designs for the upcoming season, yet he may not agree. When too many communication barriers exist, understanding may be limited.

Action is the next step. Since Jules does not agree entirely with Vera's opinion, he sends out a message of his own. He thinks up a quick response to the message (ideation), thus setting up the conditions for a dialogue to take place. He asks, "Do you mean to imply that I have not been giving free rein to my creativity lately?"

THE DIRECTION OF COMMUNICATION

Messages in organizations flow in three primary directions—downward, laterally, and upward. Additionally, they travel along a diagonal, or even a zigzag, path. Messages

[5]The physiological aspects of this model are based on William V. Haney, *Communication and Organizational Behavior,* rev. ed. (Homewood, Ill.: Richard D. Irwin, 1973), p. 154.

in any one of these directions can also be classified as being one-way versus two-way. A message sent in any direction can encounter a communications roadblock. In this section, we describe the major communication directions[6] and mention one or two unique problems associated with each one.

Downward Communication

The purpose of downward communication is to transmit information from higher to lower levels in the organization. The communication event can take place among different combinations of senders and receivers, including top management to lower-level employees, top management to lower-level managers, and manager to his or her subordinates. Through downward communication, management is able to carry out its basic functions of planning, organizing, controlling, and directing. When you receive an evaluation of your performance, you are the recipient of downward communication.

One potential problem with downward communication is that subordinates react best to those matters they judge to be of greatest personal interest to their superior, sometimes neglecting other matters. "Among the various commands, policies, practices, and suggestions that come from above, subordinates select those most in keeping with their perception of their bosses' character, personal motivation, and style and give them priority."[7]

Another problem with downward communication is that many managers overemphasize it at the expense of inviting upward communication. Messages are sent to employees, but not enough effort and time is devoted to learning if the message has been properly received. Subordinates will sometimes not react to a memo they do not understand rather than take the initiative to ask for clarification. Downward communication is sometimes misinterpreted because many employees tend to regard communications from above as indicators of dissatisfaction. The underlying belief is, "If management wrote a memo about this topic, it must be that we're doing something wrong."

Horizontal Communication

Communication among co-workers within the same department or across departments is necessary for work accomplishment. Many of these communication events are sent across informal pathways: they are not part of the formal job description, but they facilitate coordination. Thus one manager may say to a personnel specialist, "I think that one of my people should be encouraged to take early retirement. But before I even bring up the topic with him, or my boss, I would like some input from you."

A major barrier to effective horizontal communication is that workers are isolat-

---

[6]Our discussion borrows from Jitendra M. Sharma, "Organizational Communications: A Linking Process," *Personnel Administrator,* July 1979, pp. 35–37.

[7]Bruce Harriman, "Up and Down the Communications Ladder," *Harvard Business Review,* September–October 1974, p. 145.

ed from each other when they are grouped into different departments. The isolation leads to limited understanding of each other, which in turn leads to rivalry and friction.[8] As described in Chapter 13, one technique of resolving interdepartmental conflict is simply to get people talking to each other in interdepartmental meetings.

Upward Communication

The purpose of upward communication is to transmit information from lower to higher levels in the organization. Without upward communication, management works in a vacuum, not knowing if messages have been received properly or if other problems exist in the organization. The case about the trade show presented at the outset of this chapter can be explained partially as a failure in upward communication. The manager of manufacturing did not get the message across to top management about the manufacturing delay. On the positive side, upward communication is the pathway over which ideas for innovation and improvement are sent.

One barrier of note to upward communication is that many employees fear communicating their ideas up the organization. A study of 2,000 employees in eight companies discovered that a majority believed that they would be chastised if they spoke up to superiors. They also believed that the best way of gaining promotion was to agree with superiors.[9] Another barrier is that many employees see management as being both inaccessible and unresponsive. Employees often think that their bosses are too busy to be disturbed, or they simply cannot find their bosses when they are wanted. Furthermore, "If they can locate them, the manager is not responsive to what they say, which results in employees becoming very reluctant to express their ideas, opinions, and feelings."[10]

An explanation for the problems of upward communications has been offered in terms of human perception: the better the interpersonal perception, the better the communications. Upward communications encounter difficulty in most hierarchical organizations because perception downward is less acute than is perception upward. The reason offered for this difference is that people in a subordinate position must, for survival or success, develop a keen understanding of the true motives and personality of those in positions of power over them.[11]

One-Way versus Two-Way Communication

Effective face-to-face communication is *transactional.* Person A may send messages to person B to initiate communications, but B must react to A to complete the communi-

---

[8]Harold Koontz and Cyril O'Donnell, *Principles of Management: An Analysis of Managerial Functions,* 4th ed. (New York: McGraw-Hill, 1968), p. 605.

[9]A. Vogel, "Why Don't Employees Speak Up?" *Personnel Administration,* May–June 1967, pp. 19–23.

[10]Ibid., p. 22.

[11]Harriman, "Up and Down the Communications Ladder," p. 144.

cation loop. When the communication transaction is completed, communication has traveled in two directions, back and forth. One reason written messages frequently fail to achieve their purpose is that the sender of the message cannot be sure what meanings are attached to its content. Face-to-face transactions help to clarify meanings. Harold Leavitt has drawn some interesting contrasts between one-way and two-way (transactional) communication.[12]

1. *Speed* can be accomplished more readily with one-way communication. For example, a manager might call a staff meeting, announce a directive, and leave. Only fifteen minutes of his or her executive time have been consumed. Transactional communication might have taken three hours. In the long run, it is quite possible that the time advantage of one-way communication will be lost. One-way messages have a lower probability of acceptance than do two-way messages.

2. *Appearance* of one-way messages is more impressive. One-way directives appear businesslike and official. The manager above might have entered the conference room, made the announcement that there would be a 15 percent reduction in personnel, and left the room.

3. *Covering up of mistakes* is easier with one-way communication. "Then the sender will not have to hear people implying or saying that he is stupid or that there is an easier way to say what he is trying to say."[13]

4. *Protection of one's power* is more readily accomplished with one-way than with two-way communication. When mistakes occur, the sender can justify to himself or herself that the appropriate message was delivered but the intended receiver did not listen. When mistakes occur in transactional communication, the sender shares the blame, but it is also much more probable that the intended message will be communicated.

5. *Simplification of managerial life* is better accomplished with one-way than with two-way communication. Once communication becomes transactional, the manager must deal with the feelings, attitudes, and perceptions of his or her subordinates. Similarly, the subordinate must deal more directly with people when he or she attempts transactional communication. For instance, it is much simpler to write your company president a letter of complaint than to confront her with your dissatisfactions.

6. *Planfulness, orderliness, and systemization* characterize one-way communication. Managers who carefully rehearse the material they want to present to subordinates can have well-organized staff meetings. Transactional communication is much sloppier. It is difficult to predict what embarrassing questions the receiver will ask when you solicit questions and opinions.

7. *More valid communication* is possible with the two-way approach. It allows for more accurate transmission of facts and, from a systems standpoint, allows for feed-

---

[12]Harold J. Leavitt, *Managerial Psychology*, 4th ed. (Chicago: University of Chicago Press, 1978), pp. 119–24. See also the second edition of the same book, pp. 141–50.

[13]Ibid., 2nd ed., p. 144.

back and correction. A subtle result of transactional communication is that authoritarian leadership behavior is difficult to maintain. Shared authority is one consequence of the transactions that take place.

FORMAL COMMUNICATION PATHWAYS

The formal communication system refers to those pathways (channels) officially designated by the organization for transmitting information within and outside the total organization. Formal pathways between and across organizational units generally follow an upward, lateral, or downward path. Within the work group, the paths may be even more diverse, including following a circular direction. Whatever the direction, an organization functions more smoothly when communication paths are unclogged. Among the negative consequences of clogged communication channels are low-quality decision making, poor coordination, and decreased job performance. Three important determinants of the direction of communications flow over formal pathways are the official organization structure, the actual flow of work, and small-group communication networks.[14]

Organization Structure

The organization chart indicates the official direction in which messages should be sent to get work accomplished. If you want to discuss a proposal with a person of considerably higher organizational rank than yourself, it will usually be necessary to go through formal channels to schedule an appointment. If you want to send a message to someone at your level, or of lower organizational rank, you send the message by yourself or through an intermediary, in a lateral or downward direction. In short, because the formal organization chart shapes superior-subordinate-staff relationships, it dictates communication pathways. In large organizations, these pathways can be complex. Twelve levels of management are often found in major business corporations or large governmental units. The formal pathway indicates the least complicated route over which the message will be transmitted. In practice, the route may be much more circuitous. You may have to "touch base" with many people before your message is encoded by the right person several levels above you.

Work Flow

Formal communication pathways are also profoundly influenced by the actual work flow. Whether in a manufacturing, sales, or service organization, employees are forced to communicate with each other as dictated by the natural flow of work. If the quali-

---

[14]The first two follow Elmer H. Burack, *Organization Analysis: Theory and Application* (Hinsdale, Ill.: Dryden Press, 1975), pp. 180–81.

ty-control department discovers an unacceptably high number of defects in a product, that department must send a lateral message to the department that made the product. Or when a sales manager receives an inquiry from a potential customer, the sales manager will most likely initiate a downward communication to a sales representative. The latter will be asked to follow up on the lead. In some instances, the flow of work may proceed in a direction opposite to the chain of command. A person of lower organizational rank may initiate work for an employee or employees of higher organizational rank. For example, when a clerk brings a problem to the attention of the department head, in a sense the clerk is saying, "Here is a problem that I think deserves your immediate attention."

Small-Group Communication Networks

The arrangement of interpersonal contacts within the work group is often a formal arrangement, while at other times the contacts develop informally in response to work necessity or personal preferences. Whether formal or informal, these networks determine the communications flow. Four of these networks have been studied extensively in laboratory experiments (see Figure 11–2). The major difference among the networks is the degree to which they are centralized.[15] Among the major dependent variables related to centralization are speed and accuracy of problem solving and the frequency of communication.[16]

1.   In the *circle network,* communication may be initiated on either side of a group member. It is symbolic of lateral communication systems without a leader who communicates with each subordinate. In the latter situation, if a person wanted to communicate, he or she would have to speak to a superior. Experiments have shown that groups using the circle network were slow to organize, made many errors, and solved problems more slowly than did groups using any of the other networks. However, they were prolific message senders and were the most satisfied!

2.   The *chain* is a version of the circle except that there is a missing link. Each open end of the chain reduces the total volume of communication that can be initiated in the network. Because fewer messages can be sent, the communication system tends to be more efficient. Satisfaction with the communication process decreases somewhat because communication becomes more centralized. Most people prefer to have the opportunity to communicate with as many co-workers as possible.

3.   *Y networks* are similar to the chain except that one member falls outside the chain. A Y pattern is symbolic of the staff specialist who interacts with a line manager. This

    [15]H. Joseph Reitz, *Behavior in Organizations,* rev. ed. (Homewood, Ill.: Richard D. Irwin, 1981), pp. 319–23.
    [16]Leavitt, *Managerial Psychology,* 4th ed., pp. 234–43.

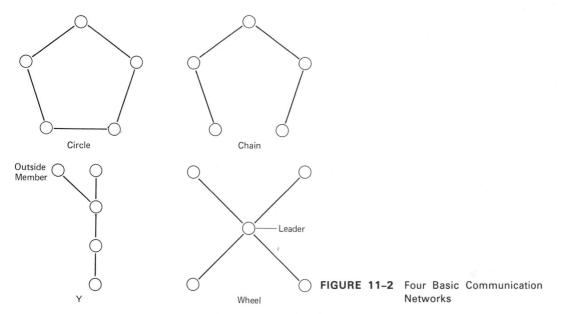

Circle

Chain

Outside Member

Y

Wheel

Leader

FIGURE 11–2 Four Basic Communication Networks

arrangement saves time and is therefore efficient, but some group members feel that they are excluded from receiving potentially valuable information.

4. Under the *wheel network,* one person sits at the communications hub; all messages must be sent through that person. Research shows consistently that the person at the hub emerges as the leader and decision maker. Even if a group member has strong personal leadership characteristics, the communications advantage held by the person at the hub gives him or her decision-making power. The wheel also offers certain advantages to management: groups using the wheel network organized the most quickly and solved problems more accurately and quickly than did groups using other networks.

An important implication of research on communication networks is that communication pathways do affect productivity and satisfaction. For example, a wheel appears to be the best network in a task-oriented environment, yet it lowers satisfaction. Still, new ideas are more likely to be generated. However, creativity and flexibility are fostered in a circle. It has been noted that "The restriction of new ideas in the wheel is often due to the person in the middle who feels that the group is already efficient and that innovations will only introduce complexity into a routine and patternized network."[17]

[17]Robert L. Trewatha and M. Gene Newport, *Management,* 3rd. ed. (Plano, Tex.: Business Publications, 1982), p. 330.

INFORMAL COMMUNICATION PATHWAYS

The information needs of people cannot be fully met by the formal communications system. As a consequence, informal (unofficial) communication pathways are built up around existing social relationships to satisfy requirements for additional information in the workplace. The combination of the formal and informal communication pathways results in a substantial number of routes over which information can travel. A comparison of the formal and informal communication systems is shown in Figure 11–3. Only a sampling of the many possible informal pathways is illustrated. For example, it is conceivable that K might approach C in the company parking lot and discuss interdepartmental matters while the two of them strolled into the plant. Thousands of potential communication links, both formal and informal, exist in any complex organization. Two major manifestations of informal communication pathways are the grapevine and the rumors it carries.

The Grapevine

The major informal communication pathway in an organization is called the grapevine, a term with a unique origin. During the Civil War, telegraph lines were loosely strung from tree to tree appearing somewhat like grapevines. As a result, messages sent along these lines were often ambiguous and distorted. It therefore became frequent practice to attribute rumor to the grapevine.[18] Keith Davis describes it in this manner: "Being flexible and personal, it spreads information faster than most management communication systems operate. With the rapidity of a burning powder train, it filters out of the woodwork, past the manager's door and the janitor's closet, through steel walls or construction glass partitions and along the corridors."[19] Related to this description, some basic characteristics of the grapevine have been identified:

1. A significant percentage of employees consider the grapevine to be their primary source of information about events within the firm. It often has a bigger impact on employees than do messages sent over formal channels.

2. It is more flexible than formal channels and embellishes information to a greater extent than do formal channels.

3. Information is transmitted along the grapevine with considerable speed; the more important the information, the greater the speed.

4. Although it has been estimated that up to three-fourths of rumors spread over the grapevine are true, the grapevine tends to produce a low level of understanding among receivers of its messages. Many rumors that start out as true become distorted as they are passed along the grapevine.

5. The oral mode of transmission, rather than written or nonverbal, is typical of the grape-

---

[18]Ibid., p. 331.

[19]This composite definition is derived from Davis's statements in Keith Davis, *Human Relations in Business* (New York: McGraw-Hill, 1957), p. 244, and "Tending the Grapevine," *Time,* June 18, 1973, p. 67.

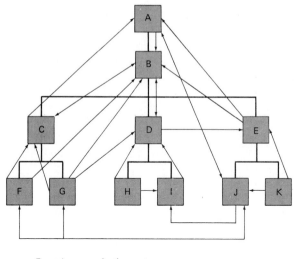

FIGURE 11–3 A Comparison of the Formal and Informal Communication Systems

———— Formal communication system

———— Informal communication system

Source: Reprinted by permission from Robert L. Trewatha and M. Gene Newport, *Management,* 3rd ed. (Plano, Tex.: Business Publications, 1982), p. 331.

vine. Yet instances have been observed of written channels being used when "word of mouth is not convenient or may be too obvious."

6. Recipients of grapevine messages usually communicate with several other individuals rather than with only one. Of those receiving messages, only about 10 percent function as liaison individuals—people who transmit information to others.[20]

7. The grapevine can be used by management as a method of transmitting information that it may not wish to transmit formally. One example would be to feed the grapevine with the news that salary increases will be very small this year. When increases turn out to be average, people will tend to be satisfied. Similarly, the grapevine can be valuable in gauging the reaction of employees to an announcement before it is transmitted through formal channels.[21]

Rumor Control

As already implied, a rumor is a message that is transmitted through the organization, usually over the grapevine, although not based on any official word. An important dysfunction of rumors is that they are capable of disrupting work and lowering morale. Rumors also can plague organizations in their relationship with customers. A story circulated at one time that the hamburgers sold by a large chain of franchise restaurants were contaminated by worms. It was also said that the firm donated some profits to the Church of Satan. Sales were adversely affected by these rumors.

The best general antidote to dysfunctional rumors is to minimize ambiguous for-

[20]The first six points are based on Trewatha and Newport, *Management,* pp. 332–33.

[21]Walter St. John, "In-House Communication Guidelines," *Personnel Journal,* November 1981, p. 877.

mal messages and to transmit valid information down and across the organization. A few practical tips for dealing with rumors have been formulated:

- First, try to wait it out. The rumor may run its course before doing too much damage.
- If the rumor persists, make it news. If you talk about the rumor and deny it, then nobody has an exclusive. Everybody has heard it.
- Ridicule the rumor. Call it preposterous, stupid, crazy. People will then ridicule those who repeat it.
- A full disclosure of the facts is the best antidote to a true or false rumor. The full truth can often be used to nip a rumor in the bud.[22]
- For countermeasures, feed the grapevine with actual information to get the facts through the informal communication channels.[23]

BARRIERS TO INTERPERSONAL COMMUNICATION

Messages sent from person A to person B (or to a group of persons) are rarely received by those people in exactly the form intended by person A. Barriers exist that complicate the process of communication.[24] As illustrated in Figure 11–4, systems theory provides a framework for understanding what transpires when messages are communicated. Input consists of messages—spoken or written—as sent by the receiver. A host of variables or conditions shapes the output of the message. Intervening variables may be related to the receiver, the sender, or the environment. For instance, the receiver might be a group of angry people, the sender might have poor communication skills, and the organizational climate might be one of distrust and suspicion. The list of intervening variables should be considered illustrative, not exhaustive.

Preconceived ideas.   The observation that "people hear what they expect to hear" concisely explains a major barrier to communication. This same principle explains why people so frequently state: "I've heard that message before." Perhaps they are only receiving the same message they received before.

Denial of contrary information.   Messages that conflict with information already accepted as valid by the receiver are often rejected or denied. (This phenomenon is one key aspect of cognitive dissonance.) An employee who believes that he or she is an outstanding performer may not receive the first message from the manager documenting his or her needs for improvement.

[22]The first four suggestions are credited to Fredrick Koenig as quoted in Jane See White, "Biggest Companies: Targets of Biggest Rumors," *Rochester Democrat and Chronicle,* April 7, 1980, p. 1C.

[23]St. John, "In-House Communication Guidelines," p. 877.

[24]One of many similar conceptions of communication barriers is James L. Gibson, John M. Ivancevich, and James H. Donnelly, Jr., *Organizations: Behavior, Structure, Processes,* 3rd ed. (Plano, Tex.: Business Publications, 1979), pp. 413–23.

Input   Intervening Variables   Output

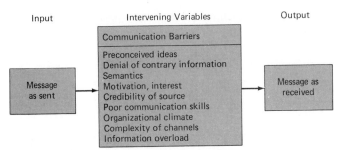

FIGURE 11–4 Barriers to Interpersonal Communication

Semantics. Words have different meanings to different people. An entire discipline—semantics—has been built around this widely accepted aspect of communications. The president of a large manufacturing company was quoted in the local newspaper as saying, "Technical competence is not dead in our society and this will be shown in our company. I see an increasing emphasis for us upon technical competence." During the next several weeks, small-group discussions were held in individual departments to discuss the implications of this statement. A perceptive personnel manager recorded some of the different meanings attached to the phrase "technical competence."

Engineers, in general, were encouraged because they interpreted "technical" to refer to engineering as opposed to administration, manufacturing, or marketing. One engineer stated, "At last, the importance of our efforts to the company is being recognized." According to a manufacturing manager, some production workers were upset by the president's statement. They interpreted it to mean that higher productivity levels would be needed to obtain the same wage rates. (This was a nonunion shop.) Two members of the management training program felt the statement implied that younger administrative employees might be cut, because the company was shifting away from administrative work and toward technical work. The industrial nurse (who overheard many concerns of employees when they visited the company medical facility) commented that the public statement was interpreted as an early warning of an impending layoff. According to this interpretation, poor performers—those considered by the company to be technically incompetent—were in jeopardy of losing their jobs.

Motivation and interest. It is difficult to get through to a person who is not interested in what you have to say. If receivers are not motivated to accept the messages sent by the sender, the communication loop will probably remain incomplete. Effective sales representatives attempt to get their messages across by appealing to an active need such as security or self-fulfillment.

Credibility of the source. Messages often do not register with receivers because the sender is not trusted. Incredible messages are literally those not believed to be true. Senders of messages, to be credible, have to earn such a reputation over an extended period of time. Reputations of low credibility, however, can be earned in a much shorter period of time. Sometimes class stereotypes create a mental set that the sender of messages must overcome. Professional politicians, for example, must work hard to establish themselves as a credible source of information because of stereotypes that a politician is an individual of low credibility.

Poor communication skills.   Substantial individual differences exist in the ability of people to communicate, representing yet another intervening variable influencing the transmission of messages from sender to receiver. Some differences in communication skills are attributable to education and training; others stem from more basic personality characteristics. For instance, articulate, persuasive, and confident people communicate more effectively.

Communications effectiveness is influenced by subtle aspects of personality such as sensitivity about the timing of messages. Poor timing is exemplified by the managers who relay important instructions to employees on the Friday afternoon before a holiday. By that time most people will be shifting their attention away from work and toward vacation. Good timing, in contrast, is exemplified by the department manager who asks for new funds after information has been released that the company has achieved its financial objectives for the year. Under these circumstances, the department manager's superior is more likely to listen to his proposition.

Receivers of messages also manifest individual differences. Some people are better listeners than others by virtue of education, training, personality characteristics, or physical characteristics (e.g., level of hearing acuity). Personal conflicts may also serve as a barrier to developing listening acuity. Anxious people sometimes are too preoccupied with their personal problems to pay an appropriate amount of attention to messages from other people. People placed under considerable organizational stress may also show some decrease in listening acuity.

Organizational climate.   The atmosphere or "personality" of an organization also influences the extent to which a message is received. Messages sent in an organization where a high degree of trust and openness exists have a higher probability of being received than do those sent in a climate of distrust and defensiveness. Another aspect of organizational climate affecting the communication of messages relates to the formality versus informality of orders and requests. In some organizations, formal orders must be issued to accomplish all but routine tasks.

Complexity of channels.   All things being equal, communications efficiency decreases with the number of baffles through which information must pass before reaching its intended receiver.[25] This partially explains why face-to-face communication works more effectively in small rather than in large organizations. Direct channels can be used more readily in small organizations because fewer layers of management have to be penetrated. For instance, if a small-company president has information to relay to a middle manager, he or she will probably feel no qualms about violating the chain of command by speaking directly to the manager in question. Large, complex organi-

[25]George Strauss and Leonard Sayles, *Personnel: The Human Problems of Management,* 3rd ed. (Englewood Cliffs, N.J.: Prentice-Hall, 1972), p. 217.

zations have heightened communications problems by the very nature of their complexity.

Information overload.   A major barrier to communication is that many people are so overloaded with information that they cannot sort out which information is worth reacting to. It has been noted that if all communications were attended to, the actual work of the organization would never take place.[26] Photocopying machines and computers have been a major contributor to information overload. Today it requires little effort for organization members to generate printed data for others to read. The large number of meetings characteristic of modern organization also contributes to information overload. In recognition of the overload problem, a number of document abstracting services have been developed for managers.

In addition to serving as a communications barrier, information overload has been identified as a source of stress and job burnout. Burnout has been a common phenomenon in firms that suffer from periodic information overload, such as public accounting firms during tax season. The accompanying box provides some suggestions for reducing information overload stress (see pages 296–297).

OVERCOMING BARRIERS TO COMMUNICATION

Despite the many barriers to interpersonal communication present in every organization, the situation is not hopeless. Many messages do get through to the receiver as intended, and many barriers to organizational communication can be overcome. The most general strategy for improving organizational communication is to be sensitive to the presence of the barriers that exist and act accordingly. Most of the barriers can be coped with if senders sharpen their skills in sending messages and perceiving the needs of the audience. Various informal techniques are available to people who want to improve their organizational communication skills.

Recognize the Receiver's Frame of Reference

It has been suggested that the manager should place himself or herself in the shoes of the receiver and attempt to anticipate personal or situational factors that will influence the symbolic interpretation or decoding of the message.[27] Similarly, a unifying point inferred from Figure 11-4 is that the receiver's point of view must be factored into the transmission of a message. One challenge in communicating with others is that their frames of reference are resistant to change. If employees, for example, have a long history of being skeptical of messages sent by management, it will take more than one trustworthy message to modify their frame of reference.

[26]Szilagyi and Wallace, *Organizational Behavior and Performance,* p. 432.
[27]Ibid., p. 433.

HOW TO REDUCE INFORMATION OVERLOAD STRESS

Martha H. Rader, a business communication specialist, has formulated some suggestions for reducing the stress that results from information overload. Her suggestions integrate principles of stress management and time management. Those strategies related most directly to handling information overload are summarized here.

Eliminate Environmental Stimuli

Think about as few things at a time as possible. Any distraction is just one more stimulus adding to your overload. Noises and visual distractions, such as telephones ringing, typewriters clattering, computer printers buzzing, and people walking by, are examples of environmental stimuli that will aggravate information overload. The open-office concept is not always an ideal setting for individuals trying to cope with information overload. Ideally, the office should provide a work setting as free from environmental distractions as possible.

Use Memory Aids

Don't clutter up your brain with trivial information such as dates, times, addresses, and telephone numbers. Make a "to do" list and look at it several times a day so you won't use your valuable shortened memory capacity for such matters. Similarly, don't waste energy and time by composing a new letter or memorandum when you have written a similar message in the past.

Delegate Tasks

Don't wait until you are suffering from information overload to decide to delegate a job to a subordinate. It frequently takes more time to explain how to do a complicated task than it does to go ahead and do it yourself, so plan ahead. Make sure you don't place your employees in an information overload situation, too, by giving them more duties than they are able to handle.

Prioritize Communications

When working under pressure, don't let yourself be diverted by low-priority communications. Message screening and prioritizing can be delegated to a secretary.

Eliminate Redundancy

Some meetings and conferences can be eliminated entirely, canceled in overload periods, or simply conducted more efficiently. Just using an agenda and a time limit can reduce information overload in staff and committee meetings. Eliminating unnecessary communication inputs is a good technique for reducing information overload. Every manager should periodically review the reports and publications that he or she receives to determine which ones can be eliminated.

Organize Your Desk

Desk clutter is a distraction; keep your desk uncluttered. Poor housekeeping is a symptom of information overload. If you make an effort to keep your desk clean, you will find that your level of frustration will be much less. Keeping only one item on your desk will encourage you to think about one thing at a time. If you can learn to think about only one problem at a time, you will probably never suffer seriously from information overload.

Try to Relax

When you are being overstimulated by too many communication inputs, try to stay away from people. If you are having a particularly hectic day, try lunching alone rather than with the usual group.

Source: Adapted and excerpted from Martha H. Rader, "Dealing with Information Overload," *Personnel Journal,* May 1981, pp. 373–75. Reprinted with the permission of *Personnel Journal,* Costa Mesa, Ca.; all rights reserved.

Utilize Verbal and Nonverbal Feedback

Systems theory indicates that communications are complete only when the sender receives feedback that the message has been received as intended. Individuals communicating to each other can receive both verbal and nonverbal feedback. (Nonverbal communication is explored later in this chapter.) Written messages afford much less opportunity for feedback. Considerable emotion and feeling has to be elicited from a written communication before a written response is made voluntarily. Feedback will provide the sender clues about the acceptance of his message. Brief, straightforward questions such as the following are helpful in eliciting feedback about the reception of a message:

> How do you feel about my statement?
> What do you think?
> Tell me how what I have said has come across to you.
> Do you see any problems with what we have talked about?

Failing to elicit verbal feedback about other people's reactions to a message paves the way toward misunderstanding or sometimes a breakdown in communications. When receivers are timid, shy, or afraid, additional effort must be invested in eliciting feedback.

Observing nonverbal cues is useful in providing insight into how the receiver feels about a message. Nonverbal signs may be at variance with the content of a person's reaction to a message. For example, a manager might ask a programmer if he or she feels confident in debugging an important program. "Yes, I'm confident" might be the verbal response, but a hand tremor and a speech stammer suggest otherwise. Feedback of this nature would serve as a signal to the manager that assistance should be provided in the more difficult portions of the assignment.

Reinforce Words with Action

Verbal statements of intent represent but a beginning to the communication process. Statements of policy or intended actions become credible only after management (or anyone else) has established the reputation of backing up words with action. Following through on the behavior suggested by a written or spoken message decreases the "credibility gap" and helps to establish a climate of trust. This elementary principle is frequently violated in the pressures of organizational life.

> One publicly held corporation issued a policy statement that the corporation would place more emphasis on participative management. To demonstrate the seriousness of this intent, a New Ventures Committee was established with representatives from all key functional areas of the business. A stated purpose of this committee was "to assist top management in making decisions about new ventures that could shape the destiny of the organization." Three months later it was announced that the corporation was negotiating to be acquired by a large electronics firm. No one on the New Ventures Committee was asked his or her opinion about the desirability of such a course of action. Future policy statements by the corporation were met with considerable skepticism.

Reinforcing words with actions helps to circumvent three barriers to communication discussed earlier. First, the credibility gap is narrowed. Second, an organizational climate characterized by trust is fostered. Third, it encourages interest in spoken or written communications because they are perceived as vital and meaningful.

Use Appropriate Language

"Written communications should be as intelligible and readable as possible" states a widely accepted principle of good communication. Every reader can think of at least one example where a written or spoken message lost (or alienated) its intended receiver because of its complexity. Exhortations about the importance of clear communications overlook one subtle consideration that deserves mention. Appropriate language is perhaps more important than simple language (although simple language is usually appropriate). Oversimplified messages can be interpreted as condescending and therefore may engender resentment.

Use Multiple Channels

Repetition also enhances communication, particularly when different channels are used to convey the same message.[28] Effective communicators at many job levels follow

---

[28]Gibson, Ivancevich, and Donnelly, *Organizations,* p. 187.

up verbal (oral) agreements with written documentation. Since most communication is subject to at least some distortion, the chances of a message being received as intended increase when two or more channels are used. It has become standard practice in several large companies for managers to use a multiple-channel approach to communicating the results of a performance appraisal. The subordinate receives a verbal explanation from his or her superior of the results of the review. The subordinate is also required to read the form and indicate by signature that he or she has read and understands the meaning of the review.

Appeal to Active Needs

A close relationship exists among communication, motivation, and perception. People attend to oral, written, and nonverbal messages that show promise of satisfying an active need. People are motivated to attend to (a perceptual process) oral, written, and nonverbal messages that show promise of satisfying an active need. An unemployed person who wants to become employed will respond attentively to any message that suggests the availability of a job for which he or she might qualify. Much advertising strategy is based upon the straightforward assumption that the most effective way in which to communicate with people is to appeal to an unsatisfied need, even if that need has to be created.

NONVERBAL COMMUNICATION IN ORGANIZATIONS

So far we have been talking mostly about verbal communication. However, communication really proceeds at two levels: the content, or the words one transmits to another, and the relationship, or the nonverbal cues that accompany these words. Nonverbal communication plays a particularly significant role in meetings and conferences. The terms "body language" and "silent messages" mean about the same thing as nonverbal communication. The process consists of many different behaviors including facial expressions, hand gestures, dilation and constriction of the pupils, and manner of dress and appearance. Eight different modes of nonverbal communication are summarized here.[29] The reader is cautioned that many of these nonverbal cues may be unreliable. For example, fist clenching may be a symptom of anger for most people, but some people clench their fists when tense for other reasons.

Head, face, and eye behavior. When used in combination, head, face, and eye behavior provide the clearest indications of interpersonal attitudes. Puffing your cheeks as you blow breath through them, for example, usually indicates dismay or ap-

[29]Our discussion is based on two sources: John E. Baird, Jr., and Gretchen K. Wieting, "Nonverbal Communication Can Be a Motivational Tool," *Personnel Journal,* September 1979, pp. 607–10, 625, and Lyle Sussman and Paul D. Krivonos, *Communication for Supervisors and Managers* (Sherman Oaks, Calif.: Alfred, 1979), Chapter 6.

prehension. Maintaining eye contact with another person improves communication with that person because it projects confidence and/or interest. To maintain eye contact, it is usually necessary to move your head and face correspondingly. Moving your head, face, and eyes away from another person is often interpreted as defensiveness or low self-confidence.

Gestures.   Another relatively reliable set of nonverbal cues is gestures. Positive attitudes toward another person (or that person's ideas) are shown by frequent gesticulation (hand movements). In contrast, dislike or disinterest usually produces few gestures. An important exception is that some people wave their hands as a symptom of anger or other negative emotion. Hand movements can also be culturally linked; some ethnic groups "talk with their hands" more than others do. The type of gesture displayed also communicates a particular message:

> Random fidgeting, such as drumming the fingers or twiddling the thumbs, is a set of gestural activities which convey extremely negative attitudes. Similarly, aggressive gestures with clenched fists and menacing postures convey hostile feelings, while frequent use of relaxed, open-palm gestures toward the other person typically convey positive attitudes.[30]

Posture.   Many messages in organizations are communicated by posture, particularly during meetings and conferences. Leaning toward another individual suggests that you are favorably disposed toward his or her messages; leaning backward communicates the opposite message. Openness of the arms and legs serves as an indicator of liking or caring. In general, people establish closed postures (arms folded and legs crossed) when speaking to people they dislike. Sitting erect presumably connotes mental alertness. Even if it doesn't, the person trying to create a favorable impression will stand and sit straight because of other people's interpretation of the meaning of good posture.

Tone of voice.   People often attach more significance to the way something is said than to what is said. When your boss says "OK" to your proposal, you probably listen attentively to the amount of enthusiasm in his or her tone. Voice tone is therefore critical, but other aspects of the voice such as volume, quality, and rate are also part of the nonverbal message (collectively called *vocalics*). As with all nonverbal cues, there is an ever-present danger of overinterpreting a single voice quality. A throat infection, for example, or general physical malaise can make a person sound lethargic even if that person is genuinely interested in the topic under discussion. Anger, boredom, and joy—three emotions that are frequently experienced on the job—can often be interpreted from voice quality in this manner:

> Anger is best perceived when the source speaks loudly, at a fast rate, in a high pitch, with irregular inflection and clipped enunciation. Boredom is indicated by moderate volume, pitch, and rate, and a monotone inflection; joy by loud volume, high pitch, fast rate, upward inflection, and regular rhythm.[31]

[30]Baird and Wieting, "Nonverbal Communication," p. 609.
[31]Ibid., p. 610.

Interpersonal distance.   The placement of one's body relative to someone else's body can be used to transmit certain messages. One study showed that people located in relatively close proximity are seen as warmer, friendlier, and more understanding than are people located farther away. The implication is that if you want to convey positive attitudes to another person, move physically close to that person. As common sense suggests, putting your arm around somebody else (or touching him or her) in a job setting is interpreted as a sign of acceptance. As with other nonverbal cues, cultural differences must be taken into account. For example, a French male is likely to stand closer to you than an English male even if they have equally positive attitudes toward you. Some guidelines have been developed for gauging how close to stand to another person.

Intimate distance ranges from actual physical contact to about 18 inches. Physical intimacy is rarely called for in organizations except that confidential information might be whispered within the intimate distance zone. *Personal distance* ranges from about $1\frac{1}{2}$ to 4 feet. The interaction that takes place in this zone typically includes friendly discussions and conversation. Occasionally, a heated argument on the job (such as that between a baseball manager and an umpire) is conducted within the personal distance zone.

Social-consultative distance is about 4 to 8 feet and is usually reserved for businesslike, impersonal interaction. We usually maintain this type of distance between ourselves and strangers such as sales representatives and purchasing agents. *Public distance* ranges from 12 feet to the outer limits of being heard. This zone is typically used in speaking to an audience at a large meeting or in a classroom. When someone violates the public distance zone by shouting across the room, it is often interpreted as a sign of rudeness or anger.[32]

Clothing, dress, and appearance.   One's external appearance plays a role in communicating messages to others. Job seekers implicitly recognize this aspect of nonverbal communication when they carefully groom themselves for a job interview. People pay more respect and grant more privileges to people whom they perceive as being well dressed and attractive. So many people are aware of the importance of dress and appearance these days that "dressing for success" may have become a defensive form of nonverbal communication. Dressing poorly has a negative impact in organizations, whereas dressing well is primarily useful in bringing one up to the norm.

Environmental cues.   The environment in which one sends a message can influence the perception of that message. Assume that an executive in your firm invites you out to lunch to discuss a work-related problem. You will think that it is a more important topic under these circumstances than if he or she met you for lunch in the company cafeteria. Other important environmental cues include room color, temperature, lighting, and furniture arrangement. A person who sits behind a large, uncluttered desk, for example, appears more powerful than does a person who sits behind a small,

[32]Sussman and Krivonos, *Communication for Supervisors and Managers,* pp. 80–81. Based on Nancy Russo, "Connotation of Seating Arrangement," *Cornell Journal of Social Relations,* Vol. 2, 1967, pp. 351–61.

cluttered desk. The presence of personal knick knacks (family photos, bowling trophies, and so forth) is said to detract from a power look.

Use of time.   Time is a precious commodity in most organizations; therefore, its use can be manipulated to emit nonverbal messages. If we are late for meetings, it might be interpreted that we are careless, uninvolved, or unambitious. However, a high-ranking official might be late for a meeting and that same amount of lateness might be perceived as a symbol of power or being busy. Treating time as a resource of little significance, such as excessive schmoozing, may be interpreted by others as lack of importance or laziness.

The study of nonverbal communication in organizations does have merit, but many of the conclusions reached may not be valid. Much of what is labeled nonverbal communication is basically an overinterpretation of minor cues. The most reliable nonverbal messages (such as moving toward or away from people) tend to be obvious and not in need of formal study.

IMPLICATIONS FOR MANAGERIAL PRACTICE

1.   Interpersonal and organizational communication is the basic process by which managers and staff specialists carry out their functions. It is therefore critical to work toward unclogging communication channels in all directions. Part of unclogging these channels is to overcome communication barriers following some of the guidelines presented in this chapter. It is particularly important to be aware of communication barriers and to recognize the receiver's frame of reference.

2.   Effective communication skills, both verbal and nonverbal, are necessary for getting work accomplished. It is therefore important to improve your oral, written, and nonverbal skills including listening ability. A wide range of programs exists for improving your written and spoken communications. Programs for improving your nonverbal skills are in shorter supply. The use of videotapes can be helpful in improving your body language. After observing your body language on tape, attempt to eliminate those mannerisms and gestures that you think detract from your effectiveness (such as moving your leg from side to side when working under pressure).

3.   In most instances of interpersonal communication, two-way communication is superior to one-way. Interact with the receiver to foster understanding. While delivering your message, ask for verbal feedback and be sensitive to nonverbal cues about how your message is getting accross. By so doing, many communication barriers (such as preconceived ideas and semantics) will be overcome.

4.   Effective communication in organizations usually involves the use of both formal and informal pathways. To improve the chances of critical information being received, it should be fed into both formal and informal channels. Often backing up written announcements with small-group discussions will aid understanding and facilitate acceptance of the message.

Summary

- Interpersonal communication is an interactive process that results in the exchange of information between people. It involves transmission and reception of verbal and non-verbal signs and symbols that come from another person and the environment of both sender and receiver. Communication serves a number of important functions including (1) emotional expression, (2) the motivation of people, (3) the transmission of data for making decisions and carrying out orders and instructions, and (4) the control of the organization's activities.

- Interpersonal communication is a process involving the steps of ideation, encoding, transmission over a medium, receiving, decoding, understanding, and taking action. Barriers to communication, or distortions, can take place at any step. The model is cyclical, since the receiver sends out a message in response to receiving one.

- Messages in organizations flow in three primary directions: downward, laterally, and upward. Through downward communication, management is able to carry out its basic functions. Lateral communications within and across departments are necessary for coordinated work activity. The purpose of upward communication is to transmit information from lower to higher levels in the organization. Also related to the directional aspect of communication, effective communication is transactional (two-way). Such communication helps to clarify meanings and ensures that understanding has taken place.

- Formal communication pathways are those officially designated by the organization for transmitting information within and outside the total organization. Three determinants of the direction of communications flow over formal pathways are (1) the official pattern of authority relationships, (2) the actual flow of work, and (3) small-group communication networks (which can be formal or informal channels). The four primary networks are the circle, chain, Y, and wheel. The wheel network appears to work best in a task-oriented environment, but the circle tends to maximize satisfaction.

- Informal communication pathways are built up around existing social relationships to satisfy requirements for additional information. The major informal communication pathway in an organization is called the grapevine. It carries both substantiated information and rumors. A significant percentage of employees considers the grapevine to be their primary source of information about organizational happenings.

- A recommended antidote to dysfunctional rumors is to minimize ambiguous formal messages and to transmit valid information down and across the organization. Also, as a countermeasure the grapevine can be fed with valid information to get the facts through the informal communication channels.

- The barriers to interpersonal communication include preconceived ideas, denial of contrary information, semantics, motivation and interest of the intended receiver, credibility of the source, poor communication skills, the organizational climate, complexity of channels, and information overload. Methods of overcoming barriers to communication include recognizing the receiver's frame of reference, utilizing verbal and nonverbal feedback, reinforcing words with action, using multiple channels, and appealing to active needs.

• The nonverbal cues that accompany words are an important part of communication in organizations. Eight categories of nonverbal behavior are head, face, and eye behavior; gestures; posture; tone of voice; interpersonal distance; clothing, dress, and appearance; environmental cues; and use of time.

Questions for Discussion

1. What symptoms of a communication problem can you identify within the organization with which you are the most familiar?
2. How would you rate your ability to communicate with others in face-to-face situations? What evidence do you have to support your rating?
3. How effective are you in receiving messages? What evidence do you have to support your opinion?
4. What nonverbal cues do members of a basketball (or football) team convey to each other during a game other than direct hand signals such as that for "time out"?
5. Many executives from a major business corporation have commented that big business does a poor job of communicating with young people. Do you have any suggestions for improving the situation?
6. Why do most fields of knowledge develop a jargon of their own?
7. What kind of organization structure do you think facilitates interpersonal communication?
8. What kind of organization structure do you think inhibits interpersonal communication?
9. Are you suffering from information overload? If so, what are your symptoms?
10. Identify a high-paying job for which communication skills are relatively unimportant. Explain why this is true.

An Organizational Behavior Problem

Why Don't They Complain to Me?

Business Equipment Corporation is a successful distributor of photocopying machines, mini-computers, typewriters, and several other varieties of small- to medium-sized office machines. The company sells the products of a number of foreign manufacturers and several domestic manufacturers. Branch units have direct responsibility for sales and machine service. Each branch manager reports to one of five regional managers. Scott, the manager of the Houston, Texas, branch, was conferring with Ned, his regional manager, who was visiting his office. Prior to this luncheon conference, Ned had chatted briefly with several of the sales and service employees in Scott's branch office. Part of the conversation between Ned and Scott took this form:

Ned: There's something I think we should talk about that's happening in your branch, Scott. Nothing serious, but it's something I want to alert you to.

Scott: Nothing too gruesome I hope. Our results have been pretty good this last quarter, haven't they?

Ned: Nothing gruesome at all. It's just a question of your style of going about things. It seems that some of your people think they don't have a big enough say in terms of who is hired into the branch.

Scott: I thought they did have a big say. Before I hire anybody, a clerk, a technical rep, or a sales rep, that person is interviewed by the people who would be working most directly with him or her.

Ned: Yes, but they think that you choose which candidates will even be interviewed. And then you make the final hiring decision.

Scott: If that's the procedure they want to follow, I guess it could be arranged. I'm concerned, though, that total participation along those lines would be cumbersome and inefficient. We would spend too much time on recruiting and selection. Besides I thought a branch manager was responsible for hiring employees.

Ned: Yes, but I think the time invested would pay off. Your people would feel much more like they are part of a team effort.

Scott: By the way. Nobody ever told me about these problems. I would have been receptive to their ideas. Why don't they complain to me instead of running to you?

Questions

1. Why is this problem included in a chapter about interpersonal communications?
2. What might Scott do in the future to encourage people to bring their problems directly to him instead of complaining to his boss?
3. Do you think the branch employees were justified in using the communication channel they did to criticize the recruiting procedure?

Additional Reading

HANEY, WILLIAM V. *Communication and Interpersonal Relations,* 4th ed. Homewood, Ill.: Richard D. Irwin, 1979.

HARPER, ROBERT D., ARTHUR N. WIENS, and JOSEPH D. MATARAZZO. *Nonverbal Communication: The State of the Art.* New York: John Wiley, 1978.

HUNT, GARY T. *Communication Skills in the Organization.* Englewood Cliffs, N.J.: Prentice-Hall, 1980.

JABLIN, FREDERIC M. "Superior-Subordinate Communication: The State of the Art." *Psychological Bulletin,* June 1979, pp. 1201–22.

MEHRABIAN, ALBERT. *Silent Messages: Implicit Communication of Emotions and Attitudes,* 2nd ed. Belmont, Calif.: Wadsworth, 1981.

ROBERTS, KARLENE H., and CHARLES A. O'REILLY. "Some Correlates of Communication Roles in Organizations." *Academy of Management Journal,* March 1979, pp. 42–57.

ROGERS, CARL R. "Barriers and Gateways to Communication." *Harvard Business Review,* July–August 1951, pp. 46–52.

Rosenthal, Robert, ed. *Skill in Nonverbal Communication: Individual Differences.* Cambridge, Mass.: Oelgeschager, Gunn & Hain, 1979.

Steil, Lyman K. "Your Listening Profile." *Success Unlimited,* September 1980, pp. 24–26.

Wycoff, Edgar B. "Canons of Communication." *Personnel Journal,* March 1981, pp. 208–212.

CHAPTER 12

Leadership in Organizations

LEARNING OBJECTIVES

1. To understand the nature of leadership.
2. To identify the three major approaches to understanding leadership.
3. To summarize three contingency theories of leadership.
4. To describe participative leadership and specify the conditions under which it will most probably be effective.
5. To describe the unique attributes of an entrepreneurial leader.
6. To acquire insight into your present or potential leadership style.

As a project manager, Larry has been asked to take a temporary foreign assignment. His present duties as manager of Project Olympia are to be assumed for a few months by the general manager, Ned. After one day of reviewing documentation about the inner workings of Olympia, Ned decided to meet with the two key personnel on the project, Jane, the director of engineering, and Mack, the director of manufacturing. Ned decided to take each person to lunch separately in order to hold a general discussion of progress on the project. Ned arranged for a Tuesday luncheon with Jane and a Wednesday luncheon with Mack.

"Jane, the reason I've invited you to lunch," explained Ned, "is that I want to get a handle on how things are going on the project. Olympia is a hot item in our company. If we do well, the heavyweights in Washington will be awarding us follow-on contracts for the next decade. Larry, of course, has kept me informed to some extent. I've also been looking at those PERT charts. But now I want a first hand discussion on what's going on."

"Well, Ned, the engineering group is doing pretty well considering the constraints we're working under. We're meeting our targets and we've only lost one or two key people so far."

"Hold on, Jane. I'm hearing some pretty strong reservations coming through on your part. What seems to be the problem?"

"Ned, please don't think I'm taking the opportunity to talk behind Larry's back just because he's out of the country. I like the guy. In some ways I admire his ability to keep on top of things. But I wonder at times if he knows how to handle professional managers. Sometimes I wonder if he is a professional manager himself."

Puzzled by Jane's comment, Ned inquired, "What do you mean? That Larry may not know how to handle professional managers or that he may not be a professional manager?"

"To Larry, the long range is three days to one week. Sometimes he makes three phone calls a day asking for answers to picky little problems. If you don't have an answer at your fingertips, he panics. He counters with a barrage of additional questions. I think he'd make a great prosecuting attorney. Maybe that's why Corporate wants him

for a troubleshooter. I try to set my objectives for several months out into the future. Sometimes I work by yearly objectives. I tackle the big conceptual issues and leave the fine points and the day-by-day details to my staff. I think a professional manager should focus more on the long and intermediate ranges than on the short range."

"But in what way does Larry's approach interfere with your professionalism as a manager?"

"I spend too much time getting ready to answer questions about the tiniest problems. I'll give you a specific example. Every Friday morning I have to spend about an hour sorting through the figures to determine if we're on budget for the week. Larry likes weekly budget figures. I'd much prefer to report on a monthly or bimonthly basis. Less time with budgets would give me more time to plan for the future."

"Thanks for your candor," commented Ned. "Now let's talk about some of the technical problems on the project."

The following day at lunch with Mack, Ned asked him how things were going. Mack eagerly responded, "Things are going great on Olympia from a manufacturing standpoint. I hope you've taken time to look at the manufacturing input to the PERT chart. We're going great guns. Please don't think I'm playing office politics while the boss is away, but Larry deserves a lot of credit for our success."

"How's that?" responded Ned.

Mack continued, "Larry is just the style of manager we needed on this project. He's got the rat-tat-tat style that a project manager must have when you're playing with big government bucks. Larry presses me for progress details almost daily. He helps keep me on my toes. Larry manages by the philosophy, 'The best way to eat an elephant is one bite at a time.' I think he's a big improvement over the past."

"What was wrong in the past?"

"Before Olympia, I worked on Project Odyssey. Our project manager was oriented toward the long range. He figured that if he set general guidelines and long-range targets, the details would fall into place automatically. To tell the truth, I think I became a little lazy working for him. I lost some of my concern for making sure all our milestones were met on time."

"Very interesting to hear your comments, Mack. Let's talk now about some of the hardware that you have been putting together."

As Mack launched into a description of the major components of the system, Ned thought to himself, "Are these two people talking about the same manager?"*

As you read this chapter, you will find an explanation for most of the leadership behavior illustrated by the opening case. Of paramount importance, Larry's experience illustrates the contingency nature of leadership. In this situation, the leadership style that was effective in dealing with Mack was ineffective in dealing with Jane.

THE MEANING OF LEADERSHIP

Successful organizations, and the units within them, consistently differ from their ineffective counterparts in one important respect—the former are characterized by dynamic and effective leadership.[1] A leader exerts influence over others, and leadership is defined as "the influential increment over and above mechanical compliance with routine directives of the organization."[2] A manager usually cannot take credit for "leading" subordinates to attend work regularly or to park their automobiles in designated areas. Also, to qualify as an act of leadership, people must be influenced to act voluntarily. Coercive acts such as physical punishment or threats of punishment are not considered to be leadership. Exerting formal authority to achieve compliance also falls outside the realm of leadership.

Leadership and management. Leading and managing are not synonymous. Leading is but one vital aspect of the managerial process, which also includes such

*Eugene H. Fram and Andrew J. DuBrin, "Time-Span Orientation: A Key Factor in Contingency Management," *Personnel Journal,* January 1981, pp. 47–48.

[1]Paul Hersey and Kenneth M. Blanchard, *Management of Organizational Behavior: Utilizing Human Resources,* 3rd ed., (Englewood Cliffs, N.J.: Prentice-Hall, 1977), p. 83.

[2]Daniel Katz and Robert L. Kahn, *The Social Psychology of Organizations,* 2nd ed. (New York: John Wiley, 1978), p. 528.

functions as planning, controlling, organizing, scheduling, and negotiating. Also, individual contributors can exercise leadership in organizations. Informal leaders—those without official sanction from the organization—emerge in many settings. Among the processes used by leaders to influence people are motivation, communication, counseling, and decision making. In short, not all managers are leaders, and not all leaders are managers.

Leadership can be multidirectional.   Leadership is typically perceived as a vertical influence process, pointing downward in the direction of formal authority. Top-level managers influence people below them, who in turn influence people below them. It is said that we look up to leaders, yet leadership is also exerted horizontally and sometimes diagonally in organizations.[3] Horizontal leadership is the use of personal power to influence people over whom the manager or staff specialist has no formal authority. In Chapter 14 we examine techniques of lateral influence in some detail.

Leadership and organizational behavior.   Topics closely related to leadership are discussed throughout this book. For example, almost all the information presented in this part of the book (understanding small groups) relates directly to influencing others. Our study of leadership in this chapter highlights several contingency theories that emphasize that effective leadership depends upon the demands of the situation. In addition, some attention is paid to the traits and characteristics of leaders themselves, including observations about entrepreneurs.

LEADER TRAITS AND CHARACTERISTICS

Early psychological studies of leadership attempted to isolate traits that would reliably differentiate leaders from nonleaders and effective leaders from ineffective leaders. Reviews of the literature on leadership suggests that there are few traits that consistently make these kinds of differentiations. Stogdill, in a widely quoted survey of leadership studies, indicated that only the traits of intelligence, scholarship, dependability and responsibility, social participation, and socioeconomic status consistently differentiate leaders from nonleaders.[4] In contrast, Gibb several years later concluded that "the numerous studies of personalities of leaders have failed to find any consistent patterns of traits which characterize leaders."[5] Negative results such as these are in part attributable to combining leadership studies from varying situations, each of which probably has different leadership demands. For example, combining a study assessing the per-

---

[3]John R. Schermerhorn, Jr., James G. Hunt, and Richard N. Osborn, *Managing Organizational Behavior* (New York: John Wiley, 1982), p. 532.

[4]Ralph M. Stogdill, "Personal Factors Associated with Leadership: A Survey of the Literature," *Journal of Psychology,* Vol. 25, January 1948, pp. 35–71.

[5]Cecil A. Gibb, "Leadership," in Gardner Lindzey, ed., *Handbook of Social Psychology,* Vol. II (Reading, Mass.: Addison-Wesley, 1954).

sonal traits of athletic coaches with a study assessing the personal traits of big-business leaders will probably be inconclusive. Leadership studies that make assessments of leaders in comparable situations are more likely to reveal characteristics that differentiate between more effective and less effective leaders.

Despite many negative research results about leadership traits, it is difficult to convince practicing managers or management consultants that there are no differences in personal makeup between successful and less successful (or effective and ineffective) leaders. A realistic view is that certain leadership traits and characteristics contribute to effective leadership in many situations. Correspondingly, similar leadership situations require similar leadership traits and behaviors. To illustrate, a person who was effective in running a production operation in a newspaper could probably run a production operation in a book bindery. There would be enough similarity among the type of subordinates and machinery to make the situations comparable. In contrast, a high school football coach might fail dismally as the managing editor of a fashion magazine. The two situations would call for dramatically different kinds of leadership.

Extensive research has been conducted about traits, characteristics, and behavior that contribute to effective leadership in a wide variety of situations. The following discussion is based on a blend of major investigations (and some systematic observations) in this area.[6,7,8]

Intelligence level is widely used in the selection of people for leadership positions. Effective leaders tend to be bright but not brilliant. They are intelligent enough to be good problem solvers, but not so intelligent that their interests lie primarily in solving abstract problems and puzzles. Leadership positions in modern organizations place a continuously increasing demand upon problem-solving ability, particularly in the areas of processing paperwork and interacting with computers.

Situation sensitivity is a leadership requirement in virtually every leadership position. An effective leader is able to size up a situation and see what leadership practice should or should not be used. A sensitive leader, for instance, would recognize that in an emergency people want unilateral, decisive leadership commands. If a company is approaching bankruptcy, its employees want a leader to say, "Follow my instructions and we'll survive." Being sensitive to situations allows a leader to adapt to different leadership roles and situations.

Effective work habits are helpful, if not essential, in most leadership situations. Even if directing the activities of artistic, free-spirited individuals, the leader contributes to organizational effectiveness if he or she is well organized. As modern organizations become more paperwork oriented (forms, budgets, and so forth), good work habits and careful organization become all the more important.

---

[6]Edwin E. Ghiselli, *Explorations in Managerial Talent* (Glenview, Ill.: Scott, Foresman and Company, 1971).

[7]Jay Hall, "What Makes a Manager Good, Bad, or Average?" *Psychology Today,* August 1976, pp. 52, 53, 55.

[8]Richard I. Lester, "Leadership: Some Principles and Concepts," *Personnel Journal,* November 1981, pp. 868–70.

Initiative is a two-faceted characteristic that helps a leader to function effectively. Initiative, on the one hand, refers to "self-starting ability," taking action without support and stimulation from others. A person aspiring toward leadership roles should recognize that initiative (or motivation and drive) is a characteristic looked for in potential leaders. If you do not appear well motivated to people above you, you probably will not be selected for a leadership position. The second facet to initiative is problem- (or opportunity-) finding ability. An effective leader looks for things that need doing or tasks that need performing and works on problems that could have a big potential payoff. An ineffective leader might spend the week performing trivial tasks.

Self-confidence is an important leadership characteristic in virtually every setting. A leader who is self-assured without being bombastic or overbearing instills confidence in his or her subordinates. Aside from being a psychological trait, self-confidence or self-assurance refers to the behavior exhibited by a person in a number of situations. It might be concluded that Maureen is a confident supervisor if (1) she retains her composure when a worker threatens to file a grievance and (2) she calmly helps a worker fix a machine failure when the department is behind schedule.

Individuality is another characteristic associated with effective leadership. It can express itself both in the unique pattern of traits possessed by the person and in work habits. The research reported here indicated that those managers who displayed the greatest individuality in the way in which they did their work were also judged to be the best managers. Individuality is important in understanding leaders because it contributes to charm or charisma.

Technical and professional competence is important for leadership, although it may be more appropriately classified as a behavior than a characteristic. It has been observed that employees will give a manager a reasonable period of time in which to become oriented to the job, but they will not respect the manager who continually relies on others in the firm to make decisions or provide guidance.

Enthusiasm is a universally desirable, if not necessary, leadership trait. Subordinates tend to respond positively to enthusiasm, and displays of enthusiasm can even be used to reinforce constructive behaviors. Enthusiasm is a desirable leadership trait because it helps to establish rapport with others. The trait can be expressed both verbally ("Way to go, team") and nonverbally through gestures, smiles, and so forth.

High ethical standards, honesty, candor, and related characteristics are essential in most leadership situations. Few modern organizations would place people in leadership positions who were known to be unethical or devious. Aside from moral considerations, the risk of public exposure of deviant behavior runs high.

Flexibility is important because it facilitates adaptive leadership behavior. A management development specialist notes that "A leader must understand that no two people or situations are ever exactly alike. Yesterday's approach may or may not be the correct approach for today or tomorrow. Effective leaders adapt their approaches to the particular person, group or problem at hand."[9]

Vision is important for leaders in top-level positions. An inspiring leader needs a

---

[9]Lester, "Leadership," p. 870.

visual image of where the organization is going and how it can get there. Effective leaders project ideas and images that excite people and develop choices that are timely and appropriate for the situation at hand.

Although the identification of traits and characteristics that are essential for leadership success has a good deal of face validity, it only explains some aspects of leadership. A more fruitful research strategy proved to be the identification of how the leader's traits matched the requirements of the situation at hand.

LEADERSHIP BEHAVIOR AND STYLES

Leadership Behavior

Following the trait approach to leadership came an attempt to understand leaders by investigating their actual activities or behavior. Rather than try to determine what effective leaders were, researchers tried to determine what effective leaders *did.* The issues to be explored included "In what manner do they lead?" "How hard do they push people?" "How much do they listen?" The dichotomy between the trait and the behavioral approach is not as clear cut as it appears on the surface. A leader's personal traits and characteristics influence his or her leadership style. For example, an easygoing, permissive person who basically cares for people will ordinarily gravitate toward a people-oriented style of leadership. Over the long run, an individual with these traits will seek out leadership situations in which such a style is appropriate, such as managing a group of professionals.

The behavioral approach to leadership led naturally to a classification of leadership styles based upon the leader's characteristic way of leading people. The style is based upon the emphasis a leader places on the functions of task accomplishment or people orientation. When we refer to the behavioral approach to leadership, we are simultaneously referring to leadership styles.

Leadership Styles

Most leadership theories incorporate two basic styles: a task-oriented style and a relationship-oriented style (also referred to as employee oriented or people oriented).[10] Task-oriented leaders direct and closely supervise subordinates to make sure that the task is being performed up to their standards. A manager with this style is more concerned about getting the job done than about developing subordinates. Employee-oriented leaders emphasize the human relationships involved in getting work accomplished. They emphasize motivating subordinates, allowing for group decision making, and listening to the problems of their people.

---

[10]Our discussion of leadership styles and the Ohio State and Michigan studies includes paraphrases from James A. F. Stoner, *Management,* 2nd ed. (Englewood Cliffs, N.J.: Prentice-Hall, 1982), pp. 471–74.

The Ohio State and Michigan Studies

Much of the thinking undergirding modern leadership theory and leadership training programs traces back to studies conducted by researchers at these universities. A number of leadership dimensions were studied at Ohio State University. The two most useful proved to be initiating structure and consideration. A basic method of classifying leadership style combines these two dimensions, as diagrammed in Figure 12–1.

> *Initiating structure* is used to describe the degree to which the leader initiates structure for subordinates by activities such as assigning specific tasks, specifying procedures to be followed, scheduling work, and clarifying expectations of subordinates. Traditional management functions such as planning, organizing, and controlling are aspects of initiating structure. *Consideration* describes the degree to which the leader creates an environment of emotional support, warmth, friendliness, and trust by engaging in such behaviors as being friendly and approachable, looking out for the personal welfare of the group, keeping the group abreast of new developments, and doing small favors for the group.[11]

It was discovered that employee turnover was lowest and job satisfaction highest under leaders who were rated high in consideration. Conversely, leaders who were rated low in consideration and high in initiating structure had high grievance and turnover rates among their employees. Research also indicated that leaders high on structure were generally rated highly by superiors and had higher-producing work groups than did leaders who scored lower in this dimension. Although high structure tends to lower job satisfaction, the relationship between these two variables is influenced by the situation. Among such findings are[12]

[11]Robert J. House, "A Path-Goal Theory of Leadership Effectiveness," *Administrative Science Quarterly,* September 1971, pp. 321–38.

[12]John R. Rizzo, Robert J. House, and Sidney E. Lirtzman, "Role Conflict and Ambiguity in Complex Organizations," *Administrative Science Quarterly,* June 1970, pp. 150–53.

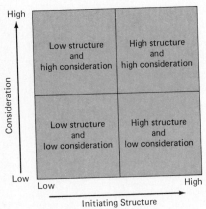

FIGURE 12–1 A Basic Method of Classifying Leadership Styles

1. Initiating structure is frequently resented by unskilled and semiskilled employees and contributes to dissatisfaction, grievance, and turnover.
2. Employees in large groups have a more favorable attitude toward structure than do employees in small groups.
3. Among high-level employees, initiating structure is positively related to satisfaction, performance, and perceptions of organizational effectiveness, but negatively related to role conflict and ambiguity.

In general, it was discovered that subordinates' ratings of their leaders' effectiveness depended more upon the situation in which the style was used than upon any of the four basic styles. To illustrate, Air Force commanders who rated high on consideration were rated as *less* effective than were task-oriented commanders. Air Force personnel are enmeshed in an organizational climate that values a high task orientation.

Researchers at the University of Michigan's Institute for Social Research also investigated differences in results obtained by production-centered and employee-centered managers. Production-centered managers set tight work standards, organized tasks carefully, prescribed the work methods to be followed, and closely supervised their subordinates' work. Employee-centered managers encouraged subordinate participation in goal setting and in other work decisions and helped to ensure high performance by engendering trust and mutual respect.

A dominant finding of these studies was that the most productive work groups tended to have leaders who were employee centered rather than production centered. It was also found that the most effective leaders were those who had supportive relations with their subordinates, tended to use group rather than individual decision making, and encouraged their subordinates to set and achieve high performance goals.[13] Despite the general consistency to the value of employee-centered leadership, some mixed findings emerged from the Michigan studies.

Later research by the Institute shed new light on the complexity of the relationships between leadership style and productivity. One group of employees in a large life insurance company was managed in an employee-centered style; another comparable group was managed in a production-centered style. Contrary to expectations, both groups showed a significant increase in productivity. However, the employee-centered leadership style produced an increase in favorable attitudes toward the supervisors and the company. In contrast, the production-centered group showed a marked decrease in favorable attitudes toward supervision and management. Based on research conducted with 20,000 employees in a firm manufacturing earth moving equipment, it was concluded that foremen with the best production records were both production and employee centered.[14]

---

[13]Arnold S. Tannenbaum, *Social Psychology of the Work Organization* (Monterey, Calif.: Wadsworth, 1966), p. 74.

[14]Robert Dubin, "Supervision and Productivity: Empirical Findings and Theoretical Considerations," in Walter Nord, ed., *Concepts and Controversy in Organizational Behavior* (Glenview, Ill.: Scott, Foresman and Company, 1972), pp. 524–25.

The Managerial Grid®

The observation that effective leaders can be both employee and production oriented became the basis for the widely used Managerial Grid.® The Grid is a comprehensive system of management and organization development and will be treated as such in Chapter 17. Attention now is directed to the five key leadership styles it portrays. Concern for production is rated on a 1 to 9 scale on the horizontal axis, while concern for people is rated similarly on the vertical axis. The Grid identifies a range of management behaviors based on the various ways in which task-oriented and people-oriented styles can interact with each other. The labels used for the five leadership styles have been changed several times by the originators of the Grid.[15] In Chapter 17 you will find slightly different labels for the same leadership styles.

Do-nothing manager (1,1).   The leader exerts a minimum of effort to get work accomplished, with very little concern for people or production. This style is sometimes referred to as *laissez-faire* management because the leader abdicates his or her leadership role.

Country club manager (1,9).   Leader gives considerable attention to the needs of people but minimum concern to task accomplishment. This behavior leads to a comfortable, friendly, and relaxed work atmosphere where nobody "makes waves." A small firm that has "cornered the market" is sometimes run in this manner.

Production pusher (9,1).   Leader achieves efficiency in operations by arranging conditions of work in such a way that human elements interfere to a minimum degree. Feelings and attitudes of subordinates, within reason, are kept from interfering with productivity. First-level supervisors in canning factories often adapt this leadership style.

Organization person (5,5).   Leader maintains adequate organization performance and morale. Mediocrity is perpetuated, but things keep "perking along." Probably most managers consciously or unconsciously utilize this leadership style.

Team builder (9,9).   Leader is able to elicit high productivity from a committed and dedicated group of subordinates. Goals of the organization and the people are successfully integrated. Leaders of this type are rare. Talented leaders and talented subordinates are required for these ideal conditions to occur. Small, technically sophisticated businesses are often characterized by a pulling together of management and employees. All members of the team are both happy and productive.

The founders of the Grid argue strongly for the value of 9,9 management. The team builder approach in almost all situations results in improved performance, low absenteeism and turnover, and high employee satisfaction. "Nine-nine" management relies on trust and respect and leads to positive outcomes because

> The engineering specifics include mutual goal-setting, openness, resolution of disagreements and conflict based on understanding and agreement, learning to change through

[15]Robert R. Blake and Jane S. Mouton, *The New Managerial Grid* (Houston: Gulf, 1978).

use of critique, and so forth. These are aspects of behavior verified in social psychology, mental health research, and clinical psychiatry as essential for a sound problem-solving relationship.[16]

Many leadership theorists argue that no one style of leadership leads to positive outcomes in all situations. However, it is difficult to argue with the logic that the best way to manage is to respond to the needs of people and attend to the task at hand. In some situations people's needs are best met by giving them considerable latitude to take care of things themselves.

System 4 Management

Rensis Likert devised a four-level model of management and organization effectiveness based in part on the leadership-style categories of task orientation and people orientation (see Figure 12–2). The four systems refer to both organization types and the styles of leadership used by managers in these organizations.[17] System 1 managers are authoritative (or authoritarian), making all the decisions and ordering their subordinates to implement them. Standards and methods of performance are also set by System 1 managers. Failure to meet the managers' goals results in threats or punishments. The managers perceive a minimum of trust or confidence in subordinates, while subordinates distrust management and feel that they have little in common with them.

System 2 managers issue orders, but employees have some freedom to comment on those orders. Subordinates are also given some flexibility to implement their assign-

---

[16]Robert Blake and Jane Srygley Mouton, "Should You Teach There's Only *One* Best Way to Manage?" *Training,* April 1978.

[17]Rensis Likert, *The Human Organization* (New York: McGraw-Hill, 1967), pp. 4–10; also based on Stoner, *Management,* p. 475.

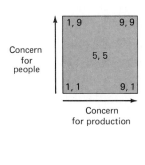

Concern for people

1, 9   9, 9

5, 5

1, 1   9, 1

Concern for production

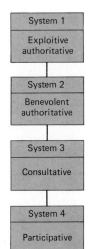

System 1
Exploitive authoritative

System 2
Benevolent authoritative

System 3
Consultative

System 4
Participative

FIGURE 12–1 The Managerial Grid® Leadership Styles and Likert's Leadership Systems

ments but within carefully prescribed limits and procedures. Subordinates who meet or exceed the managers' goals may be rewarded. In general, managers have a condescending attitude toward their subordinates, and subordinates are cautious when dealing with managers.

System 3 managers set goals and issue general orders after discussing them with subordinates (as described in the Vroom-Yetton model presented in Chapter 10). Subordinates are allowed to make their own decision about how to carry out their tasks because only broad, major decisions are made by higher-level managers. Rewards, rather than threats of punishment, are used to motivate employees. Subordinates feel free to discuss most work-related matters with their managers. Managers, in turn, believe that to a large extent subordinates can be trusted to carry out their assignments properly.

System 4, according to Likert and many other management theorists, is the ideal system toward which organizations should strive. Goals are set by subordinates and group decision making is the rule. Managers reach a decision only after incorporating the suggestions and opinions of group members. Thus, the goal they set or the decision they reach may not always be the one they personally favor. Managers rely on both external rewards and internal rewards in the form of appealing to the feelings of worth and importance among their subordinates. Performance standards exist to permit self-appraisal by subordinates rather than to provide managers with a tool to control subordinates. Interaction among managers and subordinates is frank, friendly, and trusting.

System 4 is a pure form of participative management. Other forms of participative management have gained in popularity in recent years in both Europe and the United States. Japanese management, or Theory Z (see Chapter 15), is conceptually similar to System 4.

SITUATIONAL INFLUENCES ON LEADERSHIP

Both trait and behavioral theorists agreed that leaders should adapt their style to the demands of the situation at hand. A logical extension of their thinking was the situational approach to leadership, which attempts to identify the forces in a situation indicating which particular leadership style will be effective. Our project manager, Larry, for example, may have thought that project management called for a short time-span orientation (TSO). One of his subordinates agreed and one did not. The accompanying box explains the situational factors influencing the choice of TSO (see pages 320–321).

A substantial number of factors are potentially relevant variables for choosing an appropriate leadership style. To make use of such knowledge, the manager must be aware that situational factors exist and also be able to make an appropriate diagnosis. The situational factors to be considered here are personal characteristics of subordinates, personal characteristics of the manager, environmental pressures and demands, and the prevailing work ethic.

Personal Characteristics
of Subordinates

The type of people you are leading is a major determinant of which leadership style is most effective. In general, competent subordinates—those who are well trained, intelligent, and well motivated—need a minimum of guidance and emotional support from a manager. The leader in such a situation is best advised to give considerable latitude to subordinates and play only a minor role in their social interaction. As shown in the classic diagram in Figure 12–3, the leader would move to the extreme right on the continuum of leadership behavior. Such a leader would also be classified as low-task and low-relationship.

Another subordinate characteristic that influences the optimum leadership style is the degree of authoritarianism. Authoritarian (strict, unyielding, and rigid) people have a tendency to prefer directive or authoritarian leaders. Also, they tend to dislike or even distrust a permissive or democratic leadership style. The most appropriate leadership style can also be influenced by how well subordinates think they can perform the assigned task: "The higher the degree of perceived ability relative to the task demands, the less subordinates will view leader directiveness and coaching behavior as acceptable."[18]

[18]Alan C. Filley, Robert J. House, and Steven Kerr, *Managerial Process and Organizational Behavior,* 2nd ed. (Glenview, Ill.: Scott, Foresman and Company, 1976), p. 255.

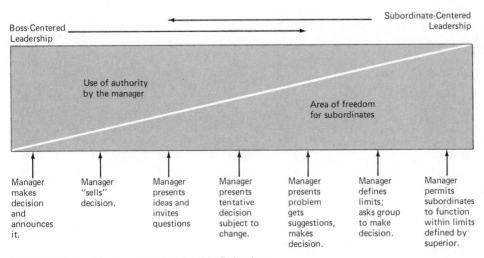

FIGURE 12–3 Continuum of Leadership Behavior

Source: Robert Tannenbaum and Warren H. Schmidt, "How to Choose a Leadership Pattern," *Harvard Business Review,* May–June 1973, p. 167. Copyright © 1973 by the President and Fellows of Harvard College; all rights reserved.

TSO AND CONTINGENCY MANAGEMENT

It is apparent that project manager Larry's two employees prefer their immediate supervisor to work with different time-span orientations. Perhaps Larry's major failure is his inability or unwillingness to communicate his TSO to Jane, the director of engineering. (We also assume here that a short TSO fits the requirements of the firm.) As implied in the case, the underlying difference between the polar ends of TSO relates to a sense of time urgency.

The leader with a short TSO thinks primarily in terms of the "here and now." The leader with a long TSO thinks primarily in terms of the long range. (Intermediate-range TSOs, of course, are also possible.) Of importance to the practicing manager is the fact that differences in TSOs lead to differences in behavior. The following summarizes several important differences in behavior we found between leaders with long and short time-span orientations.

Short-Range TSO	Long-Range TSO
Demands frequent information and feedback from employees.	Is content with infrequent information and feedback from employees.
Believes that short-range planning is more vital than long-range planning.	Believes that long-range planning is more vital than short-range planning.
Tends to exert tight controls over employees.	Tends to exert loose controls over employees.
Tends to expect results quickly from employees—even on major projects.	Content to wait a relatively long time for results on major projects.
Tends to focus more on details than on concepts.	Tends to focus more on concepts than details.
Spends considerable time in direct contact with employees.	Spends modest amount of time in contact with employees.
Works to tight deadlines.	Likes to allow a time safety margin and to have projects ready well in advance.
Works well with verbal communications.	Likes to have decisions in writing and confirming memo.

Sensitivity to TSO enhances the ability of a manager to practice contingency management. TSO is another dimension of leadership that often can be consciously altered, modified, or manipulated to meet the demands of a given leadership situation. To illustrate how TSO can facilitate contingency management, four key variables should be considered: nature of the enterprise, nature of the employee, nature of the responsibility, and extent of a crisis mode.

Nature of the Enterprise

The nature of the enterprise is an influential variable in choosing an appropriate TSO. The type of business itself will often dictate which TSO is necessary. For example, with a general merchandise retail organization, the typical budget-planning period is six months in length. It is not unusual to establish a budget only several months before it becomes operational. On the other hand, the petroleum industry must work in the long range when exploring for resources—which can take up to a decade. Of course, refinery supervisors in that same industry might have to work with very short TSOs.

Nature of Employees

Dependent and less than fully competent employees will require a shorter-range TSO from their supervisors than will their more independent and competent counterparts. Problem employees too will require a shorter TSO: they need frequent follow-up and guidance.

Line versus Staff Authority

Line units deal more frequently with short-range problems while staff units more frequently deal with a long range. Consequently, a manager of a staff unit might rely more often upon a long TSO. Yet there are specific times when a manager of a staff unit might need to operate with a very short TSO in order to be effective. One germane example is the director of a legal services department whose firm is suddenly faced with a lawsuit. He or she might then manage the department with a TSO not unlike that of a fire station captain.

The Presence or Absence of a Crisis Mode

Organizations designed to handle crises (such as hospitals and the claims office of a casualty insurance company) foster shorter TSOs among their personnel. The same is true of organizations that constantly deal in a crisis mode, although they are not designed as crisis organizations. Amusement parks are a case in point because they experience a crisis every summer season: the profits of the business are totally dependent on sales taking place during a two and a half-month period.

Personal Characteristics of the Leader

The basic personality structure with which an individual enters the leadership situation exerts a profound impact upon the leadership style that he or she chooses. The same forces may influence which style works best because it is difficult for leaders to be effective when they adapt a leadership style too foreign to their nature. As one frustrated subordinate said, "I wish my boss had never taken that seminar in participative management. He was much more believable as an autocrat."

Environmental Pressures and Demands and Group Factors

Forces related to the job itself, group characteristics, and the conditions surrounding the job are a third set of contingencies influencing the most appropriate leadership style.[19] An effective leader diagnoses these factors and takes them into account in adapting to the leadership situation.

1. *Under conditions of heavy stress, threat, or pressure,* most people want a leader to take forceful charge of the situation. In crisis situations, people are pleased to have the leader give specific orders and directives. A troubled business corporation elected a new president with a firm belief in financial controls. Although he made many enemies in the process, the company was successful in averting disaster and many employees came to appreciate this fact.

2. *Ambiguous assignments* also influence which leadership style is best. When a person cannot tolerate ambiguity (such as unclear assignments) very well, he or she would prefer to have a leader provide much structure. The result for the person would be less tension. But those who like ambiguity (so that they can provide their own structure) prefer a leader who does not meddle in their work.

3. *As the size of the work group increases,* subordinates may prefer that the leader play a more active role in coordinating activities. In addition to lowering the frustration of subordinates, clarifying and coordinating activities may improve performance. When work groups are smaller, the group members themselves can divide up responsibilities without much help from their leader.

4. *The type of technology* is another influence that helps to determine (or mediate) which leadership style is best. One extreme in technology would be the supervision of a craftlike operation, where the workers are highly skilled and self-sufficient. They would need a minimum of guidance and structure, particularly about technological matters. A leader in such a situation should therefore emphasize giving the workers autonomy. The other technological extreme is a mass-production operation where the contribution of one department is interdependent with the contribution of other departments. An automobile assembly plant would be one such operation. Deviations from standards cannot be tolerated, so the managers involved have to ensure that policies and procedures are enforced uniformly.

The Prevailing Work Ethic

When the members of a group have a strong work ethic, a leader does not have to devote much time to finding ways of motivating employees. The cultural climate is on the side of management and pride acts as a natural reinforcer. In contrast, when employees have a weak work ethic, a leader must exert considerable effort toward such matters as carefully checking up on progress toward performance goals. A high task orientation combined with a high relations orientation may be required when subordinates have a weak work ethic. In such a climate, subordinates will need more direction and encouragement.

---

[19]This discussion of environmental pressures and demands is based on Elmer Burack, *Organization Analysis: Theory and Applications* (Hinsdale, Ill.: Dryden Press, 1975), pp. 315–18.

The situational perspective on leadership led naturally to theories that attempted to specify factors upon which the most effective leadership style depended (contingency factors). Contingency theories of leadership are thus situational theories in which the "it depends" factors are well defined. Three of the most widely accepted contingency theories are presented in the next several sections of this chapter.

FIEDLER'S CONTINGENCY THEORY

The situational nature of leadership is presented with the most precision in Fiedler's contingency model. Owing somewhat to its rigor and conceptual clarity, Fiedler's theory has generated considerable attention from researchers and management writers. Its central proposition is that task-motivated (meaning the same as task-oriented) leaders are more effective when the leadership situation is very favorable or unfavorable. Relationship-motivated leaders are more effective in situations of moderate favorability. One rationale is that when conditions are favorable, the group is willing to accept a task orientation because its members do not require much in the way of emotional support. However, when conditions are unfavorable for the leader, he or she needs a task orientation to maintain control of the situation. To understand or apply this contingency theory, it is first necessary to measure one's leadership style using Fiedler's framework.[20,21]

The LPC Scale for Measuring Leadership Style

Fiedler contends that a manager's leadership style is a relatively permanent aspect of behavior and therefore difficult to modify. According to his reasoning, once you understand your leadership style, you should work in situations appropriate to that style. Or you can modify the situation so that it matches your leadership style. Similarly, managers and personnel specialists should attempt to match up leadership styles and situations. The Least Preferred Co-worker scale shown in Figure 12–4 is used to measure leadership style. It measures the degree to which a leader describes favorably or unfavorably his or her least preferred co-worker—the employee with whom the leader can work least well (or the most disliked).

The crux of the LPC scale is that a leader who describes the least preferred co-worker in a relatively favorable manner tends to be permissive, human relations oriented, and considerate of the feelings of subordinates (or relations motivated). But a person who describes his or her least preferred co-worker in an unfavorable manner

[20]Fred E. Fiedler, "The Leadership Game: Matching the Man to the Situation," *Organizational Dynamics,* Winter 1976, pp. 6–16.
[21]Fred E. Fiedler, Martin M. Chemers, and Linda Mahar, *The Leader-Match Concept* (New York: John Wiley, 1978).

Throughout your life you will have worked in many groups with a wide variety of different people—on your job, in social groups, in church organizations, in volunteer groups, on athletic teams, and in many other situations. Some of your co-workers may have been very easy to work with in attaining the group's goals, while others were less so.

Think of all the people with whom you have ever worked, and then think of the person with whom you could work *least well*. He or she may be someone with whom you work now or with whom you have worked in the past. This does not have to be the person you liked least well, but should be the person with whom you had the most difficulty getting a job done, the *one* individual with whom you could work *least well*.

Describe this person on the scale that follows by placing an "X" in the appropriate space.

Look at the words at both ends of the line before you mark your "X." *There are no right or wrong answers.* Work rapidly; your first answer is likely to be the best. Do not omit any items, and mark each item only once.

Now describe the person with whom you can work least well.

Scoring

	8	7	6	5	4	3	2	1		
Pleasant									Unpleasant	____
Friendly	8	7	6	5	4	3	2	1	Unfriendly	____
Rejecting	1	2	3	4	5	6	7	8	Accepting	____
Tense	1	2	3	4	5	6	7	8	Relaxed	____
Distant	1	2	3	4	5	6	7	8	Close	____
Cold	1	2	3	4	5	6	7	8	Warm	____
Supportive	8	7	6	5	4	3	2	1	Hostile	____
Boring	1	2	3	4	5	6	7	8	Interesting	____
Quarrelsome	1	2	3	4	5	6	7	8	Harmonious	____
Gloomy	1	2	3	4	5	6	7	8	Cheerful	____
Open	8	7	6	5	4	3	2	1	Guarded	____
Backbiting	1	2	3	4	5	6	7	8	Loyal	____
Untrustworthy	1	2	3	4	5	6	7	8	Trustworthy	____
Considerate	8	7	6	5	4	3	2	1	Inconsiderate	____
Nasty	1	2	3	4	5	6	7	8	Nice	____
Agreeable	8	7	6	5	4	3	2	1	Disagreeable	____
Insincere	1	2	3	4	5	6	7	8	Sincere	____
Kind	8	7	6	5	4	3	2	1	Unkind	____

Total _____

FIGURE 12–4 The Least Preferred Co-worker (LPC) Scale for Measuring Your Leadership Style

Source: Adapted from Fred E. Fiedler, Martin M. Chemers, and Linda Mahar, *Improving Leadership Effectiveness* (New York: John Wiley, 1976), p. 7.

tends to be task controlling, production oriented, and less concerned with the human relations aspect of the job. In short, the high-LPC person is relations motivated, whereas the low-LPC person is task motivated. To interpret your LPC score, turn to page 344.

Measuring Situation Favorability

Fiedler has identified three elements in the work situation that determine favorability: the quality of leader-member relations, the degree of task structure, and the leader's position power. The foremost determinant of situation favorability is the quality of leader-member relations, or how well the leader gets along with the group. If group members respect the manager for reasons of personality, character, or ability, the manager will not have to rely on formal rank or authority.[22]

Task structure is the second most important determinant of how favorable conditions are for the leader. When a task is highly structured, step-by-step procedures are available and many of the decisions are programmed. Managers in such situations have considerable authority. Clear guidelines exist by which to measure employee performance, and the manager can back up his or her instructions by referring to a rulebook or policy manual.

The leader's position power refers to formal authority as distinct from personal power of the leader. Some positions, such as a president of a firm or a general in the military, carry considerable power. Committee heads, on the other hand, often suffer from limited power and therefore are placed in an unfavorable leadership situation.

The most favorable situation for a leader should occur when a highly popular manager leads his or her group through a very structured, well-defined task, and he or she has considerable formal authority. Should a well-liked corporation president walk around the plant and office giving out year-end bonuses, that executive would be in a highly favorable leadership position. A hostile (poor leader-member relations), first-level (low position power) manager attempting to initiate a safety campaign (low task structure) would be in an unfavorable leadership situation.

Matching the Situation to the Leader

Fiedler classifies each group situation by taking actual measures of leader-member relations, task structure, and position power. The questions asked are straightforward and direct, such as "Is it the leader's job to evaluate the performance of subordinates?" There are eight possible combinations of these three variables in the work environment. Leader-member relations can be good or bad; tasks may be structured or unstructured; and position power may be strong or weak. A given leadership situation can be classified as belonging to one of eight cells, as shown in Figure 12–5. Cells I, II, and III are considered very favorable; cell VIII is considered very unfavorable. In addition to evaluating situation favorability (cells I through VIII), Fiedler's research studies also classify leaders as high and low LPC (or relations motivated versus task motivated).

---

[22]Some of our synthesis of Fiedler's theory is borrowed from Stoner, *Management,* pp. 482–84.

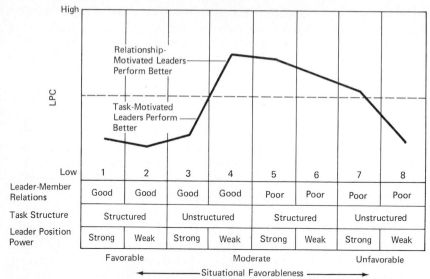

FIGURE 12–5 The Performance of Relationship- and Task-Motivated Leaders in Different Conditions of Situational Favorableness

Source: Fred E. Fiedler and Martin M. Chemers, *Leadership and Effective Management* (Glenview, Ill.: Scott, Foresman, 1974), p. 80. Copyright © 1974 Scott, Foresman and Company. Reprinted by permission.

Fiedler reviewed studies conducted in over eight hundred groups to investigate which type of leader was most effective in each situation. Among the groups studied were Air Force and tank combat crews, basketball teams, and groups of management development workshop participants. The general conclusion reached, as depicted in Figure 12-5, is that task-motivated leaders (low-LPC) were most effective in extreme situations where the leader either had a great deal of power and influence or very little power and influence. Relations-motivated (high-LPC) leaders were most effective where the leader had moderate power and influence.

Fiedler's contingency model suggests that an appropriate match of the leader's style (as measured by the LPC score) and the situation (as determined by an interaction of these three variables) leads to effective managerial performance.

Field Research on the Contingency Model

Although considered to have great promise, it would seem fair to conclude that Fiedler's model is impressive in appearance but fragile when subjected to field research. One of the many studies of the contingency model producing mixed results was conducted with careers of successful military leaders.[23] The researchers tried to ascertain

---

[23]R. E. Utecht and W. D. Heier, "The Contingency Model and Successful Military Leadership," *Academy of Management Journal,* December 1976, pp. 606–18.

whether or not the contingency model could be used as a predictor of successful military leadership. Two specific hypotheses were investigated:

1. The task-motivated successful military leader has primarily held positions of leadership in group situations classified I, II, III, and VIII in the contingency model.
2. The relationship-motivated successful military leader has primarily held positions of leadership in group situations classified IV, V, and VII in the contingency model.

The general hypothesis investigated was that the successful military leader has primarily held positions of leadership in group situations that have been favorable to his or her leadership style. The successful military leader was defined as an officer who had attended or was attending at the time of the study one of the five top-level military schools (all War Colleges). To be assigned to such a school, an officer must have demonstrated successful career progression.

Leadership style was measured with the LPC scale. Task structure information was obtained through questions about the military officer's last six leadership positions. A panel of three military judges then rated each position as structured or unstructured. Position power was judged on the basis of information about the relative ranks of the officer's immediate subordinates. The greater the difference in rank, the stronger the leader's position. Leader-member relations were measured by a group atmosphere scale that provided ratings such as friendly versus unfriendly and frustrating versus satisfying.

Mixed support was found for the general hypothesis. Hypothesis 1 concerning task-oriented military leaders was accepted. Task-oriented, successful military leaders primarily held positions in group situations classified as very favorable (I, II, III) and very unfavorable (VIII). Hypothesis 2 was not supported; there was no particular tendency for relationship-oriented military leaders to have worked in group situations of intermediate favorableness (IV, V, and VII).

Despite mixed evidence of this nature, an important practical contribution of Fiedler's contingency theory is that it helps to sensitize the leader or prospective leader to the importance of situational factors in attempting to achieve goals. A conscientious leader might ask, "What needs to be done to make this leadership situation favorable so that I can carry out my mission?" Or "What can be done to make this situation unfavorable so that my leadership style will match the occasion?"

THE PATH-GOAL CONTINGENCY THEORY

Path-goal leadership theory is a contingency theory that focuses on the leader behaviors required to motivate a subordinate to work more effectively.[24] It is based on expectancy/valence theory and several basic concepts of leadership. The role of the lead-

---

[24]See House, "A Path-Goal Theory,"; Robert J. House and Terence R. Mitchell, "Path-Goal Theory of Leadership," *Journal of Contemporary Business,* Autumn 1974, pp. 81–97; and Filley, House, and Kerr, *Managerial Process and Organizational Behavior,* Chapter 12.

er is seen as that of increasing personal payoffs to the subordinate for attaining work goals. When the subordinates clearly see the behaviors necessary to attain the payoffs (or rewards), the leader has cleared the path to goal accomplishment for the subordinate. Leader behavior is perceived as effective if it

1. Is seen by subordinates as an immediate or future source of need satisfaction.
2. Makes subordinate rewards contingent upon attaining work goals.
3. Supports goal attainment by removing roadblocks or barriers to their attainment.

Path-goal research has explored four specific styles of leadership that the leader should consider in adapting to the demands of a given situation as shown in Table 12–1. This is in sharp contrast to Fiedler's position that leadership style is relatively fixed. The path-goal leadership styles are as follows:

1. *Instrumental (or directive) leadership* emphasizes formal activities such as planning, organizing, and controlling; provides specific guidelines on standards, work schedules, rules, and regulations; and lets subordinates know what is expected of them.
2. *Supportive leadership* shows concern for subordinates' well-being and comfort and attempts to create a supportive climate; it emphasizes developing mutually satisfying relationships among members of the group.
3. *Achievement-oriented leadership* sets challenging work goals, emphasizes performance improvement, and establishes high expectations of subordinates; it expects subordinates to assume responsibility.
4. *Participative leadership* encourages subordinates' influence in decision making and sharing of information.

Contingency Factors

Each of the four leadership styles just described works well in some situations but not in others. The two sets of contingency factors that determine which style is most appropriate are subordinate characteristics and the environmental pressures and demands with which subordinates must cope to achieve work goals and job satisfaction.

TABLE 12–1 Summary of Path-Goal Relationships

Leader Behavior and	Contingency Factors		Cause	Subordinate Attitudes and Behavior
1. Directive	1. Subordinate characteristics			1. Job satisfaction
	Authoritarianism		Personal perceptions	Job → rewards
2. Supportive	Locus of control	Influence ⟩		2. Acceptance of leader
	Ability			Leader → rewards
3. Achievement oriented	2. Environmental factors		Motivational stimuli	3. Motivational behavior
	The task	Influence ⟩	Constraints	Effort → performance
	Formal authority system		Rewards	Performance → rewards
4. Participative	Primary work group			

Source: Reprinted with permission from Robert J. House and Terence R. Mitchell, "Path-Goal Theory of Leadership," *Journal of Contemporary Business,* Autumn 1974, p. 86. This journal is published by the University of Washington.

A subordinate characteristic of significance in path-goal theory is the subordinates' self-perception of their abilities. The higher the degree of perceived ability, the less willing a subordinate is to accept directive leadership. Key environmental variables include factors not within control of the subordinate yet important to task accomplishment or satisfaction. Among them are the tasks, the formal authority system of the organization, and the work group. Any of these environmental factors can motivate or demotivate employees. For example, approval of good work by other members of the work group will often act as a reinforcer.

Propositions to the Theory

The major contribution of path-goal theory is that it both specifies what leaders should do in different situations and explains the rationale for such behavior. The explanation is found in four general propositions that link performance and leader behavior through motivation:

1. Leaders perform a motivational function by increasing personal payoffs to subordinates for achieving work goals and by making the path to payoff smoother. Clarifying the path, reducing roadblocks and pitfalls, and increasing opportunities for satisfaction en route are behaviors that make the path smoother.
2. With clear paths to work goals, subordinates will be motivated because they will be more certain of how to reach goals. Role ambiguity will therefore be reduced. An effective leader would be able to detect when an employee needed help in carrying out an unfamiliar assignment.
3. Attempts by the leader to clarify path-goal relationships will be seen as redundant by employees if the work system already carefully defines the path-goal. Under these conditions, control may increase performance, but it will also result in decreased satisfaction.
4. Leader behavior aimed at need satisfaction of subordinates will increase work performance if such satisfaction increases the net positive valence of goal-directed effort. This means that if a manager provides rewards for good performance, such as choice assignments, it will only lead to higher productivity if liking for the work increases along with satisfaction.[25]

Although the several versions of path-goal theory integrate a large body of information, its complexity may lead to its lack of wide acceptance. Attempts to validate the model have been promising, but research about the theory is difficult to execute because it covers so much ground. Managers are unlikely to incorporate much of the path-goal theory into their language because it lacks the catchy phrases of leadership frameworks such as the Managerial Grid.® The primary contribution of the path-goal contingency leadership theory so far is that it helps to explain not only what type of leader is effective in a given situation, but why he or she is effective.

[25]Henry L. Tosi and Stephen J. Carroll, *Management,* 2nd ed., (New York: John Wiley, 1982), p. 369.

THE SITUATIONAL LEADERSHIP
THEORY

The contingency theory developed by Hersey and Blanchard places particular emphasis on the characteristics of the subordinates as a key situational variable. Referred to originally as the *life-cycle theory,* it is based on the idea that a leader must use the right combination of task and relationship orientations to be truly effective.

A major variable in the situational leadership theory is the *maturity* of the follower or group of followers. Maturity is defined as "the capacity to set high but attainable goals (achievement-motivation), willingness and ability to take responsibility, and education and/or experience of an individual or a group."[26] Maturity is considered specific to a situation. A bank manager might be a mature follower in a banking environment but be immature as an outfielder on the bank softball team. The psychological maturity of followers is more important than their chronological age in determining which leadership style is most likely to be effective.

Determining the Appropriate Leadership Style

The situational leadership theory contends that leader behavior, to be effective, must shift as the individual or group matures. Figure 12–6 shows the four leadership styles recommended for four different maturity levels of subordinates. According to Hersey and Blanchard, the four stages proceed in this manner: (Q 1) high-task–low-relationship behavior to (Q 2) high-task–high-relationship behavior to (Q 3) high-relationship–low-task behavior to (Q 4) low-task–low-relationship behavior. A "quadrant 4 approach" is recommended for mature individuals who do not require much technical guidance or emotional support.

Assume that a task force is drawn together to reduce the energy expenditure in a manufacturing plant. Its members are well-motivated, competent people who are working together for the first time. At the early stages of this project (Q 1), the group will need considerable structure so that the team understands its purposes and limitations. As illustrated by the bell-shaped curve in Figure 12-6, the leader shifts to a high-task and high-relationship style in Q 2. At this stage of the group's development, more attention can be made to building a good emotional relationship with the followers, although much structure is still needed. By the time the group reaches Q 3 in its maturity cycle, less task orientation is required but considerable emotional support is still important. At Q 4, the group is functioning as independent professionals who require a minimum of structure or consideration. The group proceeds about its task with a minimum of supervision. A confident leader will not "meddle" in the affairs of a highly competent, mature task force group.

[26]Hersey and Blanchard, *Management of Organizational Behavior,* pp. 162–68.

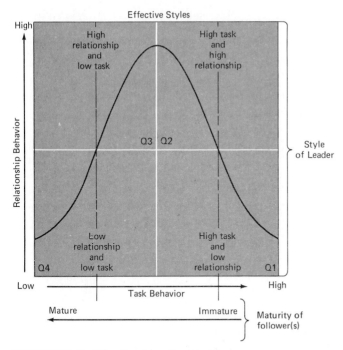

Effective Styles

FIGURE 12–6 Situational Leadership Theory

Source: Paul Hersey and Kenneth H. Blanchard, *Management of Organizational Behavior: Utilizing Human Resources,* 3rd ed. (Englewood Cliffs, N.J.: Prentice-Hall, Inc., 1977), p. 164. Reprinted by permision of Prentice-Hall, Inc.

Comment

The situational leadership theory represents a synthesis of generally well-accepted thinking about leadership and followership behavior: competent people need less leadership than do less competent people. It builds carefully upon well-researched leadership concepts and reflects the current status of research about consideration and initiating structure. A synthesis of the research about these two dimensions of leadership behavior indicates that characteristics of the followers are important in determining the right balance of consideration and initiating structure. Many variables moderate the relationships between leader behavior and various criteria including the subordinate characteristics of "Expertise, experience, competence, job knowledge, hierarchical level of occupied position, expectations concerning leader behavior, perceived organizational independence and various psychological aspects."[27]

All these factors relate directly or indirectly to the maturity level of followers. In

[27]Steven Kerr and Chester Schriesheim, "Consideration, Initiating Structure, and Organizational Criteria—An Update of Korman's 1966 Review," *Personnel Psychology,* Vol. 27, No. 4, Winter 1974, p. 567.

summary, the situational leadership theory appears valid and useful, but field studies about its utility would be helpful before reaching a final verdict.

PARTICIPATIVE LEADERSHIP STYLE

One applied value of leadership theory and research has been a recognition of the value of the participative leadership style in certain situations, particularly in managing well-motivated, conscientious employees. The essential characteristic of participative leadership or management is that subordinate workers share (or participate) in decision making, as defined in the Vroom-Yetton model. A participative leader shares both decisions and authority with subordinates. An operational definition of the meanings of participation is provided by a study that polled 157 managers about their conception of participative leadership. The ten practices most frequently cited as being participative in nature are as follows, listed in rank order of frequency:

1. Gives subordinates a share in decision making.
2. Keeps subordinates informed of the true situation, good or bad, under all circumstances.
3. Stays aware of the state of the organization's morale and does everything possible to make it high.
4. Is easily approachable.
5. Counsels, trains, and develops subordinates.
6. Communicates effectively with subordinates.
7. Shows thoughtfulness and consideration of others.
8. Is willing to make changes in ways of doing things.
9. Is willing to support subordinates even when they make mistakes.
10. Expresses appreciation when a subordinate does a good job.[28]

The use of participative management appears to be on the upswing, particularly when quality circles are considered to be a form of participative management. Up until the early 1980s, large-scale use of participative management was limited in the United States and Canada but was used widely in Europe and Japan. A study published in 1976 of about fifty large business organizations found that the preponderance of decisions were made somewhat unilaterally.[29] Formal programs of participative management include management by objectives and organization development (as described in Chapter 17). In the absence of such formal programs, many individual managers consult extensively with subordinates, depending upon both the manager's leadership style and the willingness of subordinates to participate. A large-scale

---

[28]Larry E. Greiner, "What Managers Think of Participative Leadership," *Harvard Business Review,* March–April 1973, p. 114.

[29]Donald F. Crane, "The Case for Participative Management," *Business Horizons,* April 1976, pp. 15–21.

application of participative management is illustrated by a program at Motorola involving 12,000 employees. A company executive describes it in these terms:

> At the start of the program, we identified six areas of costs employees can influence: quality of product, delivery of product, housekeeping and safety, inventory, current costs, and buy-back. We then organized manufacturing production teams so that employees could see the results of *their* efforts. As the next step, we began to post ratings of the six elements of cost—the results—each week, in each area.
>
> We organized a steering committee for the total facility to handle policy matters. This committee was comprised of representative executives. At the same time we organized an operating committee that meets to discuss cost trends and opportunities for improvement. Employees from all departments are appointed to this committee. We also developed smaller departmental teams that discuss opportunities for improvement and changes that should be made. Our participative management program is introduced in three phases: (1) the make-ready phase, (2) a simulated trial or shakedown run, and (3) the full program.
>
> Productivity improvements begin to occur during Phase One of the program's implementation. When we move on to Phase Three, the incentive phase of our program, we share the savings with employees. However, before a group, which may consist of 100 to 200 people, earns its first dollar of bonus, our costs must be acceptable. As the group increases its earnings, its benefits—and our unit costs—continue to drop.
>
> Among the positive results of the program is that we are getting a minimum of 25 percent more output from our equipment, which improves our return on net assets. In many instances, output has been up by much higher percentages. And the spirit of cooperation between employees has soared. They have extended themselves to new members of the production team and encouraged high team standards. Supervisors report that employees are learning faster and better and that safety and cleanliness has improved.[30]

Situational Variables Favoring Participative Leadership

Despite the impressive results observed at Motorola with all levels of employees, participative management has proved to be the most effective when used with professional and managerial employees. The U.S. Department of Defense commissioned the consulting and research firm of Arthur D. Little to check the validity of claims made for participative management, with particular attention given to its impact on creativity and innovation. The research strategy used was to "track the most significant technical developments of the previous decade back to the organizations and individuals from which they sprang." The results revealed that technical creativity and productivity were dramatically increased by an adaptive, democratic (participative) form of organization and inhibited by autocratic organization forms. Out of the fifty-two scientific breakthroughs studied, groups managed by a form of participative leadership produced all but one.[31]

[30]Excerpted and paraphrased from Walter B. Scott, "Participative Management at Motorola—The Results," *Management Review,* July 1981, pp. 27–28. Reprinted with permission from American Management Associations. © 1981 by AMACOM, a division of American Management Associations. All rights reserved.

[31]Robert W. Johnston, "Leader-Follower Behavior in 3-D, Part I," *Personnel,* July–August 1981, p. 39.

Consistent with this research finding, the right circumstances for participative leadership can be summarized in this way: leaders must have the required skills, subordinates must be favorably disposed toward participation, and the task must be complex, nonroutine, and require a high-quality decision and subordinate acceptance. When the opposite conditions exist, participative leadership may not be nearly as effective.[32] Additional information on the situational variables favoring participative leadership is given in Table 12–2 in reference to implications for managerial practice.

ENTREPRENEURIAL LEADERSHIP

An entrepreneur is a person who takes the risk of starting a new enterprise or introducing a new idea, product, or service to society.[33] To get the enterprise beyond the size of one or two people, the entrepreneur must exert leadership of some kind. Entrepreneurs are strongly motivated by the prospects of getting things accomplished. Such leaders help us to understand the contingency nature of leadership because they are often inspiring people who nevertheless may make poor managers.

Founders of successful enterprises often possess the personality characteristics of high enthusiasm, charisma, creativity, and persuasiveness. Often, they are perceived as being eccentric. Perhaps because of these characteristics, they tend not to be the careful planners and systematic problem solvers required and so valued within a bureaucracy. One study comparing successful entrepreneurs with successful managers found that entrepreneurs had a negative attitude toward authority, while business managers had positive attitudes in this area. It was concluded that the entrepreneurial personality is characterized by "an unwillingness to submit to authority, an inability to work with it, and a need to escape from it."[34]

Today it is widely recognized that entrepreneurial thinking is needed in all types of organizations whether in the private or the public sector. How then can bureaucratic forms of organization find situations that match the behavior of the entrepreneur? Three varieties of decentralization are now being used by some large organizations for this purpose.

1. *Divisional incorporation.* Under this system, managers become division presidents, thus satisfying their entrepreneurial urges. Also, the entrepreneurially minded manager operates more comfortably as a "president" than as a "general manager."
2. *Subsidized start-ups of new businesses.* Here the entrepreneurially minded manager (sometimes referred to as a "corporateur") has a unique opportunity to launch and maintain a new business. Younger people with strong entrepreneurial urges are attracted to large business organizations that invest in small outside businesses. Corporations investing in

[32]Filley, House, and Kerr, *Managerial Process and Organizational Behavior*, p. 229.

[33]Michael H. Mescon, Michael Albert, and Franklin Khedouri, *Management: Individual and Organizational Effectiveness* (New York: Harper & Row, 1981), p. 26.

[34]O. Collins and David Moore, *The Enterprising Man* (East Lansing: Michigan State University, Bureau of Business and Economic Research, 1964), pp. 239–40. Cited in ibid., p. 29.

TABLE 12-2 A Synopsis of Three Choices of Leadership Behavior Considering Followers' Needs and Situations

Consider Being Autocratic When . . .	Consider Being Democratic When . . .	Consider Being Laissez-Faire When . . .
Leader/manager Has complete power and no restraints on its use. Has a way of saving matters in an emergency. Has some unique knowledge. Is firmly entrenched in his or her position.	*Leader/manager* Has limited power and authority. Has restraints on use. Group might reject his or her authority and succeed at it. Has *some* existing time pressures. Has *limited* sanctions that he or she can exert.	*Leader/manager* Has no power to compel action. Has no time pressures. Possesses tenure based on pleasure of the group. Has no sanctions to exert. Has no special knowledge.
Followers Are leader-dependent persons. Are rarely asked for an opinion. Have low educational background (not always). Recognize emergencies. Are members of a "labor-surplus" group. Are autocrats themselves. Have low independence drives.	*Followers* Expect to have some control over methods used. Have predominantly middle-class values. Are physicians, scientists, engineers, managers, staff persons. Possess relatively scarce skills. Like system, but not authority. Have high social needs.	*Followers* Have more power than the leader. Dislike orders. Will rebel successfully if they so choose. Choose own goals and methods. Are volunteers, loosely organized, or in short supply. Are physicians, scientists, or others with rare skills.
Work situation Features tight discipline. Is characterized by strong controls. Is marked by low profit margins or tight cost controls. Includes physical dangers. Requires low skills from workers. Requires that frequent changes be made quickly.	*Work situation* "Umbrella" organization objectives understood. Involves shared responsibility for controls. Has some time pressures. Consists of gradual changes or regularly spaced changes. Involves actual or potential hazards occasionally. Is one in which teamwork skills are called for.	*Work situation* Has no clear purpose apparent except as the individual chooses. Is unstructured. Is one in which only self-imposed controls exist. Has no time pressures. Features few or only gradual changes. Takes place in a safe, placid environment. Requires high individual skill or conceptual ability.
Effect of autocratic leadership if carried to extreme or overused May result in poor communication, rigidity of operation, slow adaptation to changing conditions, and stunting of the growth of people.	*Effect of democratic leadership if carried to extreme or overused* May result in loss of ability to take individual initiative when necessary (in favor of group decisions); also may result in slow decision making in emergencies.	*Effect of laissez-faire leadership if carried to extreme or overused* May result in organization fragmentation, member isolation, chaos, and anarchy.

Source: Robert W. Johnston, "Leader-Follower Behavior in 3-D. Part 1." *Personnel.* July–August 1981. p. 41. Reprinted with permission from American Management Associations. © 1981 by AMACOM, a division of American Management Associations. All rights reserved.

these smaller businesses sometimes do so with the intent of acquiring them once they have grown to a size considered worthy of acquisition. At that point, it may prove useful to supplement the skills of the entrepreneur with a more bureaucratic style of manager.

3. *Venture task teams.* Teams of this type explore and enter into new business ventures, usually of a small or medium size. Since the venture begins from the concept stage, it is best led by an entrepreneurial-style manager. Product managers (individuals who have total project responsibility for a particular product such as an automobile model) have shown an eagerness to head up venture task teams.[35]

IMPLICATIONS FOR MANAGERIAL PRACTICE

1. To enhance your effectiveness as a leader, you should (a) adapt your style to the situation at hand, (b) find a situation that suits your leadership style, or (c) modify the situation so that it matches your leadership style. To accomplish any of these three ends, you will need to make an accurate diagnosis of both your leadership style and the leadership situation facing you. If you manage managers, you will have to help those managers make similar diagnoses. All the leadership theories presented in this chapter provide specific clues to determining which style matches which situation.

2. Robert W. Johnston has developed an outline for selecting the right leadership style for a given situation.[36] His model deals with the three points of the continuum of leadership behavior: autocratic, democratic, and laissez faire. As shown in Table 12-2, the model is based on a diagnosis of followers' needs and situations. We recommend Johnston's approach as a guide to selecting the appropriate leadership style (or behavior) for a given situation.

Summary

- Leadership is the process of influencing people to achieve desired objectives, provided that they are influenced to act voluntarily. The influence exerted by leadership must extend beyond mechanical compliance with routine directives of the organization. Leadership is one aspect of management and can be exerted vertically, horizontally, and diagonally.
- Certain leadership traits and characteristics contribute to effective leadership in a wide variety of situations. Correspondingly, similar leadership situations require similar leadership traits and behaviors. Among the traits and characteristics frequently as-

[35]Mack Hanan, "Make Way for the New Organizational Man," *Harvard Business Review,* July–August 1971, p. 132.
[36]Johnston, "Leader-Follower Behavior," p. 41.

sociated with effective leadership are good problem-solving ability, situation sensitivity, effective work habits, initiative, self-confidence, individuality, technical competence, enthusiasm, high ethics, flexibility, and vision.

- Two major aspects of leadership behavior are the task-oriented and relationship-oriented styles. Task-oriented leaders direct and closely supervise subordinates to ensure that the task performed is up to their standards. Relationship-oriented leaders emphasize the human relationships involved in getting work accomplished. They emphasize motivating subordinates, allowing for group decision making, and listening to the problems of subordinates.

- Leadership styles are commonly classified according to a leader's standing on task and employee orientation. One such method is the Managerial Grid®, which classifies leaders on the basis of their production and people emphasis. The ideal style is the team builder who is able to elicit high productivity from a committed and dedicated group of subordinates. The System 4 leadership concept developed by Likert recommends the participatory leadership style.

- The situational approach to leadership attempts to identify the significant forces in a situation that suggest which leadership style will be effective. Those of major importance are the personal characteristics of subordinates, personal characteristics of the leader, environmental pressures and demands, and the prevailing work ethic.

- Fiedler's contingency model is the most precise and most researched of the leadership theories. Its central proposition is that task-motivated leaders are more effective when the leadership situation is very favorable or unfavorable. Relationship-motivated leaders are more effective in situations of moderate favorability. Leadership style is measured by the LPC (least preferred co-worker scale). A relationship-motivated leader describes the least preferred co-worker in relatively favorable terms. A favorable leadership situation would be a function of good leader-member relations, high task structure, and high position power.

- The path-goal leadership theory is based on expectancy/valence theory and focuses on the leader behaviors required to motivate a subordinate to work effectively. Leader behavior is perceived as effective if it (1) is seen by subordinates as an immediate or future source of needs satisfaction, (2) makes rewards contingent upon attaining work goals, and (3) supports goal attainment by removing barriers to their attainment. The four leadership styles or behaviors in this model are directive, supportive, achievement oriented, and participative. The two sets of contingency factors that determine which style is the most appropriate are subordinate characteristics and environmental pressures and demands facing the subordinates.

- The situational leadership theory focuses on the maturity level of subordinates as the key contingency factor determining which style of leadership is the most appropriate. Immature subordinates with respect to the task at hand require a high-task and low-relationship style, whereas mature subordinates require a low-relationship and low-task.

- Participative leadership is gaining in acceptance among practicing managers. It works best when leaders have the required skills, subordinates are favorably disposed toward participation, the task is complex and nonroutine, and the decision is of high quality and must meet with high subordinate acceptance.

- Entrepreneurial leaders tend to be enthusiastic and charismatic, but they often resent authority and their managerial styles may not be suited for a bureaucracy. Several work environments have been developed within large organizations that represent a good match for entrepreneurial leadership: divisional incorporation, subsidized start-ups of new businesses, and venture task teams.

Questions for Discussion

1. What kind of group are you best equipped to lead? Why?
2. Which leadership style should a woman running a word processing center utilize? Relate your conclusion to leadership theory.
3. Describe two situations in which you think a 9,1 (production pusher) style of manager would probably be effective.
4. What kind of leadership style do you prefer to work under? Why?
5. How would you characterize the leadership style of the current president of the United States or the prime minister of Canada? the queen of England?
6. How might the situational leadership theory be applied to child rearing?
7. Which leadership style would you recommend for dealing with visually handicapped electronic assemblers? Why?
8. Identify several of the situational variables that influence the leadership style a professor should use in running a particular class.
9. Very few tests of leadership skill or potential are commercially available. What factors do you think have limited the development of such tests?
10. Would participative leadership work effectively for a field supervisor working on an oil drilling rig in the North Sea? Explain.
11. Think of any entrepreneur that you know personally, have read about, or have heard about. How do that person's traits compare with the characteristics and traits of entrepreneurs mentioned in the text?

An Organizational Behavior Problem

What Kind of Leadership and Followership Style Best Describes You?

David R. Frew has developed a unique questionnaire that provides a person tentative insight into his or her own leadership and followership style.* Taking the questionnaire might be an important first step in your development as a leader and/or follower. After completing the questionnaire, take particular note of Frew's cautionary statements.

*David R. Frew, "Leadership and Followership," *Personnel Journal,* February 1977, pp. 90–95, 97. Reproduced with the permission of *Personnel Journal,* Costa Mesa, Ca.; all rights reserved.

Leadership and Followership Style Test

Structural Leadership Profile

The following twenty statements relate to your ideal image of leadership. We ask that as you respond to them, you imagine yourself to be a leader and then answer the questions in a way that would reflect your particular style of leadership. It makes no difference what kind of leadership experience, if any, you have had or are currently involved in. The purpose here is to establish your ideal preference for relating with subordinates.

The format includes a five-point scale ranging from strongly agree to strongly disagree for each statement. Please select one point on each scale and mark it as you read the twenty statements relating to leadership. You may omit answers to questions which are confusing or to questions that you feel you cannot answer.

	Strongly Agree	Agree	Mixed Feelings	Disagree	Strongly Disagree
1. When I tell a subordinate to do something, I expect him or her to do it with no questions asked. After all, I am responsible for what he or she will do, not the subordinate.	(1)	(2)	(3)	(4)	(5)
2. Tight control by a leader usually does more harm than good. People will generally do the best job when they are allowed to exercise self-control.	(5)	(4)	(3)	(2)	(1)
3. Although discipline is important in an organization, the effective leader should mediate the use of disciplinary procedures with his or her knowledge of the people and the situation.	(1)	(2)	(3)	(4)	(5)
4. A leader must make every effort to subdivide the tasks of the people to the greatest possible extent.	(1)	(2)	(3)	(4)	(5)
5. Shared leadership, or truly democratic process in a group, can only work when there is a recognized leader who assists the process.	(1)	(2)	(3)	(4)	(5)
6. As a leader I am ultimately responsible for all of the actions of my group. If our activities result in benefits for the organization, I should be rewarded accordingly.	(1)	(2)	(3)	(4)	(5)

	Strongly Agree	Agree	Mixed Feelings	Disagree	Strongly Disagree
7. Most persons require only minimum direction on the part of their leader to do a good job.	(5)	(4)	(3)	(2)	(1)
8. One's subordinates usually require the control of a strict leader.	(1)	(2)	(3)	(4)	(5)
9. Leadership might be shared among participants of a group so that at any one time there could be two or more leaders.	(5)	(4)	(3)	(2)	(1)
10. Leadership should generally come from the top, but there are some logical exceptions to this rule.	(5)	(4)	(3)	(2)	(1)
11. The disciplinary function of the leader is simply to seek democratic opinions regarding problems as they arise.	(5)	(4)	(3)	(2)	(1)
12. The engineering problems, the management time, and the worker frustration caused by the division of labor are hardly ever worth the savings. In most cases, workers could do the best job of determining their own job content.	(5)	(4)	(3)	(2)	(1)
13. The leader ought to be the group member whom the other members elect to coordinate their activities and to represent the group to the rest of the organization.	(5)	(4)	(3)	(2)	(1)
14. A leader needs to exercise some control over his or her people.	(1)	(2)	(3)	(4)	(5)
15. There must be one and only one recognized leader in a group.	(1)	(2)	(3)	(4)	(5)
16. A good leader must establish and strictly enforce an impersonal system of discipline.	(1)	(2)	(3)	(4)	(5)
17. Discipline codes should be flexible and they should allow for individual decisions by the leader given each particular situation.	(5)	(4)	(3)	(2)	(1)

	Strongly Agree	Agree	Mixed Feelings	Disagree	Strongly Disagree
18. Basically, people are responsible for themselves and no one else. Thus a leader cannot be blamed for or take credit for the work of subordinates.	(5)	(4)	(3)	(2)	(1)
19. The job of the leader is to relate to subordinates the task to be done, to ask them for the ways in which it can best be accomplished, and then to help arrive at a consensus plan of attack.	(5)	(4)	(3)	(2)	(1)
20. A position of leadership implies the general superiority of its incumbent over his or her workers.	(1)	(2)	(3)	(4)	(5)

Structural Followership Profile

This section of the questionnaire includes statements about the type of boss that you prefer. Imagine yourself to be in a subordinate position of some kind and use your responses to indicate your preference for the way in which a leader might relate with you. The format is identical to that of the previous section.

	Strongly Agree	Agree	Mixed Feelings	Disagree	Strongly Disagree
1. I expect my job to be very explicitly outlined for me.	(1)	(2)	(3)	(4)	(5)
2. When the boss says to do something, I do it. After all, he or she is the boss.	(1)	(2)	(3)	(4)	(5)
3. Rigid rules and regulations usually cause me to become frustrated and inefficient.	(5)	(4)	(3)	(2)	(1)
4. I am ultimately responsible for and capable of self-discipline based upon my contacts with the people around me.	(5)	(4)	(3)	(2)	(1)
5. My jobs should be made as short in duration as possible, so that I can achieve efficiency through repetition.	(1)	(2)	(3)	(4)	(5)
6. Within reasonable limits I will try to accommodate requests from persons who are not my boss since these requests are typically in the best interest of the company anyhow.	(5)	(4)	(3)	(2)	(1)

	Strongly Agree	Agree	Mixed Feelings	Disagree	Strongly Disagree
7. When the boss tells me to do something that is the wrong thing to do, it is his or her fault, not mine when I do it.	(1)	(2)	(3)	(4)	(5)
8. It is up to my leader to provide a set of rules by which I can measure my performance.	(1)	(2)	(3)	(4)	(5)
9. The boss is the boss. And the fact of that promotion suggests that he or she has something on the ball.	(1)	(2)	(3)	(4)	(5)
10. I only accept orders from my boss.	(1)	(2)	(3)	(4)	(5)
11. I would prefer for my boss to give me general objectives and guidelines and then allow me to do the job my way.	(5)	(4)	(3)	(2)	(1)
12. If I do something that is not right, it is my own fault, even if my supervisor told me to do it.	(5)	(4)	(3)	(2)	(1)
13. I prefer jobs that are not repetitious, the kind of task that is new and different each time.	(5)	(4)	(3)	(2)	(1)
14. My supervisor is in no way superior to me by virtue of position. He or she simply does a different kind of job, one that includes a lot of managing and coordinating.	(5)	(4)	(3)	(2)	(1)
15. I expect my leader to give me disciplinary guidelines.	(1)	(2)	(3)	(4)	(5)
16. I prefer to tell my supervisor what I will or at least should be doing. It is I who am ultimately responsible for my own work.	(5)	(4)	(3)	(2)	(1)

Scoring and Interpretation

You may score your own leadership and followership styles by simply averaging the numbers that are included in parentheses below your answers to the individual items. For example, if you scored item number one strongly agree you will find the point value of "1" below that answer (leadership profile). To obtain your overall leadership style, add all the numerical values that are associated with the twenty leadership items and divide by twenty. The resulting average is your leadership style. Followership is measured the same way, using the sixteen items contained within Part II of the instrument.

Score	Description	Interpretations	
		Leadership Style	Followership Style
Less than 1.9	Very Autocratic	Boss decides and announces decisions, rules, orientation.	Can't function well without programs and procedures. Needs feedback.
2.0–2.4	Moderately autocratic	Announces decisions but asks for questions, makes exceptions to rules.	Needs solid structure and feedback but can also carry on independently.
2.5–3.4	Mixed	Boss suggests ideas and consults group, many exceptions to regulations.	Mixture of above and below.
3.5–4.0	Moderately participative	Group decides on basis of boss's suggestions, rules are few, group proceeds as it sees fit.	Independent worker, doesn't need close supervision, just a bit of feedback.
4.1	Very democratic	Group is in charge of decisions: boss is coordinator, group makes any rules.	Self-starter, likes to challenge new things by himself or herself.

It should be noted that scores on this instrument will vary depending upon mood and circumstances. Your leadership or followership style is best described by the range of scores from several different test times.

Compare your leadership style on this questionnaire with your LPC score. Compute the correlation coefficient between the two variables for the entire class.

Additional Reading

BASS, BERNARD M. *Stogdill's Handbook of Leadership: A Survey of Theory and Research,* rev. ed. New York: Free Press, 1981.

DRORY, AMOS, and URI M. GLUSKINOS. "Machiavellianism and Leadership." *Journal of Applied Psychology,* February 1980, pp. 81–86.

FIEDLER, FRED E., and LINDA MAHAR. "The Effectiveness of Contingency Model Training: A Review of the Validation of LEADER MATCH." *Personnel Psychology,* Spring 1979, pp. 45–62.

HOFSTEDE, GEERT. "Motivation, Leadership, and Organization: Do American Theories Apply Abroad?" *Organizational Dynamics,* Summer 1980, pp. 42–63.

JOHNSTON, ROBERT W. "Leader-Follower Behavior in 3-D, Part 2." *Personnel,* September–October 1981, pp. 50–61.

KABANOFF, BORIS. "A Critique of Leader Match and Its Implications for Leadership Research." *Personnel Psychology,* Winter 1981, pp. 749–64.

MAEHR, MARTIN L., and DOUGLAS A. KLEIBER. "The Graying of Achievement Motivation." *American Psychologist,* July 1981, pp. 787–93.

McCALL, MORGAN W., JR., and MICHAEL M. LOMBARDO. *Leadership: Where Else Can We Go?* Durham, N.C.: Duke University Press, 1978.

SCANLON, BURT K. "Managerial Leadership in Perspective: Getting Back to Basics." *Personnel Journal,* March 1979, pp. 168–71, 183–84.

————, and ROGER M. ATHERTON, JR. "Participation and the Effective Use of Authority." *Personnel Journal,* September 1981, pp. 697–703.

SCHRIESHEIM, JANET FULK, and CHESTER A. SCHRIESHEIM. "A Test of the Path-Goal Theory of Leadership and Some Suggested Directions for Future Research." *Personnel Psychology,* Summer 1980, pp. 349–70.

STAW, BARRY M., and JERRY ROSS. "Commitment in an Experimenting Society: A Study of the Attribution of Leadership from Administrative Scenarios." *Journal of Applied Psychology,* June 1980, pp. 249–60.

"Striking It Rich: A New Breed of Risk Takers Is Betting on the High-Technology Future." *Time,* February 15, 1982, pp. 36–44.

WADIA, MANECK S. "Participative Management: Three Common Problems." *Personnel Journal,* November 1980, pp. 927–28.

SCORING AND INTERPRETATION
OF LPC SCORE

To calculate your LPC score, add the numbers you placed in the right hand column, and put this total at the bottom of the page. If you scored 64 or higher you are a high LPC leader, meaning that you are relations motivated. If you scored 57 or lower you are a low LPC leader, meaning that you are task motivated. A score of 58 to 63 places you in the intermediate range. Fiedler suggests that if you score in the middle range, you should decide for yourself whether you are really a relations-motivated or a task-motivated leader.

CHAPTER 13

Conflict in Organizations

LEARNING OBJECTIVES

1. To comprehend the meaning of conflict and why it is so prevalent in organizations.

2. To explain both the functional and dysfunctional consequences of conflict in organizations.

3. To identify four major strategies for resolving conflict.

4. To describe several approaches to resolving conflict that you might be inclined to use.

5. To be able to apply a contingency viewpoint for selecting a conflict resolution technique.

One summer a group of eighteen top prison officials met for one week to improve their management skills and to design an ideal correctional institution. Half were in security positions in the institutions and half were in treatment positions. Subgroups were formed according to these specialties, and in the course of the discussion a member of the security group proposed that uniforms be eliminated in the new institution. The group then began a lengthy argument about whether or not uniforms should be worn. Finally, one of the members said, "Look, let's settle this democratically; let's take a vote." As a result, six people voted to eliminate uniforms and three voted in favor of their use.

The winning members appeared pleased, while the losing members became angry or withdrew from the discussion. In particular, one of the three losers looked at his watch and stared out the window. Another sat complaining that the others had turned into a bunch of social workers.

A group consultant present at the time suggested that the group members take another look at the situation. He asked those in favor of uniforms what they hoped to accomplish. They responded that part of the rehabilitative process in correctional institutions is teaching people to deal constructively with authority. They saw uniforms as an important way to identify authority. He then asked those opposed to uniforms what they hoped to accomplish by eliminating them. They responded that the stereotype associated with uniforms created a barrier between the guard and the inmate, making it difficult to relate with the inmate on a personal level.

The group was then asked to sug-gest ways to meet the combined goals of teaching people to deal with authority and avoiding the stereotype of the uniform. The whole group began listing alternative solutions to the problem. When members made an evaluative statement, indicating why an alternative was good or bad, they were asked to hold evaluation until all possible solutions were generated. As a result, ten solutions were suggested. The outcome was to recommend that guards wear casual clothes and nametags, while the guard captains wear uniforms. The guards were known to the inmates anyway, they said, but the captains were not, and the uniforms would serve a useful purpose in that case. The solution was acceptable to everyone and received their support. A win-lose method had been changed to win-win by identifying motives and goals, instead of two solutions, and then sequencing the discussion from problem definition to idea generation to evaluation.*

This case illustrates two major themes of this chapter: conflict in organizations is inevitable and, if handled properly, both sides can become winners. As you read this chapter, look for information in support of this theme.

THE MEANING OF CONFLICT

Conflict, in the context used here, refers to the opposition of persons or forces that gives rise to some tension. It occurs when two or more parties (individuals, groups, organizations, nations) perceive mutually exclusive goals, values, or events.[1] As origi-

*Alan C. Filley, "Conflict Resolution: The Ethic of the Good Loser," in R. C. Huseman, C. M. Logue, and D. L. Freshly, eds., *Readings in Interpersonal and Organizational Behavior* (Boston: Holbrook Press, 1977), p. 238.

[1]Definition from Center for Creative Leadership Bulletin, September 1980, p. 5. Published by the Center for Creative Leadership, Greensboro, North Carolina.

nally perceived by the two sides in the Chapter opening case, the prison guards could not simultaneously wear and not wear uniforms. Simply stated, conflict takes place when both sides believe that what each wants is incompatible with what the other wants.

Among the everyday synonyms for conflict are skirmish, battle, strong disagreement, internecine warfare, clash, and head-on collision. All these colorful terms are compatible with the idea that conflict arises out of mutual incompatibility. We clash with other departments, children, and lovers because we perceive that both sides cannot get the full share of what they want.

Conflict can occur at several levels. Intrapersonal (within-person) conflict takes place when a person has to decide between incompatible choices (Should I work on my taxes or attend the association meeting?). Conflict can also take place between and among people, among groups or organizational units, among organizations and among nations and even continents. In keeping with the intentions of this part of the book, this chapter is about interpersonal and intergroup conflict.

Substantive versus Personal Conflict

Both parties in the lead-in case to this chapter behaved rationally in their attempt to resolve conflict. Many people do not behave rationally when trying to resolve conflict, making resolution of the problem by discussion virtually impossible. The nature of the conflict heavily influences the extent to which rational problem-solving behavior is possible. People are able to solve problems much better when they face substantive rather than personal conflict. Substantive conflict refers to a real or actual issue, generally of an administrative or technical nature. One example would be a conflict over which of two models of dictating equipment is superior.

Personal conflict refers to animosities that involve deep-rooted personal feelings and attitudes. Personality clashes fall into this category. One company owner had such negative attitudes toward OSHA that he closed his business rather than implement their orders for improving plant safety. The company could afford the improvements, but the owner's feelings were so intense he would not compromise.

Many conflicts are a mixture of substantive and personal issues. Substantive issues may be present (such as which is the best geographic location for our new facility), but personal issues may also be at stake. One side may wish to "show up" the other side by choosing the winning location.

Conflict versus Competition

Some managers are concerned that resolving conflict will lead to a loss of competitive spirit in the organization. Other managers are concerned that encouraging a competitive spirit will lead to too much conflict. Both camps are partially right *and* partially wrong. With both conflict and competition, there is a basic incompatibility between goals and motives. In neither conflict nor competition can both parties come away winning entirely what they want. In conflict, one side sees an opportunity to interfere with the other's opportunity to acquire resources or perform activities. In competition, both sides try to win, but neither side actively interferes with the other.[2] A tennis match is a conflict, a golf match is a competition—unless one player tries to harass the other mentally.

Worker incentive programs are designed with competition in mind. One person striving to attain a bonus should not interfere with the activities of others trying to win the same bonus. Both sides work in parallel rather than in opposition. Nevertheless, some incentive programs designed to promote competition wind up promoting disruptive conflict. One example would be the bonus system in a retail store that encourages salesclerks to steal customers from each other.

A SYSTEMS MODEL OF INTERGROUP CONFLICT

Interpersonal and intergroup conflict can be profitably viewed from a systems perspective. Figure 13–1 presents a systems model of organizational conflict that incorporates many of the key topics to be discussed in this chapter. The underlying thesis is that conflict can be functional (helpful) or dysfunctional (harmful) depending upon the mechanisms used by the organization to handle conflict. Handling conflict refers to both its management and resolution. Part of managing conflict might be to increase conflict among members of an organizational unit that has become too lethargic. Conflict resolution refers to dealing with conflict in such a manner that the antagonism and tension between the two groups subsides and they can work together constructively from that point forward.

As implied in the model, when organizational conflict is viewed as inevitable, and is handled properly rather than suppressed, it may lead to positive outcomes for the organization and its members. In contrast, when intergroup conflict is inadequately handled, it leads to dysfunctional outcomes (lower left-hand corner of model). Negative outputs generate more conflict. For instance, if one subunit in an organization distorts goals by offering staff services whether or not they are needed, more conflict is generated. Other staff groups may feel the need to engage in similar self-protective behavior to survive.

The input section of the model mentions some of the many possible factors contributing to conflict in organizations. The list is dynamic because new contributors may arise at any time. For example, during the early 1980s, sexual harassment of both men and women was frequently observed as a source of conflict. The intervening variables section of the model refers to methods of conflict resolution which may be classified as adequate versus inadequate. Later sections of this chapter discuss these resolution methods. *Outputs* to the systems model are the positive and negative consequences of conflict in organizations. It has been estimated that managers spend

---

[2]Ross A. Webber, *Management: Basic Elements of Managing Organizations,* rev. ed. (Homewood, Ill: Richard D. Irwin, 1979), p. 448.

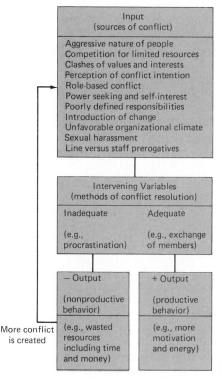

FIGURE 13–1 A Systems Model of Organizational Conflict

about 20 percent of their time resolving conflict.[3] To the extent that this function is performed well, negative consequences are minimized and the positive consequences maximized.

SOURCES OF CONFLICT

A large number of potential sources of conflict exist in organizational life. Caution must be exercised in speaking about *causes* of conflict. All conflict is ultimately caused by the feelings that people experience when an incompatibility exists between what they want and what someone else wants. For example, one occupational group might be dissatisfied with wages and seek unionization to achieve higher wages. The *source* of conflict is the competition for limited resources (management and the employees are competing for what each perceives as an equitable share of income). The cause of the conflict is the employee group's subjective feelings about being underpaid. When feelings lead to action, conflict will probably occur. Here we review the sources of conflict mentioned in Figure 13-1.

---

[3]Dennis King, "Three Cheers for Conflict!" *Personnel,* January–February 1981, p. 21.

Aggressive Nature of People

Some conflict in organizations stems from the normal need of people to find outlets for their aggressive impulses.[4] Many human beings have underlying aggressive tendencies seeking outward expression. Wars, hockey games, bull fights, muggings, homicides, and child-battering experiences provide telling evidence that humans are at least in part aggressive and hostile. It therefore follows that organizations are sometimes used as arenas for the expression of aggression, which leads to conflict. These aggressive impulses can be satisfied in a relatively socially acceptable manner by intergroup conflicts being expressed at the verbal level. Note the aggressive and hostile undertones to the following situation of intergroup conflict:

> A financial executive had just returned from an important meeting with representatives from manufacturing. Based upon some encouraging projections of increased sales, the latter requested funds for plant expansion. Prior to the meeting, the financial staff assigned to this problem had determined that the company could not afford plant expansion at this time. During the meeting, the financial executive made a persuasive appeal for his point of view. He reflected upon the meeting: "We sure nailed them to the wall. I loved the expression on their faces when Jim pointed out the holes in the marketing forecast. They know they have to play ball with us from now on to get what they want."

Competition for Limited Resources

People working in complex organizations are faced with the perpetual struggle of acquiring enough money, material, and human resources to accomplish their mission. Few organizations are in a position to provide all organizational units a "blank check" to pursue their aims. Management is thus forced to allocate resources according to the criterion of contribution to organization effectiveness. Intergroup conflict arises when various groups compete to win their share of these limited resources.[5] One financial vice president of a prominent business corporation stated that a crucial part of his job was to "do a better job of dividing up the corporate pie in order to overcome some of the gluttony that has developed around here over the years."

Another scarce resource for which groups and individuals compete is top management's time. Few executives have enough time to schedule meetings with everyone who requests a share of their time. Administrative assistants often act as buffers to prevent their bosses from being inundated with appointments. Lower-level managers gain in stature to the extent that they win out in competition for top management time.

Clashes of Values and Interests

Considerable conflict in organizations comes about simply because the values and interests of various subgroups differ. Union and management conflict represents the

---

[4]Two books on this topic are Desmond Morris, *The Naked Ape* (New York: Dell, 1969), and Konrad Lorenz, *On Aggression* (New York: Harcourt Brace, 1966).

[5]William F. Glueck, *Management* (Hinsdale, Ill.: Dryden Press, 1977), p. 525.

most readily understandable example of this basic phenomenon. A business corporation may announce publicly that profit and sales have established a new record. That same year, they might contest with labor their ability to grant a new round of wage increases. Labor interprets this behavior as both an inconsistency and a lack of interest in the economic welfare of employees. Management feels justified in arguing against a wage increase. From their viewpoint, such an increase would decrease earnings per share and make the company a less attractive investment opportunity for potential stockholders.

Conflict that so frequently takes place between engineering and manufacturing also illustrates how differences in values might underlie conflict. Engineers value technical sophistication and careful engineering. "Good" products from their standpoint are those with good technical integrity; that is, the parts work and they work for long periods of time. Manufacturing entertains slightly different values. Their mission is to produce a product at the least possible cost (within the limits of safety and customer acceptance). Manufacturing thus accuses engineering of attempting to design products that "will last for 50 years, but that customers cannot afford." Engineering accuses manufacturing of attempting to manufacture products of such limited durability that the company reputation will suffer.

Perception of Conflict Intention

Conflict is to some extent a subjective phenomenon involving both cognitive and affective components. If we formulate the belief that somebody else is out to encroach upon our share of resources, we may then feel that an adversarial relationship exists between us and that person. Recent research suggests that the extent to which a situation is defined as a conflict is related to whether the parties attribute conflict intentions to each other. "A person who perceives conflict is likely to act in a manner conveying conflict intentions."[6] In one study, data were collected from one supervisor and one subordinate in 113 park and recreation agencies. The major finding was that supervisors and subordinates who perceived conflict to exist tended to be seen by each other as using force, a strategy of conflict intention.[7]

Role-Based Conflict

Intergroup conflict sometimes surfaces because different groups occupy different roles that are antagonistic to each other.[8] Similarly, many positions in organizations are designed to have built-in conflicts. Financial analysts find themselves in frequent intergroup conflicts because their role, in the eyes of many others, represents a policing function. "I'm the cop around here. I blow the whistle when somebody is spending too

---

[6]Gary Howat and Manuel London, "Attribution of Conflict Management Strategies in Supervisor-Subordinate Dyads," *Journal of Applied Psychology,* April 1980, p. 175.

[7]Ibid., pp. 172–75.

[8]George Strauss, "Workflow Frictions, Interfunctional Rivalry, and Professionalism: A Case Study of Purchasing Agents," *Human Organization,* February 1964, pp. 137–49.

much money," said one company controller. One budget analyst, during a job satisfaction interview, made the following comment about her role:

> I'm getting a lot of kicks out of my job this year. I've become sort of a hero in financial circles around here lately. I found a hole big enough to drive a truck through in the cost estimates of that new product line. I proved to be right. I know people in manufacturing hate my guts. I don't care. I'm not getting paid to be liked. Besides that, I don't hold any grudges when people dislike me. I can only look good when they look bad.

Power Seeking and Self-interest

Interpersonal and intergroup conflicts also arise from the need to acquire power. The character traits of greed and gluttony make a similar contribution to conflict in organizations. Disputes over certain matters, such as which organizational unit shall control which other organizational units, often stem more from personal power seeking than from true concern for achieving organizational goals. Chapter 14 examines power seeking and self-interest in more detail.

Poorly Defined Responsibilities

As implied, conflict may emerge when two organizational units compete over new responsibilities. Intergroup conflict stemming from disagreements about who has responsibility for ongoing tasks is an even more frequent problem.[9] Newcomers to organizations are often struck by the ambiguity that exists about job responsibilities. Few organizations make extensive use of job descriptions or periodically update the job descriptions that do exist. (Furthermore, it is the rare manager or employee who consults his or her own job description.) Managerial and staff jobs by their very nature are difficult to structure tightly around a job description. Academic as well as other organizations are prey to the intergroup conflict that arises from poorly defined responsibilities.

Introduction of Change

Change can breed intergroup conflict. Acquisitions and mergers, for example, encourage intergroup conflict, competition, and stress. When one organization is merged into another, a power struggle often exists between the acquiring and acquired company. An attempt is usually made to minimize conflict by laying out plans for power sharing before the acquisition or merger is consummated. Frequently, the acquired company is given representation on the board of directors of the acquiring company. Nevertheless, power struggles are difficult to avoid.

> One manufacturer of high-volume, relatively low-priced toys acquired a company that made "creative," low-volume, high-priced toys for children. Shortly after the acquisition,

[9]Robert H. Miles, *Macro Organizational Behavior* (Glenview, Ill.: Scott, Foresman and Company, 1980), p. 133.

the old and new company were involved in intergroup conflict. The parent company insisted that the new company work toward increasing its volume and decreasing its unit price for products. Management of the new company insisted that this could not be done and still preserve its unique image. Ultimately, the parent company attempted to resolve the conflict by dissolving the acquired company and merging its product line into already existing facilities of its own. Within a two-year period after the acquisition, almost all the creative people (toy designers, etc.) and management of the acquired company left.

Unfavorable Organizational Climate

An organization's character, atmosphere, or climate is sometimes a contributor to or a source of intergroup conflict. Intense and frequent conflict among members of top management sets a tone that contributes to conflict at lower levels in the organization. According to the analysis of one consultant, conflict is infectious: "As contagion spreads, even distant departments are soon infected with pettiness, personal rivalries linked to different leaders and arbitrary rulings of little logic or importance."[10]

Intergroup conflict can also be related to another aspect of climate, the amount of psychological distance that organizational units maintain from each other. An extensive study of organizational conflict in colleges and universities revealed that medium amounts of *differentiation* breed the most conflict. Differentiation is defined as "the degree to which the subunits within each school have boundaries, interests, and functions separate from the other units in the institution."[11] Chairmen of academic institutions with medium differentiation found themselves in more decision-making conflict with the central administration. Negotiating faculty salaries exemplifies one area in which intergroup conflict might occur. In general, it was found that when professional groups are very much or very little distant psychologically from the administration, intergroup conflict is minimal. When the boundary between the two groups is of medium permeability, intergroup conflict tends to be highest.

Sexual Harassment

In recent years, much has been written about sexual harassment on the job. It involves any unwanted sexual advancement toward another individual, thus resulting in conflict. The harassed person faces this uncomfortable choice: "If I submit to my boss's advances, I will be compromising my morals and my sense of dignity. But if I do not submit, I may lose out" (be fired, be awarded a smaller raise, be blocked from promotion, and so forth). A conflict situation is thus created. Sexual harassment may include such actions as

> Sex-oriented verbal "kidding" or abuse (several cases have been reported of male assembly-line workers "mooning" women they wish to expel from the department).

---

[10]Alonzo McDonald, "Conflict at the Summit: A Deadly Game," *Harvard Business Review*, March–April 1972, p. 60.

[11]Gordon C. Darkenwald, Jr., "Organizational Conflict in Colleges and Universities," *Administrative Science Quarterly*, December 1971, pp. 407–12.

Subtle pressure for sexual activity.

Physical contact such as patting, pinching, or constant brushing against another's body.

Demands for sexual favors, accompanied by implied or overt promises of preferential treatment or threats concerning an individual's employment status.[12]

Sexual harassment usually takes the form of an unwanted action by a male toward a female, but may also include female against male, male against male, and female against female. Aside from being a form of organizational conflict, sexual harassment is considered to be a form of job discrimination and therefore illegal under Title VII of the Civil Rights Act. However, the federal government has ruled that if a boss sexually harasses members of both sexes, that boss is not violating the Civil Rights Act.[13] Despite this ruling, called a "bisexual exclusion," all sexual harassment, by definition, is a source of conflict.

Line versus Staff Prerogatives

A comprehensive form of conflict in large organizations is that of line generalists versus staff specialists. Some of the conflict stems from many of the sources already described in this section. Much of line versus staff (or generalist versus specialist) conflict centers on three issues: territorial encroachment, conflicting loyalties, and separation of knowledge and authority.[14]

Territorial encroachment.   In general, the staff person advises the line person. The latter may accept or reject this advice as he or she sees fit in getting things accomplished. In some instances, a staff person has considerable power. For example, if the company lawyer says a particular sales contract is absolutely illegal, management will probably draw up a more acceptable contract. At other times, a staff person may be ignored. A personnel research specialist might inform management that the firm's methods of selecting employees are unscientific and unsound. Management may ignore the advice.

An underlying reason why staff specialists and line personnel so often find themselves in dispute is that the line person may resent staff encroachment. In the personnel research example just cited, the plant manager and his or her personnel manager may say to each other, "Who does this character from the home office think he is, telling us how to select people? Our plant is running well. We have a work force of good people. We have no problems for him to solve. Why is he bothering us?"

Line people see staff people as encroaching on their territory in another important way. Whenever a staff specialist (such as an industrial engineer) makes a sugges-

[12]Excerpted from the National Labor Relations Board Policy, Administrative Policy Circular APC 80-2, issued February 21, 1980.

[13]Paul S. Greenlaw and John P. Kohl, "Sexual Harassment: Homosexuality, Bisexuality, and Blackmail," *Personnel Administrator,* June 1981, pp. 60–61.

[14]The analysis presented here follows part of the outline presented by Webber, *Management,* pp. 590–92.

tion for improvement to a manager, it automatically implies that present conditions need improvement. If the industrial engineer says "My methods will improve your efficiency," it implies that the manager is not perfectly efficient in his or her current mode of operation.

Conflicting loyalties.   Many staff specialists come into conflict with line personnel over the issue of loyalty to their discipline versus their organization. The staff person feels this role conflict because he or she may want to adhere to a professional code that conflicts with tasks assigned by the firm. An accountant in an electronics firm faced this dilemma when he disapproved of the company's earnings statement. He felt that the company was using almost fraudulent accounting practices, yet his company pressured him to approve the statement. He finally approved the financial manipulations asked for by the president but simultaneously wrote a letter of protest. His guilt about violating accounting ethics finally led him to resign from the company.

Separation of knowledge and authority.   In large organizations, few executives have sufficient knowledge to carry out their responsibilities. They are dependent upon lower-ranking staff advisors to furnish them the appropriate information. A company president usually does not even prepare his or her own speeches. In other instances, an executive may have to choose a course of action based upon technical advice that he or she does not fully understand. His or her interdependence with the staff specialist may become a source of conflict.

Another source of conflict arises when the specialist resents being evaluated by a generalist who may lack the appropriate background to evaluate fairly the specialist's work. A performance appraisal of an engineering technician by a construction superintendent led to such a confrontation. The superintendent told the technician he was performing "barely adequately" in his job. In response the technician replied, "What makes you think you are qualified to evaluate my technical work? You have no specialized background in engineering?"

CONSEQUENCES OF ORGANIZATIONAL CONFLICT[15]

Interpersonal and intergroup conflict can be functional or dysfunctional to individuals and organizations. Earlier studies of conflict within organizations focused upon the negative impact of conflict. An awareness then developed that conflict can also serve useful ends. The opinion of many behavioral scientists and managers is that an optimal level of conflict exists for every work situation. Conflict of a lesser magnitude is dysfunctional because it may lead to a feeling of lethargy that inhibits creativity and

[15]Two relevant references here are Miles, *Macro Organizational Behavior,* pp. 126–29, and Kenneth Thomas, "Conflict and Conflict Management," in Marvin D. Dunnette, ed., *Handbook of Industrial and Organizational Psychology* (Chicago: Rand McNally, 1976), pp. 891–92.

productivity. Conflict in excess of this optimum level is also dysfunctional because it may lead to negative outcomes such as a disabling stress reaction.

It is difficult to determine the optimum amount of conflict for a given situation. One strategy is to observe the consequences of conflict. When they are mostly positive, it can be assumed that the person or organizational unit is approaching an optimum amount of conflict. When the consequences are mostly negative, it is probable that conflict has reached a dysfunctional level. The summaries of the consequences of conflict presented in the listings that follow provide some clues as to whether conflict is good or bad in a given situation. When conflict brings about the conditions in the first list, it can be interpreted as productive. When conflict brings about the conditions described in the second list, it can be considered nonproductive.

Functional Consequences

1. Conflict often leads to constructive change. In fact, people sometimes enter into conflict to accomplish change. Nurses have recently entered into conflict relationships with hospital administrators and physicians to achieve gains toward improved working conditions and more professional autonomy.

2. Motivation and energy available to achieve goals may be increased under the influence of intergroup conflicts. At its best, conflict revs up both sides to the good of the organization.

3. Conflict stimulates innovative thinking. When people are forced into conflict with others to obtain their share of resources, they tend to put forth more imaginative solutions to problems. When a department is fighting with management to justify its existence, it may provide a creative explanation of what it can do for management. One community relations department faced with a serious reduction in staff sold top management on the idea of the department developing an ecology task force (which presumably was functional to society).

4. External conflict contributes to group cohesion, which may contribute to morale and productivity. The presence of a common enemy generally consolidates a group. An organizational unit that is trying to "outperform the enemy" will pull together for that purpose.

5. Old goals may be modified or replaced by more relevant goals as a result of the conflict. Engineering, for example, after having fought with manufacturing about price considerations, may decide to place less emphasis on precision in design.

6. Conflict resolution methods may become institutionalized to the advantage of the organization. After several incidents of intergroup conflict occur, outlets may be established so that people can "blow off steam" without damaging the organization. One contemporary approach to the institutionalization of conflict resolution is executive rap sessions. They are essentially informal group discussions between members of top management and lower-ranking employees.

7. Interpersonal and intergroup conflict may satisfy the aggressive urges inherent in so many people, leading to an increased feeling of well-being (although the effect may be the opposite for the recipients of their aggression).

8.   Direct expression of conflict helps to reduce accumulated tensions. "A good fight clears the air" and also provides people with the temporary mood elevation associated with expressing negative emotion such as anger and hostility.

Negative Consequences

When conflict is intense and prolonged, it is often dysfunctional for a number of reasons.

1.   Conflict acts as a stressor; therefore, the mental health of some combatants may be adversely affected. Role conflict is known to be a major source of stress in organizational life.

2.   Misallocation of resources might be the most general negative consequence of intense conflict. People waste money and time in carrying out their internecine warfare. For instance, the self-protective memos written in the heat of conflict consume time and slight amounts of money. Also, some executives call out-of-time conferences just to settle political battles.

3.   Suboptimization of parts of the system occurs when disputants push their own positions to the extreme. Literal compliance with rules and regulations illustrates this phenomenon of suboptimization. Schoolteachers in dispute with their administrations have on occasion called for a "work to rules" in which they carry out no duties not rigidly considered part of their jobs. By such tactics as leaving the school building exactly at quitting time, student welfare (for those who want extra help) is neglected.

4.   Conflict disrupts normal work flow and leads to a distortion of goals. Factions in dispute tend to focus more attention on the dispute rather than on the tasks necessary to achieve the organizational purpose. A department busy writing nasty memos to another department is often neglecting customers, clients, patients, or students.

5.   Instability and chaos often stem from extreme conflict. Organizations that appear very confused and self-destructive often achieved that state because of internal conflict.

INTERGROUP RELATIONS AND CONFLICT

Another way of analyzing the consequences of intergroup conflict is to examine what happens to relationships between and within the groups in conflict. Edgar H. Schein has provided a concise summary of replicated research in this area. The findings tend to be consistent for a variety of groups.[16]

   Within each competing group, the following effects have been observed:

- The groups become more cohesive and members become more loyal. People tend to close ranks and forget some of their internal differences.

---

[16]Edgar H. Schein, *Organizational Psychology*, 2nd ed. (Englewood Cliffs, N.J.: Prentice-Hall, 1970), p. 97.

- The group climate changes from informal to much more formal and task oriented. People become less concerned about giving psychological support to each other, but more concerned about getting the task at hand accomplished.
- As the conflict increases, the leadership climate within the group becomes more autocratic and less democratic. Group members show a willingness to accept such autocratic leadership.
- Each group shows a tendency toward becoming more tightly structured.
- Each group demands that its members put up a solid front. As a consequence, people are expected to become more loyal and conforming.

Between each competing group, the following effects have been observed:

- Each group begins to perceive the opposing group as the enemy.
- Each group undergoes some distortion in perception. It tends to see mostly strengths in itself and weaknesses in the other group. Stereotypes are formed as the animosity between the groups increases.
- The two groups become more hostile toward each other. Simultaneously, interaction and communication between the two groups decreases. Under these conditions, negative stereotypes are maintained and it becomes more difficult to correct perceptual distortions.
- When group members are forced to listen to each other (such as in a conflict resolution exercise), they tend to listen more to their own representative and less to the representative of the other group. The methods of conflict resolution described in the paragraphs that follow are designed to overcome such problems.

When conflict between persons or groups reaches dysfunctional levels, it should be resolved. Methods of resolving conflict have been around for centuries; during the last thirty years, behavioral scientists have contributed their insights and skills to the process. In the following four sections, we review both traditional and behavioral science approaches to resolving conflict. Several different methods of categorizing these resolution approaches are found in the organizational conflict literature. Our purposes are met by dividing conflict resolution approaches into four broad (and not always mutually exclusive) types: conciliation, collaboration, organization restructuring, and power tactics.

CONFLICT RESOLUTION
THROUGH CONCILIATION

Conciliation includes traditional approaches to resolving disputes such as bargaining, appeals procedures, and compromise (which is really a result of the conciliation process).[17] Conciliation approaches recognize the fact that the two parties in dispute must work together in relative harmony after the conflict is settled. Thus the United Autoworkers and General Motors work together every year to produce millions of vehicles and other products despite their periodic bargaining sessions.

---

[17]Joe Kelly, *Organizational Behavior: Its Data, First Principles, and Application,* 3rd ed. (Homewood, Ill.: Richard D. Irwin, 1980), p. 548.

Distributive bargaining is the typical form of bargaining in which resources are distributed among two or more people in conflict. What either side gains is at the expense of the other. Distributive bargaining encourages deception, since each side figures it will have to exaggerate its own claim to earn a sizable share of the resources.[18] Lawsuits often take the form of distributive bargaining. Each side begins with an offer much higher than it expects to receive or lower than it expects to grant.

Integrative bargaining is the ideal state in which both parties transcend the conflict mode and move into problem solving. As such, this strategy can properly be classified under the category of confrontation and problem solving. Under integrative bargaining, the philosophy is win-win.[19] The two groups of prison officials, aided by a group consultant, found an integrative solution to their problem. (The guards were to wear casual clothes and name tags, and the guard captains were to wear uniforms.)

Appeals Procedures

A conventional way of resolving conflict in organizations is for the people in disagreement to ask a higher authority to help them resolve their problem. As such, the process has also been labeled third-party judgment. The higher authority is ordinarily the first common boss of the people in dispute. Other arbitrators include a personnel official, a high-ranking executive, or a government official, as when a case of employment discrimination is settled outside the firm by an official of the Equal Employment Opportunity Commission.

One valid criticism of the appeals procedure is that when the higher-ranked third party settles the dispute, the person or group that has lost the decision may not be psychologically committed to the decision. However, since so many people are culturally conditioned to accept a third-party judgment, the approach often works. As in the case of a lawsuit, both sides will usually accept a judge's verdict, either that of a first judge or another judge to whom the case is appealed.

Compromise

In this popular form of conflict resolution, one party agrees to do something if the other party agrees to do something else. Compromises stem from bargaining, but often a compromise agreement is reached with a minimum of bargaining. When opposing sides in a conflict have to compete for a limited resource, compromise solutions are looked upon with favor. Each party receives a reasonable share of the resources, such as two departments being allowed to add one more employee each rather than one department being authorized to hire two employees. The criticism has been made that a compromise of this nature is sometimes suboptimal. In this illustration, the needs of the organization might have been best served if the more productive of the two departments received both new employees.

[18]Webber, *Management,* p. 464.
[19]Ibid., p. 465.

Mediation

In this approach to conflict resolution, a third party intervenes to help two parties in conflict settle their dispute. The mediator helps the parties to communicate with each other, but the mediator does not reach a binding solution to the problem. A common superior to two individuals or departments is often placed in a mediator role. Mediation is a formal step in the grievance procedure for settling management-labor disputes. If mediation fails, the grievance is passed along to arbitration—a third party who is the last resort in an appeals procedure.

CONFLICT RESOLUTION THROUGH COLLABORATION

Collaboration approaches to conflict resolution include any method that involves confrontation and resolving the underlying problem. They were developed by social psychologists and other behavioral scientists in the hopes of achieving better success than that attained through traditional resolution approaches. In collaboration, the two parties candidly lay out the real issues and then work out a viable solution to the problem. Here we describe one approach to collaboration at both the individual and group levels.

Gentle Confrontation

A general-purpose individual method of conflict resolution is to openly discuss the problem with the adversary in a tactful and nonargumentative manner. When using gentle confrontation, one makes a candid statement of the problem being faced without hinting at any "heavy-handed" approach such as giving the other side an ultimatum. If this first step in resolving conflict does not work, the individual with the conflict may try an appeals procedure. Here are two organizational examples of job-related problems amenable to gentle confrontation.

- Your job involves considerable travel; typically you are away from the office two days a week. You begin to notice that, upon your return, your office is usually in disarray and your desk has developed scratches and dents. You are told that one of your co-workers who is not assigned an office uses your office while you are away. You gently confront your co-worker about this problem, using an opening line such as "There is something bothering me that I would like to talk about."
- You notice that your boss has a consistent pattern of incorporating your ideas and suggestions into memos without giving you appropriate credit. It would seem advisable to confront your boss about this problem very tactfully.

Image Exchanging (Corporate Mirrors)

In this elaborate approach to conflict resolution, both parties come to learn how they are perceived by the other group. This exchanging of images provides understandings and insights that often lead to problem solving. The format proceeds as follows:

1. Each group prepares its self-image and its image of the other group. Groups are encouraged to write down whatever they feel or think; consensus is not mandatory. Images can be described by sentences or merely in adjectives.

2. Each group assigns a representative who presents these images to the other group. Exchanging of images provides each group data about how it is perceived by the other group and how the other group perceives itself.

3. Both groups then meet separately to discuss what kind of behavior might have led to the image formed by the other group.

4. The conclusion reached about each group's own behavior is exchanged with the other group and is jointly discussed.

5. In the final stage, specific action plans are developed that are designed to reduce the discrepancy between each group's self-image versus the image held by the other group. Usually plans cannot be developed to reduce all the discrepancies. A realistic goal is for both groups to develop methods of relating to each other which will reduce conflict and increase cooperation.[20]

Presented next is a condensed description of image exchange activity between two groups in conflict—a headquarters' personnel group and a division personnel group in the same large organization. The images exchanged portray a pressing need for improved communication and enhanced mutual respect between two groups.

1. Division personnel's image of headquarters' personnel.
    a. Too academic and theoretical. They spend time on projects that are of no help to us.
    b. They are mainly interested in keeping people happy.
    c. They have no rapport with first-line management.
    d. One-way communicators. They enjoy collecting information but are hesitant to provide information.
    e. Bright and intelligent. They keep up with new developments in the field.
    f. Basically politicos. They find out what top management is interested in and pursue those projects.
    g. Highly paid in comparison with their contribution.

2. Division personnel's image of itself.
    a. In tune to the realities of the business world: practical minded.
    b. We help the corporation turn in a profit.
    c. We have good rapport with first-line supervision.
    d. We show some impatience for getting things accomplished.
    e. Through our efforts the company is able to keep going.
    f. Our operation is lean in terms of manpower.
    g. We require very little guidance or help from headquarters to keep going.

3. Headquarters' personnel's image of division personnel.
    a. A bit narrow-minded in their approach. Automatically dismiss the value of new approaches.
    b. Limited appreciation of companywide problems.
    c. Difficult to satisfy. They ask for help, but often refuse to listen when it is given.
    d. Too identified with line management, which makes them subjective in their viewpoint.
    e. They dislike integrating their activities with corporate objectives.
    f. Nice, hard-working guys who play an important role in the company.
    g. Probably a good place for a professional personnel person to get field experience.

[20]Edgar H. Schein, *Process Consultation: Its Role in Organization Development* (Reading, Mass.: Addison-Wesley, 1969), pp. 71–72.

4. Headquarters' personnel's image of itself.
    a. Skillful at utilizing new approaches and techniques for the good of the company.
    b. Broad and progressive in our thinking.
    c. We prevent division people from thinking of only their problems.
    d. We undertake activities and programs that are designed to meet corporate objectives.
    e. Sometimes our thinking is a little too sophisticated for division people to understand.
    f. We are stretched pretty tight in terms of getting to everything that we are charged with accomplishing.
    g. Our contribution to the corporation is much greater than most people realize.

Illustrative of the kind of action plan for improvement that can be developed is the treatment of point (1a) of division personnel's image of headquarters' personnel. The issue of the headquarters' group working on projects of limited interest to the division unit came about because several times headquarters sent a detail statement in writing to the field of its plans for a new personnel program requiring implementation, without any previous informal word about the project. Twice, when these field programs were announced, the division group had been in need of assistance in quite different areas of personnel services to its management. This placed the field personnel people in the position of being perceived as uncooperative by headquarters because of their limited enthusiasm for the new project and as ineffective by line management because they were not solving the personnel problems most vexing to line management. An action plan was then developed whereby headquarters' personnel would periodically consult with division personnel to determine what problem areas they (division) felt required assistance by headquarters. These requests would then be balanced against demands from top management for corporatewide services and the judgment of the headquarters' personnel staff as to what programs they felt a headquarters' group should involve itself in. The emerged plan was helpful in modifying perceptions originally held at the time of image exchanging.

RESOLVING CONFLICT THROUGH ORGANIZATIONAL RESTRUCTURING

Interpersonal and intergroup conflict can sometimes be resolved or prevented by modifying an organization structure or by placing people in a new work environment. An example of the former would be decentralization into smaller work units so that disputes could be settled at lower levels in the organization. An example of the latter would be assigning people in conflict to serve on the same committee so they could develop a better understanding of each other's point of view. Here we look at two somewhat more complex methods of resolving conflict through organizational restructuring: unifying the work flow and interorganizational exchange.

Unifying the Work Flow

Conflict may arise when a manager or unit lacks the authority to carry out its responsibility. If managers had more control over the human and material resources they need to accomplish their task, there would be less conflict. Another contributor to this kind of conflict is that mutual dependency breeds conflict. Being dependent upon people over whom you have little control leads to many antagonisms. Managers are often forced to argue with other managers over who has priority over certain human and material resources. It has been noted that "Controlling 'everything' is probably impossible, but the system might be restructured into more logical complete work units which bring more control under one hierarchical position, thus decreasing ambiguity."[21] Costs usually increase under such decentralization, but the team spirit and decreased conflict are often worth the price.

An illustration of unifying the work flow is presented in Figure 13–2. In the situation depicted, a subsidiary of a retail store chain found itself in frequent conflict with the parent company over the use of resources. Specifically, the subsidiary wanted to control its own data processing and catalog mailings. The subsidiary sold a special line of sporting goods and clothing and thought that its problems were unique enough to warrant controlling its own catalog division. Part of the problem was that the subsidiary believed it was receiving low priority from the centralized catalog division. After considerable negotiation, the subsidiary was given control over its own catalog division. After an eighteen-month period, the new arrangement of unifying the work flow appeared beneficial.

Interorganizational Exchange

The underlying proposition to this method of conflict reduction through organization restructuring is that empathy helps to reduce conflict. One way of acquiring empathy for the other side is to work in the latter's department. Exchanging members between groups in conflict (or groups having the potential for conflict) is thus another structural approach to conflict resolution. Reassigning people in this way can achieve the ben-

[21] Webber, *Management*, p. 21.

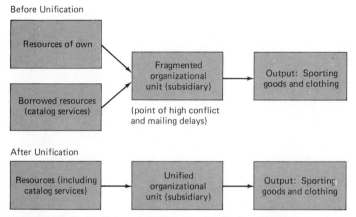

FIGURE 13–2 Unifying the Work Flow to Reduce Conflict

efit of introducing different viewpoints in the affected groups. As the group members get to know each other better, they tend to reduce some of their distorted perceptions of each other. A term for this process is interorganizational exchange activity (IO exchange).

Exchanging members as a method of conflict resolution or prevention works best when the personnel exchanged have the technical competence to perform well in the new environment. A member of a manufacturing department was transferred to a marketing department in one such exchange of members. He had limited knowledge of marketing and very little interest in learning about the discipline. The sullenness and bitterness he displayed on the job tended to intensify rather than to lessen intergroup conflict.

The president and chief executive officer of Jones & Laughlin Steel Corporation helped to execute the merger of J&L and Youngstown Steel. He attributes much of the success of that merger to the prevention of conflict by exchanging members between the two steel companies, as explained in these words:

> In our organization plan for the two salaried forces, we deliberately mixed the employees of the two companies. We now have Youngstown managers in many key operating and sales positions in J&L units and vice versa. We ended up with an outstanding team of managers, the cream of the crop from each company, and this has expedited the integration. But the people themselves contributed by their positive attitudes and dedicated efforts. There is no hint of a "we-they" syndrome. J&L and Youngstown people are working with a degree of harmony not characteristic of many mergers.[22]

CONFLICT RESOLUTION THROUGH POWER TACTICS

Power tactics in conflict resolution refer essentially to any methods whereby one side forces its will upon the other. *Domination* is a frequently used power tactic. Ross A. Webber has noted, "The simplest conceivable conflict solution is elimination of the other party—to force opponents to flee and give up the fight, or slay them."[23] Managers who express opposition to top management's policies are sometimes labeled as troublemakers and are fired. (A collaborationist approach would require that the underlying issues be resolved and then terminate the manager if that proved to be the only workable solution.) Domination sometimes takes the form of threats: "If you don't trim your expenses voluntarily, we'll make sure your budget is cut to the bone during the next budget cycle."

The formation of *coalitions* by two or more people is another manifestation of power tactics. Suppose that one executive wanted her firm to be purchased by an interested larger company. She might cultivate several allies who would then join forces

---

[22]Presentation before the New York Society of Security Analysts, March 30, 1979. Published by the LTV Corporation, Dallas, Texas.

[23]Webber, *Management,* p. 453.

to push for the acquisition. Using coalitions to win out in conflict is a common practice among legislative bodies.

Peaceful coexistence is an approach to conflict resolution that can be interpreted as a power play despite the term "peaceful." Disagreement is simply suppressed and commonalities are emphasized. The parties in conflict decide that it is better for the organization to avoid overt displays of disagreement. The consequences of open conflict are strenuously avoided. Cooperation between groups or individuals is good on the surface, but rarely do they collaborate in such a way as to maximize their joint potential.

Contingency Factors Favoring Power Plays

In general, power plays are less desirable than collaborative approaches to resolving conflict, but the case can be made for the use of power plays in some situations. It has been hypothesized, for example, that power play will be the dominant conflict management strategy for those who seek autonomy: "Power play is a secretive mode that could work in the best interests of those whose covert objective is autonomy and whose desired impression is that of being committed."[24]

Another argument for power play is that collaborating can increase one's vulnerability in competition. Collaboration (and also bargaining) assumes the exchange of information necessary to resolve a problem. In the process of exchanging information, the other side may discover you have more resources than they believed initially. Thus, they will demand more.

Another advantage of power play is that when both sides operate out of self-interest such as in many forms of bargaining, the compromise reached comes out somewhere near equity. Both sides begin with unrealistic demands and eventually a final compromise is reached. Under this procedure, there exists a sort of dynamic equilibrium that works to the advantage of both sides within the rules. "It is the dynamic interaction of finding compatible self-interests which is the substance of power-play conflict management."[25]

THE STIMULATION OF CONFLICT

When organizational conflict reaches a suboptimum level, it may be advisable for the manager to elevate conflict. In general when there is too much lethargy and lack of disagreement among people and units, conflict may be too low. Stephen P. Robbins notes that affirmative answers to one or more of the following questions may suggest a need for conflict stimulation.

[24]C. Brooklyn Derr, "Managing Organizational Conflict: Collaboration, Bargaining, and Power Approaches," *California Management Review,* Winter 1978, p. 62.
[25]Ibid.

1. Are you surrounded by "yes men"?
2. Are subordinates afraid to admit ignorance and uncertainties to you?
3. Is there so much concentration by decision makers on reaching a compromise that they may lose sight of values, long-term objectives, or the company welfare?
4. Do managers believe that it is in their best interest to maintain the impression of peace and cooperation in their unit, regardless of the price?
5. Is there an excessive concern by decision makers in not hurting the feelings of others?
6. Do managers believe that popularity is more important for the obtaining of organizational rewards than competence and high performance?
7. Are managers unduly enamored with obtaining consensus for their decisions?
8. Do employees show unusually high resistance to change?
9. Is there a lack of new ideas forthcoming?
10. Is there an unusually low level of employee turnover?[26]

Assuming an accurate diagnosis is reached that conflict should be stimulated, the next step would be to select an appropriate strategy. Considerable sensitivity to the situation would be required to increase conflict to a functional, but not a dysfunctional, level. A number of speculative stimulation techniques have been suggested, some of which are more ethical than others (see Table 13–1). The workings of one conflict stimulator, repress information, is useful in illustrating the general concept under discussion here:

> By holding back data we can quickly stimulate greater conflict. It can work as an excellent fine-tuning device because the decision on the data repressed will influence the degree of increased hostility. Most important, it has an easily available escape valve should

---

[26]Stephen P. Robbins, " 'Conflict Management' and 'Conflict Resolution' Are Not Synonymous Terms," *California Management Review*, Winter 1978, p. 73.

TABLE 13–1   Conflict Stimulation Techniques

Manipulate communication channel
   Deviate messages from traditional channels
   Repress information
   Transmit too much information
   Transmit ambiguous or threatening information

Alter the organization's structure (redefine jobs, alter tasks, reform units or activities)
   Increase a unit's size
   Increase specialization and standardization
   Add, delete, or transfer organizational members
   Increase interdependence between units

Alter personal behavior factors
   Change personality characteristics of leader
   Create role conflict
   Develop role incongruence

Source: Stephen P. Robbins, " 'Conflict Management' and 'Conflict Resolution' Are Not Synonymous Terms," *California Management Review*, Winter 1978, p. 72. © 1978 by the Regents of the University of California. Reprinted by permission of the Regents.

the intensity become too great and thus dysfunctional. A release of information should immediately initiate a reduction in conflict intensity.[27]

CHOOSING THE APPROPRIATE STRATEGY

As with most managerial tasks, a contingency approach should be taken to choosing the appropriate strategy to handle conflict. Factors related to both individual differences, the group, and the organizational climate should be taken into account in se-

[27]Ibid., p. 74.

TABLE 13–2 Conditions Favoring the Use of Selected Methods of Conflict Resolution

Technique	Favorable Conditions for Use of Technique
Distributive bargaining	Parties believe that there should be a winner and loser in conflict. Climate favors conventional bargaining.
Integrative bargaining	Parties are willing to communicate; want to explore roots of problem. Mature people are involved.
Appeals procedure	This technique is very effective in organizations where members recognize and accept authority of superiors. Adequate grievance procedures have been established.
Compromise	This technique is similar to distributive bargaining. Parties believe fundamentally in compromise. Neither party is much more dominant than the other. Temporary solution is acceptable.
Mediation	Parties are able to communicate with each other. Entertain spirit of fairness. Skillful mediator available.
Gentle confrontation	Person with gripe has adequate confrontation skills. Worth a try in almost any situation where power disparity between parties is not too great.
Image exchanging	People involved are committed so strongly to resolving conflict that they are willing to devote necessary time. Management involved has long time-span orientation.
Unifying the work flow	Organization is willing to spend money and experiment. Legitimate substantive issues are involved.
Interorganizational exchange	Parties in conflict are willing to accept job rotation. Coordination between units is necessary; requires adventuresome people.
Domination	Quick resolution of problems is called for. Working cooperatively with the loser after the conflict is not important. Secrecy about own resources is important.
Peaceful co-existence	Organization has a history of suppressing conflict. Parties are willing to "grin and bear it." Parties have some areas of joint cooperation.
Superordinate goals*	Good of the organization must be highly valued. People see link between their output and organizational performance.

*Parties are asked to look at big picture and forget petty conflicts.

lecting the best strategy for resolving conflict. At times, the decision may be made to stimulate rather than to reduce conflict. The ten questions asked in the previous section are tentative guidelines for assessing the need for conflict stimulation.

A summary guide to selecting the appropriate conflict management strategy is presented in Table 13–2. It lists all the strategies described in this chapter plus the appeal to subordinate goals.[28] In addition to making note of the specific entries in Table 13–2, several general guidelines should be kept in mind in selecting a strategy.[29] At the current state of the art of conflict resolution, it may prove more reliable to rely on general guidelines than on specific suggestions. In general, when the conflict to be resolved has a distinct legalistic aspect (such as a dispute over wages or working conditions), one of the traditional approaches would probably work the best. When it appears that the conflict is long-standing and recurring despite many attempts at resolution, changing the organization structure might be best. For instance, sales and credit might be in a perpetual conflict; unifying the work flow would probably be an effective solution.

Confrontation approaches are ideally suited to resolving conflicts among mature, responsible people who are experiencing differences of opinion involving feelings and facts. Resolving conflict through confrontation has the important advantage of not requiring changes in organization policy or design. Another guideline for practice is that collaboration and confrontation approaches should be tried first. When they do not work, it is then necessary to use traditional and organization restructuring methods. Power tactics may be necessary when intense personal issues underly the conflict and both sides want to maximize gain.

IMPLICATIONS FOR MANAGERIAL PRACTICE

1. A manager's goal should be to maintain optimum levels of conflict in his or her unit. Sometimes this will require the stimulation of conflict. At other times it will require the reduction of conflict.

2. A substantial portion of a manager's time, perhaps 20 percent, involves conflict resolution. It is therefore important for a manager (or staff specialist) to develop effective conflict resolution skills. A good starting point is to use gentle confrontation in solving a minor problem.

3. In choosing an appropriate conflict resolution strategy, it may prove helpful to consult Table 13–2. Also, some research has been synthesized about the conditions under which integrative (collaborative) methods of conflict resolution will be effective. It is advisable to alter conditions to move toward these requirements. Where such conditions are not present, the parties themselves, or a third party aiding in the process,

---

[28]The concept behind this table, plus several entries, is based on Robbins, " 'Conflict Management,' " p. 74.

[29]Derr, "Managing Organizational Conflict," p. 82.

must adjust some of the conditions to meet these requirements.[30] Realistically, all these requirements would be difficult to meet. If few of them can be met, more traditional approaches to conflict resolution should be used.

Situational requirements. Time pressures are not critical; members interact freely; information is shared; power is equalized or power differences are ignored; all parties participate.

Attitudinal requirements. Parties believe that mutually acceptable solutions are possible and desirable; parties trust each other.

Affective requirements. Parties have positive attitudes about themselves and others; parties do not feel angry, threatened, or defensive about each other.

Perceptual requirements. Parties do not make a "we-they" distinction between each other; parties perceive a cost to not agreeing.

Process requirements. Information conveyed between parties has the same meaning to both; issues are dealt with specifically and are not generalized; problems are jointly defined by the parties; feedback between the parties is specific and nonjudgmental; search for solutions is extensive; solutions are evaluated for both technical quality and acceptance; questions are asked to elicit information rather than to belittle each other; leadership is changed if needed.

Summary

- Conflict refers to the opposition of persons or forces that gives rise to some tension. It occurs when two or more parties perceive mutually exclusive goals, values, or events. Substantive conflict refers to a real or actual issue, whereas personal conflict refers to animosities that involve deep-rooted feelings and attitudes. In conflict, one side sees an opportunity to interfere with the other person's achieving a goal. In competition, both sides try to win, but neither side actively interferes with the other. Conflict can be helpful or harmful, depending upon how it is handled.

- Many potential sources of conflict are present in organizations, and the list is dynamic. The conflict sources described here are (1) the aggressive nature of people, (2) competition for limited resources, (3) clashes of values and interests, (4) perception of the intention of conflict, (5) role-based conflict, (6) power seeking and self-interest, (7) poorly defined responsibilities, (8) introduction of change, (9) unfavorable organization climate, (10) sexual harassment, and (11) line versus staff prerogatives.

---

[30]The information presented below follows closely that presented by Filley, "Conflict Resolution," pp. 49–50.

- Among the positive consequences of organizational conflict are constructive change, increased motivation and energy, innovation thinking, increased group cohesion, new and more relevant goals, establishing new methods of conflict resolution, satisfaction of aggressive urges, and tension reduction.

- Among the negative consequences of conflict are stress reactions, misallocation of resources, suboptimization of parts of the system, disruption of normal work flow, distortion of goals, and organizational instability and chaos. Dysfunctional conflict should ordinarily be resolved.

- Conciliation approaches to conflict resolution include bargaining, appeals procedures, compromise, and mediation. Bargaining can be divided into traditional forms (distributive) and integrative forms (problem solving). The different categories of conflict resolution methods show some overlap.

- Collaboration approaches to conflict resolution include those methods that involve confrontation and solving the underlying problem. Gentle confrontation is a general-purpose method of solving individual conflicts in which one candidly discusses the problem with one's adversary in a tactful manner. Image exchanging (or corporate mirrors) is an elaborate approach to conflict resolution in which both parties come to learn how they are perceived by the other group. The exchanging of images provides understandings and insights that often lead to problem solving. In the final stage of the process, specific action plans are developed that are designed to reduce the discrepancy between each group's self-image versus the image held by the other group.

- Organization restructuring is another method of resolving conflict. Unifying the work flow helps to reduce conflict by giving organizational units control over their own resources, thus reducing conflicts stemming from dependency upon each other. Interorganizational exchange attempts to reduce intergroup conflict by exchanging members among conflicting groups. By switching roles, members often gain empathy and understanding for each other's point of view.

- Conflict is often reduced or eliminated through the use of power tactics in which conflict is suppressed. Two power tactics are domination of one side by the other and the formation of coalitions. Peaceful coexistence is partially a power tactic because conflict is suppressed, even though commonalities are emphasized. Power plays are said to be helpful in some circumstances. For example, they may lead to the finding of compatible self-interests.

- When organizational conflict is at a suboptimum level, it may prove functional to stimulate conflict. Three general strategies for stimulating conflict are manipulate communication channels, alter the organization's structure, and alter personal behavior factors.

- A contingency approach should be taken in choosing the appropriate strategy to handle conflict. Factors related to individual differences, the group, and organizational climate should be given consideration. However, gentle confrontation is a low-risk strategy with a high probability of payoff in most conflict situations.

Questions for Discussion

1. What is the most pronounced intergroup conflict in the place in which you work (or at the school you attend)? Does it appear to be based on substantive or on personal issues?

2. Assume that you are the manager of a department. How would you know if conflict exists in your department? In other words, how would you diagnose the presence of conflict?

3. Identify three occupations where skill in resolving conflict is essential. Explain your reasoning.

4. Describe three positive consequences of labor-management conflict.

5. Describe three negative consequences of labor-management conflict.

6. In practice, compromise is the most typical approach to resolving conflict. What makes compromise so useful?

7. What technique do you use to resolve conflict with your boss? your spouse? or any other person with whom you are emotionally involved?

8. Which approach to stimulating conflict do you see as being unethical?

9. In your experience, which groups in business tend to be in frequent conflict with each other? What is the source of this conflict?

10. What personality characteristics and traits do you think would be an asset to a manager in resolving organizational conflict? Explain.

An Organizational Behavior Problem

The Dethroned President

When President Frank Marant gained control of Great Southern Foods from his uncle five years ago, one of his primary goals was to impose a system of financial controls over the $500 million processed foods conglomerate. The thirty-eight-year-old Marant was able to accomplish his initial objective. His controls were of some value in salvaging the company when it lost $26 million four years ago. Paradoxically, Marant's tight controls led to his recent downfall.

Insiders say controls were an obsession with Marant. He centralized his management to the point of frustrating leading executives in the company. His insistence upon checking and rechecking caused many a delay in decision making. Operations were virtually strangled in paperwork. One good example: Great Southern's most recent annual report claimed that the company would spend $5 million this year to open twenty-five more processing operations. Six months into the fiscal year, insiders report that little work has been done on the projects; because of Marant's insistence upon such a thorough analysis for each project, decisions have been postponed.

Such delayed decision making can be particularly harmful to the fast-moving field of processed foods. The continuous parade of new products in the processed foods field makes quick reaction time a necessity. An anonymous personnel director said that "Marant's situation is a textbook example of how a bungling president can mess up a company and bring about his own demise." The same personnel executive was among the fifteen people participating in a palace revolt last month when Marant was stripped of his authority.

The end for Marant came when two inside directors, Joe Palaggi and Dean Wilson, had become upset about the company's lethargy in the fall. During the same time span, a number of key managers in Great Southern had complained to Palaggi and Wilson that Marant's managerial style had been demoralizing. When it seemed that Marant was about to fire two key general managers, Palaggi and Wilson blew the whistle. They went to an outside director to explain how the company was headed toward a rapid decline. Palaggi and Wilson headed a drive to build a dossier of Marant's shortcomings as a company president.

The end for Marant came when Palaggi, Wilson, and three outside directors met in Atlanta. A special board meeting was called. Three dozen operating executives threatened to quit unless Marant was deposed from his chief executive position. The board moved swiftly, stripping Marant of his president and chief operating executive titles. He was reassigned as vice president of special projects at a $100,000 cut in pay.

Marant informed a business reporter that the whole affair was a conspiracy to remove him because he wanted to run a sophisticated, finely tuned business. A confidant of Marant said that what Marant's antagonists really objected to was his plan to bring in two new marketing-oriented executives from the outside. A countercharge issued by one of the inside directors active in Marant's dethroning was, "Frank just wasn't willing to accept the fact that you can't run a business by reading computer printouts and writing memos. If you don't get out and visit the troops, they'll eventually get rid of you."

Questions

1. What do you think of Palaggi and Wilson's method of resolving conflict between themselves and Marant?
2. What should Frank Marant do now?
3. What could have been done to resolve this conflict before it reached such drastic proportions?
4. What label (type of conflict) best fits the method of conflict resolution used by the executives who ousted Marant?
5. Do you think appointing Frank Marant as vice president of special projects will prove to be an effective compromise? Why or why not?

Additional Reading

BACHARACH, SAMUEL B., and EDWARD J. LAWLER. "Power Tactics in Bargaining." *Industrial and Labor Relations Review,* January 1981, pp. 219–33.

BRIGGS, STEVEN. "The Grievance Procedure and Organizational Health." *Personnel Journal,* June 1981, pp. 471–74.

COCHRAN, DANIEL S., and DONALD D. WHITE. "Intraorganizational Conflict in the Hospital Decision Making Process." *Academy of Management Journal,* June 1981, pp. 324–32.

DWYER, F. ROBERT, and ORVILLE C. WALKER, JR. "Bargaining in an Asymmetrical Power Structure." *Journal of Marketing,* Winter 1981, pp. 104–15.

FILLEY, ALAN C. *Interpersonal Conflict Resolution.* Glenview, Ill.: Scott, Foresman and Company, 1975.

LIKERT, RENSIS, and JANE GIBSON LIKERT. *New Ways of Managing Conflict.* New York: McGraw-Hill, 1976.

NIERENBERG, GERALD I. *The Art of Negotiating.* New York: Simon & Schuster, 1981.

RENICK, JAMES C. "Sexual Harassment at Work: Why It Happens, What to Do About It." *Personnel Journal,* August 1980, pp. 658–62.

"Teaching How to Cope with Workplace Conflicts." *Business Week,* February 18, 1980, pp. 136–39.

WELDS, KATHRYN. "Conflict in the Work Place and How to Manage It." *Personnel Journal,* June 1979, pp. 380–83.

ZEY-FERRELL, MARY. *Dimensions of Organizations: Environmental, Contextual, Structural, Process, and Performance.* Glenview, Ill.: Scott, Foresman and Company, 1979, Chapter 10.

CHAPTER 14

Organizational Power and Politics

LEARNING OBJECTIVES

1. To understand the concepts of power and politics.
2. To identify the major bases or sources of power in organizations.
3. To explain why politically oriented behavior is so frequently found in organizations.
4. To discuss several strategies for acquiring power.
5. To identify typical methods by which people attempt to influence others on the job.
6. To be aware of managerial tactics for controlling the excessive use of politics.

The director of internal audit at an industrial firm also teaches in the MBA program at two universities. He comments on his approach to teaching the applied aspects of managerial decision making:

> When teaching managerial finance and accounting courses, the author uses real-world illustrations to prove that nonquantifiable factors often dominate the managerial decision-making process—even in these otherwise quantitative courses. When lecturing on capital budgeting, the following basic techniques are presented: payback ROI (return on investment), NPV (net present value), IRR (internal rate of return), and PPP (president's pet project). A real exam-

ple is cited of a corporate president who wanted to acquire a Lear jet for his small company. Based on the actual data, students invariably reject the acquisition as nonjustifiable. They have great difficulty perceiving how, after discrediting the president's pet project, their continued employment at that firm might be considered nonjustifiable. When lecturing on product-line divestiture and segment analysis, the discussion includes the standard techniques that call for calculating the cross elasticities of demand, absorption of committed and discretionary fixed costs, and the product-line margin over direct costs. Also introduced is the real example of a product-line divestiture where all of the analyses unquestionably indicate to drop the line. The only catch is that the company president started his career as brand manager for that product and still feels a strong affinity toward it. Again, most students still vote to eliminate the product. There is not much hope for such students after graduation. With such a prodigious inability to consider nonquantifiable data, they will most likely be eliminated.*

THE MEANING OF POWER AND POLITICS

As implied from the financial executive's comments, for many people a frustrating aspect of organizations is that they are not perfectly rational systems. Few major actions are taken, or decisions made, strictly on the objective merits of the situation. Instead, almost all decisions made in organizations are influenced somewhat by political factors. The quest for power, and its related political behavior, influence minor decisions, such as which clerk gets to work overtime this Thursday evening, as well as major decisions, such as which computer system will be purchased. In recognition of these phenomena, organizational power and politics have recently become a topic of formal inquiry and research in the management and organizational behavior literature. The subject has received attention in the general business literature for several decades.[1]

Power and politics are related, but separate, concepts. Both have been defined in many ways, but a synthesis of their current usage points to these meanings:

Power is a force or store of potential influence through which events can be effected.[2] In an organizational context, power is the ability to marshal, or control, the

*Reprinted by permission from Robert F. Reilly, "Teaching Relevant Managerial Skills in the MBA Program," *Collegiate News & Views*, Winter 1981–82, p. 15.

[1]A representative example is Chester Burger, *Survival in the Executive Jungle* (New York: Macmillan, 1964).

[2]Jeffrey Pfeffer, *Power in Organizations* (Marshfield, Mass.: Pitman, 1981), p. 7.

human, informational, and material resources to get something done.[3] Politics is the study of power in action; we use political strategies and tactics to acquire power. From the standpoint of the organization theorist, "Organizational politics involves those activities taken within organizations to acquire, develop, and use power and other resources to obtain one's preferred outcomes in a situation in which there is uncertainty or dissensus about choices."[4]

Although this definition fits the state of the art in the study of organizational politics (OP), it should be noted that political activity in organizations usually refers to a special set of behaviors (not everything) for gaining power and other selected advantages. OP can therefore be defined also as an influence process in which the individual (or the group) attempts to gain advantage using tactics and strategies in *addition to merit.* The advantage sought typically is to gain power, but OP can also be used to advance one's career (a form of power), to gain affection and approval, or to avoid hard work. The information to be presented in this chapter fits both definitions of OP presented so far.

Since OP is conceptualized as the methods of acquiring power, we first discuss the sources of power in organizations, followed by an analysis of OP from five standpoints: why it exists, tactics for acquiring power, tactics for influencing others, management awareness of OP, and how to prevent political behavior from getting out of control.

SOURCES OF INDIVIDUAL AND SUBUNIT POWER

The traditional analysis of power sources differentiates between position and personal power. Position power refers to power granted to the individual by virtue of formal authority. Personal power refers to power stemming from characteristics of the individual such as charisma or expertise. A widely quoted conception of this nature lists five sources or types of social power. The first three of these power types are those granted by the organization; the fourth and fifth are derived largely from characteristics of the person.[5]

Legitimate power is also referred to as position power. People at higher levels in an organization have more power than do people below them. A chief executive officer has the right to donate money to charity. A supervisor has the right to reprimand an employee for tardiness. However, the culture of the organization helps to decide the limits to anybody's power. The C.E.O. who suggests donating most of the company

---

[3]Morgan McCall, Jr., *Power, Influence, and Authority: The Hazards of Carrying a Sword* (Greensboro, N.C.: Center for Creative Leadership, 1978), p. 5.

[4]Pfeffer, *Power in Organizations,* p. 7.

[5]John R. P. French and Bertram Raven, "The Bases of Social Power," in Darwin Cartwright and Alvin F. Zander, eds., *Group Dynamics,* 2nd ed. (Evanston, Ill.: Row, Peterson, 1960), pp. 607–23.

profits to a subversive group may find his or her decision overruled by the board of directors.

Reward power is based on the leader's ability to reward a follower for compliance. A leader can only use reward power effectively when he or she has potent rewards to dispense (as explained in the discussions of expectancy theory and positive reinforcement in earlier chapters).

Coercive power is the power to punish, or the opposite of reward power. In some situations, coercion or the threat of coercion does contribute to organizational effectiveness. Recent conceptualization on the topic suggests that properly administered, punishment can be a valuable managerial strategy.[6] The impositions of sanctions for job discrimination or drug dealing on organizational premises are two such examples.

Expert power exists when an individual possesses knowledge valuable enough to be considered a precious resource. People of low organizational rank can sometimes achieve power through providing knowledge needed at the time. A lawyer specializing in securities exerts expert power when his or her company is planning to raise new capital through stock offerings.

Referent power refers to the fact that many people identify with leaders because of the leader's personality traits and other personal characteristics. Also called charisma, this type of power is helpful in influencing people over whom the leader has no direct control. Referent power is helpful in getting elected to political office or becoming and remaining a movie star. Successful entrepreneurs are often charismatic in addition to having expert power.

Despite the utility of this power classification, it tends to oversimplify the complexity of the locus of power in organizations. Based on original research conducted at the Center for Creative Leadership and a synthesis of published information, Morgan McCall has developed a classification of power based upon the appropriateness of what is being controlled. The schema takes into account simultaneously both power derived from the individual and the organizational subunit (such as department or division). Its key proposition is that power is in large part a function of being in the right place, at the right time, with the right resources, and doing the right thing, as illustrated in Figure 14–1.

Being in the Right Place

An individual's position in the hierarchy, work flow, and communication network contributes not only to formal authority but also to the kinds of problems that that individual will be asked to handle. A theory of power called *strategic contingencies* offers this central proposition: "Those subunits most able to cope with the organization's critical problems and uncertainties acquire power."[7] In its simplest form, the

---

[6]Richard D. Arvey and John M. Ivancevich, "Punishment in Organizations: A Review, Propositions, and Research Suggestions," *Academy of Management Review,* January 1980, pp. 123–32.

[7]Gerald R. Salancik and Jeffrey Pfeffer, "Who Gets Power—And How They Hold onto It: A Strategic-Contingency Model of Power," *Organizational Dynamics,* Fall 1977, pp. 3–21.

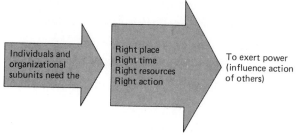

FIGURE 14-1 Sources and Origins of Power

Source: Based on information in Morgan McCall, Jr., *Power, Influence and Authority: The Hazards of Carrying a Sword,* Technical Report Number 10 (Greensboro, N.C.: Center for Creative Leadership, 1978), pp. 6-15.

strategic contingencies theory implies that when an organization faces a number of lawsuits that threaten its existence, the legal department will gain power and influence over organizational decisions.

Just being in the right place is not sufficient for acquiring power. The incumbent also has to develop the reputation of being able to cope with the contingency. For example, if the market research department develops the reputation of a place where "one can never get an answer," that department (and its manager) will not be asked to help solve critical marketing problems.

Two other important aspects of the right place as a power source are *nonsubstitutability* and *centrality*.[8] As the term implies, nonsubstitutability refers to the person's or department's uniqueness. If the expertise is important and difficult to replace, the possessor (unit or person) of that expertise gains power. A computer scientist might be powerful because he or she is the only person who understands the organization's financial system.

The centrality of a subunit is the extent to which its activities are linked into the system of organizational activities. A person or subunit has high centrality when he, she, or it is an important and integral part of the flow of work done by another person or unit (and therefore is important to the latter in terms of their work output). A sales department would have high centrality; an employee recreation association would have low centrality.

In summary, you can make some accurate predictions about the power distribution in an organization if you can identify the individuals or units that (1) cope with strategic contingencies, (2) are difficult to replace, and (3) connect with many other organizational subunits.

Being There at the Right Time

The opportunity to handle problems effectively will depend on being in a position to do something constructive when a problem comes along. The time has to be right to work on an organizational problem. For instance, introducing a new government program in Congress might not work in a period of budget tightening. At another time, that same program might be accepted.

[8]Robert H. Miles, *Macro Organizational Behavior* (Glenview, Ill.: Scott, Foresman and Company, 1980), p. 172.

The right time is closely connected to the right place. It is best to be confronted with a key organizational problem at a time when you or your department can handle the situation. One division of a company rejected a new product idea because at the time, it had too many new products in development. The idea was then transferred to a smaller division. Much to the chagrin of the larger division, that new product (a pocket calculator) became a bestseller for the company.

Having the Right Resources

The most obvious source of power is the control of resources, particularly so because power is sometimes defined as the ability to control resources. If you are in control of people, money, material, or ideas, you tend to have considerable power in the organization. As summarized by two organizational theorists, "Subunit power accrues to those departments that are most instrumental in bringing in or providing resources that are highly valued by the total organization."[9] Among these resources are control of punishments, rewards, difficult-to-find items such as silver, and the authority to influence organizational structure.

Control over resources is related to such things as one's position in the hierarchy (higher-ranking officials have more say in the commitment of resources) and location in the work flow. Information is an example of a resource that is acquired by virtue of work flow location. An assistant or secretary to a president has access to vital information. A personnel specialist who communicates freely with many different people tends to be powerful. Because the specialist "can read the organizational pulse," he or she is valuable.

A resource of particular interest to young professionals is expertise. A skillful builder of forecasting models has much expert power whenever the organization is interested in a forecasting model. Another fragile aspect of expertise as a resource is that it depends upon others' perceptions of one's expertise. Research evidence suggests that these perceptions are not always accurate. Further, once the organization has used an individual's expertise, he or she loses much of that power base. A company president of questionable ethics once commented upon the contemplated hiring of a product development specialist: "I'm not too worried about how much we pay him. Once we pick his brains, anyway, we'll get rid of him."

It is not enough to simply control a vital resource; one also has to find a suitable way of using the resource and applying it toward appropriate goals.

Undertaking the Right Action

The successful use of power leads to more power. If you displayed power by hiring an individual critical to the success of the organization, that feat would increase your power. To paraphrase a valid tautology, "People have power if they get things done; if they have the power they can get things done."[10] A fringe benefit of making good use

---

[9]Gerald R. Salancik and Jeffrey Pfeffer, "The Bases and Uses of Power in Organizational Decision Making: The Case of a University," *Administrative Science Quarterly,* Winter 1974, p. 473.

[10]Cited in McCall, *Power, Influence, and Authority,* p. 12.

of power is that it leads to the acquisition of more human resources that can help you to get more things done. Powerful bosses tend to like powerful subordinates (within limits), and people prefer working for powerful bosses. Success leads to more success, and taking powerful actions in organizations leads to more power. As the powerful subordinates accumulate, the manager accumulates more power. The draft system in professional basketball and football was purposely designed to limit this type of accumulation of power. Now the weaker teams have first pick and the strongest teams the last pick of the most powerful resources each year. These powerful resources are the college athletes of demonstrated capability and presumed potential for further success and gate appeal (or referent power).

A fitting conclusion to our discussion of the origins of power is that they are complex and diverse. A strong power base is likely to accumulate when people or units

Are in a position to deal with the important problems facing the organization.

Have control over resources perceived as valuable by others.

Are skilled or fortunate enough to bring problems and resources together at the same time.

Are centrally connected in the work flow of the organization.

Are not easily replaced or substituted.

Have successfully used their power in the past.[11]

POWER EXERCISED BY SUBORDINATES

Typically we think of power as emanating from high levels in the organization and consequently being exercised in a downward direction. In reality a good deal of power is exercised up the organization. According to the concept of legitimate authority, leaders can be only as powerful as subordinates will let them be. Subordinates are willing to take orders, within limits as described by the zone of indifference.[12] The zone refers to an area of behavior within which a subordinate is prepared to accept direction or influence. Orders of this type are seen as lawful and within the person's value system; the person is indifferent to such orders.

One company filed under Chapter XI of the bankruptcy law. Shortly thereafter, it issued a statement to employees that in the near future many checks would bounce. The reason offered was that "funds would be moving from bank to bank." In response, an employees group issued a pronouncement that its members would not tolerate this abuse of power. If more than a few checks bounced, large-scale terminations would be forthcoming. Somehow the company found ways to make the checks it issued valid.

---

[11]Paraphrased from ibid., p. 14.

[12]This concept traces back to Chester Barnard, *The Functions of the Executive* (Cambridge, Mass.: Harvard University Press, 1938), p. 167.

The concept of expert power also illustrates how power can be exercised in a vertical direction. A lower-ranking organization member with unusual skill can frequently force his or her demands upon management. One industrial supply firm tolerated the antics of an eccentric and irascible sales representative for many years before he finally retired. Although a maverick in his relations with upper management, the sales representative was well liked by most of his customers who placed large orders with him (his source of expert power).

Managers are well advised to appreciate the complexity of subordinate power. As Martin J. Gannon cautions, "If superiors do not recognize the informal power that subordinates possess, they can create many problems for themselves. It is common for a secretary working for several managers to like some and dislike others. It is also common for her to give preference to the projects of the favored managers and to be somewhat less careful when working on the projects of the less favored managers.[13]

FACTORS CONTRIBUTING TO ORGANIZATIONAL POLITICS

In general, organizational politics exists because people are in quest of the types of power described in the preceding sections of this chapter. An understanding of the OP process is served by examining this generalization in further detail.

Factors both within individuals and situations contribute to the ubiquity of political behavior. Some types of work environments are known to trigger politically oriented behavior in individuals not ordinarily prone to such tactics. A highly competitive environment is one example of a situation that fosters OP. Here we concentrate on several of the more influential factors that lead to political behavior on the part of organizational members. Most instances of politicking stem from a combination of one or more of the factors to be described.

The Need for Power

People would probably not participate in organizational power struggles if it were not for the presence of a socially acquired power motive. As with any other human need or motive, vast individual differences exist in the strength of power motives. Some people only want to control their own lives (an almost zero power need); others want to exert control and influence over vast empires (an extraordinary power need). People with strong power needs are not readily satiated, thus propelling them toward an endless display of political behavior to gain more power.

David C. McClelland has extensively studied the need for power (*n* Power) by means of projective techniques in which subjects compose stories about neutral figures. In the process of writing about others, we reveal much about our own personal-

---

[13]Martin J. Gannon, *Organizational Behavior: A Managerial and Organizational Perspective* (Boston: Little, Brown, 1979), p. 272.

ities. People with personal power concern are interested primarily in using power for their own advantage. It is these individuals who are inveterate users of power tactics on the job. In contrast, people with socialized power concern want to acquire power to help others. A person who builds a research and development laboratory for the primary purpose of developing inexpensive medicines would fit this category. The evidence, so far, suggests that *n* Power can be reliably measured in individuals.[14]

Pyramidal Organization Structures

The very shape of large organizations is the most fundamental reason for people maneuvering ("jockeying") for position and power. Only so much formal power is available to distribute among the many people who would like more of it. In the traditional hierarchy, as you move down the organization chart, each successive layer of people has less power than does the layer above. At the very bottom of the organization, people have virtually no power.

Abraham Zaleznik, an organizational theorist and psychoanalyst, makes this analysis of the inevitability of power struggles in business organizations: "Whatever else organizations may be, they are political structures. This means that organizations operate by distributing authority and setting a stage for the exercise of power. It is no wonder, therefore, that individuals who are highly motivated to secure and use power find a familiar and hospitable environment in business."[15]

Lack of Objective Standards of Performance

When managerial and individual performance can be measured objectively, political behavior becomes less necessary. For example, if a scientist employed by a pharmaceutical firm discovers a chemical cure for leukemia, he or she does not need to engage in "impression management" to achieve recognition. The scientific results speak for themselves. A staff person working in the field of strategic planning might have a much more difficult time substantiating that he or she is performing well. One alternative that the individual might pursue is to engage in job politics to achieve recognition for his or her efforts.

Emotional Insecurity

Self-confidence or emotional security is another individual variable influencing political behavior. Some people resort to office politics as a way of ingratiating themselves with superiors because they lack confidence in their talents and skills. Top-producing

[14]David C. McClelland, *Power: The Inner Experience* (New York: Irvington/John Wiley, 1976), p. 258.

[15]Abraham Zaleznik, "Power and Politics in Organizational Life," *Harvard Business Review,* May–June 1970, p. 47.

sales representatives, for example, typically do not go out of their way to curry favor with the home office. An outstanding sales record gives a personal additional self-confidence: he or she is therefore emotionally secure. In addition, that individual has acquired a large amount of expert power in the form of sales skill.

Need for Acceptance

Many employees who practice politics in the office have only modest aspirations for upward mobility or power. They simply want to be accepted and liked by others—a normal medium-order need. To accomplish this end, they conduct favors for co-workers and carry out other relatively harmless ploys. Among these techniques are supplying others with candy or coffee, running errands for others during lunch time, and bringing officemates trinkets upon return from vacation.

Work Avoidance

In an organizational subunit where people are not upwardly mobile (and/or are waiting for retirement), political maneuvers are often used to *avoid* work. The rationale for this behavior is that "If you get in good with the boss, you won't have to work so hard." One man regularly complimented his boss on her appearance. She reciprocated by not giving him difficult or unpleasant assignments. In general, using ingratiating techniques to avoid work is a ploy of the low-work-motivated individual with a low need for power.[16]

POWER ACQUISITION STRATEGIES AND TACTICS

Since almost anything done to influence another individual might be interpreted as a power tactic, the number of strategies is almost endless. One book on the subject lists over 150 methods of increasing one's power or gaining favor in an organization.[17] In general the experienced power player relies first on a casual method of influencing others such as a luncheon discussion. Stronger, more formal, methods such as "pulling rank" are used as a later resort by experienced power manipulators (used in a descriptive not an evaluative sense). In this section, we present a sampling of power acquisition strategies and tactics used in organizations. In the following section, we summarize some current research about the specifics of the influence process. Here we are concerned with broader, more diffuse approaches to attaining or retaining power.

[16]Andrew J. DuBrin, *Human Relations: A Job-Oriented Approach,* 2nd ed. (Reston, Va.: Reston, 1981), p. 122.

[17]Andrew J. DuBrin, *Winning at Office Politics* (New York: Van Nostrand Reinhold, 1978).

Maintain Alliances with Powerful People

An essential way of acquiring power is to form alliances with people who exert power themselves or influence others who exert power. Managers sometimes attempt to create a positive climate for the acceptance of their ideas by maintaining cordial relationships with a high-ranking official's secretary. Management consultants sometimes attempt to exert influence with managers by implying that they have a close working relationship with the chief executive officer. Consequently, the manager worries about losing influence with his or her immediate superior if he or she fails to cooperate with the consultant. Dramatic evidence of the importance of maintaining alliances with powerful people is found in one incident involving the Federal Bureau of Investigation. In this situation, the official who lost power also lost his job:

> William C. Sullivan, 59, a top FBI administrator and agent for 30 years, is being forced to retire after a series of policy disputes with J. Edgar Hoover. While Sullivan was on sick leave Friday, his name was removed from his office door and the locks changed. Sullivan, who was once thought to be a likely successor to Hoover, 76, was not officially informed.
>
> The FBI said that Sullivan had been under intense pressure from Hoover to leave the bureau for months but that as late as 10 P.M. Friday, Sullivan was resisting the pressure and refusing to resign. . . .
>
> Sullivan's ouster was foreshadowed about six weeks ago when Hoover appointed W. Mark Felt over Sullivan into a newly created No. 3 post in the FBI just below the director and associate director Clyde W. Tolson, 71, Hoover's long time right hand man.
>
> A former FBI official said Friday night that the downgrading of Sullivan's position was the tipoff that his days were numbered. "It's a technique the director has used for years," the official said. "You are bypassed and then ignored and, if you still don't get the idea, he just takes your name off the rolls."
>
> Justice Department sources said another cause of Sullivan's losing confrontation with Hoover was that the short, fiery Irishman had developed strong relationships with Atty. Gen. John N. Mitchell and other top Justice officials, apparently casting doubt on his loyalty to the director.
>
> The initial break between Sullivan and Hoover came during the early 1960s, ex-FBI sources said, when Sullivan argued that major domestic threat was no longer the U.S. Communist party USA, but rather the Ku Klux Klan's efforts to thwart civil rights advances in the South.
>
> "This advance was unfavorably received by the director, but Sullivan was persistent and actually made some gains in switching our emphasis," the source said. "But he lost the wholehearted backing of Hoover after that and the gap between them widened as the years went by."
>
> Sullivan reportedly was the only top FBI executive addressed by his first name by Hoover in recent years. Sullivan is described as a favorite of Hoover's for years because of his intellectual approach to his duties.[18]

[18]Ken W. Clawson, "Top FBI Official Forced Out in Policy Feud with Hoover," *Washington Post,* October 2, 1971, Section A. Reprinted with permission.

Embrace or Demolish

An historical and political analysis of the similarities between corporations and states contends that many of Machiavelli's observations about power made in the fifteenth century are still valid. Some of these observations can be translated into power acquisition strategies. For instance, the following passage quoted from *The Prince* by Niccolo Machiavelli provides guidelines for the conquest of smaller nations:

> Upon this one has to remark that men ought either to be well treated or crushed, because they can avenge themselves or lighten injuries, of more serious ones they cannot; therefore the injury that is done to a man ought to be of such a kind that one does not stand in fear of revenge.

Anthony Jay extrapolates this strategy to the situation of modern corporate takeovers: "The guiding principle is that senior executives in taken-over firms should either be warmly welcomed and encouraged or sacked; because if they are sacked they are powerless, whereas if they are simply downgraded they will remain united and resentful and determined to get their own back."[19]

Divide and Rule

Ancient in origin, this well-known political strategy often has disastrous consequences for the organization in terms of team work and coordination. Underlying the use of this power tactic is the expectation that enemies will not unite forces and form a coalition to work against you. To implement the strategy, the individual must first precipitate a rift between or among people who might form an alliance against him or her. By way of illustration, one chief engineer hoped to strengthen his position by being the person with the balance of power among the senior executives. The strategy he chose to achieve this balance of power was to deliberately stir up rivalry between the manufacturing and sales departments.

Camel's Head in the Tent

Sometimes a small beginning can be made when a total program would be unacceptable.[20] Step by step, the power actor wins his or her demands and gains power. One regional manager sought to develop her own group of staff services and rely less upon regional headquarters. The current trend within the corporation was the centralizaton of staff services, which led to her ideas being resisted. As a countermaneuver, the manager began by having her own employee training program developed because of what she insisted were "regional differences in types of people employed."

The training program was successful, thus lowering resistance to her hiring a

---

[19]Anthony Jay, *Management and Machiavelli* (New York: Holt, Rinehart and Winston, 1967), p. 6.

[20]William H. Newman, *Administrative Action: The Techniques of Organization and Management*, 2nd ed. (Englewood Cliffs, N.J.: Prentice-Hall, 1963), pp. 634–35.

market planner to work exclusively on the problems of her region. Following this, the regional manager received authorization to hire consultants to help her with a variety of local problems. Ultimately, this "camel's head" approach provided the regional manager with the autonomy she had sought in the first place.

Select a Compliant Board of Directors

Without a cooperative board, it is difficult for a chief executive officer to expand his or her power. Chief executives attempting to use the board for aggrandizing their power opt for as many inside board members as possible.[21] If you report to a president, it might seem to border on violation of your subordinate role to be openly critical of him or her in a board meeting.

Take Counsel with Caution

A classic analysis of the use of power by executives suggests a strategy that is geared more toward preventing the erosion of power already acquired than toward acquiring power. According to this analysis, the able executive must be cautious about seeking and receiving advice (contrary to the tenets of participative management). Asking advice sometimes results in decisions being made by subordinates. Although out-of-keeping with the prescriptions of participative management, the student of organizational politics and power might ponder the advice: "A vague sort of policy which states, 'I am always ready to hear your advice and ideas on anything' will waste time, confuse issues, dilute leadership, and erode power."[22]

ORDINARY INFLUENCE STRATEGIES FOR ACQUIRING POWER[23]

On a day-by-day basis, organizational members tend to use much less elaborate techniques than those just described for influencing each other and therefore attaining a mild degree of power. Research along these lines was conducted among 754 adults employed in managerial, professional, and technical positions. The tactics used by job incumbents to influence their superiors, co-workers, and subordinates were investigated in two related studies. In the first study, 165 lower-level managers were asked to

[21]Robert N. McMurry, "Power and the Ambitious Executive," *Harvard Business Review,* November–December 1973, pp. 140–45.

[22]Norman H. Martin and John H. Simms, "Thinking Ahead: Power Tactics," *Harvard Business Review,* November–December 1956, p. 28.

[23]This section of the chapter is based entirely on David Kipnis, Stuart M. Schmidt, and Ian Wilkinson, "Intraorganizational Influence Tactics: Explorations in Getting One's Way," *Journal of Applied Psychology,* August 1980, pp. 440–52.

write essays describing an incident in which they influenced their bosses, co-workers, or subordinates. By means of content analysis, 370 influence tactics, grouped into fourteen categories, were identified. The tactics ranged from a straightforward technique of rational discussion through the use of exchange (reciprocity) tactics to the use of clandestine tactics.

In a second study, the 370 influence tactics were rewritten into a fifty-eight-item questionnaire. A new sample of 754 people was asked to describe the extent to which they used each item to influence their bosses, co-workers, or subordinates. The same person answered for only one category of influence direction (upward, laterally, or downward). A factor analysis of the questionnaire items was then conducted to reduce the number of influence dimensions. Eight of these dimensions were identified:

> Assertiveness (being forthright with your demands)
> Ingratiation (getting somebody else to like you)
> Rationality (appealing to reason)
> Sanctions (using threats of punishment)
> Exchange (performing reciprocal favors)
> Upward appeal (asking for help from a higher authority)
> Blocking (engaging in work slowdowns or the threat thereof)
> Coalitions (getting the support of others)

These influence dimensions are presented in Table 14–1, along with two specific aspects of behavior that are included under each dimension. Each aspect of behavior constitutes a specific questionnaire item such as "Asked in a polite way."

Contingency and Situational Factors

So far most of the discussion in this section, and in this chapter, has dealt with generalizations about the use of power and influence tactics. We have not specified the conditions under which a particular tactic is most likely to be used. The intraorganizational research discussed here provides some new insights on this topic. By way of correlational analysis, some significant relationships were found between several factors and the choice of influence tactic.

1. *Target status.* Seven of the eight influence dimensions were associated with the status of the person trying to be influenced (the target). Basically, the findings indicated that as the status of the target person increased, employees placed more reliance on rationality tactics. Assertive tactics were used more often to influence subordinates than co-workers or superiors. The tactics of ingratiation, exchange of benefits, and upward appeal were used equally often among subordinates and co-workers but significantly less often when attempting to influence superiors. Also, participants in the study reported that they used rationality more frequently to convince superiors than co-workers or subordinates. (Appeals to reason certainly do make sense in dealing with a superior.)

TABLE 14–1 Influence Tactics and Corresponding Sample Behaviors

Dimension	Sample Behaviors
Assertiveness	a. Kept checking up on him or her. b. Expressed my anger verbally.
Ingratiation	a. Acted in a friendly manner prior to asking for what I wanted. b. Praised him or her and asked in a polite way.
Rationality	a. Wrote a detailed plan that justified my ideas. b. Used logic to convince him or her.
Sanctions	a. Gave no salary increase or prevented the person from getting a pay raise. b. Threatened him or her with loss of promotion.
Exchange	a. Did personal favors for him or her. b. Offered to help if he or she would do what I wanted.
Upward appeal	a. Made a formal appeal to higher levels to back up my request. b. Sent him or her to my superior.
Blocking	a. Engaged in a work slowdown until he or she did what I wanted. b. Ignored him or her and/or stopped being friendly.
Coalitions	a. Obtained the support of co-workers to back up my request. b. Obtained the support of my subordinates to back up my request.

Source: Based on information presented in David Kipnis, Stuart M. Schmidt, and Ian Wilkinson, "Intraorganizational Influence Tactics: Explorations in Getting One's Way," *Journal of Applied Psychology,* August 1980, pp. 445–47.

2. *Goals.* A reliable finding was that at all target status levels, the respondent's choice of influence tactic varied with the respondent's reason for exercising influence. Specifically, employees who frequently sought personal assistance from target persons used ingratiation tactics; those who frequently assigned work to target persons used assertiveness; those who frequently tried to improve a target person's performance used assertiveness and rationality tactics. Also, employees who frequently tried to persuade target persons to accept new ideas favored rationality tactics. In short, people tend to use that influence tactic that seems to best fit the end they are trying to accomplish.

3. *Subordinates as targets.* Another statistically significant finding is that the respondents showed the least variation in choice of tactics when attempting to influence their own subordinates. No matter what the reason for trying to influence subordinates, assertiveness was the influence tactic of choice. In contrast, when trying to influence co-workers and superiors, assertiveness was used much less frequently. It was reserved

for trying to assign work to, or improve the performance of, co-workers and superiors.

4. *Person's own organizational level.* The findings showed the choice of influence tactic was associated with a person's organizational level. Compared with those with low job status, people with higher job status reported more frequent use of rationality and assertiveness tactics when influencing both their subordinates and their superiors. In addition, respondents with higher job status used sanctions more frequently when influencing their subordinates.

5. *Other situational variables.* Size of work unit showed some relationship to influence tactic. In large work units, more emphasis was placed on assertiveness, sanctions, and upward appeal when influencing subordinates. The researchers note that these findings are consistent with the general idea that as the number of persons in a work unit increases, a greater reliance is placed on strong and impersonal means of control.

Unionization of the work force was also a conditional factor. If the organization was unionized, people were more likely to use ingratiating tactics to influence subordinates and blocking tactics more frequently when influencing bosses (among other findings).

Sex of the respondent was not found to be significantly related to choice of influence tactic. Men and women chose similar tactics when attempting to get their way.

MANAGERIAL AWARENESS OF POLITICAL FACTORS

Anecdotal research suggests that the vast majority of employed adults are aware that political tactics are widely used in organizations. More systematic research has also been conducted on this topic. A team of five researchers sought to answer the question, "How much do managers know about organizational politics?" The method they chose was to interview eighty-seven managerial personnel. The sample consisted of thirty chief executive officers, twenty-eight high-level staff managers, and twenty-nine supervisors. One question asked the managers was, "Organizational politics takes many forms. What are the tactics of organizational politics of which you are aware?"[24]

The managers supplied their own definitions of organizational politics (or job politics or office politics). They were not to restrict their observations to their present places of employment. The eight categories of political tactics most frequently mentioned are presented next, along with the percentage of respondents who mentioned the tactic.

- Attacking or blaming others—such as making the rival look bad in the eyes of influential organization members. As the saying goes, "When something goes wrong, the first thing to be fixed is the blame" (54.0 percent).
- Use of information, such as withholding or distorting information or using it to overwhelm another person (54.0 percent).

[24]Robert W. Allen et al., "Organizational Politics: Tactics and Characteristics of Its Actors," *California Management Review,* Fall 1979, p. 77.

- Image building/impression management—includes general appearance, dress and hair style, drawing attention to successes, and creating the appearance of being on the inside of important activities (52.9 percent).
- Support building for ideas—including getting others to understand one's ideas before a decision is made and setting up the decision before the meeting is called (36.8 percent).
- Praising others, ingratiation—supervisors used expressions such as "buttering up the boss," "apple polishing," and other more colorful, but less printable, remarks (25.3 percent).
- Power coalitions, strong allies—getting key people on your side (25.3 percent).
- Association with influential people—both business and social situations are considered important (24.1 percent).
- Creating obligations/reciprocity—the norm of reciprocity is invoked when assistance is required, "You scratch my back and I'll scratch yours" (12.6 percent).

The managers were also asked, "What are the personal characteristics of those people (the office politicians) who you feel are the most effective in the use of organizational politics?" Thirteen characteristics were mentioned as important by ten or more of the people interviewed. They are

Articulate Sensitive } 30% mention	Socially adept Competent Popular Extroverted Self-confident Aggressive Ambitious Devious } 16% mention	"Organization person" Highly intelligent Logical } 1% mention

ETHICAL CONSIDERATIONS

An inherent danger in presenting a description of political and power strategies in a management text is that the reader will interpret the discussion as an endorsement of these strategies by the author. Our discussion is intended to be descriptive, not evaluative. Each strategy and tactic must be evaluated on its merits by the ethical code of the particular individual and organization. A guiding principle, however, is to turn the tactic or strategy inward. Assume that you believe that a particular strategy (such as praise or ingratiation) would be fair and ethical to use in working with you. It would then be fair and ethical for you to use that strategy against others.

Organizational values also help to determine which political tactic or strategy is considered ethical. In most organizations, "impression management" in the form of creating a good physical appearance is considered virtually a merit factor. In some organizations, however, the technique of drawing attention to your own successes (tooting your own horn) is frowned upon; in others, it is considered to be an acceptable standard practice.

Personal values also help to determine which political tactics a person considers to be ethical. For example, if you place a high value on the concept of merit in organizations, you would tend to avoid those political tactics that you interpret as deviating from the merit system. You would much prefer to be recognized for your talents than for your ability to unduly influence others. The value system of another individual, however, might allow for using heavy doses of interpersonal influence to get ahead. According to the value system of this particular individual, being able to influence others is but one aspect of being talented.

Another perspective on the ethics of OP is to recognize that both the means and the ends of political behavior must be considered. A team of people researching the topic has commented, "Instead of determining whether human rights or standards of justice are violated, we are often content to judge political behavior according to its outcomes."[25] They suggest that when it comes to the ethics of OP, respect for justice and human rights should prevail for its own sake.

THE CONTROL OF
ORGANIZATIONAL POLITICS

If used to excess, organizational politics can be dysfunctional. To cite one adverse consequence, when political factors far outweigh merit, many competent employees may become disgruntled and quit. Another dysfunction is that overemphasis on political activity leads to an inversion of means and ends. Engaging in political behavior sometimes becomes an end in itself rather than a means of getting legitimate work accomplished. A legitimate use of organizational politics might be to help a useful department obtain an appropriate budget for the upcoming fiscal year.

As one irate subordinate complained about his boss in an organizational analysis interview, "I wish he would spend more time in the department helping us and less time running around the plant playing politics." Several organizational strategies are known to be helpful in reducing an overreliance on political behavior.

Creating an Organizational Climate
of Openness and Trust

Politically oriented behavior, at an underlying level, is in part a reaction to the fear of the consequences of revealing the truth about oneself. Many employees, for example, are hesitant to candidly criticize a superior's suggestions. When organizational members do not fear the consequences of telling the truth, they are more willing to be candid and nonpolitical. Several of the organization development strategies described later in this book include as their goal increasing openness and trust. To the extent that these OD strategies are effective, they will help to control organizational politics.

---

[25]Gerald F. Cavanagh, Dennis J. Moberg, and Manuel Velasquez, "The Ethics of Organizational Politics," *Academy of Management Review,* July 1981, p. 372.

Providing Objective Measurements of Performance

As described earlier in this chapter, less need exists to engage in political behavior when a person's contribution can be measured directly. Management-by-objective (MBO) systems are thus often the treatment of choice to reduce dysfunctional politicking. The sales manager who meets all his objectives under MBO has some factual data upon which to be promoted. Currying favor with superiors then becomes a less influential factor in his or her promotion.

Nonpolitically Oriented Behavior on the Part of Top Management

A good deal of political behavior in a given environment probably stems from modeling the actions of people in higher positions. An executive or team of executives who minimizes political behavior creates a positive model for others in the organization.

Meshing of Individual and Organizational Goals

This is perhaps the ideal antidote to excessive political behavior. When the goals, aspirations, and needs of employees can be met through their jobs, they tend to engage in behavior that will foster the growth, longevity, and productivity of their organization. In recent years, career development programs have emerged as the most logical way in which to mesh individual and organizational goals. In essence, employees are helped to develop a career path that will bring them the rewards they seek on the job. The project and matrix forms of organization structure described earlier in the book represent useful structural approaches to meshing individual and organizational goals. Such structures often provide individuals more autonomy than they would achieve in a departmental or functional arrangement. An increased feeling of autonomy, in turn, leads to increased satisfaction and less need to engage in political behavior in order to advance.

Provide for Job Rotation

Political behavior sometimes stems from a desire to protect and enlarge one's own empire. If you leave your "empire" from time to time, it follows that you will engage in fewer political squabbles to defend your empire. The empathy that results from switching assignments (or interorganizational exchange) also helps to reduce some forms of political behavior. Assume that there is intense competition between two product managers within a food company. Each may waste company resources and time in fighting political battles. Should the two product managers switch assignments, they will be better able to understand each other's point of view and recognize the value of cooperation.

IMPLICATIONS FOR MANAGERIAL PRACTICE

1. In dealing with others on the job, it is helpful to recognize that a significant portion of people's efforts will be directed toward gaining power for themselves and/or their organizational units. At times, some of this behavior will be directed more toward self-interest than toward organizational interest. It is therefore often necessary to ask the question, "Is this being done to help that person or the organization?" Your answer to this question will aid in influencing your willingness to submit to that person's demands.

2. Assuming that you want to establish a power base for yourself, a good starting point is to develop expert power. Most powerful people began their climb to power by demonstrating expertise in a particular area. Developing expertise is among the most ethical strategies of power acquisition.

3. In trying to determine if a particular set of behaviors is motivated by political or merit considerations, it is important to understand the intent of the actor. The same action might be based on self-interest or concern for others. For instance, a subordinate might praise you because he or she believed that you did something of merit. Or that same individual might praise you to attain a favorable work assignment.

Summary

- Power in an organizational context is the ability to marshal or control the human, informational, and material resources to get something done. Politics is the study of power in action; it involves those activities (in addition to merit) taken within organizations to acquire, develop, and use power and other resources to obtain one's preferred outcomes in a situation in which there is uncertainty or dissensus about choices.

- Power in organizations stems from many sources, including those granted by the organization and those derived from characteristics of the person. A traditional analysis of sources of power includes legitimate power, reward power, coercive power, expert power, and referent power (charisma). A more complex, yet overlapping, analysis of power lists the sources as (1) being in the right place, (2) being there at the right time, (3) having the right resources, and (4) taking the right action.

- Subordinates exercise power of their own in relation to superiors. One reason is that a zone of indifference exists in which subordinates will obey orders without question. Orders outside that zone will not be acceptable. Subordinates can also exert power upward through expert power; because of expert power, an individual becomes relatively indispensable.

- Political behavior in organizations is caused or contributed to, by both individual and situational factors. Among them are the psychological need for power, the fact that many organizations are shaped like a pyramid, the lack of objective standards of performance, the emotional insecurity of some people, the need for acceptance by others, and an interest in avoiding work.

- Numerous strategies have been formulated for the purpose of the acquisition of power by individuals. The ones described here are (1) maintaining alliances with powerful people, (2) embracing or demolishing, (3) dividing and ruling, (4) using the camel's head in the tent approach, (5) selecting a compliant board of directors, and (6) taking counsel with caution.

- Research on the influence process used by working adults has identified eight major influence tactics: assertiveness, ingratiation, rationality, sanctions, exchange, upward appeal, blocking, and coalitions. Situational factors help to determine which of these influence factors will be used at a given time. One example is that as the status of the target person increases, people place more reliance on rationality tactics. What goal an individual intends to achieve also bears upon which influence tactic will be chosen. It was noted that employees who frequently sought assistance from target persons used ingratiating tactics and that those who frequently assigned work to target persons used assertiveness.

- Casual observation and research evidence suggests that managers have active knowledge about organizational politics. According to an interview study, the most frequently used techniques are attacking or blaming others, use (or misuses) of information, image building and impression management, support building for ideas, ingratiation, power coalitions, association with influential people, and creating obligations/reciprocity.

- Which, if any, political strategies are chosen by an individual or organizational unit must rest on ethical considerations. A guiding principle is to use only those tactics you would consider fair and ethical if used against you.

- Strategies for organizational control of excessive political behavior include (1) creating a climate of openness and trust, (2) providing objective measures of performance, (3) adopting a nonpolitically oriented behavior on the part of top management, (4) meshing of individual and organizational goals, and (5) providing for job rotation.

Questions for Discussion

1. How might political factors influence which departments in an organization have the most power?
2. How do "bootlicking" and "apple polishing" relate to organizational politics?
3. Which sources of power are exercised by the coach of a professional athletic team?

4. What do you see as the relationship between government politics and organizational politics?

5. How do "classroom politics" relate to organizational politics?

6. What type of organizational structure do you think would minimize organizational politics?

7. At this writing, Carl Sagan, the astronomer, popular scientist, and author, is a very powerful person. What resources does he control?

8. IBM Corporation is powerful beyond question. Do a quick "power analysis" of IBM.

9. Reread the FBI case presented in this chapter. Explain specifically which power acquisition strategies and tactics the case illustrates.

10. Which of the eight influence strategies do you tend to use when your target person is somebody more powerful than yourself?

An Organizational Behavior Problem

The Political Orientation Questionnaire*

Directions. Answer each of the following statements mostly true or mostly false. We are looking for general trends; therefore, do not be concerned if you are uncertain as to whether your answer should be mostly true or mostly false to one particular question. In answering each question, assume that you are taking this questionnaire with the intent of learning something about yourself. Only you will see the results. *Do not* assume that you are taking this questionnaire as part of the screening process for a job you want.

	Mostly True	Mostly False
1. The boss is always right.	____	____
2. It is wise to flatter important people.	____	____
3. If you have an acid tongue, display it proudly at the office.	____	____
4. If you are even one-eighth American Indian, mention it on your résumé (assuming you believed it would increase your chance of getting the job you wanted).	____	____
5. I would ask my boss's opinion about personal matters (such as life insurance or real estate) even though I didn't need his advice.	____	____
6. If I had the skills, I would help the president of my company with his or her furniture-refinishing hobby on a Sunday afternoon.	____	____
7. Dressing for success is a sham. Wear clothing to the office that you find to be most comfortable.	____	____
8. If I were aware that an executive in my company was stealing money, I would use that information against him or her in asking for favors.	____	____
9. I would invite my boss to a party in my home even if I didn't like him or her.	____	____

*Reprinted from Andrew J. DuBrin, "Winning at Office Politics," *Success,* September 1981, pp. 26–28, 46.

	Mostly True	Mostly False
10. Given a choice, take on only those assignments that will make you look good.	___	___
11. I like the idea of keeping a "blunder file" about the competition for potential future use.	___	___
12. Most people at work cannot be trusted.	___	___
13. It's pointless to be concerned that people will use confidential information against you in the future.	___	___
14. Act and look cool even when you don't feel that way.	___	___
15. If I worked for a shirt or blouse manufacturer, I would never wear a competitive brand to the office.	___	___
16. Why bother cultivating the minnows in my company? It's the big fish I'm after.	___	___
17. Before taking any action at work, think how it might be interpreted by key people.	___	___
18. I would attend a company picnic even if I had the chance to do something I enjoyed much more that day.	___	___
19. If necessary, I would say rotten things about a rival in order to attain a promotion.	___	___
20. If you have important confidential information, release it to your advantage.	___	___
21. Accept advice willingly; don't obscure the issue by questioning why you are being given advice.	___	___
22. If your rival for promotion is making a big mistake, why tell him or her?	___	___
23. If I wanted to show up someone, I would be willing to write memos documenting his or her mistakes.	___	___
24. Before you write a final report to your boss, find out what he or she really wants to see included in that report.	___	___
25. I would be willing to say nice things about a rival with the intent of getting him or her transferred away from my department.	___	___
26. I have no interest in using gossip for personal advantage.	___	___
27. Don't be a complainer. It may be held against you.	___	___
28. It is necessary to keep some people in place by making them afraid of you.	___	___
29. Jack wants to be a hero, so he creates a crisis for his company and then resolves it. His strategy is at least worth a try.	___	___
30. I would go out of my way to cultivate friendships with powerful people.	___	___
31. I would never raise questions about the capabilities of my competition. Let his or her record speak for itself.	___	___
32. Power for its own sake is one of life's most precious commodities.	___	___
33. I am unwilling to take credit for someone else's work.	___	___
34. If I discovered that a co-worker was looking for a new job, I would inform my boss.	___	___
35. Even if you made only a minor contribution to an important project, get your name listed as being associated with that project.	___	___
36. It is only necessary to play office politics if you are an incompetent.	___	___

	Mostly True	Mostly False
37. There is nothing wrong with tooting your own horn.	___	___
38. I like to keep my office cluttered with personal mementos such as pencil holders and ashtrays made by my children. By doing so, my office doesn't seem so cold and businesslike.	___	___
39. Only a fool would correct mistakes made by the boss.	___	___
40. I would purchase stock in my company even though it might not be a good investment.	___	___
41. If I wanted something done by a co-worker, I would be willing to say, "If you don't get this done, our boss might be very unhappy."	___	___
42. It is much safer to be feared than loved by your subordinates.	___	___
43. Although you have to resort to speculation, make up some financial figures to prove the value of your proposal.	___	___
44. Once you become the boss, transfer from your department anyone who you suspect does not like you.	___	___
45. If you dislike a particular man in your firm, don't send him a congratulatory note when he receives a big promotion.	___	___
46. If you do somebody a favor, remember to cash in on it.	___	___
47. All forms of office politics boil down to kissing another person's backside.	___	___
48. If apple polishing helps me, I'll polish apples.	___	___
49. My primary job is to please my boss.	___	___
50. A wise strategy is to keep on good terms with everyone in your office.	___	___

Scoring. Give yourself one point for each answer you gave in agreement with the keyed answer (note that we did not use the term "correct" answer). Whether an answer is correct or not is a question of personal values and ethics. Each question that receives a point shows a tendency toward playing office politics or grabbing for power.

Question Number	Political Answer	Question Number	Political Answer
1.	Mostly true	26.	Mostly false
2.	Mostly true	27.	Mostly true
3.	Mostly false	28.	Mostly true
4.	Mostly true	29.	Mostly true
5.	Mostly true	30.	Mostly true
6.	Mostly true	31.	Mostly false
7.	Mostly false	32.	Mostly true
8.	Mostly true	33.	Mostly false
9.	Mostly true	34.	Mostly true
10.	Mostly true	35.	Mostly true
11.	Mostly true	36.	Mostly false
12.	Mostly true	37.	Mostly true
13.	Mostly false	38.	Mostly false
14.	Mostly true	39.	Mostly true
15.	Mostly true	40.	Mostly true
16.	Mostly true	41.	Mostly true

Question Number	Political Answer	Question Number	Political Answer
17.	Mostly true	42.	Mostly true
18.	Mostly true	43.	Mostly true
19.	Mostly true	44.	Mostly true
20.	Mostly true	45.	Mostly false
21.	Mostly false	46.	Mostly true
22.	Mostly true	47.	Mostly false
23.	Mostly true	48.	Mostly true
24.	Mostly true	49.	Mostly true
25.	Mostly true	50.	Mostly true

Interpreting Your Score. Your total score on the questionnaire provides you with a rough index of your overall tendencies toward being an office politician. The higher your score, the more political you are in your dealings at work. The lower your score, the less you are inclined toward political maneuvering. A more precise method of interpreting your score is to place it in one of the five categories: Machiavellian, Company Politician, Survivalist, Straight Arrow, or Innocent Lamb.

45 or more—Machiavellian. If you scored 45 or more points on the questionnaire, you have an almost uncontrollable tendency toward doing things for political reasons. A Machiavellian is a power-hungry, power-grabbing individual. People who fall into this category are often perceived by others as being ruthless, devious, and power-crazed. It would not be out of character for a Machiavellian to use electronic surveillance devices to gain advantage over rivals. Machiavellians will try to succeed in their careers at any cost to others.

A Machiavellian is often a sycophant during his or her climb to power. If it appears to be advantageous, a Machiavellian will fawn over a superior whom he or she hates. A person with a strong lust for power will voluntarily discredit the rival of a boss. One such sycophant hired a detective to uncover derogatory information about a new company manager who posed a threat to his boss.

A person falling into the Machiavellian category of our questionnaire lives in constant peril. He or she usually has created a number of enemies on the way to the top. If you are a Machiavellian, there are probably people right now who are plotting revenge. When a Machiavellian begins to slip from power, there are a number of people lurking in the background to give him or her that last definitive shove.

35 to 44—Company Politician. If you scored between 35 and 44 points, you fall into the Company Politician category. A person of this nature might be described as a shrewd maneuverer and politico—someone who typically lands on both feet when deposed from a particular situation. Many successful executives fall into this category.

A Company Politician is much like a Machiavellian, except that he or she has a better developed sense of morality. A Company Politician lusts for power, but it is not an all-consuming preoccupation. Many Company Politicians will do whatever they can to advance their cause except to deliberately defame or injure another individual. You have to be insightful to be a Company Politician. Before utilizing a political strategy such as keeping a blunder file on others, you would have to determine if the organization would tolerate such shenanigans.

25 to 34—Survivalist. A person with a score of 25 to 34 falls into the Survivalist category. If you placed here, you probably practice enough office politics to take advantage of good opportunities. You are not concerned about making any obvious political blunders such as upstaging your boss in an interdepartmental meeting. You laugh at your boss's jokes when salary-review time rolls around.

If your boss invited you to a church breakfast you would not say, "No, thanks, I'm an atheist." As a Survivalist, you probably practice enough office politics to keep out of trouble with your boss and other people of higher rank than yourself.

15 to 24—Straight Arrow. A score of 15 to 24 places you in the Straight Arrow category. Such an individual would not be perceived by others as being an office politician. Nor would he or she be seen as a person intent on committing political suicide. A Straight Arrow fundamentally believes that most people are honest, hard-working, and trustworthy. A Straight Arrow's favorite career advancement strategy is to display job competence. In the process, a Straight Arrow may neglect other important career advancement strategies such as cultivating key people.

Less than 15—Innocent Lamb. Scores of less than 15 place you in the bottom category of political savvy. An Innocent Lamb believes all organizations to be meritocracies, that good people are rewarded for their efforts and thus rise to the top. His or her only political strategy is "By Their Works Ye Shall Know Them." Thus the Lamb keeps his or her eyes focused clearly on the task at hand, hoping that someday the work will be rewarded. Innocent Lambs with an abundance of talent *do* occasionally make it to the top (star athletes and inventors are sometimes Innocent Lambs). Unless you happen to have such extraordinary aptitude, it is difficult to advance in your career by practicing the Innocent Lamb philosophy of life.

Additional Reading

BACHARACH, SAMUEL B., and EDWARD J. LAWLER. *Power and Politics in Organizations.* San Francisco: Jossey-Bass, 1980.

CULBERT, SAMUEL A., and JOHN J. McDONOUGH. *The Invisible War: Pursuing Self-interest at Work.* New York: John Wiley, 1979.

DRORY, AMOS, and URI M. GLUSKINOS. "Machiavellianism and Leadership." *Journal of Applied Psychology,* February 1980, pp. 81–86.

HUERTA, FAYE C., and THOMAS A. LANE. "Participation of Women in Centers of Power." *The Social Science Journal,* April 1981, pp. 71–86.

IZRAELI, D. N. "The Middle Manager and the Tactics of Power Expansion: A Case Study." *Sloan Management Review,* Vol. 16, 1975, pp. 57–70.

KOTTER, JOHN P. *Power in Management: How to Understand, Acquire and Use It.* New York: AMACOM, 1979.

MADISON, DAN L., et. al. "Organizational Politics: An Exploration of Managers' Perceptions." *Human Relations,* No. 2, 1980, pp. 79–100.

MURRAY, VICTOR, and JEFFREY GANDZ. "Games Executives Play: Politics at Work." *Business Horizons,* December 1980, pp. 11–23.

PFEFFER, JEFFREY. "Power and Resource Allocation in Organization," in Barry M. Staw and Gerald R. Salancik, eds., *New Directions in Organizational Behavior* (Chicago: St. Clair Press, 1977), pp. 235–65.

RAUDSEPP, EUGENE, and JOSEPH C. YEAGER. "Power: How Do You Rate on the Forcefulness Scale?" *Success Unlimited,* April 1982, pp. 48–53.

ROBBINS, STEPHEN P. "Reconciling Management Theory with Management Practice." *Business Horizons,* February 1977, pp. 38–47.

SCHEIN, VIRGINIA E. "Individual Power and Political Behavior in Organizations: An Inadequately Explored Reality." *Academy of Management Review,* January 1977, pp. 64–71.

PART FOUR

Understanding the Macro Structure

The final part of this text deals with macro organizational behavior, the study of human behavior at the level of the total organization. As with the previous three parts, there is some overlap among the individual, small-group, and organizational levels. For example, many of the techniques of "organization development" attempt to change organizational systems by changing the attitudes of people individually or in small groups. Chapter 15, Organizational Climate, deals both with the personality of total organizations and two integrated approaches to making organizations better suited to human requirements, Theory Z and quality of work life. Chapter 16, The Dynamics of Bureaucracy, explains the nature of bureaucracy and provides an objective (neither perjorative nor laudatory) analysis of its strengths and limitations.

The subject of Chapter 17, Organization Development, has become a field of study and practice of its own—how to make total organization systems more effective and efficient. Several topics that are sometimes considered to be part of OD have been presented in previous chapters. Among them are the management of stress and burnout and methods of conflict resolution.

CHAPTER 15

Organizational Climate

LEARNING OBJECTIVES

1. To understand the nature and relevance of the concept organizational climate.
2. To identify some of the factors that contribute to the uniqueness of each organization.
3. To describe the nature of a Theory Z organization.
4. To discuss what steps must be taken to create a Type Z organizational climate.

It had been a hectic day for Professor Sanchen Yang. Her day as a job candidate began with breakfast at a hotel nearby the Institute where she was applying for a position on the management science faculty of the College of Business. After breakfast, she met with the department head, Graham Benson. Then on to a meeting with the dean of the college and several other junior and senior faculty members. After attending lunch with two management science faculty members, Sanchen made a presentation to the faculty about some of her recent research on sampling techniques used in quality control.

After a few introductory remarks, Sanchen told the group, "I have brought some transparencies to help you follow my talk and to present some of my data better. As soon as I turn on the light, we'll be all set." To her embarrassment, the light did not go on. Within thirty seconds, two faculty members seated in the audience came forward to help. One said, "Even at a first-rate institution like ours, things go wrong occasionally. But I happen to have a spare overhead bulb in my office. Can you hold the presentation five minutes?" Within ten minutes, the overhead projector was back in operation, and Sanchen proceeded with her presentation.

At the end of the interviewing day, Benson asked Sanchen, "By the way, what do you think of the place?"

The candidate collected her thoughts and then commented, "I definitely like it here. I'll be quite candid. I've visited several other colleges that have more modern facilities and roomier offices. The last place I interviewed had a much larger computer system. But you offer something that's much more important to my sense of well-being. The burned-out bulb incident crystallized my thinking on the matter."

"What do you mean by that?" inquired Benson.

"The way those two professors jumped up to help me. I've noticed that all day long. There's a spirit of cooperation around here that I haven't seen elsewhere. Everybody I spoke to likes the college, and they seem to pull together as a team. It's very important to me to work in that kind of atmosphere."

"I'm glad you discovered that for yourself," said Benson. "It's the kind of thing you have to observe rather than be told directly."

INTRODUCTION

The job candidate in the chapter opening case was intuitively recognizing that organizations have a personality, uniqueness, or climate of their own. Every organization has some properties or characteristics possessed by many other organizations. However, each organization has its own unique constellation of characteristics and properties. *Organizational climate* is the term used to describe this psychological structure of organizations or their subunits. Climate is thus the feel, personality, or character of the firm's internal environment. Organization climate is also a cognition. It is a person's perception of a host of interacting variables that results in a judgment about the climate. Thus, the young professor described in the opening case reached certain conclusions based upon her observation of bits of cooperative behavior.

Since climate is one of the more intangible concepts of organizational behavior, it has been defined in many ways. Two representative definitions of organizational climate are

1. The set of characteristics that describe an organization and that (a) distinguish the organization from other organizations, (b) are relatively enduring over time, and (c) influence the behavior of people in the organization.[1]
2. A relatively enduring quality of an organization's internal environment distinguishing it from other organizations. The climate results from the behavior and policies of members of the organization; it is perceived by members of the organization; it serves as a basis for interpreting the situation; and it acts as a source of pressure for directing activity.[2]

The concept of climate is thus akin to that of human personality, because it refers to a stable uniqueness about a given organization. Also, similar to personality, climate is an abstraction. Its reality lies in how it is perceived by people, yet it does have behavioral consequences. You feel and work better in some organizational climates than in others.

Organizational Climate as an Integrating Concept

Although the concept of organizational climate is not well researched and widely accepted, it has value as an integrating concept in organizational behavior. Gibson, Ivancevich, and Donnelly write that "Organizational climate transcends individual and group dimensions and is experienced across many diverse structural units within the organization with a resulting impact on organizational performance."[3] As summarized in Figure 15–1, climate can be influenced by all the major concepts studied in Parts II, III, and IV of this book. The high job satisfaction that Professor Yang noticed among faculty members contributed to her perception of a favorable organizational climate. An organizational unit where many of the professionals and managers are burned out will have a climate different from an organization in which burnout is at a minimum. A highly political atmosphere also contributes to the organization's climate, and so do macro variables. For example, a highly bureaucratic organization will have a different climate from a System 4 organization. Organizational climate, in turn, influences outputs such as performance and satisfaction. (In previous chapters, mention was made of how organizational climate influences creativity and group decision making.)

An argument can also be advanced that the relationships in Figure 15–1 are reciprocal. Many individual, group, interpersonal, and macro factors influence climate, but climate also influences these factors. For example, creative people have an impact on an organization's climate, and climate can foster or discourage creativity.

[1]Garlie A. Forehand and B. Von Haller Gilmer, "Environmental Variation in Studies of Organizational Behavior," *Psychological Bulletin,* December 1964, p. 363.

[2]R. D. Pritchard and B. W. Karasick, "The Effects of Organizational Climate on Managerial Job Performance and Job Satisfaction," *Organizational Behavior and Human Performance,* September 1973, p. 126.

[3]James L. Gibson, John M. Ivancevich, and James H. Donnelly, Jr., *Organizations: Behavior, Structure, Processes,* 3rd ed. (Plano, Tex.: Business Publications, 1979), p. 526.

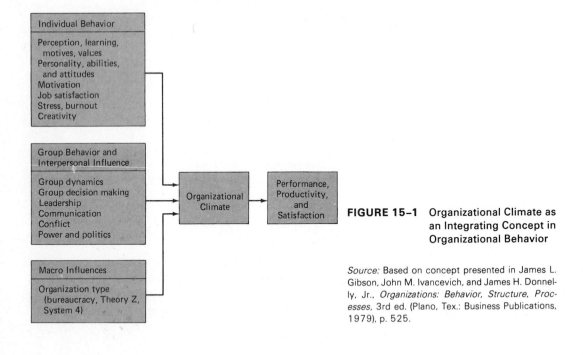

FIGURE 15–1 Organizational Climate as an Integrating Concept in Organizational Behavior

Source: Based on concept presented in James L. Gibson, John M. Ivancevich, and James H. Donnelly, Jr., *Organizations: Behavior, Structure, Processes,* 3rd ed. (Plano, Tex.: Business Publications, 1979), p. 525.

DETERMINANTS OF ORGANIZATIONAL CLIMATE

Although climate refers to the internal environment of the firm, the nature of the climate is determined by a variety of internal and external factors. The relationships shown in Figure 15–1 have already hinted at some of these determinants. In the next section, we look at several societal influences on organizational climate. Here we describe some other important determinants.

Economic conditions. Organizations develop different climates according to their position on the economic cycle. In times of prosperity—when budgets are loose rather than tight—firms tend to be more adventuresome. Risks into new ventures and new programs are taken more readily because more money is available for such purposes. Tight budgets, on the other hand, contribute to an atmosphere of caution and conservatism within an organization. Few managers are willing to suggest new programs of potential merit when mandates from above call for tight control over expenses.

Leadership style. The prevailing leadership style in an organization is a key influence on climate. If most managers use a participative style, for example, the climate would be quite different from one in which an authoritarian style predominated. One corporation has a research and development management team that is perceived by many employees as showing high concern for production and low concern for people. Much of its work is conducted on a project basis. This combination of task-oriented management and project organization produces some interesting interpretations of the organizational climate. During a business recession, one engineer in the firm made these comments:

> What an atmosphere of bad news. Most of us would quit if there were any good jobs around. When we are finished with one project, no one asks us what we would like to do next. We are shunted around like office temporaries. You never know what's coming next. On my last assignment, I had a high-level clerical job with a fancy title. This place is really unprofessional, but there is nothing I can do about it now.

Organizational policies.   Specific policies (such as "Layoffs will be used only as a last resort to cope with a business downturn") can influence organizational climate. The policy just cited will contribute to an internal environment that is supportive and humanistic.

Managerial values.   The values held by executives have a strong influence on organizational climate because values lead to actions and shape decisions. Values lead to perceptions of the organization such as impersonal, paternalistic, formal, informal, hostile, or friendly, as shown in the following brief portrait:

> Company A places a high value on providing for the welfare of people. Employees receive a much higher share of profits than the industry average. Managers are requested to visit any employee hospitalized due to an accident or an injury. Employees or dependents of employees who give birth to children receive flowers. Those who lose their jobs are provided outplacement services to help them find suitable employment elsewhere. The paternalistic values illustrated by these practices have helped to contribute to an organizational climate characterized as "warm," "friendly," and "helpful."

Organizational structure.   The design or structure of an organization influences the perception of its internal environment. A bureaucratic structure has a climate different from one organized according to a System 4 design. Some bureaucracies are perceived as "efficient," "cold," and "impersonal."

Characteristics of the members.   Organizational climate can be heavily influenced by the personal characteristics of its members. For example, organizations with a high proportion of older, less well-educated, and less upwardly mobile employees will have a climate different from an organization with many younger, highly educated, and ambitious employees.

Nature of the business.   An influential determinant of organizational climate is an organization's basic business or mission. A visitor to a meat packing company would perceive a different climate there from that of an insurance company of comparable size. The nature of the business is not an isolated variable; it influences many other organizational characteristics such as policies, characteristics of the people, and leadership style.

Organizational size. A large organization often has a different climate from a small one, even if they produce the same goods or services. It is much easier, for example, to establish a climate for creativity and innovation in a small than a large organization. Great innovations have also stemmed from small self-contained units within large organizations; Bell Laboratories of AT&T is an outstanding example of an innovative unit within a huge organization. In general, it is difficult to motivate employees when they do not perceive the link between their behavior and organizational performance.

Life stage. A firm's position on its life cycle is a subtle influence on climate. Organizations generate a different "feel" in their infancy than in adulthood. Younger organizations tend to be less formal and smaller. Mature organizations tend to be more formal and larger.

Most of the determinants of organizational climate just discussed are interrelated, and some are more pervasive than others. Degree of formal structuring (or organizational "tightness") is one such influential variable. For example, policies will be formulated to maintain tightness, and managers will adopt styles to ensure tightness, such as high task orientation.

SOCIETAL INFLUENCES ON ORGANIZATIONAL CLIMATE

An important premise of organizational behavior is that outside environmental forces influence events within organizations. A number of societal forces help to shape the organizational climate. In the list just presented, economic conditions represent one such force. Here we review briefly an additional number of societal influences on organizational climate: educational levels, diversity of the work force, technology, union contracts, government regulations, and attractiveness of nonwork.[4]

Rising educational levels. As the educational level of future and present employees increases, so do their expectations for satisfying and fulfilling work. As jobs are gradually redesigned to meet these expectations, the internal environment of the firm shows a corresponding shift toward an increased atmosphere of professionalism.

Diversity of the work force. As the work force has shifted toward a higher penetration of women and minorities into professional and managerial jobs, organiza-

---

[4]The items in this list, but not their interpretation, are from Edward E. Lawler III, "Developing a Motivating Work Climate," *Management Review,* July 1977, pp. 25–28, 37–38.

tional climates have also shifted. The internal environment of an organization where one cultural group occupies virtually all the higher-level jobs has a climate much different from that of a more diverse (and less discriminatory) organization. Many people have commented that a heterogeneous workplace is more "fun."

Technological advances.   As technology becomes more advanced, the climate tends to shift toward such perceptions as "modern," "dynamic," and "exciting." On the negative side, advanced technology can also create some negative perceptions such as "sterile," "dehumanizing," and "impersonal." Some perceptions of a manufacturing environment dominated by industrial robots have been even less flattering.

Union contracts.   Among the many provisions of union contracts that influence organizational climate are those dealing with job design and reward systems. A union that encourages job enrichment and merit pay contributes to a much different organizational climate than does a union contract that prohibits these practices. Similarly, a contract that tightens up on safety practices influences climate toward a perception of higher security.

Government regulations.   Regulations imposed on organizations by federal, state, and provincial governments all tend to decrease the organization's options. Each major regulation has a different influence on climate. One example is federal regulations increasing the mandatory retirement age from sixty-five to seventy. A firm with a large number of employees over sixty-five would develop a different climate from a firm with younger employees. Laws about employment discrimination, safety and health, and product liability all have their unique impact on climate.

Attractiveness of nonwork.   As the societal values toward recreational and educational activities become stronger, it may prove more difficult to motivate some employees on the job. As their passion for nonwork increases, they may become less passionate about job performance. Organizations would have to strengthen the potency of their reinforcers or offer more nonwork rewards for good performance. The nonwork rewards could take place during the employee's own time, such as high performers receiving membership in a health spa. Correspondingly, a firm with many leisure-oriented employees would tend to develop an organizational climate different from one with a higher proportion of work-oriented employees.

These societal trends have implications for managers attempting to foster organizational climates that result in high degrees of motivation and creativity. A team of management writers has observed that "This will become increasingly more difficult because they will be faced with a different kind of subordinate. At the same time, however, it will become increasingly more important if adequate levels of organizational performance are to be maintained."[5]

[5]Gibson, Ivancevich, and Donnelly, *Organizations,* p. 527.

DIMENSIONS OF
ORGANIZATIONAL CLIMATE

Research studies of organizational climate attempt to measure the various dimensions or factors of climate by way of questionnaires (see Figure 15–2). The questionnaire items are typically based on hunches about climate formulated during interviews of representative organization members. Fortunately there has been a reasonable degree of overlap among various studies about the contribution of certain dimensions to organizational climate. Key factors appear to arise from study to study, based upon a factor analysis of the intercorrelation among questionnaire items. For instance, the following two questions are both part of the factor (or dimension) called *support:*

> If I have a problem with my work, I know my boss will be there to help me.
> My co-workers tend to be very encouraging.

Please circle the number that indicates how you feel about each of the following statements. Number 1 means the highest agreement, while number 7 means the strongest disagreement. Number 4 means you neither agree nor disagree with the statement. Please answer every question, even if you are not sure about the way you feel on that topic.

1. Managers in my organization insist on high production.

   1   2   3   4   5   6   7

   Agree strongly   Disagree strongly

2. It is difficult to form a close relationship with most managers in my organization.

   1   2   3   4   5   6   7

   Agree strongly   Disagree strongly

3. People in this organization really pull together when the chips are down.

   1   2   3   4   5   6   7

   Agree strongly   Disagree strongly

4. We spend too much time around here shuffling papers.

   1   2   3   4   5   6   7

   Agree strongly   Disagree strongly

5. The days around here seem very long.

   1   2   3   4   5   6   7

   Agree strongly   Disagree strongly

FIGURE 15–2 A Sampling of Questionnaire Items Used to Measure Dimensions of Organizational Climate

An important distinction can be drawn between the determinants and dimensions of organizational climate. Determinants are essentially causes of climate; dimensions are the components (or factors) of climate. Similarly, one's rate of metabolism is a determinant of personality that contributes to the personality dimension called energy (or, conversely, lethargy). Organizational climate has been consistently described by seven dimensions:

1. *Individual autonomy.* The degree to which employees are free to manage themselves; to have considerable decision-making power; to not be continually accountable to higher management.

2. *Position structure.* The degree to which the objectives of, and methods for, the job are established and communicated to the individual by superiors.

3. *Reward orientation.* The degree of reward, profit, or achievement orientation fostered and reflected by managers and individual contributors. An organization that pushes people to produce and pays them for doing so will have a climate characterized by a high reward orientation.

4. *Consideration, warmth, support.* The degree to which needs for emotional support and reassurance are satisfied and nourished by other organization members, managers, and individual contributors alike.[6]

5. *Progressiveness and development.* The degree to which organizational conditions, including management practices, foster employee development and encourage the growth and application of new ideas and methods.

6. *Risk taking.* The degree to which employees perceive that they are free to experiment, innovate, and otherwise take risks without fear of reprisal, ridicule, or other forms of punishment.

7. *Control.* The degree to which control over the behavior of organizational members is formalized. In a highly bureaucratic organization, control systems are well defined. In a low-control organization, most of the controls would be self-controls; employees would monitor their own behavior. This dimension is akin to organization "tightness" versus "looseness."[7]

These seven dimensions account for most of the research findings on specific climate dimensions, but they do not account for all that is known about the topic. Other dimensions alluded to earlier in this chapter, such as paternalism and impersonality, are also meaningful. Even the popular dichotomy between a dynamic and a stagnant firm contributes much to our understanding of climate.

---

[6]The first three dimensions are from John P. Campbell, Marvin D. Dunnette, Edward E. Lawler III, and Karl E. Weick, Jr., *Managerial Behavior, Performance, and Effectiveness* (New York: McGraw-Hill, 1970), pp. 411–12.

[7]The last three dimensions are from Roy L. Payne and Derek S. Pugh, "Organization Structure and Climate," in Marvin D. Dunnette, ed., *Handbook of Organizational and Industrial Psychology* (Chicago: Rand McNally, 1976), pp. 1140–51.

The Impact of Organizational Design on Climate Dimensions

One application of the concept of climate dimensions is to use them to construct profiles that help to describe an organization, just as people can be compared on the basis of their personality profiles. Some preliminary work along these lines has been done by organization theorist Patrick Connor. He has attempted to show how organizations with radically different designs will have different climate profiles (using climate dimensions as comparison points). He contrasts two hypothetical organizations, Alpha and Beta.[8]

Alpha is a closed, stable, and mechanistic sort of enterprise. It is the type of organization that resists change by its very nature. In general, members of mechanistic organizations form close ties to their firm and its values rather than to outside reference groups such as a profession. Beta is more open, adaptive, and organic. An organic organization has the following essential characteristics:

- A close and direct relationship between the expectations of people and organizational goals, such as a hospital providing improved methods of health care.
- Continual redefining of what is expected of people through discussion with the people most intimately involved. As times change, so would job descriptions.
- Rejection of the "it's not my responsibility" response as an excuse for failures. In an effective organization, people are eager to enlarge their contribution.
- The feeling of wanting to contribute to the larger organization without having to always receive specific inducements for accomplishing specific tasks. Under these conditions, people take pride in making a worthwhile contribution.
- The presence of needed information at appropriate places in the organization. When a few key people attempt to monopolize all the information and dispense it in small doses, many inefficiencies occur.
- Emphasis on horizontal as opposed to vertical communication. People consult with each other rather than place demands on each other according to their rank.
- A strong commitment to goals that further the organization rather than to goals that involve simply maintaining what already exists. Similarly, a tendency not to be too inbred—instead, a tendency to look favorably toward outside reference groups.[9]

Design-climate profiles can be drawn for Alpha and Beta, as shown in Figure 15-3. Connor describes the profile differences between the two types of organizations in these terms: "In essence, a closed/stable/mechanistic design tends to produce a climate that is also closed and mechanistic. A design that is open/adaptive/organic, on the other hand, has the potential of fostering a climate that is equally open, innovative, and growing—for the members as well as the organization."[10]

---

[8]Patrick E. Connor, *Organizations: Theory and Design* (Chicago: Science Research Associates, Inc., 1980), pp. 408–12.

[9]John B. Miner, *The Management Process: Theory, Research, and Practice* (New York: Macmillan, 1973), p. 270.

[10]Connor, *Organizations*, p. 412.

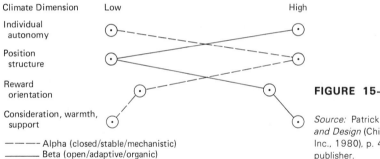

Climate Dimension	Low	High
Individual autonomy		
Position structure		
Reward orientation		
Consideration, warmth, support		

– – – – Alpha (closed/stable/mechanistic)
———— Beta (open/adaptive/organic)

FIGURE 15–3 Two Design-Climate Profiles

Source: Patrick E. Connor, *Organizations: Theory and Design* (Chicago: Science Research Associates, Inc., 1980), p. 412. Reprinted by permission of the publisher.

CHANGING THE ORGANIZATIONAL CLIMATE

Some organizational climates lead to more favorable outcomes for organization members and the organization than do other climates. Being able to change an unfavorable climate to one that is more favorable would therefore be useful. Broadly conceived, the field of organization development is a set of procedures and a philosophy for creating organizational climates that foster individual and organizational effectiveness. A career development program is one OD intervention that might improve organizational climate. To the extent that the employees participating in the program believe that management is interested in their personal welfare, the climate will move toward one of greater consideration, warmth, and support. OD is explored in some detail in the final chapter of this book.

Changing an organizational climate involves much more than the cosmetics of implementing several management development or organization development programs. Since the climate is based on deep-rooted perceptions, substantial changes in management philosophy and values are required. And these changes must stay in place over a long period of time. A change in the organizational climate is simultaneously a change in the organizational culture. The director of policy planning at the Federal Trade Commission has prepared an analysis of the type of value shifts that must take place to move an organization toward the Japanese style of collaborative management (and simultaneously changing the organizational climate):

> Morale exhortation, evangelical pep rallies, and quality circles are no substitute for the identity of interest between labor and management that occurs within an organization existing primarily and directly for its employees. American managers who try various techniques of psychological manipulation may be successful in the short run, as was Elton Mayo in his famous Hawthorne experiments. But manipulation has no staying power. Workers are not stupid, nor are managers omnipotent. Psychological manipulation invariably breaks down over the long term, resulting in more distrust and higher levels of adversarial combat.
>
> There is no art to Japanese management. There is no mystery about how to meet the Japanese challenge. While there is much about the Japanese company that we would find

abhorrent if transplanted here, there is also much that we can learn from the Japanese about the effective organization of production. Put most simply, we can learn that people are motivated to be productive not because they are well manipulated, but because they have a direct stake in future productivity.[11]

The executive making these comments may have a narrow view of motivational programs, but he does make a penetrating analysis of the necessity of a shift in values and philosophy to change the management-labor atmosphere

THE THEORY Z
ORGANIZATIONAL CLIMATE[12]

The Type Z organization is an American adaptation of the Japanese style of management. Also referred to as a hierarchical clan, the Type Z organization has a minimum of hierarchical control and a true fusion of individual and organizational goals. Theory Z, the philosophical base for the Type Z organization, arose to help American business meet the Japanese challenge of high-quality, competitively priced products, including automobiles, business machines, stereo equipment, and semiconductors. An overriding feature of the Type Z organization is that it has a unique climate characterized by a feeling of collaboration between managers and employees. American organizations exhibiting Type Z characteristics include Kodak, Procter & Gamble, Hewlett-Packard, IBM, and Rockwell International.

Essential Features

The basic properties of a Type Z organization from the standpoint of human resource management are shown in Table 15–1. A Type A organization, its opposite, represents a stereotype of the typical American corporation. The Type Z organization closely resembles the Japanese form, depending heavily on stable, long-term employment, allowing for substantial socialization into the organizational culture. The practice of moderate career specialization by rotating employees through different functions facilitates the integration of internal parts. Few people are given substantial promotions until complete socialization has taken place, which leads to natural consensual decision making.

The combination of collective decision making with a commonly shared culture reduces the need for close supervision, coordination, and evaluation. Since employees have a long-term relationship with the firm, superiors develop a holistic concern for their subordinates. Ouchi and Price observe that Type Z organizations have been able

---

[11]Robert B. Reich, "The Profession of Management," *The New Republic,* June 27, 1981, p. 32.

[12]The discussion in this section is based on two sources: William G. Ouchi and Raymond L. Price, "Hierarchies, Clans, and Theory Z: A New Perspective on Organization Development," *Organizational Dynamics,* Autumn 1978, pp. 24–44, and William G. Ouchi, *Theory Z: How American Business Can Meet the Japanese Challenge* (Reading, Mass.: Addison-Wesley, 1981). Avon Book edition also published in 1981.

TABLE 15-1 A Comparison of the Type A and Type Z Organization

Type A (typical American)	Type Z (hierarchical clan)
Short-term employment	Long-term employment
Rapid evaluation and promotion	Slow evaluation and promotion
Highly specialized careers	Moderately specialized careers
Individual decision making	Consensual decision making
Individual responsibility	Collective responsibility
Explicit, formal control	Implicit, informal control (but with explicit measures)
Segmented concern	Holistic concern

Source: William G. Ouchi and Raymond L. Price, "Hierarchies, Clans, and Theory Z: A New Perspective on Organization Development," *Organizational Dynamics,* Autumn 1978, p. 39. Reprinted with permission from American Management Associations. © 1978 by AMACOM, a division of American Management Associations. All rights reserved.

to reduce turnover, perhaps because they avoid highly volatile markets, subcontract out unstable tasks, and provide attractive working conditions.

The extremely high stability of Type Z organizations permits them to develop philosophies and cultures that approximate the features of clans in more traditional settings. A clan is an intimate association of people engaged in economic activity but tied together through a variety of bonds.[13] Because clans exist in industrialized settings, they cannot attain the levels of stability achieved by pure clans. Instead, they supplement the mechanisms of control by using some bureaucratic and some *market* mechanisms. In a market, people establish their value through competitive bidding. In a bureaucracy, employees lack a clear understanding of the value of their services. A Type Z organization, for example, calculates the profitability of each of its divisions, but it does not operate on a strict profit center concept.

The Type Z organization is intergrated into the values of society and is socially responsive. Therefore, the goals of the organization rarely conflict with the goals of individuals. Many Type Z organizations are hesitant to lay off marginal employees; they are willing to pay social costs that they do not have to. Employees at all levels experience high levels of psychological success and emotional well-being. The firms themselves experience growth rates and profitability well above the industry average.

In summary, "The ideal Type Z organization combines a basic cultural commitment to individual values with a highly collective nonindividual pattern of interaction. It simultaneously satisfies old norms of independence and present needs for affiliation. Employment is effectively (although not officially) for a lifetime; and turnover is low. Decision making is consensual, and there is often a self-conscious attempt to preserve the consensual mode."[14]

[13]Ouchi, *Theory Z,* p. 70 (Avon edition).
[14]Ouchi and Price, "Theory Z," p. 41.

STEPS FOR ESTABLISHING
A THEORY Z ORGANIZATION

The objective of moving from a Type A to Type B organization is to achieve commitment of employees to the development of a less selfish, more cooperative approach to work. Based on his consulting experience with major corporations, William Ouchi has identified thirteen steps that the executive in charge can take to achieve this goal.[15] The steps do not necessarily have to be followed in rigid sequence, and results are far from guaranteed. Nevertheless, they do represent a sound program for changing the organizational climate of a firm and, in the process, improving morale and productivity. The book, *Theory Z,* should be consulted for the full description of these steps and the changes in corporate philosophy that must be made simultaneously to produce long-range benefits.

1. *Understand the Type Z organization and your role.* Ask each manager involved to read about Type Z organizations and invite discussion of ideas. The discussion process must reflect the egalitarianism, trust, and openness and the participativeness that are the ultimate objectives of the change.

2. *Audit your company's philosophy.* Corporate philosophy should be examined because it sets forth the company's motivating spirit for all to understand. "Whether directly or indirectly, that philosophy determines how insiders and outsiders alike appraise, trust, and value the company and its products." Another value of auditing the company's philosophy is that it helps to uncover inconsistencies between word and deed.

3. *Define the desired management philosophy and involve the company's leader.* For the Theory Z philosophy to work, the leader of the firm must believe in the participative approach to management. The leader should at least specify the areas of participation that he or she is willing to submit to a fully consensual process. Participative management will tend to increase as the top executive develops a more trusting relationship with subordinates.

4. *Implement the philosophy by creating both structures and incentives.* Establishing a set of formal reporting relationships helps to prop up the "occasional lapses in information and in cooperativeness that befall humans." The incentives and the organizational groupings should be set up to facilitate smooth working relationships.

5. *Develop interpersonal skills.* Sound interpersonal skills are required in a Type Z organization because people collaborate rather than simply follow orders from higher-ranking personnel. One important skill is recognizing patterns of interaction in decision-making and problem-solving groups. Another is learning how to provide leadership so that the group can quickly identify the important issues, resolve conflicts, and arrive at high-quality, creative solutions that have everyone's support.

6. *Test yourself and the system.* It is important to verify whether or not the Z philos-

[15]Ouchi, *Theory Z,* Chapter 5.

ophy is working through such means as an informal questionnaire or asking an outside observer to audit the new management philosophy. The manager can ultimately tell that Theory Z is working if less time is needed to settle disputes and problems of coordination. A Theory Z manager may suffer some displeasures because he or she will be challenged by subordinates and have fewer operating tasks to perform.

7. *Involve the union.* In short, if the principles of egalitarianism and of equity are acceptable, then the principle of employee collective action must also be acceptable. Under Theory Z, the company and employee association or union are placed in a cooperative rather than an adversarial relationship. Also, in a truly democratic organization, employees may have less need for a union.

8. *Stabilize employment.* Some voluntary employment termination by employees can be reduced by providing a work environment characterized by equity, challenge, and participation in decision making. Unemployment due to layoffs based on poor business conditions can also be reduced by a sharing of the misfortune. Shareholders can be asked to accept lesser stock dividends; employees can accept shorter workweeks and smaller paychecks; a hiring freeze can be imposed; and perquisites can be drastically reduced. A stable work force contributes to organization growth and profitability.

9. *Decide on a system for slow evaluation and promotion.* A recommended approach for dealing with the impatience of young people for promotion is to promote them rapidly in comparison with the competition, but promote them slowly in comparison with peers so they can develop a long-range perspective. The better employees will gradually recognize that their slow early growth is an investment in their futures.

10. *Broaden career path development.* Since the North American economy is in a sustained period of slow growth, it is necessary to emphasize growth within jobs and lateral assignments as well as promotions. Research suggests that managers who continue to circulate across jobs within the firm, but without true promotion, retain their enthusiasm and productivity about as well as many "fast trackers." But managers who remain in the same position without vertical or horizontal movement quickly lose enthusiasm and commitment.

11. *Prepare for implementation at the first level.* The Theory Z management philosophy *and practice* should trickle down the organization, perhaps taking up to two years. "A lower level employee or manager cannot participate unless those above provide the invitation to do so. If an organization begins by being rigidly hierarchical, evolutionary change must begin at the top of that hierarchy."[16]

12. *Seek out areas to implement participation.* A good starting point for participation might be to hold discussion groups with employees to solicit suggestions from employees in small groups rather than from a few suggestion boxes.

13. *Permit the development of holistic relationships.* Holism refers to a concern for the employee as a "whole person," such as company involvement in helping employees to achieve a better quality of life. But holistic relationships are a consequence rath-

[16]Ibid., p. 106.

er than a cause of organizational integration. Expressions of solidarity such as wearing company uniforms or singing company songs come about as a result of employees caring about each other and the firm. If the caring is absent, the surface behavior will be meaningless.

PROBLEMS ENCOUNTERED IN A THEORY Z ORGANIZATION

Despite the glowing picture often painted of a management style akin to that in Japan, the Theory Z organization has some weaknesses. Ouchi and Price observe that because it is so homogeneous with respect to values and beliefs, the organization is hostile to deviant views. Many of the rejected views may be important for future adaptation and survival. Employees who are culturally dissimilar, such as women and minorities, tend to be excluded from the mainstream, thus experiencing feelings of alienation and psychological failure.[17]

Other problems are also encountered by managerial and professional employees in Theory Z organizations. Since most of these firms are successful and fully staffed, some employees may feel that their contribution is not vitally needed. One or two backup employees exist for each position. Many higher-level workers in such firms experience feelings of boredom and restlessness.

The compensation and job security in Theory Z firms are often so high that they lead to the "golden handcuffs" phenomenon. Many people would like to leave, but they are figuratively chained to the firm because comparable positions in other firms pay less and offer less job security. Theory Z firms also fall prey to a smugness that may lead to an overly cavalier attitude toward the competition. Some of the competitive problems General Motors has faced with Japanese automakers have been attributed to the false belief GM developed in its own vulnerability.[18] (The GM example is presented here because Ouchi classifies this automaker as a Theory Z company.)

IMPLICATIONS FOR MANAGERIAL PRACTICE

1.   Although the concept of organizational climate is general and vague, it does seem to have some important consequences in terms of productivity and satisfaction. Research has shown, for example, that providing a supportive climate for hard-core unemployed (HCU) job trainees improves their job performance. One study concluded that the work effectiveness and behavior of HCUs depends predominantly on the social climate in which they are placed and work. Increasingly, the supportiveness of this climate seems to be a major method for increasing the HCUs' performance and

[17]Ouchi and Price, "Theory Z," p. 40.
[18]John Z. DeLorean, *On a Clear Day You Can See General Motors* (New York: Avon Books, 1981).

retention.[19] Another study conducted with a similar population of people reached a similar conclusion about the impact of the right organizational climate on job performance:

> The sole factor that differentiated successful from unsuccessful HCU persons at statistically significant levels was the degree of support within the immediate organizational context in which the HCU was placed. The retention for "high support" organizations was 82 percent while that for "low support" organizations was 28 percent.[20]

2. A Theory Z or System 4 organizational climate is often associated with high levels of productivity and satisfaction. It is therefore conceivable that moving an organizational climate in the Theory Z or System 4 direction would lead to gains in productivity and satisfaction. An organization with such an organizational climate would have many of the following characteristics:

- Superiors have complete confidence and trust in all matters involving subordinates.
- Subordinates feel completely free to discuss things about the job with superiors.
- Personnel at all levels feel real responsibility for organization's goals and behave in ways to implement them.
- Considerable communication exists with individuals and groups.
- Superiors know and understand problems of subordinates.
- Very substantial cooperative teamwork is present throughout the organization.
- Employees are involved fully in all decisions related to their work.
- Goals, except in emergencies, are usually established by means of group participation.
- Quite widespread responsibility for review and control exists. Lower units at times impose more rigorous reviews and tighter controls than do top management.
- Controls are used for self-guidance and for coordinated problem solving and guidance rather than punitively.[21]

Summary

- Organizational climate refers to the psychological structure of organizations or their subunits. Climate is thus the feel, personality, or character of the firm's internal environment. Climate can be influenced by most of the major variables studied in organizational behavior, and climate itself influences outputs such as performance and satisfaction.
- The nature of the organizational climate is determined or shaped by a variety of internal and external factors, including economic conditions, leadership style, organiza-

[19]Frank Friedlander and Stuart Greenberg, "Effect of Job Attitudes, Training, and Organization Climate on Performance of the Hard-Core Unemployed," *Journal of Applied Psychology,* August 1971, p. 293.
[20]Ibid.
[21]Rensis Likert, *The Human Organization* (New York: McGraw-Hill, 1967), pp. 13–46.

tional policies, managerial values, organizational structure, characteristics of the members, nature of the business, organizational size, and life stage.

- Societal forces also influence organizational climate. Among these external factors shaping the internal environment are rising educational levels, diversity of the work force; technological advances, union contracts, government regulations, and attractiveness of nonwork.

- Organizational climate has been subdivided into many different dimensions or factors. Seven of these dimensions appear more frequently than others: individual autonomy; position structure; reward orientation; consideration, warmth, and support; progressiveness and development; risk taking; and control.

- Organizations with radically different designs will tend to have different profiles on the basis of their standing on climate dimensions. An example would be the contrast between a closed, stable, and mechanistic organization on the one hand and an open, adaptive, and organic organization on the other. The former type of organization resists change; the latter welcomes constructive change.

- To change an organizational climate in a favorable direction, far-reaching modifications of philosophy and attitudes have to be made. Modifying organizational climate can be considered an activity of organization development, with a particular emphasis on changing the organization culture.

- The Type Z organization is an American adaptation of the Japanese style of management. It has a minimum of hierarchical control and a true fusion of individual and organizational goals. The Type Z organization has a climate characterized by a feeling of collaboration between managers and employees. Its essential characteristics are long-term employment; slow evaluation and promotion; moderately specialized careers; consensual decision making; individual responsibility; implicit, informal control; and holistic concern for the individual. To move an organiztion from Type A (typical American) to Type Z involves such things as changing the management philosophy and stabilizing employment. Although most organizations labeled as Type Z are successful, they are known to experience some problems. Among them are hostility toward deviant views, some tendency (at least in the past) to exclude culturally dissimilar people from the mainstream, underutilization of some people, and a smug attitude toward the competition.

Questions for Discussion

1. Rate the organization most familiar to you as being high or low on each of the seven dimensions of organizational climate discussed in this chapter. Based on the profile you obtain, what conclusions can you reach about that organization's climate?

2. How might a policy of "promotion based mostly on seniority" affect an organization's climate?

3. Using concepts presented in this chapter, describe the organizational climate of a maximum security prison.

4. Describe how profits might influence organizational climate and also how organizational climate might influence profits.
5. What are some of the consequences of working in an organizational climate not suited to your personality?
6. Identify a successful firm that fits into the Type A pattern, and explain why you think that firm is Type A.
7. From your standpoint, do you see any potential sources of frustration in working for a Theory Z organization?
8. From your standpoint, what would be some of the rewards that result from working in a Type Z organization?
9. What would be some of the key elements in an experimental design to evaluate the effectiveness of a Theory Z organization?
10. How well suited is the process of group decision making to the Theory Z organization?

An Organizational Behavior Problem

Evaluating Organizational Climate Through Personnel Policy

An executive of the Eli Lilly Company has summarized what he thinks are some of the fundamental principles that should be followed in managing the personnel policies of the company.* Although these ideas do not exist in company manuals, they reflect many years of management practice.

Fairness. It is important that employees perceive the company as being fair. "It takes a confident individual with much tolerance, consideration, and understanding of people to help an unfortunate employee overcome a problem and develop that employee to a point where he or she will become a satisfied, happy, and contented employee."

Discharges. Department heads are not obliged to keep employees in their department they wish to leave, but only members of the personnel department can discharge an employee.

Outside Conduct. It is none of the company's concern what an employee does outside the company so long as that action does not interfere with the employee's work or with his or her associates in the business.

Decisions by Supervision. Supervisors will make occasional mistakes, but if at all possible, their decisions will be supported by the company. Following such a policy indicates that supervisors must be properly trained in the handling of people, "Otherwise a most unfortunate situation would result."

Know Everyone. Members of the personnel department should get to know as many employees as possible. One way of doing this is to appear before many groups of employees. The personnel specialist should be a friend in court of the employee.

Responsibility. "Whenever anything advantageous to the employees has been put into effect, we have always felt that this information should be given to the employees over the signature of the president, because it furthers the belief in the minds of employees that he is a fine fellow and is interested in their welfare."

*Adapted from Ouchi, *Theory Z*, pp. 218–22.

Questions

1. Based on this information, how would you characterize the organizational climate at Eli Lilly?
2. In what way does this information help to paint the picture that Lilly is a Type Z company?
3. What criticisms would you make of this statement of personnel philosophy?

Additional Reading

BATLIS, NICK C. "The Effect of Organizational Climate on Job Satisfaction, Anxiety, and Propensity to Leave." *The Journal of Psychology,* March 1980, pp. 233–40.

DEAL, TERRENCE E., and ALLAN A. KENNEDY. *Corporate Cultures.* Reading, Mass.: Addison-Wesley, 1982.

HATVANY, NINA and VLADIMIR PUCIK. "An Integrated Management System: Lessons from the Japanese Experience." *The Academy of Management Review,* July 1981, pp. 469–79.

HELLRIEGEL, DON, and JOHN W. SLOCUM, Jr. "Organizational Climate: Measures, Research, and Contingencies." *Academy of Management Journal,* Vol. 17. 1974, pp. 255–80.

MANGRUM, CLAUDE T. "Providing the Right Climate for Productivity." *Supervisory Management,* October 1981, pp. 34–40.

OUCHI, WILLIAM G. "Markets, Bureaucracies, and Clans." *Administrative Science Quarterly,* March 1980, pp. 129–41.

PASCALE, RICHARD T., and ANTHONY G. ATHOS. *The Art of Japanese Management,* New York: Simon & Schuster, 1981.

———, and MARY ANN MAQUIRE. "Comparison of Selected Work Factors in Japan and the United States." *Human Relations,* July 1980, pp. 433–55.

PEARSE, ROBERT F. "Principles of Management—2," in *AMACOM Handbook of Management* (New York: AMACOM, 1983).

SCHNEIDER, BENJAMIN. "Organizational Climates: An Essay." *Personnel Psychology,* Winter 1975, pp. 447–79.

———. "The Service Organization: Climate Is Crucial." *Organizational Dynamics,* Autumn 1980, pp. 52–65.

CHAPTER 16

The Dynamics of Bureaucracy

LEARNING OBJECTIVES

1. To appreciate the fact that bureaucracy is a form of organization design, not a perjorative term.

2. To describe the advantages of bureaucracy and the conditions favoring its use.

3. To understand some of the personality distortions and organizational problems that may occur in a bureaucracy.

4. To know how to make optimum use of the bureaucratic form of organization.

Lucy Minsky considered herself fortunate to find a position as planning manager with the United Way of Belleville County—a position that would undoubtedly provide good experience for development of her career in human services management. An important appeal of the assignment was that the job included helping the United Way develop a more efficient organization design.

After several weeks of orientation, Lucy's immediate superior, Dave Olin, went into more detail about the nature of her first big assignment. Dave spoke with considerable conviction:

"Lucy, as you know, we hired you because of a real need to make the United Way and its affiliated agencies a more efficient, more modern organization. The rest of the staff and I have been convinced for several years that there is too much duplication of function among our twenty participating agencies. The organizations we provide funds to are sometimes in competition with themselves.

"There simply isn't enough money in our budget for so many of the agencies to duplicate the same functions. We have already taken a careful look into some aspects of the problems. For instance, we discovered two years ago that there were too many social workers for the client population we serve. Two small agencies not five miles from each other had a full staff of social workers. We reassigned a few of the workers and put a three-year freeze on new hiring. By these measures we have cut down the social work staff by ten people so that, including salaries, benefits, and miscellaneous charges, we are now saving about $350,000 in annual payroll costs.

"Despite our preliminary inroads into the problem of becoming more efficient, I don't think we have approached the true magnitude of the problem. We could operate a lot more efficiently if we were more centralized. We need to figure out what services we can provide for the agencies under our jurisdiction and what services they can best provide for themselves.

"There is no doubt that we are moving toward centralization. We want your analysis of how we should best go about it, and what functions we should centralize. You're the person to recommend to us what should be done. We are making no commitment at this time that we will buy all your recommenda-

tions, but we will listen carefully to them. Our goal is to become a lean, efficient operation within two years."

"Dave, I have a suggestion," replied Lucy. "Before I sit here drawing up the grand organization plan for the social agencies of Belleville County, let me visit them and find out the thinking of their executives on this matter of centralization. I'll get their opinions and recommendations before I even begin to suggest some tentative changes."

Lucy visited all twenty of the affiliated agencies over a two-month period. She spent about two hours at each agency discussing the issue of centralizing certain aspects of community services. Two and one-half months after the planning project had begun, Lucy scheduled a conference with Dave to give an oral report of her preliminary findings.

"Dave, it looks as if the agency executives are not accepting the inevitable. They are more opposed to centralization than you and I might have guessed. They look upon our plan to streamline operations as simply another tightening of the budget, something they have lived with periodically for a long time. So far they haven't taken seriously a real move toward centralization of services. From their standpoint, our master blooper was laying off social workers and putting the freeze on new hiring. One agency head said the kindest adjective he could muster to describe that action was 'reprehensible.'

"To give you a feel for my findings, I'll review with you the observations made by Gertrude Steingut at the Bayside Settlement House. Her comments typify the reservations that most of the other agencies have about the centralization of services. She notes that a settlement house is an old-fashioned, yet much needed, institution. Most people fail to understand the vital role a settlement house plays in keeping troubled families glued together. Gertrude also thinks that the activities of a settlement house prevent hundreds of cases of drug addiction. Instead of drugs, many young people are turned on to sports and other health-sustaining activities.

"Adults drop in to speak to the settlement house staff about a wide range of problems. Bayside has been nested in a dilapidated building for thirty years. Gertrude points out that if they redecorated or modernized, they would probably lose most of their clientele.

"She may be irrational, but Gertrude believes that further centralization will lead to a modernization and upgrading of her settlement house that could be self-defeating. People in her neighborhood have come to trust the present broken-down establishment to some extent because it resembles home to them. Steingut says that Bayside policies are tied to the specific problems of its neighborhood. Centralizing policy would result in a list of policies and procedures that would not make sense for them and that would therefore be violated.

"She gave an example of a settlement house in Philadelphia that imposed a new policy of charging clients three dollars for spending the night on the premises. In the month following the imposition of this policy, the number of people accepting hostel for the night decreased from sixty to three. One of the people who was refused a night's refuge because she didn't have the three dollars returned home to be murdered by her husband that night. She had sought shelter because of a threat of violence by her husband.

"Dave, do you see the point I'm making?" asked Lucy. "We have to move cautiously in our attempts both to study the problem of centralization and to do something about it. Change is not going to be easy, especially because most of the agency executives think centralization will ruin them.*

THE NATURE OF BUREAUCRACY

In popular language, bureaucracy refers to a cumbersome organization rampant with petty rules and regulations, rigid application of these rules, slowness of operation, duplication of effort, and frustrated, ineffective functionaries (officials who carry out orders). The United Way case just presented, however, illustrates the meaning of bureaucracy as understood by an organization theorist. Bureaucracy is an authority

*Adapted from "Centralization Will Ruin Us," in Andrew J. DuBrin, ed., *Casebook of Organizational Behavior* (Elmsford, N.Y.: Pergamon, 1977), pp. 266–71.

structure designed for use with large-scale organizations and characterized by centralization of authority. Dave Olin was attempting to move the United Way affiliated agencies toward bureaucracy. A bureaucratic organization design has applicability to the public, private, and third (not-for-profit, nongovernmental agencies) sectors. Max Weber, the organizational sociologist, explained: "It does not matter for the character of bureaucracy whether its authority is called private or public. Bureaucracy as such is a precious instrument which can put itself at the disposal of quite varied—purely political as well as purely economic, or any sort of—interests in domination."[1]

Rationality and efficiency are the major attributes of the ideal form of bureaucracy. It organizes the knowledge and wisdom of large numbers of people and focuses them upon the legitimate problems to be solved. This knowledge and wisdom is controlled through the hierarchy of offices or bureaus (departments). The obedience of officials (bureaucrats) is to the impersonal order or directive, not to the individual giving the orders or directives. Weber believed strongly that bureaucratic organization results in equality of treatment, for every employee is subject to organizational policy.

Bureaucracy and power are interrelated concepts. Because bureaucracy is based on specialized knowledge and is controlled by impersonal rules of governance, the ideal type of bureaucracy is seen as a rational system of power. Being subject to the rational system of power, the bureaucrat is pressured toward efficiency. The system sustains disciplined and reliable behavior in a stable framework.[2] In Weber's ideal bureaucracy, disorder, unruliness, and personal alliances are minimized. He perceived the bureaucratic corporation as rivaled "only by the state bureaucracy in promoting rational efficiency, continuity of operation, speed, precision, and calculation of results."[3] Later in this chapter, we examine some of the ways in which many bureaucracies have departed from the ideal form.

Characteristics of a Bureaucracy

A convenient way of explaining the nature of the bureaucratic organization design is to list its identifying characteristics, several of which have already been presented in narrative form.[4]

A division of labor based on functional specialization. The bureaucratic form of organization requires task specialization. Toward this end, organizations have departments such as engineering, purchasing, manufacturing, surgery, data processing, billing, and human resource management. Employees in these departments, or other

[1]H. H. Gerth and C. Wright Mills, trans. and eds., *From Max Weber* (New York: Oxford University Press, 1946), p. 197.

[2]Our general description of bureaucracy is based on William M. Dugger, "Corporate Bureaucracy: The Incidence of the Bureaucratic Process," *Journal of Economic Issues,* June 1980, pp. 400–401.

[3]Gerth and Mills, *From Max Weber,* p. 49.

[4]Most of the information that follows is from Max Weber, *Essays in Sociology,* trans. H. H. Gerth and C. Wright Mills (Oxford: Oxford University Press, 1946). Reprinted in Joseph A. Litterer, *Organizations: Structure and Behavior* (New York: John Wiley, 1969), p. 34.

units, possess specialized information and skills that contribute to the overall effectiveness of the firm.

A well-defined hierarchy of authority.   Each lower organizational unit is controlled and supervised by a higher one. The person granted the most formal authority sits on the top of the hierarchy (chief executive officer, chairman of the board, president). As one moves down the organization chart, people at each level have less power than do those people at the levels above them. The reader is cautioned that people sometimes confuse bureaucracy with organizational hierarchy and consider them to be synonymous. Yet not all hierarchies are bureaucratic. The rational nature of a hierarchy determines whether or not it constitutes a bureaucracy. Bureaucracies were originally designed to replace feudal hierarchies.[5] The traditional authority of the feudal lord was replaced by a form of authority related to rational rules. Instead of being loyal to a feudal lord, the bureaucrat became loyal to a set of impersonal orders.

A system of rules covering the rights and duties of employees.   In a truly bureaucratic organization, each employee has a precise job description, and policy and procedure manuals are kept current and available. Employees therefore know what they can expect from the organization. For example, in a bureaucratic organization, each employee knows how much length of service is required to be eligible for how much annual vacation.

A system of procedures for dealing with work situations.   In a state or provincial motor vehicle office, each license-plate clerk knows exactly what to do when a citizen wishes to register a motor vehicle. No deviation from motor vehicle bureau policy is encouraged or allowed.

Impersonality of interpersonal relationships.   One of the original justifications for the bureaucratic form of organization is that it is supposed to overcome the favoritism found in other forms of organization. People are judged on how well they conform to organizational rules, regulations, and goals. Methods of interpersonal influence such as ingratiating oneself to a superior should not facilitate one's receiving favorable treatment in a pure form of bureaucracy. In practice, political maneuvering is no less pronounced in bureaucracies than in other forms of organization.

Promotion and selection based on technical competence.   To make this characteristic of a bureaucracy true to life, technical competence must also include managerial or administrative competence. As is true for the preceding characteristic, the individual's ability to ingratiate himself or herself with the boss should not influence the boss's evaluation of the individual. One of the many justifications for using objective tests to screen applicants for civil service jobs is that such devices decrease the chances of favoritism in selection.

---

[5]George F. Wieland and Robert A. Ullrich, *Organizations: Behavior, Design, and Change* (Homewood, Ill.: Richard D. Irwin, 1976), p. 9.

Rational decision making in every aspect of managing the enterprise. The most general way of characterizing the ideal form of bureaucracy proposed by Weber is in terms of *rationality:* the use of knowledge to relate various means to organizational ends in the best possible way. Rules, based on technical knowledge, are established with the expectation that they will regulate the organization's structure and processes so as to attain maximum efficiency.[6] One of the satisfactions of working for such a firm as Aetna Insurance Company is that most personnel and business decisions appear to be based on reason rather than on emotional or political factors.

ADVANTAGES OF A BUREAUCRACY

Bureaucracy has survived and thrived because its advantages outweigh its disadvantages. The advantages of a bureaucracy stem logically from the ideal characteristics just listed. At its best, a bureaucracy is a smooth-running organization, capable of innovation, in which all members are treated equitably. In this section we review the functional (positive contribution to the system) aspects of bureaucracy. The following two sections deal with the dysfunctional (negative contribution to the system) aspects of bureaucracy.

Advancement of Democratic Ideals

Weber's bureaucratic model was developed as a reaction against the "personal subjugation, neopotism, cruelty, emotional vicissitudes, and capricious judgment which passed for managerial practices in the early days of the industrial revolution."[7] As intended, the bureaucratic form of organization has had a significant democratizing effect in advancing certain minority interests and in implementing certain fundamental democratic principles. The principles include representation, democratic decision making, and equality. A political scientist has concluded that the federal bureaucracy, for example, is significantly more representative of the U.S. population than is Congress. Also, Congress is committed to democratic decision making (much like the Theory Z organization) characterized by consultation, negotiation, and accommodation.[8] The slowness in decision making characteristic of a bureaucracy is the inevitable trade-off incurred in pursuit of the democratic ideal.

High Levels of Accomplishment

Bureaucracy has contributed to the high levels of affluence and development in modern life. The coordinated efforts of people in complex organizations accomplish results

---

[6]Ibid., p. 8.

[7]Michael J. Wriston, "In Defense of Bureaucracy," *Public Administration Review,* March–April 1980, p. 180.

[8]Ibid.

that individuals working independently could never hope to achieve. Complex tasks can only be accomplished by complex organizations, most of which follow the bureaucratic model. As Max Weber reasoned,

> However people may complain about the evils of bureaucracy it would be sheer illusion to think for a moment that continuous administrative work can be carried out in any field except by means of officials working in offices. The whole pattern of everyday life is cut to fit this framework.[9]

Bureaucracy is almost inescapable for any society concerned with productivity, control, and efficiency. Many bureaucratic principles, such as breaking complicated problems down into smaller and more manageable tasks, are virtually indispensable. As you will see later, the real issue is not how to abolish bureaucracy but, rather, how to optimize its potential contribution.

Machinelike Efficiency

Underlying the high level of accomplishment possible in a bureaucracy is its potential for efficient operation. Weber believed that the fully developed bureaucratic mechanism compares with other organizations as does the machine with nonmechanical modes of production. A strictly bureaucratic administration is capable of precision, speed, unambiguity, continuity, discretion, and unity.[10]

IBM represents a contemporary example of what Weber envisioned when he spoke of a highly efficient organization. A purchasing agent in one company had this comment to make about IBM's penchant for thoroughness: "When we don't know where something is in our company, we call our IBM representatives. The people from IBM seem to know more about our company than we do."[11]

Personally Given Orders Become Unnecessary

A manager in a bureaucracy can point to the rulebook as the source of authority. Thus, "Any employee who fails to punch the time-recording device upon entering or leaving the office will be subject to a one-day suspension without pay." The manager can therefore not be accused of discriminating against an employee personally, nor can an employee legitimately feel that he or she was treated unjustly. Because so many rules and policies exist for controlling the behavior of employees, the manager needs to spend less time negotiating with employees than he or she might in a nonbureaucratic firm.

---

[9]J. Freund, *The Sociology of Max Weber* (New York: Pantheon Books, 1968), p. 238.

[10]Weber, *Essays in Sociology.*

[11]Andrew J. DuBrin, *Human Relations: A Job-Oriented Approach,* 2nd ed. (Reston, Va.: Reston, 1981), p. 320.

Less Need for Repetition of Orders

Since rules, regulations, and policies governing a wide range of behavior are written, managers have less need to repeat orders. A rule can be brought to the attention of an employee once. Ideally, from that point on, the employee will refer back to the rule when the same issue rises again. For example, "Any check issued for over $3,000 requires two authorized signatures."

Remote Control of People

Top management can control people from a distance when those individuals are governed by a rational set of rules and regulations. When nurses and other medical personnel are given a thorough grounding on drug security, including rules in writing, frequent on-the-spot checks should not be necessary. At the other extreme, when management has not established a clear set of rules, there is need for frequent visitation to remote areas of the organization (such as many visits by hospital officials to the wards where the drugs are stored). An effective set of rules allows people to be managed properly without constant supervision.

Legitimization of Punishment

In some instances, reprimands or punishments are necessary in a complex organization, particularly in cases of extreme rule violation such as lying, stealing, willful misallocation of resources, and the violation of health and safety codes. Since most people resent punishment, they tend to question its legitimacy. A company policy may state that "Any employee who accepts a gift from a vendor whose value exceeds $25 will be subject to reprimand." A person who accepts a pair of theater tickets from a vendor cannot cry "unjust punishment" when a formal reprimand is entered into his or her personnel file. On the basis of organizational policy, this reprimand is legitimate and thus not arbitrary.

Equitable Division of Resources

In a bureaucracy, the job that each manager and individual contributor is supposed to perform is well defined. A natural tendency exists for managers to request ample resources to carry out their missions. Most managers, if given a choice, would prefer that another staff member be added to the department. A bureaucracy usually prevents employees from overallocating resources for their own purposes. High-ranking officials try to divide up resources in an equitable fashion. Unfortunately, this advantage of a bureaucracy is sometimes subverted through the practice of empire building—adding human resources to an organizational unit more to acquire power than to contribute to the accomplishment of organizational goals.

PERSONALITY DISTORTIONS
CREATED BY A BUREAUCRACY

Despite the validity of these claims about bureaucracy at its best, bureaucracy has been accused of many evils. At the micro level, the bureaucratic form of organization is said to create distortions in individual behavior, almost to the point of a personality transformation. "Bureaucrats" are said to think and act the way they do because the organization in which they work forces them into that role. Occupying the role of a functionary gradually alters one's personality structure. A counterargument of some merit is that some personality types gravitate toward large, complex organizations because they find the organization-person match is to their liking. Here we review four behavioral or personality distortions sometimes found in a bureaucracy: rigidity of personality, modification of the conscience, bureaupathic behavior, and bureautic behavior.

Rigidity in Behavior

An unfortunate consequence of literal compliance with organizational rules and regulations is that the bureaucrat becomes rigid in his or her dealings with people and interpretations of policy and procedures. An everyday example of such rigidity took place in a state agency. An employee traveling for the state was asked to attend an after-hours meeting. Acting in a humanitarian manner, the agency head treated the employees to a buffet supper at her expense. One of the employees at the meeting suggested that he subtract the dinner from his per diem expense allowance since the buffet made it unnecessary for him to purchase dinner. The agency head said, "By no means. You either claim the full per diem or receive nothing. If you receive reimbursement for breakfast and lunch, you must accept the dinner allotment."

Merton offers an explanation for the source of some of the rigid behavior found among members of a bureaucratic organization. Clients served by the bureaucrat soon become disenchanted because the impersonal treatment offered by the bureaucracy neglects individual concerns. Faced with this dissatisfaction, the bureaucrat relies increasingly on rules, routines, and impersonality as defense mechanisms. Rules and procedures become internalized and followed in an inflexible manner, especially when the ends of the organization to which the rules are means are not considered relevant. The rigid behavior that results is ineffective in dealing with individual clients and changing circumstances.[12]

Modification of the Conscience

Ralph P. Hummel contends that the impact of bureaucracy on the human personality is so substantial that it strips one's conscience. Instead of adhering to the long-stand-

---

[12]Robert K. Merton, "Bureaucratic Structure and Personality," *Social Forces,* Vol. 18, 1940, cited in Wieland and Ullrich, *Organizations,* p. 10. The quotation is from Wieland and Ullrich.

ing values and beliefs that make up the conscience, the bureaucracy superimposes a new set of values and beliefs.[13] After being enmeshed in the bureaucratic system, the individual becomes pliable to direction from outside and above. In practice, such conscience alteration might mean that as a member of a bureaucracy, you become willing to handle people in a way that you would not have in your prebureaucratic days. For example, after being part of the system for a while, you might guiltlessly tell a job applicant that he or she is denied employment because of the lack of a valid driver's license. Hummel's analysis is based upon a psychoanalytic interpretation of personality. It may have some merit in explaining why some officials appear so cold and impersonal in disallowing exceptions to rules, yet Hummel's thinking appears speculative.

Bureaupathic Behavior

Another adverse personality consequence of working in a highly formalized organization is bureaupathic behavior. It is displayed by people who, because of emotional insecurity, feel a strong need to control subordinates or clients. The need to control leads to an increasing number of rules and a decreased tolerance for deviation from them. Bureaupathic behavior becomes more pronounced when managers have administrative responsibility over specialists whose work they do not fully understand. Simultaneously, the performance of these specialists directly influences the performance of the manager, intensifying the problem of insecurity. The bureaupathic personality responds to this insecurity by issuing more rules, regulations, and procedures, which may not improve the functioning of the organization but help the manager feel more in control.

As the superior exerts more and more control, conflict between superior and subordinate increases. An unfortunate degree of modeling may also take place. As one individual is "squeezed from above," he or she becomes more formalized in dealings with his or her own subordinates. Literally, attempts at formalizing the organization reach pathological proportions.[14]

Bureautic Behavior

While bureaupathic behavior leads to more rules and regulations, bureautic behavior is an antagonism to rules and regulations. In some cases, bureautic behavior is a backlash to bureaupathic behavior: "For whatever reasons, the bureautic individual is personally affronted by rules and procedures and acts accordingly. He or she usually acquires a reputation as a malcontent."[15] Representative bureautic behavior includes

---

[13]Ralph P. Hummel, *The Bureaucratic Experience* (New York: St. Martin's, 1977), p. 135.

[14]Thomas V. Bonoma and Gerald Zaltman, *Psychology for Management* (Boston: Kent, 1981), p. 283. The original reference is Victor Thompson, "Bureaucracy and Innovation," *Administrative Science Quarterly,* June 1965, pp. 1–20.

[15]Ibid.

refusing to use time-recording devices, disregarding inventory control forms, and parking in places reserved for people of higher rank or physically handicapped employees.

According to Bonoma and Zaltman, participative management is a useful antidote to bureautic behavior. If workers participate in the formulation of a rule or regulation, they will generally feel positive about compliance. Conversely, the less participative and consultative, the more negative attitudes will be generated when the rule is imposed.[16] Resistance to the rules will lead predictably to more rules to counteract the resistance, starting a cycle of resistance and counterresistance.

ORGANIZATIONAL PROBLEMS CREATED BY A BUREAUCRACY

Several of the problems created by a highly formalized organizational system have already been mentioned in this chapter and in Chapter 7, about stress and burnout. In addition, so many derogatory comments about bureaucracy abound that most readers are familiar with many of these dysfunctions. Here we summarize most of the major criticisms made of bureaucracy, all of which stem from a misapplication of its ideal characteristics.

Inversion of Means and Ends

Rigid adherence to rules, regulations, and policies sometimes results in a situation whereby adherence becomes more important than attaining organizational goals. Thus the means become more important than the ends. A retail store manager might spend so much time enforcing a dress code for employees that she neglects the merchandising function. The original intention of the dress code was to create an ambience in the store that would increase sales. John Knowles, an open critic of American medicine, provides another example of the inversion of means and ends: "In the teaching hospital, it has become set that the patient exists for the teaching programs, and not that the hospital exists for the patient."[17]

High Frustration and Low Job Satisfaction

Many employees find working for a bureaucracy to be frustrating and dissatisfying. Among the sources of frustration and dissatisfaction people point to are the "red tape," loss of individuality, and inability to make an impact on organizational performance. Research has been conducted about the sources of dissatisfaction often found

[16]Ibid.

[17]Quoted in David R. Hampton, Charles E. Summer, and Ross A. Webber, *Organizational Behavior and the Practice of Management* (Glenview, Ill.: Scott, Foresman and Company, 1973), p. 530.

in a bureaucracy. The subjects were seventy-eight staff employees drawn from six large manufacturing organizations in the Midwest. They represented the functions of accounting, personnel, engineering, architecture, and market research. Among the information collected were measures of the style of organization (bureaucratic, collaborative, coordinative) and job satisfaction. A major finding was that job satisfaction decreased as the bureaucratic properties of the organization increased. The authors concluded, "This can be explained by the lack of individual responsibility and control characterizing bureaucratic structures."[18]

Insensitivity to Individual Problems

As noted in our discussion of the bureaupathic personality, dissatisfaction with bureaucracy sometimes stems from its inflexibility in handling exceptions to the rule. Despite the pleas of the frustrated and perplexed client for individual consideration, the bureaucrat usually adheres to regulations. A man working for a large company requested that he receive his paycheck three days early to make a down payment on an exceptionally good buy on a used car. The company refused despite his persistence in receiving a favorable ruling on the issue. By the time the incident was over, the employee had impaired his relationship with his boss to such an extent that the employee requested and received a transfer to another department.

Avoiding Responsibility

A bureaucracy is designed to pinpoint responsibility, yet in practice many people use bureaucratic rules to avoid responsibility.[19] Faced with decisions they prefer not to make, the responsibility-avoiding functionaries will say, "That's not my job" or "That decision lies outside my sphere of influence." Closely related to avoiding responsibility is the shunning of innovation so frequently found in a bureaucracy. Rather than risk trying a new procedure, the bureaucratic (or bureaupathic) superior will say, "What you are suggesting violates tradition. Around here we don't do things that way."

Delay of Decision

Bureaucracies move painfully slowly on complex decisions. The delay comes about because a number of people have to concur before a final decision is made about issues of importance. (A Theory Z organization by its nature exhibits the same types of delays.) In one company, a manager wanted authorization to subscribe to a trade newsletter that cost $25 per year. After four weeks of memos and countermemos, the final decision was, "No, there are four months left on your present subscription." About fifteen

---

[18]Nicholas Dimarco and Steven Norton, "Life Style, Organization Structure, Congruity, and Job Satisfaction," *Personnel Psychology,* Winter 1974, pp. 581–91.

[19]This and the following disadvantage are described in Herbert G. Hicks and C. Ray Gullett, *The Management of Organizations,* 3rd ed. (New York: McGraw-Hill, 1976), pp. 380–86.

people were involved in making the decision. At one point a long-distance telephone call was made across the country about the newsletter subscription.[20]

The Peter Principle

About twenty years ago, a partly satirical explanation was advanced as to why so many incompetent people are found in hierarchies—particularly those of bureaucratic design. The now-famous Peter principle states, "In a hierarchy, every employee tends to rise to his (or her) level of incompetence."[21] In other words, many people get promoted once too often and because of it suffer deficiencies in job performance. A frequent example of the Peter principle is the promotion of competent technical or sales personnel into administrative positions for which they are ill suited by temperament. Despite the allure of the Peter principle as an explanation for so many bureaucratic ills, many well-managed complex organizations use advanced techniques of personnel selection that minimize promoting people into positions for which they are unqualified.

Isolation from Outside Evaluation and Feedback

Wriston writes that a particular weakness of a bureaucracy is its relative isolation from outside evaluation or feedback, an isolation that he attributes to the bureaucracy's monopolistic nature. According to this logic, bureaucratic monopolies are not only relatively unconcerned with profit, but they often function without a ready profit measure. Since feedback is considered vital to keeping all systems functioning properly, the lack of feedback represents a serious weakness in bureaucratic structure.[22]

Weakness in Goal Setting

Governmental bureaucracies are frequently evasive about their goals because of political factors. Power struggles are typical in government. The result is often a "maelstrom of pushing and pulling for politicians and bureaucrats alike. Under these conditions there may seem to be little, if any, personal advantage to be gained from clarifying program or policy goals."[23] Disagreements among interest groups might only be exacerbated by clarification of program goals. Although this goal-setting problem may exist at the highest levels, governmental agencies tend to have more well-developed programs of management by objectives than private organizations. One reason is that it is difficult to receive funding without a statement of objectives.

[20]Case example is presented in J. D. Donavid (pen name), "The Bureaucracy Lives," *Dun's Review,* April 1972, pp. 93–96.
[21]Laurence J. Peter and Raymond Hull, *The Peter Principle* (New York: William Morrow, 1969), p. 26.
[22]This and the following problem are from Wriston, "In Defense of Bureaucracy," p. 181.
[23]Ibid.

Inbreeding

Bureaucracies have also been criticized for perpetuating themselves by generating new sets of officials that think and behave in ways quite similar to their predecessors. Several perjorative terms have been offered for this phenomenon, including "homosexual reproduction" and "the cloning of male bureaucrats." When inbreeding, in fact, takes place, the consequence is a restriction of opportunity. People whose social origins differ significantly from those of the existing bureaucratic elite do not have an equal opportunity to rise to levels of authority.[24]

Although this criticism has been voiced in recent years, it is worth mentioning that federal, state, and provincial bureaucracies have served as pacesetters to society in providing equal employment opportunity.

Organizational Arteriosclerosis

As a consequence of several of the problems just noted, there is a tendency for many organizations to become old and rigid and to substitute a concern with means for a concern with ends. All systems tend to diversify and develop self-protecting behaviors to ensure their own survival. It is typical for even committed people to become preoccupied with their perks, power, and remuneration. As an organization's original leaders grow older, this creates a more conservative and administratively top-heavy organization. It is not unusual to find entire new agencies or departments established to accomplish program objectives that existing units have become too calcified to accomplish.[25]

OPTIMIZING THE BUREAUCRATIC ORGANIZATION DESIGN

Although bureaucracies often create problems for members and clients, it is illogical to suggest that the bureaucratic form of organization design does not serve a useful place in society. A more promising approach is to carry out selected strategies that collectively optimize the use of bureaucracy. Above all, bureaucracy should be used for its intended purpose. In addition, constructive use can be made of flexible structures, selection methods, organizational feedback, and "sunset legislation" for governmental agencies.

Use Bureaucracy for Recurring Problems

Contemporary organization theory suggests that bureaucracy is the best structure for organizations facing a stable, predictable, relatively homogeneous environment, such

[24]Dugger, "Corporate Bureaucracy," p. 403.
[25]Wriston, "In Defense of Bureaucracy," p. 403.

as the processing of thousands of insurance claims or the manufacture of beer cans. Bureaucracy is noted for its efficiency in its handling of common, recurring problems. "There is no need to reinvent the wheel each time a problem recurs. Rather, the job of the manager is simply to apply an appropriate, carefully thought-out, logical policy or rule, and the problem is solved."[26] The proper people are consulted (deferred to) when decisions are made. Because the environment is relatively stable, little need exists for quick decisions.

Use Flexible Organizational Subunits

Most bureaucracies are less rigid with respect to organization structure than their critics believe. Temporary task forces or projects are typically embedded within the larger bureaucracy to deal with problems that are not large-scale or repetitive in nature. Alan C. Filley and Robert J. House explain how research-based knowledge can be applied to design a more flexible organization structure. The appropriate form of organizational structure depends on the production technology and external environment. For example, when the environment and technology are stable and predictable, the traditional hierarchy appears to work best.[27] In contrast, when the bureaucracy is facing a dynamic situation with an unpredictable environment, a loose, nonhierarchical organization structure appears more appropriate. Most new products within a bureaucratic manufacturing organization are launched using a project (nonhierarchical) structure. Project and temporary task forces thus give the bureaucracy the flexibility of structure it requires to adapt. (See, also, parallel structures, in the next chapter.)

Valid Methods of Selection and Promotion

Several of the problems of a bureaucracy can be overcome by using valid methods of selecting and promoting people. The Peter principle, for instance, is not nearly so inevitable in organizations where people are carefully screened before being promoted. If it appears that an individual is unsuited to administrative work (because of his or her performance on temporary assignments or on the administrative portions of his or her current responsibilities), that person should not be promoted in the organization. Modern methods of personnel selection, such as the assessment center, can also improve the quality of selection.

The problems of bureaupathic and bureautic behavior can also be dealt with to prevent these people from being promoted into key positions within the bureaucracy. If managers (who themselves do not exhibit these behavior distortions) detect these characteristics early in an individual's career, that person can be appropriately counseled. Without improvement, that person can be declared ineligible for promotion.

[26]B. J. Hodge and William P. Anthony, *Organization Theory: An Environmental Approach* (Boston: Allyn & Bacon, 1979), p. 435.

[27]Alan C. Filley and Robert J. House, "Management and the Future," *Business Horizons,* August 1972, p. 14.

Organizational Feedback

Building feedback systems into bureaucracies can overcome the problems caused by insufficient feedback. The more open a bureaucracy, the easier it is to construct such systems. However, a good feedback system contributes to openness. The purpose of the feedback system is to provide a bureaucracy and its bureaucrats with specific and useful information on their performance. In the process, it provides an avenue, a direction, and a motivation for change. Outside advisory boards and consumer panels are two such feedback mechanisms.[28]

Sunset Legislation

In recent years, governmental bureaucracies have been subject to sunset legislation in selected states. "Sunset" means that when an agency's term expires it is not automatically renewed. Instead, the agency must defend its value to the public, and the legislature votes on whether or not to grant the agency another term of existence. Before voting, an arm of the state legislature, or some other outside group, evaluates the agency.[29] Professional licensing boards (such as architecture, optometry, and psychology) are among the state agencies that have been subject to sunset laws in recent years. An approach to coping with a bureaucracy from the individual's standpoint is described in the box on pages 439 to 440.

THE FUTURE OF BUREAUCRACY

In the mid-1960s, several influential social psychologists predicted the demise of bureaucracy, regarding it as an inappropriate form of organization for the future of modern society. Some of these predictions have been withdrawn by the predictors and scoffed at by their critics.[30] Nevertheless, the era of a strictly hierarchical bureaucracy seems to be over. Almost all bureaucracies combine some features of the adhocracy (special-purpose temporary organizations) within the classical bureaucratic structure.

Organization development authority W. Warner Burke predicts that bureaucracy as a form of organization will persist during the 1980s. The dominant reason is the search for cost savings through centralization. Typically, centralization leads to bigger bureaucracy. Under standardization, more people and functions must conform to the same rules and policies. Sometimes this practice frustrates managers. One AT&T executive describes it this way: "Managing is not as much fun as it used to be. Every-

---

[28]Wriston, "In Defense of Bureaucracy," p. 182.

[29]Ibid.

[30]Joe Kelly, *Organizational Behavior: Its Data, First Principles, and Applications,* 3rd ed. (Homewood, Ill.: Richard D. Irwin, 1980), p. 129. The classic prediction of the demise of bureaucracy is Warren G. Bennis, "A Funny Thing Happened on the Way to the Future," *American Psychologist,* Vol. 25, 1970, pp. 595–608.

THE GAMESMAN COPES WITH BUREAUCRACY

What kinds of people choose to work in a corporate bureaucracy, and what does it do to them? Psychoanalyst and corporate investigator Michael Maccoby has given some indication in *The Gamesman*. He emphasizes the psychological impact of the corporate institution: "Corporations like BDC and RI (fictitious names for real firms) organize more human energy of higher intellectual quality than any other institutions in America. Each year, they hire and eventually shape the character of a large percentage of the most talented college graduates, reinforcing certain human potentials and not others."

The corporate bureaucracy not only selects and then reinforces certain character traits, but also creates them, even in individuals outside the corporate world. Maccoby found that the basic orientation of the bureaucratic character is toward a career, that is, toward rising above the occupational status of one's cohorts. Careerism, reflected in the bureaucrat's desire that his home be "a springboard for success" and through his desire for successful children, has penetrated very deeply into the American character. The bureaucrat's expectations for his family are turning that fundamental institution into a new kind of "satellite industry" to supply the human support needed in the struggle for bureaucratic success.

In the psyche of the careerist, the main desire is for a rise in status, and the main emotion is fear. In careful psychological probings of individual corporate bureaucrats, Maccoby found that a generalized feeling of fear is a common character trait of managers. The reason is obvious: "He is afraid that external events beyond his control or his inability to control himself will damage or destroy his career."

To be successful, to rise to the highest levels of the corporate bureaucracy, one must become a gamesman. To cope with the fear and frustration, one must treat the climb up the bureaucratic ladder as a game. Maccoby describes the gamesman: "Unlike other business types (generally unsuccessful), he is energized to compete not because he wants to build an empire, not for riches, but rather for fame, glory, the exhilaration of running his team and of gaining victories. His main goal is to be known as a winner, and his deepest fear is to be labeled a loser."

The gamesman, in playing the game of managerial career, must design himself for success and protect himself from the fear of failure. Through constant adaptation to the changing requirements for success and through constant insulation from the fear of failure, the gamesman loses, or perhaps never has a chance to develop, the internalized norms of moral conduct. In Maccoby's words, he has an "underdeveloped heart." That is, he is readily adaptable to different external rules of the game because he has suppressed his internal directions—his conscience. Maccoby summarizes: "The gamesman will pollute the environment, unless the law is such that each corporation must clean up its mess. . . . He will produce and advertise anything he can sell unless food and drug laws or other legislation stop him. . . . Even when he believes that the Government spends too much on weapons, he will make them."

In short, the gamesman, the dominant character type selected and produced by the corporate bureaucracy, is a fundamentally irrational human being.
Certainly, he is rational in a narrow sense. He will rationally pursue a goal in order
to win. But in a larger sense, he is irrational, for he will pursue any goal, as long as
he can win. He lacks specific internal direction; he lacks internal reason. His desire to win is irrational because he has no *reason* to win, no cause to pursue. He
simply wants to win, at anything.

And he is a creation of Max Weber's so-called efficient and rational bureaucracy.

Source: Excerpted from William M. Dugger, "Corporate Bureaucracy: The Incidence of the Bureaucratic
Process," *Journal of Economic Issues,* June 1980, pp. 405–6. Reprinted from the *Journal of Economic
Issues* by special permission of the copyright holder, the Association for Evolutionary Economics. The
quotations within this insert are from Michael Maccoby, *The Gamesman* (New York: Simon & Schuster,
1976). In order they are from the Bantam Book edition, pp. 202, 100, and 122.

---

thing has to go upward through one layer of committees after another, just to make
sure we are going to do it 'the right way.' "[31]

General Motors is an example of the recent trend toward centralization (and,
therefore, bureaucratization) in industry. In the past, the purchasing function at GM
was located in each division. Gradually, each corporate unit has transferred its purchasing operations to corporate headquarters. Considerable conflict took place between the corporate purchasing function and divisional units during the transfer of
responsibility from divisions to headquarters. To the credit of GM management, the
conflict was managed well, including appealing to the superordinate goal of saving
money to stave off an even further recession in the auto industry.[32]

IMPLICATIONS FOR
MANAGERIAL PRACTICE

1.   Working in a bureaucracy does not inevitably create more frustration than satisfaction for the manager. Bureaucracy can make the manager's job easier in several
ways. Task specialization provides good organizational support because specialists are
usually available to lend their expertise to complex, nonrecurring problems. Also, employees perceive orders and punishments as stemming from the authority of the organization rather than from the whims of the manager, therefore reducing potential anger and hostility. Finally, resources tend to be allocated on the basis of need rather
than by favoritism, which facilitates the manager getting his or her task accomplished.

2.   If you work within a bureaucratic system for a prolonged period of time, it may
prove valuable to monitor your own behavior, and ask for feedback from others, to see

[31]W. Warner Burke, "Organization Development and Bureaucracy in the 1980s," *The Journal of Applied Behavioral Science,* March 1980, p. 430.
[32]Ibid.

if you are falling prey to such personality distortions as rigidity, bureaucratic behavior, and bureautic behavior.

3.   Since bureaucracies have many potential weaknesses, it is advisable to manage your organizational unit in such a way as to minimize these weaknesses. Two such optimizing strategies under the control of the manager are (1) use special-purpose task forces to solve nonrecurring problems and (2) insist on valid methods of selection and promotion for your unit. In addition, it is valuable to use the bureaucratic organization design for large-scale recurring problems.

Summary

- Bureaucracy is an authority structure designed for use with large-scale organizations, characterized by centralization of authority, rationality, and efficiency. The major characteristics of a bureaucracy are a division of labor based on functional specialization, a well-defined hierarchy of authority, a system of rules covering the rights and duties of employees, a system of work procedures, impersonality of interpersonal relationships, promotion and selection based on technical competence and rational decision making.

- Among the potential advantages of bureaucracy are advancement of democratic ideals, high levels of accomplishment, machinelike efficiency, less need to give orders personally or repeat them, remote control of people, legitimization of punishment, and equitable division of resources.

- Bureaucracy is potentially capable of producing certain distortions of personality, including rigidity in actions and thinking, modification of a portion of one's conscience, bureaupathic behavior (a strong need to control subordinates of clients), and bureautic behavior (an exaggerated antagonism to rules and regulations).

- Organizational problems sometimes created by a bureaucracy include (1) inversion of means and ends, (2) high frustration and low job satisfaction, (3) insensitivity to individual problems, (4) avoidance of responsibility, (5) delay of decisions, (6) the Peter principle (promoting people once too often), (7) isolation from outside evaluation and feedback, (8) weakness in goal setting, (9) inbreeding (perpetuation of similar-type officials), and (10) organizational arteriosclerosis.

- Suggestions for optimizing bureaucracy include (1) use it for recurring problems, (2) use flexible organizational subunits (task forces), (3) use valid methods of selection and promotion, (4) solicit organizational feedback, and (5) use sunset legislation (do not automatically renew the charter of a governmental agency).

- The future of bureaucracy has been given an impetus by the movement toward centralization in many organizations as a method of promoting efficiency and cost savings. Yet, in practice, pure bureaucracies are rare; most bureaucracies contain some features of an adhocracy (special-purpose nonhierarchical subunits).

Questions for Discussion

1. Why are some people quite content working for a bureaucracy?
2. What does the following joke used by Ronald Reagan tell us about how people perceive a bureaucracy? "A bureaucrat is somebody who likes to cut red tape—lengthwise."
3. Identify at least two forms of organization that are not bureaucratic.
4. Is a professional football team a bureaucracy? Use the characteristics of a bureaucracy presented in this chapter to help you develop your answer.
5. What impact has this chapter had on your perceptions of a bureaucracy?
6. Can you think of a large and successful organization that is not highly bureaucratic?
7. Bureaucracies were designed with efficiency in mind. What has gone wrong that makes so many bureaucracies seemingly inefficient?
8. Identify two types of enterprises for which the bureaucratic form of organization would be well suited.
9. Identify two types of enterprises for which the bureaucratic form of organization would be ill suited.
10. In what ways do bureaucracies create stress for organizational members?

An Organizational Behavior Problem

"Centralization Will Ruin Them"

Reread the lead-in case to this chapter and then answer the following questions, incorporating into your answer some of the insights you have gained from studying this chapter.

Questions

1. Why is a case about resistance to centralization included in a chapter about bureaucracy?
2. In what way did a change in organizational size contribute to the bureaucratization of the social welfare agencies?
3. What does this case tell us about some of the potential problems associated with bureaucracy?
4. What does this case tell us about some of the potential advantages of bureaucracy?
5. What strategies can you recommend to Dave and Lucy for dealing with the resistance to centralization?

Additional Reading

Abrahamsson, Bengt. *Bureaucracy or Participation: The Logic of Organization.* Beverly Hills, Calif.: Sage Publications, 1977.

Bennis, Warren G. *Beyond Bureaucracy.* New York: McGraw-Hill, 1977.

Blau, Peter M. *The Dynamics of Bureaucracy.* Chicago: University of Chicago Press, 1955.

————, and MARSHALL W. MEYER. *Bureaucracy in Modern Society,* 2nd ed. New York: Random House, 1971.

Bureaucracy in the Eighties. Special issue of *The Journal of Applied Behavioral Science,* August 1980.

CREMER, JACQUES. "A Partial Theory of the Optimal Organization of a Bureaucracy." *The Bell Journal of Economics,* Autumn 1980, pp. 683–93.

DOWNS, ANTHONY. *Inside Bureaucracy.* Boston: Little, Brown, 1967.

GORDON, LEONARD V. "Measurement of Bureaucratic Orientation." *Personnel Psychology,* Spring 1970, pp. 1–13.

GRINYER, PETER H., and MASOUD YASI-ARDEKANI. "Strategy, Structure, Size, and Bureaucracy." *Academy of Management Journal,* September 1981, pp. 471–86.

HOLZER, MARC, KENNETH MORRIS, and WILLIAM LUDWIN, eds. *Literature in Bureaucracy: Readings in Administrative Fiction.* Wayne, N.J.: Avery, 1981.

JANSEN, ROBERT B. *The ABCs of Bureaucracy.* Chicago: Nelson-Hall, 1979.

KAUFMAN, HERBERT. *Red Tape: Its Origins, Uses, and Abuses.* Washington, D.C.: The Brookings Institute, 1977.

KRAUS, WILLIAM A. *Collaboration in Organizations: Alternatives to Hierarchy.* New York: Human Sciences Press, 1980.

SCOTT, WILLIAM G., and DAVID K. HART. *Organizational America.* Boston: Houghton Mifflin, 1979.

Organization Development

LEARNING OBJECTIVES

1. To understand the meaning and purposes of organization development.
2. To know why the OD specialist occupies a sensitive role.
3. To be able to design a specific OD program such as team building or a survey feedback program for an organization.
4. To be able to offer several valid criticisms of OD.

Behavioral science consultant Bruce entered the motel conference room after the other members of the team building had arrived. Looking around the room, he commented, "It's good to see everybody here on time. It shows you aren't resisting the heavy stuff. As we agreed upon in our previous session, this morning we will look at some of the roadblocks we are facing. I want you to explain candidly to each other anything you see that one team member is doing to another that detracts from rather than enhances productivity.

"A convenient way to begin is for each of you in turn to describe how any other team member might be making it difficult for you to accomplish your job.

We'll begin with Peggy, seated here to my left."

Peggy: (Laughs nervously) You really sprung that one on me, Bruce. I wasn't prepared. But let me give it a try. I want to say something to you, Conrad. You're a fine fellow and all that, but you are very slow in getting answers back to me. You're supposed to be our resident management information systems specialist, but it takes forever to get information from you. I feel better now that I said it. (Conrad squirms, and the other members laugh.)

Gary: Bruce, have you ever thought about the problems you're creating? This touchy-feely stuff is driving me up the wall. I should be back in the office working on my budget rather than shooting the bull about team work. I'm wondering if these sessions are cost-effective.

Paul: Gary, I think your comment about Bruce tells more about you than about him. It's your insensitivity to people problems that creates a lot of difficulty. If you can't attach a number to something, you dismiss its importance. The last time I tried to get you to deal with a serious morale problem, your only concern was how the situation affected the bottom line. If you would become a little more sensitive to people, I think you would function much better as a controller.

Greg: Peggy, let me have a crack at you. Everybody around here says what a fabulous human resource specialist you are. I don't deny that you're a good personnel professional. Yet I have this vague feeling that you're a phony. There seems to be a big gap between what you say and what you are really thinking. The upshot is that if you say you agree with me on an issue, I'm not sure that you really do agree. It shows up when you don't follow through on something we agreed on.

Laura: Okay Paul, it's your turn to get a little well-intended feedback. (The group laughs.) No doubt, you're a marketing pro, and it's often fun to work with you. But you're so damn impatient, it serves as a communication block. You come across to me and others as if you would rather be doing something else. On your worst days, it seems as if you resent the time you have to spend in meetings with us. Other than that, it's a pleasure working with you.

Conrad: There's an issue with you, Laura, that I want to bring up. I hope you'll take it as a constructive suggestion. You're basically the operations manager of our chain of retail outlets. That means that you have to spend enormous amounts of time in the field, supervising operations. I accept that. What I question is whether or not you're making a contribution to our management team. You go out on your trips, but you never come back with any suggestions for improvement. I like you, but I wonder what you are doing for the firm.

This vignette is an approximate transcript from a portion of a team building session conducted with executives from a retail store chain. It illustrates an important implication to be derived from studying this chapter: personal issues are often embedded in work issues. Unless these personal and emotional issues are resolved, it is difficult to bring about constructive change in organizations.

THE MEANING OF ORGANIZATION DEVELOPMENT

As illustrated indirectly in the session just presented, any form of organization development is aimed at improving the work effectiveness of individuals, groups, and total organization systems. OD has been defined in many ways. An *ideal* definition states that "Organization development is a long-range effort to improve an organization's problem-solving and renewal processes, particularly through a more effective and collaborative management of organization culture—with special emphasis on the culture of formal work teams—with the assistance of a change agent, or catalyst, and the use of the theory and technology of applied behavioral science, including action research."[1] A leading authority in the OD movement notes that rarely do managers see OD as a long-range strategy for organizational innovation and renewal (despite the aspirations of the OD specialist.)[2]

More realistically, OD is generally taken to refer collectively to an assortment of training or therapeutic interventions whose purpose it is assumed to be improvement of the organization and its members.[3] If either the ideal or the real definition of OD is taken literally, then almost any application of behavioral science to organizations would be considered OD.

[1]Wendell L. French and Cecil H. Bell, Jr., *Organization Development: Behavioral Science Interventions for Organization Improvement* (Englewood Cliffs, N.J.: Prentice-Hall, 1973), p. 15.

[2]Michael Beer, *Organization Change and Development: A Systems View* (Glenview, Ill.: Scott Foresman and Company, 1980), p. 263.

[3]David C. Bowers, "Organizational Development: Promises, Performances, Possibilities," *Organizational Dynamics,* Spring 1976, p. 50.

Confusion exists between the concepts of OD on the one hand and other interventions such as training and development on the other. The terms overlap somewhat, but a fundamental difference between them exists. A useful distinction is that training and development are usually involved when the target of change is the individual or small group. When the organizational system is the target of change, we are referring to OD.[4] Career counseling, for example, could be part of development if it were aimed primarily at helping individuals to integrate their needs with those of the organization. If career counseling were aimed at improving total organizational effectiveness, it would be considered OD. Organization development, then, can be said to include interventions such as training and development.

A number of different techniques already described in this text may be classified as OD. Among them are positive reinforcement, job enrichment, flexitime, creativity training, and methods of conflict resolution. Five additional approaches to OD are described in this chapter: career development, team building, the survey feedback, grid OD, and quality of work life programs.

PURPOSES OF OD

Organization development activities have many different goals and purposes, some of them being linked to the particular intervention. If outplacement counseling were considered part of OD, one of its subgoals would be to help terminated employees find suitable employment elsewhere. Generally speaking, OD is aimed at overall increases in productivity, morale, and satisfaction. Among the specific purposes, goals, and objectives that might be established for any one OD program are these:

1. Increased level of trust and mutual emotional support among organization members.
2. Increased incidence of confronting rather than suppressing organizational problems.
3. Increased openness of communications in four directions: downward, upward, laterally, and diagonally.
4. Enhanced employee morale and satisfaction.
5. Movement toward a more participative, collaborative leadership style throughout the organization.
6. Increased management of, rather than suppression of, conflict.
7. Elimination of dysfunctional conflict among interdependent groups.
8. Enhanced motivation of employees at various organizational levels.
9. Decreased political behavior among managerial workers.
10. More rapid response to significant change.[5]

---

[4]Book review by Meg Gerrard and Howard Baumgartel in *Personnel Psychology,* Winter 1979, p. 781.

[5]Several items in this list are based on Wendell L. French, *The Personnel Management Process: Human Resources Administration,* 4th ed. (Boston: Houghton Mifflin, 1978), pp. 541–42. Other items on the list are based on John C. Agathon, "Management Development," in Joseph J. Famularo, ed., *Handbook of Modern Personnel Administration* (New York: McGraw-Hill, 1972), Chapter 22, p. 19.

OD STRATEGIES

As the technology of OD continues to grow, it becomes increasingly difficult to categorize and classify the variety of OD interventions. Harold J. Leavitt suggests that organizational change can be accomplished by three broad approaches—the structural, the technological, and the humanistic.[6]

The *structural* approach is brought about by modifying the formal organization. One method here would be to apply principles of classical organization design such as increasing or decreasing span of control as the situation warranted. Another method would be to decentralize an organization. A third structural approach aims at improving organizational performance by modifying the work flow (such as that proposed in Chapter 13 in relation to conflict resolution).

The *technological* approach focuses on altering the equipment, work measurement techniques, engineering methods, research techniques, or production methods. Systematic application of the technological approach to change began with the scientific management approach proposed by Frederick W. Taylor. A modern application is the installation of computer systems for such purposes as corresponding with customers.

The *humanistic* (or people) approach changes organizations by bringing about changes in organization members. Most OD practitioners are primarily involved with interventions designed to change people. In fact, the OD movement began with sensitivity training for managers, in which they learned methods of being more open with people. Most of the better known OD approaches can be classified as methods of changing people. All the methods to be described in this chapter fall into this category, owing to the OB orientation of this text.

In addition to categorizing OD interventions as structural, technological, and humanistic, it is helpful to categorize them by level: individual, small group, and organizational. A sampling of interventions at each level is listed in Table 17–1. Most of these interventions are described in this text (refer to the index) or in end-of-chapter references. In this chapter, we describe one individual intervention (career counseling), one group intervention (team building), and three organization-level interventions (survey feedback, grid OD, and QWL programs).

ROLE OF THE CONSULTANT
OR CHANGE AGENT

Many professionals apply OD concepts and techniques to organizations. Originally, OD practitioners were organizational psychologists who worked with clients on a consulting basis. Now a wide variety of human relations specialists consider themselves to

---

[6]Harold J. Leavitt, "Applied Organizational Change in Industry: Structural, Technological, and Humanistic Approaches," in James G. March, ed., *Handbook of Organizations* (Chicago: Rand McNally, 1965), pp. 1144–68.

TABLE 17–1   A Sampling of Techniques, Methods, and
Programs Sometimes Considered to Be OD
Interventions

Focus on the individual
  Counseling for ineffective performance
  Employee assistance programs (EAPs)
  Career counseling
  Positive reinforcement programs
  Job enrichment
  Transactional analysis (TA)
  Assertiveness training (AT)
  Relaxation techniques (for stress reduction)
  Performance appraisal systems
  Outplacement counseling

Focus on small groups
  Team building
  Image exchanging (organizational mirrors)
  The confrontation meeting
  Modified work schedules
  Affirmative action programs
  Leaderless group discussion (used in assessment centers)
  Synectics
  Group brainstorming
  Sensitivity training (encounter groups)

Focus on large organizational units or total organization
  Grid organization development
  Survey feedback
  Compensation programs
  Financial control systems
  Human resource accounting
  Management by objectives (MBO)
  Worker participation programs
  Quality of work life programs
  Scanlon plans
  Employee stock ownership programs

be OD consultants. Included in their ranks are over 2,000 members of the OD network, a group of practitioners who meet twice a year to keep up with the latest in OD.[7] Outside consultants have now been joined by a large group of internal consultants who practice OD exclusively with their own organizations. Many of these people have job titles such as organization development specialist.

OD practitioners are also referred to by such titles as "interventionist," "change agent," and "process consultant." Although confusing, such a diversity of titles does point to the primary roles of the OD specialist. The traditional role is that of an ob-

[7]W. Warner Burke, "Organization Development and Bureaucracy in the 1980s," *The Journal of Applied Behavioral Science,* No. 3, 1980, p. 423.

server who helps people solve their own problems. He or she does not give expert advice but encourages people to diagnose the true nature of their problems and arrive at workable solutions. Using this approach, the OD consultant will say to a client, "Here is what I see you doing. You talk to each other about budgets when the real issues are those of personality clashes. What are you going to do about it?" To be effective in such a role, the consultant must have a humanistic perspective—believe in both people's desire and capacity for constructive growth.

A newer role for the OD consultant is one of expert advisor (the traditional consulting role). He or she diagnoses the client's problems and then suggests a course of action that should remedy that problem. Acting in this role, an OD consultant might say, "My diagnosis of your problem is that your sales personnel are undermotivated. My solution is a program of job enrichment. The motivation of the sales force will increase if their jobs are made more exciting and meaningful." As W. Warner Burke notes, "The consultant himself or herself has changed from a nondirective, purely process-oriented practitioner to an authoritative specialist."[8]

Many people believe that it is difficult for OD practitioners to be effective when they are part of the power structure that they are trying to change. People are more likely to trust you when you seem to be a neutral observer. A change agent from remote company headquarters can thus work more effectively than can a person permanently assigned to that particular division. Several professors of organizational behavior have learned through experience that it is difficult to bring about organizational change in their own colleges. However, to the extent that the OD consultant deals in mostly technical areas or changes (such as redesigning jobs)—and not personal issues—being an outsider is a much less significant factor.

Michael Beer notes that no research is available about the qualities of an effective OD consultant, yet it is generally accepted that the characteristics of the consultant are as important as the particular OD techniques used. He notes that the change agent must possess behavioral science knowledge, research skills, and clinical skills. These constitute his or her "technical bag" and provide the consultant with expert power. "Additionally, he must possess the personality and interpersonal competence to use himself as an instrument of change. These are the sources of his or her referent power."[9]

CAREER DEVELOPMENT PROGRAMS

Career development programs (CDPs) are a widely used means of integrating individual and organizational goals. If employees are helped to achieve rewarding and satisfying careers within the organization, presumably the organization will also prosper.

---

[8]W. Warner Burke, "Organization Development in Transition," *The Journal of Applied Behavioral Science,* Vol. 14, No. 1, January 1976, p. 28.

[9]Michael Beer, "The Technology of Organization Development," in Marvin D. Dunnette, ed., *Handbook of Industrial and Organizational Psychology* (Chicago: Rand McNally, 1976), p. 984.

Among the ways in which CDPs help the organization (and, therefore, qualify as organization development) are the demonstration of social responsibility, the fulfillment of affirmative action and equal employment opportunity programs, the reduction of turnover and absenteeism, and the reduction of managerial and professional obsolescence.[10]

Certain elements of what is considered to be career development have been in practice for many years. Virtually any intervention or program that helps employees to manage their careers can be considered part of career development. Among such miscellaneous programs are tuition aid, career counseling with performance appraisal, human resource planning and forecasting, life and/or career planning workshops, and dual career ladders for professional personnel.

A Comprehensive Program

Ideally, career development programs should be carefully planned to integrate a number of personnel programs. It will serve the purposes of this chapter to illustrate one such program in a large insurance company. If all its elements were implemented successfully, both individuals and the organization would prosper. The career development program is divided into nine segments.[11]

1. *Human resource forecasting.* The purpose of this segment is to forecast the human resource requirements of the organization. Career development programs may become dysfunctional if people are encouraged to aspire to positions that may not exist in the future. One finding of this insurance company was that fewer first-level supervisors and clerks would be needed in the future because of expanded use of data processing.

2. *Nomination of candidates for CDP.* Although virtually all employees are eligible for some aspect of the CDP, a select group of supervisors and managers is nominated for a special career acceleration program. Nominations are accepted from all second-level managers and above plus certain high-level staff personnel. A major criterion for nomination into this elite group is that the individual must have received outstanding ratings in three of his or her last four performance evaluations.

3. *Career planning self-analysis.* Every person in the key group is asked to complete a questionnaire designed to get him or her thinking about his or her own personal development in an insightful way (see Table 17–2). The goals set by individuals are carefully reviewed by higher levels of management and a career planning specialist as a way of reality testing. People are not necessarily told to change their goals, but a frank discussion is held of their chances of achieving a long shot such as "I want to be chief executive officer of this company by age thirty-one."

---

[10]William F. Glueck, *Personnel: A Diagnostic Approach,* rev. ed. (Plano, Tex.: Business Publications, 1978), p. 263.

[11]Our program summarizes the one found in Andrew J. DuBrin, *Contemporary Applied Management* (Plano, Tex.: Business Publications, 1982), pp. 171–78.

TABLE 17–2 Some Questions Typically Found in Career Development Inventories

1. How would you describe yourself as a person?
2. What are the three most important items on your wish list?
3. What are your three biggest accomplishments?
4. Write your own obituary as you would like it to appear after the termination of your life.
5. What are your short-, intermediate-, and long-range career goals?
6. What are your personal goals? (What do you want out of life?)
7. If you could start your career all over again, what would you do differently?
8. What would be the ideal job for you?
9. What career advice can you give yourself?
10. What opportunities that exist now in your firm, or are likely to exist in the future, would you like to pursue?

4. *Assessment and feedback.* Key group members are invited to spend several days at an assessment center where they are put through a series of job-related exercises such as handling items in an in-basket. Their performance is observed and evaluated by human resource specialists and managers. After the assessment period, each participant is given feedback on his or her performance along with counseling suggestions for self-improvement and personal development.

5. *On-the-job training.* Guided job experience is an important aspect of career development. On-the-job training can take such forms as job enrichment or a superior coaching a subordinate about improved job performance. For example, a boss might urge a subordinate manager to be more methodical in preparing budgets or in taking care of paperwork.

6. *Management development programs.* Various formal management development and training programs are used to supplement on-the-job training and coaching. Management development is closely linked to career development: developing one's skills as a manager enhances one's effectiveness and contributes to developing one's career. A company executive cautions, "Before we launch a management development program, we take a careful look at the kind of skills and knowledge we think our managers should have."

7. *Performance appraisal counseling.* In both this insurance company and many other firms, some aspects of career counseling are integrated with performance evaluation. After reviewing an employee's performance, the manager is supposed to make suggestions to that person for improvement and growth. Managers are given some training in career development counseling to help them deal with this sensitive area. Managers must recognize the issues over which they should not offer advice and counseling (such as "Should I drop out of manufacturing and enter personnel?").

8. *The management inventory chart.* A highly confidential tool, the inventory chart is an organization chart with notations about the promotability of people in the boxes. To establish these notations, the vice president of human resources and the company president carefully scrutinize the performance appraisal results, the assessment center

results, and any other relevant information available about the person. The chart is updated every year so that no one's rating of potential is frozen.

9. *Evaluation of the CDP.* Ideally, evaluation of a career development program should follow the experimental method outlined in Chapter 2. The insurance company in question uses such measures as turnover rates and the ease with which key vacancies are filled internally. Most career development programs suffer from a lack of rigorous evaluation.

Career Development Programs and Organization Effectiveness

Carefully planned and managed career development programs appear to be making a contribution to individual and organizational effectiveness. Milan Moravec reports, for example, that one bank's career counseling program saved $1.95 million in one year. Based on tabulations by an industrial engineer, this estimate reflected 65 percent reduced turnover, 85 percent improvement in performance, 25 percent increased productivity, and 75 percent increased promotability.[12]

A major criticism of career development programs is that CDPs encourage wishful thinking and unfulfilled expectations. While engaging in self-analysis, many employees present a biased, unrealistic description of their personal strengths and goals. Career development inventories, such as the one shown in Table 17–2, tend to encourage such grandiose thinking. People aspire toward positions for which they are unqualified and that may not exist or are in severely limited supply. Very few aspiring vice presidents can be accommodated.

Career development programs, as a part of OD, are often sold to top management as a method of integrating individual and organizational goals. Since it is often difficult to integrate the two sets of goals the majority of times, a substitute for true integration has been developed to make career development programs more realistic. Called *career negotiation,* this concept assumes that some sort of trade-off can be reached between employee and organizational needs. Both the individual and the organization will prosper if the two parties can reach a workable compromise about organizational requirements versus individual aspirations. A workable compromise might take the following form. The organizational position is "You stay with us now, and in return, we can offer some exciting challenges in the future." The individual position is "I can accept the current job for a while longer if you can help me get into an executive career track." The negotiated transaction is that both parties agree to increase career options within organizations.[13]

By negotiating, and therefore modifying individual and organizational needs, the chances increase that a career development program will lead to improved individual

---

[12]Milan Moravec, "A Cost-Effective Career Planning Program Requires a Strategy," *Personnel Adminstrator,* January 1982, p. 28.

[13]James F. Wolf and Robert N. Bacher, "Career Negotiation: Trading Off Employee and Organizational Needs," *Personnel,* March–April 1981, pp. 53–59. The quotations are from p. 57.

and organizational effectiveness. Both the individual and the organization (in reality, its representatives) are less likely to become frustrated with each other.

TEAM BUILDING

A natural focal point for improving the functioning of a total organization is to improve the effectiveness of its basic building blocks—small work teams. Following this logic, team building has become one of the most popular OD interventions. Team building can be described as an attempt to assist the work group in becoming more adept by learning how (with the assistance of a process consultant) to identify, diagnose, and solve its own problems.[14] Two assumptions about group behavior underlie the concept of team building. First, for groups to work productively, they must cooperate and coordinate their work toward the accomplishment of specific tasks. Second, the personal welfare and emotional needs of the group must be met. Team building works on both these aspects simultaneously.[15] In short, the basic purpose of team building is to help group members examine their own behaviors and develop action plans that will improve task accomplishment.

A General Model of the Team Building Process[16]

The lead-in case in this chapter illustrated one aspect of team building, the surfacing of interpersonal issues. Here we summarize the basic features of a widely used approach to team building described by Michael Beer. Team building begins with the gathering of data about group processes and problems in two basic ways. The consultant can conduct interviews with members of the work group and/or use questionnaires. It is imperative that the team leader inform the participants about how the data will be used and with whom they will be shared. Team members are told something to this effect: "All information will be shared with everybody, but the source of the data will not be divulged."

The data discussed during team building sessions may include leadership behavior, interpersonal relationships, roles of group members, perceptions of trust, planning and decision making, goals, delegation, technical and task problems, and communication barriers.

Shortly after the data have been collected, the work group meets off the premises to avoid day-to-day pressures and interruptions. In some large work settings, a secluded conference room is chosen for team building. The duration of the meetings is highly variable. At one extreme are "retreats" that last for three days or even longer. At the

---

[14]H. Kent Baker, "The Hows and Whys of Team Building," *Personnel Journal,* June 1979, p. 367.

[15]Edgar F. Huse and James L. Bowditch, *Behavior in Organizations: A Systems Approach to Managing* (Reading, Mass.: Addison-Wesley, 1973), p. 293.

[16]This section is based on Beer, "The Technology of Organization Development," pp. 955–56.

other extreme are half-day sessions. My observations are that in recent years many team builders have moved toward briefer sessions, partially to accommodate the concerns of managers about being away too long from regular duties.

During the meeting, the team leader feeds back the data to the group. In typical fashion, problems are categorized and placed on charts or chalkboards for presentation, discussion, and priority setting. The group is empowered to decide whether to tackle interpersonal problems before planning problems or leadership problems before communication problems. Often, the consultant will encourage the group to tackle first those problems that will make subsequent discussion and problem solving easier. Each concrete discussion is followed by the development of specific action plans to accomplish a particular goal. A sample of such an action plan is "From now on, Al (the boss) will ask us first before assigning us to a corporate project."

At least one follow-up session is scheduled to review progress toward the accomplishment of action plans. Typically, some of the action plans have fallen short of full implementation. A discussion of the snags that developed during implementation can be helpful in bringing about the desired progress.

Role of the consultant.   To understand the process of team building, it is necessary to examine the role of the team leader, who is almost always an external or internal consultant. It would be extremely difficult for a regular member of the work group to serve as team leader. Throughout the team building sessions, the consultant plays at least four roles. First, he or she functions as a process consultant helping the group to analyze the process of its interactions. The leader promotes group norms conducive to confronting conflict and placing it on a problem-solving basis. If suitably trained, the consultant can serve as a resource person on questions or problems related to organizational behavior. When appropriate, he or she functions as a teacher on subjects such as leadership, group process, motivation, and conflict resolution. The team leaders may also serve as counselors to individuals during or following the team building session.

Effectiveness of Team Building

Research and opinion suggest that team building is an effective organization development intervention. Much of its success is based on its core ingredients of confronting important problems and developing action plans for their resolution. Team building is well accepted by managers because it has good face validity—it appears to be quite job related. Based upon a review of the existing empirical and theoretical evidence, Beer reached the following optimistic conclusion:

> Team development or group development is perhaps the most powerful and pervasive OD technology available to the change agent. Its design provides data for diagnosis and unfreezing, incorporates experiential learning, and provides the means for refreezing new behavior. Furthermore, the process of team development is likely to change organizational inputs (needs, values, skills) and a wide variety of group and organizational character-

istics and functions (leadership, group cohesiveness, communication, planning). Through problem identification, it can also effect immediate change in organizational outputs.[17]

THE SURVEY FEEDBACK APPROACH

A well-structured, well-organized approach to organization development with a long history of good performance is the survey feedback technique. In essence, it involves (1) taking a survey of organizational problems via questionnaire and/or interviews, (2) reporting these results back to the organization, (3) developing action plans to overcome the problems uncovered, and (4) follow-up.

Administering the survey. A survey designed by a specialist in attitude measurement is administered to a total organization, a subunit, or a representative sample of either. Both multiple-choice and write-in items are generally used on the questionnaire, as illustrated in Figure 17–1.

Feedback sessions. After an analysis of the survey results has been conducted, the information is fed back to survey participants. Both items of relevance to most organizations and a few company-specific items are included. For example, if the human relations specialist developing the questionnaire knew that tight budgets were recently imposed in the company, a question like this might appear:

Our budgets are realistic and fair.

Strongly
Disagree _____ Disagree _____ Neutral_____ Strongly
Agree _____

When is a good time to conduct an organizational survey? Experience suggests that the best time is when the organization is not undergoing a major change. Also, general conditions should not be unusually good (such as the acquisition of a major contract) or particularly bad (a major layoff). Administering the survey under "normal" conditions helps to provide data that are not basically a reaction to temporary conditions.

The opinion is often expressed that a survey should not be administered unless people in the organization trust each other. According to this reasoning, distrust leads to response bias. Although this opinion is logical, a survey-OD technique is designed to uncover such problems. Unless the survey is conducted, the distrust problem may not be resolved. The OD practitioner first meets with members of top management to discuss the findings and some of their implications. Next, meetings are held with organizational families (regular work groups such as departments) to discuss the findings.

[17]Ibid., p. 960.

Sample Objective Questions

	Strongly Disagree	Disagree	Neutral	Agree	Strongly Agree
We have a major communications problem around here.	_____	_____	_____	_____	_____
Few people listen to each other in our company.	_____	_____	_____	_____	_____
Our management makes all the decisions.	_____	_____	_____	_____	_____
Few people leave our company voluntarily.	_____	_____	_____	_____	_____

Sample Write-in Question

In your opinion, what are the two or three biggest problems facing this company? Write your answer in the space provided. Use the back of this page if necessary.

_____

_____

_____

FIGURE 17-1   Sample Questionnaire Items from an OD Survey

In years past, more emphasis was placed upon sending written summaries of the results to participants. Such an approach is devoid of emotional involvement, thus losing its effectiveness as an OD technique.

Develop action plans.   A major difference between OD and merely "conducting a survey" is contained in this step. Participants are asked their recommendations about how some of the problems uncovered in the survey should be resolved. A final report of the survey is not released until the action plans developed by people at several levels in the organization have been incorporated. At the University of Michigan Survey Research Center, a rule has been formulated that

> no report containing recommendations based solely on their own analysis of data will be given to the client. Instead, they present data in preliminary form and involve members of the client organization in interpreting the data and deciding on specific courses of action.[18]

A dominant theme uncovered in an OD survey conducted in upstate New York was that employees were unsure of the future of their company. Many people wrote in comments such as "Rumors have it that our plant will be closed within six months.

[18]George F. Wieland and Robert A. Ullrich, *Organizations: Behavior, Design, and Change* (Homewood, Ill.: Richard D. Irwin, 1976), p. 504.

That's no way to live when you have a daughter ready for college." The action plan developed by middle management was straightforward and workable. It suggested an open meeting with top management to discuss the future of the company at that location. Top management complied. In the meeting it was explained that the rumors had a grain of truth, but were essentially incorrect. The company would not close the plant, but all expansion would take place in states with lower tax rates and utility rates.

Follow-up.   OD techniques fit very well into a systems framework. Without continuous feedback and correction, OD fails or at best is a short-lived interesting experience. Several months after the OD survey is conducted, a check should be made to determine if the action plans developed in the earlier stages are being implemented. In one company an action plan was developed to realign the wage scale of first-line supervision. A three-month checkup revealed that nothing had been done. Prodding by the OD consultant and a respresentative from first-line supervision helped management to begin some long-needed changes.

GRID ORGANIZATION DEVELOPMENT

The popular Grid approach to organization development endeavors to make individuals and organizations more effective by bringing about changes in attitudes, values, and behavior. We emphasize the Grid here because of its widespread use. The Grid OD program is built upon a framework for understanding leadership styles, as shown in Figure 17–2. A summary statement of the nature of the program and its objectives is provided by the originators of the Grid.

> An effective organization is characterized by lean staffing with highly competent, committed people who, through participation and involvement, ensure an "everybody wins" situation—customers, stockholders, employees. Grid learning is directed toward achieving these kinds of results. The fundamental motivational theory is that people respond to high standards of excellence from which they derive job satisfaction and pride. Through the application of these concepts, any organization can achieve high levels of productivity and quality. The organization's objective performance demonstrates its excellence.[19]

The specific objectives of a grid organization development seminar are for participants to

- Study their organization as an interacting system and apply techniques of analysis in diagnosing its problems.
- Understand the rationale of systematic change, as contrasted to change by evolution or revolution.
- Gain insight into the strategies of Grid Organization Development for increasing productivity and quality.

[19]Brochure from Scientific Methods, Inc., Austin, Texas.

- Examine the instruments and documents used in the different phases and simulate their application to the participant's own situation.
- Evaluate the styles of leadership and techniques of participation most likely to produce high-quality results.
- Assess the effort and expense required and risks involved relative to potentials of increased profit and human effectiveness.[20]

Grid OD, as with other forms of OD, also applies to nonprofit organizations. The concept of profit for these organizations can readily be translated to "staying within budget."

Phases of Grid OD

The OD program involves two parts and six phases.[21]

Part I: Management development.   Phase 1, *study of the Managerial Grid®*, emphasizes the theory of effectiveness that underlies the grid program. Concepts about the various leadership styles depicted in Figure 17–2 are taught at this stage of the program. At the outset of the seminar, each participant's leadership style is evaluated and reviewed. Next is fifty hours of problem solving, focusing upon situations involving interactions with people and its effects upon task performance. Each group assesses its problem-solving performance.

Phase 2, *team development,* gives managers an opportunity to develop and analyze their managerial styles and group practices. The climate of openness and trust developed in the first phase is supposed to carry over into the second phase. Teams are given the opportunity to evaluate their own behavior and problem-solving abilities. An important objective of the first two phases is to build more effective relationships among groups, among co-workers at the same level, and between superiors and subordinates.

Part II: Organization development.   Phase 3, *intergroup development,* involves an examination of the interrelationships of related organizational units. An important objective here is joint problem-solving. To accomplish this end, participants are sensitized to the importance of building 9,9 group roles and norms beyond the single work group. Simulated situations are established in which tensions that typically exist between groups are identified and discussed by group members.

Phase 4, *developing a corporate model,* involves top management working with lower-ranking groups to develop an ideal model for managing the organization in the future. The development of this organization includes developing convictions about ideal management practices by testing the ones that currently exist and setting feasible

---

[20]Ibid.

[21]Robert R. Blake and Jane Srygley Mouton, *The New Managerial Grid* (Houston: Gulf, 1978). A summary of this information is Robert R. Blake and Jane Srygley Mouton, "An Overview of the Grid," *Training and Development Journal,* May 1975, pp. 29–37.

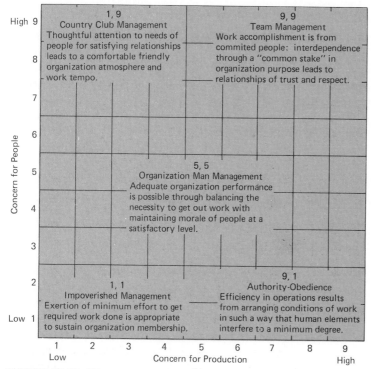

FIGURE 17–2 The Managerial Grid®

Source: Robert R. Blake and Jane Srygley Mouton, *The New Managerial Grid* (Houston: Gulf, 1978), p. 11. Reproduced by permission.

objectives within a time framework. Similar to MBO, the planned goals at each level will presumably be linked.

Phase 5, *implementing development,* follows with exercises designed to help the organization move toward the model developed in phase 4. Groups throughout the organization are given tasks that describe the problem to be solved and the goal. All group members share in the information given to the group leader. Once the information is understood and agreement is reached by group members, the group begins to work on corrective steps. One example might be "Let's draw up a specific game plan of how we can get forecasts from marketing with enough lead time to allow us to get our work accomplished."

Phase 6, *consolidation,* is the capstone. The achievements of the earlier phases are evaluated with the objective of working through problem areas and taking corrective action. It often takes about one year after the first five phases are completed to identify weaknesses in the goals and plans. Phase 6 helps to reinforce the new patterns of management learned in phases 1 through 5.

Grid OD Effectiveness

Grid OD has endured since the early 1960s. Thousands of organizations, worldwide, have devoted considerable human and financial resources to this complex, systematic method of improving organizational effectiveness. On this basis alone, it must be concluded that Grid OD must be contributing something of value to society. Two aspects of the Grid system underlie its helpfulness in an organizational setting. First, it forces management to carefully examine its own organizational problems. Second, it is based on established group dynamics and leadership theory.

A frequent criticism of Grid OD is *not* that it does not work but that not enough evidence exists that it *does* work. A number of organizations that have begun a Grid program have abandoned the effort. The same is true of virtually any encompassing program including MBO, job enrichment, and even interview training. Management often lets potentially worthwhile programs slide in the press of day-to-day business problems. A comprehensive review of OD technology concluded that "Grid OD is a major contribution to the technology of OD and, considering the state of the art, is probably a very effective and efficient tool for organization change."[22]

The Grid and Contingency Management

Critics of the Grid express concern that by espousing a 9,9 orientation, this approach to OD may be ignoring the realities of contingency management. Blake and Mouton rebut that there *is* one best way in which to manage people, and this is through the use of behavioral science principles. If 9,9 principles are used, for example, the strategy remains the same but the tactics may vary. A manager might supervise a long-term employee differently from one newly hired. The point emphasized by Blake and Mouton is that in both cases the manager can still use the basic leadership strategy of trying to maximize production and human welfare.

QUALITY OF WORK LIFE (QWL) PROGRAMS

The dual challenges of trying to improve productivity and make work a psychologically rewarding experience have given impetus to the QWL movement in North America. European approaches to QWL preceded those in America and placed more emphasis on satisfaction than productivity. QWL is ideally defined as "A process by which all members of the organization, through appropriate channels of communication set up for this purpose, have some say about the design of their jobs in particular, and the work environment in general."[23] As a consequence of this kind of organiza-

---

[22]Beer, "Technology of Organization Development," p. 982.

[23]Edward M. Glaser, "Productivity Gains Through Worklife Improvement," *Personnel*, January–February 1980, p. 72.

tional climate, suggestions, questions, and criticisms that might lead to any kind of improvement are encouraged. It has been noted that when management encourages feelings of involvement, it leads to ideas and actions for upgrading of operational effectiveness and efficiency, along with enhancement of the work environment. Increased productivity often comes about as a natural by-product of these attitudes and actions.

QWL and OD are overlapping concepts to the extent that the terms are sometimes used interchangeably. It seems logically consistent to classify QWL programs as a major subset of OD, with similar programs and methods being used to achieve both QWL and OD, as implied from Table 17–3. Here we describe one traditional QWL program and one less well-known QWL method followed by a summary of the conditions under which these programs tend to be successful. It is important to recognize that QWL in spirit is not a series of neatly packed programs. As Edward Glaser observes, "Improving the quality of worklife is a process rather than a set of specific steps, because organizations and institutions are not all alike. The improvement ideas forthcoming from a given QWL program are based on that particular firm's culture, needs, and readiness for change."[24]

Case History of QWL in a Manufacturing Firm

A manufacturing company was faced with the dual problem of labor-management friction and declining product quality. Consequently, sales suffered, half the work

[24]Ibid., p. 75.

TABLE 17–3 Features Contained in Quality of Work Life Programs

1. Reasonable compensation and fringe benefits.
2. Job security.
3. A safe and healthful work environment.
4. Recognition for achievement through promotion, pay, or other rewards.
5. Due process in the settlement of grievances, separations, or other work-related problems.
6. Participation in decision making.
7. Some responsibility for and autonomy over the immediate work process.
8. Flexible time arrangements such as flexitime or the compressed workweek.
9. Emphasis on education, training, and career development.
10. Use of nonbureaucratic forms of work organization.
11. Consideration of social aspects of life on the job.
12. Open communication and adequate feedback to employees.
13. Recognition of the competing demands of work, family, community, and leisure.
14. Redesign of work such as job enrichment.

Source: Paul Bernstein, "Career Education and the Quality of Working Life," *Monographs on Career Education* (Washington, D.C.: U.S. Department of Health, Education, and Welfare, 1980), pp. 13–16.

force was laid off or terminated, and the company was soon sold to a Japanese firm. The new president immediately called a meeting of top management and union officials to discuss the situation. His basic thrust was to solicit their suggestions on improving quality and cutting costs. The president then met with the rest of the work force and invited their ideas as well. He claimed that if appreciable business improvement could be achieved through the ideas generated, the firm would be able to rehire laid-off employees and provide improved job security.

Following the QWL format, the next step involved establishing a joint labor-management committee to analyze production problems, evaluate ideas for improvement, propose action plans, share in making decisions about the design and organization of work, and give feedback to all employees. Within nine months, business improved sufficiently to enable the company to rehire the same number of employees it had laid off. A psychological consultant involved in the program made this analysis of its success:

> The dramatic turnaround in the organization's fortunes resulted from a managerial style that enlisted the cooperation of interested personnel at all organizational levels, including local union officials, in solving problems *they* helped to identify and in devising methods of capitalizing on perceived business opportunities. In addition to instituting a responsive, collaborative management/union relationship with joint participation in various types of planning, the new owners demonstrated a readiness to adopt modernizing technical changes and a willingness to invest capital in promising business ventures.[25]

Improving Quality of Work Life Through Parallel Organizations[26]

Another macro approach to improving the quality of work life is the creation of flat, flexible, yet formal problem-solving and governance organizations that serve to supplement bureaucracy. Instead of trying to replace bureaucracy, parallel structures coexist with the former. A schematic and a verbal comparison between bureaucracy and the parallel structure is shown in Figure 17–3. Some conceptual overlap exists between the Theory Z and parallel structures, particularly in the effort made to produce flexibility in work assignments.

The parallel organization attempts to institutionalize a set of externally and internally responsible, participatory, problem-solving structures alongside the conventional line organization that carries out recurring tasks. Unlike the informal organization, the parallel organization is a second, equally formal structure. In addition to allowing for change and responsiveness, the parallel organization offers more opportunity and power for a wider range of people than is possible in a bureaucracy. "Because a sense of opportunity and power is critical to a high quality of work life, the parallel

---

[25]Ibid.

[26]This section is based on Barry A. Stein and Rosabeth Moss Kanter, "Building the Parallel Organization: Creating Mechanisms for Permanent Quality of Work Life," *The Journal of Applied Behavioral Science,* Vol. 16, No. 3, March 1980, pp. 371–88.

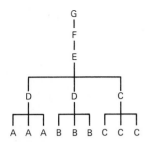

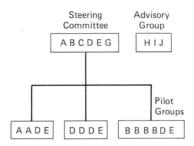

Bureaucratic Organization

- Routine operations — low uncertainty
- Focused primarily on "production"
- Limited "opportunities" (e.g., promotion)
- Fixed job assignments
- Competency established before assignment
- Long chain of command
- Objectives usually top-down
- Rewards: pay/benefits
- Functionally specialized
- Leadership is a function of level

Parallel Organization

- Problem solving — high uncertainty
- Focused primarily on "organization"
- Expandable "opportunities"
  (e.g., participation in a task force)
- Flexible, rotational assignments
- Developmental assignments
- Short chain of command
- Objectives also bottom-up
- Rewards: learning, recognition/visiblity,
  different contribution, bonus possibility,
  new contacts
- Diagonal slices — mix functions
- Leadership drawn from any level

FIGURE 17–3   A Schematic and a Verbal Representation of a Parallel Organization Structure

Source: Barry A. Stein and Rosabeth Moss Kanter, "Building the Parallel Organization: Creating Mechanisms for Permanent Quality of Work Life," *The Journal of Applied Behavioral Science,* Vol. 16, No. 3, March 1980, pp. 378, 385. Reproduced by special permission from *The Journal of Applied Behavioral Science,* copyright 1980, NTL Institute.

structure enhances individual satisfaction and effectiveness in the very act of coping with the new external pressures. The parallel structure thus forms a mechanism for building high quality of work life and environmental responsiveness *permanently* into bureaucratic organization."[27]

Parallel structures in a high-technology organization.   A research report has been published on the installation of parallel structures in Compu Corp (not its real name), a large producer of high-technology equipment. Some reorientation and evaluation of traditional company practices were thought to be in order because (1) the firm's new size had made it increasingly difficult to manage traditionally, (2) increased competition and market pressure for some products necessitated tighter control of growth and operations in these production facilities, and (3) continuing rapid developments in technology suggested a need for better anticipation of sudden product changes.

The project was launched at one plant, based on the hypothesis that "The relatively ineffective behavior and unsuitability for promotion of many of the first-level supervisors was the result of the limited opportunity and power available to them in the existing structure." It was thought that if this hypothesis were correct, the devel-

[27]Ibid., p. 373.

opment and installation of a parallel organization, by providing new sources of opportunity and power, would increase participants' effectiveness and recognition. The initial project proceeded through five stages:

1. *Initial education and planning.* Individual and group discussions were held to generate understanding of and support for the project and its theoretical framework on the part of corporate and plant management and staff.

2. *Information gathering, structural diagnosis, and hypothesis testing.* In this stage, data were gathered systematically, analyzed, and fed back to plant members. To supplement the initial interviews and observations, a formal questionnaire was administered that provided measures of the information, flexibility, opportunities, and problems that people experienced in their jobs. Preliminary results were fed back through memos and discussions. The consultants noted that the provision of written and oral feedback was an important step in convincing managers and employees that the project represented something potentially useful.

3. *Action planning.* Here construction began on elements of the parallel organization (refer to Figure 17–3). The action groups were composed of different arrangements of personnel: some were mixtures of many levels, some were existing work groups, and some were representatives of several areas. The parallel structures represented the expansion of opportunity and power through

- A chance to acquire other than strictly technical training.
- A chance to have an impact on the firm in ways other than through the regular job.
- A way in which to detour around bureaucratic structures that were not effective.
- A mechanism for managing new activities that exist outside the regular job.

4. *Implementation.* The group's own initiative and commitment shaped the implementation stage. Managers and employees were free to make key decisions about how to organize themselves, involve and inform production workers, and maintain current production levels.

5. *Integration and diffusion of the results within the system.* In this stage, various activities were carried out to mesh the accomplishments of the parallel organization into the larger system. The Steering Committee made presentations to others at the plant to inform them more fully of project activities. Participation in the project was incorporated into new job descriptions and included in performance evaluations, thus giving people credit for work in the parallel organization. The consultants report that the most effective diffusion mechanism was the link between the assembly-line pilot group and Compu Corp's QWL manager, since his part of his function was to diffuse and explore company efforts of this sort. Despite the various approaches to diffusion of results, the process did not work as thoroughly as members of the pilot project wished.

Output of the program.   Although quantified data on dependent variables such as productivity and satisfaction were not reported, it was believed that the results of the program were substantial. After six months, the pilot group completed its activities and accomplished the following:

1. A strategy was developed to increase the effectiveness of the assembly line through the use of flexible, horizontally integrated teams and to increase productivity and product quality.
2. Modules were prepared to improve various aspects of work life including performance appraisal training for supervisors, orientation programs for new and transferred employees regarding the production groups, and career path planning.
3. A report was generated on procedural inconsistencies across the production groups that hampered work coordination along with suggestions and alternatives for action and a recommendation for the establishment of a supervisors' forum (meetings of all production supervisors).
4. A set of recommendations was developed for modifying supervisory training to make the process more linked to the perceived need of the supervisors themselves.
5. In general, employees who participated in the project gained important new skills, became more productive, and consequently became more satisfied with their jobs.

Significance for QWL programs in general. Stein and Kanter believe that the parallel organization may be an important answer to the problem of reforming organizational work. Employees at all levels make the reforms themselves via participation in the parallel organization. Managers support the program because it does not undercut its members' own positions or replace their functions. Above all, "A second formal structure oriented to the quality of work life and flexibility can be erected not on the ruins of bureaucracy but on its living capacity to do what bureaucracy does best."[28]

Perhaps the researchers have reached a level of optimism not entirely warranted by their preliminary results, but the parallel organization does appear to be a large-scale OD intervention of merit. It has also been used successfully at General Motors.[29]

ILLUSTRATIVE RESEARCH ABOUT THE EFFECTIVENESS OF OD[30]

Rigorous evaluation of OD interventions is not readily accomplished. One solid attempt toward this end is an evaluation of a year-long organization development project conducted in the Communications and Electrical Division of the City of San Diego. The management of C & E and the OD consultants who conducted the project

[28]Ibid., p. 306.

[29]E. C. Miller, "The Parallel Organization Structure at General Motors: An Interview with Howard C. Carlson, *Personnel,* April 1978, pp. 64–69.

[30]This section follows closely the material in Christian F. Paul and Albert C. Gross, "Increasing Productivity and Morale in a Municipality: Effects of Organization Development," *The Journal of Applied Behavioral Science,* No. 1, 1980, pp. 59–78.

established the goals of increasing productivity, improving morale, and maintaining or improving customer satisfaction. A subgoal was that the goals of productivity and morale should not interfere with each other. An attempt was made by the experimenters to avoid the pitfalls of many program evaluation studies. A quasi-experimental design was used, care was taken to obtain high-quality comparison groups, frequent measurements were made, eclectic data collection methods were used, and appropriate statistical methods were used to analyze the data.

Method

The experimental group was the ninety employees of the C & E division. The unit is primarily a service organization that maintains several electronic systems, including traffic-signal equipment and outside lighting. The OD treatment given the experimental group followed the *action research model.* Basically, the action research model progresses through stages of gathering data, feeding information back to the participants, planning and implementing change, and evaluating the results of the intervention (much like the team building model described earlier). The data gathering phase suggested that five specific interventions might be useful to the C & E division, as described next.

Interviews.   The consultants interviewed each employee, including the superintendent, to discover employee perceptions of the organizational climate. Both open-ended questions (such as "What makes cooperation between work groups difficult?") and rating scale questions ("On a scale of 1 to 5, how satisfied are you with your job?") were included. Interviews were structured, and participants were told that their responses would be confidential. Both subjective and objective data from the interviews were used in planning later project activities.

Team building workshops.   The top management group of the division participated in a three-day team building workshop that bore little similarity to the team building approach described earlier in this chapter. Activities at the workshop included training in communication and management skills, discussion of the results of the earlier data gathering, employee attitude surveys and interviews, and formal exercises designed to identify specific organizational problems and to plan solutions for them.

Counseling.   Throughout the project, the OD team provided the top managers with individual advice and counseling on how to implement the OD program and solve problems identified in the workshop. One purpose of the counseling was to provide objective insight on the division's functioning. Another was to allow the OD consultant to expand alternatives by describing solutions to problems that had worked in other settings.

Process consultation.   Members of the OD team attended many meetings of division personnel to serve as process consultants. In this role they provided meeting participants with insights and feedback concerning decision making, problem solving, and communication within the group. By analyzing the group processes, they hoped to make the meetings more effective.

Management skills training. Participants received a series of two-hour training sessions on such topics as the city manager's expectations of supervisors, methods for conducting effective meetings, stress management, effective discipline, choosing a leadership style, work motivation, performance evaluation, solving organizational problems, time management, and labor-management relations.

In addition to imparting cognitive knowledge, the meetings were designed to lead to organizational improvement. As expressed by the authors of the research study, "To keep the training from becoming 'just a supervisory skills course' we varied the time of the meetings, set an informal participative tone, and encouraged supervisors to use the meetings to solve real-life organizational problems."[31]

Comparison groups. An attempt was taken to secure data from comparison groups (no OD programs) wherever possible. Altogether, nine comparison groups of public employees were used. These included employees from the San Diego Buildings Division, the Long Beach communications and electrical workers, traffic-signals and street-lamps crews, and miscellaneous groups of city employees. In general, the treatment and comparison groups were not appreciably different from one another on most demographic variables.

Results. The three major dependent variables were productivity, job satisfaction, and customer satisfaction, with several measures being taken of each variable. For example, six different measures were taken of job satisfaction. A few highlights of the results follow:

1. *Productivity.* Division productivity increased during the year of the OD intervention, as indicated by such measures as the number of outages repaired (494 versus 431 for the previous year). Comparison group data were unavailable for this particular measure. Productivity was also charted by several measures of efficiency. Data on the number of work hours required for the completion of specific tasks indicated that efficiency increased during the intervention period. For example, fewer hours were required for repair of both stationary and mobile FM components. Cost savings were found in such items as a 13 percent decline in the money spent to repair and maintain a signal intersection. In general, savings in time and money were made during the intervention period, and an efficiency index increased for the treatment, but not the comparison group. The efficiency index referred to here was the ratio of productive work hours to available work hours, as derived from tasks indicated on daily work cards.

2. *Job satisfaction.* The Job Diagnostic Survey, often used in measuring the need for job redesign, was used as a measure of job satisfaction. Slight increases in job satisfac-

[31]Ibid., p. 64.

tion seemed to be attributable to the interventions. Three unobtrusive measures of job satisfaction (absenteeism, turnover, and grievances) also showed some small gains.

3. *Customer satisfaction.* The OD program seemed to have no appreciable effect on direct measures of customer satisfaction, such as telephone and mail surveys. One problem appeared to be that of restriction or range: the customers were generally quite satisfied with C & E before the intervention, and therefore little gain was possible.

Discussion and Interpretation

The authors concluded that their study supports the notion that OD intervention can produce both increased productivity and increased job satisfaction in municipal government employees. The important increases in efficiency, such as a jump from 73 percent to 94 percent on rated efficiency, were not accompanied by any decrease in morale or customer service. At the beginning of the OD project, the members of the treatment group were already well satisfied with their jobs and were already performing efficiently. "Nevertheless, on a variety of measures, we found substantial improvements that may reasonably be attributed to the intervention treatment."[32]

Our interpretation of the results is that OD seemed to do much more for productivity than for satisfaction, which is the opposite of what most OB researchers would predict. A side value of this study for the student of organizational behavior is that it demonstrates the complexity of conducting field research. The experimenters were forced to use an assortment of measures for the dependent variables, and creativity had to be exercised in identifying comparison groups.

CRITICISMS OF OD

OD programs and practitioners have been subject to much criticism by both managers and management researchers. One division president passed an edict that no more OD programs would be conducted in his division. His objection was that diagnostic interviews were stirring up discontent in his division. Researchers criticize OD because not enough solid research evidence (of the type described in the previous section) supports its widespread application. However, the same criticism is made by scholars about virtually every approach to improving individual or interpersonal effectiveness. A person who skims any issue of *Administrative Science Quarterly* or the *Journal of Applied Psychology* will find ample evidence of this kind of critical commentary. Here we offer three general criticisms of OD, keeping in mind that almost any field of professional practice has received its share of criticism.

A major discrepancy exists between the ideal and the real. Most students of organizational behavior realize that change programs should receive top management support and begin at the top of the organization. Such is the party line of the OD prac-

---

[32]Ibid., p. 77.

titioner. However, in practice, OD efforts are often conducted many levels down in the organization. A top executive often endorses an OD program and then delegates the task to a project officer for planning and implementation. In such circumstances, the highest-ranking managers to become really involved with OD are middle managers.[33]

OD makes people unfit for the real organizational world.   A predominant value system of OD practitioners is one characterized by a belief in openness, trust, and the sharing of power. They are typically "up front" people. After attending OD workshops, many participants convert to such values and behaviors. But when placed back in their own organization, they are often punished rather than rewarded for such behavior. At a minimum, such open people have a difficult time competing with highly political (and sometimes devious) organization members.[34]

Resistance to change makes the attainment of OD goals unrealistic.   The deepseated resistance to change that exists in many profit and nonprofit organizations represents a serious obstacle to OD. Burack and Smith observe that such resistance begins at the top and is firmly embedded at the middle levels of management. Among the factors that contribute to such resistance are antiplanning attitudes, people who favor technical changes more than social changes, and collective bargaining to preserve outmoded jobs and technology.[35] Although an OD intervention may bring about some short-range changes, the forces of resistance soon take hold, overthrowing whatever progress has been made through OD. Morale problems are sometimes created when management pays lip service to OD, but then, after the organization development program has ended, the firm returns shortly to traditional ways of doing things.

IMPLICATIONS FOR MANAGERIAL PRACTICE

1.   A diagnostic orientation to the concept of organization development is highly recommended. OD approaches such as team building and survey feedback usually bring about positive results because any changes they recommend are based on a careful diagnosis of the need for change. It is unrealistic to state that "diagnosis should even precede intervention" because diagnosis *is* a form of intervention. As soon as you begin to ask people whether or not change of any sort is desirable, you have already begun a process of self-questioning that may lead to change.

[33]Wendell L. French, Cecil H. Bell, Jr., and Robert A. Zawacki, eds., *Organization Development: Theory, Practice, and Research* (Plano, Tex.: Business Publications, 1978), p. 476.

[34]Andrew J. DuBrin, *Human Relations: A Job-Oriented Approach,* 2nd ed. (Reston, Va.: Reston, 1981), p. 309.

[35]Elmer H. Burack and Robert D. Smith, *Personnel Management: A Human Resource System Approach* (New York: John Wiley, 1982), p. 582.

2.   Your organization, or organizational unit, has a higher chance of benefiting from OD efforts if it is organic rather than mechanistic. Very stable and status-quo-oriented organizations (mechanistic ones) tend to benefit less from OD.[36]

3.   QWL efforts sometimes fail. Organizations interested in undertaking QWL programs should consider the following conditions that are essential for successful long-term results:

- Management must be committed to an open, nondefensive style of operation that involves sharing of information and soliciting of input from below and implementing of improvement plans.
- Employees must be given opportunities for advancement.
- Managers must be trained and developed to function effectively in a less directive, more collaborative style.
- Traditional status barriers between management and individual contributors must be dismantled to allow the establishment of an atmosphere of trust and open communication.
- Employees should receive feedback on work performance and recognition for achieving superior results. Financial rewards and other forms of positive reinforcement are also important.
- Personnel should be recruited and selected who can be motivated, or who are already motivated, to strive for excellent job performance.
- Both positive and negative outcomes of the QWL program should be analyzed and evaluated, using them to improve the organizational system.[37]

Summary

- In its ideal form, organization development is a long-range effort to improve an organization's problem solving and renewal processes, particularly through a more effective and collaborative management of organization culture. Special emphasis is placed on the culture of formal work teams, with the assistance of a change agent and the use of applied behavioral science, including action research. In practice, OD is generally taken to refer to an assortment of training or therapeutic interventions whose purpose is the improvement of the organization and its members.
- Organizational change can be accomplished by three broad approaches. The *structural* approach is brought about by modifying the formal organization. The *technological* approach focuses on altering equipment, work measurement techniques, engineering methods, research techniques, or production methods. The technological approach focuses on altering the equipment. The *humanistic* approach changes organizations by bringing about changes in organization members. Most OD practitioners concentrate

[36]Jerome L. Franklin, "Characteristics of Successful and Unsuccessful Organization Development," *The Journal of Applied Behavioral Science,* Vol. 14, No. 12, December 1976, p. 491.

[37]Based on Glaser, "Productivity Gains," p. 73.

on interventions designed to change people. OD interventions can be geared to the individual, small-group, or organizational level.

- OD consultants or change agents have two primary roles. The traditional role of the OD consultant is that of an observer who helps people to solve their own problems. A newer role is one of expert advisor (the traditional consulting role). The OD consultant diagnoses the client's problems and then suggests a course of action that should remedy the problem.

- Career development programs are based on the assumption that if individuals are helped to achieve rewarding and satisfying careers within the organization, both the individual and the organization will prosper. Ideally, a CDP integrates a number of personnel programs. A nine-phase illustrative program was described in this chapter. Although CDPs have been shown to be beneficial to the organization, they also encourage wishful thinking and disappointed expectations. Career negotiation is a process of working out a compromise between employee and organizational needs to make the CDP more effective.

- Team building, the most widely used OD method, is an attempt to assist the work group to become more adept by learning how to identify, diagnose, and solve its own problems. In the model of team building described here, the process begins with the gathering of data about group processes and problems. Shortly thereafter, the team leader feeds back data to the group. After extensive discussion, action plans are formulated to overcome the problems identified. Later, one or more follow-up sessions are scheduled to review progress toward the accomplishment of the action plans. The team building consultant plays a varied role, including that of process consultant, behavioral science resource person, and counselor. Research and expert opinion suggest that team building is an effective intervention.

- The survey feedback technique is a well-structured approach to OD with a long history of good performance. In essence, it involves taking a survey of organizational problems via questionnaires and/or interviews, feeding these results back to the organization, developing action plans to overcome the problems uncovered, and follow-up.

- Grid OD endeavors to make individuals and organizations more effective by bringing about changes in attitudes, values, and behavior. It is based upon a two-dimensional framework (concern for production and concern for people) of leadership. Grid OD involves two parts and six phases. Part 1 is management development (first two phases); part 2 is organization development (phases 3 to 6). Phase 1 involves the study of the Managerial Grid®; Phase 2 is team building; phase 3 is intergroup development; phase 4 calls for designing an ideal strategic corporate model; phase 5 involves the implementation of development; and phase 6 is consolidation—aimed at reinforcing and making habitual the new patterns of management achieved in earlier phases.

- QWL and OD are conceptually similar, and in practice they overlap considerably. QWL is aptly defined as a process by which all members of the organization, through appropriate channels of communication, have some say about the design of their jobs in particular and the work environment in general. As a consequence, both job satisfaction and productivity may increase. Improving the quality of work life is a process rather than a series of specific steps because of individual differences across organizations. The improvement ideas generated by a specific QWL program are based on that particular firm's culture, needs, and readiness for change.

- Parallel organizations are a macro approach of merit to improving the quality of work life. Structurally, they are flat, flexible, yet formal, problem-solving and governance organizations that supplement bureaucratic, hierarchical structures. The parallel organization attempts to institutionalize a set of externally and internally responsive, participative, problem-solving structures alongside the conventional line organization that carries out recurring tasks.

- OD programs have been criticized because of the paucity of research about their effectiveness. (An illustration of the type of evaluation research of a comprehensive OD program for municipal employees was described in this chapter.) Other criticisms of OD include (1) OD, in practice, is rarely carried out with top management involved; (2) OD encourages attitudes and behaviors that are inappropriate for most organizational environments; and (3) organizational resistance to change makes the attainment of OD goals unrealistic in many cases.

Questions for Discussion

1. What do you imagine are the major rewards and frustrations experienced by OD specialists?
2. In what ways might "high technology in the office" contribute to the need for OD?
3. If you were in a team building session with your boss, how candid would you be in criticizing him or her?
4. Can a manager really have high concern for people and production? Do you feel that these goals are compatible in the real world of organizational life?
5. Do you consider budgeting to be an OD technique? Why or why not?
6. Describe how team building sessions might be used to make a hospital run more smoothly.
7. How honest do you think people are in responding to organization surveys? What factors do you think influence the extent to which they are honest?
8. If you were the chief executive officer of a firm during a period of tight budgets, would you eliminate an ongoing OD program? Explain your reasoning.
9. Which aspects of an organization's environment do you think would contribute the most directly to your personal quality of work life?
10. Which factors in society do you think have contributed to the popularity of QWL programs?

An Organizational Behavior Problem

The Career Development Circle

In this exercise, each participant receives one career suggestion from every other participant. Suggestions can be offered about *anything* that might possibly help a person. Examples include, "Get some hands-on manufacturing experience" or "Learn how to dress for success." The steps are as follows:

1. The class is divided into subgroups of about ten to twelve people arranged in a circle. A team leader (preferably the course instructor) joins the group. Each subgroup follows the format described here.
2. Assume that Michele is seated to the left of the team leader. Michele introduces herself to the group and makes a five-minute presentation about her background and her career plans. Beginning with the person to the left of Michele, everybody makes one suggestion to Michele (looking at her directly). A subgroup member is allowed to pass if he or she has absolutely no suggestion or comment.
3. After Michele has heard suggestions from everyone in the group, she expresses how she feels about these comments. For instance, "Thanks, folks, for all the positive feedback and for those terrific suggestions. But, sorry, I won't compromise on my goal of becoming a high-ranking government official." Michele has the opportunity to ask for clarification of any of the points raised.
4. In clockwise progression, all other participants receive their turn at hearing suggestions and giving their reactions.
5. After all the suggestions have been made, a general group discussion follows about the implications and relevance of the session. An important issue to explore after the sessions have been completed is how this exercise fits into the general concept of organization development. For example, why is this exercise included in a chapter on OD? If this activity were conducted in a firm, how might it lead to improved organizational effectiveness and adaptability to change?

Additional Reading

ALBRECHT, KARL. *Organization Development: A Total Systems Approach to Positive Change in Any Business.* Englewood Cliffs, N.J.: Prentice-Hall, 1982.

CAMDEN, THOMAS M. "Use Outplacement as a Career Development Tool." *Personnel Administrator,* January 1982, pp. 35–37.

COX, GLENN MARTHA, and JANE COVEY BROWN. "Quality of Work Life: Another Fad or Real Benefit?" *Personnel Administrator*, May 1982, pp. 49–53.

FRENCH, WENDELL L., and CECIL H. BELL, Jr. *Organization Development: Behavioral Science Interventions Organization Improvement,* 2nd ed. Englewood Cliffs, N.J.: Prentice-Hall, 1978.

GOODMAN, PAUL S., and JOHANNES M. PENNINGS. *New Perspectives on Organizational Effectiveness.* San Francisco: Jossey-Bass, 1977.

HUSE, EDGAR F. *Organization Development and Change,* 2nd ed. St. Paul, Minn.: West Publishing, 1980.

LAWLER, EDWARD E., III. "Strategies for Improving the Quality of Work Life." *American Psychologist,* May 1982, pp. 486–93.

LIPPITT, GORDON L. *Organization Renewal: A Holistic Approach to Organization Development,* 2nd ed. Englewood Cliffs, N.J.: Prentice-Hall, 1982.

MILBOURN, GENE, and RICHARD CUBA. "OD Techniques and the Bottom Line." *Personnel,* May–June 1981, pp. 34–42.

MIRVIS, PHILIP H., and DAVID N. BERG, *Failures in Organization Development and Change: Case and Essays for Learning.* New York: John Wiley, 1977.

ROBEY, DANIEL, and STEVEN ALTMAN, eds. *Organizational Development.* New York: Macmillan, 1981.

RUBINSTEIN, SIDNEY P. "QWL and the Technical Societies." *Training and Development Journal,* August 1980, pp. 76–81.

SCOBEL, DONALD, N. *Creative Worklife.* Houston: Gulf, 1981.

Glossary

Action plan   A description of the specific steps that need to be taken to achieve an objective or bring performance back to an acceptable standard.

Adhocracy   An organization in which the dominant form or structure is made up of small, special-purpose (ad hoc) groups such as task forces or project teams.

Anthropology   The behavioral science that deals with the origins, physical and cultural development, racial characteristics, social customs, and beliefs of people.

Anxiety   Generalized feelings of fear and apprehension usually resulting from a perceived threat and accompanied by feelings of uneasiness.

Appropriate reward or punishment   A positive or negative motivator that produces results with a given individual in a given situation.

Authority   The right to control the actions of others; control that is sanctioned by the organization or society.

Behavior modification   A system of motivation that aims to change individual responses and behavior by changing a person's environment through the manipulation of incentives. Desired responses are rewarded and undesired responses are sometimes punished.

Behavioral science   Any science concerned with the systematic study of human behavior such as psychology, sociology, and anthropology. According to Joe Kelly, behavioral science is the study of human behavior that uses whatever body of knowledge is most relevant.

Bureaucracy   A rational, systematic, and precise form of organization in which rules, regulations, and techniques of control are precisely defined. A bureaucracy stands in contrast to a System 4 organization.

Bureaupathic behavior   A distortion of behavior found in a bureaucracy, whereby an emotionally insecure person feels a strong need to control subordinates and clients.

Bureautic behavior   Antagonism to rules and regulations found in a bureaucracy whereby the person acquires the reputation of a malcontent.

Career development   The personnel and human resource management activity that helps organizational members to plan their careers within the enterprise, to help the enterprise achieve its objectives and the employee achieve maximum self-development.

Case   An involved description, usually based on fact, that is useful in illustrating or studying a phenomenon. This book uses a number of case histories to illustrate the concepts discussed.

Change agent   A person whose formal role is to bring about organizational (or, sometimes, individual) change. Also called an OD consultant.

Coaching The process of helping another individual to overcome a specific, immediate problem by giving him or her advice and/or encouragement.

Cognition The process or processes by which a person acquires knowledge or becomes aware, including thinking, remembering, solving problems, and creating ideas.

Cognitive Referring to the intellectual aspects of human behavior. A cognitive process is the means by which an individual becomes aware of objects and situations. It includes learning, reasoning, and problem solving.

Common sense Sound, practical judgment that is independent of specialized knowledge, training, or the like; natural wisdom not based on formal knowledge.

Communication The passage of information and/or messages between or among people (or animals) by use of words, letters, symbols, or nonverbal communication.

Conformity Behavior that is similar in form, nature, or character to that of other people in a group. Conformity can be functional or dysfunctional.

Confrontation Bringing forth a controversial topic or contradictory material with which the other party is emotionally involved. To say "Your performance is substandard" is to initiate a confrontation.

Consultant A person who, on a fee or volunteer basis, provides advice and/or technical help or aids an organization in solving its own problem. In some circumstances, consultants provide services to individuals as well as organizations.

Contingency theory of leadership effectiveness Fielder's leadership theory with the central theme that task-oriented leaders are more effective when the leadership situation is very favorable or very unfavorable. Also, relationship-oriented leaders are more effective in situations of moderate favorability. In short, leadership effectiveness depends more on the situation than on the leader.

Control group In an experiment, the group that does not receive the treatment so that the effects of the independent variable can be validly measured.

Creative climate An organizational climate that actually encourages people to seek and bring forth creative solutions to problems.

Creativity The ability to process information in such a way that the result is new, original, and meaningful.

Data Facts, statistics, or bits of knowledge from which conclusions can be drawn, thus converting them into information. Data is the plural of datum.

Decoding A mental process that a receiver uses to decipher a message and make it intelligible.

Delegation The process by which authority and work assignments are distributed downward in an organization.

Dysfunction A negative side effect; something that takes away from the proper functioning of a system.

Emergent leader A leader who, although not given the formal title of a leader, emerges from the group to assume a leadership role.

Emotional support Encouragement or morale boosting that produces positive feelings in another individual.

Empirical evidence Evidence derived from or guided by experience, direct observation, or practice in field settings.

Encoding Converting an idea into an understandable message by the sender of the message (communicator).

Encounter group A small therapy or training group that focuses on expressing feelings openly and honestly. A T group is an example of an encounter group.

Entrepreneur A person who takes the risk of starting a new enterprise or introducing a new idea, product, or service to society.

Equity theory of motivation   A theory of work motivation based on the idea that people compare their input-output ratio to other people doing comparable work or having comparable backgrounds.

Eustress   An amount of stress that makes you come alive; a positive force in the lives of people; functional stress.

Expectancy theory   Any theory of human motivation that centers on the idea that people will expend effort if they believe that that effort will lead to a desired outcome, and whether or not that outcome will lead to a reward.

Experimental design   The layout, general plan, format, or strategy used in an experiment.

Feedback   Information that tells you how well or poorly you have performed. Also knowledge of results of your behavior that helps you to judge the appropriateness of your response and make corrections where indicated.

Focal person   The central actor or person under observation or study in a given situation.

Followership   Behavior related to following the direction or order of a leader; the opposite of leadership.

Frame of reference   The assumptions a person makes; perspectives a person uses to form a "cognitive map" for interpreting and coping with his or her world.

Frustration   Denial or thwarting of motives by obstacles that lie between the organism and the goal.

Goal- or task-oriented behavior   Activities or actions that help an individual to reach goals or accomplish tasks.

Goal-setting theory   A systematic explanation of how goal setting increases productivity. The theory emphasizes the value of both difficult and specific goals.

Grapevine   The major information communication network in an organization, used in the transmission of both rumors and true information.

Group cohesiveness   The attractiveness of the group to its members, which leads to a feeling of unity and "stick-togetherness."

Group dynamics   The study of the internal workings and processes of formal and informal groups; small-group psychology.

Group process   Patterns of activity by group members and interactions among them. Communication and influence are two group processes.

Group structure   How a group is organized or the patterns of differentiation and interrelationships among roles.

Groupthink   An extreme form of consensus or agreement that may take place when the group tries too hard to be cohesive. Group opinion may be overly dogmatic as a result.

Heredity   The transmission of genetic characteristics from parent to offspring; those aspects of a person's physical and psychological makeup that are programmed by native characteristics.

Human behavior   Any actions or activities engaged in by people including both external (such as movement) and internal activities (such as thinking and feeling).

Human relations   The art and practice of using systematic knowledge about human behavior to achieve organization and/or personal objectives.

Human resource forecasting   Estimating the size and makeup of the future work force necessary to accomplish the goals of the firm. (Formerly referred to as manpower planning.)

Hypothesis   Statement or proposition usually based on observation or past information that is tested in an experiment or research study. It may be denied or supported but never proved conclusively.

Industrial and organizational psychology   The field of psychology that studies human behavior in a work environment. Overlaps considerably with the field called organizational behavior.

Integration   This term has two meanings in an organizational context: the meshing of individual and organizational goals and the avoidance of conflict among organizational members.

Interpersonal conflict   Conflict between two or more individuals, sometimes described as a personality clash.

Interaction effect   A relationship between two or more variables that is more complicated than the simple additive effects of whatever variables may be involved. For example, one type of reward might be appropriate to some kinds of people and jobs but not to others. Or age may influence the relationship of a particular variable upon the person's job satisfaction.

Intervening variable   A factor that influences a process even though it is not an intentional input into the process. For instance, a manager's mood at the time may influence his or her decision making.

Intrinsic reward   A reward that is inherent in a task rather than one that is externally imposed. For some people, problem solving is intrinsically rewarding.

Intuition   Direct perception of truth or fact that seems to be independent of any reasoning process. A keen and quick insight that can be very helpful to a knowledge worker.

Inversion of means and ends   A situation in which following orders or performing your specialized activity becomes more important than the overall goal you are trying to accomplish. A condition of suboptimization. An example would be an organization development specialist who cares more about setting up training programs than helping the company to reach its objectives.

Job enlargement   Increasing the scope of a job, usually with the intention of increasing both satisfaction and performance.

Job enrichment   A system of job design prompted by the work of Herzberg, job enrichment attempts to increase worker motivation by making the nature of the job more exciting, rewarding, challenging, or creative.

Job performance   The output of a job activity; how well a person does in meeting the demands of his or her job.

Knowledge of results   Providing feedback to people so that they know how well they are performing an assigned task. This process is a key principle of learning.

Knowledge worker   A person whose work involves primarily conceptual skill—managers, professionals, technicians, and sales representatives, for example.

Leadership style   The characteristic manner or typical approach a particular person uses in leading people. Many different leadership styles are possible, including participative, production oriented, and "middle of the road."

Liaison group   A group that acts as an intermediary or linking function between one group and another in an organization. Often used to improve communication between marketing and manufacturing.

Lifestyle   A person's typical approach to and pattern of living, including moral attitudes, clothing preferences, ways of spending money, career pursuits, and recreational pursuits. Basically the style of life one leads.

Line responsibility or line function   The activities of departments or subunits that contribute directly to the organization's production of goods or services.

Linking pin function   A concept originated by Likert that contends that every manager is a leader in his or her own group and a subordinate in another group. The leader thus represents his or her group and links it to the rest of the organization.

Linking process   A sequence of activities that joins together two or more events or situations. For instance, in a potentially stressful situation, the appraisal process links an objective situation and an individual's perception of the situation.

Locus of control   A personality characteristic that determines people's perception of how their life is controlled. *Internalizers* perceive control of their lives as coming from inside themselves; *externalizers* believe that their lives are controlled by external factors.

Machiavellianism   An attitude or orientation leaning toward manipulating and deceiving others in an organization to further one's own cause; unscrupulous, deceitful, or dishonest behavior.

Management development   Any planned effort to improve current or future manager performance.

Management by objectives (MBO)   A system of management in which people are held accountable for reaching objectives they usually set jointly with their superiors. Objectives at lower levels within the organization contribute to the attainment of goals set at the top of the organization.

Managerial Grid®   A framework for simultaneously examining the concern for production and people dimensions of leadership. Also an OD program for teaching leaders team management—getting work accomplished through committed people.

Manifest conflict   Conflict that is readily observable and thus not hidden; the opposite of latent conflict.

Mechanistic organization   An organization generally resistant to change and characterized by highly specialized job tasks, rigid authority systems, downward flow of communications, and conflict resolution by superiors.

Midcareer crisis   A general concern that career-minded people have between the ages of thirty-five and fifty-five about their level of career accomplishment, usually accompanied by feelings of dissatisfaction, boredom, and restlessness. Usually considered to be part of the midlife crisis.

Middle manager   Manager or supervisor who is organizationally placed between first-level management and top-level management (board of directors, president, vice presidents). Work of middle managers involves considerable coordination of the work of others.

Morale   The general satisfaction level of an individual or group. It is the composite of feelings, attitudes, and sentiments that contributes to a general feeling of satisfaction.

Negative reinforcement   Removing something negative (such as a penalty or uncomfortable situation) when somebody makes the desired response; part of behavior modification and instrumental learning.

Objective   A specific state or end state or condition aimed for that contributes to a larger goal; an integral part of MBO.

Office politics   Any method of gaining advantage for yourself in a job environment not strictly related to merit, such as marrying the boss's child or laughing at the boss's jokes.

Organic organization   An organization generally accepting of change and characterized by low amounts of job specialization, high degrees of superior-subordinate interaction, autonomy for employees, and a climate of participative decision making.

Organizational mental health   The general sense of well-being of an organization, including its adaptability, sense of identity, and capacity to test reality.

Path-goal theory of leadership   A leadership theory specifying that it is necessary for a leader to influence the followers' perception of work goals, paths to goal attainment, and self-development goals. The theory is based on expectancy theory.

Perceptual block   An almost rigid tendency to think of an object in a limited way. When you overcome your perceptual blocks, it often leads to a more creative solution to a problem.

Personnel system   An organized method for dealing effectively with personnel in an organization such as a performance appraisal system.

Position power   The amount of power given the leader by virtue of his or her position. A company president has considerable position power.

Positive reinforcement   A reward for making a particular response such as receiving approval from a boss for being prompt. PR is an essential ingredient of behavior modification.

Power motive   A desire for control over people and other resources. McClelland contends that *n* Power can involve helping yourself or helping others.

Process consultant   A person who helps the group to analyze how it is functioning rather than what is accomplished. The process consultant intervenes in the group's task discussion and leads the group in an analysis of the process of the discussion. After the consultant leaves, the group members should be able to analyze their own processes.

Productivity   The amount of work produced by managers and individual contributors whether the "product" is goods or services.

Psychological contract   An unwritten understanding between the individual and the organization defining how much the individual will do for the organization, providing that his or her expectations of the employer are met.

Punishment   The presentation of an undesirable or aversive consequence for a specific behavior or removing something desirable because of a particular response.

Pyramidal organization structure   Hierarchically shaped organization in which the highest level of management has the greatest amount of formal authority. Each successive lower layer has much less formal authority.

Quasi-experimental design   A major category of experiment in which the various treatment groups are formed by assigning participants to treatments in a nonrandom fashion. Less than a pure experimental design where groups are assigned randomly.

Role   Behavior expected of an individual occupying a given position within a group.

Role ambiguity   A condition that exists when a person is uncertain as to what he or she should be doing in a particular position.

Role conflict   Anxiety generated in a person when people have incompatible expectations of him or her or when two or more roles conflict with each other.

Role underload   Situation in which a person has insufficient responsibilities and duties to perform. As a consequence, the person feels underutilized and therefore experiences stress.

Scientific management   A school of management thought that emphasizes maximizing production from people through such means as proper selection, efficient job design, and financial incentives.

Scientific method   A process of inquiry following certain logical steps such as problem recognition, review of theory and the literature, development of hypotheses, selection of a methodology to study the problem, and actual observation and experiment or test of hypotheses.

Self-actualization   A need or group of needs relating to self-fulfillment or attaining one's actual potential.

Self-concept   The total view one has of oneself. A positive self-concept leads to self-confidence.

Self-discipline   Disciplining or training oneself, usually for purposes of self-improvement.

Self-insight   A process of understanding something about oneself involving an emotional component. Also implying an explanation of one's own behavior.

Sensitivity training   An intensive approach to OD in which participants share their feelings and attitudes about each other with the group; designed to foster self-understanding and personal growth. The T group is the core of sensitivity training.

Sham democracy   A manipulative device designed to create the impression that participative leadership or a democratic group process has taken place. Used frequently in meetings.

Shared decision making A situation in which a manager allows and encourages subordinates to participate in (provide inputs to) the decision-making process.

Situation clusters A group of situations in leadership that have many factors in common. Two situations in a cluster might be a bookkeeping department and a payroll department.

Situational leadership theory A leadership model based on the idea that the leader must take into account the maturity of the followers in choosing the right blend of task and relationship orientation to be truly effective. Also called the "life-cycle theory of leadership."

Sociology The behavioral science or study of the fundamental laws of social relations and group behavior.

Staff function or responsibility The activities of departments or other subunits that contribute indirectly to an organization's production of goods and services. Staff personnel generally advise line personnel.

Strain A reaction to stress implying an unfavorable reaction to the individual or organization; a change in the state of the internal system.

Stress Any demand inside or outside the person that requires the person to cope with the demand. Groups and organizations also experience stress.

Survey feedback An approach to OD in which the results of an attitude survey are fed back to management and the workers. Corrective action is taken about problems uncovered in the survey.

Synectics A group problem-solving technique in which various elements are fitted together to produce novel and creative alternatives with a view to reaching group consensus.

System 4 management A term for participative management as developed by Likert. System 4, similar to Theory Y and Theory Z, involves full participation of all organization members in decisions directly relevant to their work activities.

Systems theory An approach to understanding organizations that emphasizes the input process–output schema and the relationship between the organization and the environment.

T group A popular form of encounter group that is highly unstructured. T groups, as part of sensitivity training, were originally developed for training managers to become more open and honest with people but now are used widely in nonwork settings.

Team building (or team development) An OD technique emphasizing small discussion groups that attempts to bring about improved communication and cooperation in work groups.

Territorial encroachment A situation that occurs when one individual or group takes over responsibility that properly belongs to another individual or group. Territorial encroachment is a source of conflict between line and staff units.

Theory A systematic explanation of some phenomenon or phenomena based upon research or empirical knowledge. The popular meaning of the term "theory" refers to speculative explanations for phenomena, or impractical ideas.

Theory X Douglas McGregor's famous statement of an alternative to the traditional management view that considers people as usually lazy and needing to be prodded by external rewards. A rigid and task-oriented approach to management.

Theory Y Douglas McGregor's famous statement of an alternative to traditional management thinking. It emphasizes that people seek to fulfill higher-level needs on the job and that management must be flexible and human relations oriented.

Transactional analysis (TA) A technique for improving interpersonal relationships that looks upon every human relationship as a transaction between the ego states (parent, adult, child) of people.

Transactional communication Communication that is characterized by give and take between two or more people; two-way communication.

Type A behavior A behavior pattern characterized by impatience, compulsiveness, high tension, high energy, and a constant striving for success.

Type B behavior A behavior pattern the opposite of Type A. A relaxed, patient, relatively contented approach to life.

Unit A subpart of an organization such as a department or division; also called a subunit.

Valence A concept used heavily in expectancy theory that refers to the strength of a person's preference for a particular outcome.

Validity The extent to which a predictor measures what it purports to measure. Several different types of validity are recognized, including criterion related and content.

Woodward research studies A long-term research project conducted in England that documents the relationship between technology and a variety of managerial activities. The studies contributed to the conteingency design point of view.

Workaholic (work addict) A person addicted to work to the extent that it has adverse consequences for family and personal life. The condition may also interfere with job effectiveness as the person often loses perspective and objectivity.

Work motivation In general, physical and mental effort expended toward meeting organizational objectives.

Zone of indifference Area of behavior within which a subordinate is prepared to accept direction or influence. Orders of this type are seen as lawful and within the person's value system.

Name Index

Subject Index